PRINCIPLES OF
CRIMINAL LAW

Sixth Edition

ANDREW ASHWORTH

Vinerian Professor of English Law, University of Oxford

OXFORD
UNIVERSITY PRESS

OXFORD

UNIVERSITY PRESS

Great Clarendon Street, Oxford OX2 6DP

Oxford University Press is a department of the University of Oxford.
It furthers the University's objective of excellence in research, scholarship,
and education by publishing worldwide in

Oxford New York

Auckland Cape Town Dar es Salaam Hong Kong Karachi
Kuala Lumpur Madrid Melbourne Mexico City Nairobi
New Delhi Shanghai Taipei Toronto

With offices in

Argentina Austria Brazil Chile Czech Republic France Greece
Guatemala Hungary Italy Japan Poland Portugal Singapore
South Korea Switzerland Thailand Turkey Ukraine Vietnam

Oxford is a registered trade mark of Oxford University Press
in the UK and in certain other countries

Published in the United States
by Oxford University Press Inc., New York

© Andrew Ashworth, 2009

The moral rights of the authors have been asserted
Database right Oxford University Press (maker)

Crown copyright material is reproduced under Class Licence
Number C01P0000148 with the permission of OPSI
and the Queen's Printer for Scotland

British Library Cataloguing in Publication Data

Data available

Library of Congress Cataloging in Publication Data

Data available

Typeset by Newgen Imaging Systems (P) Ltd., Chennai, India
Printed in Great Britain
on acid-free paper by
Ashford Colour Press Limited, Gosport, Hampshire

ISBN 978–0–19–954197–3

1 3 5 7 9 10 8 6 4 2

PRINCIPLES OF CRIMINAL LAW

7 Day

PREFACE

Although only three years have elapsed since the publication of the fifth edition, there have been major developments in the criminal law. The Fraud Act 2006 has come into force, and that is discussed in Chapter 9.8 below. The provisions of the Corporate Manslaughter and Corporate Homicide Act 2007 are referred to in Chapter 5.3 and analysed in Chapter 7.5. New offences of encouraging and assisting crime have been introduced by Part 2 of the Serious Crime Act 2007, and they are examined in Chapter 11.7. Among the other statutory changes is the re-statement of aspects of the law of self-defence in section 76 of the Criminal Justice and Immigration Act 2008, discussed in Chapter 4.6. Additionally, the Law Commission has been busy in proposing reforms, and particular attention is paid in Chapter 7 to its recommendations for reform of the law of murder, manslaughter, and infanticide, and to the way in which those have been taken forward in a consultation by the Ministry of Justice, resulting in provisions in the Coroners and Justice Bill 2009, now before parliament.

As well as taking account of new developments in legislation and in judicial decisions, the opportunity has been taken for some re-writing and re-organization of the text. The context and functions of the criminal law are outlined in Chapter 1, and then there has been considerable re-writing of Chapter 2 on criminalization, and on reasons for creating or for not creating criminal laws. Chapter 3 then examines key principles and policies relevant to the criminal law. In Chapters 4, 5 and 6, the 'general part' elements of culpability, justification, and excuse are analysed, and there has been some re-organization. Chapter 4 deals generally with *actus reus* questions. Chapter 5 is now devoted to criminal capacity (insanity, infancy and corporate liability) as well as to *mens rea* issues. Chapter 6 deals with excusatory defences. Three areas of the special part of the criminal law are then selected for examination: Chapter 7 deals with homicide, Chapter 8 with non-fatal physical violations (including sex offences), and Chapter 9 with offences of dishonesty. The book concludes with Chapter 10 on complicity, and Chapter 11 on inchoate offences.

As in previous editions, the focus of the book is upon the identification and discussion of issues of principle and policy raised by the statements of the courts, Parliament, the law reform bodies, and academic commentators. The judgments of the courts continue to provide much material for discussion, and the resurgence of criminal law scholarship has continued, with the publication of important new monographs, articles, and essays. The contention is not that English criminal law is grounded in a stable set of established doctrines: on the contrary, there is ample evidence that the arguments and assumptions that influence the development of the law form a disparate group, sometimes conflicting and sometimes invoked selectively. Often there are political factors influencing the shape of legislation or the activities of law enforcement officers, and reference is made to these below. But the aim of the book is to focus on issues of principle, some of which are immanent in existing legal rules and practices, some of which are not recognized (or not fully recognized) and which are commended here on normative grounds. To conduct a full normative argument on many of these points would require greater detail, in discussing elements of moral and political philosophy or of criminology, than is possible within the confines of this book. The same applies to comparative legal material: some references are made, particularly to the American Law Institute's Model Penal Code, but it is not possible to go much further here.

In the course of preparing this edition I have again benefited from the assistance of several friends and colleagues, and I am grateful to them all. In particular, I am grateful to James Goudkamp for his careful bibliographical assistance. The processes of Oxford University Press have been splendidly efficient. I have retained the gender-specific 'he' in most parts of the book when referring to defendants and offenders, on the ground that the vast majority of them are male.

I hope that statements about the law were accurate on 1 October 2008; a few subsequent developments have been noted in appropriate places.

A.J.A.

CONTENTS

TABLE OF CASES

TABLE OF TREATIES AND CONVENTIONS

TABLE OF LEGISLATION

1

CRIMINAL JUSTICE AND THE CRIMINAL LAW

The operation of the criminal law requires little explanation in clear cases. Someone who deliberately kills or rapes another is liable to be prosecuted, convicted, and sentenced. Criminal liability is the strongest formal condemnation that society can inflict, and it may also result in a sentence which amounts to a severe deprivation of the ordinary liberties of the offender. Of course, there are other official deprivations of our liberties: taxation is one, depriving citizens of a proportion of their income, or adding a compulsory levy to commercial transactions (for example, Value Added Tax). And taxation, no less than the criminal law, may be seen as justified by the mutual obligations necessary for worthwhile community living. But the taxing of an activity does not carry any implication of 'ought not to do', whereas criminal liability carries the strong implication of 'ought not to do'. It is the censure conveyed by criminal liability which marks out its special social significance, and it is the imposition of this official censure, and the ensuing liability to state punishment ordered by the court, that requires a clear social justification.

The chief concern of the criminal law is to prohibit behaviour that represents a serious wrong against an individual or against some fundamental social value or institution.[1] This suggests, perhaps, that there are some wrongs that are not serious enough (or appropriate for) any legal liability, such as breaking a promise to a friend without good reason, or divulging information given in confidence by a friend, and there are some wrongs that are serious enough for civil liability—such as breach of contract—but not for criminal liability. But the notion that English criminal law is

---

[1] The *form* of English criminal laws is not usually that of a prohibition, however. Laws are usually written as if addressed to police, prosecutors and courts: 'a person is guilty of x if...', or 'any person who does x, y, z shall be liable to imprisonment for a term not exceeding...'

only concerned with serious wrongs must be abandoned as one considers the broader canvas of criminal liability. There are many offences for which any element of stigma is diluted almost to vanishing point, as with illegal parking, riding a bicycle without lights, or dropping litter. This is not to suggest that all such offences are equally unimportant; there are some situations in which illegal parking can cause danger to others, for example. Yet it remains true that there are many offences for which criminal liability is merely imposed by Parliament as a practical means of regulating an activity, without implying the element of social condemnation which is characteristic of the major or traditional crimes. There is thus no general dividing line between criminal and non-criminal conduct which corresponds to a distinction between immoral and moral conduct, or between seriously wrongful and other conduct. The boundaries of the criminal law are explicable largely as the results of exercises of political power at particular points in history.

The idea of a crime is that it is something that rightly concerns the State, and not just the person(s) affected by the wrongdoing. Many crimes are civil wrongs as well (torts or breaches of contract, for example), and it is for the injured party to decide whether or not to sue for damages. But the decision to make conduct into a crime implies that there is a public interest in ensuring that such conduct does not happen and that, when it does, there is the possibility of State punishment. The police and the Crown Prosecution Service take decisions on whether to prosecute someone who is reasonably suspected of committing an offence: although they should 'take into account the consequences for the victim of whether or not to prosecute', they should act 'on behalf of the public and not just in the interests of any individual'.[2] Moreover, even if an individual citizen is wronged behind closed doors, as in cases of 'domestic violence', the State has an interest:

> But whatever else is unclear about the rights and wrongs of a domestic dispute…such violence should surely not be seen as a matter for negotiation or compromise. It should be condemned by the whole community as an unqualified wrong; and this is done by defining and prosecuting it as a crime.[3]

This view is sometimes phrased in terms of crimes as 'attacks on the community as a whole', but, as Grant Lamond argues,[4] a more convincing way of understanding crimes as public wrongs is to regard them not as wrongs *to* the community but as wrongs that the community is appropriately *responsible* for punishing. That, in philosophical terms, is what is characteristic of crimes, at least of fault-based crimes. Thus it is in the public interest to provide for the punishment of the serious wrongs involved in violent acts, wherever they occur and whoever inflicts them. But in practice matters are not so clear-cut: some crimes simply cannot be prosecuted without

---

[2] Crown Prosecution Service, *Code for Crown Prosecutors* (5th edn., 2004), para. 5.12; a victim does have the right to bring a private prosecution, but under the Prosecution of Offences Act 1985 the Director of Public Prosecutions has the power to take it over and, if appropriate, to drop it.

[3] R. A. Duff, *Punishment, Communication and Community* (2001), 62.

[4] G. Lamond, 'What is a Crime?' (2007) 27 OJLS 609, at 615–20.

the victim's testimony, and so the victim's refusal to co-operate with the prosecution may be determinative.[5] Victims of crime now have the right to make a Victim Personal Statement about the effects of the offence on them, although the courts should decline to take the further step of taking account of the views of a victim or victim's family on the question of sentence.[6] Various pro-victim initiatives, and the advent of forms of restorative justice, have raised further questions about the interface between crimes as 'offences against the State' and the involvement of victims in decision-making in criminal justice.[7]

Given the variety of forms of behaviour that have been criminalized, it is no surprise that Glanville Williams ended his search for a definition of crime without identifying any criterion based on subject-matter. He concluded that only a formal definition is sustainable: 'in short, a crime is an act capable of being followed by criminal proceedings having a criminal outcome'.[8] But one consequence of the Human Rights Act 1998 is that it is no longer for Parliament to stipulate that proceedings should be regarded as civil only. Article 6 of the European Convention on Human Rights confers extra procedural rights on any person 'charged with a criminal offence'—the presumption of innocence, a right to legal aid, a right to confront witnesses, a right to an interpreter, and so forth. The European Court of Human Rights in Strasbourg has insisted that the question whether a person is 'charged with a criminal offence' is for the court to determine by looking at the substance of the situation. This amounts to what one might term an 'anti-subversion device', created by the Strasbourg Court to prevent governments from manipulating the criminal/civil boundary and thereby avoiding those extra procedural rights. The leading decisions establish that if (a) the proceedings are brought by a public authority, and (b) there is a culpability requirement, or (c) there are potentially severe consequences (such as imprisonment or a significant financial penalty), the person will be deemed to be 'charged with a criminal offence' and will be granted the full Article 6 protections.[9] The effect of deciding that particular proceedings are essentially criminal is not to alter the court in which the case should be heard, but to require the court to ensure that the defendant is accorded the full rights conferred by Article 6 on any person 'charged with a criminal offence'.[10] This is a development of particular significance, not least because it is the magnitude of the penalty (the possibility of imprisonment or a sizeable fine) that is a major factor inclining the court to declare the proceedings criminal. In this way, the idea of criminal law is firmly linked with the possibility of a significant sentence, which in turn calls for extra procedural protections for defendants.[11]

---

[5] But see n 22 below.

[6] *Practice Direction (Victim Personal Statements)* [2002] 1 Cr App R 8; the leading case is *Nunn* [1996] 2 Cr App R (S) 136.

[7] See further A. Ashworth, 'Rights, Responsibilities and Restorative Justice' (2002) 40 B J Crim 578.

[8] G. Williams, 'The Definition of a Crime' [1955] CLP 107, at 130.

[9] See e.g. *Engel v Netherlands* (1976) 1 EHRR 647, and *Benham v United Kingdom* (1996) 22 EHRR 293.

[10] For an English example, see *Han and Yau v Customs and Excise Commissioners* [2001] 1 WLR 2253.

[11] See further A. Ashworth, 'Is the Criminal Law a Lost Cause?' (2000) 116 LQR 225.

Why might governments wish to avoid allowing defendants to have the full protections appropriate to criminal proceedings? One reason is that they may wish to
use the criminal law to deal with relatively minor infractions, in a kind of stream-
lined procedure. Some European countries have instituted a separate system of
administrative offences, with low penalties, as a way of dealing swiftly, inexpen-
sively, effectively, and not unfairly with non-serious wrongdoing,[12] But English law
has not moved in that direction. Instead, the government has sought to develop a
different and more serious form of hybrid measure to regulate behaviour that is
considered 'anti-social' or that is thought to present an unacceptable risk to others.
Examples include anti-social behaviour orders, risk of sexual harm orders, foreign
travel restriction orders, and violent offender orders. These new measures, often
referred to as civil preventive orders, consist of two stages. The first is the imposition, by a court in civil proceedings, of an order prohibiting D from doing certain
things or going to certain places. The second is a criminal offence of failing without
reasonable excuse to comply with that order, usually carrying a maximum sentence of five years' imprisonment. The only element of the civil preventive order
that falls within the criminal law, according to the government and the judiciary,
is the offence of failure to comply. Even though the contents of that offence (i.e.
the prohibitions imposed on D) are determined in civil proceedings without the
protections of criminal procedure, the courts have not used their power to declare
that the two stages of proceedings are criminal in substance.[13] They have accepted
the government's device of de-coupling the two stages: the House of Lords recognized the potentially severe consequences for D of a breach of the prohibition(s),
but its only concession was the compromise of requiring the criminal (rather than
the civil) standard of proof in the civil proceedings.[14] The upshot is that a court sitting in civil proceedings can create a kind of personal criminal code for D, breach
of which renders him liable to a maximum punishment higher than that for many
ordinary criminal offences.

The best-known example of this is the anti-social behaviour order, or ASBO. It was
conceived as a means for tackling social problems that are undeniable in their effect
on the quality of others' lives, and it became the talisman of civil preventive orders
because the problem of witness intimidation and the focus of criminal proceedings
on a particular event (rather than on aggregate nuisance) was thought to render the
criminal law insufficiently effective. A court can only make an ASBO if satisfied
that D has acted in a manner likely to cause harassment, alarm or distress, and if

---

[12] Where there are separate procedures for administrative offences, fixed penalties, etc., it must be open
to the defendant to have the case heard in a criminal court (with all the safeguards) if desired: *Le Compte,
Van Leuven and De Meyere v Belgium* (1981) 4 EHRR 1.

[13] This is the power, exercised by the European Court of Human Rights, to treat the term 'criminal charge'
as having an 'autonomous meaning', i.e. the court looks at the substance of the proceedings and not at the
label placed upon it by the domestic legislature. See n 8 above.

[14] *R (McCann) v Manchester Crown Court; Clingham v Kensington and Chelsea London Borough Council*
[2003] 1 AC 787.

the prohibitions in the order are 'necessary' for the purpose of protecting persons from further anti-social acts by D (Crime and Disorder Act 1998, s 1, as amended). However, the prohibitions may include non-criminal or criminal conduct, they must last for at least two years, and about half of breach prosecutions result in imprisonment. This raises serious questions about whether this civil preventive order, and the way in which it uses the criminal law, is a lawful, fair or proportionate response to what is often—but certainly not always—conduct that may seriously diminish other citizens' quality of life.[15] More broadly, these orders may be regarded as one manifestation of a more general movement away from the paradigms of the criminal law, and the consequent side-lining the protections of criminal procedure. Thus the greater use of diversion, of fixed penalties, of summary trials, of hybrid civil-criminal processes, of strict liability offences, of incentives to plead guilty, and of preventive orders—all of these challenge the paradigm of the criminal law, and challenge the way it is traditionally presented.[16]

1.1 THE CONTOURS OF CRIMINAL LIABILITY

When we refer to criminal liability, what sort of conduct are we talking about? The answer may differ not only from one country to another, but also from one era to another in the same country. Thus in the last forty years there have been several changes in the boundaries of the law of sexual offences, and (for example) most homosexual encounters which were criminal in England before 1967 are not criminal now, whereas some forms of insider trading on the stock market and of the possession of indecent photographs have become criminal. There are certain serious wrongs which are criminal in most jurisdictions, but in general there is no straightforward moral or social test of whether conduct is criminal. The most reliable test is the formal one: is the conduct prohibited, on pain of conviction and sentence?

The contours of criminal liability may be considered under three headings: the range of offences; the scope of criminal liability; and the conditions of criminal liability. The *range* of criminal offences in England and Wales is enormous. There are violations of the person, including offences of causing death and wounding, sexual offences, certain public order offences, offences relating to safety standards at work and in sports stadiums, offences relating to firearms and other weapons, and serious road traffic offences. Then there are violations of general public interests, including

---

[15] See further E. Burney, *Making People Behave: Anti-Social Behaviour, Politics and Policy* (2005); S. Macdonald, 'A Suicidal Woman, Roaming Pigs and a Noisy Trampolinist: Reforming the ASBO's Definition of Anti-Social Behaviour' (2006) 69 MLR 183; A. Ashworth, 'Social Control and Anti-Social Behaviour: the Subversion of Human Rights?' (2004) 120 LQR 263; A. von Hirsch and A. P. Simester (eds), *Incivilities* (2007).

[16] See further A. Ashworth and L. Zedner, 'Defending the Criminal Law: Reflections on the Changing Character of Crime, Procedure and Sanctions' (2008) 2 *Criminal Law and Philosophy* 21.

offences against state security, offences against public decency, offences against the administration of justice, and various offences connected with public obligations such as the payment of taxes. A third major sphere of liability comprises violations of the environment and the proper conditions of life, including the various pollution offences, offences connected with health and purity standards, and minor offences of public order and public nuisance. Fourthly, there are violations of property interests, from crimes of damage and offences of theft and fraud, to offences of harassment of tenants and crimes of entering residential premises. And then there is a mass of financial, business, and industrial offences, often created in order to enforce a regulatory scheme, but many having maximum penalties as high as seven years' imprisonment. More will be said about these five major fields of criminal liability in Chapter 2. As in many other legal systems, there is a whole host of miscellaneous criminal prohibitions as well.

When we turn to the *scope* of criminal liability, we raise the question of the circumstances in which a person who does not actually cause one of the above harms may, nevertheless, be held criminally liable. In legal terms, the question has two dimensions: inchoate liability and criminal complicity. A crime is described as inchoate when the prohibited harm has not yet occurred. Several of the offences mentioned in the last paragraph are defined in terms of 'doing an act with intent to cause *X*', and they do not therefore require proof that the prohibited harm actually occurred. Additionally, there are the general inchoate offences of attempting to commit a crime (e.g. attempted murder), conspiring with one or more other people to commit a crime (e.g. conspiracy to rob), and encouraging or assisting crime (brought into force in October 2008). These offences broaden the scope of criminal liability considerably, by providing for the conviction of persons who merely try or plan to cause harm. Turning to criminal complicity, this doctrine is designed to ensure the conviction of a person who, without actually committing the full offence himself, plays a significant part in an offence committed by another. Thus a person may be convicted for aiding and abetting, counselling or procuring another to commit a crime, or for participating in a joint criminal venture during which another participant commits a more serious offence than planned.

The *conditions* to be fulfilled before an individual is convicted of an offence vary from one crime to another. There are many crimes which require only minimal fault or no personal fault at all. These are usually termed offences of 'strict liability': some of them are aimed at companies, but others (including many road traffic offences) are aimed at individuals. More of the traditional offences, which have been penalized by the common law of England for centuries, are said to require '*mens rea*'. This Latin term indicates, generally, that a person should not be convicted unless it can be proved that he intended to cause the harm, or that he knowingly risked the occurrence of the harm. The emphasis of these requirements has been upon the defendant's personal awareness of what was being done or omitted. However, neither the legislature nor the courts subscribe to a firm rule that any serious offence should require proof of *mens rea*: not only are most of the offences tried in magistrates' courts strict liability offences, but half of the offences triable in the Crown Court have at least one strict liability element.[17]

Beyond the *mens rea* or fault requirement, which may differ in its precise form from crime to crime, there is a range of possible defences to criminal liability, so that even people who intentionally inflict harms may be acquitted if they acted in self defence, whilst insane, whilst under duress, and so on.

The contours of the criminal law are thus determined by the interplay between the *range* of offences, the *scope* of liability, and the *conditions* of liability. Inevitably there are times when the discussion focuses on only one of the elements, but the relevance of the other two must always be kept in view if the discussion is not to lose perspective.

1.2 THE MACHINERY OF ENGLISH CRIMINAL LAW

The criminal courts in England and Wales are the magistrates' courts and the Crown Court. Those offences considered least serious are summary offences, triable only in the magistrates' courts. Those offences considered most serious are triable only on indictment, in the Crown Court. A large number of offences, such as theft and most burglaries, are 'triable either way', in a magistrates' court or the Crown Court. If a defendant decides to plead guilty to an 'either way' offence, the magistrates can proceed to sentence (or commit to the Crown Court for sentence) without further ado. If the defendant signifies an intention to plead not guilty, proceedings to determine the mode of trial are held before magistrates. The magistrates may decide (having heard representations from the prosecutor) that the case is so serious that it should be committed to the Crown Court for trial. If they decide not to commit it to the Crown Court, the defendant still has an absolute right to elect trial by jury. In practice a majority of 'either way' offences are dealt with in magistrates' courts, since neither the defendant nor the magistrates think Crown Court trial necessary, and the numbers would increase significantly if the maximum sentence that magistrates can impose for one offence were raised from six to twelve months.[18] However, the question of a defendant's 'right' to trial by jury is a perennial subject of debate, as we will see in section 1.4 below. Finally, it should be added that the great majority of prosecutions of persons under 18 are brought in Youth Courts, where hearings are less formal and take place before specially trained magistrates.

---

[17] A. Ashworth and M. Blake, 'The Presumption of Innocence in English Criminal Law' [1996] Crim LR 306.

[18] Criminal Justice Act 2003, s. 282, provides for this but no implementation date has been set.

1.3 THE SOURCES OF ENGLISH CRIMINAL LAW

The main source of English criminal law has been the common law, as developed through decisions of the courts and the works of such institutional writers as Coke and Hale in the seventeenth century, and Hawkins, Foster, and Blackstone in the eighteenth century. The bulk of English criminal law is now to be found in scattered statutes. There was a major consolidation of criminal legislation in 1861, and the Offences against the Person Act of that year remains the principal statute on that subject. In recent years Parliament has created a range of new crimes, from keeping a dangerous dog to stalking, from failing to comply with an anti-social behaviour order to intimidating witnesses. However, some offences are still governed by the common law and lack a statutory definition—most notably, murder, manslaughter, assault, and conspiracy to defraud. Many of the doctrines that determine the conditions of criminal liability are also still governed by the common law—not merely defences such as duress, intoxication, insanity, and automatism, but also basic concepts such as intention and recklessness.

The judges therefore retain a central place in the development of the criminal law. They seem to bear the major responsibility for developing the conditions and the scope of criminal liability, and also exert considerable influence on the shape of the criminal law through their interpretation of statutory offences. Moreover, the Human Rights Act 1998 bestowed on the judges further powers and duties. Section 6 requires them always to act compatibly with Convention rights; s 3 requires them to interpret statutory provisions, so far as is possible, in such a way as is compatible with Convention rights; and s 2 obliges them to take account of the jurisprudence of the European Court of Human Rights. The higher courts do have the power to make a 'declaration of incompatibility' if they cannot otherwise bring a statute into conformity with the Convention, but that power is exercised sparingly. Cases in which the courts have used their interpretive powers under the Human Rights Act will be signalled throughout the book.[19] The Convention has not had as large an effect on the criminal law as upon criminal procedure and evidence, but there are already several judicial decisions in which the Human Rights Act has made a difference.

Also of significance is European Community law, not least because it has direct effect in this country and thus (unlike the ECHR) automatically takes precedence over domestic laws. Where a rule of English criminal law unjustifiably curtails a right conferred by Community law (such as the free movement of goods), the domestic law is disapplied and the defendant should not be convicted. European Community law has not yet had great effects on English criminal law, particularly the more serious offences which occupy much of the discussion in this book, but its potential as a source of liability and of defences should not be overlooked.[20]

---

[19] For more detailed treatment, see B. Emmerson, A. Ashworth and A. Macdonald (eds), *Human Rights and Criminal Justice* (2nd edn., 2007), particularly chs 8, 10 and 11.

[20] See further E. Baker, 'Taking European Criminal Law Seriously' [1998] Crim LR 361, and S. Peers, *EU Justice and Home Affairs Law* (2nd edn., 2006), ch 8.

One obvious difference between English criminal law and that of most other European jurisdictions is the absence of a criminal code. The somewhat faltering steps taken towards the enactment of an English criminal code are described in Chapter 3.2 below. For the present, we must record that the absence of a criminal code reduces the internal consistency of English criminal law (because it has to be gathered from judicial decisions, scattered statutes and occasionally from the old institutional writers) and also makes it harder to locate the applicable law. The attraction of these practical arguments in favour of a code is powerful, but, as we shall see, there is controversy about which parts of the criminal law should be codified and in what way.

1.4 THE CRIMINAL LAW IN ACTION

It would be foolish to think that the criminal law as stated in the statutes and the textbooks reflects the way in which it is enforced in actual social situations. The key to answering the question of how the criminal law is likely to impinge on a person's activities lies in the discretion of the police and other law enforcement agents: they are not obliged to go out and look for offenders wherever they suspect that crimes are being committed; they are not obliged to prosecute every person against whom they have sufficient evidence. On the other hand, they cannot prosecute unless the offence charged is actually laid down by statute or at common law. So we must consider the interaction between the law itself and the practical operation of the criminal process if we are to understand the social reality of the criminal law.

Even before the discretion of law enforcement officers comes into play, there is often a decision to be taken by a member of the public as to whether to report a suspected offence. The British Crime Survey suggests that at least a half of all offences are not reported to the police,[21] often because they are thought to be too trivial, or because it is thought that the police would be unable to do anything constructive, or because it is thought that the police 'would not be interested'. Even where an assault results in hospital treatment, a significant proportion of victims fail to report the offence or at least to make a formal complaint.[22] Thus, if an offence is to have any chance of being recorded, either the victim or a witness must take the decision to report the offence to the authorities. About four-fifths of the offences which come to police attention are reported by the public. This means that people's (sometimes stereotyped) views on what forms of behaviour amount to criminal offences, and also on whether the police should be called, exert considerable influence on the cases entering the criminal

[21] C. Kershaw *et al.*, *Crime in England and Wales 2007–08* (Home Office Statistical Bulletin 07/08), 39, estimating that 42 per cent of crimes are reported to the police. The overall figure masks considerable variation: thefts of vehicles are the most likely to be reported (93 per cent), and theft from the person, vandalism and assault with no injury least likely (32 per cent, 35 per cent and 34 per cent in 2003–04).'

[22] See the research by C. Clarkson *et al.*, 'Assaults: the Relationship between Seriousness, Criminalisation and Punishment' [1994] Crim LR 4.

justice system. For this and various other reasons, many offences committed at work or in the home remain concealed from official eyes. As for the one-fifth of offences that come to light in other ways, most of these are observed or discovered by the police themselves. There are some crimes, such as drug-dealing and other so-called 'crimes without victims', which are unlikely to be reported and which the police have to go looking for. And there are other crimes, such as obstructing a police officer and some of the public order offences, which the police may use as a means of controlling situations—charging people who disobey police instructions about moving on, keeping quiet, etc.[23] In these contexts the police use the criminal law as a resource to reinforce their authority.

It will thus be seen that most police investigations of offences are 'reactive', that is, reacting to information from the public about possible offences. Only in a minority of cases do the police operate 'proactively'. Other law enforcement officials may have a larger proactive role. Her Majesty's Revenue and Customs investigate offences relating to taxation and smuggling. Various inspectorates are required to oversee the observance of legal standards in industry and commerce—the Health and Safety Executive (which includes seven inspectorates: Factory, Agriculture, Nuclear, Offshore, Mines, Railway, and Quarries), the Alkali Inspectorate, the Industrial Air Pollution Inspectorate, the Environmental Health Departments of local authorities, and so on. Although these inspectorates often react to specific complaints or accidents, much of their work involves visits to premises or building sites to check on compliance with the law. It is therefore proactive work: the number of offences coming to an inspectorate's attention is largely a reflection of the number of visits and inspections carried out, and the response depends on the general policies and specific working practices of that inspectorate.[24]

What happens when an offence has been reported to the police? In most cases the offence is recorded and the police may investigate it. However, the British Crime Survey suggests that about one-half of all incidents reported to the police as crimes are not recorded as such: sometimes the evidence is thought unconvincing, or the offence too minor, or the incident redefined as lost property rather than theft of property. Of those that are recorded as crimes, the police trace around 28 per cent to an offender or suspected offender. The proportion of offences thus detected is much higher for offences of violence (around one-half)—where the victim often sees and knows the offender—than for the offences where the perpetrator's identity will often be unknown (such as burglary, 13 per cent, and robbery, 20 per cent) and for offences that may be thought not to justify a great investment of police time and resources (e.g. criminal damage, 14 per cent).[25]

---

[23] See the findings of D. Brown and T. Ellis, *Policing Low-Level Disorder: Police Use of section 5 of the Public Order Act 1986* (Home Office Research Study No. 135, 1994).

[24] See K. Hawkins, *Law as Last Resort* (2002); B. Hutter, *Compliance: Regulation and Environment* (1997); and B. Hutter, *Regulation and Risk: Occupational Health and Safety on the Railways* (2001).

[25] Kershaw *et al.*, above n 21, 169.

When the police find a suspect, they will invariably try to question this person. The Police and Criminal Evidence Act 1984 and its Codes of Practice require investigators to follow certain procedures before and during any interrogation, including notifying suspects of the right to a free and private consultation with a lawyer. The tape recording of suspects' statements is a routine feature at police stations, although statements (allegedly) made elsewhere remain admissible in evidence. Many of the miscarriages of justice uncovered in the late 1980s and early 1990s, after wrongly convicted people had spent many years in prison, stemmed from misconduct by the police at this stage of the investigation, including the falsification of notes of interviews. Following the quashing of convictions in the cases of the Guildford Four and the Birmingham Six, the Royal Commission on Criminal Justice was appointed in 1991 to examine the effectiveness of the criminal justice system. In its report the Royal Commission recognized that 'confessions which are later found to be false have led or contributed to serious miscarriages of justice',[26] but one of its key proposals, on preserving the right of silence, was rejected by the then government in favour of introducing a law that permits adverse inferences from failure to answer police questions.[27]

When the police have completed their questioning, they should release the suspect if they have insufficient evidence. If they believe they have sufficient evidence, or if the suspect has admitted guilt, there are choices to be made between prosecution, one of the forms of 'caution', and no further action. In recent years young offenders have usually received a caution, in the form of either a reprimand or a final warning under the Crime and Disorder Act 1998. For some years the policy had been to delay the entry of young people into the formal criminal justice system, in the belief that cautions were no less likely to be effective in preventing further offences, and that labelling a youth as a delinquent through formal court proceedings could reinforce that person's tendency to behave like a delinquent. The system of reprimands and warnings introduced by the 1998 Act was intended to be more rigorous and more demanding of young offenders (a warning also involves referring the young offender to a youth offending team, who may require the offender to participate in a scheme designed to prevent re-offending).[28] Thus, although the emphasis remains on the prevention of future offending, the rhetoric and the method changed to confronting offenders with their behaviour and helping them to take more responsibility for their actions.[29] The emphasis of the Youth Justice Board remains on diverting most young offenders away from court, and making use of alternative approaches such as restorative conferences that may bring the offender face to face with the victim.[30] The proportion

[26] Royal Commission on Criminal Justice, *Report* (Cm 2263 (1993)), 57.

[27] Sections 34–7 of the Criminal Justice and Public Order Act 1994, the impact of which is discussed in A. Ashworth and M. Redmayne, *The Criminal Process* (3rd edn., 2005), ch 4.

[28] For discussion, see C. Ball, 'Youth Justice? Half a Century of Responses to Youth Offending' [2004] Crim LR 167.

[29] Home Office, *No More Excuses: a New Approach to Tackling Youth Crime in England and Wales* (Cm 3809 (1997)), 1.

[30] See further <www.youth-justice-board.gov.uk>.

of young offenders receiving reprimands or warnings rather than prosecution is around two-thirds for boys and four-fifths for girls in the 12–14 age group, while in the 15–17 age group the proportions are about 45 per cent for boys and some two-thirds for girls. For adults the police may also decide to caution an offender, but again the use of cautions has declined somewhat from its peak in the early 1990s, so that around 20 per cent of adult male offenders and one-third of adult female offenders receive a caution. National Standards encourage the police to prefer a formal caution to prosecution where the offence is relatively minor, where the offender is old, infirm, or suffering from mental disturbance, and in other situations where there is little blame. However, the system has now been changed by the advent of conditional cautions, introduced by the Criminal Justice Act 2003. The decision on whether to offer an offender a conditional caution is taken by the Crown Prosecution Service, in cases where there is both an admission by the offender and objectively sufficient evidence. The conditions specified may include the making of reparation or participation in a restorative justice process. The offender is required to sign a document that spells out the conditions and records his admission of the offence.[31] Substantial evidence of the operation of conditional cautions is eagerly awaited.

Standing in contrast to the preferred use of prosecutions for suspected adult offenders (as distinct from juveniles) is the long-standing preference for alternatives to prosecution among the various inspectorates and other public authorities, such as HM Revenue and Customs. Many of these agencies regard their main aim as securing compliance rather than convictions. The Environment Agency, for example, 'regards prevention as better than cure…. The purpose of enforcement is to ensure that preventative or remedial action is taken to protect the environment or to secure compliance with a regulatory system'.[32] Such agencies therefore tend to rely on informal and formal warnings as a means of putting pressure on companies, employers, taxpayers, and the like to conform to the law. The criminal law remains in the background, as the source of the pressure towards compliance which they are able to exert, and most of these agencies regard prosecution as a last resort. Thus, for example, the Revenue and Customs Prosecutions Office and its predecessor the Inland Revenue typically brought only a few hundred tax prosecutions each year, relying chiefly on warnings and on its power to impose civil penalties on tax-evaders.[33] In these contexts, then, the criminal law is very much in the background, and the criminal process is experienced by relatively few of those caught breaking the law.[34]

Where the police are involved, however, prosecution remains the normal response for persons aged 18 and over. The initial decision whether or not to charge is now taken under the 'statutory charging scheme' introduced by the Criminal Justice Act 2003. This means that, whereas previously it was the police who usually took this initial

---

[31] For fuller discussion, see Ashworth and Redmayne, above, n 27, ch 6.

[32] Environment Agency, *Enforcement and Prosecution Policy* (2003), at <www.environment-agency.gov.uk>.

[33] See J. Roording, 'The Punishment of Tax Fraud' [1996] Crim LR 240, and A. Sanders, 'Class Bias in Prosecutions' (1985) 24 Howard JCJ 176.

[34] See further Ashworth and Redmayne, above, n 27, 169–72.

decision, it is now formally the responsibility of the Crown Prosecution Service (CPS). Police and prosecutors work together at this stage, but it is now the CPS that takes the decision whether to charge and, if so, with what offence to charge the suspect.[35] One of the aspects to be considered is evidential sufficiency: is there enough evidence on each of the elements required to prove the offence, so that it can be said that there is a realistic prospect of conviction? This requires the prosecutor to consider both the amount of evidence available and its admissibility in court (e.g. whether there has been a breach of the Police and Criminal Evidence Act and its codes of practice). The second, related, factor is whether a prosecution would be in the public interest. There is a Code for Crown Prosecutors (latest version, 2004) to provide general guidance on this and other decisions which prosecutors must take, and there is detailed guidance on prosecution policy for particular types of offence.[36]

It will be apparent from the preceding paragraphs that the defendants and offences brought to court form a highly selective sample of all detected crimes. Those convicted in court are certainly a small sample of the whole: the Home Office has estimated that if one takes account of those offences not reported, not recorded, not cleared up, and cautioned rather than prosecuted, only some 2 or 3 per cent of crimes result in a conviction.[37] Although this rises to 10 per cent for crimes such as wounding, it would not be accurate to say that the cases brought to court involve the most serious offences and offenders, because:

(1) there are crimes for which a person under 18 would not be prosecuted whereas a person of 18 or over would be;

(2) fairly serious crimes committed in the home or in certain workplaces may sometimes not be reported or prosecuted,[38] whereas prosecution is often the normal response to less serious offences in the street; and

(3) some of the crimes of petty theft which are prosecuted are, by almost any measure, less serious than many crimes which HM Revenue and Customs or other regulatory agencies deal with by warnings, civil penalties, or other alternative methods.

What emerges from this is that adults suspected of committing 'traditional' offences outside their own home are much more likely to appear in court than adults known to have committed 'modern' offences such as tax evasion, pollution, having an unsafe workplace, and so on. Even leaving young people aside, then, court proceedings are a poor representation of the reality of crime in our society.

It will be evident, too, that it is not rules but discretionary decisions which characterize these early stages in the criminal process. Police decision-making is largely

---

[35] On the new arrangements, see I. Brownlee, 'The Statutory Charging Scheme in England and Wales: Towards a Unified Prosecution System?' [2004] Crim LR 896; more generally, see Ashworth and Redmayne, above, n 27, ch 7.

[36] This may be found at <www.cps.gov.uk>.

[37] Home Office, *Digest 4: Information on the Criminal Justice System in England and Wales* (1999), 29.

[38] See Ashworth and Redmayne, above, n 27, 187–90.

discretionary, structured only by the cautioning guidelines, local arrangements for dealing with young defendants, police force orders, and internal police supervision. As research into public order policing confirms, there are considerable variations in policy and practice, not just between police force areas but also among police divisions in the same force,[39] and this determines the nature and volume of cases placed before the CPS for consideration for prosecution. The same is largely true of the regulatory and other agencies which have the power to prosecute. Moreover, the elements of discretion do not stop with the decision whether or not to prosecute. A question of particular importance for our present purposes is that of determining what offence to charge. In some cases there is little choice, but there are other cases where the prosecutor can choose between a more serious and a less serious offence. If there is a prosecution for the higher offence, it is usually possible for a court to convict of a lesser offence if it does not find the higher offence proved. But this does not mean that prosecutors routinely try for the higher offence. If, for example, the lower offence is triable only summarily (i.e. in a magistrates' court), whereas the higher offence is 'triable either way' (i.e. in a magistrates' court or at the Crown Court), the prosecutor may prefer the lesser charge so as to keep the case in a magistrates' court—for various reasons, one of which may be the belief that a conviction is more likely if the case is tried by magistrates rather than by a jury.[40] If the sentencing powers of magistrates' courts are increased under the Criminal Justice Act 2003, it is likely that many more 'triable either way' cases will be heard in the magistrates' courts, although defendants retain an absolute right to elect trial in the Crown Court for such offences.

Whether the case is set down for trial in a magistrates' court or the Crown Court, the prosecution may reach an agreement with the defence to accept a plea of not guilty to the offence charged but guilty to a lesser offence, or not guilty to some offences charged and guilty to others. We have also noted that, where a defendant on an indictable charge signifies an intention to plead guilty, the magistrates' court may proceed to pass sentence (or may commit to the Crown Court for sentence). A guilty plea is often advantageous to the prosecutor, in the sense that a conviction is assured and the hazards of a trial (with the possibility that a key witness will not give evidence convincingly) are avoided. A guilty plea may also appear advantageous to the defendant, since the conviction may be for a lesser offence (or for fewer offences). The sentence should also be lower because of the guilty plea, as section 152 of the Criminal Justice Act 2003 requires. Guidelines issued by the Sentencing Guidelines Council establish a sliding scale of sentence reductions, running from a one-third discount for indicating a guilty plea at the earliest opportunity down to a one-tenth reduction for a guilty plea 'at the door of the court'.[41] These incentives could generate considerable pressure on a defendant to plead guilty even where innocence is maintained, if defence lawyers emphasize the strength of the evidence for the prosecution, etc., and there are clearly

---

[39] T. Bucke and Z. James, *Trespass and Protest: Policing under the Criminal Justice and Public Order Act 1994* (Home Office Research Study No. 190, 1998).

[40] Ashworth and Redmayne, above n 27, at 298; cf. Code for Crown Prosecutors, para. 7.

[41] Sentencing Guidelines Council, *Reduction in Sentence for a Guilty Plea: Revised Guideline* (2007).

some cases in which innocent persons feel driven to plead guilty.[42] Average prison sentences for those pleading guilty are around a third below those convicted after a trial—a striking difference. Moreover, the procedural incentives have been increased: the Criminal Justice Act 2003 gave defendants in the magistrates' courts the right to ask the court for an indication of whether the sentence will be custodial or non-custodial (the court is not obliged to give the indication), and a similar procedure has been introduced judicially into the Crown Court.[43]

Not only, then, are the cases prosecuted a selective sample of all crimes committed, but the offences for which convictions are recorded may sometimes underestimate the true seriousness of the crimes brought to court. It may be in the apparent best interests of both prosecution and defence to settle for conviction of a less serious offence. The way in which offences are defined may facilitate or constrain many of these decisions, and so the structure of the criminal law may have a greater direct influence at this point than at some earlier stages in the criminal process. However, the predominance of official discretion opens the way for other motivations, including bias and prejudice, to enter in. Although the ratio of male to female known offenders is around five to one, we have already seen that females are cautioned (rather than prosecuted) at a higher rate than men. The picture at the sentencing stage is rather complex, with some women receiving less severe sentences than comparable men, but some receiving disposals which may turn out to be more intrusive and therefore more severe.[44] There is also some evidence of racial discrimination in the pre-trial system,[45] although some of this is a form of structural bias stemming from the way in which the system imposes disincentives on those who elect Crown Court trial and who maintain a plea of not guilty.

This brief outline has, it is hoped, demonstrated some of the ways in which the criminal law in action differs from the law as declared in the statutes and in court decisions. Little has been said about the ways in which defence lawyers may sometimes construct the defence around their own working priorities as well as around reconstructed versions of the defendant's narrative,[46] but that, too, is a factor in the presentation and the outcome of cases. So far as official agencies are concerned, each case brought to court is the product of a system which is heavily reliant on victims and other members of the public for the detection of offenders and the provision of evidence,[47] and which leaves considerable discretion in the hands of the police, other law enforcement agencies, and the Crown Prosecution Service. We have seen that that discretion is exercised unevenly, in the sense that those who commit crimes on the

[42] For fuller discussion and references, see Ashworth and Redmayne, above, n 27, ch 10.

[43] See Criminal Justice Act 2003, Schedule 3, amending s. 20 of the Magistrates' Courts Act 1980; and *Goodyear* [2005] 3 All ER 117.

[44] The complexities are explored in C. Hedderman and L. Gelsthorpe (eds.), *Understanding the Sentencing of Women* (Home Office Research Study No. 170, 1997).

[45] C. Phillips and B. Bowling, 'Ethnicities, Racism, Crime and Criminal Justice' in M. Maguire, R. Morgan and R. Reiner (eds), *Oxford Handbook of Criminology* (4th edn., 2007).

[46] See generally, M. McConville *et al.*, *Standing Accused* (1994).

[47] See the fascinating study by P. Rock, *The Social World of an English Crown Court* (1993).

streets and in other public places are likely to be prosecuted, even for relatively minor incidents, whereas offenders of certain kinds ('white-collar') are rarely brought to court. This not only emphasizes that the law in practice is different from the law in the books. It also raises questions about priorities and social justice: should we not have a ranking of crimes that makes it clear which are the most serious and which are the least serious, with the greatest efforts directed at enforcement against those who perpetrate the most serious offences, and the strongest measures taken against those offenders?[48]

1.5 OUTLINE OF THE AIMS AND FUNCTIONS OF THE CRIMINAL LAW

Is the criminal law necessary at all? It has been suggested from time to time that law in general and criminal laws in particular are needed only in conflict-ridden societies, and that the establishment of a political system based on consensus would remove the sources of crime and, therefore, the phenomenon itself.[49] This view may be attacked for its simplistic assessment of the causes of crime, but it is sufficient for present purposes to state that no modern industrially developed country seems able to dispense with criminal law, and, indeed, that occasional instances of the breakdown of policing have led to increases in certain forms of criminal behaviour.[50] This suggests that one fundamental reason for having a criminal law backed by sanctions is deterrent or preventive: so long as its provisions are enforced with some regularity, it constitutes a standing disincentive to crime and reinforces those social conventions and other inhibitions which are already in place. Fundamental though this proposition is, it should not obscure the importance of two related propositions. One is that criminal prosecutions should not be regarded as a primary means of protecting individual and social interests. In terms of prevention, more can probably be achieved through various techniques of situational crime prevention,[51] social crime prevention, and general social and educational policies[52]—not least because relatively few offences lead to a court appearance and conviction. The other proposition is that the underlying deterrent rationale of the criminal law does not support the notion that changes in particular laws, or changes in sentencing levels, ought to be pursued for their deterrent

[48] See further A. Ashworth, 'Is the Criminal Law a Lost Cause?' (2000) 116 LQR 225.

[49] Anarchist theorists such as Godwin held a version of this view (see G. Woodcock, *Anarchism* (1962)), and according to Marxist theory the law would wither away on the attainment of perfect communism (see H. Collins, *Marxism and Law* (1982)).

[50] Usually cited in this connection are the police strikes in Liverpool in 1919, and Melbourne in 1918, and the incarceration of the Danish police force by the Nazis in 1944. Broadly speaking, property crimes (looting) tend to increase whereas sexual and violent crimes do not.

[51] See R. V. G. Clarke, *Situational Crime Prevention: Successful Case Studies* (2nd edn., 1997).

[52] See generally A. Crawford, 'Crime Reduction and Community Safety' in M. Maguire, R. Morgan, and R. Reiner (eds.), *The Oxford Handbook of Criminology* (4th edn., 2007), ch 26.

effects. The evidence on what is called 'marginal deterrence' is generally equivocal, and it cannot be assumed that creating a new crime or increasing the maximum punishment will lead—in a kind of hydraulic relationship—to a reduction in the incidence of that conduct.[53]

A primary justification for criminal law and sentencing is that offenders deserve punishment for their offences, and that it is therefore just (and not merely expedient) to provide that serious wrongs culpably inflicted should lead to censure and sanctions by the State. The justice of punishment for culpable and criminalized wrongdoing may be said to stem from the wrongdoer's disrespect for the value enshrined in the law, in the sense of a 'demonstrated unwillingness to be guided by that value in acting.'[54] But to speak of justice in this context raises wider questions of justification. It assumes that the applicable criminal law has an acceptable moral content and is the product of a sufficiently democratic political process. It also raises questions about the justice of punishing the types of people who tend to be convicted and sentenced— the unemployed and the otherwise disadvantaged. This is often seen as a particular drawback of sentencing systems that aspire to proportionality or 'just deserts'. Since 'proportionate' sentences are merely reinforcing existing social inequalities, this does not achieve justice so much as confirm injustice. The point is an important one, but it is an argument against most other rationales for sentencing, too. A deterrent theory seeks to reinforce the value structure inherent in the criminal law. A rehabilitative theory would attempt to mould offenders' behaviour towards compliance with the norms of the criminal law. A restorative theory might be concerned to achieve compensation or a reconciliation that restores the *status quo ante*. Moreover, a system based on desert and proportionality can be operated humanely, without escalation of penalties.[55]

The justification for criminal law and punishment should therefore be sought in two dimensions—as a deserved response to culpable wrongdoing, and as a necessary institution to deter such wrongdoing. The former suggests that the criminal law, being society's strongest form of official censure and punishment, should be concerned only with major wrongs, affecting central values and causing significant harms. We have already noted that this is not the case in practice: the criminal law is sometimes used against relatively minor kinds of harm, often because the police are available as a convenient means of enforcement. In practice, therefore, the reach of the criminal sanction is determined by a number of conflicting social, political, and historical factors. This applies chiefly to the *range* of offences, enlarged on occasion in response to a wave of political concern and without overall consideration of the proper limits of the criminal sanction (or of the European Convention on Human Rights): prominent examples are the Criminal Justice and Public Order Act 1994, the Prevention of Terrorism Act 2005, and the Serious Crime Act 2007. The *scope*

---

[53] See e.g. A. von Hirsch *et al.*, *Criminal Deterrence and Sentence Severity: an Analysis of Recent Research* (1999), and P. Robinson and J. Darley, 'Does Criminal Law Deter? A Behavioural Science Investigation' (2004) 24 OJLS 173.

[54] G. Lamond, 'What is a Crime?' (2007) 27 OJLS 609, at 622.

[55] See A. von Hirsch and A. Ashworth, *Proportionate Sentencing* (2005), chs 5 and 6.

of criminal liability also bears witness to similar conflicts (e.g. over the extent of the offence of conspiracy); the *conditions* of criminal liability barely conceal the conflicts of principle and policy which have shaped them throughout their years of development, with recurrent debate over the merits of fault requirements necessitating subjective awareness by the defendant, as against the justifications for objective standards of liability, based on what the reasonable person should have appreciated in the defendant's position.

1.6 THE CRIMINAL LAW AND SENTENCING

A person who has been found guilty of a criminal offence is liable to be sentenced by the court. A conviction may be bad enough in itself: it is a form of public censure, and many convictions (at least for non-motoring offences) make it difficult or impossible to obtain certain jobs or enter a profession. For most of the offences covered in this book, the sentence is likely to involve considerable deprivation, either of money or of liberty or both. The criminal law may therefore be said to open the way for coercive official sanctions against an offender. Indeed, we will see below that sentencing has considerable significance for the contours of criminal liability: when Parliament creates a crime it authorizes not merely the affixing of a label of censure on the perpetrator, but also the imposition of certain deprivations by means of sentence.

The range of sentences available to English courts, and the actual exercise of judicial discretion in imposing sentences, can be outlined only briefly here.[56] The law of sentencing was consolidated in the Powers of Criminal Courts (Sentencing) Act 2000, but has since been altered in major ways by the Criminal Justice Act 2003 and other legislation. In brief, an absolute or conditional discharge may be thought sufficient for the least serious crimes or where the defendant has very strong mitigation. For many offences a fine will be the normal punishment: the size of the fine should reflect the seriousness of the offence, adjusted in accordance with the means of the offender.[57] If the offence is serious enough to warrant it, the court may consider imposing a community sentence: that sentence may contain one or more of 12 separate requirements, including a requirement to do unpaid work, a requirement to undergo drug treatment, and a curfew reinforced by electronic monitoring.

The most severe sentence is a custodial one, and a custodial sentence should be imposed only where the offence or offences are so serious that neither a fine alone nor a community sentence can be justified.[58] The length of any custodial sentence 'must be for the shortest term…that in the opinion of the court is commensurate

---

[56] For fuller discussion, see A. Ashworth, *Sentencing and Criminal Justice* (4th edn., 2005; 5th edn, forthcoming 2009).

[57] Powers of Criminal Courts (Sentencing) Act 2000, s. 128.

[58] Criminal Justice Act 2003, s. 152(2).

with the seriousness of the offence'.[59] If the sentence is for less than a year, the court may suspend it and require the offender to comply with certain requirements during the supervision period. The Sentencing Guidelines Council, which is advised by the Sentencing Advisory Panel, has issued guidelines on the sentencing framework established by the 2003 Act, as well as on many other aspects of sentencing.[60] There are also many guideline judgments of the Court of Appeal, from the period before the creation of the Council in 2003. These are intended to guide the courts in setting the length of sentence for different types of offence. The high use of imprisonment continues to be a contentious issue: England and Wales have one of the highest rates of imprisonment in Europe, and in autumn 2008 the prison population stood at a record level of some 82,000 (compared with 42,000 in early 1993).

How necessary is an understanding of sentencing law and practice to a study of the criminal law? Ideally the criminal law would be studied in conjunction with the other elements of criminal justice with which it is so intimately linked in practice and in theory—prosecution policy and other aspects of pre-trial criminal process, the laws of evidence, and sentencing too.[61] This makes the case for two years of teaching in this field, or for four one-semester modules, to cover the ground. Given that this would be difficult to achieve in many institutions, because of other pressures on the curriculum, many criminal law teachers are left with a decision about the amount of sentencing or other matters to put into criminal law modules. At a minimum, the interactions between sentencing and criminal law must be kept in view. It is sentencing, largely, that gives the criminal law its bite, and so decisions on criminal liability should be viewed as decisions about the application of censure and coercion. An example of the impact of sentencing on the criminal law is that, as we shall see in Chapter 7 below, the shape of the law on murder and manslaughter has been influenced by the existence of the mandatory penalty for murder. Another area of interaction between criminal law and sentencing is where the courts or Parliament have taken a restrictive approach in defining defences to criminal liability, in the belief that circumstances which 'almost' amount to a defence might result in significant mitigation of sentence (e.g. some cases of duress and entrapment). On the other hand, courts have tended to adopt a much looser notion of responsibility at the sentencing stage than at the liability stage: for example, courts which refuse to accept social or childhood deprivation as the basis for a defence to criminal liability may be quite willing to accept it in mitigation of sentence.[62] Thus the criminal law itself proclaims individual responsibility for actions, maintaining strict standards of conduct and setting its face publicly against the idea that social or other circumstances can excuse behaviour, whilst at the sentencing stage courts

---

[59] Ibid., s. 153(2).

[60] Sentencing Guidelines Council, *Overarching Principles: Seriousness* (2004), and *New Sentences: Criminal Justice Act 2003* (2004), and generally at <www.sentencing-guidelines.gov.uk>.

[61] Cf. P. Alldridge, 'What's Wrong with the Traditional Criminal Law Course?' (1990) 10 *Legal Studies* 38.

[62] See below, Ch 6.8.

do recognize from time to time the exculpatory force of preceding or surrounding circumstances.[63]

The aims of sentencing are not simply part of the background of the criminal law: they have implications for the shape of the criminal law itself. Thus proportionality should be a key element in the structure of the criminal law. It is a major function of the criminal law not only to divide the criminal from the non-criminal, but also to grade offences and to label them proportionately. As Nils Jareborg expresses it, 'the threat of punishment is not only a conditional threat of a painful sanction. It is also an official expression of how negatively different kinds of action or omission are judged'.[64] At the level of judicial sentencing, the Criminal Justice Act 2003 requires courts to 'have regard to' some five different purposes of sentencing—punishment, deterrence, rehabilitation, public protection, and reparation.[65] Not only do these conflict among themselves, but government-sponsored research demonstrates, for example, that the evidence for the effectiveness of deterrent sentences is unpromising.[66] The Sentencing Guidelines Council has endeavoured to save sentencing practice from the inconsistency that a 'pick-and-mix' approach to the purposes of sentencing might produce by emphasizing that section 143(1) of the Act insists upon proportionality of sentencing. Thus proportionality should have a central role, not only at the legislative stage of grading offences in the criminal law, but also at the judicial stage of passing sentence in individual cases. Within 'desert' theory there is a distinction between two kinds of proportionality.[67] One is cardinal proportionality, which requires that the severity of the punishment be in proportion to the seriousness of the offence. Exactly what the level of sentences should be remains a matter for debate, taking account of criminological research and, it is submitted, of the principle of restraint in the use of custody. The second kind of proportionality, more important for our present purposes, is ordinal proportionality. This requires an assessment of the seriousness of the crime in relation to other forms of offending, so as to establish acceptable relativities. The precise meaning of 'seriousness' here will be explored in Chapters 3 and 5, for it represents a combination of the wrong or harm done or risked and of the culpability of the offender.

This book is intended as an exploration of principles of the criminal law. It does not purport to be a textbook, and does not treat all the parts of the criminal law. Nor does it attempt to convey a general description of the criminal law in action. There are perhaps over 10,000 offences in English criminal law, the bulk of them being offences of strict liability with relatively low penalties. Although strict liability offences are discussed in Chapter 5.5(a) and in other places, the focus of the book is upon offences with substantial penalties. In this book it is principles for offences and for defences that provide the vehicle of study. In Chapter 3, many of the principles which do or should inform the criminal law are drawn together for discussion: this is largely a normative

---

[63] See A. Norrie, *Crime, Reason and History* (2nd edn., 2001), ch 10.

[64] N. Jareborg, 'The Coherence of the Penal System', in his *Essays in Criminal Law* (1988).

[65] Criminal Justice Act 2003, s. 142(1).   [66] See references in n 53 above.

[67] See further A. von Hirsch and A. Ashworth, *Proportionate Sentencing* (2005), ch 9.

exercise, raising questions about what principles should or should not determine the boundaries of criminal liability. It does not purport to be descriptive or historical, although it gives considerable prominence to the European Convention on Human Rights as a source. On the other hand, any meaningful discussion of principles must be connected to the kinds of laws that have been and are introduced, and the book's approach of examining the law through principles begins in Chapter 2, where the approach to creating new crimes is discussed. The idea is to analyse essentially political decisions to create new crimes, in terms of a more principled approach to the reach of the criminal sanction. Principles which have a particular bearing on culpability and the conditions of liability are discussed in Chapters 4 to 6. They are kept in mind when analysing three different groups of offences in Chapters 7 to 9. They are also related to questions about the scope of criminal liability in Chapters 10 and 11.

There are also frequent references to research that has a bearing on criminal justice, to give some indication of the social context in which the criminal law operates. Much more coverage could be given to these contextual issues, such as enforcement policy, police powers, the pre-trial construction of cases, and sentencing, but the primary focus of this work is upon the consideration of doctrine. This means that the discussion of the criminal law is largely centred on appellate courts, as opposed to concentrating on the law as it is enforced by the police and others. There is an endeavour to recognize the constitutional responsibilities of the courts in developing the law and interpreting legislation. There is also an endeavour to remain alert to the implications for law enforcement of leaving areas of discretion when formulating laws: we saw in section 1.4 how wide this discretion often is, and how the selective policies of various enforcement agencies lead to a rather skewed sample of defendants appearing before the courts. But the centrepiece of this book is the doctrine of the criminal law, by which is meant the policies and social values which underlie decisions to increase or decrease the *range* of the criminal law, the principles and values which bear upon decisions about the *scope* of criminal liability, and the principles, policies, and values which relate to the *conditions* of criminal liability.

FURTHER READING

N. LACEY, 'Legal Constructions of Crime', in M. Maguire, R. Morgan and R. Reiner (eds), *Oxford Handbook of Criminology* (4th edn., 2007), ch 8.

A. ASHWORTH and L. ZEDNER, 'Defending the Criminal Law: Reflections on the Changing Character of Crime, Procedure and Sanctions', (2008) 2 *Criminal Law and Philosophy* 21.

G. LAMOND, 'What is a Crime?', (2007) 27 *Oxford JLS* 609.

2

CRIMINALIZATION

We have seen (Chapter 1.5) that a system of criminal law may be justified as a mechanism for the preservation of social order. As a type of law, its technique is condemnatory and censuring: it authorizes the infliction of state punishment, it requires a procedure that provides the defendant with certain safeguards, and it results in a conviction that gives D a criminal record. To criminalize a certain kind of conduct is to declare that it is a public wrong that should not be done, to institute a threat of punishment in order to supply a pragmatic reason for not doing it, and to censure those who nevertheless do it. This use of state power calls for justification—justification by reference to democratic principles, and justification in terms of sufficient reasons for invoking this coercive and censuring machinery against individual subjects. So serious are the potential consequences, and so significant the public censure, that the decision to criminalize conduct should not simply be made 'on balance'. It will be argued here, following Doug Husak,[1] that in a liberal state there is something equivalent to a right not to be punished, which should place the burden of proof firmly on those who would wish to turn non-criminal activity into an offence.

However, it is not argued or assumed here that there exists some objective benchmark of criminality, or some general theory which will enable us to tell whether or not certain conduct ought to be criminalized. The range of actual and potential crimes is so wide and varied that this seems unattainable. We should abandon:

'attempts to derive the content of the criminal law from a single master principle... [and] accept that debates about its scope will be more piecemeal, gradual affairs, more focused on particular offences (actual or suggested), and informed by a range of values, presumptions and considerations...'[2]

The chapter's purpose is to identify some general principles and values that, it is submitted, ought to be considered when deciding whether or not to make conduct

---

[1] D. Husak, *Overcriminalization* (2008).   [2] R. A. Duff, *Answering for Crime* (2007), 142–3.

criminal. Although it is true that the frontiers of criminal liability are not given but are historically and politically contingent, it remains important to strive to identify those interests that warrant the use of the criminal law and to refine notions such as harm and wrongdoing which play so prominent a part even in political discussions of these questions.

This chapter will focus on legislative decisions to extend or curtail the criminal law. Yet we must recall, as argued in Chapter 1 above, that the practical impact of the criminal law on citizens is determined not so much by the legislature as by the workings of the various law enforcement agents—chiefly police officers, but also officials from HM Revenue and Customs, the various statutory inspectorates, and so on. Thus the legislature may be said to provide the tools, resources, or authority for law enforcement agents when it creates a criminal offence, but decisions about when to invoke and when not to invoke the available powers are taken by enforcement officers. The exercise of discretionary power therefore provides the key to practical instances of criminalization.

The chapter begins with a discussion of the two fundamental principles of autonomy and of welfare. It then develops the principle of minimalism, centred on the right not be subjected to punishment and also including consequentialist considerations such as not using the criminal law when it would be ineffective or counter-productive. Then follows a discussion of the harm principle and the principle of publicly wrongful conduct, leading to an assessment of the arguments for and against punishing 'immoral' behaviour, for including paternalistic laws, and for criminalization based on remote harms.

2.1 THE PRINCIPLE OF INDIVIDUAL AUTONOMY

One of the fundamental concepts in the justification of criminal laws is the principle of individual autonomy—that each individual should be treated as responsible for his or her own behaviour. This principle has factual and normative elements that must be explored, briefly, in turn.

The factual element in autonomy is that individuals in general have the capacity and sufficient free will to make meaningful choices. Whether this is true cannot be demonstrated conclusively. Over the centuries the 'free will' argument has been contradicted by the 'determinist' claim that all human behaviour is determined by causes that ultimately each individual cannot control. There is an immense literature on these issues, which cannot be examined here.[3] Most philosophers arrive at compromise positions which enable them to accept the fundamental proposition that behaviour is not so determined that blame is generally unfair and inappropriate, and yet to accept that, in certain circumstances, behaviour may be so strongly determined (e.g. by threats

---

[3] For an accessible discussion see A. Kenny, *Freewill and Responsibility* (1978).

from another) that the normal presumption of free will may be displaced. Similar in many ways is the 'principle of alternative possibilities', according to which an individual may properly be held responsible for conduct only if he or she could have done otherwise.[4] In support of these approaches is the fact that most of everyday life is conducted on the basis of such beliefs in individual responsibility, and that in the absence of proof of determinism we should not abandon those assumptions of free will that pervade so many of our social practices. However, as Barbara Hudson has warned:

the notion of free will that is assumed in ideas of culpability…is a much stronger notion than that usually experienced by the poor and powerless. That individuals have choices is a basic legal assumption: that circumstances constrain choices is not. Legal reasoning seems unable to appreciate that the existential view of the world as an arena for acting out free choices is a perspective of the privileged, and that potential for self-actualization is far from apparent to those whose lives are constricted by material or ideological handicaps.[5]

This point may be conceded without gainsaying the fundamental assumption of free will, so long as the possibility of qualifications is recognized. Thus, for example, the capacities assumed by the law may not be present in those who are too young or who are mentally disordered. These capacities relate to what R. A. Duff terms the 'preconditions of criminal liability', preconditions that he goes on to connect with the ability to participate in a trial as a communicative enterprise.[6] The general assumption is thus that sane adults may properly be held liable for their conduct and for matters within their control, except in so far as they can point to some excuse for their conduct—for example, duress, mistake, or even social deprivation, as discussed in Chapter 6.

No less important a part of the principle of autonomy is its normative element: that individuals should be respected and treated as agents capable of choosing their acts and omissions, and that without recognizing individuals as capable of independent agency they could hardly be regarded as moral persons.[7] Some such principles lie at the centre of most liberal political theory, and can be found, for example, in Ronald Dworkin's principle that each individual is entitled to equal concern and respect.[8] The principle of autonomy assigns great importance to liberty and individual rights in any discussion of what the state ought to do in a given situation. Indeed, a major part of its thrust is that individuals should be protected from official censure, through the criminal law, unless they can be shown to have chosen the conduct for which they are being held liable.[9] This, as we shall see in section 2.3 below, is a central element in the

---

[4] For critical discussion see e.g. J. Fischer, 'Responsibility and Control' (1982) 79 Journal of Philosophy 24.

[5] B. Hudson, 'Punishing the Poor: a Critique of the Dominance of Legal Reasoning in Penal Policy and Practice', in A. Duff et al. (eds.), Penal Theory and Practice (1994), 302.

[6] R. A. Duff, 'Law, Language and Community: Some Preconditions of Criminal Liability' (1998) 18 Oxford JLS 189; see also the concept of 'moral autonomy', developed by J. Gardner, 'On the General Part of Criminal Law', in R. A. Duff (ed.), Philosophy and the Criminal Law (1998), 239–44.

[7] See D. N. MacCormick, Legal Right and Social Democracy (1982), 23–4.

[8] R. Dworkin, Taking Rights Seriously (1977), 180.

[9] For the argument that this aspect of autonomy (which he terms 'personal autonomy') does not presuppose what I term the factual element in autonomy see Gardner, 'On the General Part', 241.

'defensive' approach to criminalization advanced by Nils Jareborg and others, insisting on the importance of protecting individuals from undue state power.[10] We will also see that H. L. A. Hart's famous principle, that an individual should not be held criminally liable unless he had the capacity and a fair opportunity to do otherwise, is grounded in the primary importance of individual autonomy.[11] On the other hand, returning to the scope of criminalization, this emphasis on individual choice militates against creating offences based on paternalistic grounds, as argued in section 2.5 below. If autonomy is to be respected, the State should leave individuals to decide for themselves and should not take decisions 'in their best interests'.

In liberal theory, the principle of autonomy goes much further than this. Thus Joel Feinberg, towards the end of his discussion of autonomy, states that:

the most basic autonomy-right is the right to decide how one is to live one's life, in particular how to make the critical life-decisions—what courses of study to take, what skills and virtues to cultivate, what career to enter, whom or whether to marry, which church if any to join, whether to have children, and so on.[12]

The difficulty is to decide how far this is to be taken. Whilst the principle of autonomy gives welcome strength to the protection of individual interests against collective and State interests, it seems less convincing in other respects. The question 'whose autonomy?' must always be asked: the criminal law is often claimed to be neutral, and yet certain forms of bias—such as gender bias[13]—may be evident in the law's assumptions and reasoning. In some of its formulations the principle of autonomy pays little or no attention to the social context in which all of us are brought up (which may both restrict and facilitate the pursuit of certain desired ends) and the context of powerlessness in which many have to live.[14] The idea that individuals should be free to choose what to do cannot be sustained without wide-ranging qualifications. A developed autonomy-based theory should find a central place for certain collective goals, seen as creating the necessary conditions for maximum autonomy. Thus Joseph Raz argues that:

Three main features characterize the autonomy-based doctrine of freedom. *First*, its primary concern is the promotion and protection of positive freedom which is understood as the capacity for autonomy, consisting of the availability of an adequate range of options, and of the mental abilities necessary for an autonomous life. *Second*, the state has the duty not merely to prevent the denial of freedom, but also to promote it by creating the conditions of autonomy. *Third*, one may not pursue any goal by means which infringe people's autonomy unless such action is justified by the need to protect or promote the autonomy of those people or of others.[15]

---

[10] See section 2.4 below.

[11] H. L. A. Hart, *Punishment and Responsibility* (2nd edn., 2008), discussed in Ch 6.

[12] J. Feinberg, *Harm to Self* (1986), 54; cf. his extensive discussion of autonomy in chs 17, 18, and 19 of that work.

[13] N. Lacey, *Unspeakable Subjects* (1998), 4–14; for an example, see provocation, discussed in Ch 7.4(b) below.

[14] See the quotation from Hudson, above, n 5.   [15] J. Raz, *The Morality of Freedom* (1986), 425.

This third feature proposes a minimalist approach to the use of the criminal law, and all three features reappear when we consider the principle of welfare.

2.2 THE PRINCIPLE OF WELFARE

We have seen that an individualist principle of autonomy is too limited, and that Raz and others have therefore developed an approach which emphasizes the State's obligation to create the social conditions necessary for the exercise of full autonomy by individual citizens.[16] Modern communitarian theorists have gone further, often emphasizing the centrality of collective goals. Thus Nicola Lacey describes the principle of welfare as including 'the fulfilment of certain basic interests such as maintaining one's personal safety, health and capacity to pursue one's chosen life plan'.[17] The specification of the interests to be thus protected should be a matter for democratic (participatory) decision-making: this means both that the interests will be objectively determined, not just according to the preference of each individual, and also that individuals whose preferences are at odds with those of the majority will lose out. Both of these are familiar features of social life. But much depends on how the notion of 'community' is developed. It ought to respond to the problems of differential power and privilege raised by Hudson.[18] The danger is that the notion of 'community' may sometimes be invoked in support of policies emphasizing public safety and the need for greater measures to ensure security: much as it is important to pursue collective goals such as environmental protection, public safety, and so on, the result may be to promote an idea of community without any special weighting of individual rights. This may produce harsh and intrusive policies—a tendency against which Lacey, in her development of communitarian perspectives, issues a strong warning.[19]

Whereas the principle of autonomy seems to suggest that individual rights should be given high priority in the legal structure, the principle of welfare recognizes the social context in which the law must operate and gives weight to collective goals.[20] Clearly there are conflicts between the two principles, but that may not always be the case. If the principle of autonomy is taken to require a form of positive liberty (freedom to pursue one's goals, etc.) rather than merely negative liberty (freedom from attack, etc.), then the principle of welfare may work towards the same end by ensuring that citizens benefit from the existence of facilities and structures which are protected, albeit in the last resort, by the criminal law. Some criminalization may therefore be accepted as the only justifiable means of upholding certain social practices as 'necessary for the general good'. Matters such as the obligation to state one's income accurately for the purpose of taxation or for the receipt of benefits can hardly be analysed convincingly

---

[16] Ibid., *passim*.   [17] N. Lacey, *State Punishment* (1988), 104.   [18] Text at n 5 above.

[19] E.g. N. Lacey, 'Community in Legal Theory: Idea, Ideal or Ideology?' (1996) 15 Studies in Law, Politics and Society 105.

[20] See Feinberg, *Harm to Self*, 37–47 for discussion.

in terms of individual autonomy: once a public decision has been made about the system to be adopted, it may be justifiable for at least egregious departures from these rules to be criminalized. The same may be said of laws relating to industrial safety, food safety, environmental protection, and so on. Although it remains to be decided whether violations of these norms should be criminalized or dealt with in some other way, the legitimacy of some criminalization on the basis of welfare as well as on the basis of autonomy cannot be put in doubt.[21] Those versions of the principle of autonomy which suggest that individuals should remain free to decide these matters according to their own preferences are not sustainable.

Yet the value of individual autonomy as a restraint upon collective and state action should not be overlooked. Decisions by the wider community may threaten basic interests of individuals, unless there is recognition of a set of protected rights. The significance of the Human Rights Act 1998 is that it imported into English law a set of protected rights—those declared in the European Convention. As we will see in Chapter 3.3 below, the Convention rights are weighted differently: some are almost absolute, some are strong rights (from which derogation may be permitted in defined circumstances), and others are qualified rights, defined in a way that allows certain restrictions on them where this is adjudged 'necessary in a democratic society'. In a sense, the group of qualified rights (and, to some extent, the interpretation of the other rights) demonstrates both the inevitability of conflicts between autonomy and welfare and the possibility of devising a procedure for 'resolving' those conflicts—although the satisfactoriness of the ECHR approach will be considered in Chapter 3.3 below and at appropriate points in later chapters. On any realistic view, the principles of autonomy and welfare have a degree of mutual interdependence, which should be recognized and structured.[22] However, that should not lead to a vague notion of 'balancing' the two principles. Rather, it should lead to the development of ways of prioritizing some rights, and of the structuring of public interest arguments so as to ensure that they meet criteria such as urgency, unavoidability, effectiveness and so forth.[23]

2.3 THE HARM PRINCIPLE AND PUBLIC WRONGS

The traditional starting point of any discussion of criminalization is the 'harm principle'. Its essence is that the State is justified in criminalizing any conduct that causes harm to others or creates an unacceptable risk of harm to others. John Stuart Mill's statement of the principle was that 'the only purpose for which power can be rightfully exercised over any member of a civilized community, against his will, is to prevent

---

[21] A. Brudner, 'Agency and Welfare in the Penal Law', in S. Shute, J. Gardner, and J. Horder, (eds.), *Action and Value in Criminal Law* (1993).

[22] Ibid.

[23] For further development in the context of criminal procedure, see A. Ashworth and M. Redmayne, *The Criminal Process* (3rd edn., 2005), ch 2.4.

harm to others'. Its main thrust is as a negative or limiting principle, having the objective of restricting the criminal law from penalizing conduct that is regarded as immoral
or otherwise unacceptable but which is not harmful to others.[24] It is developed by Joel
Feinberg in his detailed rejection of 'legal paternalism' and 'legal moralism' as sufficient reasons for criminalization.[25] However, one cannot proceed far without adopting
a definition of harm: can a satisfactory line be drawn through such things as physical
harm, harm to property, harm to feelings, and indirect harm? The question is both
fundamental and somewhat intractable. As Neil MacCormick argues:

'harm' is itself a morally loaded (and essentially contested) concept.... Nothing...could be
more obviously a moral question than the question whether individual interests in private
property are always, sometimes, or never legitimate. The issue of the justice of systems
of private property is a central one in the great clash of ideologies in the contemporary
world.[26]

Thus if we wish to define harm in terms of violations of people's legitimate interests,
we must remain conscious of the moral, cultural, and political nature of the interests
recognized in a particular system. Feinberg's definition of harm as 'those states of set-
back interest that are the consequence of wrongful acts or omissions of others'[27] does
not conclude these wider issues.[28]

   If the harm principle is primarily negative in its impact, by what route can we move
forward to consider some positive principles for criminalization? Feinberg's definition
includes both harm and wrongfulness, and it is necessary to attend to both of these
elements. When it comes to stating a positive version of the harm principle, Feinberg
proposes the following definition:

It is always a good reason in support of penal legislation that it would probably be effective in
preventing (eliminating, reducing) harm to persons other than the actor *and* there is probably no other means that is equally effective at no greater cost to other values.[29]

This formulation is an important step away from the apparently exclusionary phrase-
ology used by Mill ('the only purpose...')[30] and towards the identification of a range of
relevant reasons for and against criminalization. For Feinberg, other relevant matters
are the gravity of the possible harm, its degree of probability, and the social value of
the (otherwise dangerous) conduct.[31] His definition of the harm principle also incorporates, through its references to effectiveness and cost, some of the limiting principles
encompassed by the minimalist approach described at 2.4 below.

   The other important element, in addition to harm, is wrongfulness. It is not the
causing of harm that alone justifies criminalization, but the wrongful causing of

---

[24] J. Raz, 'Autonomy, Toleration and the Harm Principle', in R. Gavison (ed.), *Issues in Contemporary
Legal Philosophy* (1987).
[25] Feinberg, *Harm to Self*, and J. Feinberg, *Harmless Wrongdoing* (1988).
[26] MacCormick, *Legal Right and Social Democracy*, 29.   [27] J. Feinberg, *Harm to Others* (1984), 215.
[28] Ibid., 31–6.   [29] Ibid., 26.   [30] See Duff, *Answering for Crime* (2007), 123.
[31] Feinberg, *Harm to Others*, ch 5.

harm—wrongful in the sense of culpably assailing a person's interests, or abusing them by using them as a means to another's satisfaction. Thus Feinberg's elaboration of the concept of harm requires, and extends only to, 'setbacks of interests that are wrongs, and wrongs that are setbacks to interest.'[32] John Gardner and Stephen Shute go further in arguing that committing a wrong against another is the essence of most serious crimes, without the necessity to establish harm.[33] In their view, the 'pure' case of rape—victim unconscious, not knowing that the rape has occurred, and not suffering any physical or psychological effects—ought to be criminalized because of the serious wrong done to the victim, the 'sheer use' of the victim by the perpetrator. This poses a difficulty for the harm principle, claiming that it is dispensable as a reason for criminalizing an admittedly serious offence such as rape. It can easily be countered that this 'pure case' is a highly atypical form of rape, and that harm is in fact a prominent feature of most rapes and most other victimizing crimes. This response does not defeat the Gardner-Shute contention that the same reason (the wrong constituted by the sheer use of another) militates in favour of criminalizing all rapes, and that harm is not integral to that; it shifts from the normative to the empirical by suggesting that what most people recognize as the deep psychological and physical consequences of most rapes are what tell most strongly in favour of criminalizing it.

A third aspect, in addition to harmfulness and wrongfulness, is the public element in wrongs. One manifestation of this consists of those general obligations of citizens that are so important that the criminal sanction may be justified to reinforce them. A core of offences against state security may be justified on these grounds, as may some offences against the taxation and benefits system, so long as the limiting effect of the minimalist principle (see 2.4 below) is kept in view. These are public wrongs, inasmuch as the victim is not an individual but the community as a whole, and it is right that the more serious among them are considered suitable for criminalization—not least where the gain or advantage obtained is as great as, or greater than, that obtained in the typical offence with an individual victim. But it is to the latter kind of offence that we must now turn, and this is where the public element becomes problematic. How can we tell which wrongs done to individuals are sufficiently 'public' to warrant the condemnation of the criminal law? As Antony Duff argues, the answer lies not in an aspect of the wrong itself, but in the public valuation of the wrong:

We should interpret a 'public' wrong, not as a wrong that injures the public, but as one that properly concerns the public, ie the polity as a whole…A public wrong is thus a wrong against the polity as a whole, not just against the individual victim: given our identification with the victim as a fellow citizen, and our shared commitment to the values that the rapist violates, we must see the victim's wrong as also being our wrong.[34]

---

[32] Ibid., 36.

[33] J. Gardner and S. Shute, 'The Wrongness of Rape', reprinted as ch 1 of J. Gardner, *Offences and Defences* (2007).

[34] Duff, *Answering for Crime* (2007), 141–2.

The public element does not have anything to do with location: unkind remarks made to a friend in public would not 'concern the public' unless they tended to provoke a breach of the peace, and a very public breaking of a promise to attend a certain event may not be regarded as sufficiently important for the polity as a whole to be required to take action. Contrast those instances with domestic violence (e.g. a substantial beating) which, even if it occurs entirely in the private realm of a home, is a moral and social wrong that the community should regard as a wrong that ought to be pursued through the public channels of prosecution and trial.[35] Thus, as Grant Lamond has argued, the question is whether the community is appropriately responsible for punishing these wrongs.[36] The supporting argument here is presumably that the state should protect and promote the basic value of security and freedom from physical attack by prosecuting assaults wherever they occur (leaving aside questions of consent and its proper limits),[37] and that the fact that an assault occurs in a domestic context should make no difference to this. It does not follow from this that adultery is a good candidate for criminalization, harmful and wrongful though it may be in many instances, since the question is whether the value of marriage as an institution is so central and fundamental to the political community that the state is expected to prosecute through the criminal law those whose conduct threatens it.

One example of the public element of a wrong is the creation of racially and religiously aggravated offences of assault, harassment, and so forth.[38] Calling someone insulting names is not usually a criminal offence, but the rationale for these crimes (which provide for greater punishment when, *inter alia*, the offence is accompanied by racist or religious insults) is clearly connected with a belief that it is proper for the state to promote the basic value of racial tolerance and that this value is so significant as to justify criminalization. Thus these offences can be regarded as harmful public wrongs. However, the argument in this section does not suggest that there are sharp dividing lines that tell us whether or not certain conduct is sufficiently harmful, or sufficiently wrong, or has a sufficiently public element, to justify criminalization. Rather, the point is that these should be recognized as the appropriate lines of argument in support of a decision to criminalize. It is submitted in the next section that those arguing in favour of criminalization should bear the burden of proof, so the contention here is that the three elements identified above—harm, wrongdoing, and the public element—are what should be proved.

Finally, there is one respect in which the notion of criminalizing harmful public wrongs is less indeterminate, and that is where the state has a positive obligation to protect certain fundamental rights. In the English context this means positive obligations under the European Convention on Human Rights. Thus the right to life is guaranteed by Article 2, and states must ensure that they protect this by having, for

---

[35] Ibid., 141. See also V. Tadros, 'The Distinctiveness of Domestic Abuse', in R. A. Duff and S. P. Green (eds), *Defining Crimes* (2005).

[36] G. Lamond, 'What is a Crime?' (2007) 27 Oxford JLS 609.   [37] See Ch 8.3(f) below.

[38] Crime and Disorder Act 1998, ss 29–32.

example, appropriately restricted rules of self-defence.[39] Article 3 declares that no-one shall be subjected to torture or to inhuman or degrading treatment, and this requires states to ensure that their laws give adequate protection, for example, to children from physical beatings (of a certain magnitude) by their parents.[40] Article 8 declares the right to respect for private life, which includes sexuality and sexual relations, and this means that the criminal law ought not to discriminate against different forms of sexual orientation and that it should provide protection from sexual molestation, particularly for the young and mentally impaired.[41]

2.4 THE MINIMALIST APPROACH

The minimalist approach is based on a particular conception of the criminal law and its relationship to the principles of autonomy and welfare and to other forms of social control. Its four main components are a) the principle of respect for human rights, b) the right not to be subjected to state punishment, c) the principle that the criminal law should not be invoked unless other techniques are inappropriate, and d) the principle that conduct should not be criminalized if the effects of doing so would be as bad as, or worse than, not doing so. Each of these is now discussed in turn.

(a) THE PRINCIPLE OF RESPECT FOR HUMAN RIGHTS

The first point is that a minimalist approach to criminalization should respect human rights protections. Thus, for example, any criminal laws should respect freedom of expression, freedom of assembly and association, freedom of thought and religion, the right of privacy, and the right not to be discriminated against in any of those four rights. Under the European Convention this does not mean that no criminal law may curtail or abridge one of those rights: the first four rights (not the right against discrimination) are all qualified rights, which means that interference with them is permissible if it is 'necessary in a democratic society' for one of the stated purposes. Thus freedom of expression may be curtailed by an offence of sending a grossly offensive message through a public communication system,[42] by offences of speech likely to stir up racial or religious hatred,[43] or by offences of inciting violence. There are bound to be difficult borderline decisions to be taken, as where an evangelical Christian was convicted under section 5 of the Public Order Act 1986 for displaying a sign saying 'Stop Immorality, Stop Homosexuality, Stop Lesbianism', the court concluding that

---

[39] See Ch 4.6 below for the argument that English law fails in this respect.   [40] See Ch 4.7 below.

[41] See Ch 8.5, 8.6 and 8.7 below. These positive obligations and others are discussed in B. Emmerson, A. Ashworth and A. Macdonald (eds), *Human Rights and Criminal Justice* (2nd edn., 2007), ch 18.

[42] *DPP* v *Collins* [2007] 1 Cr App R 5.

[43] But note s. 29J of the Public Order Act 1986 (inserted by the Racial and Religious Hatred Act 2006), re-stating freedom of expression as a value.

the interference with his rights to freedom of religion and freedom of expression was justified by the disorder and violence it provoked.[44]

(b) THE RIGHT NOT TO BE PUNISHED

Husak argues that we should recognize a right not to be subjected to state punishment, and that this flows from the social significance of the public censure involved in conviction and from the sacrifice of human rights usually entailed by the imposition of punishment.[45] What this means in practice is that the decision to criminalize, and therefore to authorize punishment, should be recognized as being of a different order from many other legislative decisions. It is different from taxation, or from the creation of a regime of administrative regulation over a certain activity, important as those kinds of decision are. The element of public censure and the overriding of other rights means that strong justifications for criminalizing conduct are called for, and that the burden of proof should lie on those who would impose criminal liability. Moreover, this is not simply a threshold decision, of whether or not to criminalize. Much stronger justifications should be required where the offence is to be punishable with imprisonment,[46] in view of the potential deprivation of the right to liberty, and even stronger justifications where the maximum sentence of imprisonment is substantial. A particular concern in this regard is the maximum sentence of five years' imprisonment typically assigned to offences of breaching the terms of a civil preventive order, such as the anti-social behaviour order.[47]

(c) CRIMINALIZATION AS A LAST RESORT

The criminal law is a censuring and preventive mechanism, but there are others. Morality, social convention, and peer pressure are three informal sources of control, and in many spheres it seems preferable to leave the regulation of certain unwelcome behaviour to those forces. Within the law itself, there are at least two other major techniques in addition to criminalization: there is civil liability, best exemplified by the laws of tort and contract, and also there is administrative regulation, which includes such measures as licensing and franchising. What considerations should determine the choice of technique? The minimalist's answer, drawing on the considerations in (b) above, would be that the law's most coercive and condemnatory technique (criminalization) should be reserved for the most serious invasions of interests.[48] Less serious misconduct is more appropriately dealt with by the civil law, by administrative

---

[44] *DPP* v *Hammond* [2004] Crim LR 851; cf. *DPP* v *Redmond-Bate* [1999] Crim LR 998, where the Divisional Court held that the interference with rights was not justified.

[45] Husak, *Overcriminalization*, 95–101.

[46] S. Colb, 'Freedom from Incarceration: Why is this Right different from all other Rights?' (1994) 69 NYULR 781.

[47] Discussed on p. 4 above.

[48] A. Ashworth, 'Is the Criminal Law a Lost Cause?' (2000) 116 LQR 225.

regulation, or even by introducing a new category of non-criminal financial levies. This approach has a straightforward utilitarian foundation, traceable back to Jeremy Bentham's injunction not to punish 'where it must be inefficacious: where it cannot act so as to prevent the mischief' and 'where the mischief may be prevented...without it: that is, at a cheaper rate'.[49] The proper approach is therefore to assess whether a particular kind of misconduct is more appropriately dealt with through a regulatory framework, or by civil liability, or by a civil preventive order. The key question of appropriateness will depend on other factors such as the public element in the wrongdoing and the magnitude of the harm or wrong involved. But the thrust of the principle—known sometimes as the principle of subsidiarity, and applied so as to ensure that a right is not infringed where the objective of the interference could be secured in some other (lesser) way—is that the criminal law should be reserved as a legislative technique of last resort, used only for seriously wrongful or harmful conduct.

(d) THE PRINCIPLE OF NOT CRIMINALIZING WHERE THIS WOULD BE COUNTER-PRODUCTIVE

The fourth component of the minimalist approach is the principle of not creating a criminal offence, or set of offences, where this might cause greater social harm than leaving the conduct outside the criminal law, or where the prohibition is unlikely to be effective.[50] This view may be challenged on the ground that, if conduct is serious or harmful enough to justify criminalization, there is at least an important symbolic reason for declaring it to be criminal. It was suggested in section 2.1 above that the purposes of the criminal law are threefold—declaratory, preventive, and censuring. The declaratory purpose may reassure some and deter others. But even if the preventive purpose is largely unfulfilled (as, perhaps, with the 30 mph speed limit on urban roads), it may achieve *some* degree of prevention or reduction of the unwanted behaviour. Thus limited efficacy is not necessarily an argument against criminalization, although it provides a good reason to search for supplementary ways of controlling the unwanted conduct. Perhaps the restrictive policy against 'ineffective' laws is a version of the argument that the inclusion of unenforceable offences may bring the criminal law into disrepute: if so, it must be established that the patchy enforcement of speed limits, for example, really does diminish people's respect for other parts of the criminal law.[51] The other thrust of this restrictive principle is more powerful: if the criminalization of certain conduct, such as the possession of 'soft' drugs or various 'vice' offences, gives rise to social consequences that are hardly better than the mischief at which the laws aim, this militates strongly in favour of decriminalization. Thus drugs and vice laws may (i) produce active 'black markets', (ii) lead the police to adopt intrusive means of enforcement, (iii) allow the police to be selective in their enforcement, and

---

[49] J. Bentham, *Introduction to the Principles of Morals and Legislation* (1789), ch 13.
[50] See Husak, *Overcriminalization*, ch 3, and J. Schonsheck, *On Criminalization* (1994), ch 3.
[51] Cf. the assertions in S. Kadish, *Blame and Punishment* (1987), 23, 57.

(iv) lead to a degree of police corruption.[52] Prohibitions that have these consequences ought to be reconsidered: there is an ongoing debate about the propriety and wisdom of penalizing drug offences at all, and certainly so severely, when it appears that the law has little effect on the scale of drug use, importation and supply.[53] There are other objections against criminalizing drug use, although some may still argue (notably in relation to 'hard' drugs) that the case for criminalization outweighs the other social consequences.[54] This leads on to a more general argument for restraint in criminalization: that, since the enforcement of the criminal law is selective and tends to bear down most heavily on the least advantaged (the enforcement of drug laws is one reason for the disproportionately high number of non-white offenders in prison in Britain and the United States), these injustices should be kept to a minimum.

The effectiveness principle has sometimes been turned on its head, so as to produce the argument that where criminalization would be productive and cost-efficient it should be used. This has been an integral element in English criminal legislation for many years: it is rarely spelt out, but underlies the creation and re-enactment every year of scores of offences with low penalties, attached to statutes on sundry matters such as the Education Act 2005 and the Inquiries Act 2005. There are two arguments of principle against this policy, however. One is that culpability is central to the notion of wrongdoing, and most of these offences contain little or no culpability requirement. The other is the minimalist principle, also expressed in the *de minimis* limitation, that the criminal law should not be used for minor wrongs. Whilst some of these 'regulatory' offences are clearly not minor, others are. As noted in Chapter 1.5 above, English law lacks a general sanctioning system which does not involve the censure of the criminal law—a system of civil violations, infractions, or administrative wrongs. This makes it even more unlikely that decisions to criminalize are preceded by a vigorous examination of whether some non-criminal sanction would be sufficient. Small wonder that this inverted form of the effectiveness principle tends to lead to over-criminalization.

2.5 MORALLY WRONG BEHAVIOUR

If certain behaviour is regarded as morally wrong, is this a sufficient element of wrongfulness to come within the principles set out in 2.3 above? This question has been the subject of vigorous debates about the proper ambit of the criminal law in the realms of sexual morality. In the notable exchanges between Lord Devlin and

[52] See ibid., 22–8, for elaboration of this argument.

[53] See, e.g. D. Husak, *Drugs and Rights* (1992), Schonsheck, *On Criminalisation*, ch 6, and UK Drugs Policy Commission reports, 18 April 2007 and 30 July 2008.

[54] Cf. the argument of Peter Alldridge, in ch 7 of his *Relocating Criminal Law* (2000), to the effect that dealers who supply drugs to addicts are committing the wrong of exploitation. His conclusion, however, is that there are powerful counter-arguments to continued criminalization.

Professor Hart,[55] Devlin's argument was that a society is entitled to use the criminal law against behaviour which may threaten its existence; that there is a common morality which ensures the cohesion of society; that any deviation from this common morality is capable of affecting society injuriously; and that therefore it may be justifiable and necessary to penalize immoral behaviour.[56] In response, Devlin's opponents have broadly followed the approach of John Stuart Mill[57] in proclaiming that the main or only acceptable reason for criminalizing behaviour is that it causes harm to others, and that supposed 'immorality' is not a sufficient reason.

Lord Devlin's argument relies on an unacceptably loose concept of morality. He assumes that immorality is to be defined and measured according to the strength of feelings of ordinary people. If certain behaviour evokes feelings of intolerance, indignation, and disgust among ordinary members of society, that is a sufficient indication that the behaviour threatens the common morality and is therefore a proper object of the criminal law. The difficulty is that these feelings of ordinary people may be more the expression of prejudice than of moral judgement. If a person's reaction to certain behaviour is to be termed 'moral', it ought to be grounded in reasons as well as in feelings, and those reasons ought to be consistent with other standards used by that individual to judge personal behaviour. A theory about morality and the criminal law must be based on a defensible definition of morality, not one which confuses it with mere feelings of distaste and disgust.[58]

Is there, then, such a thing as a common morality? On core matters such as the use of force, fear, and fraud there may well be widely shared moral views, but on sexual matters the divergences may be great. Whose morals are to be a guide? Although Devlin maintained that morals and religion are inextricably joined, he did not argue that the teachings of the established church constitute the common morality. In this he was realistic: British society contains adherents of several religions, with diverse views on abortion, prostitution, euthanasia, and so forth, and there is a large proportion of the population which professes no religion (though its moral codes may bear some traces of religious teachings). Devlin proposed that the common morality could be discovered by assembling a group of ordinary citizens, in the form of a jury, and asking them to reach decisions on certain types of behaviour. However, not only would this method confound prejudices with moral judgements, but it might also fail to elicit agreement on some subjects such as homosexual behaviour and abortion.

Devlin's opponents have tended to be in the individualistic liberal tradition, linking Mill's harm principle with Kantian ethics. According to this view, the law should respect the autonomy of each individual above all; it should treat persons as individuals and allow each to pursue his or her own conception of the good life subject only to the minimum number of constraints necessary to secure the same freedom to

---

55 The principal essays written by the protagonists are collected in H. L. A. Hart, *Law, Liberty, and Morality* (1963), and P. Devlin, *The Enforcement of Morals* (1965).

56 See ch 1 of his *The Enforcement of Morals*.   57 John Stuart Mill, *On Liberty* (1859), *passim*.

58 Dworkin, *Taking Rights Seriously*, ch 10.

other individuals.[59] This is prominent in the minimalist approach to criminalization, and in a 'defensive' criminal law policy that treats the protection of individuals from state power as one of its principal objectives.

Similarly, Feinberg argues that 'paternalistic interference is offensive morally because it invades the realm of personal autonomy where each competent, responsible adult should reign supreme'.[60] Some liberals, when discussing whether or not to criminalize the non-wearing of seat-belts and crash-helmets, for example, might have recourse to the idea of 'harm to others': they might use Mill's principle to argue that the failure to wear seat-belts may result in harm to others, in the sense that the individuals involved may become a burden to others, creating human misery and public expenditure that are easily avoidable. It is doubtful whether this style of argument succeeds. Once the concept of harm is extended to cover indirect hardship to other individuals or to the State, Mill's principle is blunted and the possibilities for criminalization are enormous. Either one must qualify Mill by adopting the strong version of paternalism criticized by Feinberg, or one must recognize frankly that there is a competing principle at work here, such as the welfare principle described earlier. The welfare argument may be that it is strongly in the interests of the community, at a time when resources are limited, to avoid unnecessary expenditure on attending to the injuries of citizens who could protect themselves with little inconvenience. But does even that consideration argue for criminalization, as distinct from requiring them to pay for any medical treatment necessitated by their voluntary assumption of risk?

It is widely recognized that some paternalism is appropriate so as to ensure the protection of the young and the mentally disordered. The value of autonomy applies primarily to adults, and there are dangers in persons below the designated age of majority participating in heterosexual or homosexual activities, in drinking alcohol in public houses, in betting and gaming, etc. (In Britain this age varies according to the activity, and questions may be raised about the justification for this.) This principle of paternalism towards the vulnerable does not imply that all these activities are 'harmful': rather, it implies that they may have potentially far-reaching consequences for the individual concerned, and that only persons who have sufficient capacity should be allowed to take their own decisions about the potential risks.

An example of the adjustment of conflicting policies and principles is provided by the report of the Wolfenden Committee on Homosexual Offences and Prostitution in 1957.[61] The Committee followed Mill's approach in asserting that 'there must remain a realm of private morality and immorality which is, in brief and crude terms, not the law's business', but it maintained also that this principle must interact with the need

---

[59] See the discussion in section 2.1 above, and also W. Wilson, *Central Issues in Criminal Theory* (2002), ch 1.

[60] Feinberg, *Harmless Wrongdoing*, p. xvii, summarizing the argument developed in Feinberg, *Harm to Self*, chs 18 and 19. For a stimulating discussion in relation to the place of consent in criminal law see P. Roberts, 'Consent in the Criminal Law' (1997) 17 Oxford JLS 389; see also Ch 8.3(g) below.

[61] Cmnd. 257 (1957).

to protect the vulnerable against exploitation and corruption, and with the policy of protecting the citizen 'from what is offensive and injurious'. The protection of the vulnerable may be a justifiable form of paternalism, but what about protecting all citizens (adults and the young) from 'offence'?

This goes beyond protection from harm on Feinberg's definition, since individuals can hardly be said to have a stake in not being shocked or offended.[62] The idea of offensive behaviour draws a public–private distinction in respect of decency and shock to feelings; what adults do in private is not the law's business, so long as harm is not inflicted non-consensually, but what they do in the public domain may be the law's business if it is likely to give serious offence to the feelings of ordinary members of the public. Feinberg's 'offence principle' is that:

It is always a good reason in support of a proposed criminal prohibition that it is probably necessary to prevent serious offence to persons other than the actor and would probably be an effective means to that end if enacted.[63]

This is not just a traditional utilitarian balancing exercise. Feinberg limits his principle to 'serious offence', but both of these words suffer from considerable indeterminacy. Andrew von Hirsch and Andrew Simester argue that the Feinberg approach is over-inclusive (many things may cause serious offence), subjective, and not clearly connected with wrongdoing. They argue for a more objective benchmark, and suggest that the essence of the wrong involved in offensiveness lies in treating others with a gross lack of respect or consideration.[64] As with other principles, this one must be mediated by allowing other values to restrain criminalization. There should be a margin of social tolerance (being called a rude name should not be sufficient); conduct that is readily avoidable should be excluded (as where an area for nude bathing is indicated or well known); and the conduct should be immediately offensive, and not simply create a risk of subsequent offence.[65] How do these criteria apply? Homosexual acts between adult men in private have not been criminal since the Sexual Offences Act 1967, but homosexual acts in public places (e.g. public lavatories) remain criminal[66] on a public-decency or 'offensiveness' rationale, although it is not clear whether the 'ready avoidability' principle is properly applied here. Another example of the public-decency and offensiveness rationale may be found in the Indecent Displays (Control) Act 1981, which criminalizes the display of any indecent matter which is visible from a public place: here, the questions concern the grossness of the lack of consideration, the margin of social tolerance, and of course the possibility that vulnerable people (particularly the young) will be exposed to the display.

---

[62] See n 29 above.   [63] Feinberg, *Offense to Others*, ch 7.

[64] A. von Hirsch and A. P. Simester, 'Penalising Offensive Behaviour' in A. von Hirsch and A. P. Simester (eds), *Incivilities: Regulating Offensive Behaviour* (2006), 120.

[65] Ibid., 124–30.   [66] Sexual Offences Act 2003, s. 71.

2.6 REMOTE HARMS

One kind of justification offered for criminalization is that certain conduct may create an opportunity for serious harm to be caused subsequently. The preventive function of the criminal law may be interpreted as licensing the state to criminalize conduct that creates the risk of a certain harm: the conduct may not be wrongful or harmful in itself, but it is criminalized because of the consequences that may flow from it. The nature of the risk is explicit when the offence is dangerous driving or careless driving. It is implicit, and more remote, in an offence such as speeding—the prohibition on driving a motor vehicle above the applicable speed limit, a law that aims to reduce the risk of death, injury, and damage to property. Another example is a prohibition of conduct based on what the individual may do subsequently, e.g. criminalizing the possession of knives or firearms on the basis that they may be used to kill, injure, or threaten unlawfully. A further example is a prohibition of conduct based on what others may be led to do subsequently, e.g. criminalizing certain processions or public demonstrations because of what others might be tempted to do in response.

Two objections to criminalizing remote harms stand out. One is that normal causal principles appear not to support liability: if conduct is criminalized on account of what it might lead another person to do, such an intervening voluntary act should relieve the original actor of criminal liability, and so it is the person who does that voluntary act who should be penalized. The other objection is that conduct that is not harmful in itself should not attract liability, or (as with the inchoate offences) at least not unless it is accompanied by an intention to encourage, assist, or commit a substantive offence.[67] This would rule out most offences of possession, which do not require evidence of any further intent. In particular, cases in which the occurrence of harm depends on a further decision by the actor or by another (e.g. to fire the gun unlawfully) are unsuitable for criminalization.

In the context of many modern societies, however, it would seem foolish to have no offences of unregistered possession of a firearm or of explosives. The social context could be used as a basis for arguing that abstaining from possession of certain dangerous articles like guns and explosives ought to be recognized as a duty of citizenship. It is, of course, a curtailment of liberty. So are all other criminal prohibitions. The question is whether it is *justified* as a curtailment of liberty to have a registration system reinforced by some criminal offences, and in answering this question one should have regard to the magnitude of the harm as well as the likelihood of its occurrence. It is considerations of that nature which tend to support offences of speeding and of drunk driving. Of course it would be possible to have only advisory speed limits, or advisory limits of consumption of alcohol or drugs, and to reserve criminal prosecution for cases where damage, injury or death is negligently caused. But in terms of prevention that may be regarded as disastrous, on the ground that far more people would be likely

---

[67] On the new inchoate offences of encouraging and assisting crime, see Ch 11.7 below.

to exceed the relevant limits and far more preventable victimization would probably occur. Thus the concern for people's welfare, in the context of the great harm that may result if no criminal laws are in place, tells in favour of criminalization.

2.7 CONCLUSIONS AND APPLICATIONS

The main determinants of criminalization continue to be political opportunism and power, both linked to the prevailing political culture of the country. Though an attempt has been made in this chapter to identify some general principles, it remains true that key concepts such as harm, wrongdoing and offensiveness may tend to melt into the political ideologies of the time, as MacCormick argues:

resort to the criminal law is always parasitic on or ancillary to an established legal order of rights and duties in the spheres of private law and public law. Such an order of rights and duties (et cetera) has to be founded on some (however muddled and patchwork) conception of a just ordering of society. The interests protected from invasion by criminal laws are interests legitimated by a given conception of a just social order. And the harm principle would be vacuous without some such conception of legitimate interests. Hence, naturally, the laws which are justified by the harm principle on a given interpretation of 'harm' do indeed coincide with widely held precepts against 'harmful' behaviour. But they do not merely coincide; the criminal law in so far as it is concerned with fending off harmful behaviour is necessarily geared to protection of what are legitimate interests according to a certain dominant political morality.[68]

Without overlooking the politically contingent nature of much criminal legislation, it is still appropriate to discuss the values and principles that ought to be relevant to criminalization decisions, since such considerations appear to play some part at various stages in the generation and refinement of reform proposals. In these concluding remarks, the approach of the chapter will be summarized, and then the possible application of the approach to certain public order offences, terrorism offences and to the enforcement of civil preventive orders will be discussed.

The approach here has been developed for a broadly liberal democratic society, and for that reason the principles of autonomy and welfare were identified as the leading considerations. No attempt was made to conceal the fact that they may conflict in many situations, and that a key issue will always be the relative weighting of those two principles. Nonetheless, the chapter went on to set out a number of other principles and values, some of them flowing from the nature of criminal law and punishment, some having social derivations. It was argued that the building blocks of criminalization decisions are that the conduct in question must be harmful, wrongful, and of public concern—three key elements which are contestable in their application to given facts, but which are crucial dimensions. Given the censuring purpose of conviction

---

[68] MacCormick, *Legal Right and Social Democracy*, 30.

and the probability of punishment, it was argued that the approach to criminalization ought to be minimalist. This means:

(a) respecting human rights when enacting criminal laws

(b) recognizing a right not to be subjected to state punishment and the rights-deprivations it often involves

(c) regarding the criminal law as a technique of last resort, after less invasive and stigmatic measures have been dismissed as inappropriate and

(d) stepping back from criminalization if its effects are likely to be worse, or no better, than adopting some other approach.

There may be a limited role for paternalistic offences, to protect the vulnerable. There may also be a limited (preventive) role for the criminalization of conduct that is more or less remotely connected with the occurrence of harmful consequences. Lastly, whenever conduct is held to be a sufficiently harmful public wrong to justify criminalization, the maximum penalty to which it exposes an offender must be proportionate to culpability and to the seriousness of the interests violated.

Fundamental to many arguments about criminalization and decriminalization are evidential issues, some of which are empirical, others predictive. Thus, for example, the principled arguments in the debate about drugs and the criminal sanction must be related to empirical evidence of the effects of drug-taking compared with the effects of alcohol, tobacco, and similar substances, and empirical evidence about the nature and volume of drug-related crimes; the debate must also be related to properly-founded predictions of the effects of changing the law. This is only one example: the evidential foundations of arguments for criminalization and decriminalization should always be addressed.

No less necessary is a properly-based prediction of the practical effect of introducing new offences, particularly in terms of selective enforcement and creative adaptation. Selective enforcement may mean that the impact falls disproportionately on certain sections of society: traditional patterns of policing may suggest this, and there is some evidence that s 5 of the Public Order Act 1986 (which criminalizes disorderly, threatening, abusive or insulting behaviour likely to cause harassment, alarm or distress) has been invoked disproportionately against members of racial minorities.[69] Creative adaptation has also been apparent as the police have reinterpreted s 5 in a way not anticipated by the legislators, using it to penalize those who swear at them, and occasions of similar adaptation were discovered in the research into the use of the public order offences introduced by Part V of the Criminal Justice and Public Order Act 1994.[70] It may be replied that these are problems for the control of discretion among police and prosecutors, not for the legislature at the stage of criminalization.

[69] D. Brown and T. Ellis, *Policing Low-Level Disorder: Police Use of Section 5 of the Public Order Act 1986* (1994), 28–34.

[70] T. Bucke and Z. James, *Trespass and Protest: Policing under the Criminal Justice and Public Order Act 1994* (1998).

However, even if the objectionable vagueness of offences such as s 5 is left aside, the question of enforcement cannot be dismissed too readily. Unless there is a prospect of rapid and significant change in on-the-ground policing, the theoretical possibility of greater control of police discretion cannot be a telling counter-argument to overbroad offences.

The Terrorism Act 2006 contains new offences extending the ambit of the criminal law.[71] How would the principles set out in this chapter apply to them? Let us first focus on the offence in section 1(2) of publishing a statement that is likely to be understood as glorifying acts of terrorism, intending to encourage others or reckless as to whether others are encouraged to commit or prepare for such acts. Several features of this offence give grounds for concern, despite the seriousness of the harm against which it is designed to protect. First, it is an inchoate offence aimed at preventing a remote harm. The offence consists of publishing a statement in the knowledge that others may be encouraged: there is no requirement that anyone is encouraged, let alone that anyone actually carries out any of the preparatory acts mentioned (s 1(5)(b)). Those acts would, on traditional principles, be the responsibility of the person carrying them out (although the encourager would also be liable).[72] Secondly, the offence does not require proof of an intention to encourage the commission of these further acts: recklessness (knowing that there is a risk of encouraging) is sufficient. That ties in with the provisions making it clear that it is enough if the statement is 'likely to be understood by some members of the public' as an encouragement (s 1(1)) and that it is enough if members of the public 'could reasonably be expected to infer that what is being glorified is being glorified as conduct that should be emulated by them in existing circumstances' (s 1(3)(b)). In other words, unlike almost all other offences in the inchoate mode, proof of intent is not required, and there are objective elements in the definition.

Two other concerns are that the key term 'glorifies' remains vague, despite the explanation in s 20(2) that it 'includes any form of praise or celebration'; and that the significance of this vagueness is enhanced by the maximum penalty for this inchoate and remote offence, which stands at seven years' imprisonment. The harm against which the offence is designed to guard is a major harm, which could be a terrorist attack causing death; the key question is how much this should be discounted in view of the considerable distance between this offence and the actual taking of steps to cause such a harm. The analysis of this offence also demonstrates how the justifications for criminalization ought to be stronger as the maximum penalty increases. It is one thing to take the decision to criminalize, and quite another to authorize imprisonment, especially for a substantial period.

Also introduced by the Terrorism Act 2006 is the offence of preparation of terrorist acts. Section 5 makes engaging in any conduct in preparation for committing acts or

---

[71] See the analysis by V. Tadros, 'Justice and Terrorism' (2007) 11 New Crim LR 658.

[72] See the offences of 'encouraging and assisting crime' introduced by Part 2 of the Serious Crime Act 2007, and discussed in Ch 11.7 below.

terrorism, or assisting another to commit such acts, with intent to commit or assist such acts, punishable with life imprisonment. The effect of this offence is to extend the ambit of attempts liability much further: whereas a criminal attempt requires conduct that is 'more than merely preparatory' to the commission of the substantive offence, this offence is committed if any conduct that can be viewed as preparatory is engaged in. The offence does require intention, and neither recklessness nor any other objective element is part of the definition. But, despite the enormous distance between the preparatory act and the causing of any harm, the maximum penalty is the highest in English law, life imprisonment.

Lastly, we saw that the minimalist approach includes principle (c), which regards the criminal law as a technique of last resort, after less invasive and stigmatic measures have been dismissed as inappropriate. Discussions of this in England and Wales are blunted by the absence of any established alternative form of regulating unwanted conduct. Although a few particular agencies have alternative methods at their disposal, English law knows no general category of 'infractions', 'violations', 'civil offences', or 'administrative offences'. There is also no unitary machinery for enforcing or adjudicating upon such a category of wrongs. In theory, the criminal law ought to be divided from civil sanctions and administrative regulation by reference to its censuring function, and by the minimalist principle. An important aspect of this is that, if a criminal offence is to be created, then the concomitants are proper safeguards for the defendant, at least those that Article 6 of the Convention treats as the minimum. If it is decided to control certain conduct by way of either regulatory or civil mechanisms, then the penalties ought to be kept very low; otherwise, the mechanism will rightly be held to be 'criminal' in substance, and all the Article 6 safeguards will have to be respected. However, the government has exploited a gap in the system of protections: the anti-social behaviour order, introduced by s 1 of the Crime and Disorder Act 1998, may be made in civil proceedings, on the application of the local authority, a social landlord or the police, and has been held not to be a 'criminal charge'.[73] Yet breach of the order (whose conditions were set in civil proceedings) is not just a criminal offence, but an offence thought serious enough to warrant a maximum penalty of five years' imprisonment—an ingenious scheme for imposing harsh punishments yet by-passing the appropriate protections at the crucial stage of the proceedings. There is a criminal offence involved here, that of breaching a civil preventive order (notably, an anti-social behaviour order), and that offence must be justified. The question here is whether this is a sufficiently serious harm and wrong to justify criminalization: one view is that, where the prohibited conduct is not a criminal offence, its inclusion in an ASBO should not be a good enough reason to open the way to a prison sentence, let alone a substantial one. The contrasting view is that, if the court is satisfied that D's conduct was likely to cause harassment, alarm or distress to others, that is enough to carry it across the threshold of harmfulness, particular where it was persistent

---

[73] *Clingham v Royal Borough of Kensington and Chelsea* [2003] 1 AC 787, and the criticism in A. Ashworth, 'Social Control and "Anti-Social Behaviour": the Subversion of Human Rights?' (2004) 120 LQR 263.

conduct. Even those who accept this, however, must be prepared to defend a maximum sentence of five years—longer than for many offences—as proportionate.

FURTHER READING

D. Husak, *Overcriminalization* (2007).

R. A. Duff, *Answering for Crime* (2007), chs 4 and 6.

W. Wilson, *Central Issues in Criminal Theory* (2002), ch 1.

N. Jareborg, 'What Kind of Criminal Law do we Want?' in A. Snare (ed), *Beware of Punishment: On the Utility and Futility of Criminal Law* (1995).

3

PRINCIPLES AND POLICIES

3.1 RULES AND PRINCIPLES

The criminal law is sometimes presented and discussed as if it were a system of rules. It will already have become apparent from Chapters 1 and 2 that this is not true. Although there are rules, and although Parliament often goes through lengthy debates before enacting rules, there is also a great deal of discretion which often enables the police, prosecutors, magistrates, judges, and juries to adopt approaches that cannot be said to have been 'dictated' by the law. Even if it is pointed out that over 90 per cent of cases in the magistrates' courts and some two-thirds in the Crown Court involve a plea of guilty and therefore no trial, it remains the case that some of those guilty pleas will have involved negotiation between prosecution and defence; and, more especially, it must be recalled that the police exercise considerable discretion in their daily encounters with citizens.[1]

---

[1] As confirmed by the Home Office research by D. Brown and T, Ellis, *Policing Low-Level Disorder: Police Use of Section 5 of the Public Order Act 1986* (1994), and by T. Bucke and Z. James, *Trespass and Protest: Policing under the Criminal Justice and Public Order Act 1994* (1998).

There is another sense in which study of the rules is unsatisfactory as the sole or primary approach to understanding the criminal law. English criminal law both is shaped and ought to be shaped by a number of principles, policies and other standards and doctrines. One of the purposes of this chapter is to draw together and to discuss critically some of the foremost principles that ought to exert an influence on the substance of English criminal law. Examples will be given to show when certain principles have been officially recognized and may therefore have played a part in the development of case-law or legislation, but the emphasis of the chapter is on the normative as well as the political. The justifications for upholding each principle are discussed, and each principle is then followed by a policy or other instrumental goal that may often run counter to the principle in practice. It is not maintained that the principles and policies discussed in this chapter exhaust the range of standards, doctrines and other arguments that may be relevant to the shaping of English criminal law:[2] indeed, particular considerations relevant to specific offences are discussed in relation to those offences in the remainder of the book. Here, the focus is on a group of defensible principles that are consistent with the principle of autonomy outlined in Chapter 2.1, as modified by a minimal commitment to the principle of welfare in order to ensure that the social arrangements necessary to enable citizens to exercise their autonomy are also supported by the criminal law where necessary. For ease of exposition, the discussion is divided into three parts: section 3.4 deals with the range of offences, recalling Chapter 2 above; section 3.6 deals with principles bearing on the conditions of liability, to some extent anticipating Chapters 4, 5, and 6 below; and section 3.5 states some procedural principles. Questions of priority will then be discussed in section 3.7.

3.2 CONSTITUTIONALITY AND CODIFICATION

We noted in Chapter 1.3 above that many offences and defences in English criminal law are still governed by the common law, giving a significant role to the court. In constitutional theory, decisions about what conduct should be criminal should be taken by the legislature, and these decisions should then be implemented by the executive and applied by the courts. This has led to a movement not only for legislative reform of the criminal law, but also for codification. Thus the Law Commission gave its general support, when putting forward its draft criminal code in 1989, to the following proposition:

because a criminal code makes a symbolic statement about the constitutional relationship of Parliament and the courts, it requires a judicial deference to the legislative will greater than that which the courts have often shown to isolated and sporadic pieces of legislation. Far from it being a possible disadvantage of codification that it places limitations upon the ability of the courts to develop the law in directions which might be considered desirable, we believe that for the criminal law this is one of its greatest merits.[3]

---

[2] Cf. the argument made against the framework adopted in previous editions by J. Gardner, 'On the General Part of the Criminal Law', in R. A. Duff (ed.), *Philosophy and the Criminal Law* (1998), 209–13.

[3] Law Com No. 177, para. 2.2, quoting from the submission of the Society of Public Teachers of Law. See also A. T. H. Smith, 'The Case for a Code' [1986] Crim LR 285.

Thus the enterprise of codifying English criminal law has been seen partly as an exercise in constitutional propriety, subjecting the contours of the criminal law to the democratic process of Parliament rather than leaving them largely to the common law and the judges. One might argue that this change would be more symbolic than practical: the parliamentary process may be democratic merely in theory, since a powerful government may push through measures not directly related to its political mandate, and the judiciary is bound to retain considerable powers through its interpretive role. Indeed, the Law Commission's draft code deliberately left a number of points open for judicial development (e.g. liability for omissions, the recognition and scope of defences), although the significance of these areas is small compared with the bulk of the code.

Constitutional propriety apart, the chief aims of codifying the criminal law would be to improve its accessibility (having a large number of offences 'set out in one well-drafted enactment in place of the present fluctuating mix of statute and case-law'[4]), its comprehensibility (adopting a simpler drafting style), its consistency (in the sense of greater uniformity of reasoning and of terminology), and its certainty (settling many issues in advance, rather than leaving judicial decisions to do so after the event).[5] The twentieth-century codification project was commenced and shaped by a small team of academic lawyers, who produced a draft code for the Law Commission in 1985,[6] and the Commission, after consultation, published its own Draft Criminal Code in 1989.[7] Influential opinion suggested that it would not be practical to try to put the whole code through Parliament as a single Bill, since it was too large for the legislative system to cope with satisfactorily,[8] and so the Commission began to come forward with some shorter Bills. The first of these dealt with non-fatal offences against the person,[9] and an amended version of it was put out for consultation by the Government in 1998.[10] Another short Bill was put forward by the Law Commission on manslaughter,[11] and that too was followed by a Government paper.[12] Absolutely nothing has happened as a result of either declaration of Government intent, although in 2003 the Government brought before Parliament the large piece of legislation that became the Sexual Offences Act—the genesis of which was within the Home Office rather than the Law Commission. In 2001 the Government had again declared itself in favour of a criminal code, but added that 'producing a core criminal code would be a long-term commitment, not least because of the heavy demands it might make on Parliament's time'.[13]

---

[4] Law Com No. 177, i, para. 2.4.   [5] See ibid., i, paras. 2.5 to 2.11 for fuller discussion.

[6] Law Com No. 143, *Codification of the Criminal Law: a Report to the Law Commission* (1985), submitted by Professors J. C. Smith, E. Griew, and I. Dennis.

[7] Law Com No. 177 in two volumes: i. report and draft Bill, ii. commentary on the draft Bill.

[8] See [1990] Crim LR 141–2. This concern, even if valid at the time, seems difficult to maintain when the Government comes forward with legislation such as the Criminal Justice Act 2003, with 339 sections and 38 Schedules.

[9] Law Com No. 218, *Legislating the Criminal Code: Offences against the Person and General Principles* (1993).

[10] Home Office, *Violence: Reforming the Offences Against the Person Act 1861* (1998).

[11] Law Com No. 237, *Legislating the Criminal Code: Involuntary Manslaughter* (1996).

[12] Home Office, *Reforming the Law on Involuntary Manslaughter: the Government's Proposals* (2000).

[13] Home Office, *Criminal Justice: the Way Ahead* (Cm 5074 of 2001), para. 3.59. The reference to a 'core' code is intended to include codes of evidence, procedure, and sentencing too—certainly a large undertaking.

The Law Commission originally aimed to complete the revision in 2004,[14] but it has subsequently been asked to undertake a range of other work such as the review of homicide law.[15] The Commission's 2008 programme announced the abandonment of the codification project, citing factors such as increased complexity and rapid changes in legislation; both the announcement and the reasons are regrettable.[16]

Despite leading judges adding their voices to the call for a criminal code,[17] it seems that the emphasis now is on accomplishing reforms of particular parts of the criminal law rather than enacting a code and amending it subsequently. This means that in the short term the criminal law is even more scattered and difficult to find: as Toulson LJ recently stated, 'to a worryingly large extent, statutory law is not practically accessible today, even to the courts whose constitutional duty it is to interpret and enforce it.'[18] Some of the Commission's recommended reforms on complicity and the inchoate offences became law quickly (in Part 2 of the Serious Crime Act 2007), but the focus of many calls for codification has been the Offences Against the Person Act 1861 and related law, on which there seems to have been absolutely no progress. Even if it is preferable to reform portions of the law rather than enacting a criminal code that contains outmoded provisions, the present exercise has signally lost some of the key objectives of codification—the largely *formal* virtues of clarity, certainty, and consistency. Reforming legislation such as the Corporate Manslaughter and Corporate Homicide Act 2007 and Part 2 of the Serious Crime Act 2007 (not to mention the Sexual Offences Act 2003, although that was not a Law Commission product) has become so technical and complex in its style as to make the original draft code proposed by the Law Commission in 1989 read like a Beatrix Potter story. However, although the style of drafting in the 1989 code has its admirers, its approach to the proper contents of a criminal code was more controversial. It had a particular slant towards 'traditional' crimes, with no aspiration to declare the most serious types of offence; strongly towards the subjective principle of criminal liability; and without any statement of general principles or canons for interpretation. That approach to codification has certainly had its critics,[19] and there ought to be reconsideration of the decision to confine the code to 'traditional' crimes. In so far as the process of codification is intended to make the law more accessible and understandable to the public, is there not an argument for trying to deal with the most serious offences,

The same case, more fully argued, was pressed by Auld LJ in his *Review of the Criminal Courts of England and Wales* (2001), 20–2.

[14] Law Com No. 275, *Thirty-Sixth Annual Report 2001* (HC 642, 2002), para. 5.1.

[15] Law Com No. 304, *Murder, Manslaughter and Infanticide* (2006), discussed in Ch 7 below.

[16] Law Com No. 311, *Tenth Programme of Law Reform* (2008); see the editional comment at [2009] Crim LR 1.

[17] See, e.g., Sir Henry Brooke, 'The Law Commission and Criminal Law Reform' [1995] Crim LR 911; Lord Bingham, 'A Criminal Code: Must We Wait for Ever?' [1998] Crim LR 694; Mrs Justice Arden, 'Criminal Law at the Crossroads: the Impact of Human Rights from the Law Commission's Perspective and the Need for a Code' [1999] Crim LR 439.

[18] *Chambers* [2008] EWCA Crim 2467, at [24], pointing out the sheer volume of law, the amount of secondary legislation, and the absence of a proper database of legislation with hyperlinks.

[19] E.g. C. Wells, 'Restatement or Reform?' [1986] Crim LR 314; G. de Búrca and S. Gardner, 'The Codification of the Criminal Law' (1990) 10 Oxford JLS 559; S. Gardner, 'Reiterating the Criminal Code' (1992) 55 MLR 839.

rather than simply the traditional ones?[20] To exclude from the code serious offences
carrying maximum penalties of seven, ten, fourteen years, or life while including
offences such as kerb-crawling and wearing a military uniform when not entitled
seems questionable, to say the least. The decision to exclude from the code an offence
such as causing death by dangerous driving was quite wrong, and the arguments for
doing so place neatness above the value of social symbolism.

The Scots tradition in criminal law has also placed reliance on common law
development. Scottish courts, it has been said, have an inherent power to punish conduct that is grossly immoral or mischievous, or is obviously of a criminal nature.[21]
This, as we will see below,[22] has led to the judicial creation of new crimes even in modern times. The justification often advanced is one of keeping the criminal law in touch
with the community, but this begs questions about the judges' ability to represent or
distil community values. On this view, as Lindsay Farmer argues, 'the community is
idealized and free of conflicts and, of course, is not represented by the legislature'.[23]
However, the Scottish Law Commission has now published a draft criminal code, prepared by a group of academic lawyers.[24] Its relative brevity is to be commended, but it
is open to similar social criticisms as its English counterpart.

3.3 HUMAN RIGHTS AND CRIMINAL LAW

If one constitutional principle is that the reach of the criminal law should be declared
by the legislature, leaving the courts to apply and to interpret the legislation, another is
that the criminal law should respect fundamental rights and freedoms. There are two
sources of fundamental rights relevant to English criminal law—European Community
law, and the European Convention on Human Rights. European Community law
is potentially more powerful, since it takes priority over domestic law. However, its
impact on English criminal law remains somewhat scattered, even if frequently underestimated.[25] The 'third pillar' of the European Union, as established by the Maastricht
treaty of 1992, relates to co-operation in the fields of justice and home affairs. The
Amsterdam treaty of 1999 defined the objective of the 'third pillar' as the creation of
an 'area of freedom, security and justice'. The EU Constitutional Treaty anticipates its
further development, and the provisions in Article III-270 envisage harmonization

---

[20] A. Ashworth, 'Is the Criminal Law a Lost Cause?' (2000) 116 LQR 225.

[21] P. W. Ferguson, 'Codifying Criminal Law: (1) A Critique of Scots Common Law' [2004] Crim LR 49.

[22] Section 3.4(g).

[23] L. Farmer, '"The Genius of our Law…": Criminal Law and the Scottish Legal Tradition' (1992) 55
MLR 25, 39.

[24] Scottish Law Commission, *A Draft Criminal Code for Scotland* (2003), discussed by P. W. Ferguson,
'Codifying Criminal Law (2): the Scots and English Draft Code Compared' [2004] Crim LR 105. The Scots
codifying team consisted of Professors E. Clive, P. Ferguson, C. Gane, and A. McCall Smith, with Professor
Sir Gerald Gordon.

[25] See Ch 1.3 above.

of criminal laws as well as harmonized procedures, to go with mutual assistance and other co-operation (such as the European arrest warrant) already in place.[26]

More important in practice has been the change wrought by the Human Rights Act 1998, which may be loosely described as having incorporated into English law the European Convention on Human Rights. Reference has already been made to some Convention rights in Chapter 2.3 and 2.4 above. For present purposes, it is sufficient to make a broad sketch of the substantive rights guaranteed by the Convention, with some indication of their relevance to English criminal law:[27]

- Article 2 (right to life): self-defence and justifiable force as exceptions; abortion; the surgical separation of conjoined twins; the right to self-determination, and assisting suicide.

- Article 3 (right not to be subjected to torture or inhuman or degrading treatment): protection through laws against sexual and physical violation; extent of defence of parental chastisement.

- Article 5 (right to liberty and security of person): the defence of insanity; arrest for breach of the peace, and the 'quality of law' test.

- Article 6.2 (presumption of innocence): the burden of proof, and (possibly) offences of strict liability.

- Article 7 (prohibition on retroactive criminal laws): judicial lawmaking, and certainty in the definition of criminal offences.

- Article 8 (right to respect for private life): sexual offences; consent to physical harm; child abduction.

- Article 9 (freedom of religion): blasphemy (also Article 10).

- Article 10 (freedom of expression): obscenity; racial hatred offences; contempt of court; incitement to disaffection; official secrets legislation; breach of the peace, and section 5 of the Public Order Act 1986.

- Article 11 (freedom of assembly): breach of the peace, and various offences under the Public Order Act 1986 and the Criminal Justice and Public Order Act 1994 concerned with processions and demonstrations.

This list does not go into detail, but there will be references to the Convention and its jurisprudence at appropriate points in the later chapters. Nor is the list an exhaustive one. What is significant is that the Convention rights operate as a source of 'higher law' that can be used as a benchmark of the constitutionality of criminal legislation. Where a court finds that the definition of an offence interferes with one of the defendant's Convention rights and (if it is a right protected by Articles 8–11) does so either without

---

[26] See further S. Peers, *EU Justice and Home Affairs Law* (2nd edn., 2006), ch 8, esp. 423–7.

[27] For fuller discussion see B. Emmerson, A. Ashworth and A. Macdonald (eds), *Human Rights and Criminal Justice* (2nd edn., 2007).

it being 'necessary in a democratic society' or proportionate to such a necessity, it may recognize this as the basis for a defence to liability.[28]

What has been the impact of the Human Rights Act on the criminal law? The reports and consultation papers issued by the Law Commission have taken considerable care to deal with possible Convention issues. The compatibility of legislation with the Convention should be assured by the procedure whereby the Minister sponsoring a Bill certifies that it is compatible with Convention rights,[29] but in fact certificates have been issued for some Bills whose compatibility has been much contested.[30] In the courts, solicitors and counsel have not been slow to scour the Strasbourg jurisprudence for decisions in support of arguments based on the Convention, and prosecution lawyers have followed suit. Section 6 of the Human Rights Act requires all public authorities (including the courts) to act in compliance with the Convention: this means that courts will be bound to overrule judicial precedents which they find to be inconsistent with the Convention. Courts also have a duty under s 2 of the Human Rights Act to 'take into account' decisions of the European Court of Human Rights and of the European Commission on Human Rights.[31] The wording of s 2 makes it clear that the Strasbourg decisions are not binding: English courts have to interpret the Convention in the light of the Strasbourg jurisprudence, and may also consider other relevant decisions which may be drawn to their attention (e.g. decisions of the Privy Council, or constitutional cases from Canada, New Zealand, the USA, or South Africa). If the English courts were to decide not to follow a decision of the European Court of Human Rights, it is relevant to note that the right of an individual to petition to Strasbourg remains available, as it was before. In some spheres, where the Convention jurisprudence is weak (such as the burden of proof and Article 6(2)), the English courts have gone further than the Strasbourg decisions and have followed the lead of other Commonwealth countries.[32]

Most powerful of all is s 3 of the Act, which requires courts to construe legislation so as to comply with the Convention, 'so far as it is possible to do so'. This confers on courts a rather different interpretative role from that assumed at common law. Judicial discussions about 'the intention of Parliament' should be less frequent in cases where a Convention right is engaged, since the primary task is to reach an interpretation which protects the rights of individuals under the Convention—which may be the rights of defendants or of (potential) victims, for example. However, in some cases the courts have used this interpretative power extravagantly, so as to hold that a legislative provision bears a meaning that seems difficult to reconcile with its wording.[33] The courts do

---

[28] *Percy* v *DPP* [2002] Crim LR 835.   [29] Human Rights Act 1998, s. 19.

[30] E.g., the Bill that became the Sexual Offences Act 2003 (on which see Ch 8.5 and 8.6 below); and the provision that became s 76 Criminal Justice and Immigration Act 2008 (on which see Ch 4.6(g) below).

[31] The Commission dealt initially with all applications to Strasbourg until its abolition in 1998, often delivering a substantial judgment.

[32] *Lambert* [2002] 2 AC 545, and *Sheldrake* v *DPP; Attorney General's Reference No. 4 of 2002* [2004] UKHL 43.

[33] Notably in *R* v *A* [2002] 1 AC 45.

have an alternative approach in such situations: if a court is unable to read a statutory provision compatibly with the Convention, it will have to proceed as normal and the defendant will then appeal. An appellate court (Court of Appeal, Divisional Court, House of Lords) has the power under s 4 to make a 'declaration of incompatibility' if it is satisfied that a statutory provision is incompatible with the Convention.[34] This may lead the Government to take remedial action (section 10), but the issue of a declaration of incompatibility itself has no effect on the continuing validity of the law or on the outcome of the proceedings in the case.

In coming to grips with the Convention and its jurisprudence, it is important to note the difference in patterns of reasoning that it requires. The rights declared in the Convention have different strengths and, where they have exceptions, the structure of the exceptions may differ markedly. One pointer to this is Article 15, which permits States to derogate from certain rights under the Convention 'in time of war or other emergency threatening the life of the nation', 'to the extent strictly required by the exigencies of the situation',[35] but specifically excludes from derogation the rights in Articles 2, 3, 4(1), and 7. One might therefore construct the following hierarchy of rights:

- *Non-derogable rights*: the right to life (Article 2), the right not to be subjected to torture, inhuman, or degrading treatment (Article 3), the prohibition on slavery (Article 4(1)), and the right not to be convicted of a crime that was not in force at the time of the conduct (Article 7). Article 2 does provide for certain exceptions, and the same exceptions should apply in some Article 3 cases.[36] But those exceptions, discussed in Chapter 4.6 below, are narrowly circumscribed.

- *Strong rights*: the right to liberty and security of person (Article 5), the right to a fair trial (Article 6), and the right to enjoy Convention rights without discrimination on any ground (Article 14). A State is permitted to derogate from these rights under the strict terms of Article 15,[37] and the Strasbourg court has in some cases been content to afford States some margin of appreciation in respect of these rights.

- *Qualified rights*: the right to a private life (Article 8), the right to freedom of thought and religion (Article 9), the right to freedom of expression (Article 10), the right to freedom of assembly (Article 11). These are qualified or *prima facie* rights, their common feature being that the first paragraph of the Article declares the right, and the second paragraph sets out the circumstances in which

---

[34] An example of its use was in *A. v Home Secretary* [2004] UKHL 56.

[35] Art. 15 was analysed by the House of Lords in *A. v Home Secretary* (last note).

[36] Now confirmed in Strasbourg by e.g. *Rivas v France* [2005] Crim LR 305.

[37] In *A. v Home Secretary* [2004] UKHL 56 the House of Lords found that the provisions for the detention without trial of suspected international terrorists were contrary to Art. 5 and were not saved by Art. 15, since, although their Lordships accepted the Government's view that there was an emergency threatening the life of the nation, they held that the powers went further than strictly necessary and that they were discriminatory, by applying to non-nationals and not to British nationals. The Government abandoned these powers and took different powers in the Prevention of Terrorism Act 2005.

the right may justifiably be interfered with. This affords considerable scope for argument, using the Strasbourg jurisprudence and other sources.[38] The right to peaceful enjoyment of possessions, declared by Protocol 1, is also subject to a 'public interest' exception which places it within this broad category.

The grounds for justifying exceptions to the qualified rights under the second paragraphs of Articles 8 to 11 are fairly broad and wide-ranging, and turn on the two requirements of 'necessary in a democratic society' and 'proportionality'. Although the Strasbourg Court does not have an entirely consistent approach to the question of proportionality, it tends to adopt a more rigorous approach than that of the English courts—which was established in a case dealing with Article 6, an article to which proportionality is only of tangential relevance.[39] In summary, the rights declared in the Convention are not extensive and were never intended as a complete statement of the limits of the criminal sanction. As expected, the impact of the Human Rights Act on the substantive criminal law (as distinct from criminal procedure and evidence) has been rather small: the issues surrounding the compatibility of the rules on self-defence and insanity have not yet come up for decision, and few of the reported cases have necessitated a re-writing of English criminal law.[40] However, there remains scope for critical discussion of the certainty of some aspects of English criminal law, as we shall see in paragraphs 3.5(g) to (j) below.

3.4 THE RANGE OF THE CRIMINAL LAW

The preceding chapter illustrated the difficulties involved in deciding which interests the criminal law should protect (to which the European Convention has some relevance), and in ranking harms so as to achieve some kind of proportionality. Clearly a primary aim of the criminal law ought to be to provide for the conviction of those who culpably cause major harms to other citizens or to the community, but it has already been noted that in practice the criminal law contains a myriad of less serious or more controversial offences. What principles and policies are relevant to the decisions to expand or contract the criminal law in these spheres? The enquiry begins by summarizing four principles and policies already discussed in Chapter 2, and then moves on to consider two other relevant principles.

---

[38] Sections 12 and 13 of the Human Rights Act require British courts to 'have particular regard to the importance of' the rights of freedom of expression and freedom of religion.

[39] See *Brown* v *Stott* [2003] 1 AC 681, criticised in B. Emmerson, A. Ashworth and A. Macdonald, *Human Rights and Criminal Justice*, at 15–95, and *O'Halloran and Francis* v *UK* (2008) 46 EHRR 406.

[40] The most significant appear to be *H* [2002] 1 Cr App R 59 on parental chastisement (Ch 4.8); *Percy* v *DPP* [2002] Crim LR 835 (s. 5 of the Public Order Act may interfere disproportionately with the defendant's Art. 10 right); and *Goldstein and Rimmington* [2005] UKHL 63 (public nuisance and Art. 7).

(a) THE PRINCIPLE OF MINIMUM CRIMINALIZATION

This principle, which was discussed in Chapter 2.4, is that the ambit of the criminal law should be kept to a minimum. It flows from the principle of autonomy and the minimalist notion of welfare already developed in Chapter 2 above. As we saw, the point is not so much to reduce criminal law to its absolute minimum as to ensure that resort is had to criminalization only in order to protect individual autonomy or to protect those social arrangements necessary to ensure that individuals have the capacity and facilities to exercise their autonomy. The principle is supported by various evidential and pragmatic conditions, so that even if it appears to be justifiable in theory to criminalize certain conduct, the decision should not be taken without an assessment of the probable impact of criminalization, its efficacy, its side-effects, and the possibility of tackling the problem by other forms of regulation and control. The present Government has stated that in deciding whether to create a new criminal offence it considers whether 'the behaviour in question is sufficiently serious to warrant intervention by the criminal law',[41] but it is not clear how rigorously that test is applied. Creation of a criminal offence has the consequence that a defendant accused of that crime has the minimum rights guaranteed by Article 6(3) of the Convention.

(b) THE POLICY OF SOCIAL DEFENCE

Perhaps the strongest arguments against minimum criminalization are thought to derive from the policy of social defence. According to this view, the criminal law may properly be used against any form of activity which threatens good order or is thought reprehensible. There are, on this view, no limits to the use of the criminal sanction apart from financial ones. It was argued in Chapter 2 that many extensions of the criminal law are examples of political posturing, a Government response to a matter of social concern about which 'something must be done'. For this reason a sceptical stance should be adopted towards claims of 'social defence', which are easy to advance. If it is claimed that the new crime is needed to protect people from certain harms, it must be asked whether the wrong involved is so serious as to justify criminalization, and whether protection cannot be supplied more effectively by other means outside the criminal law. Creating a new crime may have a welcome symbolic effect, in condemning certain activity, but criminalization may still be neither appropriate nor effective in terms of protecting people from harm.

One difficulty with the principle of minimum criminalization is, however, that it could be taken to freeze the contours of the criminal law. If it were interpreted as a barrier against further extensions of criminal law, this would be unsatisfactory, as it would take scant account of the many anomalies accumulated in English law, as in other systems, over the years. Rectification of an anomaly (for example, the old rule

---

[41] Lord Williams of Mostyn, written reply in HL Deb. vol. 602, WA 57 (18 June 1999).

that a husband could not be convicted of the rape of his wife[42]) may well lead to a new sphere of criminalization; so may the extension of the criminal law to cover a newly arising mischief, such as internet pornography,[43] or a newly publicized mischief, such as stalking, that may cause significant harm.[44] Thus the extension of the criminal law into areas such as internet pornography, stalking, and marital rape may be justified on the ground that the wrongs involved in such conduct are no less significant than those involved in many serious crimes already established. These examples are important as a corrective to extreme libertarian arguments deriving from the policy of minimum criminalization. One might well agree that we all prefer our behaviour to be subject to as few constraints as possible, but that preference must be placed in the context of our membership of a community. Certain constraints may be reasonable in the interests of the community at large, even though they restrict particular individuals, as we saw when elaborating the principle of welfare in Chapter 2.2 above.

However, the interaction between the principle of minimum criminalization and the policy of social defence may operate in undesirable ways. It may be decided to deal with significantly anti-social behaviour through the civil law, thereby avoiding the extra protections conferred by English law and by Article 6 on persons 'charged with a criminal offence'. This was the strategy behind the creation of the anti-social behaviour order: the House of Lords has confirmed, taking a narrow view of s 1 of the Crime and Disorder Act 1998, that proceedings for the imposition of an anti-social behaviour order are civil (although holding that a standard of proof indistinguishable from the criminal standard should be applied),[45] even though the consequence of a breach of such an order is the commission of a strict liability offence with a maximum penalty of five years' imprisonment. Such orders operate like a Trojan horse. They pay lip-service to the principle of minimum criminalization, whilst enabling severe punishment with no more than a token gesture towards the normal rights of the defendant.[46]

(c) THE PRINCIPLE OF LIABILITY FOR ACTS NOT OMISSIONS

This principle has often been cited, in the courts and elsewhere, as a reason for restricting the ambit of the criminal sanction.[47] In fact, Parliament has applied the policy of social defence to produce a great increase in the number of offences which penalize persons for 'failing to' fulfil certain requirements, usually concerned with motoring, business, and finance. It now seems to be accepted that there are

---

[42] See *R v R* [1992] 1 AC 599, and below, Ch 8.5(b).

[43] See e.g. Protection of Children Act 1978 and Sexual Offences Act 2003, ss. 45–50.

[44] Protection from Harassment Act 1997, below, Ch 8.3(g); see C. Wells, 'Stalking: the Criminal Law Response' [1997] Crim LR 463.

[45] *Clingham v Royal Borough of Kensington and Chelsea* [2003] 1 AC 787.

[46] See Ch 1.2 above, and A. Ashworth, 'Social Control and "Anti-Social Behaviour": the Subversion of Human Rights?' (2004) 120 LQR 263.

[47] See further Ch 4.4 below.

justifications for imposing positive duties at least on those who engage in potentially dangerous activities, such as handling radioactive substances, selling food or driving on the roads. Moreover, there is a long-standing and fundamental duty on a parent to ensure the health or welfare of her or his child.[48] The courts have also, controversially, recognized other general duties: thus a duty to care for another can be assumed by contract, or by undertaking the care of a relative, or even by undertaking the care of a stranger;[49] and a person who creates a dangerous situation, even accidentally, has a duty to take steps to avert or minimize the danger.[50] However, courts have tended to regard omissions liability as exceptional and in need of special justification. The main reason is that positive duties to act are regarded as an incursion on individual liberty: the principle of autonomy militates against omissions liability, on the ground that public duties restrict one's liberty to pursue one's own ends by requiring one to respond to events whenever they occur (e.g. by throwing a lifebelt, or assisting injured people). Negative duties, which require citizens to avoid certain behaviour, leave them free to pursue their own desires in other directions, whereas a positive duty to act prevents them from doing anything else at the time. Familial ties and voluntarily assumed obligations may be acceptable as bases for criminalizing omissions, it is argued, but it would be wrong to introduce a general duty to assist strangers or to take steps towards enforcing the law. As we will see in Chapter 4.4 below, this viewpoint is grounded in a highly individualistic version of the autonomy principle.

(d) THE PRINCIPLE OF SOCIAL RESPONSIBILITY

This countervailing principle adopts the welfare-based proposition that society requires a certain level of co-operation and mutual assistance between citizens. There are powerful arguments of welfare which support certain duties to act to protect others in dire situations. Many other European countries criminalize the failure to render assistance to another citizen who is in peril, so long as that assistance can be given without danger to oneself.[51] Three arguments are often raised against such 'extensions' of the criminal law. First, it is objected that it will inevitably be unclear what is expected of the citizen: such laws often use the word 'reasonable', and this fails to give fair warning of what should be done and when.[52] A second and consequential objection is that the exercise of prosecutorial discretion then becomes a major determinant of criminal liability. This may be criticized as weakening the rule of law, by

---

[48] Children and Young Persons Act 1933, s. 1.

[49] *Stone and Dobinson* [1977] QB 354, discussed by A. Ashworth, 'The Scope of Criminal Liability for Omissions' (1989) 105 LQR 424, at 443–5; cf. the discussion of earlier authorities by P. R. Glazebrook, 'Criminal Omissions: the Duty Requirement in Offences against the Person' (1960) 76 LQR 386.

[50] *Miller* [1983] 2 AC 161.

[51] See A. Cadoppi, 'Failure to Rescue and the Continental Criminal Law', in M. A. Menlowe and A. McCall Smith, *The Duty to Rescue* (1993); A. Ashworth and E. Steiner, 'Criminal Omissions and Public Duties: the French Experience', (1990) 10 Legal Studies 153.

[52] The principle of fair warning is discussed in Ch 3.5 below.

transferring effective power to officials.[53] Thirdly, it is argued that omissions liability
calls for much greater justification than the imposition of liability for acts. It is said
that this reflects a widely felt moral distinction: 'we do much more wrong when we kill
than when we fail to save, even when such a failure violates a positive duty to prevent
death.'[54] But even if there is such a distinction, it would only establish that omissions
are viewed less seriously than acts, not that they are unsuitable for criminalization—
and research into public attitudes suggests otherwise.[55] So long as proper attention
is paid to 'rule of law' protections such as the principle of fair warning, there may be
good arguments for criminal liability for omissions, but the requirements and the
boundaries of omissions liability need further debate and elucidation.[56] The recognition of some social duties is therefore essential if all individuals are to have a proper
capacity for autonomy, and further the imposition of duties backed by the criminal
sanction may be justifiable to safeguard vital interests (such as life and physical integrity), if this can be done without risk or hardship to the citizen. This principle of
social responsibility would therefore support, for example, an offence of failing to
render assistance to a citizen in peril, where that assistance can be accomplished
without danger to the rescuer. The critical element here is the danger to human life
and the (qualified) duty to take certain action: it is not a prescription for making
all citizens into their fellow citizens' keepers, nor need it render D liable for all the
consequences.[57] These arguments on social responsibility and omissions liability are
developed further in Chapter 4.4(c) below.

(e) CONFLICTING RIGHTS AND THE PRINCIPLE OF NECESSITY

There may be circumstances in which it is a person's right to use force on another, even
to take another's life, as is evident from the exceptions to the right to life declared in
Article 2 of the European Convention. In principle this applies only where it is necessary for the defender to use force in order to prevent the infringement of the right to
life or the right to security of person. Similarly, where it is necessary for the apprehension of a suspected offender, prevention of the escape of a person lawfully detained, or
for the protection of an individual from attack, it may be justifiable for one individual
to infringe the normal rights of the other (the aggressor). For one person to be justified
in taking another's life Article 2 requires absolute necessity. The ambit of the principle
is examined more fully in Chapter 4.6.

---

[53] See Ch 3.5(i) above, and also the particular problems of prosecutorial discretion under the Sexual
Offences Act 2003, discussed in Ch 8.6 below.

[54] M. Moore, *Act and Crime* (1993) 58; cf the broader discussion by W. Wilson, *Central Issues in Criminal
Theory* (2002), ch 3.

[55] Cf. P. Robinson and J. Darley, *Justice, Liability and Blame* (1995), 45–8, and particularly B. Mitchell,
'Public Perceptions of Homicide and Criminal Justice' (1998) 38 BJ Crim 453 at 459.

[56] L. Alexander, 'Criminal Liability for Omissions: an Inventory of Issues', in Shute and Simester (eds),
Criminal Law Theory: Doctrines of the General Part (2002).

[57] A Duff, *Answering for Crime* (2007), 109–10.

(f) THE PRINCIPLE OF PROPORTIONALITY

This principle operates so as to place limitations on the amount of force that may properly be used in conditions of necessity. No individual, even an offender, should have his or her interests sacrificed except to the extent that it is both absolutely necessary and reasonably proportionate to the harm committed or threatened. This should apply equally to law enforcement officers and to ordinary citizens. A sharper formulation of this principle would be that the principle of necessity, in cases of conflicting rights, grants the authority to inflict only the minimum harm—a version of the view that one is justified in using force only if it is a lesser evil than allowing events to take their course.[58] As we will see in Chapter 4.6 below, the Strasbourg Court has read a requirement of 'strict proportionality' into Article 2.[59] There may also be arguments for differentiating between sudden and instinctive responses and those cases where there is ample time for reflection. Further, the assumption that the user of force is innocent and the other party is the wrongdoer does not apply in all cases, as we will see in Chapter 6.4.

3.5 THE RULE OF LAW AND FAIR PROCEDURES

In this section we deal, at greater length, with those principles and policies relating to the function of the criminal law as a means of guiding the conduct of members of society and the conduct of courts and law enforcement officers. In relation to each pair of contrasting precepts, the first-mentioned principle will have the support of the European Convention of Human Rights, whereas the second is usually based on pragmatic and political considerations of the time. Three pairs deal with aspects of the principle of legality, sometimes expressed by the maxim *nullum crimen sine lege*. This fundamental principle is more frequently rendered in England in terms of 'the rule of law':

According to the ideal of the rule of law, the law must be such that those subject to it can reliably be guided by it, either to avoid violating it or to build the legal consequences of having violated it into their thinking about what future actions may be open to them. People must be able to find out what the law is and to factor it into their practical deliberations. The law must avoid taking people by surprise, ambushing them, putting them into conflict with its requirements in such a way as to defeat their expectations and to frustrate their plans.[60]

This is a fundamental principle, with both procedural and substantive implications. It expresses an incontrovertible minimum of respect for the principle of autonomy: citizens must be informed of the law before it can be fair to convict them of an offence (many of the *mens rea* and culpability doctrines discussed in Chapter 5 are

---

[58] Discussed further below, Ch 4.7 and 4.8.   [59] See e.g. *Nachova v Bulgaria* (2005) 42 EHRR 43.
[60] J. Gardner, 'Introduction' to H. L. A. Hart, *Punishment and Responsibility* (2nd edn., 2008), xxxvi.

connected to this), and both legislatures and courts must apply the rule of law by not criminalizing conduct that was lawful when done.

(g) THE NON-RETROACTIVITY PRINCIPLE

In many other jurisdictions, especially within Europe, it is usual to begin a discussion of general principles of the criminal law by stating the maxim *nullum crimen sine lege*, sometimes known as the principle of legality. However, the connotations of the principle of legality are so wide-ranging that it is preferable to divide it into three distinct principles—the principle of non-retroactivity, the principle of maximum certainty, and the principle of strict construction of penal statutes.

The essence of the non-retroactivity principle is that a person should never be convicted or punished except in accordance with a previously declared offence governing the conduct in question. The principle is to be found in the European Convention on Human Rights, Article 7: 'no one shall be held guilty of any offence on account of any act or omission which did not constitute a criminal offence under national or international law at the time when it was committed.' This principle, also enunciated in Article 1 of the United States Constitution, forbids a legislature to create a criminal offence which applies to behaviour prior to its enactment. The rationale links back to the autonomy principle and to the concept of reliance inherent in the 'rule of law' ideal: 'respect for autonomy involves respect for the ability to plan, which requires respect for the ability to rely on the law', which in turn generates the principle of non-retroactivity.[61] How does it apply to the courts? It may seem obvious to state that they should not invent crimes and then punish people for conduct which falls within the new definition. But how would the common law have developed if such a power had not been exercised? The courts have developed and extended English criminal law over the years, untrammelled by the non-retroactivity principle. To 'adapt' the law is a great temptation for a court confronted with a defendant whose conduct it regards as plainly wicked but for which existing offences do not provide.

The conflict between the non-retroactivity principle and the functioning of the criminal law as a means of social defence reached its modern apotheosis in *Shaw* v *DPP* (1962).[62] The prosecution had indicted Shaw with conspiracy to corrupt public morals, in addition to two charges under the Sexual Offences Act 1956 and the Obscene Publications Act 1959. The House of Lords upheld the validity of the indictment, despite the absence of any clear precedents, on the broad ground that conduct intended and calculated to corrupt public morals is indictable at common law. The decision led to an outcry from lawyers and others. One objection to *Shaw* is that it fails to respect citizens as rational, autonomous individuals: a citizen cannot be sure of avoiding the criminal sanction by refraining from prohibited conduct if it is open to the courts to invent new crimes without warning. What happened in *Shaw* was that a majority of the House of Lords felt a strong pull towards criminalization because they

---

[61] B. Juratowitch, *Retroactivity and the Common Law* (2008), 49.   [62] [1962] AC 220.

were convinced of the immoral and anti-social nature of the conduct—thus regarding their particular conceptions of social defence[63] as more powerful than the liberty of citizens to plan their lives under the rule of law.

But there are two more, interconnected, objections to this decision. First, the new crime was even less defensible, since it concerned a socially controversial realm of conduct (prostitution) rather than behaviour widely accepted as an evil warranting the criminal sanction: if the courts are to legislate, they should at least confine themselves to relatively uncontroversial cases. Secondly, this realm of conduct had only recently been considered by Parliament, which had introduced limited reforms in the Street Offences Act 1959; thus it could be argued that since Parliament did not then extend the law to penalize conduct such as Shaw's, the courts were usurping the legislative function when they did so. This constitutional dimension of the decision should not be underestimated. The proper procedure is for a democratically elected legislature to create new offences. What *Shaw* seems to admit is that the police and prosecution may prefer to press a hitherto unknown charge, and the courts may uphold its validity at common law. This accords great power to the executive and the judiciary, and since an offence thus created operates retrospectively on the defendant, it fails to respect the citizen's basic right that the law be knowable in advance. The criminal law embodies the height of social censure, and its extent should be determined in advance by accountable democratic processes rather than *ex post facto* by judicial pronouncement.[64]

It appears that the English courts no longer claim the power to create new criminal offences,[65] apparently accepting the force of the principle of non-retroactivity. The Scottish judiciary does still claim this power, as part of a dynamic system of common law which must be adapted to deal with changing social circumstances. In 1983 the Scottish courts in effect created a criminal offence of selling glue-sniffing equipment,[66] and in 1989 they reached their famous decision to extend the crime of rape to husbands, overturning a long-standing exception.[67] Yet the English courts, which (since *Knuller*) ostensibly adhere to the principle of non-retroactivity, took the same decision in relation to marital rape: in *R* v *R*[68] the House of Lords abolished the husband's immunity from liability for rape of his wife. There are many convincing reasons why the old rule should have been abolished,[69] but the relevant question here

---

[63] For the controversial nature of their approach to the relationship between law and morality see Ch 2.5 above.

[64] A. T. H. Smith, 'Judicial Lawmaking in the Criminal Law' (1984) 100 LQR 46.

[65] *Knuller* v *DPP* [1973] AC 435, a case in which, paradoxically, the court appeared to create the offence of outraging public decency; *Rimmington and Goldstein* [2006] 1 AC 459, per Lord Bingham.

[66] *Khaliq* v *HM Advocate*, 1983 SCCR 483.

[67] *Stallard* v *HM Advocate*, 1989 SCCR 248, discussed by T. H. Jones, 'Common Law and Criminal Law: the Scottish Experience' [1990] Crim LR 292 and by L. Farmer, 'The Genius of our Law'.

[68] [1992] 1 AC 599, on which see M. Giles, 'Judicial Lawmaking in the Criminal Courts: the Case of Marital Rape' [1992] Crim LR 407.

[69] Summarized in the first edition of this work, at 301–3.

is whether the law should have been changed by a judicial decision which operated retrospectively on the defendant, rather than prospectively by the legislature.

That question was taken to Strasbourg, alleging that the House of Lords violated Article 7 (non-retroactivity) in this case, now referred to as *SW and CR v United Kingdom*.[70] The Strasbourg Court held that the removal of the marital rape exemption by the House of Lords[71] did not amount to a retrospective change in the elements of the offence. As the European Commission put it:

> Article 7(1) excludes that any acts not previously punishable should be held by the courts to entail criminal liability or that existing offences should be extended to cover facts which previously did not clearly constitute a criminal offence. It is, however, compatible with the requirements of Article 7(1) for the existing elements of an offence to be clarified or adapted to new circumstances or developments in society in so far as this can reasonably be brought under the original concept of the offence. The constituent elements of an offence may not however be essentially changed to the detriment of an accused and any progressive development by way of interpretation must be reasonably foreseeable to him with the assistance of appropriate legal advice if necessary.[72]

The majority of the Court went on to hold that the development of the law by the English courts 'did not go beyond the legitimate adaptation of the ingredients of a criminal offence to reflect the social conditions of the time', whereas a strong dissenting opinion argued that the abolition of the marital immunity from rape prosecution was not 'mere clarification' and could not be brought under the original concept of the offence. The Court's decision was clearly affected by the subject-matter, since it purported to justify its narrow reading of Article 7 by reference to the incompatibility between 'the unacceptable idea of a husband being immune against prosecution for rape of his wife' and the 'respect for human dignity' that is a fundamental objective of the Convention.[73] This decision implants a degree of flexibility into what ought to be a fundamental rule-of-law protection for individuals: it is not that the law ought to exist before the conduct took place, but that it ought to have been foreseeable (if necessary, with legal advice) that the law would be changed in a particular direction.

Some may argue that, as a result of this decision, the ordinary development of the common law by the courts is unlikely to be held to breach Article 7. However, it is arguable that Article 7 ought to be interpreted as placing some outer limits on judicial creativity. In the light of s 6 of the Human Rights Act it is no longer lawful for the courts to reach decisions such as those in *Shaw v DPP*[74] and *Knuller v DPP*.[75] Where, as in *Tan*,[76] the prosecution is described as 'novel', there may be good reason for mounting an Article 7 challenge.

It may be expected that questions of retroactivity will arise more frequently in the context of statutory interpretation, since there are few common law crimes remaining.

---

[70] (1995) 21 EHRR 363; for analysis, see Juratowitch, *Retroactivity and the Common Law*, 127–38.
[71] [1992] 1 AC 599.
[72] (1995) 21 EHRR 363, at 390 cf. the even more doubtful decision in *C* [2005] Crim LR 238.
[73] Ibid., at 402.   [74] [1962] AC 220.   [75] [1973] AC 435.   [76] [1983] QB 1053.

However, the judicial creation of new defences is a possibility, although the courts have sometimes deferred to the legislature on this matter.[77] The principle of non-retroactivity did not feature prominently in Lord Lowry's reasoning in *C v DPP*,[78] when he articulated five criteria for judicial lawmaking:

(1) if the solution is doubtful, the judges should beware of imposing their own remedy;

(2) caution should prevail if Parliament has rejected opportunities for clearing up a known difficulty, or has legislated leaving the difficulty untouched;

(3) disputed matters of social policy are less suitable areas for judicial intervention than purely legal problems;

(4) fundamental legal doctrines should not lightly be set aside;

(5) judges should not make a change unless they can achieve finality and certainty.

These are important principles, focusing on the constitutional aspects of judicial lawmaking that had been neglected in *Shaw v DPP* (which would fall foul of (2) and (3), at least). Lord Lowry's criteria were cited when the Court of Appeal declined to change and to broaden the basis of corporate criminal liability.[79] However, the criteria fail to give explicit recognition to the significance for individuals of the principle of non-retroactivity, and Article 7 should now be given greater weight in this context. As Lord Bingham put it in *Jones* (2007), 'it is for those representing the people of the country in Parliament, and not the executive and not the judges, to decide what conduct should be treated as lying so far outside the bounds of what is acceptable in our society as to attract criminal penalties.'[80]

Even if English law were codified, it seems likely that courts would retain some power to develop defences to liability by creating new rules and extending old ones. Mental states such as insanity and intoxication are inconsistent with the kind of reliance presupposed by the idea of fair warning. These excusatory elements in the criminal law constitute rules of adjudication for the courts rather than rules of conduct to guide citizens, in contrast to the definitions of offences and of the justificatory defences (e.g. self-defence, prevention of crime), which may be relied on by citizens in planning their behaviour. It therefore follows that the usual 'reliance' arguments against judicial creativity do not apply in the sphere of excusatory defences.[81] It may be thought, too, that the constitutional arguments are less troublesome when the courts are dealing with excusatory defences: even if it is not proper for the courts to pursue their own conception of social defence, it may be proper for them to exercise creative power in

---

[77] See nn 83–4 below.   [78] [1996] AC 1, at 28.

[79] In *Attorney-General's Reference (No. 2 of 1999)* [2000] 2 Cr App R 207, *per* Rose LJ at 218.

[80] [2007] 1 AC 136, at [29]; cf. also Lord Bingham in *Rimmington and Goldstein* [2006] [2006] 1 AC 549 at [33] and *Norris v Government of USA* [2008] UKHL 16, at [55–6].

[81] See P. H. Robinson, 'Rules of Conduct and Principles of Adjudication' (1990) 57 U Chic LR 729, and P. Alldridge, 'Rules for Courts and Rules for Citizens' (1990) 10 Oxford JLS 487. Cf. Law Com No. 177, cl. 4(4).

giving effect to considerations of individual culpability.[82] An example of this was the judicial creation of a defence of 'duress of circumstances' in the late 1980s,[83] although some years later the House of Lords declined to approve the creation of a defence of involuntary intoxication on the ground that the task was one for Parliament.[84]

If courts are granted wider powers in relation to excusatory defences, should they be permitted to create and extend them but not to abolish or restrict them at a later stage? One of the criticisms of the decision of the House of Lords in *Howe* (1987),[85] which reversed a previous authority and held that duress could not be a defence to murder either as a principal or as a secondary party, was that it effectively breached Article 7: what D did was not an offence when he did it, since at that stage duress was a defence and he would have been acquitted. On this view, once a court has created a defence it cannot abrogate it without falling foul of the principle of non-retroactivity.[86] The argument is even stronger in relation to *Elbekkay*,[87] where the Court of Appeal held that it was no defence for a man to argue that his impersonation of the victim's boy-friend was insufficient to negate the woman's apparent consent. This decision was all the more remarkable because s 142 of the Criminal Justice and Public Order Act 1994 had recently redefined rape but had repeated the reference to rape by impersonating a husband (without extending the reference to a partner, etc.), and because the Court commented that no previous decision or statute required it to hold otherwise.[88] It can be argued that this development of the law by the courts (as distinct from the legislature) was not reasonably foreseeable: whereas in the case of marital rape there had been a series of lesser decisions suggesting that the courts were moving in the direction of criminalizing all rapes of wives by husbands, there was nothing in the law prior to *Elbekkay* to suggest that a change might be imminent. It is therefore suggested that this is the type of case in which it can be argued that the contraction of a defence would be contrary to Article 7.[89] The question may occasionally arise whether a purportedly retrospective provision that is favourable to the defendant should be upheld, and both the Strasbourg Court and the Privy Council have held that a defendant should have the benefit of such a law.[90]

---

[82] See the views of Dworkin and Williams, discussed in section 3.4(l) below.

[83] See *Willer* (1987) 83 Cr App R 225 and the decisions summarized in *Hasan* [2005] UKHL 22, discussed in Ch 6.3 below.

[84] *Kingston* [1995] 2 AC 355, discussed in Ch 6.2(d) below.

[85] [1987] AC 417, discussed below, Ch 6.3.

[86] G. Fletcher, *Rethinking Criminal Law* (1978), 574, quoted by Smith, 'Judicial Lawmaking', 64–5.

[87] [1995] Crim LR 163.

[88] The decision in *Elbekkay* came a few months before Lord Lowry laid down his propositions about judicial lawmaking in *C v DPP*, above, n 78 and accompanying text.

[89] It might be argued that a well-drawn defence of reasonable mistake of law should be introduced to protect defendants from conviction in such cases, but the argument here is that it would be unlawful for a court to reach such a decision at all.

[90] See, respectively, *Kokkinakis v Greece* (1993) 17 EHRR 397 and *Chan Chi-hung v R* [1996] AC 442. The question received a similar answer under European Community law in Cases C–358/93 and C–416/93 *Aldo Bordessa* [1995] ECR I–361: see E. Baker, 'Taking European Criminal Law Seriously' [1998] Crim LR 361, at 366–8, 376–7.

(h) THE 'THIN ICE' PRINCIPLE

A counterpoint to the non-retroactivity principle is provided by what may be called the 'thin ice' principle, following Lord Morris's observation in *Knuller* v *DPP* (1973) that 'those who skate on thin ice can hardly expect to find a sign which will denote the precise spot where he [*sic*] will fall in'.[91] The essence of this principle seems to be that citizens who know that their conduct is on the borderline of illegality take the risk that their behaviour will be held to be criminal. Another popular phrase for this would be 'sailing close to the wind'. On occasions the courts have applied this principle both to the creation of a new offence and to the extension of an existing offence.[92] The arguments in favour of it seem to combine moral/social and political elements. The social element may be that courts should be able to penalize conduct which is widely regarded as, and which D ought to be aware is, on the boundaries of illegality; the political element may be that when citizens indulge in anti-social conduct that lies close to an existing offence, they ought also to know that there is a risk of criminal liability being extended to cover activities on the fringe of illegality. There are obvious counter-arguments. The principle appears to assume that it may be right for courts to extend the criminal law by analogy, whereas that has frequently been held to be contrary to Article 7 of the Convention.[93] Extension (as opposed to interpretation) should constitutionally be the province of the legislature. The 'thin ice' principle also neglects the role of the criminal law as a censuring institution whose convictions may result in both punishment and considerable stigma and social disadvantage, and overlooks the violation of the principle of autonomy caused when a citizen is convicted on the basis of a law that did not clearly cover the conduct at the time it took place.

It is unacceptable for Article 7 to be trumped by the 'thin ice' principle: Article 7 is an absolute right under the Convention, from which (according to Article 15) no derogation is possible. The days of new crimes created at common law ought to be long gone. However, the elasticity of the Strasbourg Court's decision in *CR and SW* v *United Kingdom*,[94] with its notion of the 'reasonable foreseeability' of the law continuing its development in a particular direction, leaves some leeway for the 'thin ice' principle to exert an influence.

(i) THE PRINCIPLE OF MAXIMUM CERTAINTY

The next principle—maximum certainty in defining offences—embodies what are termed the 'fair warning' and 'void for vagueness' principles in United States law.[95] All these principles may be seen as constituents of the principle of legality, and there

---

[91] [1973] AC 435.

[92] For the former see *Shaw* v *DPP* [1962] AC 220; for the latter see *Tan* [1983] QB 1053.

[93] E.g. recently by the Grand Chamber in *Korbely* v *Hungary* (judgment of 19 September 2008), at [70]; see also the excerpt from the *Kokkinakis* judgment in section (i) below.

[94] Above, n 70 and accompanying text.

[95] See, e.g., *Kolender* v *Lawson* (1983) 103 S Ct 1855; the Supreme Court of Canada applied the principle in *Prostitution Reference* (1990) 77 CR (3d) 1.

is a close relationship between the principle of maximum certainty and the non-retroactivity principle. A vague law may in practice operate retroactively, since no one is quite sure whether given conduct is within or outside the rule. Thus Article 7 of the Convention is relevant here, since it is:

not confined to prohibiting the retrospective application of the criminal law to an accused's disadvantage. It also embodies, more generally, the principle that only the law can define a crime and prescribe a penalty (*nullum crimen, nulla poena sine lege*) and the principle that the criminal law must not be extensively construed to an accused's detriment, for instance by analogy: it follows from this that an offence must be clearly defined in law. This condition is satisfied where the individual can know from the wording of the relevant provision and, if need be, with the assistance of the courts' interpretation of it, what acts and omissions will make him liable.[96]

However, the Strasbourg Court has also recognized that some vagueness is inevitable in order 'to avoid excessive rigidity and to keep pace with changing circumstances', and that a reasonable settled body of case-law may suffice to reduce the degree of vagueness to acceptable proportions.[97] It is for this reason that the court refers to access to legal advice in order to determine the precise ambit of a law.

The test applied under Article 7 is the same as that applied as the 'quality of law' standard elsewhere in the Convention. Whenever a member state seeks to rely on a provision in the Convention in order to justify its actions—whether the arrest or detention of a citizen (Article 5), or interference with one of the qualified rights in Articles 8–11—it must establish that its officials acted 'in accordance with the law'. This means a valid law, and this requires the State to show that the relevant rule satisfies the 'quality of law' standard. As the Court stated in the *Sunday Times* case:

Firstly, the law must be adequately accessible: the citizen must be able to have an indication that is adequate in the circumstances of the legal rules applicable to a given case. Secondly, a norm cannot be regarded as a 'law' unless it is formulated with sufficient precision to enable the citizen to regulate his conduct: he must be able—if need be with appropriate advice—to foresee, to a degree that is reasonable in the circumstances, the consequences which a given action may entail.[98]

The standard has been applied in a number of subsequent decisions. In *Hashman and Harrup* v *UK* (2000)[99] the applicants had been bound over to keep the peace and be of good behaviour after disturbing a fox-hunt by blowing horns. The Strasbourg Court held that their Article 10 right to freedom of expression had been breached by the binding over, since the interference with their right was not 'prescribed by law' inasmuch as the relevant law did not meet the 'quality of law' standard. The applicants had been bound over after a finding that they acted *contra bonos mores*, which was

---

[96] *Kokkinakis* v *Greece* (1994) 17 EHRR 397, para. 52.   [97] Ibid., para. 40.
[98] *Sunday Times* v *UK* (1979) 2 EHRR 245, para. 49; see generally B. Emmerson, A. Ashworth and A. Macdonald, *Human Rights and Criminal Justice*, Ch 10.
[99] (2000) 30 EHRR 241.

defined as behaviour that is 'wrong rather than right in the judgment of the majority of contemporary citizens'.[100] The Court held that this did not meet the standard because it failed to describe the impugned behaviour at all, whereas other provisions (such as conduct likely to provoke a breach of the peace) are acceptable because they describe behaviour 'by reference to its effects'.[101]

It remains unclear how far the 'quality of law' standard may be used to challenge various offences under English law. Many offences in the Theft Acts include a requirement that the defendant acted dishonestly, a concept that plainly does not 'describe behaviour by reference to its effects'. The Court in *Hashman and Harrup* stated that the offences turning on dishonesty were different because dishonesty 'is but one element of a more comprehensive definition of the proscribed behaviour'.[102] Even if that is true following recent House of Lords decisions,[103] it would hardly apply to a new general offence of dishonesty or of deception, as the Law Commission concluded.[104] There is considerable uncertainty of definition in common law offences such as cheating[105] and perverting the course of justice (although the conduct is defined by reference to its effects),[106] and they should be scrutinized urgently in the light of Article 7's requirements. When the House of Lords scrutinized the offence of public nuisance in *Rimmington and Goldstein* (2006),[107] it narrowed the definition of the offence in order to avoid uncertainty, and Lord Bingham approved the statement (in a case of perverting the course of justice) that, if the ambit of a common law offence is to be enlarged, it 'must be done step by step on a case by case basis and not with one large leap'.[108] This is consistent with the Strasbourg position outlined in paragraph (g) above.

Why should such emphasis be placed on certainty, predictability, and 'fair warning'? As with the principle of non-retroactivity, a person's ability to know of the existence and extent of a rule is fundamental: respect for the citizen as a rational, autonomous individual and as a person with social and political duties requires fair warning of the criminal law's provisions and no undue difficulty in ascertaining them. The criminal law will also achieve this respect more fully if its provisions keep close to moral distinctions that are both theoretically defensible and widely felt:[109] this suggests a connection between fair warning and fair labelling (on which see 3.6(s) below). A connected reason in favour of the principle of maximum certainty is that, if rules are vaguely drafted, they bestow considerable power on the agents of law enforcement:[110]

---

[100] *Hughes v Holley* (1988) 86 Cr App R 130.

[101] *Steel v UK* (1999) 28 EHRR 603 thus upheld the definition of 'breach of the peace', even though there remains some uncertainty in the definitions offered by the courts.

[102] (2000) 30 EHRR 241, para. 39.   [103] See the discussion of *Gomez* and *Hinks* in Ch 9.2 below.

[104] Law Commission Consultation Paper (LCCP) No. 155, *Fraud and Deception* (1999), Parts V and VI; cf. the proposals in Law Com No. 276, *Fraud* (2002), which led to the Fraud Act 2006 (see Ch 9.8 below), and which seek to avoid this problem by deploying an inchoate mode of drafting.

[105] *Pattni et al.* [2001] Crim LR 570.   [106] *Cotter* [2002] Crim LR 824.

[107] [2005] UKHL 63, [2006] Crim LR 153.

[108] Ibid., para. 33, quoting from *Clark* [2003] 2 Cr App R 363, para. 12.

[109] J. Gardner, 'Rationality and the Rule of Law in Offences Against the Person' [1994] Camb LJ 502.

[110] See the two Home Office studies of policing practice, above, n 1.

the police or other agencies might use a widely framed offence to criminalize behaviour not envisaged by the legislature, creating the very kind of arbitrariness that rule-of-law values should guard against. Similarly, when the law gives the court power to make an anti-social behaviour order in response to conduct 'likely to cause harassment, alarm or distress', this gives little warning to citizens about the type of conduct that may be prohibited with the threat of criminal conviction for repetition.[111] It will be noticed, however, that the principle is stated in a circumscribed form—the principle of *maximum* certainty, not *absolute* certainty—which indicates the compromise already inherent in the principle. In its pure form, the 'rule of law' would insist on complete certainty and predictability, but this is unattainable—'vagueness is ineliminable from a legal system, if a legal system must do such things as to regulate the use of violence...'[112] Unless the criminal law occasionally resorts to such open-ended terms as 'reasonable' and 'dishonest', it would have to rely on immensely detailed and lengthy definitions which might be extremely complicated and which might then restrict the intelligibility of the law. As Timothy Endicott argues, neither vagueness nor discretion is necessarily a deficit in the rule of law, so long as the law can perform its function of guiding behaviour.[113] Thus those who adhere to the principle of maximum certainty would insist that the use of such vague terms should be reinforced by other definitional elements, guidelines, or illustrative examples which structure the court's discretion.[114]

Any claim that a derogation from maximum certainty is necessary for the practical administration of the law must be scrutinized carefully. As the US Supreme Court put it in *Conally* v *General Construction Co* (1926): 'a statute which either forbids or requires the doing of an act in terms so vague that men of common intelligence must necessarily guess at its meaning and differ as to its application, violates the first essential of due process of law'.[115] Whether the Strasbourg Court's interpretation of the non-retrospectivity principle in Article 7 or the more general 'quality of law' requirement has been overly conservative is open to debate, but the decision in *Hashman and Harrup* demonstrates that the principle can bite, and it will do so in this country if the courts take it as seriously as the Law Commission appears to have done.

(j) THE POLICY OF SOCIAL DEFENCE

The policy of social defence runs counter to the principle of maximum certainty. It maintains that some vagueness in criminal laws is socially beneficial because it enables the police and the courts to deal flexibly with new variations in misconduct without having to await the lumbering response of the legislature. The policy of social defence thus supports the same aims as the 'thin ice' principle. It also suffers from similar

---

[111] A. P. Simester and A. von Hirsch, 'Regulating Offensive Conduct through Two-Step Prohibitions', in A. von Hirsch and A. P. Simester (eds), *Incivilities* (2007), at 186–7.

[112] T. Endicott, 'The Impossibility of the Rule of Law' (1999) 19 OJLS 1, 6.   [113] Ibid., 17–18.

[114] E.g. the problem of defining the conduct element in attempts: see Ch 11.3 below.

[115] (1926) 269 US 385, at 391.

defects, such as differing opinions of the social interests to be defended by means of the criminal law. The interests of the powerful are thus likely to prevail.

The policy of social defence would support the enactment of laws vague enough to leave room for the law enforcement agents to apply them to new forms of anti-social action—for example, the public order offences in the Acts of 1986 and 1994,[116] the power to make an anti-social behaviour order, and the common law offence of conspiracy to defraud.[117] To the objection that such crimes delegate far too much *de facto* power over citizens' lives to law enforcement agents, proponents of social defence would reply that this should be tackled by means of internal guidelines and police disciplinary procedures rather than by depriving the police and courts of the means of invoking the criminal sanction against conduct which arouses social concern. The offences themselves appear to be worded objectively and neutrally—although they suffer from what the Americans call over-breadth—but their use may be selective.[118] The policy of social defence therefore favours considerable low-level discretion, conferred (in effect) by broadly-phrased offences, and often supported by the use by politicians and journalists of imagery that depicts certain groups as the enemies of society against whom new powers are 'necessary' for 'public safety'.[119]

Social defence arguments are sometimes used to support the argument that ignorance of the criminal law should be no excuse. Thus English law authorizes the conviction of persons who were unaware of the existence of a crime, even in circumstances where it would have been difficult for them to find out that they were committing it.[120] This derogation from the notions of maximum certainty and fair warning is usually supported in terms of social defence by suggesting that, if the defence were allowed, everyone would claim it and there would be large-scale acquittals. Such arguments are unpersuasive in theory and in practice.[121]

The policy of social defence may be used to point out a distinct social dysfunction of the principle of maximum certainty. If members of society can rely upon criminal laws being drafted precisely and upon enforcement agents and the courts keeping within those boundaries, it is open to resourceful citizens to devise ways of circumventing those laws—conforming to the letter of the law, whilst dishonouring its spirit. Where this kind of activity is pursued in a systematic way, with powerful financial support, it may be regarded as a distinct threat to the values that the criminal law seeks to uphold. It is said that there are those in the financial and business worlds who make their living on these fringes of legality, exploiting the principle of maximum certainty as a shield to protect them from conviction.[122] Can these people be

---

[116] See above, n 1.

[117] Subject to the remarks of the House of Lords in *Norris v Government of USA* [2008] UKHL 16.

[118] See the studies at n 1 above.

[119] See further, on 'public order', N. Lacey, C. Wells and O. Quick, *Reconstructing Criminal Law* (2003), ch 2.

[120] Discussed below, Ch 6.5.

[121] See *Cambridgeshire and Isle of Ely CC v Rust* [1972] 2 QB 426; cf. *Lim Chin Aik v R* [1963] AC 160, discussed below, Ch 6.5.

[122] See D. McBarnet and C. Whelan, 'The Elusive Spirit of the Law: Formalism and the Struggle for Legal Control' (1991) 54 MLR 848.

distinguished from Shaw, Knuller, Tan,[123] and others? It is doubtful whether a distinction between sexual and financial morality would be sufficient to justify a difference in approach. The proper response is that the principle of legality, and in particular of maximum certainty, would accept that there is a distinction between avoidance and evasion, and that mere avoidance must be tackled by legislative amendments to the law rather than by *ex post facto* stretching by the courts. The fact that the wide common law offence of conspiracy to defraud remains in full vigour, with the result that financial misdealers are not safe from its elastic clutches, should not be viewed with approval: the offence ought to be abolished and replaced with discrete offences that comply in both letter and spirit with the principle of maximum certainty.[124]

(k) THE PRINCIPLE OF STRICT CONSTRUCTION

Two of the principles which are often brought under the umbrella of the principle of legality have already been discussed (non-retroactivity, maximum certainty); the principle of strict construction is the third. The difference here is that whereas the non-retroactivity principle applies to the lawmaking activities of Parliament and the courts, this principle relates to the courts' task in interpreting legislation. The formulation of the principle is a matter for debate. In its bald form, it appears to state that any doubt in the meaning of a statutory provision should, by strict construction, be resolved in favour of the defendant. One justification for this may be fair warning: where a person acts on the apparent meaning of a statute but the court gives it a wider meaning, it is unfair to convict that person because that would amount to retroactive lawmaking. Historically speaking, the principle seems to have originated either as a means of softening the effect of statutes requiring capital punishment, through the notion of construction *in favorem vitae*,[125] or as a response to statutory incursions into the common law—which in turn led Parliament to enact more detailed, subdivided offences of the kind that still survive in the Offences Against the Person Act 1861.[126]

The status of the principle of strict construction is unclear. It has some connection with Article 7 of the Convention in that, as we saw earlier, the Court has held that the non-retroactivity principle requires that the criminal law must not be extensively construed to an accused's detriment, for instance by analogy.[127] However, it is not clear how and when the Court would apply this principle. References to a principle of strict construction have been fitful both in England and the United States, leading to the claim that it is invoked more to justify decisions reached on other grounds than as

---

[123] See section 3.4(g) above.   [124] See Ch 9.9 below.

[125] L. Hall, 'Strict or Liberal Construction of Penal Statutes' (1935) 48 Harv LR 748. Similar reasoning (deriving more from the value of liberty than from capital punishment) may underlie the principle of giving the benefit to the accused when the Court of Appeal is faced with conflicting precedents: *Taylor* [1950] 2 KB 368.

[126] See Ch 8.3 below.   [127] *Kokkinakis* v *Greece* (1994) 17 EHRR 397, para. 52, cited at n 96 above.

a significant principle in its own right.[128] There is certainly no difficulty in assembling a list of cases in which it appears to have been ignored.[129] But it may be that it was not properly understood in its more sophisticated form in England, since it is relatively recently that a sequence of principles to be applied when interpreting criminal statutes has been established. According to the House of Lords, the proper approach is not to be bound by any particular dictionary definition of a crucial word in a statute, but rather to construe a legislative provision in accordance with the perceived purpose of that statute.[130] In order to assist in ascertaining that purpose, a court may consult a Hansard report of proceedings in Parliament, a government White Paper, or the report of a law-reform committee so as to ascertain the gap in the law which the legislation was intended to remedy.[131] If a Convention point arises, however, it is not a question of seeking the intention of Parliament but rather of applying s 3 of the Human Rights Act 1998 and interpreting the statute, so far as possible, so as to comply with the Convention.

Those who disagree with the principle have sought to ridicule it by arguing that no system of criminal law can function adequately if absolutely every ambiguity has to be resolved in favour of the defendant.[132] But this line of attack misunderstands the true role of the principle, which has now been reasserted in the courts. Its proper place is in a sequence of points to be considered by a judge when construing a statutory offence. It will be an important advance in the development of English criminal law if other courts routinely follow the approach now established by the House of Lords, although the evidence suggests that neither courts nor counsel consider statutory interpretation to be a discrete subject with its own approach and its own precedents.[133] However, there are further important questions of interpretation to which no authoritative approach has been established. For example, uncertainty still prevails over the proper approach to interpreting statutory offences which do not include a fault requirement in their definition: the courts are still without a coherent approach to the question of strict liability, and no sooner is a high-sounding ('constitutional') principle declared than other courts ignore or circumvent it.[134]

What is the argument in favour of the more sophisticated version of the principle of strict construction? The 'fair warning' argument undoubtedly plays a part, in so far as it respects the idea of citizens as rational, choosing individuals, but the primary argument is constitutional. In terms of interpreting statutes the courts are the

---

[128] J. C. Jeffries, 'Legality, Vagueness and the Construction of Penal Statutes' (1985) 71 Virginia LR 189.

[129] E.g. *Gomez* [1993] AC 442 and *Hinks* [2001] 2 AC 241 in the House of Lords, and many Court of Appeal decisions.

[130] *Attorney-General's Reference (No. 1 of 1988)* (1989) 89 Cr App R 60, affirming the Court of Appeal's decision at (1989) 88 Cr App R 191.

[131] Cf. *Black-Clawson International* v *Papierwerke Waldhof-Aschaffenber AG* [1975] AC 591 with *Pepper* v *Hart* [1993] AC 593.

[132] Jeffries, 'Legality, Vagueness and the Construction of Penal Statutes', and Law Com No. 177, para. 3.17.

[133] For fuller discussion see A. Ashworth, 'Interpreting Criminal Statutes: a Crisis of Legality?' (1991) 107 LQR 419.

[134] See below, Ch 5.5(a).

authoritative agency. Just as the principles of non-retroactivity and maximum certainty ought to be recognized by the legislature, so they should be recognized by the courts when engaging in interpretation. Indeed, the argument is even stronger for the courts, for they are the ultimate agency for determining the practical limits of the law, and yet they are an unelected group. Parliament should retain the main responsibility for the extent of the criminal law, and, indeed, it has the right to determine the courts' approach towards the task of interpretation (for example, by including some canons of interpretation in the Criminal Code[135]). The practical implication of this approach is that the courts should exercise restraint in their interpretive role, favouring the defendant where they are left in doubt about the legislative purpose.

(l) A BROADER PURPOSIVE APPROACH

Militating against the principle of strict construction is a broader purposive approach which relies on the aims of the criminal law as a whole rather than on a particular legislative purpose. Why should the courts allow those who indulge in obviously antisocial behaviour to escape conviction by reference to a principle which assumes that citizens take care to ascertain the law beforehand (which they usually do not), and which also assumes that the government and Parliament can be left to deal promptly with behaviour which is seen as a social problem (which they usually cannot, because of pressures on parliamentary time)? Indeed, the argument goes further. Citizens who do act in reliance on a particular view of the law could be excused by means of a defence of ignorance or mistake of law.[136] As for the constitutional argument, the assumption seems to be that the principle of legislative supremacy is all-powerful. Important it may be, but there are other political and fundamental values that also have a claim to be taken into account. If one purpose of the criminal law is the deterrence of significant culpable wrongdoing and the punishment of those who engage in it, does this not supply a reason for courts to interpret criminal laws so as to achieve this end? An argument of this kind leaves a great deal to be debated—in Chapter 2 we saw how controversial the boundaries of criminalization can be[137]—but its kernel is that, as with the 'thin ice' principle, it may not be unfair to penalize someone who has positioned himself on the margins of lawfulness. This may be seen as a rationalization of the appellate courts' tendency to stretch the interpretation of statutes so as to criminalize people who, they think, have manifestly committed a serious wrong.[138] As John Bell has argued, 'if the law exists to promote collective goals, as well as to

---

[135] Cf. Law Com No. 177, para. 3.17, criticized by Ashworth, 'Interpreting Criminal Statutes', 425–7.

[136] See below, Ch 6.5.

[137] Cf. Smith, 'Judicial Lawmaking', 58: 'it may be doubted whether it is possible to formulate any organising principles according to which conduct is seen to be deserving of condemnation as criminal'.

[138] J. R. Spencer, 'Criminal Law and Criminal Appeals: the Tail that Wags the Dog' [1982] Crim LR 260. Another example, which illustrates how some of these cases occur because the prosecutor chose the wrong charge and the Court cannot bring itself to acquit or quash the conviction, is *Gomez* [1993] AC 442, discussed in Ch 9.2 below.

protect individual rights, it cannot be altogether unexpected that both of these aspects should come into the resolution of hard cases'.[139]

Two counter-arguments are often heard, in addition to the principle of legislative supremacy. One is the practical point that courts have only rarely put the legislature to the test by refusing to extend existing offences to new forms of anti-social behaviour and leaving the task to Parliament. There are some isolated examples,[140] but in general the courts have not established a tradition of strict construction. If they had either brought in acquittals or quashed convictions in every case where the application of a statutory provision left some room for doubt, then the government would have been highly likely to set up a regular system for redrafting and amending criminal laws. A typical course of events was that in the case of *Charles* (1976):[141] the Court of Appeal favoured the acquittal of a man who, in spite of his bank's prohibition, had deliberately and substantially overdrawn on his bank account, because the Court found it difficult to bring the conduct within the definition of the offence charged. Bridge LJ recognized that social defence might be better served by a conviction, but he did not regard it as the Court's function to stretch the words of the statute. The House of Lords had no such compunction: it did stretch the statutory wording, and restored the conviction.[142] Had the House of Lords adopted the same approach as the Court of Appeal, then the government and Parliament would have been left to decide on the need for an amendment to the law. In the meantime, Charles and a few others would have gone free. It is this consequence which some judges, regarding themselves as custodians of the public interest, have sought to avoid by adopting broad interpretations of statutes. Doubts have been expressed about whether appellate courts are in a proper position to assess the consequences of thus extending the law,[143] and there are more recent cases in which the courts decided that it was both too difficult and inappropriate to attempt to repair defective legislation.[144] Thus in *Preddy*[145] the House of Lords declined to adopt an interpretation of the Theft Act 1968 which would have upheld the appellant's conviction, and Parliament did move quickly to rectify the anomaly by passing the Theft (Amendment) Act 1996 within five months; but, even then, Lord Goff could not resist a passing gibe at 'the so-called principle of legality, which has a respectable theoretical foundation but can perhaps be a little unrealistic in practice'.[146]

A second counter-argument is that the judicial function is to uphold individual rights, leaving broader issues of social policy to Parliament. Thus Ronald Dworkin has argued that judges ought to ground their decisions in reasons which uphold individual rights and ought not to take account of policies, goals, or overall social welfare.[147]

---

[139] J. Bell, *Policy Arguments in Judicial Decisions* (1983), 222.

[140] E.g. *Oxford v Moss* (1979) 68 Cr App R 183 and *Gold and Shifreen* [1988] AC 1063: the Computer Misuse Act 1990 may be seen as a legislative response, at least to the latter decision.

[141] (1976) 63 Cr App R 252.   [142] [1977] AC 177.

[143] See Smith, 'Judicial Lawmaking', 52–4, and also Lord Lane CJ, on credit card frauds in *Clarke* (1982) 75 Cr App R 119.

[144] *Savage, Parmenter* [1992] 1 AC 699, discussed in Ch 8.3 below.   [145] [1996] AC 815.

[146] Ibid., at 831.   [147] R. M. Dworkin, *A Matter of Principle* (1985), ch 1.

Glanville Williams has advanced a similar argument specifically in relation to criminal law.[148] It may be argued, however, that this adopts a particularly one-sided view of the criminal law. Principles of individual fairness are important, and some of them are absolutely fundamental, but this should not be allowed to obscure the wider sense of autonomy advocated in Chapter 2 above—one which emphasizes the need to provide social conditions and facilities in which a broader range of choices is available. This is not to suggest that courts should be allowed a free rein to draw on whatever social principles they wish. It is to argue that, if it proves possible to establish some general principles of criminal law, perhaps based on arguments in this chapter and Chapter 2, these may be used as an interpretive framework no less legitimately than those existing principles based on individual fairness[149]—provided always that Convention rights are duly respected.

(m) THE PRESUMPTION OF INNOCENCE

The principle that a person should be presumed innocent unless and until proved guilty is a fundamental principle of procedural fairness in the criminal law. Its justifications may be found in the social and legal consequences of being convicted of a crime, in which context the principle constitutes a measure of protection against error in the process,[150] and a counterweight to the immense power and resources of the State compared to the position of the defendant. The opposite rule—a presumption of the guilt of all those prosecuted for an offence—would impose an oppressive burden on individual citizens, and would place great power in the hands of the state officials who decide on prosecution. Article 6(2) of the Convention declares that 'everyone charged with a criminal offence shall be presumed innocent until proved guilty according to law', but the Strasbourg Court has not developed the presumption of innocence with any vigour. Indeed, in the leading decision of *Salabiaku* v *France*[151] the Court found no violation of Article 6(2) in an offence (carrying a prison sentence) that placed the onus of proof on the defendant, stating merely that the reverse onus must be 'within reasonable limits which take into account the importance of what is at stake and maintain the rights of the defence'. The English courts, on the other hand, are feeling their way towards a more robust promotion of the presumption. The famous declaration of Lord Sankey LC in *Woolmington* v *DPP* (1935)[152] that 'throughout the web of the English criminal law one golden thread is always to be seen—that it is the duty of the prosecution to prove the prisoner's guilt', had

---

[148] E.g. G. Williams, 'Statute Interpretation, Prostitution and the Rule of Law', in C. Tapper (ed.), *Crime, Proof and Punishment* (1981); 'Criminal Omissions—the Conventional View' (1991) 107 LQR 86, at 96.

[149] See, e.g., P. H. Robinson, 'Legality and Discretion in the Distribution of Criminal Sanctions' (1988) 25 Harvard J on Legislation 393; Z. Bankowski and D. N. MacCormick, 'Statutory Interpretation in the United Kingdom', in D. N. MacCormick and R. S. Summers (eds.), *Interpreting Statutes: a Comparative Study* (1991), 397.

[150] See the judgment of Brennan J in the US Supreme Court in *Re Winship* (1970) 397 US 358.

[151] (1988) 13 EHRR 379.   [152] [1935] AC 462.

increasingly been regarded as empty rhetoric as the numbers of statutory exceptions multiplied. However, in *Lambert* (2001)[153] the House of Lords used the power of interpretation in s 3 of the Human Rights Act to reinterpret a reverse onus provision in s 28 of the Misuse of Drugs Act 1971 so as to impose merely an evidential burden (not the burden of proof) on the defendant. A majority of their Lordships held that the severity of the potential penalty rendered this reverse onus a disproportionate burden on D. The House of Lords adopted the same approach to an anti-terrorism offence in *Attorney-General's Reference No. 4 of 2002*,[154] although in the conjoined appeal in *Sheldrake v DPP* their Lordships held that it would be easier to rebut the presumption for an offence with a low maximum penalty.[155]

(n) THE POLICY OF EASE OF PROOF

The presumption of innocence has been much neglected by the legislature: many offences are defined in such a way that the prosecution has to prove little, and then the defence bears the burden of exculpation. Section 101 of the Magistrates' Courts Act 1980 places on the defendant the burden of proving any excuse, exemption, proviso, or qualification in the definition of an offence tried summarily, a regime that is usually justified on grounds of expediency and economy. Neglect of the presumption is not confined to so-called regulatory offences: some 40 per cent of offences triable in the Crown Court—i.e. the most serious offences in English law—appear to violate the *Woolmington* principle by placing a burden of proof on the defendant.[156] It seems that the presumption has been so insignificant to policy-makers and legislators that often they have not even regarded it as necessary to give a reason for placing a burden on the defence.

However, there is evidence of change since *Lambert*: in the Sexual Offences Act 2003, there were several reverse onus provisions in the Bill, which were removed after the House of Commons Home Affairs Committee pointed out the conflict with the presumption of innocence.[157] Sometimes an attempt is made to justify a reverse burden by claiming that it is right to expect the defendant to prove elements relating to a defence. One difficulty here is that there is no satisfactory analytical distinction between offence and defence.[158] Legislative draftsmen do not follow a single drafting rule, and it may often be a matter of chance whether a given element is expressed as

---

153 [2001] 3 WLR 206.   154 [2004] UKHL 43.

155 For further discussion, see A. Ashworth, 'Four Threats to the Presumption of Innocence' (2006) 10 *Evidence and Proof* 241.

156 A. Ashworth and M. Blake, 'The Presumption of Innocence in English Criminal Law' [1996] Crim LR 306.

157 See J. Temkin and A. Ashworth, 'Rape, Sexual Assaults an the Problems of Consent' [2004] Crim LR 328, at 342–4.

158 See the discussions by Glanville Williams, 'Offences and Defences' (1982) 2 Legal Studies 233; Paul Robinson, 'Criminal Law Defenses: A Systematic Analysis' (1982) 82 Columbia LR 199; and Kenneth Campbell, 'Offence and Defence', in I. Dennis (ed.), *Criminal Law and Criminal Justice* (1987).

a defence or is rolled up into the definition of the crime.[159] A more reliable argument is that certain matters are much easier for one party to prove than the other: it is generally far easier for a defendant to prove that he or she had a licence or permit than for the prosecution to prove the absence of one.[160] However, this should not be allowed to shade into the far less persuasive argument that D should prove any matter that 'lies within his own peculiar knowledge',[161] a proposition that might equally apply to intention, knowledge, and many other core elements of crimes, and would thus undermine the presumption of innocence completely.

The policy of ease of proof does not merely manifest itself through the imposition of burdens on the defence. Parliament has within its control the definition of offences too, and frequently inserts strict liability elements into statutory offences. This is inconsistent with the principle of *mens rea* and with the rule of law (see 3.6(o) below), but it does not contravene the presumption of innocence enshrined in Article 6(2) of the Convention. That presumption is procedural, not substantive, and so applies only to the burden of proof.[162]

3.6 PRINCIPLES RELATING TO THE CONDITIONS OF LIABILITY

Setting the conditions for criminal liability raises further questions about 'rule of law' requirements[163] and the principle of individual autonomy (outlined in Chapter 2.1). We have already seen how these standards underlie the principle of legality in its three manifestations: the principles of non-retroactivity, maximum certainty, and strict construction. Unless a person can know what the criminal law prohibits, it is unfair to impose a conviction. Both the rule of law and the principle of autonomy emphasize respect for individuals as deliberative, choosing persons. This is often taken to suggest, as we shall see in some of the detailed principles below, that an individual should be held criminally liable only for consequences that were knowingly brought about or knowingly risked. Whatever the merits of civil liability for other consequences, an individual should not be liable to censure and punishment for them. In contrast, the principle of welfare insists that the need for social co-operation and community life may create strong arguments for extending the ambit of the criminal law and the conditions of liability—by, for example, imposing duties to take care in certain

---

[159] As demonstrated by A. A. S. Zuckerman, 'The Third Exception to the *Woolmington* Rule' (1976) 92 LQR 402.

[160] See the House of Lords decision in *Hunt* [1987] AC 352, discussed by J. C. Smith, 'The Presumption of Innocence' (1987) 38 NILQ 223, and by P. Roberts and A. A. S. Zuckerman, *Criminal Evidence* (2004), ch 8.

[161] Unfortunately even Lord Bingham in *Sheldrake* v *DPP* [2004] UKHL 43 relied on this flawed argument.

[162] As decided by the House of Lords in *G.* [2008] UKHL 37.

[163] On which see the quotation from Gardner, n 60 above.

types of situation and making the negligent liable to conviction. However, it will be argued below that this does not undermine the principle of autonomy if the appropriate conditions are fulfilled, notably that there is fair warning of the imposition of a duty of care reinforced by the criminal sanction, and that there is an exception for those incapable of attaining the required standard. All these points are taken further in Chapter 5 below: the purpose here is to express schematically the kinds of argument used.

(o) THE PRINCIPLE OF *MENS REA*

In order to satisfy rule of law standards, an offence must have a (subjective) *mens rea* requirement in order to alert D to the fact that he is about to violate the law: some element of *mens rea* is needed in order to give fair warning, which would be absent if offences could be committed accidentally. The principle of autonomy may be interpreted as taking the point further, arguing that the incidence and degree of criminal liability should reflect the choices made by the individual. The principle of *mens rea* expresses this by stating that defendants should be held criminally liable only for events or consequences which they intended or knowingly risked. Only if they were aware (or, as it is often expressed, 'subjectively' aware) of the possible consequences of their conduct should they be liable.[164] The principle of *mens rea* may also be stated so as to include the belief principle, since in some crimes it is not (or not only) the causing of consequences that is criminal but behaving in a certain way with knowledge of certain facts. Thus where the defence is one of mistaken belief, the principle of *mens rea* would state that a person's criminal liability should be judged on the facts as D believed them to be. All these aspects of the principle of *mens rea* are discussed further in Chapter 5.4 and 5.5 below. Although much of the principle's strength derives from the rule of law and the value of autonomy, this does not mean that negligence liability cannot be supported on the same basis: so long as there is an exception for incapacity, as argued below, this may be fair.

(p) THE POLICY OF OBJECTIVE LIABILITY

In spheres of activity that are perceived to be particularly dangerous, it is often thought that there are sufficient justifications for going beyond subjective liability and imposing liability for failure to fulfil a duty of care. Perhaps the clearest example of this may be found in road traffic legislation: long-standing offences such as dangerous driving and careless driving make drivers criminally liable for the degree to which they fall below the standards expected of a competent motorist.[165] Among the justifications for this is the principle of welfare, which in this respect favours the imposition of standards of behaviour on citizens because their behaviour as motorists can so easily impinge on others, with disastrous consequences.

---

164 Adopted in LCCP 177, *A New Homicide Act?*, para. 2.101.   165 See Ch 7.6 below.

In industrial contexts there is a whole host of offences based on negligence, particularly where hazardous substances or dangerous conditions are involved. Moreover, in many commercial settings the criminal law imposes strict liability on those who sell defective products or unwholesome foodstuffs, convicting them in many situations where the fault is small or non-existent. The case for extending the criminal law to relatively minor harms is based on expediency, and has already been criticized in Chapter 2.4(c) above. Strict liability itself is often supported by reference to considerations of welfare, 'policy considerations', or 'social concern', but it will be argued in Chapter 5.5(a) below that the justifications for going beyond negligence liability to strict liability are unpersuasive. Criminal liability for negligence, however, so long as it is founded on clear and well-publicized standards and duties for people performing certain activities, may be compatible with the rule of law and with the principle of autonomy. Thus, as will be argued in Chapter 5.5(f) below, there may be certain spheres in which criminal liability can properly be based on a form of negligence—taking proper account of the seriousness of the harm, the need to warn citizens of their duties, and the need to exempt those who lack the capacity to conform their conduct to the required standard.

(q) THE PRINCIPLE OF CORRESPONDENCE

Another implication of the principle of individual autonomy (with its emphasis on choice and control) and the 'rule of law' ideal (with its emphasis on the ability of individuals to plan) is the principle of correspondence. Not only should it be established that the defendant had the required fault, in terms of *mens rea* or belief; it should also be established that the defendant's intention, knowledge, or recklessness related to the proscribed harm. Thus, if the conduct element of a crime is 'causing serious injury', the principle of correspondence demands that the fault element should be intention or recklessness as to causing serious injury, and not intention or recklessness as to some lesser harm such as a mere assault. Another example, as we shall see,[166] is the law of murder: in English law a person may be convicted of murder if he either intended to kill or intended to cause grievous bodily harm. However, the latter species of fault breaches the principle of correspondence:[167] the fault element does not correspond with the conduct element (which is, causing death), and so a person is liable to conviction for a higher crime than contemplated. In effect, murder and other crimes that breach the correspondence principle are constructive crimes. They reduce 'rule of law' protections and respect for autonomy by rendering D liable to conviction for a more serious offence than intended or knowingly risked; and, to that extent, the

---

[166] Below, Ch 7.3.

[167] The Law Commission accepted this, using this as a basis for its proposed reforms: LCCP 177, *A New Homicide Act?*, paras. 3.15–18; but it subsequently discarded the principle in order to achieve greater consensus: Law Com 304, *Murder, Manslaughter and Infanticide* (2006), para. 254ff, discussed in Ch 7.3 below.

offence of conviction turns on the chance element of whether or not the more serious (unintended and unforeseen) harm results.[168]

(r) CONSTRUCTIVE LIABILITY

The argument for the extended fault element in murder, as described in the previous paragraph, favours constructive liability.[169] This has a Latin tag, *versari in re illicita*,[170] and in its widest form it argues that anyone who decides to transgress the criminal law should be held liable for all the consequences that ensue, even if they are more serious than expected. This may be termed the 'unlawful act theory', insofar as it holds that the commission of any crime against another supplies sufficient culpability to justify conviction in respect of whatever harm results. The decision to commit a crime is the crucial moral threshold: once D has knowingly crossed this, he should be liable for the resulting harm. This broad doctrine has now given way to what might be termed 'moderate constructivism', which accepts 'the requirement of subjective *mens rea* introduced by the obligation to respect the rule of law'[171] but argues that by intentionally attacking another D changes normative position, 'so that certain adverse consequences and circumstances that would not have counted against one but for one's original assault now count against one automatically, and add to one's crime.[172] In most forms this is a more moderate doctrine than the broad 'unlawful act theory'—it confines liability to resulting harms in the same 'family of offences' (usually, violence); and it does not necessarily justify the current English law of constructive manslaughter,[173] since some of its supporters restrict liability to cases where there is some 'proportionality' or alternatively 'no great moral distance' between the intended attack and the resulting harm.[174] However, these restrictive principles only come into play if the fundamental intuition of 'moderate constructivism' is conceded. Why is a minor assault vested with such high moral importance that it is thought to justify liability for injuries much more serious than foreseen? Why should such a large slice of luck enter into the assessment of criminal liability, with the result that D is labelled as having committed a significantly worse wrong than he intended or knowingly risked? John Gardner originally argued that if the criminal law puts D on notice

---

[168] See Ch 5.4 below, and J. Horder, 'A Critique of the Correspondence Principle' [1995] Crim LR 759; B. Mitchell, 'In Defence of the Correspondence Principle' [1999] Crim LR 195; J. Horder, 'A Reply' [1999] Crim LR 206; and V. Tadros, *Criminal Responsibility* (2005), 93–8.

[169] For a fuller version of the argument in this paragraph, see A. Ashworth, 'A Change of Normative Position: Determining the Contours of Culpability in Criminal Law' (2008) 11 New Crim LR 232.

[170] J. Hall, *General Principles of Criminal Law* (2nd edn., 1960), 6.

[171] J. Gardner, 'On the General Part of the Criminal Law', in A. Duff (ed), *Philosophy and the Criminal Law* (1998), 244.

[172] J. Gardner, 'Rationality and the Rules of Law in Offences Against the Person' (1994) 53 Camb LJ 502, 509.

[173] See Ch 7.5(a) below.

[174] See particularly J. Horder, 'A Critique of the Correspondence Principle' [1995] Crim LR 759, 763 and 766.

that this will be the consequence, the requirements of the rule of law are fulfilled.[175] However, giving fair warning of an unfair rule does not turn it into a fair rule, so we still await a justification for attributing such high moral importance to the change of normative position inherent in a common assault.[176] The existing law of offences against the person, stemming from an 1861 statute, is replete with examples of constructive liability, and the offences of murder and manslaughter are perhaps the best-known instances in English law. The 'change of normative position' argument seems to depend on the strength of a particular intuition—that morally the most significant element in given conduct is a decision to use force on another, and that there is insufficient moral weight in the plea, 'I only intended to punch/kick/wound slightly, not to cause injuries of *that* magnitude'.[177] This is surely to adopt an unduly narrow view of moral responsibility. It attributes too little importance to the full context of the actor's decision, and allows a person's criminal liability to turn partly on luck.[178] This argument is pursued further in the next two sections.

(s) THE PRINCIPLE OF FAIR LABELLING

This principle is chiefly applicable to the legislature. Its concern is to see that widely felt distinctions between kinds of offences and degrees of wrongdoing are respected and signalled by the law, and that offences are subdivided and labelled so as to represent fairly the nature and magnitude of the law-breaking.[179] As James Chalmers and Fiona Leverick argue in their detailed study, labels are important chiefly to *describe* D's offending behaviour for the general public and to *differentiate* that behaviour for the purposes of those working within the criminal justice system.[180] One good reason for respecting these distinctions is proportionality: one of the basic aims of the criminal law is to ensure a proportionate response to law-breaking, thereby assisting the law's educative or declaratory function in sustaining and reinforcing social standards. Fairness demands that offenders be labelled and punished in proportion to their wrongdoing; the label is important both for public communication and, within the criminal justice system, for deciding on appropriate maximum penalties, for evaluating previous convictions, for classification in prison, and so on. 'In fairness both to offenders and to others with a relevant interest, there is a need for offence labels to convey sufficient information to criminal justice professionals to enable them to make

---

[175] Gardner, above n 171, 244.

[176] See the discussion of my criticisms in J. Gardner, *Offences and Defences* (2007), 246–8.

[177] It is not clear that the counter-argument by Gardner, 'On the General Part of the Criminal Law', 236–9, deals satisfactorily with this point.

[178] For fuller discussion and references, see Ch 7.5 below on manslaughter.

[179] A. Ashworth, 'The Elasticity of Mens Rea', in C. Tapper (ed.), *Crime, Proof and Punishment* (1981); G. Williams, 'Convictions and Fair Labelling' [1983] Camb LJ 85; J. Horder, 'Rethinking Non-Fatal Offences against the Person' (1994) 14 Oxford JLS 335; B. Mitchell, 'Multiple Wrongdoing and Offence Structure: a Plea for Consistency and Fair Labelling' (2001) 64 MLR 393.

[180] J. Chalmers and F. Leverick, 'Fair Labelling in Criminal Law' (2008) 71 MLR 217, at 246.

fair and sensible decisions.'[181] Similar information may also be helpful to employers and potential employers, for example.[182]

Another justification for the principle of fair labelling does have a more direct connection with common patterns of thought in society. It is that where people generally regard two types of conduct as different, the law should try to reflect that difference. This argument was raised against the possibility of combining the crimes of theft and obtaining by deception into a single offence: people regard stealing and swindling as distinct forms of wrongdoing, and the law should not obscure this.[183] Although this proposal was not pursued, English criminal law does contain some extremely wide offences. Theft is a single offence with a maximum of seven years' imprisonment, whereas in many other jurisdictions it is subdivided into greater and lesser forms (e.g. a form of petty theft, for offences below a certain monetary value, with a lesser maximum penalty). Criminal damage is a single offence with a maximum of ten years' imprisonment, with no subdivisions to reflect the type of property damaged or the magnitude of the damage inflicted. Perhaps the clearest example is robbery, an offence with a maximum sentence of life imprisonment which conjures up an armed raid by masked men seeking substantial money or property, and yet which in English law is fulfilled by a slight push in order to snatch a purse or handbag.[184] It is regarded as axiomatic that offences of violence are sub-divided so as to distinguish different levels of injury etc.,[185] and yet robbery is not subdivided to reflect the very different degrees of force used or threatened in different cases.

What aspects of the offence should be reflected in the label? Four points may be raised in answer to this question.

First, it was noted in sections (q) and (r) above that some offences apply a much more serious label than D intended or knowingly risked—typically, the offence of manslaughter by unlawful act, for which the only fault element is in respect of the relatively minor offence of assault. The label describes the result but not the fault. This argument is examined elsewhere,[186] and controversy has recently been re-kindled by the new offences of causing death by careless driving and causing death by driving while disqualified, unlicensed or uninsured, for which the fault element is a long way below the tragic result.[187]

Secondly, dividing an offence into degrees may be sufficiently informative for criminal justice professionals but may be opposed by others, including defendants and (perhaps) the public. Thus the Law Commission's recommendation that the English law of homicide be divided into murder in the first degree, murder in the second degree and manslaughter may appear to be a triumph for fair labelling, until it is noted that provoked killings are classified not as manslaughter but as murder in the second degree—which some might regard as a misuse of the 'ultimate' label. Defendants and

---

[181] Ibid., 234.   [182] Ibid., 234–5.   [183] Below, Ch 9.2(a).
[184] A. Ashworth, 'Robbery Reassessed' [2002] Crim LR 851.
[185] Admittedly English law does not do this well: see Ch 8.3(m) below.
[186] In Ch 5.4 and Ch 7.5 below.   [187] See the discussion in Ch 7.7 below.

victims may disagree about this, but the issue is one of labelling.[188] If juries were to prove unwilling to return a verdict with the word 'murder' in it, this would create problems for the proposed scheme.

Thirdly, there are good reasons for applying the principle of fair labelling to defences. Chalmers and Leverick make the point that the same reasons favour fair labelling of justificatory defences as offences, since they may guide conduct and provide a moral assessment of conduct; for excusatory defences, it may still be important to signify why a particular verdict has been reached.[189] Similar points have been raised by those who opposed the Law Commission's proposal for a relatively narrow definition of the partial defence of provocation, on the ground that it forced some defendants (often, women) to argue their case on a defence that reflects less well on their capacity and motivation (i.e. diminished responsibility).[190]

Fourthly, and separately from the above considerations, there may be a good social reason for creating a separate offence with a separate label in order to draw public attention to the wrongness of a particular course of action. Examples of this would be the creation of racially or religiously aggravated versions of certain offences, where the aggravating feature becomes part of the offence label rather than merely a matter that affects sentencing; or, as a more long-standing example, the separate offence of assault on a police officer. How far this can and should be carried is a matter of much dispute, as for example in relation to the separate offences of causing death by driving— why are they phrased in terms of 'causing death by' rather than 'manslaughter by' or 'culpable homicide by'? Why is there no similar offence of 'causing death by medical negligence'?[191] Each of the four points above demonstrates the complex and contestable issues involved in implementing the principle of fair labelling.

(t) EFFICIENCY OF ADMINISTRATION

Economic arguments would tend to favour broader drafting of offences, leaving appropriate distinctions in culpability to be made at the sentencing stage. A welcome reduction in public expenditure on the court system would follow. The labels given to offences are regarded as less important than the actual assessment of culpability, and this can be done expeditiously at the sentencing stage. A further efficiency argument stems from the limitations of juries and lay magistrates: the criminal law must be kept as simple as possible so as to avoid confusing lay people and producing erroneous verdicts, and this argues against finely graded offences which necessitate complex instructions on the law. Many of the reforms brought about by the Theft Act 1968 and the Criminal Damage Act 1971 involved broader offences with high maximum penalties, favouring efficiency of administration at the expense of the principle of fair labelling. However, as already noted, some respect was shown for fair labelling by,

---

[188] For detailed discussion, see Ch 7.3 below.   [189] Chalmers and Leverick, 'Fair Labelling', 244–6.
[190] See further Ch 7.4 below.
[191] See A. Ashworth, 'Manslaughter: Generic or Nominate Offences?', drawing from several other essays in C. Clarkson and S. Cunningham (eds), *Criminal Liability for Non-Aggressive Death* (2008).

for example, retaining the separate offences of theft and deception, when it would have been possible to combine the two.[192] The common law offence of conspiracy to defraud is the prime example of allowing administrative efficiency to prevail—prosecutors greatly prize its flexibility—and, as noted below, the government departed from the Law Commission's recommendation and has retained this broad 'blunderbuss' offence despite the enactment of the new offences in the Fraud Act 2006.[193] Although the Sexual Offences Act 2003 was drafted so as to include many differentiated but overlapping offences, many of those offences are drafted over-broadly and rely on prosecutorial discretion for the exclusion of cases—such as sexual familiarities between young people—that ought not to be criminalized. This creates a problem of mis-labelling when prosecutorial discretion is not exercised appropriately and results in conviction for an unduly harsh offence.[194] In fact, the whole ethos of 'efficient administration' needs to be questioned. 'Efficiency' and 'practicality' are presented as neutral concepts, when they often boil down to the convenience of prosecutors. Rarely does one hear reference to the efficiency of a rule in protecting individual rights.

(u) THE PRINCIPLE OF CONTEMPORANEITY

Part of the basic doctrine of criminal law, as described by Hall among others,[195] is that not only must the defendant cause the prohibited consequence and have the required fault, but that conduct and fault must co-exist at the same time. This is the principle of contemporaneity. We will see in Chapter 5.4(c) below that the analysis of cases in the light of this principle can become rather difficult where there is a series of acts or a continuing act and where the fault element is only present for part of the time.

(v) THE DOCTRINE OF PRIOR FAULT

Even though the defendant did not have the required fault when performing the prohibited conduct, the doctrine of prior fault may be invoked to hold him liable—by fastening on to the defendant's fault at an earlier stage, which then led to an absence of fault at the time when the prohibited conduct took place. The title of Paul Robinson's seminal article, 'Causing the Conditions of One's Own Defence',[196] explains the rationale of the doctrine. A person should not be allowed to rely on an exculpatory condition (e.g. lack of fault through automatism or intoxication) if he or she had deliberately or even negligently brought about that condition (e.g. by failing to take proper medication or by drinking alcohol to excess). Thus the doctrine operates by way of exception to—or, some would say, it conflicts with—the principle of contemporaneity. The doctrine, which shares some of the roots of constructive liability, is discussed further in Chapter 5.4(d) below.

---

[192] Criminal Law Revision Committee, 8th Report, *Theft and Related Offences*, Cmnd 2977 (1966), para. 38.

[193] See Ch 9.8 and 9.9. below.   [194] E.g. *G.* [2008] UKHL 37, discussed in Ch 8.5 below.

[195] J. Hall, *General Principles of Criminal Law* (2nd edn., 1960).   [196] (1985) 71 Virginia LR 1.

3.7 CONCLUSIONS

The purpose of this chapter has been to identify and to examine critically some of the theoretical and practical arguments for lawmaking and interpretation in the criminal law. The discussion has focused on arguments of principle, but this normative dimension has been linked to the practical issues that arise in the tasks of proposing legislation, interpreting statutes, and developing the common law. When referring to 'principles' the reference has been chiefly one of aspiration: it is not suggested that any of these principles is recognized as authoritative in English criminal law, and we have seen how often pragmatic or political arguments have held sway. Indeed, some of the normative propositions referred to here as 'principles' are not even regarded as sufficiently important to call upon legislators or judges who wish to depart from them to justify the departure. And even when a principle is recognized, its wording may be so indeterminate (e.g. *maximum* certainty, *fair* warning, *fair* labelling) as to impose only loose constraints.

The Human Rights Act has not brought major changes. The Convention does not have widespread relevance to the substantive criminal law, but it has had some effect on approaches to defining offences and to judicial decision-making. Although the potential significance of Article 7 was diluted by the Strasbourg Court in *CR and SW v United Kingdom*,[197] there has been some willingness to apply the 'quality of law' standard when the government is trying to justify interference with the rights in Article 5 and Articles 8–11, for example.[198] The judiciary has taken Convention rights seriously in some high-profile decisions, on such matters as reverse burdens of proof,[199] certainty of definition in the offence of public nuisance,[200] and of course the detention without trial of terrorist suspects.[201]

Although political forces often hold sway in lawmaking, it is vital that principled arguments continue to be pressed, and this supplies a good reason for an assessment of appropriate principles of aspiration. As we have seen, some paradoxes emerge from the different pairs of principles. For example, the advocates of a degree of constructive liability rely on the occurrence of significant harm, however unexpected, as a reason for increasing the grade of an offence; yet they may not place such importance on resulting harm when accepting criminal liability for attempts, incitement, and other inchoate offences. The main thrust of this chapter has been to argue for greater attention to the rule of law and to the principle of autonomy when determining the conditions of criminal liability. Thus the subjective principles, the non-retroactivity principle, the principle of maximum certainty, the principle of strict construction, the principle of fair labelling, and the presumption of innocence—all of them tend to emphasize the value of fair warning and predictability in the law, the importance of respecting choices made by autonomous individuals, and the need to control the

---

[197] (1996) 21 EHRR 363.   [198] See above, Ch 3.5(i).   [199] See above, Ch 3.5(m).
[200] *Goldstein and Rimmington* [2005] UKHL 63.   [201] *A v Home Secretary* [2004] UKHL 56.

exercise of power by state officials. They are at the heart of legality, of the rule of law, and of what has been termed 'defensive criminal law'.[202] Whereas welfare-based principles and policies of social defence are more relevant to criminalization decisions, the rule of law and the principle of autonomy should have priority in relation to the conditions of liability, qualified only by a minimalist welfare principle. In some situations it will be justifiable to impose duties of citizenship reinforced by the criminal law, but in section 3.4(c) above it was argued that this could be done in certain circumstances without compromising the principle of autonomy. This debate, and others connected with it, is taken forward in the context of criminal conduct in the next chapter.

FURTHER READING

J. Gardner, *Offences and Defences: Selected Essays in the Philosophy of Criminal Law* (2007), 33–56 and 246–8.

J. Chalmers and F. Leverick, 'Fair Labelling in Criminal Law' (2008) 71 MLR 217–46.

B. Juratowitch, *Retroactivity and the Common Law* (2008), 43–60, 127–38, 183–97.

Law Commission Consultation Paper No 177, *A New Homicide Act for England and Wales?* (2005), 45–8.

[202] N. Jareborg, 'What Kind of Criminal Law do We Want?', *Beware of Punishment* (1995), discussed in Ch 2.4(a) above.

4

CRIMINAL CONDUCT: *ACTUS REUS*, CAUSATION AND JUSTIFICATION

4.1 THE GENERAL PART OF THE CRIMINAL LAW

This chapter and the following two chapters discuss what is usually known as the general part of the criminal law. It has been traditional for writers on English criminal law to approach the analysis of offences by means of two concepts with Latin names, *actus reus* and *mens rea*: the *actus reus* consists of the prohibited behaviour or conduct, including any specified consequences; the *mens rea* is usually described as the mental element—the intention, knowledge, or recklessness of the defendant in relation to the proscribed conduct. Whether this distinction is given Latin names or is expressed, as preferred here, in terms of conduct elements and fault elements, the distinction is nothing more than an analytical tool, and at that a rather 'rough and ready' one. It does have implications—for example, if the absence of lawful justification for conduct is treated as an element of the *actus reus*, this indicates that a defendant who was mistaken about the facts giving rise to the justification should not be criminally liable if the offence requires *mens rea* or fault.[1] It also has some manifest shortcomings: many of the accepted 'defences' to crime cannot be explained in terms of absence of fault or lack of *mens rea*—such defences as duress and even intoxication require a more complex account. Moreover, it can be strongly argued that what is often portrayed as 'the

---

[1] See the further discussions of this principle in Ch 5.5(d) below.

general part' of English criminal law is no such thing: with thousands of strict liability offences[2] and many other variations of liability, what many writers refer to as the general part is no more than a set of aspirational principles—and others argue that we should even abandon the aspiration, and admit appropriate variations in liability according to the context.[3]

Recognition of the inadequacy of the traditional *mens rea/actus reus* distinction has led to a search for more helpful ways of constructing a framework for criminal law.[4] German law has long adopted a threefold distinction between wrongdoing, absence of justification, and culpability,[5] but a more elaborate structure is probably needed if it is to be faithful to the inevitable complexity of modern criminal law.[6] There is no space here to examine these issues more extensively, and the classification adopted may be said to be less important than an enquiry into that which it might obscure, i.e. 'what the preconditions to criminal liability really are, and how far they really reflect the principles they are commonly supposed to encapsulate'.[7] For convenience of exposition the conditions of criminal liability may be divided into four working groups:

(i)   act and causation requirements;

(ii)   absence of justification;

(iii)   capacity and fault requirements;

(iv)   excusatory defences.

Chapter 5 below has been expanded in this edition to deal with the requirements of criminal capacity (the doctrines of insanity, infancy and corporate liability) as well as traditional *mens rea* requirements, i.e. the range of possible fault elements which the prosecution has to establish in order to construct a case for the defence to answer. Chapter 6 will discuss excusatory defences, mostly based on the absence of fault elements which do not correspond with positive *mens rea* requirements and of which the defendant has to provide some evidence in order to raise them as live issues in a case. Although these positive and negative fault requirements fall into the general part of the criminal law, it should not be assumed that they apply invariably and to all offences. We will see that there are controversial issues about the propriety of the many strict liability offences, and about the unavailability of certain defences to those charged

---

[2] See Ch 5.5(a) below.

[3] J. Gardner, 'On the General Part of the Criminal Law', in R. A. Duff (ed.), *Philosophy and the Criminal Law* (1998).

[4] See the critical essay by P. H. Robinson, 'Should the Criminal Law Abandon the Actus Reus/Mens Rea Distinction?', in S. Shute, J. Gardner, and J. Horder, (eds.), *Action and Value in Criminal Law* (1993).

[5] See G. P. Fletcher, *Rethinking Criminal Law* (1978).

[6] P. H. Robinson, *Structure and Function in Criminal Law* (1997).

[7] A. T. H. Smith, 'On Actus Reus and Mens Rea', in P. R. Glazebrook (ed.), *Reshaping the Criminal Law* (1978), 95.

with particular crimes. There are also some defences that do not fit easily into any recognized category.[8]

This chapter deals with both (i) act and causation requirements and (ii) absence of justification. It is fundamental to the characterization of certain conduct as criminal that it is not justified. Although some offences are drafted so as to exclude justifiable conduct, the most usual approach is to define offences without reference to the possibility that the conduct may be justified under certain circumstances. This leaves the justifications in the general part of the criminal law. Perhaps it is for this reason that they are often classified as 'general defences', since they arise only when the defendant raises them. They may be said to function like defences, but their significance is more fundamental. Conduct which is justified is right, or at least permissible, in the circumstances. This is quite different in theory from the operation of defences which are excuses (e.g. duress, intoxication, mistake), discussed in Chapter 6 below. There the act is wrongful, but the defendant is excused on account of his lack of culpability at the time. Where the defendant's act is regarded as justifiable (e.g. self-defence), the act is not wrongful—even though in most situations, where no justification applies, it would be.[9] Justifications therefore negate criminal conduct. They also afford some guidance to citizens on the circumstances in which they are permitted or right to use force, cause damage, etc., and therefore they ought to comply with standards of fair warning.[10]

The chapter begins with an exploration of the doctrines of voluntariness, acts, omissions, and causation. To proceed to conviction without proof of voluntary conduct would be to fail, in the most fundamental way, to show respect for individuals as rational, choosing beings. More generally, if people were liable to conviction despite doing nothing, or because something had been done *to* them, this would fail to respect their autonomy (see Chapter 2.1) and would certainly not give them fair warning of the incidence of the criminal sanction, unless reasonable duties had been made plain to them.[11] Similarly, where it cannot be established that the defendant (D) was responsible for the conduct or consequence prohibited by the crime, there should be no conviction.

Some such requirements are needed to protect individual autonomy by ensuring that both Parliament and the courts preserve fair warning and fair opportunities to choose not to offend. The chapter begins with the notion of involuntary conduct, the limits of which are examined in section 4.2. We then turn in section 4.3 to various challenges to the 'voluntary act' requirement—where is the act if the law criminalizes the occurrence of a state of affairs, or mere possession? Section 4.4 considers how

---

[8] A. Ashworth, 'Testing Fidelity to Legal Values: Official Involvement and Criminal Justice' (2000) 63 MLR 633.

[9] Cf. J. Gardner, *Offences and Defences* (2007), ch 4.

[10] P. Robinson, 'The Modern General Part: Three Illusions', in S. Shute and A. P. Simester (eds.), *Criminal Law Theory: Doctrines of the General Part* (2002); because the justifications guide conduct, M. Moore (*Placing Blame*, (1997), ch 1) goes so far as to state that they belong to the 'special part'.

[11] This caters for criminal liability for omissions, discussed in section 4.4 below.

the voluntary act requirement relates to crimes of omission. We then turn to causation, and later deal with the circumstances in which conduct may be recognized as justifiable.

4.2 INVOLUNTARY CONDUCT

(a) AUTOMATISM AND AUTHORSHIP[12]

Automatism is often regarded as a defence to crime rather than as an essential component of criminal conduct. Certainly the discussion that follows has more in common with the treatment of various excuses in Chapter 6 than with the rest of this chapter, and illustrates the heterogeneity of the concept of *actus reus*. Its appearance here, however, reflects its fundamental nature. Automatism is not merely a denial of fault: its import runs far deeper than a claim that conduct was accidental or unintentional.[13] It is more of a denial of authorship, a claim that the ordinary link between mind and behaviour was absent; the person could not be said to be acting as a moral agent at the time—what occurred was a set of involuntary movements of the body rather than 'acts' of D. The usual examples of this are behaviour following concussion, being physically overpowered by another person, and being attacked by a swarm of bees whilst driving.

The theory is that automatism prevents liability for all crimes. One way of rationalizing this within the traditional framework of *actus reus* and *mens rea* is to maintain that automatism negates *actus reus*, since it shows that the conduct or omission was not the result of the defendant *acting* but of something *happening to* the defendant. Since all crimes require a form of conduct, even if some of them do not require fault, it follows that automatism may lead to acquittal on any and every charge. Many of the early cases concerned motoring offences for which strict liability is imposed, and to which automatism is one of the few routes to acquittal. However, since automatism operates as such a powerful exculpatory factor, the courts have attempted to circumscribe its use, defining it fairly narrowly and developing three major doctrines of limitation.

Although it is common to refer to automatism as a 'defence', in practice voluntary conduct is assumed in all cases. Where, exceptionally, a defendant brings credible evidence to raise the possibility of involuntariness, the prosecution must establish beyond reasonable doubt that the accused was not in a state of automatism when the conduct occurred. In some cases, only expert medical evidence will be sufficient to provide a foundation for the judge to leave the issue to the jury, or the magistrates

---

[12] See generally R. D. Mackay, *Mental Condition Defences in the Criminal Law* (1995), ch 1; R. F. Schopp, *Automatism, Insanity, and the Psychology of Criminal Responsibility* (1991).

[13] Thus in *Attorney General's Reference (No. 4 of 2000)* [2001] Crim LR 578 a driver claimed that when he put his foot down to the brake pedal he pressed the accelerator instead and the bus shot forward out of his control; this was truly a claim of accident and not of involuntary conduct.

to dismiss the charge.[14] Thus, when it is said that 'voluntary action is a fundamental requirement of criminal liability', it should not be overlooked that it is rare for the issue to arise in court.

(b) THE ESSENCE OF AUTOMATISM

Examples of forms of involuntariness which might amount to automatism include convulsions, muscle spasms, acts following concussion, physically coerced movements, etc. Criminal lawyers used to express the legal position in terms of a requirement of a voluntary act, going on to say that an act is voluntary if it is willed.[15] One criticism of this is that it does not explain how the act of will itself occurs, and suggests an infinite causal regress;[16] another is that it misrepresents and exaggerates our awareness of the movements involved in our behaviour.[17] These criticisms led Hart to propose a 'negative' definition, describing involuntary actions as 'movements of the body which occurred though the agent had no reason for moving his body in that way'.[18] This switches attention to rare occasions of involuntariness, of which two types may be identified—behaviour which is uncontrollable, and behaviour which proceeds from severely impaired consciousness. Uncontrollable behaviour may be illustrated thus: D is physically overpowered by X and is made to stab V. In these circumstances it is fair to say that this was not D's *act* but something which *happened to* D: the same view might be taken of a person brought to this country by ferry and then forced to leave the ferry and step on to British soil.[19] Further examples may be conduct during an epileptic fit, and reflex actions. Turning to behaviour proceeding from a lack of consciousness, this can be illustrated by things done during a hypoglycaemic episode (which may be the result of taking insulin to correct diabetes). Both types of automatism should apply equally to offences of omission, excusing those who fail to fulfil a legal duty through physical incapacity arising from inability to control behaviour or through significantly reduced consciousness.[20]

Those final words bring us to an unresolved question. Must a court be satisfied beyond reasonable doubt that the defendant had a total lack of consciousness or of control over his behaviour, or will a lesser impairment suffice? In the first place, we should recall that the prosecution bears the burden of proof, ultimately, and all that the defence need do is to bring credible evidence. In *Broome v Perkins* (1987),[21]

---

[14] *Cook v Atchison* [1968] Crim LR 266.

[15] The classic statement is that of J. Austin, *Lectures on Jurisprudence* (5th edn., 1885), 411–24. For an excellent application of the philosophy of action to criminal responsibility see R. A. Duff, *Criminal Attempts* (1996), chs 9–11.

[16] A. I. Melden, 'Willing', in A. R. White (ed.), *The Philosophy of Action* (1968), 77.

[17] H. L. A. Hart, *Punishment and Responsibility* (2nd edn., 2008), 103.

[18] Ibid., 255–6, reformulating (in response to criticism) the passage appearing at 105.

[19] The facts of *Larsonneur*, discussed in the text accompanying n 53 below.

[20] See Model Penal Code, art. 2.01(1), draft Criminal Code (Law Com No. 177) cl. 33(2), and A. Smart, 'Responsibility for Failing to Do the Impossible' (1987) 103 LQR 532.

[21] (1987) 85 Cr App R 321; see also *Isitt* (1978) 67 Cr App R 44.

upholding a conviction for careless driving even though the defendant had been in a hypoglycaemic state, the Divisional Court held in effect that the defence must adduce credible evidence that the defendant was exercising no control over his bodily movements at the time. A similarly stringent test was applied in *Attorney General's Reference (No. 2 of 1992)*,[22] where there had been expert evidence about a condition known as 'driving without awareness', but the Court held that automatism requires a 'total destruction of voluntary control on the defendant's part', and that the alleged condition did not establish this. These decisions are inconsistent with earlier cases in which the defendant's consciousness was significantly reduced but not totally absent, and yet where this was held sufficient for an acquittal;[23] both *Broome* and the *Reference* case concerned road traffic offences, and it is possible that a more restrictive view is taken there because of the risk of false claims, but that is hardly a convincing reason for such a significant distinction in the application of the involuntariness requirement.

What, then, should be the extent of the involuntariness doctrine? Hart's definition depends upon the absence of a reason for the movements of the body ('the mind of a man bent on some conscious action'[24]) whereas the cases seem to have more to do with an absence of capacity. Glanville Williams, taking this point, argued that movements are involuntary if D is unable to avoid them.[25] Not only does this involve a shift of emphasis to capacity, but it also strikes an unusual note in asking not only whether D did control the movements (were they uncontroll*ed*?), but whether D could have controlled them (were they uncontroll*able*?). Williams's approach is preferable here, as the draft Code recognizes; Hart's test dwells on cognition, whereas the essence of automatism is lack of volition. But there is no concealing the questions of judgement it leaves open. The draft Code includes within automatism any movement which '(i) is a reflex, spasm or convulsion; or (ii) occurs while he is in a condition (whether of sleep, unconsciousness, impaired consciousness or otherwise) depriving him of effective control of the act'.[26] The key concept here is 'effective control', and this, combined with 'impaired consciousness', shows how difficult it is to eliminate questions of degree even from such a fundamental aspect of criminal liability. The *essence* of automatism lies in D's inability to control the movement (or non-movement) of his body at the relevant time, but it may be thought unduly harsh to restrict the doctrine to cases of apparently total deprivation. The phrase proposed by the Law Commission, 'depriving him of effective control', would expressly empower the courts to evaluate and judge D's worthiness for a complete acquittal, whereas if the decisions in *Broome v Perkins* and *Attorney General's Reference (No. 2 of 1992)* represent the law (at least within the sphere of road traffic offences) the doctrine of automatism is unavailable whenever the court believes that there was a residual element of control in the defendant's behaviour at the time. The advantage of the Law Commission's formula would be to allow sensitivity to the

---

[22] (1993) 97 Cr App R 429.   [23] E.g. *Charlson* [1955] 1 WLR 317; *Quick* [1973] QB 910.
[24] Hart, *Punishment and Responsibility*, 106.
[25] G. Williams, *Textbook of Criminal Law* (2nd edn., 1983), ch 29.   [26] Law Com No. 177, cl. 33(1).

special facts of unusual cases; its disadvantage would lie in the freedom left to courts to incorporate extraneous considerations into their judgments.

At common law the courts have imposed at least three major limitations on the doctrine of automatism—by excluding cases involving insanity, intoxication, and prior fault—and it is to these developments that we must now turn.

(c) INSANE AUTOMATISM

Even if D's bodily movements are uncontrollable or proceed from unconsciousness, the doctrine of automatism will not be available if the cause of D's condition was a mental disorder classified as insanity.[27] The courts originally developed this policy for reasons of social defence, since it ensured that those who fell within the legal definition of insanity were subject to the special verdict and (at that time) to indefinite detention rather than being allowed to argue that their condition rendered their acts uncontrollable, and that they should therefore have an unqualified acquittal on the grounds of automatism.

The social policy behind this judicial approach is expressed most clearly in Lord Denning's speech in *Bratty v Attorney-General for Northern Ireland* (1963).[28] D based his defence to a murder charge on psychomotor epilepsy, but the trial judge ruled that automatism was not available, holding that the true nature of the condition was a disease of the mind and that therefore insanity was the only defence. The House of Lords upheld the trial judge's approach, and Lord Denning affirmed that 'it is not every involuntary act which leads to a complete acquittal'. D's behaviour may have been involuntary, 'but it does not give rise to an unqualified acquittal, for that would mean that he would be left at large to do it again'. The proper verdict is one of insanity, 'which ensures that the person who suffers from the disease is kept secure in a hospital so as not to be a danger to himself or others'. Moreover, Lord Denning was inclined to give 'mental disease' a broad definition for this purpose, so as to include 'any mental disorder which has manifested itself in violence and is prone to recur'. This decision confirmed the dominance of the policy of social defence over considerations of individual responsibility.

In practice, the effect of this strict approach has not been greatly to swell the numbers of people pleading insanity. Typically, if a defence is based on automatism but the judge rules that, since the origin of D's condition was a 'disease of the mind', the defence should be treated as one of insanity, many defendants decide to plead guilty to the charge rather than to persist with an insanity defence. The Criminal Procedure (Insanity and Unfitness to Plead) Act 1991 grants courts a discretion to choose committal to hospital, absolute discharge, a guardianship order, or a supervision order, if there is an insanity verdict.[29] This still places considerable emphasis on social defence,

---

[27] Discussed in detail in Ch 5.2 below.   [28] [1963] AC 386.
[29] For further discussion see Ch 5.2(c) below.

and may not be an attractive option if the defendant's condition bears little relation to the common understanding of insanity.

In recent years the courts have tended to transfer more varieties of involuntariness out of automatism and into insanity. The leading case is *Quick* (1973),[30] where D's defence against a charge of causing actual bodily harm was that the attack occurred during a hypoglycaemic episode brought on by the use of insulin and his failure to eat an adequate lunch. The defence relied on automatism, whereas the prosecution sought and obtained a ruling that the condition amounted to insanity. The defendant then pleaded guilty and appealed. The Court of Appeal, quashing the conviction, held that a malfunctioning of the mind does not constitute a 'disease of the mind' within the insanity defence if it is 'caused by the application to the body of some external factor such as violence, drugs, including anaesthetics, alcohol, and hypnotic influences'. This 'external factor' doctrine was accepted by the House of Lords in *Sullivan* (1984),[31] where it was also restated that 'diseases of the mind' include both permanent and transitory conditions. Thus, where the malfunctioning of the mind is caused by an external factor, the legal classification is automatism rather than insanity, and the prosecution must disprove D's claim; where it arises from an internal cause, the classification is insanity, and the burden of proof lies on D. This leads to the apparently strange result that a hypoglycaemic episode (resulting from the taking of insulin to correct diabetes) falls within automatism, whereas a hyperglycaemic episode (resulting from a high blood-sugar level which has not been corrected) falls within insanity, since it is an internal condition rather than a condition caused by an external factor.[32] Epilepsy falls within insanity for the same reason.

The courts have also applied the internal–external distinction to cases of somnambulism. In *Burgess* (1991)[33] the Court of Appeal held that, since there is no external cause of sleepwalking, this condition must be regarded as arising from internal causes and therefore classified as insanity, following *Quick* and *Sullivan*. The defendant in *Burgess* had not changed his plea to guilty but succeeded on a plea of insanity. Now, under the Criminal Procedure (Insanity and Unfitness to Plead) Act 1991, it would be open to a judge to grant a conditional discharge in these circumstances. However, the 'insanity' label might be unwelcome to many such defendants, and English law has no satisfactory means of dealing with cases involving both danger and an absence of responsibility.[34] The case for an urgent review of the 'external factor' doctrine is strong.[35]

---

[30] [1973] QB 910.   [31] [1984] AC 156.

[32] *Hennessy* (1989) 89 Cr App R 10; *Bingham* [1991] Crim LR 433.

[33] [1991] 2 QB 92; cf. *Bilton, The Daily Telegraph*, 20 July 2005, where a person who carried out serious sexual acts while sleepwalking was apparently acquitted entirely.

[34] For an illuminating discussion, see I. Embrahim *et al.*, 'Violence, Sleepwalking and the Criminal Law: the Medical Aspects' [2005] Crim LR 614, and W. Wilson *et al.*, 'Violence, Sleepwalking and the Criminal Law: the Legal Aspects' [2005] Crim LR 624.

[35] R. D. Mackay and B. J. Mitchell, 'Sleepwalking, Automatism and Insanity' [2006] Crim LR 901.

One type of condition that has not yet been classified authoritatively in England is 'dissociation', which is often marked by a short period of uncharacteristic behaviour accompanied by some degree of memory loss. In *Rabey* (1978)[36] the Supreme Court of Canada ruled, in the case of a defendant who attacked a woman who had rejected his admiration for her, that the dissociative state in which he acted could not be classified as automatism. Although D's rejection by the woman might be regarded as an external factor, 'the ordinary stresses and disappointments of life which are the common lot of mankind do not constitute an external cause constituting an explanation for a malfunctioning of the mind which takes it out of the category of a "disease of the mind"'. Thus the rejection was an external factor but not the primary cause of the dissociative state: the Supreme Court thought that this lay in the defendant's 'psychological or emotional make-up'. That approach left open the possibility that an utterly extraordinary event might suffice as an external cause, and a trial judge so ruled in *T* (1990).[37] Here the defendant had been raped three days before she joined two others in a robbery, during which she said 'I'm ill, I'm ill' and then stabbed a bystander. Her defence was one of automatism arising from post-traumatic stress disorder caused by the rape. The judge ruled that the rape was a sufficient external cause to place the case within the doctrine of automatism rather than insanity.

(d) AUTOMATISM THROUGH INTOXICATION

Although the Court of Appeal in *Quick* held that automatism arising from intoxication does not fall within the definition of insanity, this does not mean that a person who causes harm whilst in such an intoxicated state as to have significantly reduced consciousness or to be unable to control movements of the body should be brought within the doctrine of automatism. If the cause of the involuntariness is intoxication, then the courts treat the case as falling within the ambit of the intoxication doctrine. It is rare for the evidence to be strong enough to raise a reasonable doubt that D was sufficiently intoxicated as to be in a state of automatism, but this seems to have been accepted in *Lipman* (1970),[38] where D had taken drugs and believed that he was fighting off snakes and descending to the centre of the earth, whereas he was actually suffocating his girlfriend. A defence of automatism was refused, and the case was treated as one of intoxication,[39] drawing on the doctrine of prior fault discussed in (e) below. However, if D's condition appears to have arisen through intoxication followed by concussion resulting from a bump on the head, the court may have to establish the dominant cause of the condition and subsequent behaviour.[40]

---

[36] (1978) 79 DLR (3d) 414, on which see R. D. Mackay, 'Non-Organic Automatism—Some Recent Developments' [1980] Crim LR 350.

[37] [1990] Crim LR 256 (Snaresbrook Crown Court).   [38] [1970] 1 QB 152.

[39] On which see below, Ch 6.2. If English law were to abandon the *Majewski* approach and adopt the Antipodean solution (see p. 215 below), cases of involuntariness through intoxication would fall to be dealt with by the general rules on automatism.

[40] *Stripp* (1979) 69 Cr App R 318.

(e) PRIOR FAULT

The aim of the doctrine of prior fault[41] is to prevent D taking advantage of a condition if it arose through D's own fault. In relation to automatism, the point was first made in *Quick* (1973),[42] where Lawton LJ held that there could be no acquittal on this ground if the condition 'could have been reasonably foreseen as a result of either doing or omitting to do something, as, for example, taking alcohol against medical advice after using certain prescribed drugs, or failing to take regular meals whilst taking insulin'. According to this view, the question of prior fault is resolved by applying the test of reasonable foreseeability, the test of the reasonably prudent person in D's position. But in *Bailey* (1983)[43] the Court of Appeal held that a person should not be liable to conviction if the condition of automatism arose through a simple failure to appreciate the consequences of not taking sufficient food after a dose of insulin, even if the reasonably prudent person would have realized it. The defence of automatism should be available unless it can be shown that D knew that his acts or omissions were likely 'to make him aggressive, unpredictable and uncontrolled with the result that he may cause some injury to others'. On this view, prior fault requires awareness of risk, sometimes called subjective recklessness.[44]

The conflict between the doctrine of prior fault and the principle of contemporaneity of conduct and fault is discussed elsewhere.[45] The question here is whether the doctrine should apply at all in automatism cases. Consider the approach of trying to avoid the conflict with the contemporaneity principle by convicting D in respect of conduct at an earlier point in time, when there was fault. In *Kay* v *Butterworth* (1945)[46] D fell asleep while driving home from night-work, and his car collided with soldiers marching down the road. It was held that he could be convicted of careless driving—not in respect of the collision (when he was asleep and therefore involuntarily omitting to exercise due care), but in respect of his earlier failure to stop driving when he felt drowsy. Even on its own terms, this approach is possible only where the offence is of a continuing nature, and where the charge can be appropriately worded. But one advantage of this approach is that it recognizes that the driving was at one stage involuntary, and that involuntary movements cannot be the subject of criminal liability. The application of prior fault in cases such as *Quick* fails to take this point, in the sense that criminal liability still depends on, or is traced through, the involuntary movements.[47] Only if one maintains that the doctrine of prior fault is so fundamental to our notions of responsibility that it trumps ordinary causal principles, as well as the principle of contemporaneity, can the law's position be rationalized.

---

[41] Discussed above, Ch 3.6(v), and below, Ch 5.4(d).

[42] [1973] QB 910; for discussion of this development see A. J. Ashworth, 'Reason, Logic and Criminal Liability' (1975) 91 LQR 102.

[43] (1983) 77 Cr App R 76.   [44] On which see below, Ch 5.5(c).

[45] See above, Ch 3.6(u), and below, Ch 5.4(d).   [46] (1945) 173 LT 191.

[47] See C. Finkelstein, 'Involuntary Crimes, Voluntarily Committed', in S. Shute and A. P. Simester (eds.), *Criminal Law Theory: Doctrines of the General Part* (2002).

(f) REFORM

The proposition that people should not be held liable for conduct that is involuntary is fundamental, and the common law on automatism has developed from it. However, even accepting that cases of prior fault should continue to be excluded from automatism and that cases resulting from intoxication should be classified under the intoxication rules, one major unsatisfactory feature of the law on automatism is the line drawn between this doctrine and the defence of insanity. Since the courts have flexible powers of disposal under the 1991 Act, it may be argued that judicial persistence with the internal/external distinction does not have drastic implications for defendants. None the less, there can be no sense in classifying hypoglycaemic states as automatism and hyperglycaemic states as insanity, when both states are so closely associated with such a common condition as diabetes. The difference in burdens of proof (prosecution must disprove automatism, defence must prove insanity) compounds the anomaly. The proper boundaries of the defence of insanity will be examined further in Chapter 5.2(c), but it is apparent from the discussion here that the present scope of the phrase 'disease of the mind' is too wide. There are many states in which the functioning of the mind is affected but which should not sensibly be included within the concept of insanity. On the other hand, it is difficult to arrive at a clear definition of automatism: the draft Code refers to 'impaired consciousness...depriving him of effective control of the act'.[48] This rightly recognizes that total absence of control should not be required, but it therefore leaves us with a test dependent on a judgement of degree and value ('effective'), and does so without identifying the relevance of the defendant's capacity rather than awareness and 'choice'.[49]

4.3 ACTS, STATES OF AFFAIRS, AND POSSESSION

Accepting that a person should not be held liable for things which occur whilst he or she is in an involuntary state amounting to automatism, should there be a further requirement that liability should be based on acts? At first blush it seems wrong that people should be held liable for things that happen to them, or for doing nothing. Do legal systems succeed in avoiding the creation of offences that do not require an act? Should they try to avoid such offences?[50]

Before sketching answers to those two questions, we must make the point that not all criminal offences are formulated so as to require proof of a particular *type* of act. For some offences, such as wounding and rape, the definition specifies an act and it is

---

[48] Ch 5.2(d).

[49] Compare Law Com No. 177, paras. 11.3–11.4, with the discussion of the case of *T* by J. Horder, 'Pleading Involuntary Lack of Capacity' (1993) 52 Camb LJ 298, at 312–15.

[50] Cf. M. Moore, *Act and Crime* (1993), with Duff, *Criminal Attempts*, chs 9–11, and A. P. Simester, 'On the So-Called Requirement for Voluntary Action' (1998) 1 Buffalo Crim LR 403.

clearly a wrongful act. For some offences, such as doing an act with intent to impede the apprehension of a person who has committed an arrestable offence,[51] and all crimes of attempt, the definition requires an act, but not one that is in itself wrongful: the intention with which the act is done is critical, but the act requirement still functions so as to exclude involuntary movements. (Whether ordinary acts should be penalized simply because of the actor's intentions is discussed elsewhere.[52]) For other offences, the definition refers only to a result (e.g. causing death), and the act requirement is implicit. Any kind of act suffices. Those offences have a tendency to raise questions of causation (did D's act cause the death?), which draws attention to another feature of the act requirement: what is necessary is not merely an act, but an act that causes the conduct or consequence specified in the definition of the offence. This should rule out cases in which D's act is superseded by the voluntary intervening act of some third party—where it is the intervening act, and not D's original act, that is the cause. The troublesome decisions on voluntary intervening acts are reviewed in section 4.5 below.

There are three types of offence that appear to challenge the requirement of an act. First, there are offences relating to states of affairs: is it right that a person should be liable to conviction in respect of a state of affairs that happens to him, and is not his act? Secondly, most criminal codes contain offences of possession, and it is questionable whether these require any act. Thirdly, and most obviously, there are offences of omission. The essence of these offences is that they penalize a person for doing nothing when he or she should have done something. We examine in the next section whether, and to what extent, offences of omission can be justified. In the remainder of this section, states of affairs and offences of possession are considered.

(a) SITUATIONAL LIABILITY

Are there good reasons for convicting a person simply because a state of affairs exists, without the person 'doing' anything? The leading case is *Larsonneur* (1933),[53] where D left England because the duration of her permitted stay had come to an end. She went to Ireland, from where she was deported back to this country. On her return, she was convicted of 'being found in the United Kingdom' contrary to the Aliens Order 1920. Her appeal, based on the argument that her return to England was beyond her control, was dismissed by the Court of Criminal Appeal. The case is widely criticized: her return to this country was not her own act, and was contrary to her will and desire. The Court might have held that there was no voluntary act by the defendant, since it appears that various officials compelled her return to this country. It might then have given consideration to the degree of any prior fault on her part.[54] The judgment fails to discuss these points of principle, and the decision hardly shines as a beacon of common law reasoning. However, *Larsonneur* does not stand alone. In *Winzar* v *Chief*

---

[51] Criminal Law Act 1967, s. 4.   [52] See Ch 11, below.   [53] (1933) 149 LT 542.

[54] Cf. the analysis by D. J. Lanham, '*Larsonneur* Revisited' [1976] Crim LR 276, suggesting that the decision may have been based on prior fault (see below, Ch 5.4(e)).

Constable of Kent (1983)[55] the Divisional Court confirmed a conviction for being found drunk on a highway, in a case where the defendant had been taken from a hospital on to the highway by the police. Another similarly worded offence is that of being drunk in charge of a motor vehicle, and there are many other offences that impose what Peter Glazebrook has termed 'situational liability'.[56]

We will see in Chapter 5.3(b) below how, in certain situations, the courts have imposed 'vicarious liability' on shop owners and employers by construing statutory words so as to achieve convictions. In effect, these individuals and companies are being held liable simply for states of affairs—for the fact that an employee sold American ham as Scottish ham, for example, even though the shop owner had specifically warned against this.[57] However, Andrew Simester has argued that in all these cases it is not the absence of a required act that is objectionable, but the absence of a fault element.[58] The proper approach, he submits, is evident from two New Zealand prosecutions of visitors for staying after the expiration of a visitor's permit. In *Finau* v *Department of Labour* (1984)[59] the conviction was quashed because D was pregnant and no airline would carry her. In *Tifaga* v *Department of Labour* (1980)[60] the conviction was upheld because D was at fault in running out of money, with the result that he could not afford a ticket. The offence did not require an act (or an omission), but rather a state of affairs for which D was responsible. Thus, as argued in Chapter 5.3(b) below, it may be defensible to impose situational liability if the law is so phrased as to ensure that defendants are in control of their activities and know about their duty to avoid certain situations. This insists on a voluntariness requirement, but not an act requirement. So long as fair warning is given of the standards expected of those embarking on certain activities or enterprises, the principles of legality or 'rule of law' are satisfied and autonomy is respected.[61] The English legislature, unfortunately, sees no objection to creating state-of-affairs offences such as 'being found' or 'being drunk in charge' without any voluntariness requirement—not even exceptions to cover the person who has been manhandled into the position in which he or she is found or the person who has been rendered drunk by the stratagem of others.[62] The courts have failed to develop the common law so as to provide a defence of compulsion or to insist on proof that D was responsible (i.e. voluntarily) for the conduct, result, or state of affairs proscribed.

(b) OFFENCES OF POSSESSION

English law contains several offences of possession, relating to such items as offensive weapons,[63] any articles for use in a burglary, theft, or deception,[64] and controlled

---

[55] *The Times*, 28 March 1983.

[56] P. R. Glazebrook, 'Situational Liability', in Glazebrook (ed.), *Reshaping the Criminal Law* (1978), 108.

[57] As in *Coppen* v *Moore* [1898] 2 QB 306.

[58] Simester, 'On the So-Called Requirement for Voluntary Action', at 410–13.

[59] [1984] 2 NZLR 396.   [60] [1980] 2 NZLR 235.   [61] See Ch 3.5(g) above.

[62] Cf. *Kingston* [1995] 2 AC 355, below, Ch 6.2.   [63] Prevention of Crime Act 1953.

[64] Theft Act 1968, s. 25.

drugs.[65] Sometimes possession is the basic element of a crime in the inchoate mode, such as possessing drugs with intent to supply.[66] In ordinary language one might agree that it is possible to possess an item without any act on one's part. Are offences of this kind therefore contrary to principle? Most of the difficulties with the concept of possession have arisen in drugs cases. The leading decision is that of the House of Lords in *Warner v Metropolitan Police Commissioner* (1969),[67] but neither the speeches of their Lordships nor subsequent cases have rendered the law clear or principled. The first proposition is that a person is not in possession of an item that has been slipped into her bag or pocket without her knowledge. The second proposition is that if a person knows that an article or container has come under her control, she is deemed to be in possession of it even if mistaken about its contents, unless the thing is of a wholly different nature from what was believed.[68] The exception is extremely narrow: Warner believed that certain bags contained scent when in fact they contained cannabis, but that was held not to be a sufficiently fundamental mistake, and his knowledge that he had the bag was sufficient. In *Warner* Lord Pearce stated that the mistake would not be sufficiently fundamental if D thought the containers held sweets or aspirins when in fact they held heroin.[69] The narrowness of this exception to the second proposition throws attention back to the first proposition, but that has also been confined tightly. In *Lewis* (1988)[70] it was held that D was rightly convicted of possessing controlled drugs when they were found in a house of which he was tenant but which he rarely visited. His defence was that he neither knew nor suspected that drugs were on the premises. The Court of Appeal appeared to hold that, since he had the opportunity to search the house, he should be held to possess items that he did not know about but could have found. In effect, this reduces the first proposition almost to vanishing point. Surely it could equally be said, of the person into whose bag drugs are slipped by some third party, that she could have searched her bag and found them? Probably this is another example of the so-called 'war against drugs' resulting in the distortion of proper legal standards.

The reason for enacting offences of possession is that they enable the police to intervene before a particular wrong or harm is done: in effect, these offences extend the scope of criminal liability beyond the law of attempts.[71] One ground for questioning possession offences is that they may criminalize people at a point too remote from the ultimate harm, not allowing for a change of mind. Another pertinent question is whether they depart from the voluntariness requirement. Although taking possession of an article will often (but not always) involve some act of the defendant, it is surely wrong to regard the conduct as *voluntary* if D was substantially mistaken as to its contents. Thus the first proposition in *Warner* is right in suggesting that possession is not purely a physical matter but does have a mental component,

---

[65] Misuse of Drugs Act 1971, s. 5(2).   [66] Ibid., s. 5(3).   [67] [1969] 2 AC 256.

[68] These propositions were restated by the Court of Appeal in *McNamara* (1988) 87 Cr App R 246.

[69] [1969] 2 AC, 256, at 307.

[70] (1988) 87 Cr App R 270, with commentary by J. C. Smith at [1988] Crim LR 517.

[71] See the discussion in Ch 11.9(c) below.

although wrong in restricting that fault element to the mere realization that some item or container has arrived in one's pocket, bag, or house. The Court of Appeal has been pressed to broaden the fault element, notably in *Deyemi and Edwards* (2008),[72] chiefly by reference to those House of Lords decisions such as *B v DPP* and *K*,[73] which stated that the presumption of *mens rea* is a constitutional principle. The Court felt itself bound by previous decisions on possession of firearms, which follow the *Warner* approach, but certified a point of law of general public importance for the House of Lords. Until the decision in *Warner* is revisited, it remains objectionable that the English courts have failed to adhere to any basic voluntariness requirement, and have also ridden roughshod over normal principles of causation, which would operate so as to relieve D from liability when the voluntary act of a third party had brought about the possession.

4.4 OMISSIONS

Omissions are controversial for two main reasons—first, whether and to what extent it is justifiable to criminalize omissions rather than acts;[74] and secondly, whether liability for omissions violates the 'act requirement' in criminal law. Pursuing the second point here, much has been made above of the importance of requiring proof that the defendant voluntarily did something to produce the prohibited conduct or consequence. In so far as this can be termed an 'act requirement', are omissions a true exception to it?[75] If they are, is this another argument against criminalizing them?

One much-discussed preliminary question is the distinction between acts and omissions.[76] Sometimes it is argued that certain verbs imply action and therefore exclude liability for omissions, and that the criminal law should respect the distinctions flowing from this. English courts have often used this linguistic or interpretive approach. It has led to a variety of decisions on different statutes,[77] without much discussion of the general principles underlying omissions liability. The Law Commission's draft Criminal Code may be said to signal the continuation of this approach, by redefining the homicide offences in terms of 'causing death' rather than 'killing', and redefining the damage offences in terms of 'causing damage', rather than 'damaging', so as 'to leave fully open to the courts the possibility of so construing the relevant (statutory) provisions as to impose liability for omissions'.[78] The draft code would therefore remove any linguistic awkwardness in saying, for example, that

---

[72] [2008] 1 Cr App R 25.

[73] [2000] 2 AC 428 and [2002] 1 AC 462 respectively, discussed in Ch 5.5(a) below.

[74] On which see Ch 3.4(c) and (d) above.

[75] See Simester, 'On the So-Called Requirement for Voluntary Action', 427.

[76] See Duff, *Criminal Attempts*, 317–20.

[77] With different interpretations of words such as 'cause': see G. Williams, 'What should the Code do about Omissions?' (1987) 7 Legal Studies 92.

[78] Law Com No. 177, ii, para. 7.13; see generally paras. 7.7–7.13.

a parent killed a child by failing to feed it; but it does so in this specific instance, and without proclaiming a general principle that the act requirement may be fulfilled by an omission if a duty can be established. Attachment to the vagaries of the language is no proper basis for delineating the boundaries of criminal liability.

In some situations the courts, following the linguistic approach, have nevertheless found themselves able to impose omissions liability. In *Speck* (1977)[79] the defendant was charged with committing an act of gross indecency with or towards a child. The evidence was that an 8-year-old girl placed her hand on his trousers over his penis. He allowed the hand to remain there for some minutes, causing him to have an erection. The Court of Appeal held that the defendant's failure to remove the hand amounted to an invitation to the child to continue with the act, and that the offence would then be made out. In effect, the Court either held that his inactivity in those circumstances constituted an invitation which amounted to an act, or it created a duty in an adult to put an end to any innocent touching of this kind, with omissions liability for not fulfilling the duty. The analysis is similar to that in *Miller* (1983),[80] where D fell asleep whilst smoking, woke up to find the mattress smouldering, but simply left the room and went to sleep elsewhere. He was convicted of causing criminal damage by fire, on the basis that a person who initiates a sequence of events innocently and then fails to do anything to stop the sequence should be regarded as having caused the whole sequence. On this view the conduct constitutes a single, continuing act; Miller caused the damage because he took no steps to extinguish the fire he had innocently started. It must be doubted whether these efforts to find an act which then coincides in point of time with the defendant's knowledge or intention are convincing.[81] Surely the courts are imposing liability for an omission in these cases, by recognizing that a duty arises. *Speck* is a little different from *Miller* since the original act in *Speck* was that of the girl, and the duty must therefore amount to the recognition of an obligation on an adult to put an end to an indecent yet innocent touching by a child. In so far as these decisions appear to extend the statutory wording, are they objectionable on grounds of retro-activity and lack of fair warning, or defensible as applications of existing common law doctrine to new situations?

In other situations it seems possible to offer plausible reasons for regarding the same event as either an act or an omission, and in some cases the courts have sought to exploit this ambiguity when dealing with problematic medical issues.[82] Yet it is one thing to say that a healthcare professional who decides not to replace an empty bag for a drip-feed has made an omission, whereas switching a ventilator off is an act; it is another thing to maintain that the act–omission distinction should be crucial to any determination of the criminal liability in the two situations. In *Airedale NHS Trust v Bland* (1993)[83] the House of Lords held that it would be lawful for a doctor to withdraw treatment from a patient in a persistent vegetative state, even though

---

[79] (1977) 65 Cr App R 161.   [80] [1983] 2 AC 161.

[81] See the criticisms by J. C. Smith [1982] Crim LR 527 and 774, and D. Husak, *Philosophy of Criminal Law* (1987), 176–8.

[82] See I. M. Kennedy, *Treat Me Right* (1988), 169–74.   [83] [1993] AC 789.

death would inevitably be hastened by that conduct. The House held that the with-drawal of treatment would constitute an omission, and thus regarded the duties of the doctor as the central issue. The decision was that a doctor has no duty to continue life-supporting treatment when it is no longer in the best interests of the patient, hav-ing regard to responsible medical opinion.[84] However, the Court of Appeal declined to adopt this subterfuge in *Re A (Conjoined Twins: Surgical Separation)*,[85] holding that the surgical separation of the twins would undoubtedly be an act, and subsequently deciding that carrying out an operation which would result in the death of one twin in order to save the life of the other could be justified on grounds of necessity. This required the Court, in effect, to recognize a new defence of 'balance of evils' in English law—which was what the House of Lords tried to avoid in *Bland*, by construing the withdrawal of treatment as an omission and then focusing attention on the existence of a duty.

The question thus arises again: is there any clear means of distinguishing acts from omissions? It has been argued that conduct should be classified as an omission if it merely returns the victim to his or her 'natural' condition, or the condition in which she would have been but for D's attempt to carry out treatment, or a rescue.[86] Disconnecting a life-support machine would therefore not be classified as an act because it merely returns the patient to the condition in which he or she would have been without any treatment. This view is open to several objections, notably that of deciding what the 'original condition' is in relation to each actor, and the implication that a person who has saved a non-swimmer from drowning could, on discovering that the non-swimmer is an enemy, leave him in the water.[87] However, one advantage of categorizing the conduct as an omission is that it then makes liability depend on the recognition of a duty—which would be straightforward in the case of the rescued non-swimmer. This approach may therefore offer comfort to those who insist that the act–omission distinction should not be used to avoid or foreclose moral arguments about the proper limits of criminal liability. But it is not a clear distinction, since it remains open to manipulation in different situations. The conclusion must therefore be that, although there are some clear cases of omission and some clear cases of act, there are many ambiguous cases in which the act–omission distinction should not be used as a cloak for avoiding the moral issues.[88]

This demonstration of the fragility of the act–omission distinction and of the vagar-ies of the English language indicates that it may be simplistic to oppose omissions liability in principle. There are some clear cases of omission in which it is desirable

---

[84] Cf. now the Mental Capacity Act 2005, especially s. 4, and also M. Wilks, 'Medical Treatment at the End of Life—a British Doctor's Perspective', in C. Erin and S. Ost (eds), *The Criminal Justice System and Health Care* (2007).

[85] [2000] 4 All ER 961.

[86] J. Rachels, 'Active and Passive Euthanasia' (1975) 292 New England J of Medicine 78, as restated by M. Moore, *Act and Crime*, 26.

[87] Ibid., 27.

[88] Cf. N. Lacey, C. Wells, and O. Quick, *Reconstructing Criminal Law* (3rd edn., 2003), 680–95.

to have criminal liability, such as the parent who neglects to feed her or his child or neglects to protect it from abuse.[89] Omissions can be involuntary or not, in the same way as acts; and, provided that the harm resulted because D failed to intervene, it can be argued that omissions are also causes.[90] Omissions liability may therefore satisfy the principle that no-one should be held liable for bodily movements that he or she did not and could not direct. It may also satisfy the principle that no person should be held liable for conduct or consequences that he or she did not cause. But one point of the act requirement is to exclude liability for mere thoughts that do not result in some bodily movement, and omissions fall foul of that.[91] They do so for a good reason—that certain positive duties to act are so important that they can rightly be made the subject of criminal liability. Of course, such a duty should also be defined with sufficient certainty and made known to those affected by it. So long as these formal requirements are fulfilled there can be no fairness objection to holding a person liable, provided that he or she is capable of taking some steps to carry out the duty.

4.5 CAUSATION

At the beginning of this chapter it was stated that causation is one of the most basic requirements of criminal liability. Whereas for those offences that merely require conduct the voluntariness requirement (automatism) is crucial, for the many crimes which specify consequences the requirement of causation assumes a central place. Just as it seems wrong to impose criminal liability in the absence of voluntary conduct by the defendant, so it seems wrong to convict a person who did not cause the consequence or state of affairs specified in the offence. Of course, as we shall see in Chapter 5, the law often goes further and insists not only that the defendant voluntarily caused the offence but also that he did so knowingly, intentionally, and so on. Here, however, the concern is to explore the minimum conditions for criminal liability.

The reason for requiring that the defendant should be shown to have causal responsibility for the conduct, consequence, or state of affairs lies in the principle of individual autonomy, discussed in Chapter 2.1 above. That principle respects individuals as capable of choosing their acts and omissions. It follows from this that they should be regarded as agents responsible, at the very least, for the normal consequences of their behaviour. Respect for individual autonomy and responsibility for conduct and consequences go hand in hand. Thus the approach of the criminal law is to affix causal responsibility to the last individual whose voluntary behaviour impinged on the situation. To take two simple examples, if A wounds V in a way that will surely cause V's death within minutes, and B (unconnected with A) then comes along

---

[89] E.g. *Emery* (1993) 14 Cr App R (S) 394, and the new duty imposed by the Domestic Violence, Crime and Victims Act 2004, discussed in Ch 7.6 below.

[90] See R. A. Duff, *Answering for Crime* (2007), 111, and the discussion in section 4.5 below, on Causation.

[91] Duff, ibid., 112–3.

and shoots V dead, causal responsibility for the death rests with B. His is the last voluntary act. It supersedes A's or, in other language, breaks the causal chain between A's act and V's subsequent death. A may be liable for attempted murder, but not for a homicide offence. The second example concerns a man of 25 who commits an armed robbery: why should not his grandparents, aged 75, also be held to have caused the offence on the basis that their act of intercourse some fifty years earlier was the original or 'true' causal root of his lawbreaking? The conventional answer to this is that a person of 25 is an autonomous individual who should be treated as responsible for his decisions and their consequences. There may be many earlier events that shape his behaviour—his upbringing, his experiences at school, the influence of other young men in his locality, the fact that he was offered £5,000 to commit the robbery—but, in the absence of an excuse strong enough to amount to a legal defence, his decision to commit the offence was sufficiently free to make it fair to ascribe causal responsibility to him.

Before looking further into the common law approach, two other possibilities must be mentioned. First, one might wish to develop an approach to causation which placed particular emphasis on a person's *wrongful* act. A simple example would be where D stabs V and V then receives inappropriate medical treatment and dies. While a straightforward application of the autonomy principle would make the doctor causally responsible for the death, one might wish to say that D should be held liable for the death because it was his conduct that led to the doctor having to treat the victim: but for D inflicting the wound, the doctor would not have been called upon. One problem with this is that it may seem to produce the kind of infinite regress that would have held the grandparents causally responsible for robbery in the earlier example. But that problem can be avoided if one were to specify a wrongful or, better, a criminal act. This would at least allow the courts to convict D and others who inflict life-threatening injuries, despite any medical errors that happen to supervene. A second possibility is to point to the extraordinary narrowness of the approach to causation grounded in autonomy. In the discussion of the principle of welfare in Chapter 2.2 above, we saw that it would be both artificial and undesirable to think of social life in terms of individuals pursuing their own ends in isolation from one another. On the one hand, many decisions are influenced and constrained by others; on the other hand, it is right that certain restrictions are placed on individual freedom in order to maximize the freedom of others to pursue their preferences. The principle of welfare has a clear impact on decisions to criminalize, and there are some occasions on which it rightly influences judgments of culpability,[92] but it seems to be ignored in the field of causation.[93] The criminal law picks out the individual who performed the last voluntary act and places causal responsibility there, without reference to the antecedents and wider social setting of the event. If it were a question of determining the causal responsibility

---

[92] See Chs 5 and 6, below.

[93] For a critical argument along these lines, see A. Norrie, *Crime, Reason and History* (2nd edn., 2001), ch 7.

for an industrial dispute or a particular wave of social unrest, it is unlikely that anyone would be content to attribute it to a single individual. The causal strength of various contributing factors would be assessed. The traditional approach in criminal law is to ignore these other factors, except in so far as they are relevant later to the issue of culpability, and to focus on the individual. It is not clear how a system of criminal law could function otherwise, but that does not provide a convincing justification for continuing as we are. Moreover, as we will see below, the traditional approach has to be stretched and distorted in order to deal with some types of case.

(a) THE GENERAL PRINCIPLE

The definitions of many crimes require that D caused a result (e.g. murder, grievous bodily harm, criminal damage) or that he caused a result by certain means (e.g. causing death by dangerous driving). In cases where it is clear that D either intended to cause the result or knowingly risked causing it, the causal enquiry is likely to be brief because no court will see much merit in the argument that the result was highly unlikely in the circumstances and probably a coincidence. Thus the dictum 'intended consequences are never too remote' is one expression of the strong effect which culpability has in hastening a finding of causation and overlooking restrictive policies which might otherwise be invoked. Where the culpability element does not overshadow the issue—and particularly in crimes of strict liability, where no culpability may be required—the question arises what minimum connection must be established between D's conduct and the prohibited result. Although courts have occasionally succumbed to the temptation to say that causation is a question of fact for the jury or magistrates,[94] there ought to be guidance on the principles to be applied when assessing the significance of those facts. Some decisions have attempted to articulate principles, but how coherent they are is a matter of debate.

The general principle is that causation is established if the result would not have occurred *but for* D's conduct. Of course there may be many other 'but for' causes of the result, but an explanation has already been offered for the law's concentration on voluntary human behaviour—the principle of individual autonomy. Yet the 'but for' test does appear to be rather undemanding, and it may be consciousness of this which has led English courts to refer to further (though often uncertain) parameters. In *Cato* (1976),[95] for example, the Court of Appeal expressly stopped short of the 'but for' test. D had been convicted of the manslaughter of V, whom he had injected with a heroin compound at V's request. On the issue of whether D's injection of the heroin could be said to have caused V's death, the Court stated that: 'as a matter of law, it was sufficient if the prosecution could establish that it was *a* cause, provided it was a cause outside the *de minimis* range, and effectively bearing upon the acceleration of the moment of the

---

[94] E.g. *Alphacell Ltd* v *Woodward* [1972] AC 824, but cf. the slightly more definite approach in *National Rivers Authority* v *Yorkshire Water Services* [1995] 1 AC 444. See generally N. Padfield, 'Clean Water and Muddy Causation' [1995] Crim LR 683.

[95] (1976) 62 Cr App R 41.

victim's death'.[96] The Court later stated that the cause must be 'a cause of substance', although it held that the term 'substantial cause' would be putting the requirement too high.[97] Clearly, the Court was reluctant to accept 'but for' causation here, fearing that the link between D's conduct and V's death might be too tenuous.

Notorious examples of the puissance of culpability over causality are provided by the medical cases. At the celebrated trial of Dr Bodkin Adams (1957), charged with murdering a patient by administering excessive doses of morphine, Devlin J stated the orthodox view that to shorten life by days and weeks is to cause death no less than shortening it by years, but he added that a doctor 'is still entitled to do all that is proper and necessary to relieve pain and suffering even if the measures he takes may incidentally shorten life'.[98] This direction to the jury might be thought compatible with the principle subsequently espoused in *Cato*, that a *de minimis* contribution (i.e. a minimal cause which 'people of common sense would overlook'[99]) is not a sufficient cause in law. However, this probably does not capture the precise point of the *Adams* direction, which is rather that a doctor's administration of drugs in order to relieve pain, founded upon clinical judgement, will not be regarded as causing death so long as it remains within reasonable bounds. Those bounds were transgressed in the case of Dr Cox, who administered a drug in order to stop the patient's suffering by causing her death, not simply to relieve pain.[100] The Adams approach was followed in Dr Moor's case (1999),[101] where the trial judge again drew a distinction between administering drugs with intent to kill the patient and administering drugs as proper treatment to relieve pain and suffering. What the courts appear to be doing here is to deny that there is causation in the latter instance, in order to avoid the need to confront the question whether a doctor can have a valid defence to an intentional killing.[102] The orthodox proposition that shortening life involves causing death is neglected, and the courts apply a version of the doctrine of double effect to argue that the doctor does not cause death if the primary intention is to relieve pain, even though it is well known that this will shorten the patient's life. This is perhaps best characterized as a covert recognition, in causation doctrine, of some form of defence based on clinical medical necessity.[103]

To summarize, the *Cato* principle is that it is sufficient if D's conduct was a 'but for' cause which was more than minimal: it need not be a substantial cause,[104] but it seems

---

[96] Ibid., 45.   [97] Ibid., 46; cf. *Cheshire* [1991] 1 WLR 844, referring to a 'significant contribution'.

[98] [1957] Crim LR 365.

[99] H. L. A. Hart and T. Honoré, *Causation in the Law* (2nd edn., 1985), 344–5.

[100] See (1992) BMLR 38.   [101] A. Arlidge, 'The Trial of Dr. Moor' [2000] Crim LR 31.

[102] The subsequent case of *Re A (Conjoined Twins: Surgical Separation)* [2000] 4 All ER 961 (above, n 85, and accompanying text) is one of the few to confront this question.

[103] See S. Ost, 'Euthanasia and the Defence of Necessity', in C. Erin and S. Ost (eds), *The Criminal Justice System and Health Care* (2007). and below, section 4.8(b).

[104] There are isolated exceptions: see Corporate Manslaughter and Corporate Homicide Act 2007, s. 1(3), stating that 'an organisation is guilty of an offence under this section only if the way in which its activities are managed or organised by its senior management is a *substantial element* in the breach' (my italics). See further Ch 7.5(c) below.

that a mere 'but for' cause will rarely be sufficient,[105] and it might be best to require D's conduct to be a 'significant cause.'[106] The principle has been illustrated here in relation to 'result-crimes' but the same approach should be adopted to crimes that penalize conduct or possession, although for those crimes the difficulties will usually concern the exceptions in (b) below.[107] The draft Criminal Code re-states the general principle in terms of 'an act which makes more than a negligible contribution to its occurrence',[108] and the Model Penal Code deals with the issue by excluding causes which are too remote to have a just bearing on responsibility.[109] The requirement of 'but for' causation is sometimes termed 'factual causation', which is then contrasted with 'legal causation'—not only to suggest that the law requires something more than 'but for' causation, but also to indicate that there are other aspects of the doctrine to be considered.

(b) INTERVENTIONS BETWEEN CONDUCT AND RESULT

The principle of individual autonomy presumes that, where an individual who is neither mentally disordered nor an infant has made a sufficient causal contribution to an occurrence, it is inappropriate to trace causation any further. This is taken to justify not only picking out D's conduct from other possible causes and regarding that conduct as operating on a 'stage already set',[110] but also declining to look behind D's conduct for other persons who may be said to have contributed to D acting as he or she did. The principle, then, is that voluntary conduct acts as a barrier in any causal enquiry in criminal law: by and large, D's voluntary conduct will usually be regarded as the cause of an act or an omission if it was the last human conduct before the result. Concurrent causes are possible, as where two people inflict injury or damage at the same time, so long as each of their acts passes the minimum threshold by way of contribution.[111]

A natural event occurring after D's conduct may be treated as terminating D's causal responsibility if it is a coincidence, but not if it could reasonably be expected.[112] The contrast would be between D, whose assault victim catches scarlet fever in hospital and dies (which should be treated as a 'visitation of Providence' and as negativing any causal connection between D and the death), and E, who leaves his assault victim lying on a tidal beach, where he later drowns (this is within the risk which was reasonably

---

[105] The old law on obtaining by deception (now replaced by the Fraud Act 2006, on which see Ch 9.8) provided a possible example of 'but for' causation: see p. 125 of the fifth edition of this work.

[106] This was how Lord Bingham paraphrased *Cato* in *Kennedy (No. 2)* [2008] UKHL 1 AC 269, at 274.

[107] See the discussion of crimes of possession in Ch 4.3(b) above.

[108] Law Com No. 177, cl. 17(1)(a).   [109] American Law Institute, *Model Penal Code*, s. 2.03.

[110] See Hart and Honoré, *Causation in the Law*, ch 1 and *passim*, and the derivative discussions by S. Kadish, *Blame and Punishment* (1987), ch 8, and H. Beynon, 'Causation, Omissions and Complicity' [1987] Crim LR 539; cf. also Williams, *Textbook of Criminal Law*, ch 14.

[111] E.g. *Attorney-General's Reference No. 4 of 1980* (1981) 73 Cr App R 40.

[112] Hart and Honoré, *Causation in the Law*, 342; the draft Criminal Code refers to an intervening act 'which could not in the circumstances have been reasonably foreseen', Law Com No. 177, cl. 17(2).

foreseeable, and therefore not a sufficient coincidence to prevent causal responsibility for the death).

What if D's act is followed by another human act, which intervenes before the result occurs? Because traditional causal theory does not review the entire situation but tends to focus on the last human act, one might expect an intervening human act to negative D's causal responsibility. But in at least three sets of situations—(i) the non-voluntary conduct of third parties; (ii) the conduct of doctors; and (iii) the conduct of the victim—this is not so, raising questions about what is the general rule and what the exception.

(i) *'Non-Voluntary' Conduct of Third Parties:* since the general principle is said to be that the voluntary intervening act of a third party severs or supersedes the causal connection between D's act and the prohibited result, the courts have developed exceptions in cases where the third party's intervention would not be described as voluntary. If the third party is an infant or is mentally disordered, this lack of rational capacity may be regarded as sufficient to discount the third party's act in causal terms. The same applies if D sets out to use a responsible adult as an 'innocent agent', giving false information to that person in the hope that he or she will act upon it. The behaviour of the person who has been tricked is discounted as non-voluntary for these purposes. The case of *Michael* (1840)[113] illustrates the principle. D's child was in the care of a foster-mother, and D, wishing her child dead, handed a bottle of poison to the foster-mother, saying that it was medicine for the child. The foster-mother saw no need for the medicine and placed it on the mantelpiece, from which her own 5-year-old child later removed it and administered a fatal dose to D's child. The intended result was therefore achieved through the unexpected act of an infant rather than through the mistakenly 'innocent' act of an adult, but neither of these intervening acts was regarded as sufficient to relieve D of causal responsibility.[114]

A similar approach may be taken where the intervening act is one of compulsion, necessity, or duty. If the third party brings about the prohibited harm whilst under duress from D, then D may be regarded as the legal cause of the result.[115] The same analysis can be applied where D creates a situation of necessity, or where D's behaviour creates a duty to respond in the third party. Thus in *Pagett* (1983)[116] D was being pursued by the police and took his pregnant girlfriend hostage, holding her in front of him as a shield whilst he fired shots at the police. The police fired back at D, but killed the girlfriend. The Court of Appeal upheld D's conviction for the manslaughter of his girlfriend, even though the fatal shots were fired by the police and not by him. The Court offered two reasons in support of this conclusion: first, the police officer's conduct in shooting back at D was necessary for his self-preservation and therefore was not a voluntary act; and, secondly, that the police officer was acting from a duty to prevent crime and to arrest D. Both these reasons beg important questions: did

---

[113] (1840) 9 C and P 356; cf. G. Williams, *'Finis* for *Novus Actus'* [1989] Camb LJ 391.

[114] Cf. *Cogan and Leak* [1976] 1 QB 217, on 'semi-innocent agency', discussed in Ch 10.6 below.

[115] *Bourne* (1952) 36 Cr App R 125; see also below, Ch 10.6.

[116] (1983) 76 Cr App R 279; see Hart and Honoré, *Causation in the Law*, 330–4.

a necessity exist? Was there a duty? They contain no reference to a duty to avoid harm to the person being held hostage: should not the liberty to act in self-preservation be subject to this qualification?[117] These points ought to have been explored at least. Perhaps a better rationale for this decision may be found in a doctrine of 'alternative danger': where D places a person in the position of having to choose between two drastic courses of action, one threatening self-danger and the other threatening danger to another, the result should be attributed causally to the creator of the emergency, and not to the unfortunate person who has to choose. This leaves open the possibility of finding that a trained police officer ought to have acted with greater circumspection towards the hostage on the facts of *Pagett*, if that is a fair judgment on the facts of that case, since the law might justifiably expect more of a trained official than of a hapless citizen caught up in extreme events.[118]

Whatever one might say about the Court of Appeal's attempts to rationalize the causal responsibility of Pagett for his girlfriend's death, at least they kept some faith with the fundamental principle that a voluntary intervening act breaks the causal chain. This cannot be said of one aberrant decision of high authority, *Environment Agency v Empress Car Co (Abertillery)* (1999).[119] In this case the company had fixed an outlet from its diesel tank which would drain towards a river, governed by a tap that was not locked. An unknown person opened the tap and the river was polluted. The company denied that it caused the polluting matter to enter controlled waters, contrary to the Water Resources Act 1991, and on normal principles one would expect the deliberate act of a third party to negative its causal responsibility. However, the House of Lords held that if the company 'did something which produced a situation in which the polluting matter could escape but a necessary condition of the actual escape which happened was also the act of a third party or a natural event, [the court] should consider whether that act or event should be regarded as a normal fact of life or something extraordinary'.[120] In this way the House of Lords discarded the general principle that a voluntary intervening act breaks the causal chain in favour of the distinction 'of fact and degree' between ordinary and extraordinary interventions. The conviction in this case is a clear policy decision, aimed at imposing stringent duties on companies to take steps to prevent pollution, and convicting them for omissions to fulfil those duties. When the House of Lords returned to the subject in *Kennedy (No. 2)*, Lord Bingham held that the *Empress Car* decision is to be confined to its facts.[121] In *Kennedy No. 2* (2005)[122] D handed V a syringe of heroin with which V then injected himself and died. Overruling the Court of Appeal's strained judgment in favour of a

---

[117] Art. 2 of the ECHR suggests so: see below, Ch 4.6(b).

[118] See further Ch 6.4 below; cf. the arguments of P. A. J. Waddington, ' "Overkill" or "Minimum Force"?' [1990] Crim LR 695, with the implications of Art. 2 of the ECHR.

[119] [1999] 2 AC 22, overruling *Impress (Worcester) Ltd v Rees* [1971] 2 All ER 357.

[120] *Per* Lord Hoffmann at 36.

[121] [2008] 1 AC 269, at 276, adding that the House 'would not wish to throw any doubt on the correctness of the *Empress Car* case'.

[122] [2005] 2 Cr App R 348; the Court's first decision in this case was also much criticized, see *Kennedy* [1999] Crim LR 65.

conviction for manslaughter, Lord Bingham recognized the criminal law's approach of treating individuals as autonomous beings, giving rise to the principle that 'D is not to be treated as causing V to act in a certain way if V makes a voluntary and informed decision to act in that way.' Thus the House of Lords unanimously held that there should be no conviction for manslaughter because D did not cause V to take the heroin: it was self-administered.

(ii) *Conduct of Doctors:* The decision in *Pagett* contains more than a hint that the court was far more concerned about convicting a morally culpable person than about the refinements of causation, and similar leanings may be found in cases involving doctors. In cases where medical attention is given to a victim, there is rarely any doubt that it may properly be described as 'voluntary': doctors work under pressure, occasionally having to make rapid decisions, but they are trained and trusted to exercise clinical judgement in these circumstances. Doctors act under a duty to treat patients, but they surely do so voluntarily.

However, the courts have drawn a distinction between (a) cases where the injury inflicted by D remains a substantial and operating cause of death despite the subsequent medical treatment, in which case D remains causally responsible even if the medical treatment is negligent; and (b) those where the original wound becomes merely 'the setting in which another cause operates', in which case D's responsibility may be negatived by subsequent aberrant medical treatment.[123] The reference to an 'operating and substantial' cause may be regarded as more favourable to D than the general principle of causation, unless the term 'substantial' is read as meaning, simply, 'more than minimal'. This is confirmed by the statement in *Cheshire* (1991)[124] that a significant contribution is all that is required, and that the defendant's act does not need to be the sole or even the main cause:

Even though negligence in the treatment of the victim was the immediate cause of his death, the jury should not regard it as excluding the responsibility of the accused unless the negligent treatment was so independent of his acts, and in itself so potent in causing death, that they regard the contribution made by his acts as insignificant.[125]

No clear reason is offered for discounting the voluntary intervening act of the doctor. If the doctor administers a drug to which the patient is known to be intolerant, or gives some other wrong treatment, surely the inappropriateness of the medical treatment should affect the causal enquiry. The courts' reluctance to discuss the causal significance of the medical treatment probably stems from a desire to ensure the conviction of a culpable offender, and this suggests a strong attachment to a 'wrongful act' approach to causation, deciding the issue by reference to broader judgements of innocence and culpability. This appears to overlook the fact that D, who inflicted the original wound which gave rise to the need for medical attention, will still be liable for attempted murder or a serious wounding offence even if the medical treatment is

---

[123] *Smith* [1959] 2 QB 35, distinguishing *Jordan* (1956) 40 Cr App R 152; cf. the critical attack of Norrie, *Crime, Reason and History*, 147–8.
[124] [1991] 1 WLR 844.   [125] Ibid., 852.

held to negative his causal responsibility for the ensuing death. For adherents of the 'wrongful act' approach this would be insufficient: they want to see responsibility for the ultimate result pinned on the defendant. However, a court which declares that it is not the doctor who is on trial but the original wrongdoer[126] is merely offering an unconvincing rationalization of its failure to apply the ordinary causal principle that a voluntary intervening act which accelerates death should relieve the original wrongdoer of liability for the result. If that causal principle is thought unsuitable for medical cases, should we not be absolutely clear about the reasons, and then look closely at a doctrine of clinical medical necessity?[127]

(iii) *Conduct or Condition of the Victim:* The general principle that the law approaches causation by considering the effect of an autonomous individual's conduct upon a 'stage already set' is usually taken to extend to cases where the victim has some special condition which makes him or her especially vulnerable. This is sometimes known as the 'thin skull' principle, or the principle that defendants must take their victims as they find them. If D commits a minor assault on V, and V, who is a haemophiliac, dies from that assault, the principle applies to render D causally responsible for the death.[128] Now this principle of causation may have little practical effect on its own, since most of the serious criminal offences require proof of *mens rea* (proof that D intended or foresaw the risk of causing, say, serious injury), and it will usually be possible to show that the *mens rea* was lacking because D was unaware of V's special condition. However, where an offence imposes constructive liability (such as manslaughter in English and American law),[129] the 'thin skull' principle reinforces the constructive element by ensuring that there is no causal barrier to convicting D of an offence involving more serious harm than was intended or foreseen. The objections to constructive manslaughter are set out in Chapter 7.5 below. The objection to the 'thin skull' principle is that such physical conditions are abnormal and that much of the standard analysis of causation turns on distinctions between normal and abnormal conditions.[130]

What principles should apply to the causal effect of the victim's conduct after D's original act? Should V's conduct be subject to the normal rules of voluntary intervening acts? *Roberts* (1972)[131] was a case in which D, while driving his car, made suggestions to his passenger, trying to remove her coat, at which point she opened the door and leapt from the moving car, suffering injury. The Court of Appeal upheld D's conviction for assault occasioning actual bodily harm, on the basis that a victim's 'reasonably foreseeable' reaction does not negative causation. Whether 'reasonable foreseeability' is an accurate way of expressing the point in question must be doubted; one might well say that the prospect of the woman jumping from the moving car was relatively unlikely. Surely it would be better to consider the principle of 'alternative

[126] *Per* Lord Lane CJ, in *Malcherek* (1981) 73 Cr App R 173.   [127] Section 4.7 below.

[128] A clear example, on these facts, is the American case of *State* v *Frazer* (1936) 98 SW (2d) 707.

[129] See below, Chs 5.4(a) and 7.7.

[130] See the criticism of Hart and Honoré by Norrie, *Crime Reason and History*, 149–50.

[131] (1972) 56 Cr App R 95; see also *Corbett* [1996] Crim LR 594.

danger': D's conduct had placed V in a situation of emergency in which she had to make a rapid choice about how to react. One might then say that any reaction which cannot be regarded as wholly abnormal or 'daft'[132] should remain D's causal responsibility. In this sense, V's reaction is non-voluntary.

What if the victim refuses to accept medical treatment for the injury inflicted by D? The question presented itself starkly in *Blaue* (1975).[133] D stabbed V four times, piercing her lung. V was advised that she would die from the wounds unless she had a blood transfusion, but, adhering to her faith as a Jehovah's Witness, she refused to undergo this treatment. She died. The Court of Appeal held D to be causally responsible for her death. Her intervening decision not to accept the 'normal' treatment did not negative D's causal responsibility, because, the Court argued, the situation was analogous to that covered by the 'thin skull' rule. Stating that 'those who use violence on other people must take their victims as they find them', the Court added that this 'means the whole man [*sic*], not just the physical man. It does not lie in the mouth of the assailant to say that his victim's religious beliefs which inhibited him [*sic*] from accepting certain kinds of treatment were unreasonable.'[134] Is this another example of a court stretching the principles of causation so as to ensure the conviction of a wrongdoer? The 'thin skull' principle applies only to pre-existing physical conditions of the victim. The principle of individual autonomy suggests that, in general, any subsequent act or omission by V should negative D's causal responsibility. Exceptions to this are where V's subsequent conduct falls within the 'reasonable foreseeability' notion in *Roberts*[135] or, perhaps, within the principle of 'alternative danger'. D's actions in *Blaue* can certainly be said to have caused a situation of alternative danger and emergency, and so then the question would be whether V's reaction should be classified as wholly abnormal. In a statistical sense it surely was: it must be rare to refuse a blood transfusion knowing that death will follow that refusal. To accept this would be to make no distinction between one who refuses treatment for religious reasons and one who refuses out of spite. It could be argued that the standard of normality should be informed by social values rather than enslaved to statistical frequency, that religious beliefs are a matter of conscience which should be respected, and therefore that acts or omissions based on religious conviction should not be set aside as abnormal.

So whilst it is possible to construct arguments in favour of D's causal responsibility for the death, this may be more a question of legalistic ingenuity than social appropriateness. It would have been possible to convict Blaue of attempted murder or wounding with intent to cause grievous bodily harm, both offences which carry a maximum sentence of life imprisonment. No doubt there was much sympathy and respect for the victim, courageously adhering to her religious beliefs in the face of death, generating the argument that it would not be appropriate to hold her causally responsible for her own death. Perhaps this is, at root, another example of the 'wrongful act' approach. Lawton LJ in *Blaue*[136] clearly regarded this as the common law approach,

---

[132] (1972) 56 Cr App R 95, at 97.   [133] (1975) 61 Cr App R 271.   [134] *Per* Lawton LJ, ibid., 274.
[135] (1972) 56 Cr App R 95.   [136] (1975) 61 Cr App R 271.

and evidently it is closely related to the maxim that anyone who knowingly does a wrongful act should take the consequences, discussed in Chapter 5.4(b) below in the context of fault requirements. Certainly it is difficult to give a convincing explanation of the judicial approach, here as in the medical cases, without referring to the 'wrongful act' approach or at least, as tentatively suggested above, to some principle of 'alternative danger'.

There is also a long line of cases in which V has aggravated his or her condition by failure to attend to injuries or wounds, or even by deliberately re-opening them. The judicial approach is to hold that D can still be convicted if his conduct made an operative and substantial contribution to the result, even if V's own act or omission also contributed.[137] Once again, the more rigorous approach of recognizing that V's own act broke the causal chain, and that D should therefore be convicted of an attempt or other offence, has been found unattractive by the courts.

(c) CAUSATION AND OMISSIONS

One of the difficulties sometimes raised about imposing criminal liability for omissions, in addition to those already discussed in section 4.4 above, is the problem of causation. How can an omission be said to cause harm? Or are these cases exceptions to the causal requirement?[138]

Starting with the most basic question, is it possible to say that, but for an omission, a harm would not have resulted? The existence of a duty justifies calling it an omission, and the non-performance of that duty in a situation where it arises can be said to cause the result. To take an extreme example, a parent who makes no attempt to save her or his child from drowning in shallow water can be said to cause the child's death: but for the parent's inaction, the child would almost certainly have lived. It is no answer to say that the child would have drowned anyway if the parent had not been there, because in that eventuality there would have been no duty and hence no omission. On the facts as they were, the parent was present, and but for non-performance of the duty the child would not have died. When dealing with causation by acts, we have seen that the courts have used terms such as 'significant' and even 'substantial' in some cases, chiefly to rule out remote or minimal causes, but this should create no special difficulty for omissions. One counter-argument is that this approach may sometimes lead to the conclusion that many people caused a result: if, in a jurisdiction which imposes a duty of easy rescue, twenty or more people stand by without offering any help or raising the alarm, the conclusion must be that all these people caused the harm that occurred. This is true, and is hardly an argument against the causation approach. Nor would it be a counter-argument to say that but for several omissions in

---

137 See also *Dear* [1996] Crim LR 595.

138 For discussions see Husak, *Philosophy of Criminal Law*, ch 6; A. Leavens, 'A Causation Approach to Omissions' (1988) 76 Cal LR 547; H. Beynon, 'Causation, Omissions and Complicity' [1987] Crim LR 539.

the past many crimes would not have been committed: this is really no different from the argument against tracing causation to grandparents, mentioned earlier.

This is not to suggest that the application of causal arguments to cases of omission is without difficulty. For example, if A stabs V it is obvious that but for A's act V would not have suffered this wound; but if a parent makes no effort to save a child drowning in a pool, it is possible that the duty might have been fulfilled by summoning help (which might have caused delay, and the child's life might have been lost), or that the parent might not have been able to save the child's life anyway (if it had already been in the pool some time before the parent arrived). The point of these examples is that the 'but for' clause may be less concrete in some omissions cases, and may occasionally require a judgement to be made. However, at the very least there are many clear cases where ordinary causal analysis creates no more problems than it does in relation to acts.

(d) CAUSING OTHER PERSONS TO ACT

Can it ever be held that one person caused another to act in a certain way? The notion would seem to be inconsistent with the general principle of individual autonomy, emphasized above by reiterating the principle that a voluntary intervening act removes or displaces the previous actor's causal responsibility. Yet we have already noted one case in which a person can be said to cause another to act—the case of innocent agency, where the third party lacks rationality or has been tricked. Further cases arise in the law of complicity, that branch of the criminal law which holds people liable for helping or encouraging others to commit crimes, which will be discussed at length in Chapter 10.

One example of the type of case under discussion is where D goes to P and offers P money to injure or kill V:[139] the law will hold D liable for counselling and procuring P's subsequent offence, and one might say that D *causes* the offence, in some sense. Clearly, however, D did not cause P to act as an innocent agent: P was not, we assume, lacking in rational capacity, and so on the general principle of individual autonomy P would be regarded as causally responsible for the result. D cannot, therefore, be held to have caused that result in the usual sense, but one might follow Hart and Honoré in suggesting that D may be said to have given P a reason for committing it.[140] This is a dilution of the general approach to causation, aimed specifically at rationalizing the criminal liability of certain accomplices.

But it is not only those who 'counsel or procure' who are brought within the English law of accomplice liability. It is also persons who 'aid and abet' others to commit offences. Advice, information, and other acts of assistance and encouragement may be great or small, and may be readily obtainable from others if this would-be accomplice

---

[139] *Calhaem* [1985] QB 808.

[140] Hart and Honoré, *Causation in the Law*, 51; cf. G. Williams, 'Finis for *Novus Actus*' [1989] Camb LJ 391, at 398.

had declined. So, as an element of causal contribution to P's offence, D's 'aiding' may be insignificant indeed—certainly well below the 'but for' threshold, even in the extended sense adopted by the notion of 'occasioning'. Many writers now acknowledge that the element of causation is absent from some cases of 'aiding and abetting'.[141] This brings us to a reconsideration of the role of causation.

(e) CONCLUSION

Causation is a complex topic, with which we have been able to deal only briefly here. Proof of causation is often said to be an essential precondition of criminal liability, but there is reason to doubt the generality of that requirement, notably in respect of accomplice liability (just discussed) and vicarious criminal liability.[142] Rather than insisting on a universal requirement of causation, it may be preferable to argue that liability should be negatived, in general, by the voluntary intervening act of another. Several criticisms of the judicial approach to three exceptional categories of case have been advanced above. Often the explanations given by the courts are unconvincing. Whilst traditional or standard causal theory emphasizes the significance of the last voluntary act, there is no reluctance to look wider or to massage the term 'voluntary' in certain situations, especially where D clearly started the sequence of events by doing a wrongful act. The challenge is to re-examine the intuitions that lead judges and others to their conclusions (e.g. the wrongful act theory, the approach to medical mistakes, etc.), with a view to constructing a law that ensures that the courts respect the various principles outlined in Chapter 3.

4.6 SELF-DEFENCE AND JUSTIFIABLE FORCE

Many offences include a qualification such as 'without lawful excuse', 'without lawful authority or reasonable excuse', and so on. We are not concerned here with the different shades of meaning attached to such phrases,[143] nor with the legislature's frequent use of the word 'excuse' to refer to justifications, but rather with some general doctrines which operate as justifications for conduct which would otherwise be criminal. Self-defence is the best known of these justifications, but there are others concerned with the prevention of crime, the arrest of suspected offenders, the protection of property, and so forth.

Lawyers frequently speak of these doctrines as defences, e.g. 'the defence of self-defence', and procedurally that is how they function. If there is evidence, usually

---

[141] J. C. Smith, 'Aid, Abet, Counsel and Procure', in P. R. Glazebrook (ed.), *Reshaping the Criminal Law* (1978); Kadish, *Blame and Punishment*, ch 8; cf. Part 2 of the Serious Crime Act 2007, discussed in Ch 11.7 below.

[142] See Ch 5.3(b) below.

[143] See R. Card, 'Authority and Excuse as Defences to Crime' [1969] Crim LR 359, 415.

raised by the defendant, that the conduct may have been justifiable, the prosecution bears the burden of proving beyond reasonable doubt that the conduct was *not* justifiable or lawful. 'If the prosecution fail to do so, the accused is entitled to be acquitted because the prosecution will have failed to prove an essential element of the crime, namely that the violence used by the accused was unlawful.'[144] The consequences of presenting the justifications as the element of unlawfulness required in all crimes will not be taken further here.[145] Neither this, nor the procedural device of treating them as defences, should deflect attention from the fundamental significance of the doctrine of justification. There are certain situations when individuals have a right, or at least a permission, to do things which would generally be prohibited because they cause harm or damage. The most extreme occasions are those on which the law justifies one person in killing another. It is sometimes said that justified conduct is right conduct, but in a penetrating study Suzanne Uniacke argues that justified conduct is conduct that one has a right to do—it is permissible in the situation, even if it is not necessarily a matter for congratulation.[146] Two other preliminary points flow from this: first, it is not permissible to resist justified conduct; and, secondly, the rules of justification should respect the various principles of legality and 'rule of law' for the same reason that offence-definitions should, that is, because they may be relied upon to guide behaviour.[147]

(a) SELF-DEFENCE AND INDIVIDUAL AUTONOMY[148]

It is hardly surprising that decisions on self-defence formed an important and frequent element in the development of the English common law in days when there was no organized policing and when the carrying of deadly weapons was common. The issues here concern the basic right to life and physical safety. An individual who is either attacked or threatened with a serious physical attack must be accorded the legal liberty to repel that attack, thus preserving a basic right. A well-regulated society will provide a general protection, but it cannot guarantee protection at the very moment when an individual is subjected to sudden attack. The criminal law cannot respect the autonomy of the individual if it does not make provision for this dire situation.

(b) THE PROBLEM OF CONFLICTING RIGHTS

In terms of individual autonomy, one difficulty with this position is that these situations involve two individuals (at least). If the law gives the person attacked the

---

[144] *Per* Lord Griffiths in *Beckford* v *R* [1988] AC 130, at 144.

[145] See Ch 6.4 below, and cf. R. H. S. Tur, 'Subjectivism and Objectivism: Towards Synthesis', in S. Shute, J. Gardner, and J. Horder (eds.), *Action and Value in Criminal Law* (1993).

[146] S. Uniacke, *Permissible Killing: the Self-Defence Justification of Homicide* (1994), 26 and ch 2 generally.

[147] See section 4.1 above, and n 9.

[148] For detailed studies of the law on self-defence and the theory underlying it, see F. Leverick, *Killing in Self-Defence* (2006), and B. Sangero, *Self-Defence in Criminal Law* (2006).

liberty to wound or kill the aggressor, what happens to the aggressor's right to life and physical safety? The answer to this question must have as its starting point the European Convention on Human Rights, Article 2 of which declares the right to life in these terms:

1. Everyone's right to life shall be protected by law. No one shall be deprived of his life intentionally save in the execution of a sentence of a court following his conviction of a crime for which this penalty is provided by law.[149]

2. Deprivation of life shall not be regarded as inflicted in contravention of this Article when it results from the use of force which is no more than absolutely necessary:

   a. in defence of any person from unlawful violence;

   b. in order to effect a lawful arrest or to prevent the escape of a person lawfully detained;

   c. in action lawfully taken for the purpose of quelling a riot or insurrection.

Articles 3 and 5 of the Convention protect a citizen's freedom from inhuman treatment and security of person, but, unlike Article 2, they contain no explicit exceptions in favour of the justifiable use of force, and the Court has had to imply such exceptions.[150] As for the exceptions to Article 2, two of them appear rather strange. To suggest that causing death may be absolutely necessary 'to effect an arrest' (Article 2.2b) is somewhat absurd since, as Sir John Smith has pointed out, one cannot arrest a dead person.[151] A justifiable killing to prevent a riot or insurrection (2.2c) is barely conceivable. However, Article 2 has no exception for killings in the prevention of any other non-violent crime. Thus, for example, a householder who kills a burglar ought to have no defence, if Article 2 is applied, unless the circumstances can be said to have involved the defence of a person from unlawful violence. The acquittal of the householder, in a case where physical violence had not been offered by the burglar, might suggest that English law does not respect the right to life in Article 2.[152]

The approaches of other legal systems differ considerably. Some maintain that an innocent person's rights are absolute and thus recognize few limitations on those rights, even when that person is repelling a minor assault or defending property.[153] This suggests that the aggressor forfeits the normal rights when he embarks on an attack, and that it is his misconduct in starting the conflict which justifies the law in giving preference to the liberty of his victim. The idea of forfeiture is not objectionable in itself,[154] but it should be carefully circumscribed lest it allows the person attacked

---

[149] Note that Protocol 6 to the Convention requires the abolition of the death penalty. Several European States, including the UK, have agreed to this protocol, which is also brought into English law by the Human Rights Act 1998.

[150] *Rivas v France* [2005] Crim LR 305 and *RJ and M-J D v France* [2005] Crim LR 307.

[151] J. C. Smith, 'The Right to Life and the Right to Kill in Law Enforcement' (1994) NLJ 354.

[152] For a similar argument, accepted by the European Court, see *A v UK*, discussed in section 4.8 below.

[153] Fletcher, *Rethinking Criminal Law*, 862–3; cf. A. Dershowitz, *Preemption* (2006), 197–9.

[154] Uniacke argues that there is no conceptual difficulty with the notion of forfeiture so long as we accept that the right to life, like many other rights, is conditional on our conduct: *Permissible Killing*, 201 and ch 6 generally.

to stand fast and use whatever force is necessary to protect his rights of ownership and liberties of passage. The forfeiture approach bears some similarity to the 'wrongful act' analysis in causation[155] and to the theory of constructive liability,[156] in that it attributes great significance to the wrongfulness of a person's initial act. However, the focus should be on the right to life, as the jurisprudence of the European Convention establishes.[157] Initial wrongfulness should only be taken to permit the proportionate use of force: the innocent subject of an attack should not be free to use whatever force is necessary to vindicate his threatened rights. Such an analysis would assign no value to the rights of the attacker. If the criminal law is committed to ensuring that everyone's life is protected and that force is inflicted as rarely as possible, it cannot accept a vindicatory approach which would allow the infliction of gratuitous, or at least disproportionate, harm. Forfeiture of life to protect a person from some minor hurt, loss, or damage would promote honour above respect for life and limb. The tendency of the English courts to reach for the concept of reasonableness, without setting out the relevant rights first, is an unfortunate aspect of legal culture.

(c) THE RULES AND THE PRINCIPLES

Self-defence is a long-standing defence in English law,[158] but it must be considered in the light of two statutory provisions. Section 3 of the Criminal Law Act 1967 states that 'a person may use such force as is reasonable in the circumstances in the prevention of crime...'. The section was not intended to supplant the common law rules on self-defence,[159] and the courts have continued to develop those rules. It is true that in most situations of self-defence it could be said that the person was preventing crime (i.e. preventing an attack which constituted a crime), but that would still leave certain cases untouched—notably, attacks by a child under 10, by a mentally disordered person, or by a person labouring under a mistake of fact. Such aggressors would commit no offence, and so it is the law of self-defence, not the prevention of crime, which governs.[160]

A more recent statutory provision is section 76 of the Criminal Justice and Immigration Act 2008, which 'is intended to clarify the operation of the existing defences' (s 76(9)), notably self-defence. It is rare for legislation to state on its face that it is for clarification: this curious notion must mean that the common law defence is not abolished,[161] but that the new provisions supersede the common law to the extent that they apply. However, as will appear from the following paragraphs, section 76 deals with only a few of the many issues of principle arising in the law of self-defence.

Section 76(2) states that the section applies to the common law on self-defence and to section 3 of the Criminal Law Act, which deals with force used in the prevention of

---

[155] Above, section 4.5.   [156] See Ch 3.6(r).   [157] See n 207 below and accompanying text.
[158] A. Ashworth, 'Self-Defence and the Right to Life' [1975] CLJ 282.   [159] Ibid., 285.
[160] See the judgment of Ward LJ in *Re A (Conjoined Twins: Surgical Separation)* [2000] 4 All ER 961.
[161] Cf. s. 59 of the Serious Crime Act 2007 ('the common law offence of inciting the commission of another offence is abolished'), discussed in Ch 11.6 below.

crime or in effecting a lawful arrest. When the Law Commission considered the issue some years ago, it identified other possible justifications for the use of force (such as the prevention or termination of trespass on property), and these must not be forgotten.[162] The principles should be the same as for the other justifications. However, where the force used is not physical but consists of damage another's property, the legal principles are different. The justifiable damaging of another's property requires only that D believed that 'the means of protection adopted... would be reasonable having regard to all the circumstances'.[163] This hardly embodies a legal standard at all, since it turns on D's beliefs as to what is reasonable. One feature of the draft Criminal Code was that it would abolish the different rule for property damage.

(d) THE PROPORTIONALITY STANDARD

The law of self-defence has two elements: necessity and proportionality. The requirement that the use of force must be necessary (or, where the right to life is involved, 'absolutely necessary') is combined with a further requirement that the amount of force must be proportionate to the value being upheld. This shows respect for the rights of the attacker in self-defence cases, and for the rights of suspected offenders in relation to the other justifications. Even though the necessity element has subjective elements, as we shall see, the reasonableness of the force used depends not on D's beliefs but on an objective assessment.[164] Thus where D misjudges the amount of force which is reasonable, e.g. to insist on passing along a path barred by another, to eject a trespasser, or to detain a poacher, this is a mistake of law rather than of fact. The Court of Appeal has confirmed that D's view of the amount of force that was reasonable is not determinative: the magistrates or jury should assess whether, in the circumstances existing at the time, the amount of force was reasonable.[165] The standard cannot be a precise one: section 76 of the 2008 Act states that the force must not have been 'disproportionate', i.e. not out of proportion to the amount of harm likely to be suffered by the defendant, or likely to result if a forcible intervention is not made. What is crucial is that it should rule out the infliction or risk of considerable physical harm merely to apprehend a fleeing non-violent offender,[166] to stop minor property loss or damage, etc. As a nineteenth-century Royal Commission remarked, a law whose only requirement was necessity 'would justify every weak lad whose hair was about to be pulled by a stronger one, in shooting the bully if he could not otherwise prevent the

---

[162] Law Com No. 177, cl. 44, mostly re-stated in Law Com No. 218, *Legislating the Criminal Code: Offences Against the Person and General Principles* (1993), cl. 27.

[163] Criminal Damage Act 1971, s. 5(2).   [164] See e.g. *Jones, Milling et al* [2007] 1 AC 136.

[165] *Owino* [1996] 2 Cr App R 128, not following *Scarlett* (1994) 98 Cr App R 290. See also *Tudor* [1999] 1 Cr App R (S) 197. Cf. the controversy surrounding the US case of *People* v *Goetz* (1986) 68 NY 2d 96, where D had shot and wounded four youths on the New York subway after they had demanded five dollars from him.

[166] As the European Court of Human Rights held in *Nachova* v *Bulgaria* (2006) 42 EHRR 933.

assault'.[167] On this view, the proper approach is to compare the relative value of the rights involved, and not to give special weight to the rights of (say) a property owner simply because the other party is in the wrong (i.e. committing a crime).[168] Thus in *Rashford* (2006)[169] the Court of Appeal rightly held that self-defence should not be ruled out simply because D was the initial aggressor. If V's response to D's aggression was out of all proportion, D would be justified in using sufficient force to protect himself. If, however, D had intended to provoke V into attacking him, in order to then use fatal force on V, it is well established that self-defence would be unavailable.[170]

Although Article 2 of the Convention does not specify a proportionality requirement, the Strasbourg Court has emphasized that the use of deadly force must be both absolutely necessary and strictly proportionate if it is to come within an exception to the right to life.[171] The American Model Penal Code provides that deadly force is not justified 'unless the actor believes that such force is necessary to protect himself against death, serious bodily harm, kidnapping or sexual intercourse compelled by force or threat'.[172] It is debatable whether this goes too far in allowing the lawful sacrifice of a life to prevent certain non-fatal assaults,[173] and it should be noted that Article 2 of the Convention is vague on this question. Deadly force may be justified 'in defence of any person from unlawful violence', but how serious a violent attack? The Strasbourg jurisprudence is no more precise than English law on this point, and the Model Penal Code formulation might be a worthwhile starting-point for analysis and argument.

Should the judgment of proportionality be affected by the fact that the force was used against a law enforcement officer? Since English law renders an arrest lawful if the police officer has reasonable grounds for suspicion (even if the grounds turn out to be erroneous), this may be of importance. There are English decisions which draw a distinction between resisting a lawful—but mistaken—arrest (which is not justified), and repelling the unlawful use of violence by police (which is justified),[174] and this principle is to be found both in the Model Penal Code and the draft Criminal Code.[175] It permits individuals to defend themselves against excessive force by the police, whilst requiring them not to use force against police who are effecting an arrest for which the officer may believe there are reasonable grounds (even if the arrestee believes otherwise).

---

[167] Report of the Royal Commission on the Law Relating to Indictable Offences (1879, C. 2345), note B, at 44; see at 11 for an assertion of the principle that 'the mischief done by, or which might reasonably be anticipated from, the force used is not disproportioned to the injury or mischief which it is intended to prevent'.

[168] See Leverick, *Killing in Self-Defence*, ch 6. For a different view see the judgment of the German Supreme Court, set out in P. H. Robinson, *Fundamentals of Criminal Law* (2nd edn., 1995), 488–90.

[169] [2006] Crim LR 546.

[170] For the 18th century authorities, see Ashworth, 'Self-Defence and the Right to Life', 299–301.

[171] E.g. in *Andronicou and Constantinou v Cyprus* (1998) 25 EHRR 491, at para. 171; *Gül v Turkey* (2002) 34 EHRR 719, at para. 77; *Nachova v Bulgaria* (2006) 42 EHRR 933.

[172] Model Penal Code, s. 3.04.

[173] J. C. Smith, *Justification and Excuse in the Criminal Law* (1989), 109 and ch 4; Leverick, *Killing in Self-Defence*, ch 7.

[174] *Fennell* [1971] 1 QB 428; *Ball* [1989] Crim LR 579.

[175] Model Penal Code, s. 3.04(2)(a)(i); Law Com No. 177, cl. 44(4).

(e) ASPECTS OF THE NECESSITY REQUIREMENT

The necessity requirement forms part of most legal regimes on justifiable force. The first question to be asked is: necessary for what? We have seen that force may be justified for any one of several lawful purposes. The necessity must be judged according to the lawful purpose which the defendant was trying to pursue: for self-defence, purely defensive force will often be all that is necessary; in order to apprehend a suspected offender, on the other hand, a police officer or citizen will need to behave proactively. These differences may become particularly important in cases where there is a suspicion or allegation that the force was used by way of revenge or retaliation rather than in pursuit of a lawful purpose. What was the defendant's purpose? Could the conduct be said to be necessary for that purpose?

Does this reference to 'purpose' mean that there is a mental element in the justifications, such that a person cannot rely on a particular justification if he or she is ignorant of the basic facts needed to support that justification? In *Dadson* (1850)[176] a constable shot a fleeing thief. Such force was justifiable only against 'felons', and a thief was a felon if he had two previous convictions. This thief had previous convictions and so was a felon, but the constable fired at him without knowing this. It was held that the constable could not rely on the justification of using force to apprehend a felon because he was unaware of the basic fact needed to constitute the justification. The Northern Irish case of *Thain* (1985)[177] takes this point further, since D, a soldier on duty, stated from the outset that he did not fire the shot in order to apprehend V (who was running away at the time) and said that he shot in reaction to a sudden movement by V. It seems that D might have succeeded if he had maintained that his intention was to arrest, but he proffered another reason and was convicted of murder. This decision holds that there is an element of belief or motive whenever a justification is relied upon, and this is surely right. In many circumstances a greater use of force might be justifiable for law enforcement than merely for defence.[178]

In most cases, where no problem of the mental element arises, the main issue is necessity. The English courts have continued to develop the common law, but without always relating the issues to any general themes and without explicit reference to the primacy of the right to life. An attempt is made here to organize the decisions around six aspects of necessity, referring to section 76 of the 2008 Act where relevant.

(i) *Imminence:* Although section 76 is silent on the matter, there is authority that the use of force can be necessary only if the attack is imminent.[179] If there is time to warn the police, then that is the course which should be taken, in preference to the use

---

[176] (1850) 4 Cox CC 358.   [177] [1985] NI 457.

[178] Cf. *Nachova v Bulgaria*, above, n 166 and text thereat; see also n 182 below. For controversy over the *Dadson* principle, see R. Christopher, 'Unknowing Justification and the Logical Necessity of the *Dadson* Principle in Self-Defence' (1995) 15 Oxford JLS 229, and P. H. Robinson, 'Competing Theories of Justification: Deeds v. Reasons' with J. Gardner, 'Justifications and Reasons', both in A. P. Simester and A. T. H. Smith (eds.), *Harm and Culpability* (1996).

[179] E.g. *Attorney-General for Northern Ireland's Reference* [1977] AC 105; *Chisam* (1963) 47 Cr App R 130.

of force by a private individual.[180] But this apparently does not mean that it is unlawful to prepare or keep armaments for an anticipated attack. In the *Attorney-General's Reference (No. 2 of 1983)*[181] D's shop had been looted during rioting which the police had struggled to control; D made some petrol bombs with which to repel any future attack, and the question was whether these were in his possession 'for a lawful object'. It was held that they were, if the jury accepted that D intended to use them only against an attack on his premises which the police could not control. This is an unusually indulgent approach for the criminal courts—a conviction followed by a discharge would be more normal, since it does not signal that such conduct is permissible—but it was a response to a particular type of situation. If the police are unable to offer protection and attack is imminent, the rationale for justifiable force is made out—although objects so lethal as fire-bombs should rarely be approved as lawful means of defending business premises, as opposed to defending a home or human beings.

This decision leaves a number of questions about the 'imminence' requirement unresolved. Where a woman who has been habitually subjected to physical abuse by her male partner has a reasonable fear that he may kill her next time, does this satisfy the 'imminence' requirement if she then kills him whilst he is asleep? True it may be that 'a "reasonable person" does not fear immediate death from a sleeping person',[182] but that reference to immediacy is surely too strict, and it may be argued that the real issue is whether the woman reasonably fears a danger to her life that she will be unable to avoid.[183] Another problem concerns the lawfulness of carrying a gun or an offensive weapon in order to repel an anticipated attack: the authorities would seem to suggest that, although the use of the weapon might be lawful if an attack takes place, its possession beforehand remains an offence.[184] A further unresolved question arises where a law enforcement officer shoots a fleeing suspect on the basis that the suspect is likely, if allowed to escape, to commit violent offences: must it be shown that those offences might or would be committed sooner rather than later?[185]

(ii) *A Duty to Avoid Conflict?*: One of the most technical but most significant elements in the common law of self-defence was the duty to retreat. Its technicality lay in its careful wording and its exceptions; its significance was that, from an early stage, the common law recognized limitations on the forfeiture principle and on the primacy of the non-aggressor's autonomy in these situations. However, the duty has now

---

[180] See *Jones, Milling et al* [2007] 1 AC 136; see also Lord Bingham's judgment on duress and the duty to avoid using force in *Hasan* [2005] 2 AC 467, discussed below in Ch 6.3.

[181] [1984] QB 456; see also *Cousins* [1982] QB 526.

[182] J. Dressler, 'Battered Women who Kill their Sleeping Tormentors' in S. Shute and A. P. Simester (eds.), *Criminal Law Theory* (2002), 269.

[183] J. Horder, 'Killing the Passive Abuser', in Shute and Simester, ibid., at 292–3; Leverick, *Killing in Self-Defence*, ch 5. Cf. also the proposal to create a new partial defence (in murder cases) for situations where D acted during a loss of self-control stemming from D's fear of serious violence from V, discussed in Ch 7.4(b) below.

[184] See *Evans v Hughes* [1972] 3 All ER 412; Smith, *Justification and Excuse*, 117–23; and now D. J. Lanham, 'Offensive Weapons and Self-Defence' [2005] Crim LR 85.

[185] A point left open by the European Commission in *Kelly v UK* (1993) 74 DR 139.

disappeared as such. In *Julien* (1969)[186] it was rephrased as a duty to demonstrate an unwillingness to fight, 'to temporize and disengage and perhaps to make some physical withdrawal'. In *Bird* (1985)[187] the Court of Appeal accepted that the imposition of a 'duty' is too strong. The key question is whether D was acting in self-defence or in revenge or retaliation. Evidence that D tried to retreat or to call off the fight might negative a suggestion of revenge, but it is not the only way of doing so. The modification of the law seems to derive from the suggestion in Smith and Hogan's textbook that the 'duty' as described in *Julien* is inconsistent with the liberty to make a pre-emptive strike.[188] It is not. The liberty to make a pre-emptive strike can easily be cast as an exception to the general duty to avoid conflict, and, as such, it is no more inconsistent with the rule than any other exception to a rule. The difficulty with regarding the duty to avoid conflict as merely one consideration to be borne in mind here is that it says nothing about the circumstances which might outweigh it. If the law is to protect everyone's right to life and to pursue the minimization of physical violence, the avoidance of conflict—or what Fiona Leverick refers to as the 'strong retreat rule'[189]—must be right in principle. Section 76 is silent on this.

(iii) *Protection of the Home:* One long-standing exception to the duty to retreat is that a person attacked at home has no duty to withdraw. This may be regarded as one remaining bastion of the autonomy-based view, regarding the individual's home as sacrosanct. Undoubtedly many citizens feel that way about their homes today,[190] but there are two questions to be resolved. The first is whether an exception to the duty to avoid conflict should be recognized here: *should* there be any obligation to 'temporize and disengage' if a person enters one's home unlawfully, manifesting an intent to steal property or to carry out an unlawful eviction? Much depends on the situation and on D's purpose in acting. If D believes there is a threat only to personal property in the home and that there is no danger to D, reasonable force may be used to detain the intruder,[191] but not aggressive force. If D believes that the threat is to evict him, it can be argued that D should have resort to the civil courts rather than using what may be considerable violence to defend his possession. If D believes there is a threat of violence from the intruder, as will often be the assumption,[192] then surely life should be placed before property and D should retreat rather than (if this is possible) using a weapon against the intruder. Although popular sentiment appears to be otherwise, any other approach would value property interests more highly than life and limb. But

---

[186] [1969] 1 WLR 839.   [187] [1985] 1 WLR 816.

[188] J. C. Smith and B. Hogan, *Criminal Law* (5th edn., 1983), 327, quoted by the Court of Appeal in *Bird* [1985] 1 WLR 816; see now *Criminal Law* (12th edn., by D. Ormerod, 2008), 368.

[189] Leverick, *Killing in Self-Defence*, 82, and ch 4 generally.

[190] P. Robinson and J. Darley's subjects strongly maintained that there should be no duty to avoid conflict when attacked at home (and also declined to find full criminal liability when a person failed to retreat in a non-home setting): *Justice, Liability and Blame* (1995), 60.

[191] *Faraj* [2007] 2 Cr App R 25.

[192] See the Irish decision in *DPP v Barnes* [2006] IECCA 165 for an examination of the householder's rights and those of the burglar, concluding that the crime of burglary is itself an act of aggression, and that under the Irish Constitution there can be no duty to retreat from the home.

in several cases in which a firearm, sword, or knife has been used against a burglar with fatal results, the householder has been either acquitted or not prosecuted.[193] It must be recalled that Article 2 of the Convention does not allow an exception to the right to life in favour of the prevention of crime, unless the crime is 'unlawful violence' or a riot.[194] English law therefore violates the deceased's right to life in so far as it allows the acquittal of a householder who uses fatal force against an offender who has not done or threatened 'unlawful violence', although it must be said that there seems to be strong popular support in this country and elsewhere for such an approach.[195] Finally, what about cases in which unlawful violence is used, and the violence is by one occupant of the home against another? In modern times no clear view has been taken on this 'domestic violence' point by the English courts, but it can be argued strongly that a woman who reasonably fears further violence from her partner should be able to defend herself without in any way being obliged to leave.[196]

(iv) *Freedom of Movement:* English law also recognizes an exception to the duty to avoid conflict (if such a duty exists) in those cases where D is acting lawfully in remaining at, or going to, a place, realizing that there is a risk that someone will force a violent confrontation there. The authority for this is *Field* (1972),[197] where D was warned that some men were coming to attack him. D stayed where he was, the men came and made their attack, and in the ensuing struggle D stabbed one of them fatally. The Court of Appeal quashed his conviction, holding that he had no duty to avoid conflict until his attackers were present and had started to threaten him. The American case of *State v Bristol* (1938)[198] takes the point further, holding that D had no duty to avoid entering a bar where he knew his adversary (who had threatened him with attack) to be drinking. The American court declined to lay down a rule which might 'encourage bullies to stalk about the land and terrorize citizens by their mere threats'. These two decisions appear to promote the value of freedom of movement above any duty to avoid conflict in advance by, for example, informing the police of the threat.[199] However, in *Redmond-Bate v DPP*[200] the Divisional Court held that the defendant's right to preach should be protected, as an exercise of the right to freedom of expression under Article 10 of the Convention, and it was only if the words spoken were likely to provoke violence in others that it would have been proper to arrest her: if her

---

[193] D. J. Lanham, 'Defence of Property in the Criminal Law' [1966] Crim LR 368, 426; Smith, *Justification and Excuse*, 109–12; and Leverick, *Killing in Self-Defence*, 83–5.

[194] Above, section 4.6(b). Cf. the strong public feeling aroused by the case of Norfolk farmer Tony Martin, who shot a burglar dead (see *Martin* [2002] 1 Cr App R 27, and next note).

[195] A private member's Household Protection Bill was put forward in 2005. See generally S. Skinner, 'Populist Politics and Shooting Burglars' [2005] Crim LR 275.

[196] A. McColgan, 'In Defence of Battered Women who Kill' (1993) 13 Oxford JLS 508, at 516 and 525, developed by Horder, 'Killing the Passive Abuser'; cf above, para. (i), and Leverick, *Killing in Self-Defence*, ch 5.

[197] [1972] Crim LR 435.   [198] (1938) 53 Wyo 304.

[199] Cf. Lord Mance in *Jones, Milling et al.* [2007] 1 AC 136, with the arguments of F. McAuley and J. P. McCutcheon, *Criminal Liability: a Grammar* (2000), 760–1.

[200] [1999] Crim LR 998; cf. *Beatty v Gillbanks* (1882) 9 QBD 308 and *Nicol and Selvanayagam v DPP* [1996] Crim LR 318.

words were not provocative of violence, only those who used or threatened violence should have been arrested. This suggests a small qualification of a subject's right to freedom of expression, and there are surely strong arguments for this. Should not the minimization of physical violations (implicit in Article 5) take precedence over freedom of expression (Article 10) and movement? Is there not some analogy with omissions to assist in saving life, where a citizen's general liberty should also be outweighed by a specific social duty?[201] These remarks concern self-defence and the defence of property only; clearly, a person who acts with the purpose of preventing crime or arresting a suspected offender cannot be expected to avoid conflict, and so the proportionality standard ought to assume primacy there.

(v) *Pre-Emptive Strike:* The use of force in self-defence may be justifiable as a pre-emptive strike, when an unlawful attack is imminent.[202] This is a desirable rule, since the rationale for self-defence involves the protection of an innocent citizen's vital interests (life, physical security), and it would be a nonsense if the citizen were obliged to wait until the first blow was struck. The liberty to make a pre-emptive strike is not inconsistent with a duty to avoid conflict (if it were recognized), but it should be read as being subject to that duty. In other words, it would be possible and desirable to have a law which imposed a general obligation to avoid conflict but, where this was not practical, authorized a pre-emptive strike.[203] A law which allows pre-emptive strikes without any general duty to avoid conflict runs the risk, as Dicey put it, of over-stimulating self-assertion.[204]

(vi) *Necessity, Proportionality and Law Enforcement:* The point has already been made that a police officer or citizen whose purpose is to prevent a crime or to apprehend a suspected offender must behave proactively. The primary legal restriction on such conduct has been the standard of proportionality, in relation to the purpose that the actor was aiming to achieve.[205] How serious an offence was being or had been committed? Is there a danger of serious offences in the near future? Applying Article 2 of the Convention, not only must the justification fall within paragraph 2(a), (b), or (c) of the Article, but the force must be shown to have been 'absolutely necessary' and 'strictly proportionate'—the adverbs emphasizing the sharper formulation of the tests under the Convention. This should be the benchmark for scrutinizing the so-called 'shoot-to-protect' policy adopted by the Association of Chief Police Officers in 2003 and defended after the London bombings. Although its details have not been made public, the Metropolitan Police Commissioner referred to shooting to kill 'a deadly and determined bomber who is intent on murdering many other people'.[206] Much then depends on whether reasonable grounds should be required for the belief that V is such a person.

---

[201] See above, section 4.4.   [202] E.g. *Beckford* v *R* [1988] AC 130, at 144.

[203] See n 188 above, and accompanying text.

[204] A. V. Dicey, *Introduction to the Study of the Law of the Constitution* (8th edn., 1923), 489.

[205] See the discussion of *Thain* above, n 177 and text thereat.

[206] Sir Ian Blair in oral evidence to the House of Commons Home Affairs Committee, *Counter-Terrorism*, 13 September 2005, Qs 59–60.

Some of the leading European decisions are not uncontroversial. In *McCann and others* v *UK* (1996)[207] the European Court of Human Rights held (by a ten to nine majority) that the UK had violated the right to life of three suspected IRA terrorists who were shot dead by security forces in Gibraltar. The most important ruling was that Article 2 requires law enforcement operations to be organized so as to 'minimize, to the greatest extent possible, recourse to lethal force'. The Court found that the planning of the operation failed to show the required level of respect for the suspects' right to life. It did not find that the soldiers who fired the shots violated Article 2, although it did state that their reactions lacked 'the degree of caution in the use of firearms to be expected from law enforcement personnel in a democratic society, even when dealing with dangerous terrorist suspects'.[208] In *Andronicou and Constantinou* v *Cyprus* (1998)[209] the Court (by a five to four majority) held that Article 2 was not violated when Cypriot security forces stormed a house where a hostage was being held, firing machine guns in all directions and killing both the gunman and the hostage. This decision appeared to leave a considerable gap between the strict formulation of the tests and their application to the facts, but the Court distinguished it in *Gül* v *Turkey* (2002).[210] The Court noted that in the *Cyprus* case the hostage-taker was known to be in possession of a gun, which he had fired twice already. In the *Turkey* case, there was insufficient reason to believe that Gül had a gun, and 'the firing of at least 50–55 shots at the door was not justified by any reasonable belief of the officers that their lives were at risk'.[211] It is fair to say that the Strasbourg judgments, particularly when applied to the facts of the cases, leave some scope for debate about what Article 2 actually requires.[212]

(f) MISTAKEN BELIEF AS TO NECESSITY

In English law the rule has become established that a person who purports to use justifiable force should be judged on the facts as he or she believed them to be.[213] Section 76(3) of the 2008 Act confirms that this subjective test represents English law, and section 76(4) goes on to state that the reasonableness of the belief may be considered when

---

[207] (1996) 21 EHRR 97; for analysis of the ECHR case-law, see Leverick, *Killing in Self-Defence*, ch 10, and B. Emmerson, A. Ashworth, and A. Macdonald (eds), *Human Rights and Criminal Justice*, 748–57.

[208] Cf. P. A. J. Waddington, '"Overkill" or "Minimum Force"?' [1990] Crim LR 695, for the argument that if officers do not shoot to kill they risk the possibility that an injured suspect might still be able to kill or wound someone—in which case, shooting to kill might be justifiable in the first place.

[209] (1998) 25 EHRR 491.   [210] (2002) 34 EHRR 719.   [211] Ibid., para. 82.

[212] However, it is widely recognized that the State has a positive duty to ensure that the right to life of all its citizens is protected, and to ensure that its police and military personnel conduct their operations with due respect for Article 2. Passages in several judgments (e.g. *Isaveya* v *Russia* (2005) 41 EHRR 791, at para. 175) suggest that there may be grounds for charging senior police officers with negligent manslaughter if they fail in this duty. See also *Juozaitiene* v *Lithuania* (2008) 47 EHRR 1194.

[213] By the Privy Council in *Shaw* v *R* [2002] 1 Cr App R 10; cf. *Martin* [2002] 1 Cr App R 27, where the Court of Appeal nevertheless held that psychiatric evidence to assist the jury to understand D's likely perceptions was not admissible.

assessing whether it was genuinely held.[214] However, in cases of killing under Article 2, the Strasbourg Court has insisted on several occasions that the actions of those who take life should be judged on the basis of the facts that 'they honestly believed, *for good reason*, to exist'.[215] This is clearly an objective test which, in effect, places such a high value on the right to life as to require law enforcement officers to make reasonable attempts to ascertain the true facts before using lethal force. It is easy to argue that this may not always be possible; but a more telling point is that, where it is possible, it ought to be done so as to respect the right to life. For this reason, previous editions of this work have contended that it should be a principle of English law; the arrival of the Convention jurisprudence strengthens that case. The fact that the Strasbourg cases on Article 2 deal only with law enforcement officers should not be crucial, since it is the State's duty to ensure that the law protects the lives of all victims, no matter who threatens them.[216] However, in *Bubbins* v *UK* (2005)[217] the Strasbourg Court appeared to modify its position, reiterating the requirement of an 'honest belief, for good reason' but then softening it considerably by emphasizing the actual belief of the police officer at the time he shot V.[218] It is true to say that the Strasbourg Court has had ample opportunity to point out any incompatibility between the English law of self-defence and the Convention, and has not done so.[219] Yet, as the Joint Committee on Human Rights has pointed out, adopting the same argument as this book, the preponderance of Strasbourg jurisprudence favours the objective test of reasonable belief, and 'the very minimum required by human rights law' in order to protect the right to life of ordinary citizens is that the test of belief 'for good reason' should be introduced 'when force is used by state agents.'[220]

(g) JUSTIFIABLE FORCE AND THE EMOTIONS

The foregoing paragraphs have examined principles which might produce outcomes that consistently uphold human rights in those varied situations in which a claim of justifiable force might arise. Some might regard those principles as too mechanical for the sudden and confused circumstances of many such cases. It is well known that a sudden threat to one's physical safety may lead to strong emotions of fear and panic, producing physiological changes which take the individual out of his or her 'normal self'. According to this view, the most just law is the simplest: was the use of force an innocent and instinctive reaction, or was it the product of revenge or some manifest fault?

---

[214] S 76(5) states that voluntary intoxication should be left out of account. General discussions of mistaken beliefs will be found in Ch 6.4 and of intoxication in Ch 6.2, below.

[215] *McCann et al.* v *UK* (1996) 21 EHRR 97, at para. 200; *Andronicou and Constantinou* v *Cyprus* (1998) 25 EHRR 491, at para. 192; *Gül* v *Turkey* (2002) 34 EHRR 719, at paras. 78–82 See Leverick, *Killing in Self-Defence*, ch 10.

[216] See n 212 above. [217] (2005) 41 EHRR 458. [218] Ibid., paras. 138–9.

[219] Per Collins J in *R (Bennett)* v *HM Coroner for Inner London* [2006] EWHC Admin 196; see also the Government response to the Joint Committee, printed as Appendix 7 to the report below.

[220] Joint Committee on Human Rights, *Legislative Scrutiny* (15th report, session 2007–08), para. 2.35.

This simple approach may have the great advantage of recognizing explicitly the role of the emotions in these cases. It is surely right to exclude revenge attacks from the ambit of justifiable force.[221] It is also consistent with the doctrine of prior fault for the law to construe the standards of reasonableness and necessity strictly against someone whose own fault originally caused the show of violence.[222] The question then is how much indulgence should be granted to the innocent victim of sudden attack who reacts instinctively with strong force. In the leading case of *Palmer* (1971)[223] Lord Morris stated that it is 'most potent evidence' of reasonableness that the defendant only did what he or she 'honestly and instinctively thought necessary'. The Strasbourg Court, despite its insistence on the requirement of 'good reason', deferred in *Bubbins* to the beliefs of 'an officer who was required to act in the heat of the moment to avert an honestly perceived danger to his life'.[224] Section 76(7) of the 2008 Act now gives legislative authority to this approach, by providing that a court should take account, when assessing reasonableness, of the considerations:

(a) that a person acting for a legitimate purpose may not be able to weigh to a nicety the exact measure of any necessary action; and

(b) that evidence of a person's having done only what the person honestly and instinctively thought was necessary for a legitimate purpose constitutes strong evidence that only reasonable action was taken by that person for that purpose.

The additional flexibility of this approach suggests that it is more accurate to state the law's requirement in terms of a 'not disproportionate' use of force rather than a proportionate response, but even then there must be limits. It cannot be right for absolutely any reaction 'in a moment of unexpected anguish' to be held to be justifiable,[225] particularly in the case of a trained firearms officer, even if it is right for the courts to consider 'how the circumstances in which the accused had time to make his decision whether or not to use force and the shortness of the time available to him for reflection, might affect the judgment of a reasonable man'.[226] To the extent that the law has moved away from objective standards towards indulgence to the emotions of innocent citizens, the rationale of justification becomes diluted by elements of excuse.[227]

The fairness of this concession to what Blackstone termed 'the passions of the human mind'[228] is often supported by reference to the famous dictum of Holmes J, namely,

---

[221] As the Law Commission has recommended their exclusion from the partial defence of provocation: see Ch 7.5(b) below.

[222] See Ashworth, above n 158, and Leverick, *Killing in Self-Defence*, ch 6.

[223] [1971] AC 814, at 832.   [224] *Bubbins* v *UK* (2005) 41 EHRR 458, at para. 139.

[225] A phrase from *Palmer*, above n 223; see also the insistence of the Joint Committee on Human Rights (above, n 220), para. 2.24, that allowing force which is not 'grossly disproportionate' would go too far and breach the state's obligations under Article 2.

[226] *Per* Lord Diplock, in *Attorney-General for Northern Ireland's Reference* [1977] AC 105.

[227] On which see J. Horder, *Excusing Crime* (2004), 48–52.

[228] *Commentaries on the Laws of England*, iii, 3–4.

that 'detached reflection cannot be demanded in the presence of an uplifted knife'.[229] This dictum is significant for its limited application: it concerns cases of an 'uplifted knife', i.e. typically, sudden and grave threats or attacks; it has no application to cases where the attack is known to be imminent and the defendant has time to consider his position. Nor should it necessarily be conclusive in relation to those who are trained to deal with extreme situations, such as the police and the army.[230] As the element of sudden and unrehearsed emergency recedes, the social interest in the minimal use of force becomes a firmer precept again. In this type of situation, the law ought to give consideration to the relative importance of the sanctity of life and the physical safety of all persons, including offenders, when compared with such other interests as the free movement of citizens. The aphorism about the 'uplifted knife' should not be used to prevent the principled resolution of cases to which it does not apply.

(h) CONCLUSIONS

The law relating to self-defence and justifiable force depends on resolution of a clash between two aspects of the right to life—the individual's autonomy and right to protect life by using even fatal force if necessary, and the right to life of every citizen (including offenders). English lawyers have generally been reluctant to discuss the issues in these terms, and the government has rarely acknowledged its positive obligation under Article 2 of the Convention to have in place laws that give maximum protection to the right of life of all citizens. The relevant law—whether on self-defence or the other forms of justification—is mostly common law, and the enactment of section 76 of the Criminal Justice and Immigration Act 2008 to 'clarify' the common law is a disappointment, a missed opportunity to legislate at the detailed level rightly recommended by the Law Commission[231] and to engage with Article 2 of the Convention and its requirements. An urgent re-assessment of the law on justifiable force is called for, taking full account of the issues discussed above.

4.7 CHASTISEMENT OF CHILDREN

For centuries it has been the common law that a parent is justified in using reasonable force to discipline her or his child.[232] For example, in *Smith* (1985)[233] a mother had asked the defendant (her partner) to smack her 6-year-old child for disobedience, and

---

[229] *Brown v United States* (1921) 256 US 335, at 343.

[230] Cf., however, the use of the concession in the *Andronicou* case, above, n 215, and in *Bubbins*, above, n 224.

[231] In the draft criminal code, Law Com No. 177, cl. 44; however, on some of the issues, this book differs from the Commission's particular recommendations.

[232] *Hopley* (1860) 2 F and F 202; see generally H. Keating, 'Protecting or Punishing Children: Physical Punishment, Human Rights and English Law Reform' (2006) 26 LS 394.

[233] [1985] Crim LR 42.

he gave the child two strokes with his belt. Although it upheld the man's conviction for assault, the Court of Appeal recognized that the defence of reasonable chastisement exists and held that the prosecution must prove that D 'did more than inflict moderate and reasonable chastisement on the child'. However, in *A v United Kingdom* (1998)[234] the European Court of Human Rights held that the ill-defined nature of this defence failed to discharge the government's duty to ensure that the child's rights under Article 3 of the Convention were protected. Article 3 declares that no person shall be subjected to 'inhuman and degrading treatment or punishment'. In this case the 9-year-old applicant had been beaten with a garden cane on several occasions by his stepfather, leaving marks that were visible several hours later. The judge had left the jury to decide on the reasonableness of the chastisement, and they had acquitted the man. The Strasbourg Court's finding of a violation of Article 3 in this case did not require the criminalization of all smacking of children by parents, but rather a tightening of the law. The Government accepted that it has a duty to ensure that the criminal law is so framed as to prevent degrading punishment, and that the then law failed to achieve this, and it conducted a public consultation on the matter.[235] Most of those working with children argued that the defence of reasonable chastisement should be abolished, as in Sweden and 13 other European countries.[236] Some argue that the present law contributes to the cycle of violence and (as the United Nations Committee on the Rights of the Child has put it) fails to 'promote positive and non-violent discipline.'[237] The European Commissioner for Human Rights regards such consequentialist arguments as less powerful than the consideration that 'the existence of special exceptions for violent ill-treatment of children in otherwise universally applicable laws against assault breaches the principle of equal protection under the law.'[238] However, the consultation suggested that a majority of members of the British public favoured retaining the defence (castigated by the European Commissioner as a 'disreputable legal concept') in order to allow parents to carry out their duty to bring up their children properly. These strong conceptions of parental duty prompt reflections on the rationale for this defence, which remains obscure[239] and may reside (historically, at least) in some form of delegation by the State of its power to punish, or in an approach that permits parents to determine (within limits) what is in the 'best interests' of the child.

The law has now been changed by s 58 of the Children Act 2004, which states that 'reasonable punishment' cannot be a defence to any offence under ss 47, 20 or 18 of the Offences Against the Person Act 1861, or to the offence of child cruelty under s 1 of

---

[234] (1999) 27 EHRR 611.

[235] Department of Health, *Protecting Children, Supporting Parents* (2000); this paper and the responses are helpfully analysed by J. Rogers, 'A Criminal Lawyer's Response to Chastisement in the European Court of Human Rights' [2002] Crim LR 98.

[236] Commissioner for Human Rights, *Children and Corporal Punishment: 'the Right not to be Hit', also a 'Children's Right'* (2006) 43 EHRR SE17.

[237] UNHCHR, *Concluding Observations of the Committee on the Rights of the Child: United Kingdom* (2002), UN Doc CRC/C/15/Add.188, para. 35. See further Keating, *Protecting or Punishing Children.*

[238] Above, n 236, at 228.   [239] Cf., ibid., at 106–12, who discusses an analogy with duress.

the Children and Young Persons Act 1933. This leaves it open for D to raise the defence to a charge of battery. The implication is that only minor hurts such as smacking will come within the defence, but there are two problems with the new law. First, the line between battery and assault occasioning actual bodily harm is crucial to the ambit of s 58, but it has not been sharply drawn by the courts. Indeed, it can be suggested that the line is actually drawn in the wrong place, and that many offences are prosecuted as battery when a conviction under s 47 would be a realistic prospect.[240] Secondly, the Strasbourg jurisprudence on Article 3 makes it clear that the reasonableness of any 'punishment' should depend not only on the duration of the assault, its physical and mental consequences in relation to the child, the age and personal characteristics of the child, as recognized by the Court of Appeal in *H.* (2002),[241] but also on such matters as whether an instrument was used and whether marks were left on the child's body.[242] In order to ensure compliance with Article 3, magistrates who try these cases[243] must ensure that they take account of all these factors in deciding whether a particular battery amounted to reasonable chastisement.

4.8 JUSTIFICATIONS, NECESSITY, AND THE CHOICE OF EVILS

The discussion so far has focused on self-defence and the justifications relating to law enforcement and the prevention of crime. Generally speaking, the justifications relating to self-defence may be linked directly to the principle of autonomy, in the basic sense of self-preservation, whereas the justifications relating to law enforcement may be linked to the principle of welfare, although that principle should also be interpreted so as to insist on the minimal use of force. In some situations, however, the principle of individual autonomy is compromised because it may not be possible to protect the autonomy of all persons involved. These are the 'choice of evils' cases, which must now be discussed.

(a) NECESSITY AS A JUSTIFICATION

English law contains limited defences of duress and necessity, which apply when a person commits an otherwise criminal act under threat or fear of death or serious harm. The relevant law is examined in a later chapter,[244] where it will become apparent

---

[240] See further Ch 8.3(d) and (e) below.   [241] [2002] 1 Cr App R 59, at [31].

[242] Cf. the more certain terms of the Criminal Justice (Scotland) Act 2003, s 51, which requires courts to give special consideration to assaults involving a blow to the head, shaking or the use of an implement (although it does not regard such assaults as necessarily unjustifiable).

[243] By removing s. 47 offences from the ambit of the defence, the new law ensures that all such cases will now be tried in magistrates' courts.

[244] See below, Ch 6.3.

that many statements about the ambit of the defences (especially in the courts) are ambivalent or even indiscriminate as to whether their basis lies in justification (D had a right to use this force) or excuse (the use of force was unjustifiable, but D did not behave unreasonably in the dire circumstances). One apparently clear statement came when the House of Lords, in rejecting duress as a defence to murder, held in *Howe* (1987)[245] that, even if D's own life is threatened, it cannot be justifiable to take another innocent life. What this means is that one innocent person who stands in danger of imminent death cannot be justified in killing another innocent person. To kill an aggressor in self-defence is one thing, but to kill an uninvolved third party, even if this were the only means of preserving one's own life, could not be right—even though it might be excusable, as we shall see elsewhere.[246] But what about the possibility of justifying the killing of an innocent non-aggressor when this will save two or more other lives? One example of this emerged from the inquest into the deaths caused by the sinking of the ferry *Herald of Free Enterprise* in 1987.[247] At one stage of the disaster several passengers were trying to gain access to the ship's deck by ascending a rope-ladder. On that ladder there was a young man, petrified, unable to move up or down, so that nobody else could pass. People were shouting at him, but he did not move. Eventually it was suggested that he should be pushed off the ladder, and this was done. He fell into the water and was never seen again, but several other passengers escaped up the ladder to safety. No English court has had to consider this kind of situation:[248] are there circumstances in which the strong social interest in preserving the greater number of lives might be held to override an individual's right to life?

Any residual justification of this kind must be carefully circumscribed. It involves the sanctity of life, and therefore the highest value with which the criminal law is concerned. Although there is a provision in the Model Penal Code allowing for a defence of 'lesser evil',[249] it fails to restrict the application of the defence to cases of imminent threat, opening up the danger of citizens trying to justify all manner of conduct by reference to overall good effects.[250] The moral issues are acute: 'not just anything is permissible on the ground that it would yield a net saving of lives'.[251] Yet there may be situations in which the sacrifice of a small number of lives may be the only way of saving a much greater number of lives, as where a dam is about to burst (flooding a whole town) unless a sluice-gate is opened (flooding a less densely

---

[245] [1987] AC 417.

[246] Cf. J. J. Thomson, 'Self-Defense' (1991) 20 Philosophy and Public Affairs 283, with R. Christopher, 'Self-Defense and Objectivity' (1998) 1 Buffalo CLR 537; on necessity as an excuse see below, Ch 6.3(a).

[247] Smith, *Justification and Excuse*, 73–9.

[248] Cf. *Dudley and Stephens* (1884) 14 QBD 273, the case in which two men saved themselves by killing and eating the weakest member of a threesome who had been adrift in a boat for many days; but they were rescued the following day, and some have questioned the necessity of their act. See A. W. B. Simpson, *Cannibalism and the Common Law* (1984), and below, Ch 6.4(a).

[249] Model Penal Code, s. 3.02; cf. G. P. Fletcher, *Rethinking Criminal Law* (1978), 788–98.

[250] Cf. the remarks of the House of Lords in *Jones, Milling et al* [2007] 1 AC 136.

[251] Thomson, 'Self-Defense', 309; see also J. Finnis, 'Intention and Side-Effects', in R. G. Frey and C. W. Morris (eds.), *Liability and Responsibility* (1991), for the argument that it is never morally right to choose (intend) to take another's life.

populated area). Could a doctrine of necessity justify the intentional killing of people in the latter area in order to save the greater number, if there were no alternative? There are strong arguments in favour of recognizing some such extreme situations of justifying necessity, but there are those who would oppose this and would insist that there can never be a justification for intentionally taking life—although it may be acceptable to recognize a (partial) excuse in such cases.

Some situations give rise to the further moral problem of 'choosing one's victim', which arises when, for example, a lifeboat is in danger of sinking, necessitating the throwing overboard of some passengers,[252] or when two people have to kill and eat another if any of the three is to survive.[253] To countenance a legal justification in such cases would be to regard the victim's rights as morally and politically less worthy than the rights of those protected by the action taken, which represents a clear violation of the principle of individual autonomy. Yet it is surely necessary to make some sacrifice if the autonomy of everyone simply cannot be protected. A dire choice has to be made, and it must be made in a way that fairly minimizes the overall harm. A fair procedure for resolving the problem—perhaps the drawing of lots—must be found. But here, as with self-defence and the 'uplifted knife' cases,[254] one should not obscure the clearer cases where there is no need to choose a victim: in the case of the young man on the rope-ladder, blocking the escape of several others, there was no doubt about the person who must be subjected to force, probably with fatal consequences.

(b) MEDICAL NECESSITY

Is it ever justifiable for a doctor to act contrary to the letter of the law for clinical reasons? There has been little direct discussion of this by the courts or the legislature. The summing-up in *Bourne* (1939)[255] is sometimes cited as authority that a doctor may not be convicted (there, for carrying out an abortion) if it is necessary to save the life of the patient, but that particular area of the law is now subject to express statutory provisions.[256] More common in recent times has been the acceptance of 'concealed defences' of medical necessity, by means of stretching established concepts.[257] For example, we saw how Devlin J in the *Adams* trial modified the general proposition that any acceleration of death satisfies the conduct element for unlawful homicide.[258] And the next chapter will show how the House of Lords in *Gillick v West Norfolk and Wisbech Area Health Authority* (1986)[259] deviated from the general proposition that intention includes foresight of virtual certainty. In these decisions the desired effect

---

[252] *United States v Holmes* (1842) 26 Fed Cas 360.   [253] *Dudley and Stephens* (1884) 14 QBD 273.

[254] See *Brown v United States* (1921) 256 US 335, and the text accompanying n 229 above.

[255] [1939] 1 KB 687.   [256] Abortion Act 1967.

[257] Smith, *Justification and Excuse*, 64–70; A. Ashworth, 'Criminal Liability in a Medical Context: the Treatment of Good Intentions' in A. P. Simester and A. T. H. Smith (eds.), *Harm and Culpability* (1996).

[258] See above, section 4.6(a), on the cases of Dr Adams and Dr Moor; see also the 'medical' exception to the principle that a voluntary intervening human act negatives causal responsibility in section 4.6(b)(ii) above.

[259] [1986] AC 112, discussed in Ch 5.5(b).

was to avoid the conviction of a doctor who acted in the 'best interests' of the patient, and the chosen method was to distort established concepts rather than to confront the problem openly.

One way of bringing the issues into the open would be to create a special defence, which might (following Paul Robinson's suggested draft) provide a justification for reasonable treatment for the promotion of the patient's health.[260] The definition would be quite elaborate, and much would turn on the criteria of reasonableness—some would contend that 'reasonableness' should be determined by reference to practices 'accepted at the time by a responsible body of medical opinion',[261] whereas the ultimate determination ought surely to be that of the court.[262] Alternatively, the judges could be left to develop a defence at common law. One of the first English judges to confront some of the issues was Lord Goff in his speech in *Re F* (1990),[263] where he distinguished three forms of necessity—public necessity, private necessity, and necessity in aid of another. The last category was not merely confined to medical cases (e.g. acting to preserve the life of a person who is in a condition that makes it impossible to give consent) but also extends to other cases of action to protect the safety or property of a person unable to give consent. The key element of the decision in *Re F* was that the necessity was determined by reference to the patient's best interests. It might be possible to reconcile the result of *Bourne*[264] with this approach, but the reasoning in that case was that the interests of the young mother should be allowed to override those of the foetus. That kind of balancing of interests was ruled out in *Dudley and Stephens*, but it underlies the reasoning of Brooke LJ in *Re A (Conjoined Twins: Surgical Separation)*,[265] where he distinguished *Dudley and Stephens* on the ground that in *Re A* there was no doubt about the person whose life should be sacrificed and why (that she was incapable of separate existence, and that a failure to operate would hasten the death of both twins). This frank approach to the problem is preferable to the distorting effect of some of the earlier decisions,[266] but there remains the question of how exactly a serviceable defence of justified necessity should be drafted.

(c) NECESSITY AND OTHER JUDICIAL DEVELOPMENT OF JUSTIFICATIONS

In the past almost all justifications have been developed by the judges. If the criminal law is to be codified, should an exhaustive list of justifications be included? The Law Commission thinks not. Its draft Criminal Code includes provisions on duress and

---

[260] P. Robinson, *Criminal Law Defences* (1984), ii, 173.

[261] *Airedale NHS Trust v Bland* [1993] AC 789, *per* Lord Browne-Wilkinson at 883.

[262] As Lord Mustill argued in the *Bland* case.

[263] [1990] 2 AC 1; see S. Gardner, 'Necessity's Newest Inventions' (1991) 11 Oxford JLS 125.

[264] Above, n 284.

[265] [2000] 4 All ER 961, on which see J. Rogers, 'Necessity, Private Defence and the Killing of Mary' [2001] Crim LR 515.

[266] See S. Ost, 'Euthanasia and the Defence of Necessity', in C. Erin and S. Ost (eds), *The Criminal Justice System and Health Care* (2007).

on justifiable force, but clause 45(4) provides that a person does not commit an offence by doing an act that is justified or excused by 'any rule of common law continuing to apply by virtue of section 4(4)'.[267] The intended effect is to preserve the power of the courts to develop defences, including justifications. There is an evident need for flexibility in responding to new sets of circumstances, but on the other hand the courts are not suited to the kind of wide-ranging review that ought to be carried out before a justification is recognized or even taken away.[268] A code should go as far as it can in formulating the justifications for what would otherwise be criminal conduct, even if it must rely on terms such as 'reasonable' at various points. This may mean the open discussion not merely of hitherto concealed defences such as medical necessity,[269] but also of broader concepts of necessity. Thus in *Shayler* (2001)[270] (disclosure of official secrets in order to expose alleged failures by the security services to protect citizens adequately) and again in *Jones, Milling et al* (2006)[271] (damage to an airbase in order to impede aircraft leaving for the invasion of Iraq), the appellate courts took a highly restrictive approach to the prospect of a justificatory defence of necessity, whereas decisions such as *Re A (Conjoined Twins: Surgical Separation)*[272] demonstrate a possible category of justificatory necessity. In those two cases the courts were urged to apply it to what may be termed 'political necessity', to justify acts aimed at preventing a greater evil. The conditions for such a defence ought to be tightly circumscribed, but that is no reason to deny its existence.[273]

(d) STATUTORY RECOGNITION OF JUSTIFICATORY PURPOSES

There is an increasing tendency to insert into legislation some specific justificatory defences. Long-standing examples are s 5(4) of the Misuse of Drugs Act 1971, allowing a defence to drugs charges if D's purpose in keeping the possession of the drugs was to prevent another from committing an offence or to hand them over to the authorities, and section 87 of the Road Traffic Regulation Act 1984,[274] creating exemptions from speed limits for emergency vehicles. Sections 1 and 4 of the Protection from Harassment Act 1997 both include defences for persons whose course of conduct (which might otherwise amount to 'stalking') was 'pursued for the purpose of preventing or detecting crime'.[275] Section 73 of the Sexual Offences Act 2003 states that

---

[267] For discussion see Law Com No. 177, ii, para. 12.41.

[268] See particularly the two articles by Rogers, on reasonable chastisement (above, n 235) and on necessity and private defence (above, n 265), and the discussion of 'the democracy problem' by Gardner (above, n 263).

[269] See Ch 5.3(c) below.

[270] [2001] 1 WLR 2206; the case went to the House of Lords on other grounds: [2003] 1 AC 247.

[271] [2007] 1 AC 136.   [272] See n 265 above and text thereat.

[273] S. Gardner, 'Direct Action and the Defence of Necessity' [2005] Crim LR 371; cf. C. Clarkson, 'Necessary Action: a New Defence' [2004] Crim LR 81, arguing against a separation of justificatory necessity from its excusatory counterpart.

[274] As amended by s. 19 of the Road Safety Act 2006.

[275] See further A. Ashworth, 'Testing Fidelity to Legal Values: Official Involvement and Criminal Justice', in Shute and Simester (eds.), *Criminal Law Theory*, at 322–30.

a person cannot be convicted of aiding, abetting or counselling a child sex offence if he acts 'for the purpose of (a) protecting the child from sexually transmitted infection, (b) protecting the physical safety of the child, (c) preventing the child from becoming pregnant, or (d) promoting the child's emotional well-being by the giving of advice'.[276] The presence of the justification depends here on the purpose or motive for which D acts, a point underlined by the further requirement that D does not act for the purpose of sexual gratification or in order to encourage sexual activity. Now section 50 of the Serious Crime Act 2007 provides a 'defence of acting reasonably' to a person who would otherwise be guilty of encouraging or assisting crime,[277] and, again, one of the factors to be considered in assessing reasonableness is 'any purpose for which he claims to have been acting' (s 50(3)(b)). Thus central to all these justificatory defences is the purpose for which the act was done.

4.9 CONCLUSIONS

This chapter has dealt with various issues relevant to criminal conduct. It began by examining the extent to which the law reflects the principle of individual autonomy through its requirements of voluntary act and of causation. Not only is the reflection imperfect, but we found that discussion of these conduct elements in criminal liability (sometimes labelled *actus reus*) involves mental elements and fault elements at several points, e.g. involuntariness, omissions, causation, and purpose in cases of justification. The chapter then turned to the requirement that the conduct be unlawful, in the sense of unjustified, and once again we saw that the boundaries of justification depend on conflicting considerations which are often not openly or fully analysed. The true significance of many of these issues will not become apparent until Chapters 5 and 6, or later, but three points may be signalled at this stage.

First, this chapter has provided ample evidence of the importance, in shaping the criminal law, of conflicts between the principle of individual autonomy and principles of welfare. For example, even in relation to the voluntariness requirement—the veritable sanctum of individual autonomy—there are the marks of welfare-based limitations where the rules on insanity, intoxication, and prior fault impinge. Similar conflicts appear clearly in the legislative and judicial approaches to liability for omissions. Even in the justifications for force, the strong individualism which favours the 'innocent' defendant has occasionally come into conflict with the underlying social goal of minimizing force in these situations.

A second general point is that most of the doctrines considered yield, at crucial junctures, to malleable terminology which leaves considerable discretion to those

---

[276] See also the similar defence for principals in s. 14 of the Sexual Offences Act 2003 (facilitating the commission of a child sex offence).

[277] For the Law Commission's approach, see Law Com No. 300, *Inchoate Liability for Assisting and Encouraging Crime* (2007), 82–8.

who apply the law. This is at its plainest with the ubiquitous term 'reasonable' in the justifications, although there is now some evidence of a more principled approach. Discretion is also conceded by the proposition that the boundaries of omissions liability turn on the interpretation of particular words in statutes, by various concepts in the sphere of causation (e.g. *de minimis*, 'voluntary'), and by such notions as prior fault and 'external factor' in automatism. The presence of these open-ended terms does not empty the rules of their significance, but it raises doubts about the law's commitment to the values upheld by the principle of maximum certainty outlined in Chapter 3.5(i). It is one thing to leave the rules open-ended when persons are unlikely to rely on them (as with the excusatory defences discussed in Chapter 6), although even there the value of consistent judicial decisions should not be overlooked. It is another thing to leave the rules open-ended when citizens as well as courts may rely on them: thus the Law Commission's recognition that the law on self-defence can be structured more explicitly is a welcome step away from universal deliverance to 'reasonableness', and the enactment of section 76 of the Criminal Justice and Immigration Act 2008 is almost an irrelevance, and certainly a sorely missed opportunity.

Thirdly, in this chapter we have seen the first signs of the impact of the European Convention on English criminal law. More still needs to be done to bring the terms of the defence of reasonable chastisement of children into line with Article 3, and there is a strong case for going further and abolishing the defence entirely. The effects of Article 2 on the various rules on the justification for force are more difficult to gauge, partly because the leading Strasbourg decisions are not as clear as some would maintain. However, before Parliament accepted the amendment that became section 76 of the 2008 Act there should have been a proper public assessment of the positive obligations stemming from Article 2: the Government's rather late and cursory treatment of the issue suggests less than full commitment to the Human Rights Act.

FURTHER READING

R. A. Duff, *Answering for Crime* (2007), ch 5.

R. D. Mackay, *Mental Condition Defences in the Criminal Law* (1995), ch 1.

H. L. A. Hart and T. Honoré, *Causation in the Law* (2nd edn., 1985), chs XII and XIII.

F. Leverick, *Killing in Self-Defence* (2006), *passim*.

B. Sangero, *Self-Defence in Criminal Law* (2006), *passim*.

V. Tadros, *Criminal Responsibility* (2005), ch 10.

C. Erin and S. Ost (eds), *The Criminal Justice System and Health Care* (2007), chs 6–12.

5

CRIMINAL CAPACITY, *MENS REA* AND FAULT

5.1 THE ISSUES

In Chapter 4 we examined some of the fundamental requirements of a crime that are usually embraced by the notion of *actus reus*—voluntary act, causation, and absence of justification. One feature of that discussion was how frequently a kind of fault element was to be found playing a role in the *actus reus*: for example, the doctrine of prior fault in automatism (5.2(e)), compassionate purpose in causation (4.5(a)), and elements of prior fault in the principles of justifiable force (4.6(d) and (e)). In this chapter we deal first with another fundamental requirement of a crime, criminal capacity. It is a precondition of criminal liability that the defendant is a person with sufficient capacity to be held responsible, and this leads to an examination of infancy and insanity as barriers to criminal responsibility (5.2), and then to corporate criminal liability (5.3).

Having established that the defendant meets the preconditions for criminal responsibility, we then move to the fault requirements, or *mens rea* (as criminal lawyers often call them). The paradigm fault requirement is intention, as required in major crimes such as murder, rape and robbery. The presence of a fault element does not mean that D was necessarily culpable: that is an all-things-considered judgment, taking account of whether D's conduct was justified (Chapter 4 above) or was excused (Chapter 6 below). But, those considerations apart, the fault element normally indicates culpability, and in 5.4 below we explore some of the reasons for and against the criminal law requiring proof of fault. We then go on, in 5.5, to give detailed consideration to the principal varieties of fault requirement in the criminal law. In broad terms there is a hierarchy of fault requirements: intention is the paradigm and most demanding, followed by recklessness, and then by negligence. However, the majority of crimes in English law impose strict liability, being offences for which neither intention, nor recklessness, nor negligence needs to be proved. Most of these are summary offences, triable only in the magistrates' courts and carrying relatively low penalties, but around half of the offences triable in the Crown Court have a strict liability element.[1] It is therefore important, throughout this chapter, to distinguish between normative claims about the principles the law should observe and the realities of the law as it is. It may be argued that criminal conviction should always be founded on proof of fault, but that is far from being empirically true. In order to underscore this point, part 5.5 of this chapter begins with a discussion of strict liability, before turning to intention, recklessness and negligence.

Two further points must be made at this stage. One is that it is not unusual for an offence to have two or more different fault elements, relating to different aspects of the *actus reus*: the point may be illustrated by considering the several different elements in 'abuse of trust' offences in sections 16–19 of the Sexual Offences Act 2003, which include the various requirements that D intentionally does the sexual activity, that D knows or could reasonably be expected to know of the circumstances by virtue of which he is in a position of trust in relation to the victim, and which requires no knowledge as to age if the victim is under 13 but requires reasonable belief that the victim is 18 if in fact he or she is aged 13–17. It is much clearer if crimes such as these are analysed in terms of their separate elements—e.g. conduct, circumstances, result—so as to ascertain what form of fault is required in respect of each element.[2] This leads to the second point: as we go through the specific offences in Chapters 7, 8, and 9 we will see that it is not just the terminology of fault requirements that is diverse (many statutes contain words such as 'maliciously' and 'wilfully') but also their substance (e.g. requirements such as 'dishonestly' and 'fraudulently'). The discussion in this chapter does not purport to cover all fault terms and is confined to positive fault requirements, in other words, the mental attitude specified in (or implied within) the offence and which the prosecution must establish. Selected for analysis below are core fault terms such as intention, recklessness, knowledge, and negligence, together with offences that use other terminology which has been held to impose a form of 'strict' or no-fault liability. One difficulty in focusing on a small range of fault terms is that the existing variety of approaches to fault is not captured, and that any generalization on the basis of a few fault terms may lead to inaccurate conclusions.[3] We will return to that difficulty at the end of the chapter, after laying some foundations for wider discussion.

---

[1] A. Ashworth and M. Blake, 'The Presumption of Innocence in English Criminal Law' [1996] Crim LR 306.

[2] P. H. Robinson, *Structure and Function in Criminal Law* (1997), ch 3.

[3] For debate see J. Gardner and H. Jung, 'Making Sense of Mens Rea: Antony Duff's Account' (1991) 11 Oxford JLS 559; J. A. Laing, 'The Prospects of a Theory of Criminal Culpability: Mens Rea and Methodological Doubt' (1994) 14 Oxford JLS 57; J. Gardner, 'Criminal Law and the Uses of Theory: a Reply to Laing' (1994) 14 Oxford JLS 217.

5.2 AGENCY, CAPACITY, AND MENTAL DISORDER

One of the fundamental presumptions of the criminal law and criminal liability is that the defendant is 'normal', i.e. is able to function within the normal range of mental and physical capabilities. Many of the principles of individual fairness discussed in Chapter 3 presuppose an individual who is rational and autonomous: otherwise he does not deserve to be liable to criminal punishment. A person who is mentally disordered may fall below these assumed standards of mental capacity and rationality, and this may make it unfair to hold him responsible for his behaviour. It is for this autonomy-based reason that most systems of criminal law contain tests of 'insanity' which result in the exemption of some mentally disordered persons from criminal liability. A similar rationale may be given for the voluntariness requirement, discussed in Chapter 4.2 above. There is also the prior question of whether the defendant is fit to be tried—whether the person can participate in the trial in a sufficiently meaningful sense. It is an essential precondition of a fair trial, as Antony Duff has argued,[4] that the defendant is a responsible citizen who is answerable before the court. The doctrine of 'unfitness to plead', discussed in paragraph (b) below, embodies a procedural attempt to deal with this in relation to mentally disordered defendants. Once it has been decided that a person is fit to plead, there is still the question whether at the time of the alleged act D was a sufficiently responsible moral agent: the defence of insanity, discussed in paragraphs (c) and (d) below, addresses this issue. Before, that, however, a few words must be said about young children, where legitimate concerns about answerability to the court and moral agency have received an unsatisfactory response from English lawmakers.

(a) THE MINIMUM AGE OF CRIMINAL RESPONSIBILITY

In England and Wales the minimum age of criminal responsibility is 10, substantially lower than the minimum age in many other European countries, where teenage children are dealt with in civil tribunals up to the age of 13 (France), 14 (Germany), 15 (Scandinavia) or 16 (Spain and Portugal). At common law the presumption of *doli incapax* applied to children under 14, requiring the prosecution to establish that the child knew that the behaviour was seriously wrong before the case could go ahead. The presumption was much criticized,[5] some arguing that children who failed to realize the wrongness of their behaviour were more in need of conviction and compulsory treatment,[6] and it was abolished by s 34 of the Crime and Disorder Act 1998.[7] However, it remains important to think about fundamental issues in relation to the

---

[4] E.g. R. A. Duff, 'Law, Language and Community: Some Preconditions of Criminal Liability' (1998) 18 Oxford JLS 189.

[5] Notably by the House of Lords in *C v DPP* [1996] AC 1.

[6] An argument expressed strongly by Glanville Williams, 'The Criminal Responsibility of Children' [1954] Crim LR 493, at 495–6.

[7] For discussion of whether a defence of *doli incapax* still exists, see *DPP v P* [2006] 4 All ER 628 and *T.* [2008] 2 Cr App R 17.

responsibility of young offenders. Are they fit to stand trial at the age of 10? Do they have sufficient understanding of the proceedings to participate meaningfully in them? In what sense are they responsible citizens at that age? Can it be said that, when they do criminal things with the required fault element, they are acting as moral agents, in a sufficiently full sense?[8] The first two points were discussed by the European Court of Human Rights in *V and T v United Kingdom* (1999),[9] drawing on the United Nations Convention on the Rights of the Child, which does not lay down a minimum age of criminal responsibility but does declare several other relevant standards.[10] The Court held that, although the trial process to which the two 11-year-old applicants were subjected did not amount to 'inhuman and degrading treatment' within Article 3 of the Convention, the trial did violate Article 6 in its failure to ensure that the boys understood the proceedings and had the opportunity to participate, and in the failure to reduce feelings of intimidation and inhibition. A subsequent Practice Direction sets out the steps that trial judges should take in these unusual cases in order to comply with Article 6,[11] but the Strasbourg Court has held that this gives insufficient priority to the need to ensure that all young children have adequate opportunity to participate meaningfully in the criminal trial.[12]

The European Commissioner on Human Rights has specifically recommended that consideration be given to raising the age of criminal responsibility 'in line with norms prevailing across Europe', on the grounds that children of 10, 11 or 12 cannot have sufficient consciousness of the nature and consequences of their actions.[13] The cognitive abilities of young children may not be sufficiently developed; their self-control may not yet have developed adequately; and they may be particularly susceptible to peer pressure at that age.[14] These are all aspects of moral development and, since childhood and adolescence are the time when moral reasoning and self-control should be learnt, it is not reasonable for the criminal law to demand as much from children as from adults.[15] The case for raising the minimum age of criminal responsibility in England and Wales is overwhelming.[16]

(b) UNFITNESS TO STAND TRIAL[17]

The common law has developed tests for determining whether persons are unfit to stand trial through mental disorder or (in some cases) through being deaf mute. The

---

[8] J. Horder, 'Pleading Involuntary Lack of Capacity' (1993) 52 Camb LJ 298, at 300–2.

[9] (1999) 30 EHRR 121.

[10] G. van Bueren, *The International Law on the Rights of the Child* (1995), ch 7.

[11] *Practice Direction: Crown Court (Trial of Children and Young Persons)* [2000] 1 Cr App R 483.

[12] *SC v United Kingdom* (2005) 40 EHRR 226.

[13] Office of the Commissioner of Human Rights, *Report by Mr Alvaro Gil-Robles, Commissioner for Human Rights, on his visit to the United Kingdom* (Comm DH (2005) 6), paras. 105–7.

[14] F. Zimring, 'Toward a Jurisprudence of Youth Violence', in M. Tonry and M. Moore (eds), *Youth Violence*, (1998), 447.

[15] A. von Hirsch and A. Ashworth, *Proportionate Sentencing* (2005), ch 3.

[16] See further H. Keating, 'Reckless Children' [2007] Crim LR 546.

[17] R. D. Mackay, *Mental Condition Defences in the Criminal Law* (1995), ch 5.

leading case is *Pritchard* (1836),[18] where Alderson B held that the question was whether
the defendant 'was of sufficient intellect to comprehend the course of the proceedings
in the trial so as to make a proper defence'. Pritchard was deaf and dumb, and not
surprisingly the Court's statement dwelt on matters of cognition and understanding.
The modern version is that the defendant must be capable of giving, receiving, and
understanding communications relating to a criminal trial—on matters such as chal-
lenging jurors, deciding on a plea, understanding the evidence, instructing counsel,
and so forth.[19]

The statutory procedure in these cases is as follows. Under the Criminal Procedure
(Insanity) Act 1964, when there are doubts about a defendant's fitness to plead, this
should be the first issue to be determined, before any evidence about the alleged offence
is heard. However, the 1964 Act gave the judge a discretion to postpone the issue of
fitness to plead until the end of the prosecution case, and this discretion would tend to
be exercised where there was doubt about whether the defendant had committed the
offence anyway. The Criminal Procedure (Insanity and Unfitness to Plead) Act 1991
engrafted a further procedure on to those established by the 1964 Act.[20] It provides
that, wherever a court has decided that a defendant is unfit to plead, it must then
conduct a 'trial of the facts'. The judge's discretion to postpone the issue of fitness to
plead remains, but it seems likely that almost all cases will now adopt the 1991 Act's
approach. Evidence of fitness to plead will be examined first. If the defendant is found
fit to plead, the case will proceed. If the defendant is found unfit to plead, another jury
will be empanelled and there will be a trial to determine whether the defendant 'did
the act or made the omission charged against him as the offence'. This formula was
intended to separate the conduct or *actus reus* from the fault elements of an offence,[21]
but formerly that approach did not apply in murder cases, where committal to hospital
without limit of time was mandatory on a finding that the act was done. In *Antoine*
(2001)[22] the House of Lords held that evidence of diminished responsibility may not
be considered if the charge is murder, and in *Grant* (2002)[23] the Court of Appeal
took the same view of provocation since that qualified defence is 'intimately bound up
with the defendant's state of mind'. However, Lord Hutton's speech in *Antoine* leaves
open the possibility that evidence of mistake, accident, or self-defence might be considered on a trial of the facts. Since mistake and accident are usually simple denials
of *mens rea*, this is confusing and suggests that Parliament or the courts will need to
revisit this important issue.

If the court is not satisfied that D did what was alleged, an acquittal must follow. If the court is satisfied that D did the act, the 1991 Act gives the judge a choice
between admission to hospital with or without: a restriction order; a guardianship

---

[18] (1836) 7 C and P 303.   [19] *Robertson* [1968] 1 WLR 1767, *Friend* [1997] 2 All ER 1012.

[20] For the origin of the reforms see *Report of the Committee on Mentally Abnormal Offenders* (chairman:
Lord Butler) (1975), ch 3.

[21] For analysis of this and other provisions of the 1991 Act see S. White, 'The Criminal Procedure
(Insanity and Unfitness to Plead) Act' [1992] Crim LR 4.

[22] [2001] 1 AC 340.   [23] [2002] Crim LR 403.

order; a supervision and treatment order; or an absolute discharge. Formerly this discretion was not available where the charge was murder, but section 24 of the Domestic Violence, Crime and Victims Act 2004 now extends the choice of orders to murder cases, in line with Article 5(1)(e) of the Convention.[24] However, committal to hospital should not be permitted at all unless there is a recognized medical condition warranting hospital confinement.[25] The annual total of findings of unfitness to plead declined to some thirteen per year during the late 1980s, but in the years following the 1991 Act the numbers began to rise, so that between 1999 and 2001 the annual average was some 75 cases. It is also clear that the courts are using the full range of disposals.[26]

The Convention provides two strong reasons for reform of the law on unfitness to stand trial. First, compliance with Article 5.1(e) requires that any detention of a mentally disordered person must be justified on the grounds of objective medical expertise, and this indicates both that the current English test may be too wide (in including deaf mute persons) and too narrow (in excluding some relevant forms of mental disorder).[27] Secondly, the emphasis of the Strasbourg Court on the requirement of 'effective participation' in trials[28] should lead to a broadening of the test for unfitness, so that it encompasses what Mackay has termed 'decisional competence' in the broad sense. Recent proposals in Scotland[29] and, more specifically, in Jersey[30] point in this direction.

(c) THE SPECIAL VERDICT OF INSANITY[31]

If the defendant is thought fit to stand trial, then the issue of mental disorder may be raised as a defence; namely, that at the time of the alleged offence D was too disordered to be held liable. Medical evidence will be crucial in determining this,[32] but it is for the law to lay down the appropriate test. Mental disorder is a broad concept under the Mental Health Act 1983, as amended by the Mental Health Act 2007, and few would maintain that all those who fall within one of the four classes of disorder under that Act should be exempted from criminal liability. The criminal law has settled on a much

---

[24] Section 24 inserts a new s. 5 into the 1991 Act, giving the court some discretion on disposal but requiring it to impose a hospital order with restrictions, in murder cases, if the conditions for that order are fulfilled.

[25] R. Mackay, 'On Being Insane in Jersey: Part Two' [2002] Crim LR 728.

[26] R. D. Mackay, B. J. Mitchell and L. Howe, 'A Continued Upturn in Unfitness to Plead' [2007] Crim LR 530.

[27] Mackay, 'On Being Insane in Jersey: Part Two'; for earlier discussion, see D. Grubin, 'What Constitutes Fitness to Plead?' [1993] Crim LR 748; cf. R. A. Duff, 'Fitness to Plead and Fair Trials' [1994] Crim LR 419 and reply by Grubin, [1994] Crim LR 423.

[28] Notably in the context of young children: see section 6.2(a) of this chapter.

[29] Scottish Law Commission, *Report on Insanity and Diminished Responsibility* (Scot Law Com No. 195, 2004), ch 4 and draft Bill, cl. 4.

[30] See the valuable analysis by R. D. Mackay, 'On Being Insane in Jersey: Part Three' [2004] Crim LR 291, discussing the *O'Driscoll* decision.

[31] Mackay, *Mental Condition Defences in Criminal Law*, ch 2.

[32] S. 1(2) of the Criminal Procedure (Insanity and Unfitness to Plead) Act 1991 requires the evidence of two doctors, at least one of them an experienced psychiatrist.

narrower conception of 'insanity', proof of which should lead to a verdict of 'not guilty by reason of insanity'. In order to understand how this defence functions, however, it is important to bear in mind that until the Criminal Procedure (Insanity and Unfitness to Plead) Act 1991 came into force, the result of a successful defence of insanity was mandatory and indefinite commitment to mental hospital. Whilst research revealed that about one-fifth of defendants thus committed were released within nine months,[33] there was no certainty of, or entitlement to, early release and the potentially severe effect of the insanity verdict was enough to lead many defendants to plead guilty and to hope for a more favourable disposal at the sentencing stage. The 1991 Act gave the court the same discretion after an insanity verdict (except, formerly, in murder cases) as it has after a finding of unfitness to plead: hospital order, guardianship, supervision, absolute discharge. This still leaves the possibility that the court will order deprivation of liberty, even though the defendant has 'succeeded' on a 'defence': insanity defences remain rare, with an average of 15 per year from 1999–2001, but around half of the disposals are community-based, i.e. supervision or absolute discharge.[34]

The possible legal consequences of the insanity verdict show the tension between considerations of individual autonomy and policies of social welfare in this sphere, and the same tension is manifest in the evidential and procedural provisions.[35] Insanity is the only general defence where the burden of proof is placed on the defendant,[36] a paradox when one reflects that the consequence of a successful defence may be a court order favouring social welfare rather than the defendant's own interests. The prosecution may raise insanity if the defendant pleads diminished responsibility in response to a murder charge,[37] and, according to one view, can do so in all cases where D puts state of mind in issue.[38] The prosecution bears the burden of proving insanity here, which is much more appropriate given the consequences of the verdict of 'not guilty by reason of insanity'.

The requirements of the defence of insanity were laid down by the judges in *M'Naghten's Case* as long ago as 1843:[39]

to establish a defence on the ground of insanity, it must be clearly proved that, at the time of committing the act, the party accused was labouring under such a defect of reason, from

---

[33] R. D. Mackay, 'Fact and Fiction about the Insanity Defence' [1990] Crim LR 247.

[34] R. D. Mackay, B. J. Mitchell and L. Howe, 'Yet More Facts about the Insanity Defence' [2006] Crim LR 399.

[35] See A. Loughnan, '"Manifest Madness": Towards a New Understanding of the Insanity Defence' (2007) 70 MLR 379, proposing a reinterpretation of the exceptional procedural and evidential provisions relating to insanity.

[36] T. H. Jones, 'Insanity, Automatism and the Burden of Proof on the Accused' (1995) 111 LQR 475; a challenge to this under Art. 6.2 of the Convention now seems unlikely to succeed, following the Court of Appeal's decision in *Lambert, Jordan and Ali* [2001] 1 Cr App R 205 to uphold the reverse onus in diminished responsibility.

[37] Criminal Procedure (Insanity) Act 1964, s. 6.

[38] *Per* Watkins LJ, in *Dickie* (1984) 79 Cr App R 213, at 219.

[39] (1843) 10 Cl and Fin 200; see generally N. Morris, *Madness and the Criminal Law* (1982), and I. Potas, *Just Deserts for the Mad* (1982).

disease of the mind, as not to know the nature and quality of the act he was doing; or, if he did know it, that he did not know he was doing what was wrong.

A 'defect of reason' means the deprivation of reasoning power, and does not apply to temporary absent-mindedness or confusion.[40] It is, however, limited to cognitive defects, and therefore excludes from the insanity defence those forms of mental disorder that involve significant emotional or volitional deficiencies. Although in that respect the definition of insanity is very narrow,[41] in other respects it is so wide as to go well beyond even the general definition of mental disorder in the Mental Health Acts 1983–2007. Thus the phrase 'disease of the mind' has been construed so as to encompass any disease which affects the functioning of the mind—whether its cause be organic or functional, and whether its effect be permanent or intermittent—so long as it was operative at the time of the alleged offence.[42] This means, as we saw in Chapter 4.2(c) above, that any condition which affects the functioning of the mind and which results from an 'internal' rather than an 'external' cause will be deemed to be a 'disease of the mind', and if D relies on it in his defence he will be held to be raising the defence of insanity. The 'internal factor' doctrine has resulted in epilepsy,[43] sleepwalking,[44] and hyperglycaemia[45] being classified as insanity. This shows that the policy of social protection has gained the upper hand, and that the judiciary has been prepared to overlook the gross unfairness of labelling these people as insane in order to ensure that the court has the power to take measures of social defence against them. Even then, the policy of protection has not been carried to its logical conclusion, since the law now perpetrates the absurdity of classifying *hyper*glycaemia as insanity (protective measures possible under the 1991 Act) whilst, because of the external/internal distinction, classifying *hypo*glycaemia as automatism (resulting in an outright acquittal unless prior fault can be shown).[46] More will be said about this below.

Where it is established that there was a defect of reason due to disease of the mind, it is then necessary to show that it had one of two effects. First, the defence is fulfilled if D did not know the nature and quality of the act—in other words, did not realize what he was doing. In most cases this would show the absence of intention, knowledge, or recklessness; but since this mental state arises from insanity, considerations of welfare are held to require the special verdict rather than an ordinary acquittal. Secondly, the defence is fulfilled if D did not know that he was doing wrong. English law appears ambivalent about the proper approach to this requirement: the Court of Appeal has recently confirmed that 'wrong' bears the narrow meaning of 'legally wrong',[47] although there is evidence that in practice courts sometimes act upon the Australian interpretation of 'failure to appreciate that the conduct was morally wrong'

---

[40] *Clarke* (1972) 56 Cr App R 225.   [41] See paragraph (d) below.
[42] *Per* Lord Diplock, in *Sullivan* [1984] AC 156.   [43] *Sullivan* [1984] AC 156.
[44] *Burgess* [1991] 2 QB 92, overlooked in the rape case of *Bilton, Daily Telegraph*, 20 December 2005.
[45] *Hennessy* (1989) 89 Cr App R 10.   [46] See, more fully, Ch 4.2 above.
[47] *Johnson* [2008] Crim LR 132, applying *Windle* [1952] 2 QB 826, which had been followed by the majority of the Supreme Court of Canada in *Schwartz* (1979) 29 CCC (2d) 1.

(usually, where D believes that he must, for some distorted reason, do the act).[48] This is unsatisfactory, but it seems that legislative reform would be required to introduce the broader 'moral wrong' test. The fact that these limbs of *M'Naghten* are alternatives ought to mean that insanity may be a defence to strict liability crimes too, since the second test is applicable there, and a Divisional Court ruling to the contrary is difficult to support.[49]

(d) REFORM

Two major issues concerning defences of mental disorder emerge from the above discussion: the question of definition and the question of protective measures. In the past the latter has often driven the former, in that the definition has been expanded to include persons against whom compulsory measures are thought to be necessary. The 1991 Act altered the balance somewhat, since committal to a mental hospital is now only a possible and not an inevitable consequence of a special verdict of not guilty by reason of insanity. But the label 'insane' remains, and it is manifestly unsuitable for those whose behaviour stemmed from epilepsy, somnambulism, or diabetes.[50]

  Defence lawyers will rightly challenge aspects of the insanity doctrine under the Human Rights Act. Article 5.1(e) of the European Convention allows that 'persons of unsound mind' may lawfully be deprived of their liberty, but the leading decision in *Winterwerp* v *Netherlands*[51] lays down three further requirements. First, there must be a close correspondence between expert medical opinion and the relevant definition of mental disorder: that can hardly be said of a test formulated in 1843 and subsequently held to encompass epilepsy, hyperglycaemia, and sleepwalking.[52] Secondly, the court's decision must be based on 'objective medical expertise', a requirement that could be used in conjunction with the 1991 Act to hold that psychiatric reports to the court should be accorded more weight than under the restrictive M'Naghten test.[53] Thirdly, the court must decide that the mental disorder is 'of a kind or degree warranting compulsory confinement', and until the law was changed in 2004 the court had no opportunity to make such a determination in murder cases.[54]

---

[48] *Stapleton* v *R* (1952) 86 CLR 358; research evidence from R.Mackay and G. Kearns, ('More Facts about the Insanity Defence [1999] Crim LR 714 and Mackay, Mitchell and Howe, ('Yet More Facts about Insanity', at 406–7) shows that many psychiatrists interpret 'wrongness' in this wider sense, and that courts seem to accept this.

[49] *DPP* v *H* [1997] 1 WLR 1406, analysed critically by T. Ward, 'Magistrates, Insanity and the Common Law' [1997] Crim LR 796.

[50] R. D. Mackay and G. Reuber, 'Epilepsy and the Defence of Insanity—Time for Change?' [2007] Crim LR 782; see also the discussion on automatism in Ch 4.2(f) above.

[51] 2 EHRR 387 (1979).

[52] P. J. Sutherland and C. A. Gearty, 'Insanity and the European Court of Human Rights' [1992] Crim LR 418.

[53] E. Baker, 'Human Rights, M'Naghten and the 1991 Act' [1994] Crim LR 84.

[54] A new s. 5 of the 1991 Act, inserted by s. 24 of the Domestic Violence, Crime, and Victims Act 2004, gives courts a choice of orders following the special verdict in a murder case, but requires it to make a hospital order if the conditions are fulfilled.

A Convention challenge to the M'Naghten Rules has already met with some success in Jersey.[55]

Although arguments based on Article 5 only have purchase at the stage where D is deprived of liberty, they are relevant in many cases and it would be best if the defence of insanity itself were reformed sensibly before piecemeal challenges are mounted under the Human Rights Act. The M'Naghten Rules are widely recognized to be outmoded. They refer only to mental disorders which affect the cognitive faculties, i.e. knowledge of what one is doing, or of its wrongness, whereas some forms of mental disorder impair practical reasoning and the power of control over actions. This is now recognized in the 'diminished responsibility' doctrine in manslaughter,[56] which includes cases of 'irresistible impulse', and it should clearly be recognized as part of a reformed mental disorder defence. The Model Penal Code accomplishes this by referring to mental disorders which result in D lacking 'substantial capacity either to appreciate the wrongfulness of his conduct or to conform his conduct to the requirements of the law'.[57] The Butler Committee proposed to take this into account in a different way—by ensuring that one ground for a mental-disorder verdict is that, at the time of the alleged offence, D was suffering severe mental illness or handicap.[58] In other words, if the mental disorder was severe in degree, there should be no need to establish that it affected D's cognition: so long as the court is satisfied that the conduct was attributable to that disorder, the special verdict should be returned. It therefore includes both cognitive and volitional deficiencies, and places the insanity verdict more squarely on the ground of incapacity.[59] In doing so, however, it takes a somewhat static view of mental disorder, confining it more or less to the major psychoses. It fails to recognize the variety of mental disorders, and the fact that some of them may substantially impair the patient's practical reasoning even though the diagnosis contains some prominent evaluative elements. Psychiatry has been attacked for these inevitably contestable elements of evaluation, but the proper response is to recognize and discuss the evaluations rather than to deny their relevance to criminal liability.[60]

Only to a small extent is this conservative approach to mental disorder mitigated by the second limb of the Butler proposals, also to be found in a revised form in the draft Criminal Code.[61] This provides for evidence of mental disorder to be adduced to show that D lacked the mental element for the crime. The Law Commission, unlike the Butler Committee, would limit the type of mental disorder that may be relied upon here to 'severe mental illness' and 'incomplete development of mind'. The Commission cited the danger of allowing too wide a definition, which would sweep

---

[55] R. D. Mackay and C. A. Gearty, 'On Being Insane in Jersey' [2001] Crim LR 560.

[56] Homicide Act 1957, s. 2; see below, Ch 7.4(e).   [57] Model Penal Code, s. 4.01.

[58] Butler Report, para. 18.30.

[59] Cf. Scottish Law Commission, *Report on Insanity and Diminished Responsibility* (2004), paras. 2.52–2.63, rejecting any volitional component in the insanity defence.

[60] K. W. M. Fulford, 'Value, Action, Mental Illness, and the Law', in S. Shute, J. Gardner, and J. Horder (eds.), *Action and Value in Criminal Law* (1993).

[61] Law Com No. 177, cll. 34–40.

in too many defendants.[62] However, the proposed definition is framed so as to include cases of 'pathological automatism that is liable to recur', and again classifies diabetes and epilepsy within mental disorder for reasons of social defence.[63] This is both contrary to the principle of fair labelling[64] and in violation of the European Convention, and should be abandoned. A separate form of defence should be devised for this group of conditions. Of course this leads to the problem of drawing a definitional line between 'insanity' and 'automatism', and it was the difficulty of doing so that led the Law Commission to bring these cases within the mental disorder defence, believing that this would be less 'offensive' and 'preposterous' than the insanity label.[65] Even if that answers the fair labelling argument, it leaves the European Convention challenge unaffected unless it is provided that no person with those conditions shall be deprived of liberty—and that, again, would require a separate definition.

5.3 CORPORATE LIABILITY

(a) NATURAL AND CORPORATE PERSONALITY

Most discussion of criminal liability is concerned with individual defendants as authors of acts or omissions, raising questions of respect for the autonomy of individuals. We saw in Chapter 2.1 and 2.2 that a developed notion of autonomy is not solely about negative liberty, i.e. protecting individuals from harm, but also involves elements of positive liberty or welfare, i.e. providing facilities and social arrangements whereby individuals can exercise autonomy more fully. By providing a framework for individuals to form companies and corporations, the legal system contributes to this end. Corporate activities now play a major part in social life—through companies as employers, as providers of goods and services, as providers of transport and of recreational facilities, and so forth. The criminal law has made increasing inroads into these spheres in recent years: the courts have developed doctrines of vicarious and corporate liability, and the legislature had introduced new offences directed specifically as corporate activities in the financial and commercial sphere (e.g. Financial Services and Markets Act 2000, and the Companies Acts 1985–9). Yet historically the criminal law has developed around the notion of individual human beings as the bearers of rights and duties. It is still somewhat trapped in that framework, even though the idea of companies as separate legal entities from their shareholders and their management was established in the nineteenth century. A limited liability company has even been treated as a separate legal entity from the one man who controlled it.[66]

The present theory, then, is that corporate personality attaches to companies just as natural personality attaches to individuals (with certain modifications). But does

---

[62] Law Com No. 177, para. 11.27.   [63] Ibid., ii, para. 11, 28.   [64] See above, Ch 3.6(s).
[65] Law Com No. 177, para. 11.28(c).   [66] *Salomon v Salomon* [1897] AC 22.

this theory, which has a firm hold in company law, mean that companies can be convicted of offences? The courts moved slowly in this direction in the mid-nineteenth century. Although still doubting whether companies could be said to *do* 'acts', the courts overcame any reluctance to hold companies liable for *failing* to act[67] and for committing a public nuisance.[68] The driving force behind these innovative decisions, both concerning railway companies in the early days of rail travel, was not legal theory but pragmatism: 'there can be no effective means of deterring from an oppressive exercise of power, for the purpose of gain, except the remedy by an indictment against those who truly commit it, that is, the corporation acting by its majority'.[69] And from there the law developed towards criminal liability for companies, acting through their controlling officers.[70]

(b) TOWARDS CORPORATE CRIMINAL LIABILITY

This subject was given a pressing social importance in the late 1980s by the series of disasters connected with corporate activities and involving considerable loss of life—for example, the Piper Alpha oil rig explosion, the Clapham rail disaster, the King's Cross fire, the sinking of the *Marchioness*, and in 1987 the capsize of the ferry *Herald of Free Enterprise*. It does not make sense to present each of these, and the string of subsequent transportation disasters, as the responsibility of a few individuals. Indeed, enquiries into the disasters have tended to emphasize the role of deficiencies in the systems of corporate management and accountability. Major disasters apart, the newspapers offer evidence of a constant stream of incidents of industrial pollution, unsafe working conditions, impure foods, and unfair business practices which impinge upon, or threaten to impinge upon, the lives of individual citizens.

Growing recognition of the significance of corporate harm-doing has not, however, been accompanied by substantial alteration of the framework of criminal liability. The trend, as we shall see, has been to attempt to fit corporate liability into the existing structure rather than to consider its implications afresh. And, more important in social terms, there has been little change of approach at the level of enforcement. It is one thing to have a set of laws which penalizes corporate wrongdoing as well as individual wrongdoing. It is quite another thing to have a balanced machinery of enforcement which strives to ensure the proportionate treatment of individuals and companies according to the relative seriousness of their offences: present arrangements seem to draw a strong line between frequent police action against individuals and the relatively infrequent action of the various inspectorates, government departments, etc.

---

[67] *Birmingham and Gloucester Railway Co* (1842) 3 QB 223.
[68] *Great North of England Railway Co* (1846) 9 QB 315.   [69] *Per* Denham CJ at 320.
[70] Another landmark case was *Mousell Bros v London and North-Western Railway Co* [1917] 2 KB 836. For discussion of the history see L. H. Leigh, *The Criminal Liability of Corporations in English Law* (1969), ch 2, and C. Wells, *Corporations and Criminal Responsibility* (2nd edn., 2001), ch 5.

against companies.[71] However, the social calculation cannot be presented simply as an imbalance in treatment between 'crime in the streets' and 'crime in the suites'. We must also take into account the finding of social surveys that it is street crimes that cause real harm and fear to people, not least to those who are already among the most disadvantaged in society.[72] It is therefore a question for discussion whether devoting large resources to the detection and prosecution of corporate harm-doers would be either defensible or socially acceptable.

There are some straightforward applications of the doctrine that a company is a legal person, separate from the individuals involved in its operations. Thus, for example, two principal provisions of the Health and Safety at Work Act 1974 are as follows:

s 2 (1) 'It shall be the duty of every employer to ensure, so far as is reasonably practicable, the health, safety and welfare at work of all his employees.'

s 3 (1) 'It shall be the duty of every employer to conduct his undertaking in such a way as to ensure, so far as is reasonably practicable, that persons not in his employment who may be affected thereby are not thereby exposed to risks to their health and safety.'

These provisions, in conjunction with s 33 of the Act (which creates an offence of failing to discharge either duty), are clearly directed at companies no less than at individual employers.[73] Thus in *British Steel plc*[74] the company was convicted of failing to discharge its duty under s 3 of the Act. During an operation to re-locate a steel platform, under the supervision of a British Steel employee, an unsafe method of working led to the collapse of the platform and a sub-contracted worker was killed. The Court of Appeal upheld the conviction, on the basis that it was the employer on whom the duty was imposed, and it had clearly not been discharged. Similar reasoning can be used to hold companies liable for a whole range of offences of strict liability: they can cause pollution, sell goods, fail to submit annual returns, etc. An offence of strict liability is one which requires no fault for conviction: any person may be found guilty simply through doing or failing to do a certain act.[75] Thus, if a company owns the business or premises concerned, it may be convicted of failing to control emissions of pollutants, or for causing polluting matter to enter a stream.[76]

---

[71] See A. Ashworth, 'Is the Criminal Law a Lost Cause?' (2000) 116 LQR 225, and the discussion by D. Nelken, 'White Collar Crime', in M. Maguire, R. Morgan, and R. Reiner (eds.), *The Oxford Handbook of Criminology* (4th edn., 2007).

[72] T. Jones, D. Maclean, and J. Young, *The Islington Crime Survey*; M. Gottfredson, *Fear of Crime* (Home Office Research Study No. 84, 1986).

[73] *Associated Octel* [1996] 1 WLR 1543, a decision of the House of Lords. See also *Gateway Foodmarkets Ltd* [1997] Crim LR 512, imposing a duty under s. 2 of the Act on the employer in respect of the acts of all employees, not just those who were 'controlling minds' (see below).

[74] [1995] 1 WLR 1356; compare the much more restrictive approach in *Seaboard Offshore Ltd* v *Secretary of State for Transport* [1994] 1 WLR 541.

[75] See above, *Birmingham and Gloucester Railway Co*, n 67 and the discussion of strict liability in Ch 5.5(a).

[76] See the conviction under s. 85 of the Water Resources Act 1991 upheld in *Environment Agency* v *Empress Car Co (Abertillery)* [1999] 2 AC 22, criticized above at p. 107.

(i) *The Possibility of Vicarious Liability:* Outside the criminal law there have been further developments, and the law of torts has established a doctrine of vicarious liability of employers for the conduct of their employees.[77] There is no such general doctrine in the criminal law, but various exceptions and quasi-exceptions are gaining a foothold. One is the 'delegation principle': where a statute imposes liability on the owner, licensee, or keeper of premises or other property, the courts will make that person vicariously liable for the conduct of anyone to whom management of the premises has been delegated.[78] This applies whether the defendant is an individual or a company. The underlying reason for this principle seems to lie in the assumption that such offences would otherwise be unenforceable, since delegation would remove responsibility from the person in effective control. The second exception revolves around the interpretation of such key words in statutes as 'sell', 'use', and 'possess'. The clearest example is where a statute prohibits the selling of goods in certain circumstances. *Coppen* v *Moore (No. 2)* (1898)[79] held the shop owner liable as the person who sold the goods in law, even though he was away from the shop at the time and an assistant carried out the transaction—in breach of the instructions left by the owner. So long as the assistant is acting as an agent rather than as a private individual, 'vicarious' liability is imposed.[80] In effect, a similar result flowed from the application of s 3 of the Health and Safety at Work Act 1974 in the *British Steel* case, since the company was held liable for the inadequate supervision by its own employee.[81] A third exception or quasi-exception arises where a statutory offence penalizes conduct that appears to require a personal act, such as 'using' a motor vehicle with defective brakes: in *James & Son* v *Smee*[82] the Divisional Court held the company liable, on the basis that the use of the vehicle by an employee in the course of employment constituted use by the employer.

These examples of vicarious liability in the criminal law may appear not to respect the principle of individual autonomy, in so far as they hold people (or a company) liable for something that was not their own voluntary act or omission. They can be justified only on the principle of welfare and, even then, they should be made to respect 'rule of law' values by ensuring fair warning of the standards expected. Fair warning is not assured if decisions are made by way of statutory interpretation in the courts, rather than clearly by the legislature.

(ii) *The Identification Principle:* We now return to corporate liability as such. Most of the instances discussed so far concern offences of strict liability, where it is often easier to construe a statute so as to impose direct liability on a company. In 1944 the courts began to develop a new doctrine which imposes liability on companies for

---

[77] P. S. Atiyah, *Vicarious Liability in the Law of Torts* (1967).

[78] Cf. *Allen* v *Whitehead* [1930] 1 KB 211 with *Vane* v *Yiannopoullos* [1965] AC 486; see P. J. Pace, 'Delegation: A Doctrine in Search of a Definition' [1982] Crim LR 627.

[79] [1898] 2 QB 306.

[80] A. P. Simester and G. R. Sullivan, *Criminal Law: Theory and Doctrine* (3rd edn., 2007), 252, argue that this is not an example of vicarious liability because the owner does the *actus reus* himself since he is the seller. However, the physical act is that of his employee, so at least it is a form of quasi-vicarious liability.

[81] Above, n 74 and accompanying text.

[82] [1955] 1 QB 78, discussed by Simester and Sullivan, *Criminal Law*, above, n 80, 253.

offences requiring a mental element. In *DPP v Kent and Sussex Contractors Ltd*[83] the defendant company was charged with two offences—making a statement which was known to be false, and using a false document with intent to deceive. The Divisional Court held that the company could be convicted of both offences, on the basis that its officers possessed the required 'knowledge' and 'intent to deceive', and that those states of mind could therefore be imputed to the company itself. As Viscount Caldecote CJ held, 'a company is incapable of acting or speaking or even thinking except in so far as its officers have acted, spoken or thought.' Thus the company is identified with those officers who are its 'directing mind and will' for these purposes.[84] This identification principle was applied in the leading case of *Tesco Supermarkets v Nattrass* (1971),[85] where the company had been convicted of offering to sell goods at a higher price than indicated, contrary to the Trade Descriptions Act 1968. A shop assistant at a local Tesco store had failed to follow the manager's instructions, with the result that the goods were offered at a higher price than advertised. The House of Lords quashed the conviction, holding that the manager of one of the company's supermarkets was not sufficiently high up in the organization to 'represent the directing mind and will of the company'. The identification principle is therefore fairly narrow in its scope. It allows large companies to disassociate themselves from the conduct of their local managers, and thus to avoid criminal liability. Moreover, where a large national or multi-national company is prosecuted, the identification principle requires the prosecution to establish that one of the directors or top managers had the required knowledge or culpability. Managers at such a high level tend to focus on broader policy issues, not working practices. Thus it may be considerably easier to achieve convictions in respect of the activities of small companies than of large corporations.[86]

The seeds for an expansion of the *Tesco v Nattrass* test have been sown by Lord Hoffmann, speaking for the Privy Council in *Meridian Global Funds Management Asia Ltd v Securities Commission* (1996).[87] Courts should be prepared to go beyond the people who represent the 'directing mind and will' of a company, and to enquire, in the context of the particular offence, 'whose act (or knowledge, or state of mind) was *for this purpose* intended to count as the act, etc., of the company?' The reach of this extension is unclear, since much turns on the statutory context. In this case it enabled the conviction of the company on the basis of the knowledge of two investment managers that they were making unlawful investments. When the Court of Appeal was invited to extend the identification principle along these lines in *Attorney-General's*

---

[83] [1944] KB 146.

[84] Two other cases decided in the same year confirmed this approach: *ICR Haulage Ltd* [1944] KB 551, and *Moore v I Bresler Ltd* [1944] 2 All ER 515.

[85] [1972] AC 153.

[86] Cf. *JF Alford (Transport) Ltd* [1997] 2 Cr App R 326 (below, Ch 10.3(b)), and the conviction of manslaughter of a small outdoor pursuit company and its managing director in respect of the deaths of young canoeists sent out in poor weather with inadequate training and supervision (*OLL Ltd and Kite, The Times,* 9 December 1994), with the difficulty of identification in *Redfern* [1993] Crim LR 43.

[87] [1995] 2 AC 500.

Reference (No. 2 of 1999),[88] a case arising from the Southall train crash, it declined to do so. Rose LJ held that:

The identification theory, attributing to the company the mind and will of senior directors and managers, was developed in order to avoid injustice: it would bring the law into disrepute if every act and state of mind of an individual employee was attributed to a company which was entirely blameless.[89]

The terms of this statement beg a number of questions, but it was clear from the judgment that the Court of Appeal thought that any significant extension of the judge-made identification principle should be left to Parliament.

(c) INDIVIDUALISM AND CORPORATISM

The history of legal developments in this sphere suggests a somewhat slow progress towards integrating corporations into a legal framework constructed for individuals, with few gestures towards the differences between corporations and individual human beings.[90] There are those who argue that this is only right: social phenomena can only be interpreted through the actions and motivations of individuals, and abstractions like corporations constitute barriers to proper understanding.[91] Only individuals can *do* things, and so the law is right to concentrate its attentions upon them. Indeed, any other view might threaten the principle of individual autonomy by holding people liable when they did no voluntary act.

The weakness of this argument is that individual actions can often be explained fully only by reference to the social and structural context in which they were carried out. When the managing director of a company is announcing a commercial strategy, he or she is acting not merely as an individual but also as an officer of the company. Without reference to the structure and policies of the company and to that person's role within it, there can be no proper explanation of what was said and done. The argument, therefore, is that the behaviour of individuals is often shaped by their relationship to groups and collectivities—'shaped' in a meaningful sense, not 'determined' in the sense that individual autonomy is lost in the process (since individuals normally have some liberty to disengage themselves from the corporation). The thrust is that companies often acquire a momentum and a dynamic of their own which temporarily transcend the actions of their officers. Perhaps the clearest application of this can be found in offences of omission, particularly those involving strict liability. In a case like *Alphacell Ltd v Woodward (1972)*,[92] where polluting matter escaped from the company's premises into a river, it seems both fairer and more accurate to convict the

---

88 [2000] 2 Cr App R 207.   89 Ibid., 211.

90 See Wells, *Corporations and Criminal Responsibility*, ch 3, and G. R. Sullivan, 'The Attribution of Culpability to Limited Companies' (1996) 55 Camb LJ 515.

91 Cf. S. Lukes, *Individualism* (1973), ch 17.

92 [1972] AC 824; cf. the early decision in *Birmingham and Gloucester Railway Co* (1842) 3 QB 223.

company rather than to label one individual as the offender: where the law imposes a duty, the company should be organized so as to ensure that the duty is fulfilled.

None of this is meant to suggest that individuals within a corporation should not bear personal responsibility for their conduct. In appropriate cases they should do so, provided that they had fair warning of any special duties attached to the activities of the company.[93] The important point is that companies should be open to both criminal and civil liability, since it is they who create the structural context for the individual's conduct *qua* company officer. The corporation appoints the individual and sustains him in this position—the individual is in that place, doing that thing, because of the corporation—and so it is right that the corporation should bear primary liability, or at least concurrent liability with its officer. This does not mean that legality and 'rule of law' principles should be neglected: companies are run by individuals, who ought to receive fair warning of their duties. All these arguments may need adjusting for small, even one-person, companies and also for non-profit organizations. Moreover, they leave open the question whether the criminal law in its traditional form is the most appropriate means of dealing with corporate harm-doing.

(d) CHANGING THE BASIS OF CORPORATE LIABILITY

The theoretical arguments in favour of corporate criminal liability seem strong, but developments at common law have been slow. The 'identification principle' in *Tesco Supermarkets* v *Nattrass*[94] has a relatively narrow sphere of operation, and there has been little judicial enthusiasm for the greater flexibility proposed in the *Meridian* case.[95] A small number of statutes impose direct or vicarious liability on companies, the Health and Safety at Work Act 1974 being an example, but there is no such general approach. An alternative strategy of placing the emphasis on individual liability would be unlikely to work with larger companies: any particular individual might be dispensable within a corporation (e.g. the 'Company Vice-President responsible for going to gaol'), allowing the company to continue on its course with minimal disruption; or it might be difficult to identify the individual responsible, not least because the lines of accountability within companies are sometimes unclear. But with smaller companies, which are far more numerous, this might be workable.

A number of different approaches have been canvassed in recent years. Celia Wells, whilst emphasizing the need to re-assess the socio-political role of corporations and of individuals within them, lends support to an approach that depends partly on a version of aggregation, whereby a company's culpability should be constructed out of the knowledge and the attitudes of employees as a whole,[96] and partly on the need to ensure that individual company officers are prosecuted where appropriate. Another, complementary approach would be to use company policies, or their absence, as the

---

[93] Wells, *Corporations and Criminal Responsibility*, 160–3; cf. J. Gobert and M. Punch, *Rethinking Corporate Crime* (2003), ch 8, with their discussion of companies as accomplices in ch 2.

[94] [1972] AC 153.   [95] Above, n 111.

[96] Wells, *Corporations and Criminal Responsibility*, 164–8.

basis for liability. This follows the approach of Brent Fisse and John Braithwaite, and in particular their concept of 'reactive fault'.[97] In their view, rather than expending prosecutorial energy and court time trying to disentangle the often convoluted internal structures and policies of corporations, the law should require a company which has caused or threatened a proscribed harm to take its own disciplinary and rectificatory measures. A court would then assess the adequacy of the measures taken. The concept of fault would thus be a *post hoc* phenomenon. Rather than struggling to establish some antecedent fault within the corporation, the prosecution would invite the court to infer fault from the nature and effectiveness of the company's remedial measures after it has been established that it was the author of a harm-causing or harm-threatening act or omission. The court would not find fault if it was persuaded that the company had taken realistic measures to prevent a recurrence, had ensured compensation to any victims, and had taken the event seriously in other respects. But the whole orientation of the system would be different: every death caused, whether purely accidental or not, would be treated as potentially a serious offence until the company established otherwise.[98]

Following a lengthy process of discussion and negotiation, a new form of corporate liability has now been introduced in the limited (but high profile) area of homicide.[99] The Corporate Manslaughter and Corporate Homicide Act 2007 introduces a new offence of corporate manslaughter, which can be committed only by 'organizations' and not by individuals. The legislative framework of the new offence is highly technical, but for present purposes we can focus on the mechanism by which liability is imposed. Section 1 of the 2007 Act provides:

An organisation...is guilty of an offence if the way in which its activities are managed or organised—

(a) causes a person's death, and

(b) amounts to a gross breach of a relevant duty of care owed by the organisation to the deceased.

Three features of the new Act's approach stand out. First, it applies to 'organizations', which include companies, partnerships, and various associations and government departments. This is controversial, but is not pursued here. Secondly, the offence is only committed if 'the way in which its activities are managed and organized by its senior management is a substantial element in the breach' of duty. This focus on 'senior management' is developed by section 1(4), which provides that senior managers must be persons who 'play significant roles' in either decision-making or managing the whole or a substantial part of the organization's activities. This shows that the model of corporate liability adopted in the 2007 Act has not strayed far from the 'identification principle' that has developed at common law. It is, to be blunt, doubtful

---

[97] B. Fisse and J. Braithwaite, *Corporations, Crime and Accountability* (1993).

[98] See the analysis by G. R. Sullivan, 'Expressing Corporate Guilt' (1995) 15 Oxford JLS 281.

[99] See the detailed discussion in Ch 7.5(c) below.

if the manager of a large Tesco superstore plays a significant role in managing a sub-stantial part of Tesco's activities. If the company is to be prosecuted under the 2007 Act, it must be shown that people at a higher level in a large organization organized the relevant activities in such a way as to amount to a substantial element in the breach. Thirdly, however, section 8 of the Act directs the jury to consider any alleged breach of health and safety legislation, and permits the jury to take account of evidence of 'atti-tudes, policies, systems or accepted practices within the organization that were likely to have encouraged' any failure to meet safety standards. This suggests that evidence of corporate culture may be determinative in some cases.

Whether this new approach will be thought to achieve justice in homicide cases remains to be tested. Certainly it seems to be a rather narrow approach to serve as a model for corporate criminal liability generally, and so the quest for a fairer set of prin-ciples must go on. The new approach also serves to raise the wider question of whether it is the conviction of organizations that is the most important aspect, or whether the sentencing of organizations should be regarded as important too. A company can hardly be imprisoned, moderate fines can be swallowed up as business overheads, and swingeing fines may have such drastic side-effects on the employment and livelihoods of innocent employees as to render them inappropriate. Fisse and Braithwaite have proposed a range of special penalties, some of which are rehabilitative (putting cor-porations on probation to supervise their compliance with the law), some of which are deterrent (punitive injunctions to require resources to be devoted to the develop-ment of new preventive measures), and others of which have mixed aims (e.g. com-munity service by companies).[100] In their view, the primary search should be for a regime which ensures maximum prevention. The 2007 Act provides for three types of sentence—publicity orders (requiring the organization to make it known that it has been convicted of this offence); remedial orders (requiring the offender to remedy the causes of the homicide); and fines (which may prove problematic for the reasons given above, and which are questionable insofar as they may have deleterious effects on the level of public service provided by organizations such as hospital trusts and the police).

5.4 FAULT AND *MENS REA*: GENERAL PRINCIPLES

(a) CHOICE AND THE SUBJECTIVE PRINCIPLES

The principle of *mens rea* has already been outlined in Chapter 3.6(o) above, together with the related principles of correspondence (Chapter 3.6(q)) and of fair labelling (Chapter 3.6(s)). The essence of the principle of *mens rea* is that criminal liability

---

[100] Fisse and Braithwaite, *Corporations, Crime and Accountability*; cf. Gobert and Punch, *Rethinking Corporate Crime*, ch 7.

should be imposed only on persons who are sufficiently aware of what they are doing, and of the consequences it may have, that they can fairly be said to have chosen the behaviour and its consequences. This approach is grounded in the principle of autonomy (Chapter 2.1 above): individuals are regarded as autonomous persons with a general capacity to choose among alternative courses of behaviour, and respect for their autonomy means holding them liable only on the basis of their choices.[101] The principle of *mens rea* may also be claimed to enhance the constitutional values of legality and rule of law, by reassuring citizens that they will be liable to conviction, and to the exercise of state coercion against them, only if they knowingly cause or risk causing a prohibited harm. If this were achieved, the criminal law would ensure that 'each person is guaranteed a greatest liberty, capacity and opportunity of controlling and predicting the consequences of his or her actions compatible with a like liberty, capacity and opportunity for all'.[102] What this liberal view rejects is an approach which holds people criminally liable solely on the ground that liability and punishment would have a general deterrent effect in preventing further harms. That approach, associated with utilitarian theories,[103] looks to the probable social effects of liability and punishment, denying the individual defendant any special status in the matter: if the punishment of people in D's position would have an overall deterrent effect, then D should be punished, even though he or she cannot be said to have *chosen* to cause the harm. Deterrent theories therefore tend to give priority to welfare. Theories of punishment in the liberal tradition may recognize the relevance of welfare, at least at the level of justifying the criminal law itself and justifying the criminalization of certain conduct, but at the level of individual liability to conviction and censure they insist that respect for the principle of individual autonomy has superior value to general calculations of social utility. (This means that they must either denounce strict liability offences, or find some plausible argument in their favour.)

The principle of *mens rea* also encompasses the belief principle, which holds that criminal liability should be based on what defendants believed they were doing or risking, not on actual facts which were not known to them at the time. Also flowing from the principle of *mens rea*, as we saw in Chapter 3.6(q) above, is the principle of correspondence, which insists that the fault element for a crime should correspond to the conduct element specified for the crime. Thus, if the conduct element is 'causing serious injury', then the fault element ought to be 'intention or recklessness as to causing serious injury'; a lesser fault element, such as 'intention or recklessness as to a mere assault', would breach the principle of correspondence. This makes the point that the

---

[101] Cf. A. Brudner, 'Agency and Welfare in Criminal Law', in S. Shute, J. Gardner, and J. Horder (eds.), *Action and Value in Criminal Law* (1993), and R. Lippke, *Rethinking Imprisonment* (2007), 84–98.

[102] D. A. J. Richards, 'Rights, Utility and Crime', in M. Tonry and N. Morris (eds.), *Crime and Justice: An Annual Review* (1981), iii, 274.

[103] Notably those of Bentham: for extracts and discussion see von Hirsch, Ashworth and Roberts, *Principled Sentencing* (3rd edn., 2009), ch 2.

notion of choice is not an abstract phenomenon, but should in principle be linked to the circumstances or consequences specified in the definition of each crime.

Do the notions of fault and choice that underlie the principle of *mens rea* have a wider application? While the principle of *mens rea* supports only criminal liability for intention, knowledge and (subjective) recklessness, there are serious questions about whether gross negligence, or even negligence, can be said to involve sufficient fault and choice to justify the imposition of criminal liability. English law contains several offences of negligence, whereas the tendency of commentators has been to regard them as aberrant and calling for special justification. This discussion will be taken further in paragraphs 5(f) and 5(g)below.

(b) CONSTRUCTIVE LIABILITY AND 'MORAL LUCK'

We have already seen, in Chapter 3.6(q) above, that subjectivists tend to place high value not only on the principle of mens rea and on the belief principle (that D should be judged on the facts as he believed them to be), but also on the principle of correspondence (that in relation to each conduct element of an offence, the fault requirement should be at the same level). We also noted, in Chapter 3.6(p), that this is disputed by advocates of constructive liability, arguing that once D has crossed a significant moral threshold he should be held liable for whatever consequences follow. We will see in later chapters that among the examples of constructive liability are manslaughter by unlawful act (Chapter 7.5) and unlawful wounding (Chapter 8.3). Offences of this kind allow what is termed 'moral luck' to play a significant role in determining the level of criminal liability. As elaborated in Chapter 3.6(q) and (r) above, subjectivists tend to oppose the intrusion of moral luck into criminal liability. The argument is that the criminal law should blame people for what they intended or foresaw and for what lay within their control: it should draw a straight line through the vicissitudes of life and the vagaries of fortune when determining the extent of criminal liability.[104] A different view is taken by moderate constructivists.[105] Like subjectivists, moderate constructivists accept that the criminal law should respect the rule of law and should maintain 'clear and certain offence definitions, good publicity, and conformity between announced rule and adjudicative standard.'[106] However, moderate constructivists reject the principle of correspondence between the level of the conduct element and the level of the fault or *mens rea*, and instead argue that, so long as D intentionally commits a relevant offence, that fault is sufficient to justify conviction for a more

---

[104] For further argument, compare A. Ashworth, 'Taking the Consequences', in Shute, Gardner, and Horder (eds.), *Action and Value in Criminal Law* (1993) and V. Tadros, *Criminal Responsibility* (2005), 90–8, with R. A. Duff, *Criminal Attempts*, ch 12, and R. A. Duff, 'Whose Luck is it Anyway?', in C. Clarkson and S. Cunningham (eds), *Criminal Liability for Non-Aggressive Death* (2008).

[105] See Ch 3.6(r) above; compare the different framing of the same debate in German and French laws: J. R. Spencer and A. Pedain, 'Strict Liability in Continental Criminal Law', in A. P. Simester (ed), *Appraising Strict Liability* (2005), 275–81.

[106] J. Gardner, 'On the General Part of the Criminal Law', in R. A. Duff (ed), *Philosophy and the Criminal Law* (1998), 243.

serious offence in the same family if an unanticipated and more serious consequence results.[107] This is because:

By committing an assault one changes one's normative position, so that certain adverse consequences and circumstances that would not have counted against one but for one's original assault now count against one automatically, and add to one's crime.[108]

This is John Gardner's statement of the doctrine of 'change of normative position:' as he accepts, to assert that such a change takes place when D intentionally commits a relevant offence does not supply a justification for imposing moderately constructive liability on D.[109] More work needs to be done if the 'change of normative position' argument is to be a convincing rationale for moderate constructivism. In the meantime, as argued in Chapter 3.6(r), the criminal law should give precedence to the principle of correspondence.

(c) THE PRINCIPLE OF CONTEMPORANEITY

As we saw in Chapter 3.6(u), the principle of contemporaneity states that the fault element must coincide in point of time with the conduct element in order to amount to an offence. This forms part of the ideology that the function of the criminal law is not to judge a person's general character or behaviour over a period of time; its concern is only with the distinct criminal conduct charged. According to this view, whether or not criminal conviction is deserved depends on D's conduct and mental attitude at the relevant time. But this narrow statement of the principle, if indeed it ever represented a complete statement of the law,[110] has been progressively abandoned in the face of intuitions to the contrary exemplified in leading cases. In the famous case of *Fagan* v *Metropolitan Police Commissioner* (1969)[111] D accidentally drove his car on to a policeman's foot, and then deliberately left it there for a minute or so. The defence to a charge of assault was that the conduct element (applying force) had finished before the fault element began; the act and the intent never coincided. The Divisional Court held that D's conduct in driving the car on to the foot and leaving it there should be viewed as a continuing act, so that the crime was committed when the fault element (D's realization of what had happened and decision to leave the car there) came together with the continuing conduct. This is not the only occasion on which the courts have invoked the notion of a 'continuing act' to expand the time-frame of a crime and thus the application of the principle of contemporaneity.[112] However, a different approach

---

[107] Ibid., at 244; see also Ch 3.6(r) above.

[108] J. Gardner, 'Rationality and the Rules of Law in Offences against the Person' (1994) 53 Camb LJ 502, at 509.

[109] J. Gardner, *Offences and Defences* (2007), 246–7, replying to A. Ashworth, 'A Change of Normative Position: Determining the Contours of Culpability in Criminal Law' (2008) 11 New Crim LR 232.

[110] An early general statement was that of Lord Kenyon CJ in *Fowler* v *Padget* (1798) 7 Term Rep 509.

[111] [1969] 1 QB 439.

[112] E.g. in rape (*Kaitamaki* v *R* [1985] 1 AC 147, now confirmed by the Sexual Offences Act 2003, s. 79(2)) and in theft (on appropriation, *Hale* (1978) 68 Cr App R 415). Cf. the critique by M. Kelman, 'Interpretive

was taken by the House of Lords in *Miller* (1982),[113] the case in which a squatter was smoking in bed, accidentally set the mattress on fire, but simply moved to another room without attempting to remedy the problem, with the result that the house caught fire. Although Lord Diplock did not reject the view that the fire was a continuing act that began accidentally but could then be connected with D's fault when he realized that the mattress was on fire, he expressed a preference for the 'duty' analysis, whereby the accidental creation of danger gave rise to a duty (a continuing duty to avert the danger caused) which in this case D knowingly failed to discharge.

The continuing act approach seems to exert an influence in another area. In *Thabo Meli v R* (1954)[114] the plan was to kill V in a hut and then throw his body over a cliff: this was what D believed he was doing, but in fact V died from the fall down the cliff and not from the beating in the hut. The argument for the appellant was based on the lack of contemporaneity (this time it was intent first, death later), but the Privy Council rejected this, holding that the beating and the disposal over the cliff formed part of a planned series of acts which should be regarded as a single course of conduct. On this analysis, the presence of the fault element at any stage during the planned sequence would suffice. That reasoning was extended in *Church* (1966)[115] to cover a series of acts which had not been planned but which simply followed one after the other. Subsequently, in *Le Brun* (1991),[116] the Court of Appeal had to deal with a case in which D had assaulted his wife, and then when he tried to move her unconscious body dropped her, causing her to suffer a fractured skull from which she died. The Court held that the conduct and the fault elements 'need not coincide in point of time' so long as they formed part of a 'sequence of events', particularly in a case such as this where D's later acts were attempts to conceal his initial offence. All these cases could have resulted in convictions for other offences (attempted murder in *Thabo Meli*, grievous or actual bodily harm in the last two cases), but the courts apparently took the view that since the consequence—death—resulted from D's original culpable conduct, homicide convictions ought to be registered. A similar analysis would be possible in non-homicide cases. The decisions therefore take a rather elastic view of the contemporaneity principle, and seem to be motivated by considerations akin to constructive liability.[117]

It is convenient to deal here with one more awkward situation relating to the link between conduct and fault. In *Attorney-General's Reference (No. 4 of 1980)* (1981),[118] it appeared that D was arguing with his female partner at the top of a flight of stairs, that he pushed her away and she fell backwards down the stairs, that he concluded she was dead, and then dragged her back to their flat with a rope around her neck and cut up her body. The Court of Appeal held that there could be a conviction on these facts, even though it was not clear which of D's acts caused death. So long as the jury was

Construction in the Substantive Criminal Law' (1981) 33 Stanford LR 591, and the defence by M. Moore, *Act and Crime* (1993), 35–7.

[113] [1983] 2 AC 161, discussed in Ch 4.4 above.   [114] [1954] 1 WLR 228.   [115] [1966] 1 QB 59.
[116] [1992] QB 61.
[117] Cf. the felony-murder rule and constructive manslaughter, section 5.4(b) above.
[118] [1981] 1 WLR 705.

satisfied that D had sufficient fault for manslaughter when he pushed her backwards, and sufficient fault for manslaughter when he cut up her body,[119] it was immaterial which act caused death. The facts of this case are somewhat stronger than the facts of *Thabo Meli*, *Church*, and *Le Brun*, since in all of those cases it was clear that it was not D's initial act that caused death. Surely in the *Reference* case it should have been possible to convict D if the court was satisfied that there was a sequence of events and that D had the required fault element at some stage; the actual facts, however, were taken not to raise this point.

(d) THE DOCTRINE OF PRIOR FAULT

We saw in Chapter 3.6(v) above that the principle of contemporaneity conflicts in certain situations with the doctrine of prior fault—the principle that a person should not be allowed to take advantage of any defence or partial defence to criminal liability if the relevant condition or circumstances were brought about by his or her own fault. Whilst the contemporaneity principle insists that the criminal law is concerned with the prohibited event itself, not with its antecedents or its sequels, the doctrine of prior fault points to circumstances in which the antecedents of the event ought (by way of principled exception) to affect a proper moral evaluation of D's conduct. Two examples of the doctrine's operation may be given. First, a person who deliberately drinks to excess in order to stoke up the courage to do a certain act will not be allowed to rely on that intoxication by way of defence because it arose from prior fault.[120] Secondly, if D taunts another in the hope of inducing the other to attack him, D should not be able to rely on provocation or self-defence as a defence to a charge of murder, because the attack on D will be regarded as self-induced.[121] Examples of the doctrine of prior fault in operation were noted in Chapter 4, in relation to automatism and self-defence, and will be seen in abundance in Chapter 6 (on intoxication, duress, necessity, etc.).

One remaining question concerns the amount of 'fault' required for the doctrine to take effect. A study by Paul Robinson revealed considerable diversity of provisions in the Model Penal Code and in American laws generally,[122] and a similar diversity appears in England.[123] Should *any* causal contribution by D make a defence unavailable, or should it be a lack of proper care (for example, drinking alcohol when its possible effects are widely known,[124] joining a gang which is known to use violence[125]), or should the doctrine require proof that D foresaw the possibility that certain conduct might follow? The differences between these approaches ought not to be regarded

---

[119] An intention merely to assault would suffice: see the discussion in 5.4(b) above.

[120] See *Attorney-General for Northern Ireland* v *Gallagher* [1963] AC 349, and below, Ch 6.2.

[121] Cf. *Edwards* v *R* [1973] AC 648, with *Johnson* (1989) 89 Cr App 148, and below, Ch 6.7.

[122] P. H. Robinson, 'Causing the Conditions of One's Own Defence: A Study in the Limits of Theory in Criminal Law Doctrine' (1985) 71 Virginia LR 1.

[123] Cf. the different wording in the draft Criminal Code (Law Com No. 177) on automatism (cl. 33(1)(b)) and on duress (cl. 42(5)), for example.

[124] See below, Ch 6.3(c).   [125] *Hasan* [2005] 2 AC 467, and below, Ch 6.5(c).

as unimportant, since the withdrawal of a *defence* simply on the grounds of some small amount of fault on D's part is equivalent to a principle of constructive liability for *offences*. One way of avoiding this difficulty would be to devise a range of offences to cover 'faulty' acts (e.g. excessive consumption of alcohol), and then convict D of an offence of that kind—whilst not removing any defence to the substantive crime which might otherwise be open.[126] This would introduce further complexities into the law, but at least it attempts a fair solution of a difficult problem.

5.5 VARIETIES OF FAULT

Having introduced the subjective principles and some problems of contemporaneity of conduct and fault, we now move to the core fault elements. First to be considered is strict liability, for which there may be little or no fault at all. One reason for considering these offences first is that they are the most numerous, a fact that belies the prominence often given to intention and recklessness in the rhetoric of English criminal law. We then turn to the *mens rea* terms of intention, recklessness, and knowledge, before exploring the little-used concept of negligence.

(a) STRICT LIABILITY[127]

There is no clear convention about when criminal liability should be classified as 'strict'. We will use the term here to indicate those offences of which a person may be convicted without proof of intention, knowledge, recklessness, or negligence. Some offences prescribe liability without fault but allow the defendant to avoid liability on proof of 'due diligence'. There is dispute about whether offences with such provisos are properly termed 'strict liability' offences,[128] but for our present purposes they will be included within the concept of strict liability. This corresponds with the Canadian approach, which separates strict liability (where a defendant can avoid liability by establishing that there was no negligence) from absolute liability (where the only defences available relate to fundamental elements of capacity or necessity).[129] The term 'absolute liability' has its own difficulties, however, since one can argue that liability should only be described as absolute where there is no defence available at all to someone who is proved to have caused the prohibited event. What this shows, above all, is that there is no settled terminology to give simple expression to the numerous permutations of conditions for liability. If one takes account of the device of shifting

---

[126] Robinson, 'Causing the Conditions of One's Own Defense'.

[127] See the searching exploration of this topic in A. P. Simester (ed.), *Appraising Strict Liability* (2005).

[128] See the study by L. H. Leigh, *Strict and Vicarious Liability* (1982).

[129] There is ample authority that automatism is a defence to strict liability offences, but some disagreement on whether insanity may afford a defence: cf. *Hennessy* (1989) 89 Cr App R 10 with *DPP v H* [1997] 1 WLR 1406, discussed in Ch 5.2(c).

the burden of proof on to the defendant, then the permutations range from requiring *mens rea*—with the burden of proof on the prosecution—to defining special defences or provisos with an evidential burden on D, defining special defences or provisos with a legal burden of proof on D, requiring proof of negligence by the prosecution, creating a no-negligence defence to be proved by D, imposing liability with no due diligence defence at all, and even to a dispensation from proving an element of the offence.[130]

(i) For and Against Strict Liability: Let us leave aside the complexities introduced by changes in the burden of proof, and formulate a central question: what are the arguments for imposing criminal liability with no due diligence defence available? The main argument is a form of protectionism or 'social defence'. It maintains that one of the primary aims of the criminal law is the protection of fundamental social interests. Why should this function be abandoned when the violation of those interests resulted from some accident or mistake by D? Surely, Wootton argued, '*mens rea* has got into the wrong place': it should be relevant not to the actual conviction, but to the appropriate means of dealing with the offender after conviction. 'If the object of the criminal law is to prevent the occurrence of socially damaging actions, it would be absurd to turn a blind eye to those which were due to carelessness, negligence or even accident. The question of motivation is in the first instance irrelevant.'[131] At a time when victims' interests are receiving greater recognition, arguments of this kind may find considerable support. The infliction of the prohibited harm would become the trigger for state action, aimed at minimizing the risk of the harm being repeated.

The strength of the argument lies in its concern for the welfare of citizens in general. Its weakness is to suggest that this is a justification for using the *criminal law* in *this* way. There are two major questions to be answered here: would it be fair? Would it be effective? The fairness issue is one which runs through this chapter and, indeed, through the whole book. The criminal law is society's most condemnatory instrument, and, as argued in Chapter 2.1, Chapter 3.6, and section 5.4(a) above, respect for individual autonomy requires that criminal liability be imposed only where there has been choice by D. A person should not be censured for wrongdoing without proof of choice (as distinct, perhaps, from being held civilly liable). This is a fundamental requirement of fairness to defendants. Indeed, it is not only unfair to censure people who are not culpable, but also unfair to punish them for the offence. Moreover, in so far as the criminal trial has a communicative function, strict liability impairs this by severely limiting D's ability to explain, excuse or justify the conduct and by requiring a conviction in all but exceptional circumstances.[132]

---

[130] A. Ashworth, 'Towards a Theory of Criminal Legislation' (1989) 1 Criminal Law Forum 41.

[131] B. Wootton, *Crime and the Criminal Law* (2nd edn., 1981) 47. Note that a few pages later Baroness Wootton advocates 'a wider concept of responsibility... in which there is room for negligence as well as purposeful wrongdoing' (50), which is less an argument for strict liability than for negligence liability. Support for negligence liability is also found in the landmark decision of *Sweet v Parsley*, discussed in the text at n 154 below.

[132] See, for example, the contributions of J. Horder and R. A. Duff in Simester (ed.), *Appraising Strict Liability*.

Opponents of subjectivism may dismiss this as a mere matter of convention—and outmoded convention at that. The criminal law should simply be regarded as an efficient social resource for the prevention of harm,[133] with conviction carrying no special moral connotations of 'guilt' or 'blame'. Is there not something incongruous, in a world in which avoidable deaths and injuries are much too frequent and cause much grief and insecurity, for the State meticulously to observe the 'intent' and 'belief' principles, the presumption of innocence, and other fairness principles so as to facilitate the acquittal of clumsy, ignorant, but nevertheless dangerous people?[134] One answer to this challenge is to reassert that the prevention of harm is neither the sole nor the overriding aim of the criminal law, and that the criminal law is not the only official means of preventing harm. Even Bentham, whose general approach was to transcend individual considerations and to weigh the social benefits against the social disadvantages of criminal liability, argued that criminal punishment is an evil which should be reserved for the worst cases, and that legislators should turn first to education, regulation, and civil liability as means of preventing harms.[135]

The subjective principles reflect the value of individual autonomy, but many of the harms which afflict, or threaten to afflict, citizens today are the result of the acts or omissions of corporations. Pollution, defective products, food and drugs, safety at work, transport systems—all these sources of danger are dominated by corporate undertakings. We saw in part 3 of this Chapter that the traditional doctrines of the criminal law have various shortcomings when applied to corporate decision-making and responsibility. Once a secure basis for corporate liability is found, the next question would concern the appropriate conditions of liability for companies. Some corporations operate in spheres of such potential social danger, and wield such power (in terms of economic resources and influence), that there is no social unfairness in holding them to higher standards than individuals when it comes to criminal liability—so long as fair warning is given, since companies are run by individuals. This is particularly so when companies operate in spheres where public safety may be at risk. However, the same cannot generally be said of individuals, save in exceptional categories such as road traffic offences, where a licence to drive is required and safety is a central issue. It can therefore be argued that the conflict between social welfare and fairness to defendants should be resolved differently according to whether the defendant is a private individual or a large corporation. On the other hand, those two categories do not exhaust the range of defendants: a substantial proportion of British businesses have a sole proprietor, and, although their duties may well be more extensive, their criminal liability should follow the model for private individuals.[136] That

---

[133] Cf. the nuanced argument of G. Lamond, 'What is a Crime?' (2007) 27 Oxford JLS 609, at 629–31, suggesting that strict liability may have a proper role in regulating conduct that increases the risk of violations of significant public or private interests, as in road traffic law, health and safety, and food standards.

[134] J. Braithwaite, *Corporate Crime in the Pharmaceutical Industry* (1984), ch 9.

[135] *Introduction to the Principles of Morals and Legislation*, ch XIII.

[136] See J. Horder, 'Strict Liability, Statutory Construction and the Spirit of Liberty' (2002) 118 LQR 458, at 472–4.

model should reject strict liability for individuals on grounds of unfairness and lack of respect for autonomy: negligence should be the minimum requirement.

Moving to the second question, whether criminal liability without fault is a particularly efficacious means of preventing harm, it is important to keep in mind the differences between individual behaviour and corporate activity. At least two aspects of efficacy arise: the ease of enforcing no-fault offences, and the preventive effects of liability without fault. Ease of enforcement may be thought obvious: it must be less trouble to prepare a prosecution in which fault is not relevant than to prepare one in which proof of fault is needed. Indeed, the Court of Appeal has quashed convictions on the basis that evidence of fault is inadmissible, because not relevant, if adduced by the prosecution on a strict liability charge.[137] For the more serious offences, however, evidence of fault will be needed at the sentencing stage if the courts are to pass sentence on a proper basis.[138] This means that the prosecution will have to prepare some evidence on the point, which in turn diminishes any procedural benefit of strict liability. But there may still be benefits to the prosecutor in not having to prove fault for minor offences, and there may also be indirect benefits as a result of being able to use the threat of prosecution and conviction in order to secure compliance. Many of the regulatory agencies with the power to invoke 'strict liability' offences adopt what may be termed a 'compliance strategy' towards law enforcement—that is, aiming to secure conformity to the law without the need to process and penalize violators.[139] Regulatory activities focus on obtaining compliance, and prosecution is reserved for the few cases where either the violator is recalcitrant or the violation is so large that public concern can only be assuaged by a prosecution. This may also mean that prosecutions tend to be brought only in cases where there is fault: indeed, there are regulatory agencies which pursue such a policy, even though they have no-fault offences at their disposal.[140] There is little evidence among the regulatory agencies of a 'deterrence strategy', using criminal prosecution as a primary means of preventing breaches of the law. That approach to law enforcement is more typical of the police, who rarely occupy themselves with the so-called regulatory offences aimed at commercial and industrial safety etc.

It is therefore difficult to reach a firm conclusion about the preventive efficacy of strict liability. It is probably an overstatement to regard it as a 'means of prevention', since the no-fault offence usually forms one part of a broad regulatory scheme. Some argue that the availability of a no-fault offence strengthens the regulator's hand in ensuring compliance and, therefore, prevention. It enables regulators to use lesser measures, and then to prosecute when there is real fault.[141] Others argue that no-fault offences which

[137] *Sandhu* [1997] Crim LR 288.

[138] Cf. *Lester* (1976) 63 Cr App R 144 with *Hill* [1997] Crim LR 459.

[139] A. Reiss, 'Selecting Strategies of Social Control over Organizational Life', in K. Hawkins and J. M. Thomas (eds.), *Enforcing Regulation* (1984).

[140] The leading study is K. Hawkins, *Law as Last Resort* (2003). For shorter reviews, see G. Richardson, 'Strict Liability for Regulatory Crime: The Empirical Research' [1987] Crim LR 295, and R. Baldwin, 'The New Punitive Regulation' (2004) 67 MLR 351.

[141] See Hawkins, *Law as Last Resort*; B. S. Jackson, '*Storkwain*: a Case Study in Strict Liability and Self-Regulation' [1991] Crim LR 892, discussing the role of the Pharmaceutical Society in regulating pharmacists.

are followed by low penalties on conviction are almost counterproductive, resulting in
the imposition of derisory fines on large organizations. Indeed, if regulation in such
spheres as industrial safety had been harnessed to relatively serious offences requiring
proof of fault, then those offences might now be taken much more seriously, integrated
into people's thinking about offences against the person rather than being regarded as
'merely regulatory' and 'not real crime'.[142] This is, of course, part of a much wider issue
about the conventional concepts of crime (as now embodied, for example, in the draft
Criminal Code)[143] and about conventional approaches to enforcement which regard
some offences as police matters and some not. Much turns on the agency through
which enforcement takes place, the style of enforcement adopted, and the elements of
discretion in choosing and following a style of enforcement.

Is it an argument in favour of, or against, strict liability that the offence is a minor one
or a grave one? The English courts have used both triviality and gravity as arguments
in favour of strict liability. Many offences with low penalties are, or have been held to
be, offences requiring no proof of fault.[144] This reasoning derives some justification
from an economic argument based on ease of prosecution: such trivial offences are
not worth the public expenditure of prosecution and court time in proving fault. There
is hardly any stigma in being convicted of such offences, and so it is thought to be in
the public interest to dispose of them quickly (although the result may be to dilute the
moral legitimacy of the criminal law). But none of this can apply to serious offences.
Principles of individual fairness, even if overridden by economic considerations in
respect of minor offences, should surely be central to the question of conviction for
serious offences. One clear benchmark here is the availability of imprisonment as a
punishment. The American Model Penal Code proposes that imprisonability should
be a conclusive reason against strict liability.[145] In Canada the Supreme Court has
held that an offence of strict liability which carries the possibility of a custodial sentence is contrary to the Charter of Rights, unless there is a no-negligence defence.[146]
However, the jurisprudence of the European Court of Human Rights is equivocal on
the matter.[147]

---

[142] Cf. decisions such as *Seaboard Offshore Ltd v Secretary of State for Transport* [1994] 1 WLR 541,
British Steel [1995] 1 WLR 1356, *Associated Octel* [1996] 1 WLR 1543, and *Gateway Foodmarkets Ltd* [1997]
Crim LR 512.

[143] Cf. the justifications for confining the English codification initiative to 'traditional' offences by the
Code Team (Law Com No. 143, paras. 2.10–2.13 and Appendix A) and by the Law Commission (Law Com
No. 177, paras. 3.3–3.6), with the critical remarks of C. Wells, 'Restatement or Reform' [1986] Crim LR 314
and A. Ashworth, 'Is the Criminal Law a Lost Cause?' (2000) 116 LQR 225.

[144] *Alphacell Ltd v Woodward* [1972] AC 824, following the notion of 'quasi-crimes' outlined by Lord Reid
in *Sweet v Parsley* [1970] AC 132.

[145] Model Penal Code, s. 6.02(4). For discussion in the context of the US Constitution see A. Michaels,
'Constitutional Innocence' (1999) 122 Harv LR 829.

[146] *References re Section 94(2) of the Motor Vehicles Act* (1986) 48 CR (3d) 289; see D. R. Stuart, *Canadian
Criminal Law* (4th edn., 2001).

[147] Whether the presumption of innocence ought to have any implications for strict criminal liability is
a matter that has been debated extensively. See e.g. the contribution by Sullivan in Simester (ed.), *Appraising
Strict Liability*; V. Tadros and S. Tierney, 'The Presumption of Innocence and the Human Rights Act' (2004)
67 MLR 402; and A. Ashworth, 'Four Threats to the Presumption of Innocence' (2006) 123 SALJ 62.

(ii) The Development of Strict Liability: No presumption against the imposition of no-fault liability for imprisonable offences has been enunciated in this country; indeed, English law contains several examples of courts using the seriousness of the offence as an argument in favour of strict liability—a course of reasoning which inevitably results in no-fault liability for some imprisonable crimes. The nadir of such judicial reasoning was probably reached in *Howells* (1977),[148] where D was charged with possessing a firearm without a certificate, an offence contrary to s 1 of the Firearms Act 1968, with a maximum penalty of three years' imprisonment. D sought to rely on s 58 of the Act, which exempted 'an antique firearm which is...possessed as a curiosity or ornament'. When evidence was given that the gun was not an antique but a reproduction, D then put the point that he believed it to be an antique, since it had been sold to him as such. This would be a defence only if some requirement of knowledge or belief could be read into the statute. The Court of Appeal ruled this out and upheld strict liability:

First, the wording would, on the face of it, so indicate. Secondly, the danger to the community resulting from the possession of lethal firearms is so obviously great that an absolute prohibition against their possession without proper authority must have been the intention of Parliament when considered in conjunction with the words of the section. Thirdly, to allow a defence of honest and reasonable belief that the firearm was an antique and therefore excluded would be likely to defeat the clear intentions of the Act.[149]

This is poor reasoning. The powerful expression of the second point, the danger to the community, gives no weight at all to the argument against rendering a person liable to imprisonment without proof of fault; indeed, the argument seems not to have been mentioned. The 'danger to the community' argument is surely questionable in itself. Is it really being contended that the more serious the (potential) harm, the stronger the argument for strict liability? Would this support strict criminal liability for all killings? Moreover, the assertion about the original intention of Parliament is unsupported: there is no reference in the judgment to the history of this part of the Firearms Act. The third point in the quotation merely restates the assertion. Everything depends on whether Parliament, by failing to include any fault terms in the relevant section of the Act, did intend to exclude fault, or whether it was merely leaving the issue to be determined by the courts.[150] This brings us back to the first point, that the wording 'on the face of it' favours strict liability. This is a monumentally unhelpful statement, which calls for some discussion of the respective functions of the legislature and the courts in these matters.

Part of Parliament's function in defining offences should be to state any fault requirement for liability. It discharges this function in many statutory provisions, but in many others it remains silent, merely enacting a provision that penalizes an act or an omission without any reference to fault. Over the years the courts have had to

---

[148] [1977] QB 614. See also *Bradish* [1990] 1 QB 981.   [149] *Per* Browne LJ, at 626.
[150] P. Devlin, *Samples of Lawmaking* (1970), esp. 71–3.

'interpret' these provisions on many occasions, deciding whether or not to insert a fault requirement. Not only do strict liability crimes account for over half of some 10,000 offences in English criminal law, but half of the offences serious enough to be tried in the Crown Court have a strict liability element too.[151] The courts' approach to interpretation has not been a model of consistency. In some cases they avoid the substantive issue by proceeding as if it were merely a linguistic matter. In others they make high statements of principle, which may raise hopes that a consistent framework is to be established. This is the present position, the House of Lords having recently handed down two decisions that extol the presumption of *mens rea* as a 'constitutional principle'.[152] In the past, any hopes of a more consistent judicial approach have usually been dashed, as the supposed principle is progressively whittled away or, more damningly, simply ignored. Consistency does not, of course, rule out the possibility of reasoned exceptions. But, as the following small selection from the enormous variety of offences (including many in the field of road traffic) shows, there is little evidence of consistency on any level.

One of the earliest statements of principle was that of Wright J in *Sherras* v *de Rutzen* (1895),[153] who stated that: 'there is a presumption that *mens rea* . . . is an essential ingredient in every offence; but that presumption is liable to be displaced either by the words of the statute creating the offence or by the subject-matter with which it deals, and both must be considered'. What 'subject-matter' displaces the presumption? One example given by Wright J was 'acts which are not criminal in any real sense', where the criminal penalty is attached to acts which are not regarded as morally wrong. This was a reference to offences involved in regulating the sale of tobacco, food, alcohol, and so forth. There were a number of judicial decisions in the 1960s which held persons liable for quite serious drug offences without proof of any fault, in the belief that public policy demanded this, but this trend was arrested in what is probably the leading case, *Sweet* v *Parsley* (1970).[154] The case involved a schoolteacher who was prosecuted for being concerned in the management of premises used for the purpose of smoking cannabis; she had rented her farmhouse to a group of students who, unbeknown to her, smoked cannabis there. The case went up to the House of Lords on the question whether any fault had to be proved. If one takes the language 'on its face', to refer back to the quotation from *Howells*,[155] it suggests liability without fault. The premises were used for smoking cannabis, and D was concerned in their management. But their Lordships were unanimous in holding that the statute should be construed in the light of the presumption that *mens rea* is required. They took the view that the courts had no power to impose negligence liability in such cases: the choice lay between *mens rea* and strict liability, and the presumption should be in favour of the former.

---

[151] Ashworth and Blake, 'The Presumption of Innocence'.

[152] *B* v *DPP* [2000] 2 AC 428 and *K* [2002] 1 AC 462, discussed on pp 172–4 below. The decisions were applied by the Court of Appeal in *Kumar* [2005] Crim LR 470.

[153] [1895] 1 QB 918.   [154] [1970] AC 132.   [155] See n 148 above.

This presumption did not fare well during the next decade. It was soon held to be displaced in another House of Lords case, *Alphacell Ltd v Woodward* (1972),[156] where a company was convicted of causing polluted matter to enter a stream. Three reasons played a part—the linguistic one, that the word 'cause' was thought to favour strict liability; that the low maximum penalty favoured dispensing with fault; and the assumption that pollution offences were not criminal in a real sense. The decision in *Howells*[157] is hard to reconcile with *Sweet v Parsley*, as is *Pharmaceutical Society of Great Britain v Storkwain Ltd* (1986),[158] where the House of Lords held that a person may be liable to conviction for selling drugs without a valid prescription, contrary to the Medicines Act 1968, without proof of fault. The decision was reached by analysing the statute, with scant reference to any presumption of *mens rea* and without giving weight to the fact that the offence carried a maximum sentence of two years' imprisonment.

(iii) A New Constitutional Principle? The new millennium brought an apparent change of direction. In *B v DPP* (2000)[159] the House of Lords had to decide whether, in the offence of indecency with a child under 14 contrary to the Indecency with Children Act 1960, there was strict liability as to the age of the child or the prosecution had to establish knowledge of the child's age. The House unanimously held that 'the common law presumes that, unless Parliament has indicated otherwise, the appropriate mental element is an unexpressed ingredient of every offence'.[160] Not only does this decision apply the presumption stated in *Sweet v Parsley* in preference to the older view that, in sexual offences, it is morally justifiable to impose strict liability as to age,[161] but Lord Steyn accepted the description of the presumption of *mens rea* as a 'constitutional principle' that is not easily displaced by a statutory text.[162] The same approach was taken by the House of Lords in *K* (2002),[163] where the charge was indecent assault on a girl under 16. The defence was that the girl had told D that she was 16. The question was whether this section of the Sexual Offences Act should continue to be regarded as imposing strict liability as to age, or whether the presumption of *mens rea* applied. Again, not only did the House of Lords find unanimously in favour of the presumption of *mens rea*, but both Lord Bingham and Lord Steyn described the presumption as a 'constitutional principle'.[164]

(iv) Exceptions to the Constitutional Principle? What does the term 'constitutional principle' mean? It is clearly intended as a principle of judicial interpretation. Whether

---

[156] [1972] AC 824; see also *Environment Agency v Empress Car Co* [1999] 2 AC 22, discussed in Ch 4.5(b) above.

[157] Above, n 148 and accompanying text.   [158] (1986) 83 Cr App R 359; cf. Jackson n 141 above.

[159] [2000] 2 AC 428.   [160] *Per* Lord Nicholls at 460.

[161] *Prince* (1875) LR 2 CCR 154; cf. R. Cross, 'Centenary Reflections on Prince's Case' (1975) 91 LQR 520 and J. Horder, 'How Culpability Can, and Cannot, Be Denied in Under-age Sex Crimes' [2001] Crim LR 15.

[162] *Per* Lord Steyn at 470, borrowing the expression from Sir Rupert Cross, *Statutory Interpretation* (3rd edn., 1995, by Bell and Engle), at 166.

[163] [2002] 1 AC 462.

[164] Lord Bingham at [17], Lord Steyn at [32]. Lord Bingham made similar remarks in the recklessness case of *G.* [2004] 1 AC 1034, discussed in 5.5(c) below.

it is a principle of which Parliament ought to take account is another matter: in the Sexual Offences Act 2003 it certainly did not, overruling the effect of both the House of Lords decisions.[165] Even for the judges, it is a principle and not a rule. Thus, for example, Lord Nicholls held in *B v DPP* that courts may rebut the presumption of *mens rea* by reference to 'the nature of the offence, the mischief sought to be prevented, and any other circumstances which may assist in determining what intent is properly to be attributed to Parliament when creating the offence'.[166] One might comment that if the presumption can be rebutted so easily it may prove to be worth little. It may be justifiable to rebut the presumption for minor offences which may be described as 'not criminal in any real sense', but the failure to regard the possibility of imprisonment as a crucial distinction is a major weakness.[167] A powerful example of this is *Gammon v Attorney-General for Hong Kong* (1985).[168] Following the collapse of a building, the defendants were charged with offences against the construction regulations which carried high fines and a maximum prison sentence of three years. Lord Scarman, giving the opinion of the Privy Council, reaffirmed the presumption of *mens rea* laid down in *Sweet v Parsley*, and added that 'the presumption is particularly strong where the offence is "truly criminal" in character'. He went on:

the only situation in which the presumption can be displaced is where the statute is concerned with an issue of social concern; public safety is such an issue.... Even where a statute is concerned with such an issue, the presumption of *mens rea* stands unless it can also be shown that the creation of strict liability will be effective to promote the objects of the statute by encouraging greater vigilance to prevent the commission of the prohibited act.

The last few words support the principle that strict liability should not be imposed where there is nothing more a defendant could reasonably be expected to do in order to avoid the harm.[169] This means that liability is tethered, however loosely, to the defendant's control; liability is not completely strict in these cases. However, the earlier part of the quotation demonstrates how muddy the waters still are. In some cases the courts say that strict liability is appropriate for minor offences which are not truly criminal.[170] Yet they also seem to hold, as in *Gammon*, that it is appropriate where offences relate to public safety or social concern—a description which (as pointed out earlier) could extend to large areas of the criminal law. That the *Gammon* decision was cited by the House of Lords in *B v DPP* without any attempt to confront this problem indicates a pessimistic outlook for the 'constitutional principle.'

In a search for principled exceptions, let us examine two areas of the law—firearms, and sexual offences—where the courts have taken a different view. The decision of

---

[165] See the discussion of sexual offences in Ch 8.5 below.   [166] [2000] 2 AC at 463–4.

[167] In addition to *Howells* and *Muhamad*, see also decisions such as *Storkwain* (above, n 158), *Gammon v Attorney-General for Hong Kong* [1985] AC 1 and *R v Wells Street Magistrates' Court and Martin, ex p Westminster City Council* [1986] Crim LR 695.

[168] [1985] AC 1 at 14.   [169] See *Lim Chin Aik v R* [1963] AC 160.

[170] For an example, see *Harrow LBC v Shah* [2000] 1 WLR 83 (selling lottery tickets to a person under 16: strict liability as to age approved so as to help enforcement).

the Court of Appeal in *Deyemi and Edwards* (2008)[171] is of particular importance, since the defence placed strong reliance on the 'constitutional principle' of *mens rea*. The defendants were found in possession of an article that they believed to be a large torch but which was in fact a stun-gun. They were convicted of possessing a prohibited weapon, contrary to section 5 of the Firearms Act 1968 and the judge, having examined the facts, gave them a conditional discharge. The Court of Appeal recognized the significance of the House of Lords decisions establishing the 'constitutional principle', but held that it was bound by a long line of authority (including *Howells*, above) to hold that this is a strict liability offence. The House of Lords decisions were each 'concerned with the proper meaning of the statutory provisions in question', held Latham LJ, a dismissal that confines their sphere of influence to statutory provisions that have not yet been the subject of an authoritative interpretation. On the substantive issue, presumably the argument is that strong reasons of public policy require the courts to impose strict liability in firearms cases, otherwise measures of control would be weakened. But the outcome here—conditional discharges for the two defendants—suggests that an acquittal in this kind of case would not weaken the law. The convictions were unfair, as the sentences indicate. The line of firearms cases which the Court applied ought to be overruled.

Turning to sexual offences, the decision of the House of Lords in *G.* (2008)[172] confirms that the offence of rape of a child under 13 in section 5 of the Sexual Offences Act 2003 imposes strict liability as to age. The House was unwilling to accept human rights arguments to the effect that this breaches the presumption of innocence in Article 6(2) and breaches the Article 8 rights of the accused (who was aged 15 only).[173] The majority view, expressed by Baroness Hale, was that strict liability is necessary here in order to ensure the protection of children from the sexual attentions of others. The implication is that allowing a defence of reasonable mistake (a negligence standard) would reduce that protection unacceptably; on this view, the unfairness and stigma of convicting a mistaken defendant of this serious offence is less important, even when that defendant is also below the age of consent (and could have been charged with a lesser offence). Both the empirical and the normative strands in that attempted justification call for close examination.

(v) Conclusion: Despite pronouncements of high authority on the existence of a 'constitutional principle' requiring fault, English law remains in an unsatisfactory state. The judgments in *B. v DPP* and in *K* refer to the possibility of rebutting the principle or presumption; there are decisions since 2000 that show how easy it is for a court to find a reason for rebutting the presumption;[174] and it seems that courts will follow precedents on the precise statute rather than resorting to the broader authorities on

---

[171] [2008] 1 Cr App R 25.   [172] [2008] UKHL 37.

[173] For fuller discussion of the decision, see Ch 8.6(a) below.

[174] E.g. *Muhamad* [2003] QB 1031 (offence of materially contributing to insolvency by gambling); *Matudi* [2003] EWCA Crim 697 (offence of importing products of animal origin, not citing either *B v DPP* or *K*).

the 'constitutional principle'.[175] So long as different statutes are promoted by different government departments without an overall grammar or standard, progress towards a consistent approach will be hampered. The first move should be for Parliament, probably prompted by the Law Commission, to establish a principled way of proceeding. If there are persuasive economic and social arguments in favour of strict liability for minor offences—and those arguments must be rigorously evaluated—then this may be permitted so long as imprisonment is not available. There should be recognition of the principle that no person should be liable to imprisonment without proof of sufficient fault.[176] This principle should inform the distinction between minor and non-minor offences. The classification of an offence as 'regulatory', whatever that may mean, should be irrelevant to the imposition of strict liability: if imprisonment is available as a sanction, then fault should be required whether it is called 'regulatory' or not. Similarly, the 'public safety' test stated in the *Gammon* case should be discarded, not least because it points in exactly the wrong direction by arguing in favour of strict liability for more serious offences.

(b) INTENTION

The term '*mens rea*' has conventionally been used to connote four fault requirements: intention or recklessness as to a specified consequence, and knowledge of, or recklessness as to, a specified circumstance. In discussing offences of strict liability, we have considered the main arguments in favour of requiring fault as a condition of criminal liability, chiefly arguments of choice and fair warning. Now we move to the more detailed and specific question of drawing distinctions between the four main forms of fault which generally fall under the umbrella of *mens rea*. The task is important, because of the key role of intention in serious crimes. Sometimes the intent is the essence of an offence, as in doing an act with intent to impede the apprehension of an offender, all crimes of attempt, and offences defined in terms of 'doing x with intent to do y' (such as burglary: entering as a trespasser with intent to steal).[177] Sometimes the law uses intention as the main method of grading offences: both the murder-manslaughter distinction and the dividing line between wounding under s 18 of the Offences against the Person Act 1861 (maximum penalty of life imprisonment) and wounding under section 20 (maximum penalty of five years' imprisonment) turn on the presence or absence of intention.

---

[175] As in *Deyemi and Edwards* (n 171 above). See also the speculation of Colin Manchester on how the Licensing Act 2003 will be interpreted, in 'Knowledge, Due Diligence and Strict Liability in Regulatory Offences' [2006] Crim LR 213.

[176] See further R. A. Duff, *Punishment, Communication and Community* (2001), 149–51.

[177] Burglary is discussed below, Ch 9.5. On intent-based crimes see generally A. Ashworth, 'Defining Criminal Offences without Harm', in P. F. Smith (ed.), *Criminal Law: Essays in Honour of J. C. Smith* (1987), and J. Horder, 'Crimes of Ulterior Intent', in A. P. Simester and A. T. H. Smith (eds.), *Harm and Culpability* (1996).

(i) *Intention in Principle*: It is quite possible—indeed, quite normal—to do things with more than one intention in mind. I can demolish a fence with the simultaneous intentions of making way for a new fence, providing wood for the fire, pleasing my partner (who has repeatedly asked me to demolish the fence), and so on. The approach of the criminal law, however, is generally not to ask with what intentions D committed the act, but to ask whether one particular intention was present when the act was committed. The law, generally speaking, is interested in the presence or absence of one particular intention—that specified in the definition of the offence charged—and not in conducting a general review of D's reasons for the behaviour in question. Did D intend to kill the crew of the aircraft on which he placed a bomb, as well as intending (as he admits) to claim the insurance money on the cargo? Did D intend to assist the enemy by his actions, as well as intending (as he admits) to save his family from a concentration camp?[178]

The law's approach in selecting one intention, and then abstracting it from D's other reasons and beliefs at the time, calls for careful consideration. It is essential to keep in mind the particular intent required by the definition of the offence. It is quite possible to say 'D pulled the trigger of the gun intentionally', without implying that D intended to kill V when he pulled the trigger. The offence of murder turns (broadly)[179] on the presence or absence of an intention to kill; whether the trigger was pulled intentionally or accidentally may be an important part of the case, but the legally required intention is that D *intended to kill* V. Loose references to whether D 'acted intentionally' can blur this distinction: it is unhelpful to refer to intention without relating it to a particular object or consequence, which in a legal context means the intent specified in the indictment or information.[180]

This approach to intention may avoid some philosophical errors, but the proper definition of intention remains the subject of theoretical debate and judicial disagreement. The core of 'intention' is surely aim, objective, or purpose; whatever else 'intention' may mean, a person surely acts with intention to kill if killing is the aim, objective, or purpose of the conduct that causes death. When drafting, however, it may be best to avoid the term 'purpose' (which may give rise to confusion with D's ultimate purpose in doing the act), and instead to define intention in terms of 'acting in order to bring about' the result.[181] Similarly in *Mohan* (1976)[182] James LJ defined intention as 'a decision to bring about [the proscribed result], in so far as it lies within the accused's power, no matter whether the accused desired that consequence of his act or not'. This definition has the advantage of stating that desire is not essential to intention (one may act out of feelings of duty, for example, rather than desire); it has the disadvantage of referring to a 'decision', whereas in many offences of violence and other crimes the

---

[178] See the discussion of *Steane* below, n 198 and accompanying text.   [179] See below, Ch 7.3(c).

[180] For further study see R. A. Duff, *Intention, Agency and Criminal Liability* (1990), chs 3, 4, and 6, critically discussed on this point by A. P. Simester, 'Paradigm Intention' (1992) 11 Law and Philosophy 235.

[181] LCCP 177, *A New Homicide Act?*, paras. 4.36–37, adopting the argument of A. Khan, 'Intention in Criminal Law: Time to Change?' (2002) 23 Statute LR 235.

[182] [1976] QB 1.

events happen so suddenly and rapidly that a fleeting realization of what one is doing may be the most that time allows. In law this fleeting realization is enough for intention, rendering the term far less concrete than is sometimes assumed.[183]

The *Mohan* case involved an attempted crime, and intention is thought to be crucial to attempts, because one cannot be said to *attempt* to produce a result unless one *intends* to produce it (see below, Chapter 11.3(a)). The decision in *Mohan* goes some way towards stating the core of the concept of intention, i.e. acting in order to bring about a result. One intends consequences that one chooses to produce: thus the death of another person is intended if it is chosen as an end in itself, or as a means to an end.[184] This reference to choosing something as a means to an end is important, because otherwise D could always avoid liability by pointing to some ulterior motive for the action: 'it was not my purpose to kill V, because my real purpose in shooting at V was to inherit V's money after V's death'. Such a purported detachment of the means from the end is quite unconvincing. Both are part of the intention with which D fired the shot, and the criminal law is interested only in whether the killing was intentional.

Should the concept of intention be more extensive than that, in the context of criminal liability? Lawyers have tended to assume that intention includes not only acting in order to bring about *x* but also acting with foresight of certainty that *x* will result—that D can be said to have intended a result if he or she realized that the result was certain to follow from the behaviour in question. An early example of this may be found in Bentham's writings, and his distinction between direct and oblique intention is one way of expressing the point.[185] One might say that a consequence is *directly* intended if D acts in order to produce it, and that it is *obliquely* intended if it is not D's aim but is known to be certain.[186] To regard both these mental attitudes as forms of intention is to make a moral point. It is not necessarily being claimed that ordinary people in their everyday language use the term 'intention' in this way.[187] The claim is that the person who foresees a consequence as certain should be classified as having intended that result rather than as having been merely reckless towards it—and the claim is being made in the knowledge that some killings would thus be classified as murder rather than manslaughter, some woundings described as 'with intent' rather than merely as unlawful, and so on. As soon as the argument moves from the moral to the legal, such questions of classification arise. What has to be established is not that all cases of foresight of certainty are socially or morally as bad as all cases of purpose, but that it is more appropriate to classify them with 'intention' than with 'recklessness'.

[183] R. Cross, 'The Mental Element in Crime' (1967) 83 LQR 215.

[184] Compare J. Finnis, 'Intention and Side-Effects', in R. G. Frey and C. W. Morris, *Liability and Responsibility* (1991), 32, with A. P. Simester, 'Why Distinguish Intention from Foresight?', in Simester and Smith (eds.), *Harm and Culpability* (1996).

[185] Bentham, *Introduction to the Principles of Morals and Legislation*, ch VIII, on direct and oblique intent. Bentham's definition of oblique intent was wider than that described here, a point discussed by Glanville Williams, 'Oblique Intent' (1987) 46 Camb LJ 417.

[186] Ibid.   [187] See the discussion of 'ordinary language' below, p. 175.

If we pursue the moral part of the argument further, we find that the shorthand phrase 'foresight of certainty' is perhaps too brief in this context. Few future events in life are absolutely certain, and a reference to consequences as 'certain to follow' would generally mean 'practically certain to follow' or 'certain, barring some unforeseen intervention'.[188] A familiar example is D, who places a bomb on an aircraft with the aim of blowing it up in mid-flight in order to claim the insurance money on the cargo. D knows that it is practically certain that the crew of the aircraft will be killed as a result of the explosion. One might say that D's *purpose* is to claim the insurance money, but if the charge is murder, that is irrelevant. The key question is whether D intended *to kill*. Let us assume that D did not act in order to kill, i.e. that he had not chosen the death of the air-crew as the means to his end. Should the law extend the definition beyond direct intent to cover D's awareness of the practical certainty that the crew would be killed? The argument in favour of this is that D's behaviour shows no respect for the value of human life at all: D knows that the crew will die, and yet he still pursues the aim of blowing up the aircraft. There is little social or moral difference between that and planning the explosion in order to kill the crew. It is sometimes thought that the 'test of failure' argues against this:[189] since D would not regard the explosion as a failure if the cargo were destroyed but the crew were not killed, this serves to differentiate him from someone whose purpose is to kill. But to establish that a philosophical distinction exists between D and the purposeful killer is not to conclude the matter: to transfer the argument from morality to law, it has to be decided whether the person who foresees death as virtually certain should be bracketed with the directly intentional killer (murder) or treated as merely reckless (manslaughter).[190] Recklessness, as we shall see below, includes the taking of relatively small risks. There is a strong argument that someone who takes a risk of death that amounts to a virtual certainty comes very close to the person who chooses someone's death as the means to an end. They both show no respect at all for human life. The Law Commission accepts this, preferring a definition that includes not only the person who acts in order to bring about the prohibited consequence but also the person who 'thought that the result was a virtually certain consequence of his or her action'.[191]

(ii) *Intention in the Courts*: At present there is no legislative definition of intention. How have the courts approached the question? The leading decisions concern the crime of murder, to be discussed in a later chapter,[192] but their effect can be summarized here. The first of the leading cases is *Moloney* (1985),[193] in which the House of Lords held that judges should generally avoid defining the term 'intention', beyond explaining that it differs from 'desire' and 'motive'. Only in exceptional cases should the judge depart from this golden rule, notably, where the essence of the defence is that D's purpose was only to frighten, not to harm, the victim. Here the jury should

---

[188] The phrase of Lord Lane CJ, in *Nedrick* (1986) 83 Cr App R 267.

[189] Duff, *Intention, Agency and Criminal Liability*, ch 3.

[190] For extensive discussion, see I. Kugler, *Direct and Oblique Intention in the Criminal Law* (2002).

[191] Law Com No 304, *Murder, Manslaughter and Infanticide* (2007), para 3.27.

[192] Ch 7.3(c).   [193] [1985] AC 905.

be instructed to decide whether D foresaw the prohibited consequence as 'a natural consequence' of the behaviour: if the answer was yes, they could infer intention from that. In the course of his speech Lord Bridge gave hints of the sort of cases he meant to include—cases where the consequence was a 'little short of overwhelming', or 'virtually certain'—but unfortunately the centrepiece of his speech was the term 'natural consequence'. When this was used by the judge to direct the jury in *Hancock and Shankland* (1986),[194] it was held to be unsatisfactory. The House of Lords overruled its own test of 'natural consequence', and Lord Scarman stated that juries should be told that 'the greater the probability of a consequence the more likely it is that the consequence was foreseen, and that if that consequence was foreseen the greater the probability is that that consequence was also intended'.

These decisions left unclear the precise legal meaning of intention and the proper approach to directing a jury, and Lord Lane CJ attempted to synthesize the House of Lords decisions when presiding in the Court of Appeal in *Nedrick* (1986):[195]

Where the charge is murder and in the rare cases where the simple direction is not enough, the jury should be directed that they are not entitled to infer the necessary intention, unless they feel sure that death or serious bodily harm was a virtual certainty (barring some unforeseen intervention) as a result of the defendant's actions and that the defendant realized that such was the case.

This direction now has the authority of the House of Lords. In *Woollin* (1999)[196] the House disapproved a direction in terms of whether D had realized that there was a 'substantial risk' of serious injury, and held that the *Nedrick* formulation should be followed—with one modification. Where *Nedrick* states that if D foresaw the relevant consequence as virtually certain the court is 'entitled to infer' intention, *Woollin* states that the court is 'entitled to find' intention.[197] This change has little practical significance, and it leaves open the possibility that, if courts are 'entitled' but not required to find intention in these cases, then there may occasionally be cases where they may lawfully decide not to find intention despite foresight of virtual certainty.

In English law, therefore, intention is not defined in terms of (a) acting in order to bring about a result or (b) acting in the knowledge that the result is virtually certain to follow. The indirect or oblique element, (b), is said to be something on the basis of which intention can be found, and not a species of intention. The reluctance of the judiciary to commit themselves to a particular definition of intention confirms that they see the need to preserve an element of flexibility so that they can continue to allow occasional divergences from the 'standard' (a) or (b) definition. Appellate decisions over the years reveal a variety of departures from what might be termed the 'standard definition' of intention. Thus in *Steane* (1947)[198] the Court of Criminal Appeal quashed D's conviction under wartime regulations for the offence of doing acts likely to assist

---

[194] [1986] AC 455.   [195] (1986) 83 Cr App R 267.   [196] [1999] AC 82.

[197] Applied by the Court of Appeal in *Matthews and Alleyne* [2003] 2 Cr App R 30, although Rix LJ commented that 'there is very little to choose between a rule of evidence and one of substantive law'.

[198] [1947] KB 997.

the enemy, with intent to assist the enemy. The Court held that if D's acts were as consistent with an innocent intent (such as saving his family from a concentration camp) as with a criminal intent, the jury should be left to decide the matter. This diverges from the standard definition, since it was never discussed whether D knew that it was virtually certain his acts would assist the enemy. The Court could probably have used the defence of duress to quash the conviction, but it evidently thought that adopting a narrow definition of intention provided a simpler route to the desired result. Similarly, in the civil case of *Gillick* v *West Norfolk and Wisbech Area Health Authority* (1986)[199] the House of Lords held that a doctor who gives contraceptive advice to a girl under 16 for clinical reasons, whilst realizing that this would facilitate sexual activity, is not guilty of aiding and abetting the offence of sexual activity with a child. The decision might well have been placed on some such ground as 'clinical necessity',[200] but instead Lord Scarman explained that 'the bona fide exercise by a doctor of his clinical judgement must be a complete negation of the guilty mind'. With this sweeping statement it was held that the doctor did not have the intention required for aiding and abetting, even though it may be assumed that prescribing the contraceptives was foreseen as virtually certain to assist the commission of an offence.

To set alongside these two decisions which favour a narrow definition of intention it is not difficult to find decisions pointing in a different direction. In *Smith* (1960)[201] D had offered a bribe to an official, solely in order to demonstrate that the official was corrupt. The Court of Criminal Appeal upheld his conviction for corruptly offering an inducement to an official, holding that D had an intention to corrupt so long as he intended the offer to operate on the mind of the offeree. In this case D's law-abiding motivation was held to count for nothing. Similarly in *Chandler* v *DPP* (1964),[202] the defendants' convictions of acting 'for a purpose prejudicial to the safety or interests of the State' were upheld by the House of Lords. They had infiltrated a military airfield, and this was regarded as prejudicial to the State's interests. The defendants' argument that their own purpose was to promote the safety and interests of the State (by promoting peace), rather than to prejudice them, was discounted.

What these decisions demonstrate is that the courts do not adhere to a single definition of intention. Various observations may be made about this. One common reaction is to treat it as evidence for a 'realist' interpretation of how courts behave: they decide on the desired result, and then define the law in whatever way happens to achieve it. But the evidence is limited to a small number of appeal court decisions, and may not reflect the everyday operation of the criminal courts. Even if it were true to some degree (and few suggest that the courts have an absolute freedom in these matters), what is it that leads courts to adopt these reasons for reaching these particular results? Judges in the appellate courts are fond of referring to 'ordinary language' as a justification for their decisions, but this often appears to be a camouflage

---

[199] [1986] AC 112.   [200] See the discussion in Ch 4.8(b) above.
[201] [1960] 2 QB 423; see also *Yip Chiu-Cheung* [1995] 1 AC 111, discussed in Ch 11.5 below.
[202] [1964] AC 763.

for moral judgements. Critical writers have made much of the tensions revealed by the varied judicial approach. Thus Nicola Lacey scrutinizes the shifting language of the appellate judges and argues that this reflects their attempt to keep the law fairly close to popular conceptions (and thereby to enhance its legitimacy) whilst trying to ensure that the interests of the powerful are not significantly challenged.[203] Alan Norrie, focusing on the way in which courts sometimes regard the defendant's motive as a reason for concluding that the result was not 'intended' (*Steane, Gillick*) and sometimes do not (*Smith, Chandler*), argues that contemporary criminal law is trapped by a set of concepts stemming from a desire to separate 'legal judgment from substantive moral issues', which means that in difficult cases the courts find themselves 'excluding and re-admitting substantive moral issues into a technically conceived set of fault categories'.[204] Thus a model direction stating that, where a court is satisfied that D foresaw a result as virtually certain, it is 'entitled to find' that D intended the result, may operate so as to allow the courts to expand and contract the definition so as to reflect other factors, including moral judgements of a defendant's background and situation.

(iii) *Intention Concluded*: In delivering the unanimous judgment of the House of Lords in *Woollin*, Lord Steyn observed that the appeal concerned the crime of murder and that 'it does not follow that "intent" necessarily has the same meaning in every context in the criminal law'.[205] However, the variable approaches to intention described in the previous paragraphs have not been explained by judges on an offence-specific basis, and there would surely need to be particular arguments in favour of adopting a different definition for a certain crime or class of crimes. The *Woollin* definition may therefore be treated as established, and yet we have seen that the House of Lords left the door ajar: the phrase 'entitled to find' preserves an element of 'moral elbow-room' which many judges believe to be essential to doing justice. The Law Commission accepts this view: in recommending that 'an intention to bring about a result may be found if it is shown that the defendant thought that the result was a virtually certain consequence of his or her actions,'[206] the Commission argues that this element of flexibility is 'the price of avoiding the complexity' needed if a comprehensive definition were attempted, and that broad terms such as 'extreme indifference' would create greater uncertainty. The reason judges adopted variable meanings of intention in the decisions discussed above is largely that the standard definition, in combination with the range of available defences to liability, sometimes fails to capture moral distinctions which are thought important. The term 'intent'—sometimes the determinant of liability, sometimes a primary way of grading offences—is not one that necessarily incorporates elements of moral evaluation, unlike the other *mens rea* term 'reckless' (discussed below).[207] Thus when faced with a strong moral pull towards exculpation the courts have sometimes, as in *Steane* and in *Gillick*, manipulated the

---

[203] N. Lacey, 'A Clear Concept of Intention: Elusive or Illusory?' (1993) 56 MLR 621.

[204] A. Norrie, *Crime, Reason and History* (2nd edn., 2001), 58.

[205] [1999] AC 82, at 90; see the observations of V. Tadros, 'The System of the Criminal Law' (2002) 22 LS 448, at 451–5.

[206] Law Com No. 304, para 3.27; see generally paras 3.18–3.26.   [207] See p. 178.

concept of intention rather than developing a defence to criminal liability. However, it would surely be better to adopt a tighter definition of intention, excluding the permissive words 'may be found' in the Law Commission's recommended definition, and to place greater emphasis on appropriate defences. Under the criminal code the courts would have a power to develop new defences,[208] so as to ensure that what they regard as important moral distinctions are marked appropriately.

(c) RECKLESSNESS

Much of the preceding discussion about the proper limits of the concept of intention in the criminal law has inevitably concerned the dividing line between recklessness and intention. The argument was that there are some cases in which D knows the risk of the prohibited consequence to be so very high (i.e. practically certain) that it is more appropriate to classify his mental attitude within the highest category of culpability (intention) rather than in the lesser category of recklessness. We may note that some would draw the dividing line lower, arguing that if D foresaw the prohibited consequence as a *probable* result, this should be classified as intention, leaving only the lesser degrees of risk within the category of recklessness.[209] We will now move away from these arguments, but they do remind us that debates about the boundaries of intention relate to the grading of culpability and so of offences. The same is true of the lower boundary between recklessness and negligence: when criminal lawyers refer to offences as requiring '*mens rea*', they usually mean that either intention or recklessness will suffice for liability but that negligence will not. Thus, once again, the debate concerns not so much language as the limits of criminal liability.

An abiding difficulty in discussing the legal meaning of recklessness is that the term has been given several different shades of meaning by the courts over the years. In the law of manslaughter, 'reckless' has often been regarded as the most appropriate adjective to express the degree of negligence ('gross') needed for a conviction:[210] in this sense, it means a high degree of carelessness. In the late 1950s the courts adopted a different meaning of recklessness in the context of *mens rea*, referring to D's actual awareness of the risk of the prohibited consequence occurring:[211] we shall call this 'advertent recklessness'. Controversy was introduced into this area in the early 1980s, when the House of Lords purported to broaden the meaning of recklessness so as to include those who failed to give thought to an obvious risk that the consequence would

---

[208] Expressly preserved by cll. 4(4) and 45(4) of the draft Criminal Code. See now *Re A (Conjoined Twins: Surgical Separation)* [2000] 4 All ER 961, discussed below, Ch 7.2; and more generally, A. Ashworth, 'Criminal Liability in a Medical Context: the Treatment of Good Intentions', in Simester and Smith (eds.), *Harm and Culpability* (1996).

[209] This was one of the views expressed in *Hyam* v *DPP* [1975] AC 55, by Lord Diplock (not dissenting on this point); see J. Buzzard, 'Intent' [1978] Crim LR 5, with reply by J. C. Smith at [1978] Crim LR 14.

[210] See *Andrews* v *DPP* [1937] AC 576 and *Adomako* [1995] 1 AC 171, discussed below in Ch 7.5.

[211] *Cunningham* [1957] 2 QB 396, adopting the definition offered by C. S. Kenny, *Outlines of Criminal Law* (1st edn., 1902; 16th edn., 1952).

occur:[212] as we shall see in paragraph (ii) below, the House of Lords has now reversed itself on this point.[213] The law of manslaughter will be left for discussion later:[214] here we will focus on the other meanings of recklessness.[215]

(i) *Advertent Recklessness*: It was in *Cunningham* (1957) that the Court of Criminal Appeal held that, in a statute, the term 'malicious' denotes intention or recklessness, and that recklessness means that 'the accused has foreseen that the particular kind of harm might be done and yet has gone on to take the risk of it'.[216] There are essentially three elements in this definition, and they are the same ones found in the Model Penal Code's definition of recklessness as 'the conscious taking of an unjustified risk'. First, it requires D's actual awareness of the risk;[217] this is why it is referred to as 'advertent recklessness', and it is regarded as the key element in bringing recklessness within the concept of *mens rea*. A person should be held to have been reckless about a particular result only if the court is satisfied that he or she was aware of the risk at the time. The second element is that a person may be held to have been reckless if he or she was aware of *any degree* of risk: we have seen that when the risk is so high as to be a practical certainty, D may be classed as intending the consequence, but any risk, however slight, may be sufficient as a minimum for recklessness, so long as D is aware of it and it materializes. In its recommendations for reform of the law of homicide, the Law Commission proposes a narrower definition of recklessness—that D must be aware of a 'serious risk', i.e. one that is 'more than insignificant or remote.'[218] It is not clear whether this would alter the outcome of many cases, but it is right that an offence such as murder should be more tightly defined. The third element is that the risk which D believes to be present must be an unjustified or unreasonable one. This is an objective element: courts have rarely discussed it, but it exerts a significant background influence. A typical example of the objective element is the surgeon who carries out an operation knowing that death will probably result.[219] Thus 'the responsibility line is drawn according to an evaluation of the nature of the activity and the degree of the risk'.[220] This evaluative task has rarely been performed by the courts but, as Alan Norrie rightly points out, this is because prosecutors have often made their own evaluations at an early stage and no prosecution (or at least no prosecution for a serious offence such as manslaughter) has been brought in most such cases.[221] Thus we have scant judicial authority relating to the objective element in recklessness.

---

[212] *Caldwell* [1982] AC 341, and *Lawrence* [1982] AC 510.   [213] In *G.* [2004] 1 AC 1034.

[214] Ch 7.5(b).

[215] A further meaning of recklessness was adopted in sex cases (see *Kimber* [1983] 1 WLR 1118, *Satnam S and Kewal S* (1984) 78 Cr App R 149), but the enactment of the Sexual Offences Act 2003 relegates this to a matter of historical interest only.

[216] See above, n 211.   [217] Model Penal Code, s. 2.02(s)(c).

[218] Law Com No 304, paras 3.36–3.40, relating to first degree murder and to reckless murder (second degree); for further discussion, see Ch 7.3(c) below.

[219] Criminal Law Revision Committee, 14th Report, *Offences against the Person* (1980), 8.

[220] D. J. Galligan, 'Responsibility for Recklessness' (1978) 31 CLP 55, at 70.

[221] Norrie, *Crime, Reason and History*, 78–80. For example, prosecutions for offences of recklessness have been unusual in respect of large-scale transportation disasters.

The justifications for the advertent definition of recklessness are grounded in the principle of individual autonomy and the importance of respecting choice, outlined above.[222] The distinction between recklessness and negligence turns on D's awareness or unawareness of the risk. In both cases there is an unreasonable risk taken, but D should only be held to have been reckless if he or she was aware of the risk. A person who is aware of the risk usually chooses to create it or to run it, and therefore chooses to place his or her interests above the well-being of those who may suffer if the risk materializes. Choosing to create a risk of harmful consequences is generally much worse than creating the same risk without realizing it. Moreover, holding a person reckless despite unawareness of the risk would result in a conviction in a case like *Stephenson* (1979).[223] D, a schizophrenic, made a hollow in a haystack in order to sleep there; he felt cold, and so lit a small fire, causing the whole haystack to go up in flames, and resulting in damage of some £3,500. The defence relied on medical evidence that D may not have had the same ability to foresee the risk as a mentally normal person. The Court of Appeal, quashing D's conviction, held that the definition of reckless-ness clearly turned on what this defendant actually foresaw, and the medical evidence should have been taken into account on this point. This decision, then, strongly affirms the element of individual fairness in the advertent or subjective definition. An entirely objective test would exclude this.

Does concentration on the element of awareness always produce decisions in accord with fairness? There are at least two types of awkward case for a test of liability which requires the court to be satisfied that the defendant actually saw the risk, however briefly. One is where a person acts impulsively in the heat of the moment. This is often expressed in ordinary speech by saying 'I acted without thinking', or 'I just didn't think'. D denies that he or she was aware of the risk at the time of acting. In *Parker* (1977)[224] D tried unsuccessfully to make a telephone call from a payphone; in his frustration he slammed down the receiver and broke it. The Court of Appeal upheld his conviction for causing criminal damage recklessly, despite his defence that it did not occur to him that he might damage the telephone. The Court held that he must have known that he was dealing with breakable material, even if that fact was not at the forefront of his mind when he slammed the receiver down. He had 'closed his mind to the obvious', or suppressed this knowledge at the time of the act.[225] It is quite evident that this decision involves some stretching of the awareness element which is thought to be central to advertent recklessness. In effect, it broadens the time-frame from the moment of the act itself to an earlier and calmer time, when D would almost certainly have answered the question: 'What might happen if you slammed down a telephone receiver?', by saying: 'It might break'. The reason for thus broadening the time-frame is presumably to prevent bad temper resulting in an acquittal, since this would be

---

[222] See above, section 5.4(a).   [223] [1979] QB 695.   [224] [1977] 1 WLR 600.

[225] See the discussion by Geoffrey Lane LJ in *Stephenson* [1979] QB 695, and M. Wasik and M. P. Thompson, 'Turning a Blind Eye as Constituting Mens Rea' (1981) 32 NILQ 328, at 339. In *Booth v CPS* (2006) 170 JP 305 the Divisional Court upheld a finding of recklessness on the basis that D had 'closed his mind' to the obvious.

socially undesirable: people should control their tempers. But it does sully the subjective purity of this definition of recklessness.

The second problem is the 'couldn't care less' attitude: D might not have thought
about a particular consequence, because it was irrelevant to his interests. If this version of events is accepted, D must be acquitted on the advertent definition of recklessness. Antony Duff has argued that these cases can and should be included within
the meaning of recklessness, by invoking the concept of 'practical indifference'. This
is 'a matter, not of feeling as distinct from action, but of the practical attitude which
the action itself displays'. Moreover, it may include cases in which D fails to advert to
certain aspects of the situation: 'what I notice or attend to reflects what I care about;
and my very failure to notice something can display my utter indifference to it'.[226] The
argument is that people who are practically indifferent to certain key features of a
situation may be just as much to blame as those who do advert to them. This argument
was put strongly in relation to the pre-2003 law of rape, contending that judgements of
practical indifference should be made on the basis that men *ought* to consider the victim's interests in such cases. Defensible as that approach is,[227] the question is whether
it is subjective, since it brings within the concept of recklessness some defendants
who do not actually advert to these matters. Duff's response is that requiring practical indifference is just as subjective, and just as respectful of individual autonomy,
as requiring awareness of risk. The practical indifference test looks to D's attitude at
the time, on the basis of his acts and words. In practice, it is likely that juries applying
the test of advertent recklessness would convict such defendants on the basis that they
must have realized the risk; but that merely suggests that it may be unnecessary to confront Duff's point, not that it is wrong.

Thus there are at least two types of situation in which the 'awareness' requirement,
the centrepiece of advertent recklessness, is problematic (on some views) and may fail
to yield an acceptable grading of blameworthiness. One is the person who acts impulsively or in a temper, 'without thinking'. The other is the person who fails to think
about the consequences out of indifference to them. A third possibility would be where
D states that he was so preoccupied with other aspects of what he was doing as to give
no thought to a particular consequence (although the courts might be reluctant to
accept such a defence).[228]

(ii) *Caldwell Recklessness*: in *Caldwell* (1982)[229] the House of Lords introduced a
new objective definition of recklessness that, incidentally, would encompass the three
types of situation with which the traditional definition does not deal convincingly.
It was heavily criticized, and for all practical purposes the subsequent decision in G.
(2004)[230] overrules it. Nonetheless, a brief discussion is appropriate here, in order to

---

[226] Duff, *Intention, Agency and Criminal Liability*, 162–3.

[227] The Sexual Offences Act 2003 alters the definition of rape in this direction: by introducing a reasonableness test of belief in consent, it ensures that practically indifferent defendants should be convicted. See
Ch 8.5 below.

[228] See G. Williams, 'The Unresolved Problem of Recklessness' (1988) 8 Legal Studies 74, at 82.

[229] [1982] AC 341. The case of *Lawrence* (n 140) was decided on the same day.

[230] [2004] 1 AC 1034.

identify some of the issues of principle raised by the *Caldwell* decision and 28 years of applying it (mostly in criminal damage cases, since it was never accepted throughout the criminal law).[231] In *Caldwell*, Lord Diplock formulated the following model direction: a person is guilty of causing damage recklessly if:

(i) he does an act which in fact creates an obvious risk that property would be destroyed or damaged and (ii) when he does the act he either has not given any thought to the possibility of there being any such risk or has recognized that there was some risk involved and has nonetheless gone on to do it.

It will be noticed that this definition includes the advertent element (by referring to the person who recognizes the risk and takes it), but then goes further, extending to all those who fail to give any thought to the possibility of a risk which may be described as obvious. The formulation in the reckless driving case of *Lawrence* goes a little further by requiring proof that the risk was 'obvious and serious', the latter term implying that the ordinary prudent person would not have considered the risk negligible.[232] Lord Diplock's primary justification for thus expanding the definition of recklessness was that it may be no less blameworthy for a person to fail to foresee an obvious risk than it is to see the risk and knowingly to take it. In other words, Lord Diplock challenged the common law distinction between recklessness and negligence on the ground that it fails to draw the line in the right place. It will be observed that Lord Diplock did not appear to be altering the balance between individual responsibility and social protection. He did not argue that the definition of recklessness should be widened because a person who fails to give thought to an obvious risk is just as *dangerous* as the person who realized the risk. Rather, he attacked fundamental conceptions of responsibility by arguing that the idea of *mens rea*, as encompassing intention and subjective recklessness, is unsatisfactory because it omits some equally culpable cases.[233] As we have seen, some of the supporters of advertent recklessness accept that it is underinclusive, in that they have attempted to stretch it to include actions during fits of temper and actions out of indifference.

A major problem with Lord Diplock's test of what would have been obvious to the reasonable person was that it admitted of no exceptions. The effect was to convict young children and mentally impaired defendants by applying to them an objective standard of foreseeability that they could not meet.[234] Thus, even if the *Caldwell* test were to be regarded as an improvement because it extended to thoughtless and inconsiderate wrongdoers, the absence of a capacity exception produced unfair convictions in some cases. The case of *G*.[235] involved two children aged 11 and 12 who set fire to

---

[231] For a fuller discussion, see the 4th edition of this work, 183–7.

[232] [1982] AC 510 at 527, reiterated in the reckless driving case of *Reid* (1992) 95 Cr App R 391.

[233] Lord Goff in *Reid* (1992) 95 Cr App R at 405–6 took the same view, arguing that unawareness of risk stemming from drink, rage, an attitude of indifference, or wilful blindness ought to be regarded as culpable and as reckless.

[234] See e.g. *Elliott v C.* (1983) 77 Cr App R 103 (mentally handicapped girl of 14), *Stephenson* [1979] QB 695 (man with schizophrenia).

[235] [2004] 1 AC 1034.

some newspapers beneath a rubbish bin and then left, after which the fire spread and caused major damage to nearby shops. The House of Lords considered whether to preserve the *Caldwell* test and engraft a capacity exception on it so as to exempt those (such as children and the mentally disordered) who might be incapable of attaining the objective standard; but this solution was rejected on the ground that the *Caldwell* test was already complicated and that this would over-complicate it to the extent of risking confusion among juries and magistrates.[236] The leading speech by Lord Bingham accepts the substance of the criticisms of *Caldwell*—the lack of legal foundation for the decision, the unfairness of its effects in some cases—and marks a reversion to the traditional, more subjective definition of recklessness based on the defendant's awareness of the risk. This closes one of the common law's less distinguished chapters,[237] and more or less returns the criminal law to a single definition of recklessness. But it does not advance the debate about the types of case that strictly fall outside that traditional definition of recklessness—the indifferent D who appears not to have thought of the risk at all, and D who acts in sudden rage or temper and claims not to have realized the risk of harm.[238]

(d) KNOWLEDGE AND BELIEF

In general terms, the requirement of knowledge is regarded as having the same intensity as that of intention, except that knowledge relates to circumstances forming part of the definition of the crime, and intention relates to the consequences specified in the definition of the crime. This is probably acceptable as a dividing line, even though the distinction between circumstances and consequences is not without difficulty when applied to the definitions of some offences.[239] Requirements of knowledge, belief, and variations on these terms are widespread in the criminal law:[240] for example, the Licensing Act 2003 created several offences of 'knowingly' allowing a licensable activity to be carried on without authorization (section 136), knowingly selling alcohol to a person who is drunk (section 141), and so forth.[241]

---

[236] *Per* Lord Bingham at para. 38. For substantive argument, see V. Tadros, 'Recklessness and the Duty to Take Care', in S. Shute and A. P. Simester (eds.), *Criminal Law Theory: Doctrines for the General Part* (2002), at 255–7.

[237] For the detailed history of the rise and fall of *Caldwell* recklessness, and suggestions for further development, see A. Halpin, *Definition in the Criminal Law* (2004), ch 3.

[238] On this point one may compare German criminal law, which also adopts this broader form of recklessness with a capacity exception—the question being whether D would or should have foreseen the risk, given his intellectual capacities and knowledge at the time. See J. R. Spencer and A. Pedain, 'Strict Liability in Continental Criminal Law', in A. P. Simester (ed), *Appraising Strict Liability* (2005), 241.

[239] See the instructive study by S. Shute, 'Knowledge and Belief in the Criminal Law', in Shute and Simester (eds.), *Criminal Law Theory*, esp. at 172–8.

[240] For discussion of the potential problems see G. Williams, 'The Problem of Reckless Attempts' [1983] Crim LR 365, R. J. Buxton, 'Circumstances, Consequences and Attempted Rape' [1984] Crim LR 25, and R. A. Duff, 'The Circumstances of an Attempt' (1991) 50 Camb LJ 100. The issue is discussed in Ch 11.3 below.

[241] See C. Manchester, 'Knowledge, Due Diligence and Strict Liability in Licensing Offences'.

It is instructive to approach the question by means of the basic definition of the offence of criminal damage—damaging property belonging to another with intent to damage property belonging to another: Criminal Damage Act 1971, s 1(1).[242] One can argue that the only fault element required here is intention—does D intend to damage property belonging to another? But it is also possible to divide the fault element into two: Does D intend to damage property? Does D know that the property belongs to another? The knowledge relates to a fact or circumstance: although it will usually be relevant to D's reasons for acting, one can separate it analytically from the result which D intends. Such an analysis is essential for those crimes which require no result or conduct, such as possessing a controlled drug, where knowledge becomes the key element in the crime.[243] The matter is absolutely clear in the many offences which include the term 'knowingly' in their definition, such as being knowingly concerned in the importation of prohibited goods into the country.[244] There are also some offences in which the requirement is extended slightly, such as handling stolen goods knowing or believing them to be stolen, where the reference to 'believing' is taken to include people who may not *know* that the goods are stolen but may have no substantial doubt that they are.[245]

It is at this point, however, that a significant difference opens up between intention and knowledge as fault requirements. One can intend a result, whether or not it actually occurs: D can intend to kill by, say, shooting at V; if D's shot missed, then D still intended to kill and may be convicted of attempted murder. If the intention fails to come to fruition, it is none the less an intention. But this does not apply to knowledge. If we return to the basic offence of criminal damage as described above, we can consider the facts of *Smith (D R)* (1974):[246] D was renting a flat, and during the course of his tenancy he fixed some panelling to the walls to conceal the wires of his stereo equipment. When his tenancy ceased, he took down and destroyed the panelling—which he had put up for his own convenience. He was charged with criminal damage, on the basis that, in law, the panelling became the property of the landlord once it was fixed to the walls. The Court of Appeal quashed his conviction for criminal damage, pointing out that although he did intend to damage property, he believed that the property was his own, and therefore he lacked the fault element for the crime. If D had been asked whether the panelling was his own, he would surely have replied: 'Yes'. Yet it would be inaccurate to say that he *knew* this, since it was not in fact true. It is more accurate to say that he *believed* the panelling to be his own; this belief should not be described as knowledge, because it does not accord with the true position. Although one can intend something which does not come to fruition, one cannot know something which is not in fact (or in law) true.

---

242 The offence may also be committed recklessly, but that is not relevant here. See more fully D. W. Elliott, 'Criminal Damage' [1988] Crim LR 403.

243 See the discussion of possession offences above, Ch 4.3(b).

244 Customs and Excise Management Act 1979, s. 170; see e.g. *Taaffe* [1984] AC 539.

245 See *Hall* (1985) 81 Cr App R 260, and the discussion below, Ch 9.6.   246 [1974] QB 354.

It is relatively unusual for the element of 'knowledge of circumstances' to be contested in serious crimes. Neither murder nor manslaughter is committed if D does not know that the object against which he uses force is a human being, but it is rare for a defendant to argue that the target was believed to be a dummy.[247] In rape, before the Sexual Offences Act 2003, it was necessary for the prosecution to prove that D knew V was not consenting or knowingly risked the possibility that V was not consenting, and the landmark decision in *DPP* v *Morgan* (1976)[248] held that D should be acquitted where the jury was left in reasonable doubt whether D mistakenly believed that V was consenting. Lord Hailsham stated that as a matter of 'inexorable logic' the absence of the necessary knowledge (because of a mistaken belief) must lead to an acquittal, since the prosecution has not proved its case. This decision has effectively been reversed by the 2003 Act,[249] but the 'inexorable logic' has been pursued by the courts in other cases.

Thus offences of assault and wounding are defined not just in terms of the use of force against another, but the *unlawful* use of force. As we saw in Chapter 4.6, force may be lawful if it is used in self-defence or the prevention of crime, for example. The 'logical' argument is that, if D used force in the belief that he was preventing a crime, when in reality this was not so, D would lack the knowledge that the use of force was unlawful and should therefore be acquitted of the offence.[250] However, as argued in Chapter 6.4 below, the 'inexorable logic' does not stand unchallenged, and there are powerful arguments for creating exceptions and for introducing requirements of 'reasonable belief' into certain offences and defences. This may be seen as running counter to the subjective thrust of some recent decisions of high authority, particularly those proclaiming a 'constitutional principle' that, unless Parliament indicates otherwise, 'the appropriate mental element is an unexpressed ingredient of every offence.[251] The justifications for departing from that principle are examined in Chapter 6.4 below. The important point here is that, where the term 'knowingly' appears in an offence or where knowledge is otherwise required, it requires subjective awareness by D of each of the facts or circumstances in the definition of the crime to which it applies.

(e) RECKLESS KNOWLEDGE

Just as recklessness as to consequences is often an alternative form of *mens rea* to intention, so recklessness as to circumstances is sometimes an alternative form of fault to knowledge. What may, for convenience, be called 'reckless knowledge' exists where D believes that there is a risk that the prohibited circumstance exists, and goes on to take that risk. It is therefore a subjective requirement, on the same level as advertent recklessness as to consequences (discussed in paragraph (c)(ii) above). However, in some cases it has been held to include 'wilful blindness', i.e. where D knows that there is a risk that a prohibited circumstance exists, but refrains from checking it.

---

[247] See G. Williams, 'Homicide and the Supernatural' (1949) 65 LQR 491.   [248] [1976] AC 182.
[249] See below, Ch 8.5(i).   [250] *Williams (Gladstone)* (1984) 78 Cr App R 276.
[251] *B* v *DPP* [2000] 2 AC 428 and *K.* [2002] 1 AC 426, discussed in part 5(a)(iii) of this chapter, above.

An example is *Westminster City Council* v *Croyalgrange Ltd* (1986),[252] where D was charged with knowingly permitting the use of premises as a sex establishment without a licence. The House of Lords held that:

it is always open to the tribunal of fact, when knowledge on the part of a defendant is required to be proved, to base a finding of knowledge on evidence that the defendant had deliberately shut his eyes to the obvious or refrained from enquiry because he suspected the truth but did not want to have his suspicion confirmed.[253]

It will be seen that Lord Bridge used the language of inference here, suggesting that a court might infer knowledge from wilful blindness in the same way as he suggested that intention might be inferred from foresight of virtual certainty.[254] There is well-known authority to the effect that wilful blindness should be treated as actual knowledge.[255] However, D does not *know* the relevant circumstance in such cases, since he has refrained from finding out, and it may not be easy to establish that he had an overwhelmingly strong belief (that it is virtually certain) that the prohibited circumstance exists. Wilful blindness should therefore be treated as a form of reckless knowledge, and relevant only when reckless knowledge is sufficient, unless it can be shown that D refrained from making inquiries because he was virtually certain that his suspicion would be confirmed.[256]

(f) NEGLIGENCE

Traditionally, books dealing with English criminal law afford an extremely brief discussion to negligence as a standard of liability. Among the common law crimes, only manslaughter rests on liability for (gross) negligence,[257] and careless driving and dangerous driving are among the few common offences based on negligence. Yet there are many offences of negligence among the statutory offences regulating various commercial and other activities, often taking the form of an indictable offence of doing an act 'with intent' to contravene the regulations, supported by a summary offence of negligence in committing an act in such a way as to 'have reason to believe' that the regulations will be contravened.[258] Moreover, other systems of law tend to have a larger group of offences of negligence, and may look askance at a set of laws which penalizes negligence where death is caused but does not penalize it where serious injury or suffering is caused or risked.

One reason for the opposition of many English text-writers to criminal liability for negligence is that it derogates from the subjective principles stated at the beginning

---

252 (1986) 83 Cr App R 155; see also the draft Criminal Code, Law Com No. 177, cl. 18(a).

253 *Westminster City Council* v *Croyalgrange Ltd* (1986) 83 Cr App R 155.

254 See *Moloney* [1985] AC 905; cf. *Woollin* [1999] 1 AC 82, above, n 196.

255 The classic statement is that of Devlin J, in *Roper* v *Taylor's Garages Ltd* [1951] 2 TLR 284, at 288.

256 Contrast the differing views of Shute (above, n 239, at 196–8) and G. R. Sullivan, 'Knowledge, Belief and Culpability' and V. Tadros, 'Recklessness and the Duty to Take Care', in Shute and Simester (eds.), *Criminal Law Theory*, at respectively 213–14 and 252–4.

257 See below, Ch 7.5(c).   258 Some examples are collected at [1980] Crim LR 1.

of this chapter.[259] The doctrine of *mens rea*, as expressed in the requirements of intention and recklessness, makes liability depend on proof that D chose the harm, in the sense of intending it or at least being aware that it might result. These elements are missing where mere negligence is sufficient: there is no need to prove that D adverted to the consequences at all, so long as the court is satisfied that a reasonable person in that situation would have done so. To have negligence as a standard of liability would therefore move away from advertence as the foundation of criminal responsibility, and in doing so might show insufficient respect for the principle of autonomy. The counter-argument to this might challenge the relevance to culpability (and to the public censure of criminal conviction) of 'the distinction between foreseen effects and effects that were unforeseen only because the agent was not paying as much attention as he could and should have paid.'[260] The proposition that human actions are sufficiently free to make blame and punishment defensible underlies most of the criminal law,[261] and it might be argued that a person who negligently causes harm could have done otherwise—he could have taken the care necessary to avoid the harm. So long as the individual had the capacity to behave otherwise, it is fair to impose liability in those situations where there are sufficient signals to alert the reasonable citizen to the need to take care. Autonomy is a fundamental principle, but this does not mean that advertence should always be required so long as there is fair warning and a fair opportunity to conform to the required standard.

Three features of this counter-argument should be noted. First, its focus on capacity should not be dismissed as 'objective', for that would be an undiscriminating use of the term. As Hart has shown, it is perfectly possible to allow exceptions for those who cannot be expected to attain the standard of foresight and control of the reasonable citizen. One only has to supplement the question, 'did D fail to attain a reasonable standard of care in the circumstances?', with the further question; 'could D, given his mental and physical capacities, have taken the necessary precautions?'[262] Negligence liability need be 'objective' only in so far as it holds liable those who fail to take precautions when they could reasonably have been expected to do so. Liability can be termed subjective in so far as it takes account of the limited capacities of the particular person. Taking objective and subjective aspects together, the blameworthiness may be expressed as 'the culpability of unexercised capacity'.[263] As Andrew Simester puts it:

Without external standards, judgement is impossible. Without reference to the defendant, judgement cannot lead to blame. The device of the reasonable man is, in a sense, one means by which the law seeks to reconcile the impersonal with the humane.[264]

---

[259] See above, section 5.4(a).

[260] J. Gardner, 'Introduction' p. xxxv, summarizing the views of H. L. A. Hart, *Punishment and Responsibility* (2nd edn., 2008).

[261] Discussed above, Ch 4.2.

[262] This is the argument of Hart, *Punishment and Responsibility*, chs 2 and 5. The absence of an incapacity exception was a major argument against the *Caldwell* test.

[263] See the detailed discussion by M. S. Moore, *Placing Blame* (1997), ch 9 and 588–92.

[264] A. P. Simester, 'Can Negligence be Culpable?', in J. Horder (ed.), *Oxford Essays in Jurisprudence* (4th Series) (2000), at 106.

In addition, empirical research suggests public support for some such individualization of negligence liability.[265] Secondly, negligence liability may also derogate from any principle of contemporaneity, in the sense that the culpable failure to take precautions often pre-dates the causing of the harm: the rail worker failed to check the signals or the track, so that a crash occurred later; D misunderstood the mechanism of the gun, so that when he later pulled the trigger it killed someone. The enquiry into capacity and opportunity necessitated by negligence liability widens the time-frame of the criminal law, giving precedence to the doctrine of prior fault over the principle of contemporaneity.[266] Thirdly, the argument is in favour of negligence liability, not strict liability. Existing law imposes obligations on people who engage in various activities: the obligations of those operating systems of public transport; or the obligations of driving a motor vehicle; or the obligations of owning or managing a factory; or the obligations of engaging in a particular trade or business. Strict liability was criticized in paragraph (a) above. Negligence liability, on the other hand, is not open to the same objections.

The discussion thus far should have established that people who cause harm negligently may be culpable, in so far as they fail to take reasonable precautions when they have a duty and the capacity to do so. What it does not establish is that negligence is an appropriate standard for criminal liability, for it must be borne in mind that criminal liability is the law's most condemnatory form, and in principle it should be reserved for serious wrongs.[267] How might it be argued that the English doctrinal tradition of drawing the line of criminal liability below intention and recklessness, and above negligence (at least for 'conventional' crimes, such as those in the draft Criminal Code)[268] is ill-founded? One approach would be to establish that some cases of negligence manifest greater culpability than some cases of subjective recklessness—the principal justification for the *Caldwell* decision. Thus it could be claimed that a person who knowingly takes a slight risk of harm is less culpable than another person who fails to think about or recognize a high risk of the same harm: D, a shotgun champion, fires at a target, knowing that there is a slight risk that the bullet will ricochet and injure a spectator, which it does; E, who rarely handles guns, is invited to participate in a shooting party and fires wildly into bushes, failing to consider the possibility of others being there, and one is injured. Is D manifestly more culpable than E? A different comparison would be between someone who knowingly takes the risk of a small harm occurring and someone who fails to recognize the risk of a serious harm occurring: a criminal law which convicts the former and not the latter could be said to be transfixed by the notion of a 'consistent' general part. Why maintain that negligence is never an appropriate standard of criminal liability, even where the harm is great and the risk obvious?

The argument is therefore moving towards the conclusion that negligence may be an appropriate standard for criminal liability where: (i) the (potential) harm is great;

---

[265] Robinson and Darley, *Justice, Liability and Blame*, 123.   [266] See above, section 5.4(f).
[267] A. Ashworth, 'Is the Criminal Law a Lost Cause?' (2000) 116 LQR 225.   [268] See Ch 3.2 above.

(ii) the risk of it occurring is obvious; (iii) D has a duty to try to avoid the risk; and (iv) D has the capacity to take the required precautions. This opens up further debates on various points. The thesis is that negligence may be an appropriate standard where there are well-known risks of serious harm. This argues in favour of negligence as a standard of liability for certain serious offences against the person, including some serious sexual offences,[269] and also for some serious offences against the environment and property. But it must be debated whether liability for serious crime should be confined to *gross* negligence, not simple negligence. And it would be vital to protect 'rule of law' expectations, and thus to ensure that people receive fair warning of any duties that may form the basis of criminal negligence liability.[270] The spread of negligence liability would not have to result in the broadening of the traditional category of *mens rea*: negligence could be admitted as a form of fault, whereas intention and recklessness would remain the two forms of *mens rea*. It would be perfectly possible for a criminal code to provide separate crimes of negligence, with lower maximum sentences, at appropriate points in the hierarchy of offences. A further issue is whether the offences of negligence should be in the inchoate mode—'failing to take reasonable precautions'—or should be tied to the occurrence of the particular harm. Careless driving is of the former type, manslaughter of the latter, and this point will be pursued further in connection with crimes of endangerment.[271]

Even granted this argument in favour of criminalizing certain instances of negligence, what would be the point of doing so? This takes us back to the aims of the criminal law, discussed earlier.[272] It might be tempting to maintain that the general preventive aim of the criminal law cannot be served by offences of negligence: the notion of deterrence presupposes rational reflection by D at the time of offending, whereas the distinguishing feature of negligence is that D failed to think (when a reasonable person would have done). However, it can be argued that crimes of negligence may exert a general deterrent effect, by alerting people to their duties and to the need to take special care in certain situations. The practical prospects of deterrence here seem no less propitious than in relation to offences requiring intention or recklessness. The principal justification, however, would be that negligent harm-doers deserve criminal conviction because and insofar as they are sufficiently culpable. This is a question of degree and of judgement, on which views may differ.[273]

(g) OBJECTIVE VERSUS SUBJECTIVE

Much of the discussion of the law in this section of the chapter has concerned the interplay of subjective and objective factors in the definition of the core fault terms.

---

[269] As now adopted in the Sexual Offences Act 2003, discussed in Ch 8.5 below.

[270] On this and other points, see J. Horder, 'Gross Negligence and Criminal Culpability' (1997) 47 U Toronto LJ 495.

[271] See Chs 7.6, 7.7, and 8.3(f).   [272] See Ch 1.3.

[273] Some 'subjectivists' might accept a case for some criminal negligence liability, while insisting that it is categorically different from liability based on choice: see Moore, above, n 263.

It has been suggested that in crimes where strict liability is imposed on individual defendants, the courts have generally placed insufficient emphasis on respect for individual autonomy and the importance of requiring fault. When dealing with recklessness and mistake, however, the tendency of some text-writers and judges has been to regard the advertent or subjective approach as axiomatic, thus excluding from conviction certain people who may be no less culpable than those who are convicted. The *Caldwell* test could be seen as a way of supplementing the narrow conception of moral fault embodied in advertent recklessness, but it was flawed in other respects (notably, the absence of an incapacity exception) and it perished.[274] An alternative is Duff's test of practical indifference, which relies considerably on objective judgements as evidence of a person's attitude when behaving in a particular way. A further alternative would be to introduce more offences of negligence and, in respect of mistaken belief, more objective limitations on defences to criminal liability—a task on which the legislature embarked in the Sexual Offences Act 2003. It is evident that, in many cases examined in this chapter, an approach that focuses solely on advertence fails to capture some moral distinctions and to satisfy all social expectations.[275] Subjective tests heighten the protection of individual autonomy, but they typically make no concession to the principle of welfare and the concomitant notion of duties to take care and to avoid harming the interests of fellow citizens. However, if we are to move towards greater reliance on objective standards, at least two points must be confronted. First, objective tests must be applied subject to capacity-based exceptions. This preserves the principle of individual autonomy by ensuring that no person is convicted who lacked the capacity to conform his or her behaviour to the standard required. Secondly, any improved moral 'fit' obtained by moving more towards objective standards must be weighed against the greater detraction from the principle of maximum certainty that is likely to result.[276] Objective standards inevitably rely on terms such as reasonable, ordinary, and prudent. They appear much more malleable and unpredictable than subjective tests that ask whether or not a defendant was aware of a given risk, and they explicitly leave room for courts and even prosecutors to make social judgements about the limits of the criminal sanction.

5.6 THE VARIETY OF FAULT TERMS

Although the focus so far has been upon intention, recklessness, and knowledge, an examination of criminal legislation in force—some modern, some from the nineteenth century—reveals a diversity of fault terms. Even if the draft Criminal Code were to

---

[274] See the discussion in section 5.5(c) above.

[275] Cf. Gardner's view that 'once we go beyond the paradigm of intention…the mentalities of crime quickly fragment and lack any intelligible ordering': J. Gardner, 'On the General Part of the Criminal Law', in R. A. Duff, *Philosophy and the Criminal Law* (1998), 231.

[276] Norrie, *Crime, Reason and History*, 66.

be enacted, its provisions would not be restricted to the core fault terms discussed so far. Moreover, the Code would cover only some 200 out of perhaps 10,000 criminal offences, so the diversity will inevitably remain for some years. A full survey of the different fault terms cannot be offered here, but some general remarks may be worthwhile.

Nineteenth-century legislation such as the Offences against the Person Act 1861 makes considerable use of the term 'maliciously'.[277] It is now settled that this term should be interpreted to mean intention or recklessness, which simplifies the criminal lawyer's task.[278] Unfortunately, certain other terms have not been interpreted consistently in line with the core terminology. Many statutory offences, both ancient and modern, rely on the term 'wilfully': although in *Sheppard* (1981)[279] the House of Lords held that the term meant 'intentionally or recklessly' in the context of the crime of wilful neglect of a child, there are other offences in which 'wilfully' has been held not to require full *mens rea*.[280] Many offences are defined in terms of 'permitting', a word that has usually been interpreted as requiring full knowledge but has sometimes been held to impose strict liability, even on individuals.[281]

More to the point, however, is the fact that many major criminal offences rely on fault terms that bear little relation to any of those discussed so far. Theft and several other Theft Act offences rely on the term 'dishonestly', which, as we shall see,[282] encompasses a mixture of elements of subjective awareness and motivation with elements of objective moral judgement. Some fraud offences turn on whether the act or omission was done 'fraudulently'. And a number of public order and racial hatred offences impose liability where a certain consequence is 'likely' to result from D's conduct, without reference to whether D is aware of this likelihood. Thus, for example, a person commits the offence of 'fear or provocation of violence' by threatening, abusive, or insulting words or behaviour *either* with intent to cause another person to believe that immediate unlawful violence will be used, *or* 'whereby that person is likely to believe that such violence will be used or it is likely that such violence will be provoked'.[283] Similarly, the offence of publishing or distributing racially inflammatory material is committed if *either* D intends thereby to stir up racial hatred *or* 'having regard to all the circumstances racial hatred is likely to be stirred up thereby'.[284] Offences that rely on the court's assessment of the probable effect of certain conduct may be said to impose a form of strict liability, or at least liability for negligence, if it is assumed that the defendant ought to have known what effect was likely. However, suffice it to say that criminal offences in English law vary in their use of fault terms. The arguments for and against the core terms, examined in this

---

[277] See the discussion of specific offences in Ch 8.3.
[278] *Cunningham* [1957] 2 QB 396; *Savage, Parmenter* [1992] AC 699; above, section 5.3(c).
[279] [1981] AC 394.
[280] See J. A. Andrews, 'Wilfulness: a Lesson in Ambiguity' (1981) 1 Legal Studies 303.
[281] Compare, e.g., *James and Son v Smee* [1955] 1 QB 78 with *Baugh v Crago* [1976] Crim LR 72.
[282] In Ch 9.2.   [283] Public Order Act 1986, s. 4(1); see Ch 8.3.
[284] Public Order Act 1986, s. 19(1).

chapter, should provide a framework for considering the justifications for most other fault terms that may be encountered.

5.7   THE REFERENTIAL POINT OF FAULT

To say that a certain crime should require intention or recklessness is not enough. One must enquire: intention (or recklessness) as to what? It might be said loosely that 'the crime of manslaughter requires proof of intention or recklessness': the reason this is a loose statement is that the intent or recklessness required may be the same as that for assault or some other criminal act, whereas the liability imposed is that for homicide. Close analysis of the elements of the crime will show that the required fault and the result specified in the definition are not on the same level. This is what the principle of correspondence, outlined above, aims to eliminate.[285] Whenever one is discussing intent or recklessness, its referential point should always be established.

(a) FAULT, CONDUCT, AND RESULT

The argument may be carried further by considering the width or narrowness of the definitions of offences. It would be far easier to establish intent for a broad offence— such as intentionally causing physical harm to another—than to establish intent in a system with a hierarchy of graded offences—such as attempted murder, causing serious injury intentionally, causing injury intentionally, and common assault—which would require proof of more specific mental states. Similarly, a law which includes a general offence of intentionally causing damage to property belonging to another makes it far easier to establish the intent than a law with a series of offences differentiated according to the type of property damaged. Do these different legislative techniques have significant implications for the subjective doctrines of fault? Surely they do: one could argue that a single broad offence of 'intentionally causing physical harm to another' would obliterate the distinction between intending a minor assault and intending a major injury, and that a single broad offence of 'intentionally damaging property belonging to another' obliterates the distinction between intending damage to a cheap item and intending damage to an expensive item.[286] Any tendency towards broader offence definitions, evident in criminal damage[287] but not in sexual offences,[288] would give greater weight to the 'malice principle' of liability for the consequences of any wrongdoing (section 5.4(b) above) than to the principle of correspondence (section 5.4(a) above). To that extent, it would detract from the elements of choice and control

---

285   See above, section 5.2(b).

286   Cf. the facts of *G.* [2004] 1 AC 1034, where the two children set fire to paper beneath a dustbin, and the ultimate result was damage to buildings costing around £1 million.

287   See Law Com No. 29, *Offences of Damage to Property* (1970), and the Criminal Damage Act 1971.

288   Sexual Offences Act 2003, discussed in Ch 8.5 below.

which are fundamental to the subjective approach. But how should this problem be solved?[289] It is hardly practical to allow each person to nominate those factors which he or she regarded as significant in any particular event: who is to say whether fidelity to individual choice and control requires two or twenty grades of criminal damage, or two or four grades of offences of violence? Nonetheless, the implications for fault principles of these labelling decisions[290] should be kept firmly in mind.

The argument may be taken still further, for there are cases where it is plain that D intended to cause a different result from the one which actually occurred. How ought the law to deal with such cases? Should it respect D's choice, and provide for a conviction of attempting to do X (which was what D intended to do)? Or should it regard the result as the dominant factor, ignore the difference in D's intention, and convict on the basis of 'sufficient similarity' between the intention and the result? English law adopts the latter, more pragmatic approach. The Law Commission, in introducing a provision into the draft Criminal Code which follows the traditional approach, confirms the emphasis on results by stating that a conviction for attempt would be 'inappropriate as not describing the *harm done* adequately for labelling or sentencing purposes'.[291] The traditional English approach rests on three doctrines—unforeseen mode, mistaken object, and transferred fault.

(b) UNFORESEEN MODE

When D sets out to commit an offence by one method but actually causes the prohibited consequence in a different way, the offence may be said to have been committed by an unforeseen mode. Since most crimes penalizing a result (with fault) do not specify any particular mode of commission,[292] it is easy to regard the difference of mode as legally irrelevant. D intended to kill V; he chose to shoot him, but the shot missed; it hit a nearby heavy object, which fell on V's head and caused his death. Any moral distinction between the two modes is surely too slender to justify legal recognition. To charge D with *attempting* to kill V when he *did* kill him seems excessively fastidious. Pragmatism is surely the best approach here, and English law is generally right to ignore the unforeseen mode.[293]

(c) MISTAKEN OBJECT

When D sets out to commit an offence in relation to a particular victim but makes a mistake of identity and directs his conduct at the wrong victim, the offence may be said to have been committed despite the mistaken object. The same applies if D intends to

---

[289] See A. Ashworth, 'The Elasticity of *Mens Rea*' in C. Tapper (ed.), *Crime, Proof and Punishment* (1981), and Moore, *Placing Blame*, ch 11.

[290] See the discussion of the principle of fair labelling in Ch 3.6(s).

[291] Law Com No. 177, ii, para. 8.57 (my italics).

[292] The offences of fraud form an exception: see below, Ch 9.7.

[293] See Ashworth, 'The Elasticity of *Mens Rea*', 46–7.

steal one item of property but mistakenly takes another. So long as the two objects fall within the same legal category, it may be said that any moral distinction between them is too slender to justify legal recognition. However, much depends on the breadth of definition of the relevant offence: there is surely some moral significance in the plea: 'I thought the picture I damaged was just a cheap copy; I had no idea that a valuable painting would be kept in that place'.[294] English law favours the pragmatic answer of reflecting shades of moral culpability at the sentencing stage, but one might argue on principle that to convict this person of intentionally or recklessly damaging a valuable painting is a gross mislabelling of the wrong. In one sphere, English law's general approach of ignoring mistake of object within the same offence is not followed. This is the law of complicity: where A gives assistance to D who plans to kill X, and then D decides to kill Y, there is long-standing authority to the effect that A cannot be convicted for aiding and abetting D's murder of Y.[295] The complexities of the moral distinctions drawn here are discussed in Chapter 10.5 below, but if it is accepted that the identity of the victim is so important in this type of case, one may enquire more widely whether there really is inadequate moral significance in the plea: 'I intended to kill my enemy, X, and never meant any harm to the poor innocent, Y'. The pragmatic approach adopted elsewhere in the criminal law (apart from complicity) may fail to mark significant moral distinctions in some cases, and many might be dissatisfied if the only conviction were for attempting to murder X.

(d) TRANSFERRED FAULT

When D sets out to commit an offence in relation to a particular person or a particular property but his conduct miscarries and the harm falls upon a different person or a different property, English law regards D's intent as transferred and the offence as committed against the actual victim or property. When the fault is transferred, any defence which D may have is transferred with it.[296] As with unforeseen mode and mistaken object, the fault may only be transferred within the same class of offence.[297] Thus, if D throws a brick at some people, intending to hurt them, and the brick misses them and breaks a window, the intent to injure cannot be transferred to the offence of damaging property.[298] In this situation, the possible offences are an attempt to cause injury, and recklessly damaging property. As with the doctrine of mistaken object, the breadth of definition of the offence has some importance here. It is one thing to accept that D, who swung his belt at W and struck V, should be convicted of injuring V;[299] it is quite another thing, in moral terms, to accept that E, who threw a stone at a window, should be convicted of intentionally damaging a valuable painting which, unbeknown to him, was hanging inside. Yet English law would convict E, applying the

---

[294] See ibid., 47.　　[295] See Law Com No. 177, ii, para. 8.31, and below, Ch 10.5(a).

[296] *Gross* (1913) 23 Cox CC 455 (partial defence of provocation transferred).

[297] See A. Ashworth, 'Transferred Malice and Punishment for Unforeseen Consequences', in P. Glazebrook (ed.), *Reshaping the Criminal Law* (1978).

[298] *Pembliton* (1874) 12 Cox CC 607.　　[299] As in the leading case of *Latimer* (1886) 17 QBD 359.

broad wording of the Criminal Damage Act 1971 (any 'property belonging to another'), without any need to rely on the doctrine of transferred fault.[300] Thus the ambit of all three doctrines is much affected by the breadth of each offence definition.

The doctrine of transferred fault and its relationship with conceptions of subjective guilt remain sources of considerable controversy.[301] Rather surprisingly, in view of its long pedigree in English law, the doctrine was denounced by Lord Mustill in the House of Lords for 'its lack of any sound intellectual basis'. In *Attorney-General's Reference (No. 3 of 1994)*[302] D stabbed his girlfriend in the stomach, knowing that she was pregnant. Two weeks later the child was born prematurely, and because of its grossly premature birth it failed to thrive and died after four months. The House of Lords held that on these facts D could not be convicted of murder, holding that transferred malice could have no application because the foetus had no separate existence at the time the mother was attacked. The facts of this case are unusual, thankfully, but the House of Lords failed to deal convincingly with the relevance of the doctrine of unforeseen mode (should it matter that the child's death resulted from the premature birth, not from any direct wound?) and with the relevance of the extended principle of contemporaneity (if the death was part of an unbroken sequence of events following the stabbing, should not D's original intent be connected with the ultimate death?).[303] It could be argued that it would go too far if three artificial doctrines (transferred fault, unforeseen mode, and extended contemporaneity) were combined to find someone guilty of the highest crime in the land. Indeed, Jeremy Horder argues that the law should recognize a further restrictive principle, the remoteness doctrine, so as to ensure that there is no conviction of an offence (e.g. murder) if the way in which the death of the unanticipated victim occurred was so remote from what D intended or anticipated that to convict D of murdering the actual victim would be an unrepresentative label.[304]

(e) ESTABLISHING THE REFERENTIAL POINT

A system of criminal law which succeeded in reflecting the varying degrees of importance which people attribute to aspects of their intention (the mode of execution, the identity of the victim, the value of the property) might be a 'law professor's dream', but it is clearly not practical. Such an individuated or fine-grained approach to fault has to give way, at least in some respects, to claims of administrative efficiency. But that does not establish that the traditional English approach is the most appropriate. The draft Criminal Code provides for the continuation of the pragmatic approach, arguing that

---

[300] See Ashworth, 'Transferred Malice and Punishment', 89–93.

[301] Cf. e.g., D. Husak, 'Transferred Intent' (1996) 10 Notre Dame J Law, Ethics and Public Policy 65, with A. M. Dillof, 'Transferred Intent: an Inquiry into the Nature of Criminal Culpability' (1998) 1 Buffalo Crim LR 501.

[302] [1998] 1 Cr App R 91.   [303] See the discussion of this principle in section 5.4(c) above.

[304] J. Horder, 'Transferred Malice and the Remoteness of Unexpected Outcomes from Intentions' [2006] Crim LR 383.

this is simpler for prosecutors and that an attempt conviction in the above situations would ignore the harm actually done.[305] Does its pragmatism stretch too far? Would it not be better to analyse some of these cases in terms of an unfulfilled intention, combined with an accidental (or perhaps reckless) causing of harm? Some would argue that the present law of inchoate offences would not ensure a conviction in all these cases of miscarried intent and miscarried recklessness:[306] according to this view, the three doctrines are not merely effective in returning convictions and symbolically right in their emphasis on results,[307] but also necessary if justice is to be done in all cases. There is, it may be argued, no serious distortion of 'desert' or proportionality involved in the three doctrines, since the doctrines do not misrepresent the class of harm that D set out to commit. Yet there remains the law's ambivalence about the importance of a victim's identity: if this really is significant to offenders and people's judgements of them, as the law of complicity implies, should not prosecutors make more use of the law of attempts, where it is clearly applicable?[308]

FURTHER READING

H. L. A. HART, *Punishment and Responsibility* (2nd edn., 2008), chs 2 and 5.

J. GARDNER, 'Introduction', to Hart (above).

R. A. DUFF, *Answering for Crime* (2007), ch 3.

— 'Whose Luck is it Anyway?', in C. Clarkson and S. Cunningham (eds), *Criminal Liability for Non-Aggressive Death* (2008).

V. TADROS, *Criminal Responsibility* (2005), ch 8.

A. P. SIMESTER (ed), *Appraising Strict Liability* (2005).

A. ASHWORTH, 'A Change of Normative Position: Determining the Contours of Culpability in Criminal Law' (2008) 11 *New Crim LR* 232.

---

[305] In effect, cl. 24 of the draft Criminal Code is a 'deeming' provision: see Law Com No. 177, ii, paras. 8.57–59.

[306] G. Williams, 'Convictions and Fair Labelling' [1983] CLJ 85.

[307] Cf. the discussion of luck and results in section 5.4(b) above.

[308] Cf Horder, 'Transferred Malice and Remoteness', with A. P. Simester and G. R. Sullivan, *Criminal Law: Theory and Doctrine* (3rd edn., 2007), 156–8.

6

EXCUSATORY DEFENCES

6.1 EXCUSES AND OTHER DEFENCES

Criminal lawyers sometimes speak and write as if criminal guilt turns on the presence or absence of *mens rea*, but observations in previous chapters have already hinted that matters are not so simple. The notions of fault and culpability go further and deeper than *mens rea* and require a discussion of other doctrines broadly termed 'defences'. It is technically incorrect to use the term 'defence' when referring to the 'defence of mistake' or the 'defence of accident', since these (along with intoxication) are simply 'failure of proof' arguments; 'mistake' or 'accident' is merely a way of explaining why the prosecution has failed to prove the required knowledge, intention, or recklessness in respect of a particular ingredient of an offence.[1] Defences of various kinds have been discussed in earlier chapters. The requirement of a voluntary act (Chapter 4.2) is often referred to as the defence of automatism. The various justificatory defences, such as self-defence, were analysed in Chapter 4.6, 4.7 and 4.8. Defences of lack of capacity, particularly insanity, were discussed in Chapter 5.2. In the present chapter the focus is on excuses and potential excuses for wrongful acts, the essence of which is that D 'lived up to normative expectations' when responding to testing circumstances[2]— typically duress (section 6.3), but also to some extent intoxication (section 6.2), reasonable mistake and putative defences (section 6.4) and mistake of law (section 6.5). Last, there is a miscellany of possible defences, chiefly entrapment (section 6.6) but

---

[1] See P. H. Robinson, 'Criminal Law Defenses: A Systematic Analysis' (1982) 82 Columbia LR 199, *Structure and Function in Criminal Law* (1997), ch 5, and *Criminal Law Defences* (1984), for a five-fold classification of defences: (i) failure of proof defences; (ii) offence modifications (e.g. withdrawal in complicity); (iii) justifications; (iv) excuses; and (v) non-exculpatory public-policy defences (e.g. time limitations). This chapter is concerned with (iv) and with some forms of (i).

[2] J. Gardner, *Offences and Defences* (2007), ch 6.

also some forms of mistake of law (section 6.5) that are based on elements of excuse and other public-policy arguments. We will return, at the end of the chapter, to take stock of the various rationales.

6.2 INTOXICATION

Research confirms that many of those who commit crimes of violence and burglary (at least) have taken some kind of intoxicant beforehand.[3] Alcohol is probably the most widely used of intoxicants, but narcotic or hallucinogenic drugs are involved in some cases, too, and our discussion will relate to those who have taken alcohol, drugs, or a combination of the two. The usual effects are a loosening of inhibitions and, perhaps, a feeling of well-being and confidence. It is well known that people who have taken intoxicants tend to say or do things which they would not say or do when sober, and, in that sense, intoxicants may be regarded as the cause of such behaviour. But, as we saw in Chapter 5, the criminal law's conception of fault has tended to concentrate on cognition rather than on volition. Thus the approach to intoxication has not been to examine whether D's power to choose to cause the prohibited harm was substantially reduced, but has been to focus on its relation to *mens rea*. However, the law has been reluctant to allow intoxication simply to negate *mens rea*: instead, rather like its approach to automatism (see Chapter 4.2 above), it has drawn on arguments of prior fault and social defence in order to prevent the simple acquittal of those who cause harm and who lack awareness at the time because of intoxication. This, as we shall see, has caused various doctrinal difficulties for English criminal law.

(a) THE ENGLISH INTOXICATION RULES

From what was said earlier about the doctrine of prior fault,[4] it is not surprising to find that a person who deliberately drinks himself into an intoxicated state in order to carry out a crime will have no defence. As Lord Denning declared in *Attorney-General for Northern Ireland* v *Gallagher* (1963):[5]

If a man, whilst sane and sober, forms an intention to kill and makes preparation for it . . . and then gets himself drunk so as to give himself Dutch courage to do the killing, and whilst drunk carries out his intention, he cannot rely on this self-induced drunkenness as a defence to a charge of murder.

Cases such as this are rare and hard to believe: can a person be totally drunk and yet carry out a plan? More frequent are cases in which D has become intoxicated

---

[3] G. Dingwall, *Alcohol and Crime* (2006); the British Crime Survey reports that 45 per cent of victims of violent incidents believed the offender(s) to be influenced by alcohol and 19 per cent believed their offender(s) to be influenced by drugs: C. Kershaw *et al.*, *Crime in England and Wales 2007/08* (2008), 76–7.
[4] See Ch 5.4(d) above.   [5] [1963] AC 349, at 382.

'voluntarily', i.e. where there is no reason to regard it as 'involuntary',[6] and has then done something which, he argues, he would not have done but for the alcohol or drugs.

It could be said that there is an 'inexorable logic'[7] that if *mens rea* is not present, whether through intoxication or otherwise, D should not be convicted. However, considerations of social welfare have led the courts to introduce an unusual distinction. The decision in *DPP* v *Majewski* (1977)[8] divides crimes into 'offences of specific intent' and 'offences of basic intent', and allows intoxication as a 'defence' to the former but not to the latter. Murder and wounding with intent are crimes of specific intent, and there is no great loss of social defence in allowing intoxication to negative the intent required for those crimes when the amplitude of the basic intent offences of manslaughter and unlawful wounding lies beneath them—ensuring D's conviction and liability to sentence. Various theories have been advanced in an attempt to explain why those offences (together with theft, handling, and all crimes of attempt, for example) are crimes of 'specific intent' whereas others are not, but none is satisfactory.[9] For example, to assert (as did Hughes LJ in *Heard* (2008))[10] that crimes of specific intent require proof of purpose is unconvincing, since that is not true of murder.[11] Moreover, many crimes contain some elements for which only intent will suffice and others for which recklessness is sufficient.[12] However, this rather ramshackle law has proved workable. The courts have thus restricted the operation of the 'inexorable logic' of *mens rea* to the few offences of specific intent and, since most of them are underpinned by a lesser offence of 'basic intent', no great loss of social defence has occurred.

The policy expressed in *Majewski* through the idea of 'offences of basic intent' was expressed slightly differently in *Caldwell* (1982)[13] in terms of 'recklessness'. Thus, where recklessness is a sufficient fault element for the crime, evidence of intoxication is irrelevant because anyone who was intoxicated is deemed to have been reckless. This is a simpler rule to apply, although it appears not to have displaced the *Majewski* test.[14] It is subject to an exception, as we shall see in section 6.2(d) below, in cases where the intoxication can be regarded as to some degree 'involuntary'. Section 6(5) of the Public Order Act 1986, which applies only to offences in that Act, reads as follows:

a person whose awareness is impaired by intoxication shall be taken to be aware of that of which he would be aware if not intoxicated, unless he shows either that his intoxication was not self-induced or that it was caused solely by the taking or administration of a substance in the course of medical treatment.

---

[6] See the discussion in section 6.2(d) below.

[7] The phrase of Lord Hailsham in *DPP* v *Morgan* [1976] AC 182, at 214, criticized in Ch 5.5(d) above and section 6.5 below.

[8] [1977] AC 443.

[9] Their inadequacy is demonstrated by G. Williams, *Textbook of Criminal Law* (2nd edn., 1983), 428–30, and A. Ward, 'Making Some Sense of Self-induced Intoxication' [1986] CLJ 247.

[10] [2008] QB 43, on which see D. Ormerod, [2007] Crim LR 654.   [11] See Ch 7.3 below.

[12] S. White, 'Offences of Basic and Specific Intent' [1989] Crim LR 271.   [13] [1982] AC 341.

[14] The discussion of 'drunken accidents' in *Heard* (above, n 10) pays little regard to the possibility of recklessness in certain situations.

This provision, though couched in the terminology of awareness instead of advertent recklessness, may be thought to express the law's general approach.[15]

The effect of all these rules is that voluntary intoxication rarely functions as a ground of exculpation. Here, as with automatism and some mistakes, the 'logic' of the standard doctrines of *actus reus* and *mens rea* has been subordinated to considerations of welfare and social defence. Thus where it is alleged that intoxication induced a state of automatism, the case is treated as one of intoxication (the cause) rather than automatism (the effect).[16] The same approach has been quite vigorously pursued in cases of intoxicated mistake, bringing them under the rules of intoxication (the cause) rather than mistake (the effect). In *O'Grady* (1987),[17] where the defence took the form of a drunken mistaken belief in the need for self-defence, the Court of Appeal held that D could not rely on his mistake if it stemmed from intoxication. This means, in effect, that where the subjective rule for mistake clashes with the objective rule for intoxication, the latter takes priority. The Court of Appeal confirmed this in *Hatton* (2006),[18] declining an invitation to depart from *O'Grady* and confirming a conviction for murder of someone who made an intoxicated mistake in self-defence.[19] This leads to the extraordinary result that in crimes of specific intent—notably murder, with its mandatory sentence of life imprisonment—intoxication may negative *mens rea* whereas an intoxicated mistake must be discounted. The *O'Grady* approach should surely be confined to crimes of basic intent or recklessness, although one of the few decisions on such crimes went the other way. This was *Jaggard* v *Dickinson* (1980),[20] where the Divisional Court was so mesmerized by the wording of the Criminal Damage Act 1971 (which does not deal expressly with intoxication) that it paid no heed to the general principles relating to defences of intoxication. At least *O'Grady* recognized the clash of approaches between mistake and intoxication, although it resolved the conflict wrongly in respect of crimes of specific intent.

(b) THE ATTACK ON THE ENGLISH APPROACH

The approach of the English courts has been attacked on several grounds. The distinction between 'specific intent' and 'basic intent' is ill-defined, even if it does have some moral coherence. The approach of deeming intoxicated persons to be reckless rests on a fiction, and the attempts of Lord Elwyn-Jones in *DPP* v *Majewski* to argue that intoxicated persons really are reckless because 'getting drunk is a reckless course of conduct'[21] involve a manifest confusion between a general, non-legal use of the term

---

[15] *Aitken* (1992) 95 Cr App R 304, *Richardson and Irwin* [1999] 1 Cr App R 392.

[16] *Lipman* [1970] 1 QB 152; see Ch 4.2 above.

[17] (1987) 85 Cr App R 315; there is debate about whether this ruling was merely *obiter dictum*, but it has now been applied in *O'Connor* [1991] Crim LR 135 and in *Hatton*, below.

[18] [2006] 1 Cr App R 16.   [19] See also *Fotheringham* (1989) 88 Cr App R 206, on rape.

[20] [1981] QB 527.   [21] [1977] AC 443, at 475.

'reckless' and the technical, legal term, which denotes (for almost all offences)[22] that D was aware of the risk of the result which actually occurred. In most cases it is far-fetched to argue that a person in the process of getting drunk is aware of the type of conduct he or she may later indulge in.

These criticisms of the courts' attempts to stretch the established meaning of 'intent' and of 'recklessness' in order to deal with the problems of intoxication have been joined by other arguments. Some have held that the intoxication rules are inconsistent with s 8 of the Criminal Justice Act 1967, which requires courts to take account of all the evidence when deciding whether D intended or foresaw a result:[23] but the effect of *DPP v Majewski* is to deny that evidence of intoxication is relevant unless the crime is one of specific intent, and s 8 extends only to legally relevant evidence.[24] Another argument is that the intoxication rules are inconsistent with the principle of contemporaneity, in that they base D's conviction (of an offence of basic intent) on the antecedent fault of voluntarily taking intoxicants:[25] but the principle of contemporaneity itself conflicts with the doctrine of prior fault, as we have noted,[26] and there seems no reason why contemporaneity should be an absolute principle. The question is whether it is appropriate to apply the rival doctrine of prior fault to intoxication cases.

Whatever the merit of these criticisms, it is undeniable that the intoxication rules in English law rest on fictions and apparently illogical legal devices. Is it the policy of restricting the defence of intoxication which is wrong, or merely the legal devices used to give effect to the policy?

(c) INTOXICATION, CULPABILITY, AND SOCIAL POLICY

One may concede that, in fact, a person may be so drunk as not to know what he or she is doing when causing harm to others or damage to property, and yet maintain that there are good reasons for criminal liability. What might these reasons be? At the root of the 'social defence' or 'public protection' arguments is the proposition that one of the main functions of the criminal law is to exert a general deterrent effect so as to protect major social and individual interests, and that any legal system which allows intoxication to negative *mens rea* would present citizens with an easy route to impunity. Indeed, the more intoxicated they became, the less likely they would be to be held criminally liable for any harm caused. As a matter of human experience, it is far from clear that this argument is soundly based. There are several common law jurisdictions which have declined to follow the English approach and which simply

---

[22] See above, Ch 5.5(c), for discussion.

[23] See J. C. Smith, 'Intoxication and the Mental Element in Crime', in P. Wallington and R. Merkin (eds.), *Essays in Honour of F. H. Lawson* (1987).

[24] [1977] AC 443, at 475; see C. Wells, 'Swatting the Subjectivist Bug' [1982] Crim LR 209.

[25] Voiced by majority judges in the High Court of Australia, in *O'Connor* (1980) 146 CLR 64.

[26] See Ch 5.4(d) and (e).

regard intoxication as one way of negativing *mens rea*.[27] Two comments may be made here. First, these jurisdictions can be taken to be reinforcing the important and often neglected point that it is extremely rare for a defendant to be able to raise even a reasonable doubt that he was unaware of what he was doing. All that is required for proof of intent or recklessness is a momentary realization that property is being damaged or that a person is being assaulted, etc. Thus, even if evidence of intoxication were relevant, D's condition would not usually be acute enough to prevent conviction. Secondly, and alternatively, the rarity of acquittals based on intoxication in these jurisdictions may simply be because juries and magistrates are applying a normative test rather than a purely factual test. Thus the confidence of the majority judges in the High Court of Australia that juries and magistrates will not be too readily persuaded to acquit in these cases[28] may derive less from the rarity of acutely intoxicated harmdoers than from a belief that the courts will simply decline to return verdicts of acquittal where D is regarded as unworthy or culpable in some general way. This would suggest that both the English and the Australian approaches are unsatisfactory in their method— the English because it deems intoxicated harmdoers to be 'reckless' when they are not, the Australian because it relies on juries to make covert moral assessments and not simply the factual assessment that the law requires—even if they usually produce socially acceptable outcomes.

There remains the question of individual culpability. What distinguishes evidence of intoxication from many of the other explanations for D's failure to realize what most ordinary people would have foreseen is the element of prior fault. It was D's fault for taking drink or drugs to such an extent as to lose control over his behaviour. Does this mean that, in order to support a finding of culpability, it must be established that D knew of the likely effects of the intoxicants upon behaviour? Probably not, for it would be regarded as perfectly fair to assume that all people realize the possible effects of taking alcohol or drugs (apart from the exceptional situations to be discussed in paragraph (d) below). 'It is common knowledge that those who take alcohol to excess or certain sorts of drugs may become aggressive or do dangerous or unpredictable things.'[29] This is plainly an objective standard, but it is so elementary that it should not be regarded as unfair on anyone to assume such knowledge. Thus there is an element of culpability in intoxication cases which serves to distinguish them not only from insanity cases (which arise without fault) but also from many cases of simple absence of *mens rea*. The point was put more strongly and more directly in early modern times, when temperance was regarded as a virtue and excessive drinking as an 'odious and loathsome sin'.[30]

---

[27] See *Keogh* [1964] VR 400, and *O'Connor* (1980) 146 CLR 64 in Australia, and *Kamipeli* [1975] 2 NZLR 610 in New Zealand: compare G. Orchard, 'Surviving without *Majewski*—a View from Down Under' [1993] Crim LR 426 with S. Gough, 'Surviving without *Majewski*?' [2000] Crim LR 719.

[28] Cf. S. Gough, 'Intoxication and Criminal Liability: the Law Commission's Proposed Reforms' (1996) 112 LQR 335, at 337.

[29] *Bailey* (1983) 77 Cr App R 76, *per* Griffiths LJ at 80.

[30] J. Horder, 'Pleading Involuntary Lack of Capacity'(1993) 52 Camb LJ 298, at 308–9.

But in what does the culpability consist? Specifically, is D to blame for becoming intoxicated or for causing the proscribed harm? It is fairly simple to establish culpability for becoming intoxicated if there is no evidence that it was 'involuntary'. It is fairly difficult to establish culpability for causing the proscribed harm if we follow normal principles: we must assume acute intoxication at the time of the act, and if we look back to the period when D was becoming intoxicated, it is unlikely that one could establish actual foresight of the kind of harm eventually caused. Perhaps some people who regularly assault others when drunk may realize that there is a risk of this occurring, but in order to encompass the majority of cases, it would be necessary to rewrite the proposition about 'common knowledge' so as to maintain that people should realize that, when intoxicated, they are likely to cause damage or to assault others. The culpability, in other words, is somewhat unspecific—as in many instances where prior fault operates to bar a defence.[31] Sentencing decisions suggest that intoxication may mitigate on the first occasion it is raised, if the offence can be portrayed as 'out of character', but it will not mitigate any subsequent offences committed in an intoxicated state.[32]

(d) VOLUNTARY AND NON-VOLUNTARY INTOXICATION

We have already noted that non-voluntary intoxication may constitute an exception to the general intoxication rules, and we saw that s 6(5) of the Public Order Act 1986 recognizes an exception where the intoxication was not 'self-induced'. There is, however, no sharp distinction between the voluntary and the non-voluntary: rather, there is a continuum of states in which D has more or less knowledge about the properties of what he is consuming. The English courts, consistently with their generally restrictive approach, have been reluctant to exempt defendants from the intoxication rules. Thus in *Allen* (1988),[33] D's argument was that he had become intoxicated because he had not realized that the wine being given to him had a high alcohol content. The Court of Appeal held that, so long as a person realizes that he is drinking alcohol, any subsequent intoxication is not rendered non-voluntary simply because he may not know the precise strength of the alcohol he is consuming. In some circumstances this might be quite a harsh ruling, but in broad terms it is compatible with judicial statements about the unpredictability of alcohol.

A different problem arose in *Hardie* (1985),[34] where D took a quantity of Valium tablets 'for his nerves' and later set fire to an apartment. The Court of Appeal quashed his conviction. The main distinguishing factor here was that Valium is widely regarded as a sedative or soporific drug, and is not thought likely 'to render a person aggressive or incapable of appreciating risks to others'. This suggests that one basis

---

[31] See P. H. Robinson, 'Causing the Conditions of One's Own Defence' (1985) 71 Virginia LR 1, at 50–1, discussed above, in Ch 5.4(e).

[32] For the uncompromising judicial response to repeated offences of drunken violence, see *Sheehan and O'Mahoney* [2007] 1 Cr App R (S) 149 and *McDermott* [2007] 1 Cr App R (S) 145.

[33] [1988] Crim LR 698.   [34] (1985) 80 Cr App R 157.

for the distinction between voluntary and non-voluntary intoxication is a division of intoxicants into those that are sedative and others that may have aggressive effects. The Court in *Hardie* added that none the less D would be treated as reckless if he had known, contrary to general beliefs, that Valium might have disinhibiting rather than sedative effects.[35] It should be noted that s 6(5) of the Public Order Act 1986, set out above, allows D a defence where the intoxication 'was caused solely by the taking or administration of a substance in the course of medical treatment'. In line with the general approach, this should be confined to cases where D was not warned of the possible effects, or where those effects were not widely known.

The question of non-voluntary intoxication is raised most directly by *Kingston* (1995).[36] The evidence suggested that certain sedative drugs had been introduced into D's coffee, and that he had then carried out indecent sexual acts on a sleeping boy. The Court of Appeal quashed D's conviction, holding that if D had been placed in an altered mental state by the stratagem of another, and this led him to form an intent that he would not otherwise have formed, he should have a defence. This approach accepts that D may have had the mental element required for the crime, but looks to the *cause* of that condition: in effect, a doctrine of prior lack of fault. The House of Lords restored the conviction. If the non-voluntary intoxication is so acute as to negative *mens rea*, then it may lead to an acquittal of any offence requiring *mens rea*, whether of specific or basic intent. Where non-voluntary intoxication is not so acute as to negative *mens rea*, Lord Mustill held that there is no basis for an acquittal unless the courts were to create a new defence.[37] This the House was unwilling to do, because their Lordships could see no significant moral difference between this case and *Allen*, and because the opportunity for false defences was considerable. The matter was one for the Law Commission and Parliament.

What, then, is the position? If the intoxicant is in the soporific category, it seems from *Hardie* that D may have a defence if he can show that he lacked the mental element required for the crime. The general rule would prevent evidence of intoxication being adduced to show that he was not reckless but, if the intoxication was non-voluntary, evidence of the intoxication should be admitted. However, where the intoxicant is not so powerful as to remove D's awareness of what he is doing, it seems immaterial whether it is in the soporific or the 'aggressive' category. *Kingston* holds that there is no defence available and D is therefore convicted on the basis of his intention or recklessness. Even if D can establish that the intoxicant was administered without his awareness—the 'laced' or 'spiked' drink[38]—this appears insufficient to alter the analysis, even though one might think that this presents a stronger argument than *Hardie*. The House of Lords in *Kingston* overlooked D's absence of fault in bringing

---

[35] This follows the reasoning in *Bailey* (1983) 77 Cr App R 76 on diabetes and automatism: see above, Ch 4.2.

[36] [1995] 2 AC 355.

[37] His Lordship concluded that the few distant authorities in favour of the defence were unpersuasive, and so the House of Lords (rightly) considered the issue afresh.

[38] For an example see *Blakely and Sutton* [1991] Crim LR 763.

about the condition, and adopted an implausibly narrow view of excuses premised on the presence or absence of *mens rea*. For these reasons, the decision should be reversed, but it is doubtful whether one should go further, as G. R. Sullivan has argued, and allow courts to look to D's character and destabilized condition in order to determine whether or not he was blameworthy, and to find a defence if D is not adjudged blameworthy.[39]

(e) FINDING A LEGAL SOLUTION

A simple solution compatible with the ordinary logic of the liability rules is to regard evidence of intoxication as relevant on issues of *mens rea*, following various decisions in New Zealand and in the non-Code states of Australia.[40] There will only rarely be acquittals, and these may be regarded as part of a small price for respecting the principle of individual autonomy—like occasional acquittals of clumsy and thoughtless individuals. In practice the behaviour of most defendants who allege intoxication will show some elements of intention, knowledge, or awareness.[41] However, an objection to the Antipodean approach is that it seems to yield the anti-social maxim 'more intoxication, less liability', and public outcries at certain acquittals have led some Australian states to abandon the simple 'logical' approach.[42] It gives no weight to the elements of choice and risk involved in getting drunk. Usually the choice is to loosen one's self-restraint rather than to commit a crime, let alone a particular kind of crime; but the retention of control over one's behaviour might fairly be regarded as a social duty, and its abandonment as a form of wrongdoing.[43] This argument may be weakened where D is addicted to alcohol or drugs, since the element of choice may have been exhausted long ago.[44]

In this country the various proposals for reform seem to fall into one of two different camps. On the one hand there are those who argue that the essence of the wrongdoing in most cases lies in becoming intoxicated, and that it is unfair to label a defendant as a certain kind of offender (wounding, indecent assault, etc.) if he really was so intoxicated as not to realize what he was doing. Along these lines was a Consultation Paper issued by the Law Commission in 1993, proposing that courts be allowed to take account of evidence of intoxication on any issue of fault (following the Antipodean approach), but also introducing a new offence of causing harm whilst intoxicated—a 'state of affairs' offence designed to achieve a measure of social defence

---

[39] G. R. Sullivan, 'Making Excuses', in A. P. Simester and A. T. H. Smith (eds.), *Harm and Culpability* (1996). For discussion of character-based theories of excuse, see Ch 6.7(b) below.

[40] See n 27 above.

[41] R. Shiner, 'Intoxication and Responsibility' (1990) 13 Int J Law and Psychiatry 9; C. N. Mitchell, 'The Intoxicated Offender—Refuting the Legal and Medical Myths' (1988) 11 Int J Law and Psychiatry 77.

[42] Gough, 'Surviving without *Majewski*?', also discussing the Canadian decision in *Daviault* (1995) 118 DLR (4th) 469 and its consequences.

[43] Gough, 'Intoxication and Criminal Liability'.

[44] Cf. H. Fingarette, 'Addiction and Criminal Responsibility' (1975) 84 Yale LJ 413 with J. Tolmie, 'Alcoholism and Criminal Liability' (2001) 64 MLR 688.

without unfair labelling of the offender (in line with German law).[45] However, the prevailing approach to reform is an adaptation of the common law, and the latest version is to be found in a draft Bill of 1998:[46]

For the purposes of this Act a person who was voluntarily intoxicated at any material time must be treated—

(a) as having been aware of any risk of which he would have been aware had he not been intoxicated; and

(b) as having known or believed in any circumstances which he would have known or believed in had he not been intoxicated.

The first part of this means that in most cases an intoxicated actor will be deemed reckless, which is not far from the present law and its distinction between specific and basic intent.[47] The 1998 Bill also deals with intoxicants taken on medical advice, and includes a definition of voluntary intoxication. It does not provide a separate defence of involuntary intoxication, and indeed creates a presumption that intoxication was voluntary. All of this might be described as 'workable', although it ignores the moral arguments made by those who favour the modified German-Antipodean approach to which the Law Commission was temporarily attached in 1993. The case for a purely subjective approach to intoxication seems unconvincing, but the arguments about how the intoxicated wrongdoer should be labelled and sentenced remain keenly contested.[48]

6.3 DURESS AND NECESSITY

This part of the chapter deals with cases in which D's behaviour fulfils the conduct element and the positive fault requirements of an offence, but in which D acted in response to threats from another person (sometimes called 'duress *per minas*'), or in order to avert dire consequences (called 'necessity' or 'duress of circumstances'), or, unusually, in circumstances of marital coercion. We have already seen, in Chapter 4.8,

---

[45] Law Commission Consultation Paper No. 127, *Intoxication and Criminal Liability* (1993). German law adopts this approach, allowing intoxication to negative intention (applying the 'inexorable logic') but then applying an offence of 'dangerous intoxication' that consists of committing the conduct element of another offence while culpably intoxicated: see J. R. Spencer and A. Pedain, 'Strict Liability in Continental Criminal Law' in A. P. Simester (ed)., *Appraising Strict Liability* (2005), 244–5.

[46] Home Office, *Violence: Reforming the Offences Against the Person Act 1861* (1998), draft Bill, cl. 19, based on the criminal code proposals in Law Com No. 177, draft Bill, cl. 22. An intervening report from the Law Commission, Law Com No. 229, *Legislating the Criminal Code: Intoxication and Criminal Liability* (1995), was not adopted in its central recommendations.

[47] Sir John Smith rightly questioned (b), which might have unexpected consequences in attributing to people beliefs they did not hold: 'Offences Against the Person: the Home Office Consultation Paper' [1998] Crim LR 317, at 321.

[48] Cf. A. Ashworth, 'Intoxication and the General Defences' [1980] Crim LR 556 with Gough, 'Intoxication and Criminal Liability'.

that some cases of necessity might give rise to a claim that the use of force was *justified*, but those are likely to be rare cases where there is a net saving of lives. In focussing here on the *excusatory* defences of duress and necessity, we will find that the development of the common law has been characterized by conflicts between recognizing the pressure to which D was subject and upholding the rights of victims, and occasionally by mixing justificatory with excusatory reasons.

(a) REQUIREMENTS OF THE DEFENCES

The courts have generally held that the requirements of duress by threats and of duress of circumstances (which has largely taken over from necessity) are in parallel.[49] Although both defences require some danger external to D,[50] they arise in different factual circumstances, and it might be best to illustrate this by contrasting two cases. In *Hudson and Taylor* (1971)[51] two teenagers were prosecution witnesses at a trial for wounding. They testified that they did not know the man charged and could not identify him as the culprit. The man was acquitted but the young women were charged with perjury. They admitted that they gave false evidence, but said that they were under duress, having been threatened with violence by various men, one of whom was in the public gallery at the original trial. The Court of Appeal quashed their convictions because the defence of duress had been wrongly withdrawn from the jury. In *Conway* (1989)[52] two men approached D's car, whereupon D, urged on by his passenger, drove off at great speed and in a reckless manner. D's explanation was that he knew that his passenger had recently been threatened by two men who had fired a shotgun. D feared that these two men intended harm, and his driving was in response to that emergency. The Court of Appeal quashed the conviction for reckless driving because the trial judge had failed to leave the defence of duress of circumstances to the jury. The difference emerging from these two cases, then, is that for the defence of duress itself there should typically be a direct threat aimed at persuading D to commit a particular offence, whereas for duress of circumstances there will typically be a situation of emergency (involving perceived danger but not direct threats) that leads D to do something that would otherwise be an offence.

What, then, are the general requirements of the two defences? They appear to be restricted to cases where D acted as he did out of fear of death or serious injury.[53] Threats to property or to reputation have been held to be insufficient,[54] but there was a dictum in *Steane* (1947)[55] that a threat of false imprisonment would suffice. In a sense it seems strange that the degree of threat or danger should be fixed in this

[49] See *Willer* (1986) 83 Cr App R 225, *Conway* (1988) 88 Cr App R 159, *Martin* (1989) 88 Cr App R 343, discussed by D. W. Elliott, 'Necessity, Duress and Self-Defence' [1989] Crim LR 611.
[50] *Rodger and Rose* [1998] 1 Cr App R 143 (D's own suicidal tendencies cannot found either defence).
[51] [1971] 2 QB 202.   [52] [1989] 3 All ER 1025.
[53] *DPP for Northern Ireland v Lynch* [1975] AC 653; *Bowen* [1996] 2 Cr App R 157.
[54] In, respectively, *DPP v Lynch* [1975] AC 653 at 687, and *Valderrama-Vega* [1985] Crim LR 220.
[55] [1947] KB 997.

way, since the seriousness of the crimes in respect of which duress is raised may vary considerably. A dire threat should be necessary to excuse a person who caused a grave harm, but it does not follow that some lesser threat should not be sufficient to excuse a lesser offence. However, the courts have continued to insist on threats of death or serious harm as the standard requirement and, additionally, that the threats must be such that 'a sober person of reasonable firmness' would not have resisted them.[56] This objective condition has been tested in cases in which there have been attempts to introduce evidence to the effect that D's personality rendered him or her particularly susceptible to threats. In *Bowen* (1996)[57] the Court of Appeal held that the question is whether D responded 'as a sober person of reasonable firmness sharing the characteristics of the defendant would have done'. In applying this test a court should not admit evidence that D was more pliable, vulnerable, timid, or susceptible to threats than a normal person, and characteristics due to self-abuse (alcohol, drugs) should also be left out of account. But the Court did suggest that it would be proper to take account of age, sex, pregnancy, serious physical disability, or a 'recognized psychiatric condition'.[58] In view of the re-affirmation of the objective standard of self-control in provocation,[59] this broadening of the ambit of duress may appear anomalous. However, the comparison with the operation of a partial defence to murder (i.e. provocation) is not an apt one, since duress operates as a complete defence to offences other than murder. Whereas the objective standard in provocation can be maintained in the expectation that mentally disordered defendants will have resort to the partial defence of diminished responsibility, the possibility of relaxing the requirements of duress for mentally disturbed defendants can only be realized through a complete defence or conviction followed by mitigation of sentence.[60]

In some cases the question of mixed threats and mixed motives has arisen: in *Valderrama-Vega* (1985),[61] a case in which D was both under severe financial pressure and subject to blackmail threats, the Court of Appeal held that duress would be available if the jury found that D would not have acted as he did but for the death threats he had received. The other pressures may have exerted an influence, but so long as the threats were causally significant, this was sufficient.

The threats need not be addressed to D personally:[62] the defence is available if the threats are against D's family or friends, but it now seems that there must be some

---

[56] *Graham* (1982) 74 Cr App R 235, confirmed by the House of Lords in *Howe* [1987] AC 417.

[57] [1996] 2 Cr App R 157.

[58] For the suggestion that this phrase has wider implications than the Court realized, see A. Buchanan and G. Virgo, 'Duress and Mental Abnormality' [1999] Crim LR 517.

[59] *Attorney-General for Jersey* v *Holley* [2005] 2 AC 580, overruling *Smith (Morgan)* [2001] 1 AC 146, and discussed in Ch 7.4(b) below.

[60] See further J. Horder, *Excusing Crime* (2004), 183–5.

[61] [1985] Crim LR 220; P. Alldridge, 'Developing the Defence of Duress' [1986] Crim LR 433.

[62] *Valderrama-Vega*, n 61 above; *Gill* (1963) 47 Cr App R 166; and Law Com No. 83, *Defences of General Application* (1977), 2–3.

connection with D.[63] In the unusual case of *Shayler* (2001),[64] the defence was that D revealed official secrets because he believed that (unidentified) people were placed in danger by MI5's activities. The Court of Appeal held that, for the defence to be available, the threat or danger must be to D himself or 'towards somebody for whom he reasonably regarded himself as being responsible'.[65]

The threat must be 'present' and not a remote threat of future harm, but how long an interval may elapse? In *Hudson and Taylor*,[66] the facts of which were outlined above, the Court of Appeal held that it is not necessary that the threat would be carried out immediately, so long as its implementation was imminent. The same approach was taken in *Abdul-Hussain et al.* (1999),[67] where a group of Shiite Muslims from Iraq had hi-jacked an aircraft to Stansted airport. When they surrendered, they claimed that they had acted out of fear of persecution and death at the hands of the Iraqi authorities. The trial judge withdrew the defence from the jury on the ground that the threat was not sufficiently close and immediate, but the Court of Appeal held that imminence is sufficient and that the execution of the threat need not be immediately in prospect. However, in *Hasan* (2005)[68] Lord Bingham opposed the drift towards the looser concept of 'imminence' and held that older authorities in favour of a requirement of immediacy should be restored: there is a duty to take evasive action where possible, particularly where the threat 'is not such as [D] reasonably expects to follow immediately or almost immediately on his failure to comply with the threat'.[69] Lord Bingham regarded *Hudson and Taylor* as wrongly decided, commenting that he could not accept 'that a witness testifying in the Crown Court at Manchester has no opportunity to avoid complying with a threat incapable of execution there and then'. This strong line suggests, further, that the concession to the defendants' youth in *Hudson and Taylor*—'having regard to his age and circumstances, and to any risks to him which may be involved in the course of action relied upon'[70]—should also be removed from the law on duress. Lord Bingham's conception of duress evidently finds no place for those who cannot measure up to reasonable expectations.

Another objective element is that the defendant is not entitled to be judged on the facts as he believed them to be. Contrary to the generally subjective approach to mistaken beliefs,[71] the Court of Appeal in *Graham* (1982)[72] held that the test for duress is

---

[63] However, it has been held that the defence is unavailable where D himself is the source of the danger, through his (conditional) determination to commit suicide: *Rodger and Rose* [1998] 1 Cr App R 143.

[64] [2001] 1 WLR 2206.

[65] Lord Bingham in *Hasan* [2005] 2 AC 467 approved this formulation as 'consistent with the rationale' of duress (para. 21(3)).

[66] See above, n 51, and accompanying text.   [67] [1999] Crim LR 570.

[68] [2005] 2 AC 467. The decision is also known as *Z*.   [69] Ibid., para. 28.

[70] [1971] 2 QB 202, at 207.

[71] See Ch 5.5(d) above and Ch 6.4 below; the Divisional Court erroneously applied this general approach to duress in *DPP* v *Rogers* [1998] Crim LR 202.

[72] (1982) 74 Cr App R 235; much of Lord Lane's judgment proceeds on an analogy with provocation, even though the preponderance of authority favours a subjective test for belief in provocation cases—see Ch. 6.4 below, and W. Wilson, 'The Structure of Criminal Defences' [2005] Crim LR 108.

whether, as a result of what D *reasonably* believed that the duressor had said or done, he had *good cause* to fear death or serious injury. Lord Lane offered no convincing reasons for departing from the subjective orthodoxy of the time, and in *Safi* (2003)[73] the Court of Appeal appeared to favour a subjective approach, although the point was not argued to a clear conclusion.[74]

Both duress and necessity are subject to the doctrine of prior fault.[75] In *Sharp* (1987)[76] D joined a gang of robbers participating in crimes where guns were carried, but when he tried to withdraw he was himself threatened with violence. The Court of Appeal held that the defence of duress is unavailable to anyone who voluntarily joins a gang 'which he knows might bring pressure on him to commit an offence and was an active member when he was put under such pressure'. In *Shepherd* (1987)[77] the Court added that: 'there are certain kinds of criminal enterprises the joining of which, in the absence of any knowledge of propensity to violence on the part of one member, would not lead another to suspect that a decision to think better of the whole affair might lead him into serious trouble'. The doctrine of prior fault does not only operate in the context of joining criminal enterprises: it also applies where drug users become indebted to drug dealers who have a reputation for violence. The leading decision now is *Hasan*,[78] where D associated with a man who was known to use violence, and who allegedly forced D (by threats) to carry out two burglaries. Lord Bingham held that there should be an objective test, based on the foreseeability of violence being threatened by the people with whom D was associating, and not requiring foresight of coercion to commit crimes of a particular kind:[79]

The policy of the law must be to discourage association with known criminals, and it should be slow to excuse the criminal conduct of those who do so. If a person voluntarily becomes or remains associated with others engaged in criminal activity in a situation where he knows or ought reasonably to know that he may be the subject of compulsion by them or their associates, he cannot rely on the defence of duress to excuse any act which he is thereafter compelled to do by them.[80]

Thus the subjective element in *Sharp*, 'which he knows…', is superseded by the strongly objective approach running through Lord Bingham's speech in *Hasan*. However, Baroness Hale's speech favours the subjective approach in *Sharp*, and also argues that the foreseen threat must have been a threat to commit crimes rather than a general threat of violence.[81] The latter point is surely right: the likelihood of being subjected to violence or threats thereof is different from the foreseeability of threats being used to force D to commit crimes, and the latter should be required.

---

[73] [2003] Crim LR 721.

[74] It is tolerably clear from the strong objectivism of Lord Bingham's speech in *Hasan* [2005] 2 AC 467, notably at para. 38, that he would support the *Graham* test.

[75] Discussed in Ch 5.4(d) above.   [76] [1987] QB 853.   [77] (1988) 86 Cr App R 47.

[78] [2005] 2 AC 467.   [79] Overruling *Baker and Ward* [1999] 2 Cr App R 335 on this point.

[80] [2005] 2 AC 467, at para. 38; see also *Ali* [2008] EWCA 716.   [81] Ibid., para. 77.

(b) THEORETICAL FOUNDATIONS FOR THE DEFENCES

Why should defences of duress be allowed? One argument is that acts under duress or necessity are justified in the sense that they constitute a lesser evil than the carrying-out of the threat: the credentials of this rather narrow justificatory argument were discussed in Chapter 4.8. In general the courts have tended to mix arguments of justification with those of excuse, without noticing the distinction. How strong are the arguments for excusing D rather than justifying the act? It is fairly clear that duress and necessity do not negative intent, knowledge, or recklessness: D will know only too well the nature and consequences of the conduct. It also seems unlikely that they negative the voluntary nature of D's conduct: the elements of unconsciousness and uncontrollability of bodily movements which are regarded as the hallmark of involuntary behaviour[82] are not typically to be found in duress cases. Two separate rationales, with somewhat different implications, warrant further discussion—the first seeing duress as characterized by moral involuntariness, the second regarding it more as a reasonable response to extreme pressure.

Although conduct in response to duress or necessity is not *in*voluntary, it may be described as *non*-voluntary. The argument is that there is a much lower degree of choice and free will in these cases than in the normal run of actions. George Fletcher has termed this 'moral or normative involuntariness', arguing that the degree of compulsion in these cases is not significantly less than in cases of physical involuntariness.[83] The phrases used by the Court of Appeal in *Hudson and Taylor*—'effective to neutralize the will of the accused', and 'driven to act by immediate and unavoidable pressure'— have been repeated in many subsequent decisions. Even though 'neutralizing the will' puts it rather too strongly, the idea of moral involuntariness seems to encapsulate the approach of English judges, who also draw on a supposed analogy with provocation. Full acceptance of the 'moral involuntariness' rationale might lead to an entirely subjective version of duress, in which the degree of pressure experienced by D would be the main issue. In fact English law imposes a standard of reasonable steadfastness, but of course that could be explained as a means of avoiding false defences (as courts and reform committees often state) rather than a rejection of the basic rationale.[84]

An alternative rationale is to regard the successful duress defence as recognition that D responded in a reasonable way to the pressure of circumstances which involved extreme danger. It is important not to over-sell the element of reasonableness here. It is not being claimed that D had a right to respond as he did, save perhaps in the small group of cases where a net saving of lives is in prospect.[85] Duress usually operates as an excuse, recognizing the dire situation with which D was faced and limiting the

---

[82] See Ch 4.2.

[83] G. P. Fletcher, *Rethinking Criminal Law* (1978), 803, adopted by Dickson J in the Supreme Court of Canada in *Perka v R* (1984) 13 DLR (4th) 1. For discussion see C. Wells, 'Necessity and the Common Law' (1985) 5 Oxford JLS 471.

[84] Acceptance of the 'moral involuntariness' rationale might also raise questions about the law's rejection of social and financial pressures as grounds of defence: see section 6.8(b) below.

[85] Discussed in Ch 4.8 above.

defence to cases where D responded in a way that did not fall below the standard to be expected of the reasonable citizen in such circumstances. On this rationale the person of reasonable firmness assumes a central role, not so much in announcing a standard that should be followed, or reducing the risk of false defences, but rather in recognizing that D was not lacking in responsibility for what was done.[86] D is excused for giving way to the threat or danger when resistance could not reasonably be expected in the circumstances—which means that self-sacrifice is required in certain (lesser) situations. There is thus a pale reflection of doctrines of self-defence, which requires a proportionate response to the threatened harm if D is to be acquitted.[87] Two further issues must then be resolved. The first is whether the idea of 'moral involuntariness' is at all relevant on this rationale: is it necessary to show, to any degree, that D's will was overborne at the time? The answer must be negative, and it is instructive that no such requirement forms part of English law on duress—even though the judiciary often refers to it.[88] If 'moral involuntariness' merely embodies a recognition that D was faced with dire circumstances of danger, then so be it; but if it suggests that it is necessary to show that D was in some form of disturbed condition at the time, that is surely unsustainable. The defence should be accorded to someone whose response to the extreme situation was as cool as a cucumber, so long as the other requirements are fulfilled.

That leaves the issue of citizens who, for one reason or another, cannot attain the standard of reasonable firmness in these situations. We saw that in *Bowen*[89] the Court of Appeal recognized a small group of conditions which might be allowed to modify the standard of reasonable firmness, whilst maintaining that the standard should be upheld for those falling outside that short list. Arguments of this kind have been encountered in other contexts,[90] but they have recently been rejected by the House of Lords for provocation cases.[91] The 'moral involuntariness' rationale argues in favour of including these people in the defence of duress, on the basis of the severe reduction of their free will. But they fall outside the 'reasonable response' rationale, to which the standard of reasonable steadfastness is central, and so the most appropriate form of defence would ideally be one that rests on diminished capacity or extreme mental or emotional disturbance.[92]

---

[86] Gardner, *Offences and Defences*, ch 6; Horder, *Excusing Crime*, 99–109.

[87] See the argument of C. Clarkson, 'Necessary Action: a New Defence' [2004] Crim LR 81.

[88] For two cases using the language of reasonableness rather than that of moral involuntariness see *Pommell* [1995] 2 Cr App R 607 and *DPP v Harris* [1995] 1 Cr App R 170. For fuller analysis see K. J. M. Smith, 'Duress and Steadfastness: in Pursuit of the Unintelligible' [1999] Crim LR 363.

[89] [1996] 2 Cr App R 157, above, n 57 and accompanying text.

[90] E.g. where negligence is the fault element for crimes (see Ch 5.5(d) above), and to a small extent in self-defence (see Ch 4.6(g) above).

[91] *Attorney-General for Jersey v Holley* [2005] 2 AC 580, overruling *Smith (Morgan)* [2001] 1 AC 146, and discussed in Ch 7.4(b) below. However, age is recognised as a factor to be taken account in provocation cases (*DPP v Camplin* [1978] AC 705) and also in duress (*Bowen*, above). Cf. *Wilson*, n 108 below and accompanying text.

[92] Cf. Horder, *Excusing Crime*, 183–5, and the discussion in section 6.7 below.

A more radical approach would be to argue that, since there are so many questions of degree in duress and necessity cases (degree of threat, degree of immediacy, seriousness of crime), they are much more appropriate for the sentencing stage than the liability stage.[93] On that view, the duress defences should be abolished altogether. At present English law takes the view (except in murder cases) that there is a point at which threats or an emergency may place so much pressure on an individual that it is unfair to register a conviction at all, so long as the individual does not fall below the standard of reasonable firmness, but that in lesser situations claims of duress sound only at the sentencing stage. Mitigation may be right if 'desert' is the basis for sentence, but supporters of deterrent sentencing have a particular problem. Their general approach is to maintain that the stronger the temptation or pressure to commit a crime, the stronger the law's threat should be in order to counterbalance it.[94] The law and its penalties should be used to strengthen the resolve of those under pressure. Yet Bentham also accepted that criminal liability and punishment are inefficacious where a person is subject to such acute threats (e.g. death, serious injury) that the law's own threat cannot be expected to counterbalance it: in these cases, he said, there should be a complete defence.[95] The difficulty with this analysis is that it suggests heavy deterrent sentences for all cases except the most egregious, where it prescribes no penalty at all—a distinction with momentous effects but no clear reference point. There is surely a sliding scale of intensity of duress and necessity. If, in the dire circumstances that confront D, he or she responds in such a way that one could not reasonably expect more of a citizen, then surely neither conviction nor punishment is deserved. Mitigation of sentence should be available for less extreme cases, to reflect strong elements of pressure that did not amount to the full defence.

(c) DURESS, NECESSITY, AND THE TAKING OF LIFE

Although most of the elements of these defences seem to be based on a rationale of excusing a person's understandable submission to the threat, the troubled issue of whether the defences should be available to murder has led the courts to draw on justification-based rationales. The tone was set in the late nineteenth century with *Dudley and Stephens* (1884),[96] where two shipwrecked mariners killed and ate a cabin-boy after seventeen days adrift at sea. Lord Coleridge CJ held that no defence of necessity was available in a case of taking another person's life. In the first place, he argued, there is no *necessity* for preserving one's own life, and there are circumstances in which it may be one's duty to sacrifice it. Then, secondly, if there were ever to be a similar case, who would judge which person is to die? (This point might be overcome by drawing lots.) So he concluded that, terrible as the temptation might be in this kind of case, the law should 'keep the judgment straight and the conduct pure'. The

---

[93] See below, section 6.8(a), and M. Wasik, 'Duress and Criminal Responsibility' [1977] Crim LR 453.

[94] J. Bentham, *Introduction to the Principles of Morals and Legislation* (1789), ch XIV, para. 9.

[95] Ibid., para. 11.   [96] (1884) 14 QBD 273.

sentence of death was later commuted to six months' imprisonment, thus emphasizing the obvious conflict between the desire to reaffirm the sanctity of life and the widely felt compassion for people placed in an extreme situation.

In *DPP* v *Lynch* (1975)[97] the House of Lords accepted, by a majority of three to two, that duress by threats should be available as a defence to an accomplice to murder, reflecting the law's compassion towards a person placed under such extreme pressure. But then the Privy Council in *Abbott* v *R* (1977)[98] held that duress was unavailable as a defence to the principal in murder, and in *Howe* (1987)[99] the House of Lords had to decide whether to perpetuate this distinction between principals and accomplices. Their Lordships decided not to do so, unanimously favouring a rule which renders duress and necessity unavailable as defences in all prosecutions for murder.[100] The primary reason for their decision was that the law should not recognize that any individual has the liberty to choose that one innocent citizen should die rather than another. All duress cases involve a choice between innocents, D and the intended victim, and the law should not remove its protection from the victim. Thus D is required to make a heroic sacrifice. A secondary argument, similar to that employed a century earlier in *Dudley and Stephens*, was that executive discretion could take care of deserving cases—either by releasing D on parole at an early stage or even by refraining from prosecution.[101]

Both these arguments are open to criticism. The argument based on protection for the innocent victim seems to assume that duress is being advanced as a justification for killing: this enables the judges to assume that, because the killing of an innocent person is unjustified, duress should not be a defence. It was argued earlier that a killing under duress might be justifiable if there were a net saving of lives,[102] but that is not the issue here. Where it is a question of liability for taking one innocent life to save another, the rationale must be one of excuse, not justification. It can therefore be put alongside other situations in which a killing may be excused in whole or in part (e.g. mistaken self-defence, intoxication, provocation), without being justified.[103] Utilitarians might argue that a rule denying duress as a defence to murder is preferable because over the years it might achieve a net saving of lives:[104] this not only fails to take the defendant's interests into account, but also assumes that persons under duress will know of the law's approach and will be influenced by it, an assumption which will rarely be true (except perhaps in some terrorist cases). The second argument, in favour of convicting the person under duress and then invoking executive clemency to reduce the punishment, also smacks of an unrealistic utilitarian solution. For one thing, there

---

[97] [1977] AC 653.

[98] [1977] AC 755; cf. I. Dennis, 'Duress, Murder and Criminal Responsibility' (1980) 96 LQR 208.

[99] [1987] AC 417.

[100] The House of Lords held in *Gotts* [1992] 2 AC 412 that, by logical extension, duress should not be available as a defence to attempted murder.

[101] *Per* Lords Griffiths and Mackay, at 446 and 457.   [102] Above, Ch 4.8.

[103] P. Alldridge, 'The Coherence of Defences' [1983] Crim LR 665.

[104] A. Kenny, *Freewill and Responsibility* (1978), 38.

can be no certainty that the Parole Board will view these cases more favourably than others. For another, if we are satisfied that D was placed under extreme pressure, we ought to declare that publicly either by allowing a defence or, if not, by allowing a partial defence to murder on an analogy with provocation. The argument in favour of merely a partial defence should not be understated: as Chapter 7.4(c) will show, it is possible both to recognize the sanctity of life as a fundamental value and to demonstrate compassion.

In its 2005 Consultation Paper the Law Commission proposed that duress should only be available as a partial defence to first degree murder, reducing it to second degree murder, and that the *Bowen* test of relevant characteristics should be tightened so as to run in parallel to the partial defence of provocation.[105] There were other, complicated proposals about how this approach should be adapted to defences of duress to second degree murder and to manslaughter, but the consultation process persuaded the Commission to abandon this whole approach. Although recognizing that consultees were 'more divided on duress' than on any other aspect, the Commission has now reverted to its earlier view that in principle it would be morally wrong to convict of any crime a defendant who satisfies the stringent requirements of the defence of duress, having reacted as a person of reasonable fortitude might have done.[106] The Commission recognizes that recommending duress as a partial defence might have been a compromise acceptable to many, but it states that the argument against a complete defence based on the sanctity of life is not conclusive because of cases of 'ten year olds and peripheral secondary parties becoming involved in killing under duress.'[107] The reference to age is sharpened by the subsequent decision in *Wilson* (2007),[108] where a boy of 13 was pressed by his father into helping with the killing of a neighbour and no defence of duress was available on the charge of murder, despite considerable evidence that he was so frightened that he could not disobey his father. The Law Commission's principal argument is that as a matter of moral principle a person who is found by a jury to have reacted to extreme circumstances as a reasonable person might have done 'should be completely exonerated despite having intentionally killed,' adding that youth is a relevant factor in determining reasonableness.[109] Thus the Commission insists that the threat must be believed to be life-threatening, and that D's belief that the threat has been made is based on reasonable grounds. The argument for adopting the *Graham* approach is that, compared with provocation and self-defence (which have no such requirement of reasonable belief), there is a less immediate temporal or physical nexus between the threat and the killing in duress cases.[110] This also becomes the primary argument in favour the Commission's recommendation that the

---

[105] LCCP 177, *A New Homicide Act?* (2005), Part 7.

[106] Law Com No 304, *Murder, Manslaughter and Infanticide* (2006), Part 6; the earlier report adopting the same approach was Law Com No. 218, *Legislating the Criminal Code: Offences against the Person and General Principles* (1993).

[107] Ibid., para 6.46.   [108] [2007] QB 960.   [109] Law Com No 304, paras 6.53 and 6.142–3.

[110] Ibid., para 6.79.

burden of proof be reversed where duress is raised as a defence to homicide[111]—that the separation of the threat from the killing creates extra difficulties for the prosecution. However, the Commission supports the tightening of the law by the House of Lords in *Hasan*, one aspect of which was the replacement of the former 'imminence' requirement with one of immediacy; so the temporal separation cannot be great, and reference to 'time to reflect' takes insufficient account of the great emotional turmoil brought about by threats of this kind.[112]

(d) MARITAL COERCION

Section 47 of the Criminal Justice Act 1925 provides that 'on a charge against a wife for any offence other than treason or murder it shall be a good defence to prove that the offence was committed in the presence of, and under the coercion of, the husband'. This defence is rarely raised, and the burden of proving it lies on the defendant/wife. It does not require proof of any threats or danger of death or serious bodily harm: although it should be shown that the wife's will was overborne, it seems that evidence of tormenting and persistent badgering might be sufficient to support the defence.[113] The Law Commission has taken the view that the defence is inappropriate in modern times, especially the restriction to wives, and has recommended that these cases be subsumed within the duress defences and mitigation of sentence.[114]

6.4 REASONABLE MISTAKE AND PUTATIVE DEFENCES

For the first three-quarters of the twentieth century, the approach of the common law to mistake was that if the defendant wished to rely on this defence it must be shown that he had reasonable grounds for his mistaken belief. The leading case was *Tolson* (1889),[115] where the Court for Crown Cases Reserved held that a mistake of fact on reasonable grounds would be a defence to any criminal charge. Despite being cited as the leading case, the ambit and status of *Tolson* were never clear, since Stephen J devoted much of his judgment to the proposition that if the mental element of the crime is proved to have been absent, the crime so defined is not committed.[116] Certainly it

---

[111] For criticism of this recommendation, see A. Ashworth, 'Principles, Pragmatism, and the Law Commission's Recommendations on Homicide Law Reform' [2007] Crim LR 333, at 340–2.

[112] The Ministry of Justice's Consultation Paper 19 on *Murder, Manslaughter and Infanticide: Proposals for Reform of the Law* (2008), much discussed in Ch 7 below, does not cover the duress recommendations.

[113] *Shortland* [1996] 1 Cr App R 116.

[114] Law Com No. 83, *Defences of General Application* (1977), para. 3.9.   [115] (1889) 23 QBD 168.

[116] Compare E. Griew, 'States of Mind, Presumptions and Inferences', in P. F. Smith (ed.), *Criminal Law: Essays in Honour of J. C. Smith* (1987), with A. P. Simester, 'Mistakes in Defence' (1992) 12 Oxford JLS 295, and R. H. S. Tur, 'Subjectivism and Objectivism: Towards Synthesis', in Shute, Gardner, and Horder (eds.), *Action and Value in Criminal Law* (1993).

is authority for the proposition that reasonable mistake is a defence to crimes of strict liability.[117] It is also authority on the crime of bigamy, and was expressly preserved by the House of Lords in *DPP* v *Morgan* (1976)[118] when it introduced (or, in the light of Stephen J's judgment, reintroduced) the proposition that if the mental element is missing in respect of one of the conduct elements specified in the definition of the crime, then as a matter of inexorable logic D should be acquitted even if the mistake was wholly unreasonable.

The 'inexorable logic' argument may be accepted as a starting point, but the question is whether considerations of moral fault indicate that in certain types of case it should be abandoned. We have already seen that the 'inexorable logic' has not been followed in respect of intoxication (where special restrictive rules have been created) and does not apply in duress. When the House of Lords in *Morgan* opted for the 'inexorable logic' approach, treating the claim of mistake as a mere denial of the required mental element, it expressly left undisturbed two different rules—the *Tolson* principle (above), as applied to bigamy, and the requirement that mistakes relating to a defence should be reasonable. This second requirement relates to 'defences' resting on justification or on consent: if there is a mistake about the circumstances giving rise to the justification or the consent, this makes it a putative defence (i.e. an *excuse* rather than a *justification*, because the circumstances for justification were absent and D merely believed they were present). The persistence of the objective approach to mistake in these cases owed more to assumption and repetition than to principled argument. Its chief application was in self-defence, where courts had tended to require that any mistake about the circumstances should be based on reasonable grounds.[119] But this reasonable mistake doctrine, left intact in *Morgan* itself, was swept away by decisions of the Court of Appeal and Privy Council in the 1980s.[120] Thus a putative defence will succeed wherever the prosecution fails to prove that D knew the relevant facts (i.e. that D did not hold the mistaken belief claimed), no matter how outlandish that belief may have been. Thus in *Williams* (1984)[121] V saw a man, X, snatch a bag from a woman in the street; V ran after X and forcibly detained him; D then came upon the scene and asked V why he was punching X; V said, untruthfully, that he was a police officer; D asked V for his warrant card, and when V failed to produce the card, D struck V. D was charged with assaulting V, and his defence was that he mistakenly believed that his actions were justifiable in the prevention of crime. It is plain that his

---

[117] Confirmed by the House of Lords in *Sweet* v *Parsley* [1970] AC 132.

[118] [1976] AC 182, discussed in Ch 5.5(d) above.

[119] The leading cases were probably *Rose* (1884) 15 Cox CC 540 and *Chisam* (1963) 47 Cr App R 130. The only careful analysis was that of Hodgson J in the Divisional Court in *Albert* v *Lavin* (1981) 72 Cr App R 178. Cf. however the subjective approach to mistake in provocation cases: *Letenock* (1917) 12 Cr App R 221, *Wardrope* [1960] Crim LR 770.

[120] *Kimber* (1983) 77 Cr App R 225, followed by *Gladstone Williams* (1984) 78 Cr App R 276 and by *Beckford* [1988] 1 AC 130.

[121] (1984) 78 Cr App R 276.

actions were not in fact justified, since V was acting lawfully in trying to detain X.[122] The law requires the prosecution to satisfy the court that D was aware of the facts which made his action unlawful, and he was not. He was mistaken. The Court of Appeal held that his conviction should be quashed: 'The mental element necessary to constitute guilt is the intent to apply unlawful force to the victim. We do not believe that the mental element can be substantiated by simply showing an intent to apply force and no more.'

The courts in *Williams* and *Beckford*[123] presented this as an application of the 'inexorable logic' approach in *Morgan* (overlooking the fact that *Morgan* left this aspect of the law unchanged), reasoning as follows:

(i) unlawfulness is an element in all crimes of violence;

(ii) intention, knowledge, or recklessness must be proved as to that element; and therefore;

(iii) a person who mistakenly believes in the existence of circumstances which would make the conduct lawful should not be criminally liable.

The crucial step is the first: how do we know that unlawfulness is a definitional element in all crimes?[124] Not all crimes are defined explicitly in this way. So it is, rather, a doctrinal question. Andrew Simester has argued that unlawfulness cannot be an ingredient of the *actus reus*, since only when there is *actus reus* with *mens rea* can we conclude that conduct was unlawful.[125] Might this not be a question of terminology? Some would argue, as we saw in Chapter 4.6, that there is no *actus reus* where the conduct is justified. If 'absence of justification' is substituted for 'unlawfulness' in the above reasoning, does not the difficulty claimed by Simester disappear? A stronger argument is that, irrespective of the definitional boundaries of the *actus reus*, there is a need to confront the moral issue whether there should not be some duty to reflect before using force against another. Using force is *prima facie* wrongful and should put a citizen on notice to examine the grounds for doing so—if, of course, time and circumstances permit. This distinguishes cases of putative defence from other cases of mistake in which D does not think what he is doing is wrongful or dangerous.[126]

Rather than relying on the logic of steps (i), (ii), and (iii) above, the law should adopt this more context-sensitive approach, taking some account of the circumstances of the act, of D's responsibilities, and of what may reasonably be expected in such situations.[127] The consequence may be not to require knowledge of a certain circumstance in the definition of the offence, but to require reasonable grounds for a belief. In rape

---

[122] S. Uniacke, *Permissible Killing* (1994), discussed in Ch 4.6 above, would say that D's conduct was agent-perspectivally justified but not objectively justified.

[123] n 120 above.

[124] Cf. the discussion by S. Yeo, *Compulsion in the Criminal Law* (1991), 198–208.

[125] Simester, 'Mistakes in Defence'; see also Gardner, *Offences and Defences*, ch 5.

[126] *McCann v UK*, discussed in Ch 4.6(g) above; see also Simester, above, n 125, 307.

[127] Cf. A. Brudner, 'Agency and Welfare in the Penal Law', in Shute, Gardner, and Horder (eds.), *Action and Value in Criminal Law*, 35 and 43.

cases these considerations militate in favour of a requirement of reasonable grounds for any mistake, as the Sexual Offences Act 2003 now provides;[128] reasonable grounds should also be required in respect of age requirements for consensual sexual conduct, although in this respect the 2003 Act goes further and imposes strict liability in some circumstances;[129] and in principle it is right to require reasonable grounds before allowing the acquittal of a police officer with firearms training, as in *Beckford* v *R* (1987).[130] Of course, any such infusion of objective principles must recognize the exigencies of the moment, and must not demand more of D than society ought to expect in that particular situation.[131] That is a necessary safeguard of individual autonomy. The general point, however, is that there may be good reasons for society to require a certain standard of conduct if the conditions were not such as to preclude it, particularly where the potential harm involved is serious. These arguments may be no less strong in many cases of putative defences of duress and necessity, where a reasonableness requirement has been imposed.[132] Any move in the direction of requiring reasonableness may have the effect of raising the question whether cases of mistaken belief in justification are necessarily cases of excuse, or whether they may be treated as forms of justification.[133] In fact they have elements of both: Antony Duff proposes that this is best expressed by describing D's conduct as wrong but warranted—wrong because there is no objective reason for it, but warranted because D (reasonably) believed in the existence of circumstances that would have made it the right thing to do.[134]

English law currently takes variable approaches to these questions. In recent years the judges have often seemed to be firmly in the embrace of the 'inexorable logic' approach to mistake,[135] but there have been some deviations which perhaps suggest recognition of the complexity of the issues. As noted in the discussion of duress in section 6.3(a) above, the poorly-reasoned decision in *Graham*,[136] holding that a mistake about the nature of the threat must be a reasonable one if the defence of duress is to be available, has now been championed on strong welfarist grounds by Lord Bingham in *Hasan* and adopted by the Law Commission.[137] However, although the objectivist approach in the Sexual Offences Act suggested a more context-sensitive

---

[128] See Ch 5.5(d) above and Ch 8.5(c) below.

[129] See Ch 8.6(d) below, discussing *G*. [2008] UKHL 37.

[130] Compare *Beckford* [1988] AC 130 with *McCann* v *UK*, above, Ch 4.7(f)(vi); cf. J. Horder, 'Cognition, Emotion and Criminal Culpability' (1990) 106 LQR 469. The High Court of Australia has required 'reasonable grounds' in all cases of mistaken self-defence: *Zecevic* v *R* (1987) 162 CLR 645.

[131] See, e.g. the provision in s 76(7) of the Criminal Justice and Immigration Act 2008, that in determining whether force was reasonable in self-defence a court should take account of 'what the person honestly and instinctively thought necessary', discussed in Ch 4.6(g) above.

[132] As discussed in section 6.3(c) above, the Law Commission has recommended a subjective test of mistake for duress. However, it moved towards an objective approach, at least in relation to mistaken belief in consent in rape cases, in its Consultation Paper No. 139, *Consent in the Criminal Law* (1995), ch 7.

[133] See J. Horder, 'Killing the Passive Abuser', in S. Shute and A. P. Simester (eds.), *Criminal Law Theory: Doctrines of the General Part* (2002).

[134] R. A. Duff, *Answering for Crime* (2007), 270–6.

[135] For recent affirmations see *B* v *DPP* [2000] 2 AC 428 and *K* [2002] 2 AC 462 discussed in Ch 5.5(a) above.

[136] (1982) 74 Cr App R 235.   [137] [2005] 2 AC 467, discussed in part 3(a) of this chapter.

treatment of mistake and putative defences, such considerations were neglected in the drafting of the self-defence provisions in section 76(3) of the Criminal Justice and Immigration Act 2008, which confirms a wholly subjective test of belief with no variations between trained police or military personnel and ordinary citizens caught up in a sudden incident.[138]

6.5 IGNORANCE OR MISTAKE OF LAW

(a) THE ENGLISH RULES

English criminal law appears to pursue a relatively strict policy against those who act in ignorance of the true legal position, but the maxim *ignorantia juris neminem excusat* (ignorance of the law excuses no one) is too strong as a description. Ignorance or mistake as to civil law, rather than criminal law, is capable of forming the basis of a defence; indeed, the crimes of theft and criminal damage explicitly provide for defences where D believes that he has a legal right to take or to damage property.[139] But it would be unsafe to state the rule by reference to a distinction between matters of civil law and criminal law, because offences are often defined in such a way as to blur the two. Whether goods are classified as 'stolen' for the purposes of the offence of handling stolen property seems to be a question of criminal law, so if D knows all the facts but misunderstands their legal effect this is irrelevant. Whether an auditor is disqualified from acting for a certain company seems to be a question of civil law, so where D was unaware of the relevant law, his conviction for acting as an auditor knowing that he was disqualified was quashed.[140] One difference between these two offences is that the latter contains the word 'knowingly', whereas the crime of handling includes the words 'knowing or believing'; it is certainly true that a number of English decisions have allowed mistake or ignorance of the law to negative 'knowingly',[141] but this cannot explain all the decisions.[142] English law does recognize that the obligations are not all on one side. The state has duties to declare and to publicize laws and regulations: non-publication of a Statutory Instrument will usually afford a defence to any crime under that Instrument to a person unaware of its existence,[143] and failure to publish a government order in respect of a particular person will also afford a defence to that person if he or she is unaware of the order.[144]

---

[138] See the discussion in Ch 4.6(f) above.

[139] Theft Act 1968, s. 2(1)(a); Criminal Damage Act 1971, s. 2.5(2)(a).

[140] *Secretary of State for Trade and Industry* v *Hart* [1982] 1 WLR 481.

[141] Williams, *Textbook of Criminal Law*, ch 20.

[142] E.g. *Grant* v *Borg* [1982] 1 WLR 638, *Jones, The Times*, 19 August 1994.

[143] Statutory Instruments Act 1946, s. 3(2).

[144] *Lim Chin Aik* v *R* [1963] AC 160; see also Toulson LJ in *Chambers* [2008] EWCA Crim 2467.

(b) INDIVIDUAL FAIRNESS AND PUBLIC POLICY

It could be argued that individual fairness demands the recognition of ignorance or mistake of law as an excuse: a person who acts in the belief that conduct is non-criminal, or without knowing that it is criminal, should not be convicted of an offence. Although ignorance of the law may not negative the fault requirements of a particular offence, respect for individual autonomy supports the excuse in its own right: a person who chooses to engage in conduct without knowing that it is criminal makes a choice which is so ill-informed as to lack a proper basis. The counter-arguments are based on conceptions of intrinsic wrong and of social welfare. One is that it can fairly be assumed that people know that certain morally wrong conduct is criminalized, even if they are unaware of the precise terms of the law.[145] The utilitarian argument that it is desirable to encourage knowledge of the law rather than ignorance, and any rule which allowed ignorance as a defence would therefore tend to undermine law enforcement.[146] This does not establish that ignorance of the law is always wrong, merely that it may be socially harmful. Another is the argument that, if we judge defendants on their *particular view* of the law rather than on the law as it is, we are contradicting the essential objectivity of the legal system.[147] This is, to say the least, an exaggeration: so long as the court states what the law is, the law's objectivity remains unimpaired. It would also seem to suggest that for a court to allow any excuse amounts to a denial of the offence. This not only confuses the element of excuse with the element of wrongdoing,[148] but also overlooks the value of a publicized trial, where reasonable mistake of law is allowed, as a means of public education.

Is it generally wrong to be ignorant or mistaken about the law? It may be argued that it is a duty of citizenship to know the law. Thus, to convict a person despite ignorance of the law is not to attack the principles of choice and individual autonomy which were identified earlier as fundamental to the principles of fairness.[149] Rather it is to forsake an atomistic view of individuals in favour of a recognition of persons as social beings, with both rights and responsibilities within the society in which they live.[150] It has already been argued that in many situations it is fair to expect citizens to take care to enquire into the surrounding circumstances before they act, and the case for requiring some mistakes to be reasonable has been put.[151] A similar line of argument might support a duty on each citizen to take reasonable steps to become acquainted with the criminal law. There are few problems in making the duty known, since 'ignorance of the law is no excuse' is a widely-known

---

[145] *Christian v R.* [2006] 2 AC 400 (defendants from Pitcairn Island knew rape and sexual abuse were seriously wrong and criminal, though unaware of terms of English law); see H. Power, 'Pitcairn Island: Sexual Offending, Cultural Difference and Ignorance of the Law' [2007] Crim LR 609.

[146] O. W. Holmes, *The Common Law* (1881), 48.

[147] J. Hall, *General Principles of Criminal Law* (1960), 388, and above, Ch 4.1.

[148] Fletcher, *Rethinking Criminal Law*, 734, and above, Ch 4.1.   [149] See above, Ch 5.4(a).

[150] J. Raz, *The Morality of Freedom* (1987), 206–7, and above, Ch 4.2 and 4.3.

[151] In Ch 5.5(d) and in section 6.4 above.

principle even now.[152] The duty should not be an absolute one, however. First, there is often uncertainty in the ambit of the law. Sometimes the legislature acknowledges the difficulty of stating the law by allowing D's own standards as a benchmark of lawfulness, as in the crime of blackmail.[153] Sometimes it resorts to a broad standard such as 'reasonable' or 'dishonest', leaving the courts to concretize the norm after each event, which goes against the principles of maximum certainty and fair warning.[154] This is not to suggest that every case in which the courts change the law should inevitably give the defendant a defence of ignorance of the law; indeed, the European Court of Human Rights has held not only that judicial extensions of the law conform to Article 7 if they are 'reasonably foreseeable', but also that the application of that test varies according to the subject-matter of the law and that 'a law might still satisfy the requirement of foreseeability even if the person concerned had to take legal advice' to determine its practical scope.[155] A second reason for not making the policy absolute is the possibility that the State has not fulfilled its duties in respect of making a new offence known and knowable.[156] The State clearly has this duty when it seeks to impose criminal liability for an omission,[157] and the duty applies generally to the publication of laws. This, indeed, is an aspect of the principle of legality, requiring both certainty of definition and fair warning.[158]

One way of maintaining the general duty to know the law, whilst allowing exceptions based on respect for individual autonomy, would be to provide that a mistake of law may excuse if it is reasonable. This, in combination with the argument in section 6.4 above, would have the advantage of narrowing the present gulf, wide and difficult to defend, between the effects of ignorance of law (no general defence) and ignorance of fact (frequently negativing liability).[159] Ignorance of the law would clearly be reasonable if fair warning of a prohibition had not been given: this would accommodate the second point above. Mistake or ignorance of law might also be reasonable if D had no cause to suspect that certain conduct was criminal, or if D had been misinformed or wrongly advised about the law (see (c) below), or perhaps in other circumstances.[160] Ignorance and mistake would be unlikely to be held reasonable if D was engaging in a business or an activity (such as driving a car) that is known to have changing

---

[152] Cf. D. Husak, 'Ignorance of Law and Duties of Citizenship' (1994) 14 Legal Studies 105, 110: 'the problem arises from the fact that few persons are likely to be aware of the existence of the alleged duty to know the law'.

[153] Theft Act 1968, s. 21(1), discussed below, Ch 9.4.   [154] See above, Ch 3.5(h).

[155] Cantoni v France (1997) VIII HRCD 130, on the French offence of selling prohibited pharmaceutical products; cf. Ch 3.5(g) above on Art. 7.

[156] Husak, 'Ignorance of Law', at 115, rightly emphasizes that the state has duties as well as citizens.

[157] See the American case of Lambert v California (1957) 355 US 225 on omissions (and above, Ch 4.4(c)).

[158] See Lord Bingham in Rimmington and Goldstein [2006] 1 AC 459 at [30]; and above, Ch 3.5(i).

[159] Cf. D. Husak and A. von Hirsch, 'Culpability and Mistake of Law', in Shute, Gardner, and Horder (eds.), Action and Value.

[160] See ibid., proposing that the only way of avoiding unfairness is to allow courts to assess the moral legitimacy of D's beliefs. Cf. the remark of Brooke LJ in R (on application of W) v DPP [2005] EWHC Admin 1333, that a boy of 14 'might well not know what was a criminal offence and what was not'.

rules;[161] but the merit of a reasonableness requirement is that it would not absolutely rule the defence out. A defendant would be able to argue that there were special circumstances warranting exculpation. To rebut the claim that such an excuse might be raised so often as to impede the administration of the criminal law, one has only to refer to the lengthy experience of Scandinavian countries in providing for defences of this kind.[162]

The draft Criminal Code states that 'ignorance or mistake as to a matter of law does not affect liability to conviction for an offence except (a) where so provided, or (b) where it negatives the fault element of the offence'.[163] This is traditional, inflexible, and unsatisfactory: it would prevent the courts from developing a wider defence, and would relegate most of these matters to mitigation of sentence.[164] Moreover, exception (b) hardly corresponds to any general moral distinction. The legislature has not pursued a consistent policy in deciding whether or not 'knowingly' should form part of the definitions of offences, and it certainly cannot be assumed that Parliament had considered whether particular offences justify an exception in favour of ignorance or mistakes of criminal law (including unreasonable ones). The courts have veered between allowing ignorance of law to negative 'knowingly' and declaring that this approach would be 'wholly unacceptable'.[165] There is a need to adopt a clear principle (a duty with circumscribed exceptions) and then to interpret statutory offences in the light of it. The same approach should be adopted where the offence includes a phrase such as 'without lawful excuse' or 'without reasonable excuse'.[166]

(c) THE RELIANCE CASES

Another benefit of moving away from the relatively strict English policy against defences based on mistake or ignorance of criminal law towards a 'reasonable grounds' defence would be to deal more fairly with the 'reliance' cases. In *Cooper v Simmons* (1862)[167] an apprentice absented himself from his apprenticeship after the death of his master, having sought the advice of an attorney and having been counselled that he was no longer bound. The Court nevertheless convicted him of unlawfully absenting

---

[161] Thus the distinction drawn by Brudner, 'Agency and Welfare', 36, between ignorance of 'true crimes (as distinct from welfare offences)' is not convincing, since there may be strong duties in the latter category too.

[162] J. Andanaes, '*Error Juris* In Scandinavian Law', in G. Mueller (ed.), *Essays in Criminal Science* (1961); cf. generally P. Brett, 'Mistake of Law as a Criminal Defence' (1966) 5 Melb U LR 179.

[163] Law Com No. 177, cl. 21.

[164] As in *Thomas* [2006] Crim LR 71, where D was unaware that the Sexual Offences Act 2003 had changed the law by criminalizing sexual acts by foster-parents with former foster children under 18 (not 16).

[165] Cf. *Secretary of State for Trade and Industry v Hart* [1982] 1 WLR 481, with *Grant v Bord* [1982] 1 WLR 638, two decisions of the House of Lords in the same year; see generally A. T. H. Smith, 'Error and Mistake of Law in Anglo-American Criminal Law' (1984) 14 Anglo-American LR 3. Cf. *Attorney-General's Reference (No. 1 of 1995)* [1996] 2 Cr App R 320, where the absence of 'knowingly' was one factor in the Court's decision to hold that ignorance of the law was no excuse.

[166] See R. Card, 'Authority and Excuse as Defences to Crime' [1969] Crim LR 359 and 415.

[167] (1862) 7 H and N 707, discussed by Brett, 'Mistake of Law as a Criminal Defence'.

himself from his apprenticeship, and Pollock CB stated that 'it would be dangerous if we were to substitute the opinion of the person charged...for the law itself'. In *Arrowsmith* (1975)[168] D had on occasions distributed leaflets urging British soldiers not to serve in Northern Ireland. In the past the Director of Public Prosecutions had declined to prosecute her under the Incitement to Disaffection Act 1934, but now she was charged with an offence under that Act. One line of defence was that she reasonably believed, as a result of a letter from the Director, that her conduct did not contravene the Act. The Court of Appeal upheld her conviction, stating that 'a mistake as to the law would not avail the appellant except perhaps in mitigation of sentence'. Both these cases would surely be better analysed in terms of reasonable reliance. If it is established that D relied on advice from officials with regard to the lawfulness of the proposed conduct, that ought to be sufficient to support reasonable grounds for the mistake of law.

Confusion may arise about the entitlement of a particular agency or official to advise a member of public about the law, as one English case vividly demonstrates,[169] but since reasonable mistake of law would be an excuse, the key question is whether D reasonably assumed that the person giving the advice was duly authorized. In the element of reliance, these cases can call upon a kind of estoppel reasoning—the State and the courts should not convict a person whom they or their officers have advised otherwise.[170] Thus the Control of Pollution Act 1974, s 3(4)(a), specifically creates a defence to the crime of unlicensed waste-disposal where D 'took care to inform himself from persons who were in a position to provide information', recognizing both individual fairness and an estoppel on officials. Thus, even if one were persuaded by the argument that allowing mistake of law as a general defence would encourage ignorance of the law, the reverse of that argument applies here: to recognize officially-induced error as a defence would signal the value of citizens checking on the lawfulness of their proposed activities. Indeed, all the values that support the principle of fair warning militate in favour of recognizing officially induced error, since a citizen who seeks advice is showing respect for the law.[171]

One reason for the rarity of appellate cases on mistake of law may be that it is often accommodated in other ways. An appeal is unlikely if a person receives substantial mitigation of sentence, perhaps an absolute or conditional discharge. On some occasions a person who acted on a mistaken view of the law might not be prosecuted at all, or the prosecution might be discontinued.[172] In one case a company was advised by members of the local council's planning department that the erection of advertising boards would not require planning consent. The company erected the boards, and the council then brought a prosecution. The Divisional Court held that the

---

[168] [1975] QB 678.   [169] *Cambridgeshire and Isle of Ely CC v Rust* [1972] 1 QB 426.

[170] A. Ashworth, 'Excusable Mistake of Law' [1974] Crim LJ 652.

[171] A. Ashworth, 'Testing Fidelity to Legal Values' in Shute and Simester (eds.), *Criminal Law Theory*, and the refinements proposed by Horder, *Excusing Crime*, 270–6.

[172] *Code for Crown Prosecutors* (5th edn., 2004), para. 5.10(c) ('genuine mistake or misunderstanding').

prosecution should have been stayed as an abuse of process,[173] Schiemann LJ stating that it is 'important that the citizen should be able to rely on the statements of public officials'. The council had argued that these were junior officials and that the company was wrong to rely on their opinion, but the Divisional Court replied that 'it was not as though they had requested planning advice from one of the council's gardeners'. This is a significant decision, employing the powerful procedural approach of staying the prosecution where a mistaken view of the law has been implanted by an official. The courts might well decline to recognize a substantive defence of officially-induced error of law,[174] but it can be argued that staying the prosecution is a more appropriate remedy inasmuch as D might not have brought himself within the offence definition at all if the official advice had not been given.

Should the doctrine extend to acting on the advice of a lawyer? Glanville Williams, although a strong supporter of a defence of reasonable reliance on official statements, pointed out the danger that allowing reliance on a lawyer's advice (rather than official advice) might open up a broad route to exculpation for corporate defendants in particular.[175] On the other hand, for an individual to take legal advice might be even more reasonable, in terms of citizenship duties, than to rely on the advice of a junior official.[176]

6.6 ENTRAPMENT

There are cases in which the police arrange either for one of their own officers or for some other person to approach D and tempt him to commit an offence. If D commits the offence after the officer or *agent provocateur* has over-stepped the boundary of permissible conduct, should there be a defence of entrapment? Some jurisdictions admit such a defence. Until 2001 English law relied merely on the exclusion of evidence or mitigation of sentence in such cases. Now, following the decision of the House of Lords in *Looseley; Attorney-General's Reference No. 3 of 1999*,[177] proof of entrapment leads to a stay of the prosecution.

What amounts to entrapment? The House of Lords held that where 'the police conduct preceding the commission of the offence was no more than might be expected from others in the circumstances' it is acceptable.[178] This is the 'unexceptional opportunity test': if all that the official does is to offer D an unexceptional opportunity, this is

---

[173] *Postermobile v Brent LBC, The Times*, 8 December 1997, discussed at [1998] Crim LR 435, and by Ashworth, 'Testing Fidelity to Legal Values', at 303.

[174] Cf. *Kingston* [1995] 2 AC 355, discussed in section 6.3(d) above, where the House of Lords held that it must be for Parliament to decide whether or not to introduce a new defence.

[175] G. Williams, 'The Draft Code and Reliance on Official Statements' (1989) 9 Legal Studies 177, at 186–7; the Model Penal Code, s. 2.04(3), also allows reliance on official advice, but not a lawyer's advice, as a defence.

[176] See further Ashworth, 'Testing Fidelity to Legal Values', at 306–7.   [177] [2002] 1 Cr App R 29.

[178] *Per* Lord Nicholls at [23].

permissible conduct. If the official goes further than that—as by inciting, instigating, persuading, or pressurizing—it would be a case of entrapment. Where there are reasonable grounds for suspecting a particular individual, or individuals frequenting a certain place, of involvement in a type of offence (e.g. drug dealing), it seems that it is permissible to test the person(s) by approaching them and making an enquiry.[179] The rationale of this approach to entrapment seems to have two strands. First, the courts are concerned to prevent abuse of executive power: it would be a misuse of power for the State's agents to lure citizens into breaking the law and then to prosecute them for doing so. Secondly, entrapment must be prevented in order to protect the integrity of the criminal justice system—which would be undermined if the courts allowed the prosecution of crimes created by state officials.[180] These rationales led the House of Lords in *Looseley* to adopt the procedural remedy of staying the prosecution for abuse of process, rather than allowing the trial to proceed and according D a defence to criminal liability. This approach is consistent with that of the Strasbourg Court in *Teixeira de Castro* v *Portugal*,[181] which held that the entrapped applicant had been 'deprived of a fair trial from the outset', and therefore that Article 6 had been violated.

The Supreme Court of the United States still upholds an entrapment defence,[182] and the Model Penal Code includes one.[183] The Supreme Court's version focuses on whether D would have committed the offence otherwise, which then becomes a question of whether he was 'pre-disposed' to commit such offences. This notion is also to be found in the Strasbourg decision in *Teixeira de Castro*, but it shifts the enquiry back towards the character and previous record of the person incited—and into dangerous waters. The House of Lords was wise to reject the notion of predisposition in its *Looseley* judgment, but it remains to be seen whether its requirement of 'reasonable suspicion' that the person targeted was involved in that type of offending will be any more robust.

The rationale and remedies for entrapment just described are dependent on the involvement of the State and its officials in instigating crime. No such rationale would apply if it were a private individual who, on his or her own initiative, incited D to commit the offence: the fact that one person incites another does not relieve the other of criminal liability, since the law regards each of them as autonomous individuals who are able to choose what to do. However, there is an argument that few people would wish to live in a society where they were liable to have their virtue tested unexpectedly (by, for example, journalists in search of a story), and that therefore the exclusion of evidence ought to be available in egregious cases of private entrapment.[184] The courts seem to accept this to some extent, in that they seem to have made little of the distinction between official entrapment and private entrapment (typically engineered by

---

[179] See the discussion by A. Ashworth, 'Re-Drawing the Boundaries of Entrapment' [2002] Crim LR 161, and in 'Testing Fidelity to Legal Values', at 310–22.

[180] See, e.g., Lord Nicholls at [1] and Lord Hoffmann at [39–40].   [181] (1999) 28 EHRR 101.

[182] *Jacobson* v *US* (1992) 112 S Ct 1535.

[183] S. 2.13 (official inducement of offence; not available if offence involves bodily injury).

[184] K. Hofmeyr, 'The Problem of Private Entrapment' [2006] Crim LR 319.

journalists), although there has been no case in which a stay of prosecution on grounds of private entrapment has been ordered and upheld.[185]

6.7 REVIEWING THE NON-JUSTIFICATORY DEFENCES

In Chapter 4 we dealt with justifications for the use of force, often regarded as defences, and also with involuntary conduct. Justifications are clearly separate from the exculpatory doctrines in this chapter, but the reason for placing involuntariness (automatism) in Chapter 4 is that it relates to the basic requirement of a voluntary act. From the functional point of view, however, automatism tends to operate as a defence, and its rationale belongs properly with the capacity requirements (expressed in terms of infancy and insanity) discussed in Chapter 5.2. Reference will be made below to these incapacity 'defences', as we consider some general questions about the rationales, functions, and appropriate responses to the various conditions discussed in this chapter. First, we shall examine the implications of the threshold question: should a suggested excuse be recognized as a defence, or merely as a mitigating factor in sentencing, or even marked in a different way? Secondly, we consider the roots of fault and the excuses in conceptions of individual responsibility. Thirdly, we go on to examine the arguments in favour of policies of social defence and social responsibility. Whether it is possible to travel beyond a demonstration of the conflicting policies and principles and to achieve a unifying theory is then the question which remains.

(a) THE RECOGNITION OF EXCULPATORY DOCTRINES

In moral and social terms there is probably a scale of exculpation, running from the most acute forms that affect agency itself by denying responsibility (such as insanity and automatism) to mere matters of difficulty and extra pressure at the other extreme. Most forms of exculpation can be manifested to a different degree (strong or weak circumstances of duress, mild or acute mental disorder). During the course of the chapter it has often been remarked that the courts strive to keep the ambit of a particular 'defence' as narrow as possible, so as to capture only the full or extreme cases. This approach leaves other cases which have exculpatory elements to be dealt with in some other way. In some spheres of criminal law it is not simply a question of whether there is a defence or not. Provocation and diminished responsibility[186] are available as partial defences to murder, reducing the crime to manslaughter, and there is no

---

[185] Cf. the decision of the Court of Appeal in *Shannon* [2000] 1 Cr App R 168 with that of the Strasbourg Court in *Shannon v UK* [2005] Crim LR 133; see also Ashworth, 'Re-Drawing the Boundaries of Entrapment', at 175–6.

[186] See Ch 7.4(b) and (e), below.

procedural reason why they and other partial defences should not be granted a wider application—wherever there is a ladder of offences, the partial defence might serve to reduce the higher to the lower.[187] There are obvious counter-arguments, grounded in the increased complexity and length of trials of cases where the unique stigma of 'murder' is not present,[188] but these concede rather than weaken the moral/social arguments for allowing the reduced culpability in, say, provocation cases to be signi-fied by a reduction in the offence of conviction. This may be regarded as an example of fair labelling:[189] just as there is a 'scale of excuse, running downwards from excusing conditions, through partial excuses to mitigating excuses',[190] so the law should reflect these gradations through complete defences, partial defences, and then mitigation of sentence.

In some spheres, English courts have faltered and have refused to recognize a defence at all, leaving all degrees of exculpation to be reflected by procedural means, chiefly at the sentencing stage. This has been the predominant approach to entrapment,[191] and for many years it was the courts' approach to excuses based on necessity.[192] Indeed, the House of Lords has gone further by proposing executive discretion as a desirable way of mitigating the effective punishment of those who kill under duress.[193]

It would be procedurally possible to deal with all excuses, and, indeed, with all fault requirements, by excluding them from the criminal trial and dealing with them at the sentencing stage. As we saw in Chapter 5.4(a), one could create a strict liabil-ity system in which proof of conduct and causation was sufficient for conviction, and fault would then be considered at the sentencing stage as a pointer to the most appropriate means of state intervention to prevent any repetition. The objection to this is that a criminal conviction is rightly regarded as condemnatory: it is unfair to apply this official censure when the absence of fault is so high on the 'scale of excuse' that there should be no formal blame. Supporters of strict liability, such as Baroness Wootton, would reply that on their system a conviction would not carry such a stigma, since it would not imply culpability.[194] Such an approach would sacri-fice the underlying deterrent and censuring elements of the criminal law, as well as reducing the protection of individual autonomy by reducing the individual citizen's ability to plan and to predict the law's interventions. So long as the criminal law is the principal censuring institution, conviction should carry the moral connotation of culpable wrongdoing, and so there ought to be the possibility of recognizing com-pelling excuses by means of acquittal.

---

[187] As proposed by the Criminal Law Revision Committee in its 1976 Working Paper, 'Offences against the Person'.

[188] See M. Wasik, 'Partial Excuses in the Criminal Law' (1982) 45 MLR 515, and Horder, *Excusing Crime*, 143–52.

[189] See above, Ch 3.5(l).   [190] Wasik, 'Partial Excuses', 524.   [191] See above, section 6.6.

[192] See above, section 6.3(c).

[193] See *Howe* [1987] AC 417, but cf. the discussion in section 6.3(c) above.

[194] The views of Baroness Wootton were discussed above, Ch 5.5(a).

Even if defences to criminal liability are recognized for 'strong' exculpatory factors, it will remain necessary to deal appropriately with 'weak' or imperfect cases of exculpation. This is where mitigation of sentence should be the principal tool. Unless the penalty is mandatory (as, in English law, for murder), courts will be able to reflect the strength of the excuse in the sentence they pass. However, there are two difficulties in treating this as an ideal way of reflecting the defendant's desert. First, there is the question of establishing the factual basis for mitigation. Sometimes this will have emerged during a trial, if a trial has taken place,[195] but more often it will be necessary to lay a foundation after conviction and before sentence. Procedures to ensure proper fact-finding are still developing, but there has been insufficient recognition of the importance of ensuring that defendants have the same evidential safeguards as they would have had in a criminal trial.[196] Secondly, there is no clear recognition that mitigation of sentence is a right. It is often presented as discretionary, suggesting that courts may withhold a reduction in sentence if they wish to do so.[197] This is unsatisfactory, and reflects the general lack of structure of English sentencing law in respect of mitigating factors.

If defences to liability and mitigation of sentence should be the two principal responses to excuses, what should be the role of procedural remedies? The most powerful procedural approach is not to prosecute at all. Thus prosecutors are expected to take account of the likely line of defence in a particular case, and they might therefore bring no prosecution if convinced that a certain defence is probable to succeed. Where they are not so convinced, they may still decide that a prosecution would not be 'in the public interest'. The *Code for Crown Prosecutors* mentions cases where 'the offence was committed as a result of a genuine mistake or misunderstanding', and cases where 'the defendant is elderly or is, or was at the time of the offence, suffering from significant mental or physical ill health'.[198] Both of these factors are to be weighed against the seriousness of the offence. In practice, non-prosecution and discontinuance of prosecution are responses to many cases involving mentally disordered persons, who may then be admitted to hospital or a treatment programme informally. However, a deeper issue is whether a prosecution should be stayed once it has been commenced. This powerful remedy has been held appropriate in cases of entrapment[199] and in one case of officially-induced mistake of law:[200] the reason it is particularly appropriate in these types of case is that the involvement of officials in 'creating' the offence makes it wrong for the prosecution to be heard by the courts at all. Providing a defence to liability would not be enough: it is so fundamentally wrong for the state to prosecute that D should not be put to the trouble of defending himself.

---

[195] See Ch 1.4 above on the prevalence of guilty pleas.

[196] See A. Ashworth, *Sentencing and Criminal Justice* (4th edn., 2005), 342–6.   [197] Ibid., Ch 5.7.

[198] Crown Prosecution Service, *Code for Crown Prosecutors*, discussed in Ch 1.4 above.

[199] *Looseley; Attorney General's Reference No. 3 of 1999* [2002] 1 Cr App R 29, discussed in section 6.6 above.

[200] *Postermobile plc* v *Brent LBC, The Times*, 8 December 1997, discussed in section 6.5(c) above.

(b) INDIVIDUAL RESPONSIBILITY

It was shown in Chapter 5.4(a) that the roots of the conception of individual responsibility which underlies the principle of *mens rea* lie in respect for the autonomy of the individual. Thus defendants who did not have the capacity to choose—who were not responsible moral agents—should be dealt with by means of the denial-of-responsibility 'defences' of infancy, insanity, and automatism. Those who were responsible moral agents should then be judged, if they raise defences such as duress, necessity, or reasonable mistake, according to the standard of what we ought reasonably to expect of a person in that situation. These defendants are, as John Gardner puts it, 'asserting their responsibility' (in the sense that they are claiming to have the capacities of a normal citizen of full age and sound mind) but claiming an excuse on the ground that their response to a testing situation 'lived up to expectations in a normative sense'.[201] Thus, as we saw in section 6.3 above, the standard of the person of reasonable firmness is central to the defences of duress and necessity. Now in one sense this might be thought to be indulgent to D—there is no requirement that he should have felt totally deprived of his freedom of action, merely that a reasonably steadfast citizen would have found the pressure intolerable.[202] But that may be explained on the ground that this is not a denial of responsibility but an excuse, where a high but reasonably achievable standard is more appropriate than perfectionism.[203]

In another sense, however, the standard of 'normative expectations' may be thought insufficiently indulgent to D: it precludes actual enquiry into the pressures experienced by this defendant. Even if D felt totally overwhelmed by the pressures, the law would not allow a defence of duress unless a reasonably steadfast person would also have been seriously affected. In other words, there is no scope for a plea of diminished personal capacity, based on D's inability to meet the normative expectations. In the past the courts have been reluctant to lower the standard, because of a fear of false defences if the law were totally subjective, or a fear of a significant loss in the deterrent effect of the law, or perhaps for other social reasons. But in more recent years, as we have seen, courts have occasionally been willing to lower the standard in order to take account of certain individual susceptibilities and conditions.[204] Lowering the standard blurs the rationale, however. Strictly speaking, if D lacks the capacity to attain the standard normatively expected, then the essence of plea is not that D behaved as a responsible citizen might be expected to, but rather that D is to some extent denying responsibility for what was done. Acknowledging this difference, Jeremy Horder argues for an intermediate category of cases where the essence of D's response is diminished capacity.[205]

---

[201] Gardner, *Offences and Defences*, 124.

[202] See *Hasan* [2005] 2 AC 467, and the theoretical discussion by A. Brudner, 'A Theory of Necessity' (1987) 7 Oxford JLS 338.

[203] E. Colvin, 'Exculpatory Defences in Criminal Law' (1990) 10 Oxford JLS 381, 395.

[204] In duress, see the loosening in *Bowen* [1996] 2 Cr App R 157 and the tightening in *Hasan* [2005] 2 AC 467, above, section 6.3(a); in provocation, see the loosening in *Smith (Morgan)* [2001] 1 AC 146 and the tightening in *Attorney General for Jersey* v *Holley* [2005] UKPC 23, below, Ch 7.4(b).

[205] Horder, *Excusing Crime*, ch 3; R. Lippke, *Rethinking Imprisonment* (2007), 88–101.

This would reduce the grade of liability for defendants who to a significant extent felt coerced, compelled, or 'pressured' to do what they did and where there is evidence of an underlying condition to explain this. It might, for example, be open to those who narrowly fail to satisfy the requirements of a defence of insanity, and could include such conditions as pre-menstrual syndrome.[206] It would also deal with those unable to attain the standard of reasonable steadfastness in duress and necessity.[207] In order to preserve the distinct grounds for different complete excuses (such as duress), and to respect fair labelling, it would be preferable to articulate as many discrete defences as possible, and to have any defence or partial defence of diminished capacity in a kind of residual or 'sweeper' role. Whether its availability would unduly complicate trials is for careful enquiry and debate. There is no need for citizens to have fair warning of its existence,[208] but it is important to ensure that the courts exercise their power fairly and consistently as between similarly or equivalently situated defendants.

Some have put the case for a defence of 'social deprivation' or 'rotten social background' on the basis of diminished capacity. Thus it has been argued that social deprivation should excuse because it causes criminal behaviour; that socially deprived people may find themselves under pressure to commit crime, or in a situation where crime is the 'lesser evil'; or that socially deprived people who have been abused and maltreated by others have already suffered and therefore should not be punished further, or at least fully, for their own crimes.[209] To connect this with the rationale offered earlier, it could be argued that some of these people are trapped in a criminal lifestyle, with scarcely more capacity for free choice than the person under duress, and that therefore society has no warrant for expecting them to achieve the normative expectations appropriate to others.[210] Critics suggest that this confuses explanation with excuse: research may demonstrate a causal link between social deprivation and offending behaviour, but this does not deny the capacity or a fair opportunity to behave otherwise.[211] Judge Bazelon, a strong proponent of the 'social deprivation' defence, subscribed to the diminished capacity argument but put greater weight on the state's responsibility for the defendants' predicament: 'It is simply unjust to place people in dehumanizing social conditions, to do nothing about those conditions, and then to command those who suffer, "Behave—or else!" '[212] This locates the reasoning much closer to the 'normative expectations' argument, though suggesting that for this group the normative expectations should be lower; and the reference to the

---

[206] P. Taylor and G. Dalton, 'Pre-Menstrual Syndrome: a New Criminal Defense?' (1983) 19 Cal WLR 269; *Sandie Smith* [1982] Crim LR 531; and J. Dressler, 'Reflections on Excusing Wrongdoers: Moral Theory, New Excuses and the Model Penal Code' (1988) 19 Rutgers LJ 671, 707.

[207] See section 6.3(b) above.   [208] See Ch 3.5(i) above.

[209] See the judicious but critical assessment of these arguments by S. Morse, 'Deprivation and Desert', in W. C. Heffernan and J. Kleinig (eds), *From Social Justice to Criminal Justice* (2000).

[210] For deeper discussion, see N. Lacey, C. Wells and O. Quick, *Reconstructing Criminal Law* (3rd edn., 2003), 408–12.

[211] M. Moore, 'Causation and the Excuses' (1985) 73 Cal LR 1091; S. Kadish, *Blame and Punishment* (1987), 102–6; Dressler, 'Reflections on Excusing Wrongdoers'.

[212] D. Bazelon, 'The Morality of the Criminal Law' (1976) 49 S Cal LR 385.

state's role and responsibility chimes more with the rationales for defences of entrapment (6.6) and reliance on official advice (6.5), a kind of muted estoppel.[213] However, reference to the state's role may also suggest that there are other and preferable ways of tackling these inequalities than through the introduction of a criminal law defence, although some would contend that they are only preferable because they leave the logic of liberal criminal law untarnished and not preferable because they are likely to be particularly effective.

(c) SOCIAL RESPONSIBILITIES AND SOCIAL DEFENCE

In practice, the objective standard of the person of reasonable firmness in excuses such as duress and necessity may be sustained less by the doctrine of 'normative expectations' or Hart's 'fair opportunity' rationale than by judicial fear of false defences.[214] The latter may also be a prominent reason for the presence of restrictive conditions in intoxication (the limitation to crimes of 'specific intent') and in ignorance or mistake of law (the virtual denial of such a defence). There are, however, stronger social arguments for restrictions. One is the importance of taking compulsory measures against persons shown to be capable of causing harm in their condition. This is a major plank of the 'special defence' in insanity cases, where absence of capacity leads to a special verdict which, in turn, may give rise to compulsory measures of social protection. Yet we saw in Chapter 5.2 that the terms of the defence are not designed to demonstrate that D is a dangerous person, likely to cause further serious harm if given a simple acquittal. The same might be said of the restrictions placed on intoxication as a defence (section 6.2), where beliefs about future dangerousness may play some part, but probably the chief reason for restricting the defence is the belief that people who do harm whilst intoxicated are blameworthy.[215]

One argument often mobilized against the infiltration of objective requirements into excusing defences is 'logic'. We have noted this in relation to intoxication (section 6.2(b) above) and particularly mistake of fact (section 6.4). Consistency of approach to excusing conditions would certainly seem to be an element in fairness, but it does not follow that the excuses should be consistently and utterly subjective in their requirements. The subjective principles have their foundation in the principle of individual autonomy, and its emphasis on choice, control, and fair warning. But we have seen that modern liberal philosophy has begun to emphasize that individuals should be viewed as members of society with mutual obligations rather than as abstracted and isolated individuals. The subjective principles and the contemporaneity principle,[216]

---

[213] See also the contribution by B. Hudson, 'Punishing the Poor', in Heffernan and Kleinig, *From Social Justice to Criminal Justice*.

[214] In *Hasan* [2005] 2 AC 467, Lord Bingham's primary reason for taking a restrictive, objectivist approach to the duress defence was one of 'public policy', including (para. 22) fear of false defences.

[215] For other arguments in favour of taking coercive measures against those acquitted on certain grounds, see Colvin, 'Exculpatory Defences', 392.

[216] See above, Ch 5.4(a) and (d).

ingrained as they are in much academic writing in the common law world, in some judicial pronouncements, and in many Law Commission proposals, seem premised on an atomistic view of individual behaviour.[217]

An alternative approach would spell out certain duties of citizenship which should form part of membership of a legal community and which might have some bearing on issues of criminal responsibility. One such duty might be to show reasonable steadfastness in the face of pressure, and to avoid uncontrolled behaviour that might lead to harm to others. This might be applied to cases of intoxication, based on the general social proposition that persons who take large amounts of alcohol or certain drugs constitute a greater and well-known risk of causing harm. A similar argument might be used to justify the refusal to admit provocation as a general defence, rather than as a partial defence to murder. In principle no exceptions should be admitted to the principle that citizens should control their tempers. However, certain provocation cases contain strongly exculpating elements, in terms of justified anger or fear combined with a disturbed emotional state, and these make a convincing case for provocation as a qualified defence.[218]

How might the 'duties of citizenship' approach apply to mistake cases? Citizens may surely be expected to make reasonable efforts to acquaint themselves with the contours of the criminal law, but this does not support the refusal of the English courts and legislature to recognize a general excuse based on ignorance or mistake of law. On the contrary, the citizen's duty is fulfilled by making reasonable enquiries, and this would support a defence of reasonable ignorance or mistake of law. Indeed, where there is reasonable reliance on official advice the prosecution should be stayed, since D has acted as a good citizen should.[219] Strangely, the English courts erred in the opposite direction in cases of mistake of fact, seduced by the allure of what Lord Hailsham described as 'inexorable logic'. The courts have failed to show proper sensitivity to the rights of others in particular situations which ought to alert the citizen, but Parliament has now intervened in relation to sex cases. Thus, rather than regarding the defendant in a rape case as abstracted from the situation of close proximity to the victim and subject only to the momentary and 'inexorable' logic of the question: 'did he at that time realize that there was a risk that she was not consenting?', the law now requires that D reasonably believed that the other party consented.[220] Similarly, rather than applying broad subjective principles to a defendant who alleges mistake as to the age of a young person with whom he had (consensual) sexual relations, the law now requires a reasonable belief that the child is 16 or over where the actual age is 13–15 (inclusive),[221] although it goes further and (controversially) imposes strict liability as to age where the child is under 13.[222] Would it not also be proper to require higher

---

[217] M. Kelman, 'Interpretive Construction in the Substantive Criminal Law' (1981) 33 Stanford LR 591.

[218] Horder, *Excusing Crime*, Ch 4, and below, Ch 7.4(b).   [219] Above, section 6.5(c).

[220] Sexual Offences Act 2003, s. 1(1)(c), and below, Ch 8.5(i).

[221] Cf. Sexual Offences Act 2003, s. 9(1)(c) with the decisions of the House of Lords in *B v DPP* [2000] 2 AC 428 and *K.* [2002] 2 AC 462, discussed in Ch 5.5(a) above.

[222] E.g. Sexual Offences Act 2003, ss 5–8, interpreted in *G.* [2008] UKHL 37 and criticised below, Ch 8.6.

standards of those trained for special roles? Thus, rather than regarding a police officer as abstracted from his or her training and knowledge of alternative means of resolving a situation and subject only to the momentary and 'inexorable' logic of the question: 'did he at that time believe that his life was in danger from V?', the law should ask whether he took care (so far as possible) to ensure that V was armed, before injuring V or taking V's life.[223]

The drift of this argument is towards the idea of duties of citizenship which relate in part to control of one's own passions or 'vices'[224] and in part to one's respect for the rights of others in situations which obviously concern those rights (e.g. sexual intercourse, the use of deadly force). The doctrine of prior fault should prevail over the principle of contemporaneity, as the various duties tug the enquiry away from the momentary conduct towards a broader consideration of the situation and its antecedents. Those wedded to traditional theory will doubtless regard this as the spread of negligence liability, and so it is. In this sense, it is compatible with much of what was said by Lord Diplock in *Caldwell*,[225] in that failure to give thought to those matters which the reasonable citizen might regard as obvious may be just as culpable as momentary advertence to such matters. But the idea of duties of citizenship does not require full adherence to the *Caldwell* doctrine. Two modifications are particularly important. First, the general notion that citizens with ordinary powers of perception and self-control should exercise those powers must be subject to an exception in favour of persons incapable of attaining that general standard.[226] But it was argued above that it would be conceptually and socially clearer to deal with such persons separately under a (partial) defence of diminished capacity, rather than to distort the general 'normative expectations' of citizens. Secondly, a full-blown notion of individual responsibility should be responsive to the relative magnitude of the wrongs or harms. The paradox of *Caldwell* is that it applied chiefly to criminal damage, an offence which is, in most instances,[227] well down the scale of seriousness. A socially sensitive doctrine would impose greater duties of care on citizens in situations where serious harm is widely known to be possible (e.g. use of firearms, fire-raising, irregular driving), where great harm is a possibility (e.g. the operation of transport systems, sports stadiums), and particularly where the means of avoiding the wrong or harm are relatively simple (as in sexual intercourse, enquiring about the other's willingness). It will be evident that these arguments do not promise a simplified system of fault and excuses, but Chapters 5 and 6 should have demonstrated that the present system is far from simple. Conflicts between 'pure' individual responsibility and questions of social responsibility are endemic in this sphere. The allure and 'logic' of orthodox subjectivism need re-appraisal in the light of considerations of welfare and social responsibility, and a proper adjustment of the different claims debated.

---

[223] See *McCann v UK*, discussed in Ch 4.6(f)(vi) above, and Gardner, *Offences and Defences*, 128–30.

[224] Fletcher, *Rethinking Criminal Law*, 514; V. Tadros, *Criminal Responsibility* (2005), Ch 3.3.

[225] [1982] AC 341, discussed in Ch 5.3(c) above.

[226] See the discussion in Lippke, *Rethinking Imprisonment*, 88–101.

[227] Cf. criminal damage by fire, which is often serious.

Lastly, discussion of citizens' responsibilities should not lead one to neglect the positive duties of the State in these matters. The obligation to publicize new criminal laws is one such duty, particularly strong in respect of duties to act. It is also time to recognize more fully the wrongness of entrapping citizens into committing offences (section 6.6) and the wrongness of convicting those who rely on official advice (section 6.5). And then there is the more general issue of the State's responsibility for social conditions which foster crime. This is not an outrageous notion: the preamble to the European Convention on Compensation for Victims of Crimes of Violence refers to the idea that the State's duty to provide compensation arises from its failure to prevent crimes,[228] and this suggests at least an obligation to take reasonably determined measures to reduce crime. One such measure is to relieve those criminogenic social conditions of poverty, bad housing, unemployment, lack of social facilities, and so forth which have an established link with law-breaking.[229] Even if we are not prepared to go so far as to accept social deprivation as an excuse for crime,[230] it may be regarded as significantly reducing an offender's 'desert', and also as an example of state neglect of a duty towards its citizens.[231]

(d) EXCULPATION AND 'DESERT'

Modern writings on the criminal law have made substantial advances in uncovering and criticizing the reasons for admitting, rejecting, and shaping the various fault requirements in criminal liability. Some 'defences' are essentially denials of capacity and responsibility (notably infancy, insanity, and automatism); others are denials of the positive fault requirements of offences (usually, of intention, recklessness, or knowledge). Another important conceptual distinction is that between justification and excuse, which improves the clarity of analysis and might avert confusions in the courts.[232] However, once the conceptual distinction is made, it must be recognized that some defences (or partial defences) contain elements of both,[233] and that some others rest on neither rationale—for example, principles of integrity and coherence support a decision to stay the prosecution if there is a finding of entrapment or reliance on official advice. It is probably true that defendants would prefer to be acquitted on grounds of justification (recognizing that the conduct was acceptable in the circumstances) rather

---

[228] Council of Europe, *European Convention on Compensation for the Victims of Crimes of Violence* (1984).

[229] For reviews, see D. Farrington, 'Childhood Risk Factors and Risk-Focused Prevention', and D. Smith, 'Crime and the Life Course', in M. Maguire, R. Morgan, and R. Reiner (eds.), *Oxford Handbook of Criminology* (4th edn., 2007).

[230] See text at nn 209–212 above.   [231] N. Lacey, *State Punishment* (1988), ch 3 and 140–1.

[232] See, e.g., the discussion of *Howe* above, Ch 6.3(d).

[233] For an introduction to the literature, see Fletcher, *Rethinking Criminal Law*, ch 10; K. Greenawalt, 'The Perplexing Borders of Justification and Excuse' (1984) 84 Columbia LR 1897; J. Dressler, 'Justifications and Excuses: a Brief Review of the Concept and the Literature' (1987) 33 Wayne LR 1155; G. Williams, 'The Theory of Excuses' [1982] Crim LR 732; W. Wilson, *Central Issues in Criminal Theory* (2002), chs 10 and 11; R. A. Duff, *Answering for Crime* (2007), ch 11.

than on grounds of excuse (conduct unacceptable, but D insufficiently culpable), and indeed that many defendants would prefer to be acquitted on grounds of excuse than on grounds of denial of responsibility (D lacking capacity at the time, not acting as a responsible moral agent).[234] This is one reason women defendants may be unwilling to accept a diminished responsibility defence when they claim provocation.[235]

The search for a unifying theory of excuses has been less productive, partly because different authors set out to rationalize different groups of defences (some including denials of capacity, others excluding them).[236] Hart's influential doctrine, that a person should be held criminally liable only if he or she had the capacity and a fair opportunity to act in conformity with the law,[237] captures the essence of individual autonomy in the importance of having fair warning and being able to plan and predict. However, it leaves much work to be done on appropriate criteria of the 'fairness' of opportunities. Gardner's theory of 'normative expectations' is clear about its rationale,[238] but of course requires interpretation in practice. However, both Hart and Gardner recognize that the enquiry should not be entirely subjective, and that there are good grounds for expecting people to attain certain standards of behaviour. The idea of duties of citizenship, aired in the previous section, might thus be developed to broaden out the concept of desert. Although some of the objective requirements mentioned in this chapter are based on principles of welfare, it should not be thought that all of them are derogations from a properly social theory of individual autonomy.[239]

Desert theory—maintaining that individuals should be liable to punishment only when they deserve it, and to the extent that they deserve it[240]—may find its application in one of three forms in modern writings.[241] One is the character theory, which argues that D's 'desert' is 'gauged by his character' and therefore that 'a judgment about character is essential to the just distribution of punishment'.[242] Behaviour should be excused when it does not reflect D's true character, but D should be held responsible whenever the behaviour can be regarded as genuinely expressive of his dispositions.[243] The Court of Appeal came close to espousing this theory in *Kingston*,[244] when it held that D should not be held liable for acts done whilst involuntarily (but not totally) intoxicated. Full espousal of the theory would have excused D if he had no general disposition to paedophilia but would have convicted him if paedophilia was part of his general character. There are several difficulties with this approach, one of which is

---

[234] See D. Husak, 'The Serial View of Criminal Law Defences' (1992) 3 Crim L Forum 369, developed by Horder, *Excusing Crime*, ch 3.

[235] See further Ch 7.5 below.

[236] P. Westen, 'An Attitudinal Theory of Excuse' (2006) 25 *Law and Philosophy* 289, 330.

[237] H. L. A. Hart, *Punishment and Responsibility* (2nd edn., 2008), chs 2 and 7, and the re-assessment in J. Gardner's 'Introduction', xxxiv–liii.

[238] Gardner, *Offences and Defences*, ch 5.   [239] See Ch 4.1 above for discussion.

[240] See Ch 1.5 above.   [241] See Westen, 'Attitudinal Theory of Excuse.'

[242] Fletcher, *Rethinking Criminal Law*, 800.

[243] For analysis and discussion, see Lacey, *State Punishment*, 65–78; Horder, *Excusing Crime*, ch 1; Tadros, *Criminal Responsibility*, ch 1.

[244] Discussed in section 6.2(d) above; see further Sullivan, 'Making Excuses'.

the breadth of the conception of character it employs (although that, in turn, raises the question of one's responsibility for one's character), and another is its lack of sharpness in distinguishing between acceptable and unacceptable excuses.[245] Fletcher's attempt to limit the theory to the particular act charged, by reference to the principle of legality and the value of privacy, is unconvincing.[246] A second approach is choice theory, emphasizing respect for D's autonomy and for the choices he or she made and not imposing liability for conduct which cannot be said to be chosen. Gardner's 'normative expectations' theory falls into this category, as does much of Hart's famous doctrine of fair opportunity. A third strand may be found in capacity theory, which focuses on D's capacity to conform conduct to the law's requirements. Although some regard this as a general rationale, Horder has argued for its place as a supplement to choice theory, not denying or altering 'normative expectations' theory but adding to it a further ground of (partial) defence for those unable to attain the objective standards inherent in the 'normative expectations' approach.[247] Acknowledging that there are some who cannot attain the general normative standards requires an assessment of other principles, facts and rationales, as we have seen (for example) when examining the case for a defence based on social deprivation. But this is not to reject a framework based on desert, however, since that would be to reject the foundations for many of the safeguards and protections for individuals that are constructed out of respect for autonomy, and that is not the road we should go down.

FURTHER READING

H. L. A. Hart, *Punishment and Responsibility* (2nd edn., 2008), chs 2 and 7, and Introduction by J. Gardner.

S. Kadish, *Blame and Punishment* (1987), ch 5.

J. Gardner, *Offences and Defences* (2007), chs 4, 6 and 7.

J. Horder, *Excusing Crime* (2004), ch 3.

V. Tadros, *Criminal Responsibility* (2005), chs 10 and 11.

R. A. Duff, *Answering for Crime* (2007), ch 11.

P. Westen, 'An Attitudinal Theory of Excuse', (2006) 25 *Law and Philosophy* 289.

---

[245] Cf. Dressler, 'Reflections on Excusing Wrongdoers', 692–701, with Tadros, *Criminal Responsibility*, ch 11.

[246] Fletcher, *Rethinking Criminal Law*, 800, criticized by Brudner, 'A Theory of Necessity', 344–7.

[247] Horder, *Excusing Crime*, ch 3.

7

HOMICIDE

This chapter deals with the approach of the criminal law to behaviour which causes death or risks causing death. Murder, manslaughter, and several other homicide offences are discussed, and one recurrent issue here is fair labelling: does English law respond proportionately to the different degrees of culpability manifested in cases where death is caused?

7.1 DEATH AND FINALITY

For practical purposes, the culpable causing of another person's death may fairly be regarded as the most serious offence in the criminal calendar. There is an argument that treason is a more serious offence, since it strikes at the very foundations of the State and its social organizations, but in any event treason is rarely prosecuted. The harm caused by homicide is absolutely irremediable, whereas the harm caused by many other crimes is remediable to a degree. Even in crimes of violence which leave some permanent physical disfigurement or psychological effects, the victim retains his or her life and, therefore, the possibility of further pleasures and achievements, whereas death is final. This finality makes it proper to regard death as the most serious harm that may be inflicted on another person, and to regard the culpable causing of death without justification or excuse as the highest wrong.

Although many deaths arise from natural causes, and many others from illnesses and diseases, each year sees a large number of deaths caused by 'accidents', and also a number caused by acts or omissions which amount to some form of homicide in English law. In 2000, for example, the statistics showed that there were some 13,000 accidental deaths, of which some 3,200 occurred on the roads and the remainder either at work or in the home.[1] By comparison, the number of deaths recorded as criminal homicide is much smaller, although it has been rising gradually (from around 600 per year at the start of the 1990s to around 700 per year in the early years of this century).[2] This includes all the murders and manslaughters, but it leaves further questions to be confronted. For example, are we satisfied that the 700 deaths recorded as homicide are in fact more culpable than all, or even most, of the deaths recorded in other categories? In other words, does English criminal law pick out the most heinous forms of killing as murders and manslaughters, or are the boundaries frozen by tradition? For example, the number of offences of causing death by dangerous driving and causing death by careless driving whilst intoxicated has hovered around 300 per year for the past decade: many of these offences result in sentences more severe than those handed down for some forms of manslaughter,[3] which prompts the question whether these offences should be brought into manslaughter or other offences should be removed from that category.

We will see below that Parliament has created four new homicide offences in the last few years. For one of them (corporate manslaughter) it has used the term manslaughter. For the others it has either used the terminology of 'causing death by' (the two offences introduced by the Road Safety Act 2006)[4] or provided no label at all (the offence under section 5 of the Domestic Violence, Crime and Victims Act 2004).[5] Various questions may be raised: are these labelling decisions acceptable? Are these extensions of homicide law defensible, or is the distance between the defendant's fault and the consequent death too remote? What implications, if any, should the different labels have for sentence levels? These and other problems in the reform of homicide law will be examined below, after the contours of the present law have been discussed.

7.2 THE CONDUCT ELEMENT: CAUSING DEATH

English law distinguishes between the offences of murder and manslaughter, as we shall see, but the two crimes do have a common conduct element. It must be proved that the defendant's act or omission caused the death of a human being. The requirements of causation in the criminal law were discussed in Chapter 4.5 above, and already some problems came to light. Thus, the standard doctrine is that to shorten

---

[1] *Social Trends 2000* (2001).

[2] This excludes the year 2002–03, when the actual figures were inflated by the inclusion of some 172 murders by Dr Harold Shipman which came to light during the public inquiry into that case: see T. Dodd *et al.*, *Crime in England and Wales 2003–2004* (2004), 78.

[3] Sentencing Guidelines Council, *Causing Death by Driving* (2008); M. Hirst, 'Causing Death by Driving and Other Offences: a Question of Balance' [2008] Crim LR 339.

[4] See below, at Ch. 7.7.   [5] See below, at Ch. 7.6.

life by days is to cause death no less than shortening it by years, and this raises questions about the liability of doctors who administer drugs which they know will have the effect of shortening life, even though their primary purpose is to relieve pain. We noted that, in the rare trials of doctors for murder, the approach has been to direct the jury (in effect) to determine whether the doctor's primary motive was to relieve pain or to accelerate the patient's death[6]—an approach that conflicts with the orthodox approach to intention. It would be more consistent with prevailing doctrine for the courts to accept that a doctor intends to cause death in that situation, and therefore fulfils both the conduct and fault elements for murder, and then to deal with the case through a suitably refined defence of clinical necessity.[7]

At what points does an organism start and cease to be a person within the protection of the law of homicide? The current view, both in English law and in that of many other European countries,[8] is that a foetus is not yet a person and therefore cannot be the victim of homicide. Thus in the difficult case of *Attorney-General's Reference (No. 3 of 1994),*[9] where D had stabbed his pregnant girlfriend, also injuring the foetus, and the child was born prematurely and died some four months later from the wound, the House of Lords held that the doctrine of transferred intention could not be applied because it could only operate to transfer intention from one person to another, and not from a person to (what was then) a foetus. Only when the child is born alive and has an existence independent of its mother does it come within the protection of the law of homicide, although there are other serious offences capable of commission before birth, notably child destruction (which carries a maximum of life imprisonment).[10] The point at which the protection of the law of homicide begins was a crucial factor in the case of *Re A (Conjoined Twins: Surgical Separation).*[11] The twins were conjoined and both would have died within months if left conjoined, but the stronger twin had good prospects of survival if surgical separation was performed. The Court of Appeal held that the weaker twin was sufficiently capable of independent breathing to be classed as a human being: she was independent of her mother, even though she was dependent on the vital organs of her twin for survival. Once it was decided that she was a person within the protection of the law of homicide, it followed that the operation to separate the twins would constitute the conduct element of murder in relation to the weaker twin (who would inevitably die shortly afterwards)

---

[6] Cf the cases of Dr Bodkin Adams, Dr Moor and Dr Cox, discussed in Ch 4.5 above.

[7] See below, n 11 and accompanying text, where the Court of Appeal adopted this approach in the somewhat analogous 'conjoined twins' case.

[8] See the discussion by the European Court of Human Rights in *Vo v France* (2005) 40 EHRR 259, holding that a foetus does not come within the protection of Article 2 of the Convention, which guarantees the right to life. Cf. E. Wicks, 'Terminating Life and Human Rights: the Fetus and the Neonate', in C. Erin and S. Ost (eds), *The Criminal Justice System and Health Care* (2007).

[9] [1998] AC 245; the doctrine of transferred intention, and the impact of this decision on it, was discussed in Ch 5.5(d) above.

[10] Essentially, the killing of a foetus capable of being born alive: Infant Life Preservation Act 1929, s. 1.

[11] [2000] 4 All ER 961.

unless there was some legal justification for the homicide, which the Court, invoking a version of necessity, held there was.

It seems that a person will be treated as dead if he or she has become irreversibly 'brain dead', the definition of brain death being largely left to medical practice.[12] Thus switching off the life support machine of someone who already fulfils the criteria of brain death would not amount to the conduct element of murder. What if the patient does not fulfil those criteria, but is in a persistent vegetative state? This was the situation in the case of Tony Bland, who was being kept alive by food from a naso-gastric tube and by occasional administrations of antibiotics.[13] The House of Lords held that it would be lawful to discontinue treatment, thus allowing the patient to die. The elements of criminal homicide would not be present, they held, because discontinuing treatment was not causing death: it was allowing the patient to die of his pre-existing condition. Discontinuing treatment was properly regarded as an omission, not an act, and it was not a criminal omission because there was no duty to treat the patient, since there was no hope of recovery and it was no longer in his best interests to be kept alive. The controversial aspects of this decision cannot be pursued here.[14]

At common law there was also a rule that a person could only be convicted of a homicide offence if the death occurred within a year and a day of the accused's act or omission. Advances in medical science now make it possible for some victims to be kept alive for years after being injured or wounded, and the argument that the passage of years should not prevent a homicide prosecution was accepted by Parliament in the Law Reform (Year and a Day Rule) Act 1996, which abolished the old rule. The Act relies on prosecutorial discretion to prevent oppressive or unfair prosecutions: section 2 provides that, where more than three years have elapsed since the injury and the defendant has already been convicted of a non-fatal offence, a prosecution for homicide may only be instituted with the Attorney-General's consent. It would be helpful to see the publication of some principles or guidelines on which this discretion should be exercised.

7.3 DEFINING MURDER: THE INCLUSIONARY QUESTION

(a) THE PROCEDURAL CONTEXT

If causing death is to be regarded as the most serious harm, it would seem to follow that the most blameworthy form of homicide (the greatest wrong) should result in the most severe sentences imposed by the courts. Indeed, many systems of criminal law

---

[12] *Malcherek and Steel* (1981) 73 Cr App R 173.   [13] *Airedale NHS Trust v Bland* [1993] AC 789.
[14] Cf Ch 4.4 above, and J. Coggon, 'Ignoring the moral and intellectual shape of the law after *Bland*' (2007) 27 LS 110.

impose a mandatory sentence for murder (or whatever the highest form of homicide is called in that system). In some jurisdictions this is a mandatory sentence of death.[15] In the United Kingdom the penalty for murder is the mandatory sentence of life imprisonment.[16] The existence of the mandatory sentence has a significant impact on the shape and content of the remainder of the law of homicide: as we shall see, the dividing line between murder and manslaughter may be affected by the inability of courts to give different sentences for murder, and there are those who believe that the strongest reason for retaining provocation as a partial defence to murder is that otherwise a judge could not reflect degrees of culpability in the sentence (for murder).

The mandatory sentence of life imprisonment is divided into three portions: the first is now known as the minimum term (formerly, the tariff period), and is intended to reflect the relative gravity of the particular offence. It is a term that is served in full, and the early release provisions applicable to all determinate custodial sentences do not apply here. Once the minimum term expires, the second part consists of imprisonment based on considerations of public protection, and a murderer who is thought still to present a danger may be detained until the Parole Board decides that it is safe to order release. The third portion is after release from prison: the offender remains on licence for the rest of his life. Although until 2003 the Home Secretary had the final say on the minimum term and ultimate release, those decisions have now passed to the courts and the Parole Board respectively.[17] However, the Government wished to fetter the judges so as to ensure that minimum terms were not set too low. Thus section 269 of the Criminal Justice Act 2003 requires a court, when setting the minimum term to be served by a person convicted of murder, to have regard to the principles set out in Schedule 21 of the Act. The structure of that Schedule is to indicate three starting points:

- a whole life minimum term for exceptionally serious cases, such as premeditated killings of two people, sexual or sadistic child murders, or political murders;

- 30 years for particularly serious cases such as murders of police or prison officers, murders involving firearms, sexual or sadistic killings, or murders aggravated by racial or sexual orientation;

- 15 years for other murders not falling within either of the higher categories.

It should be borne in mind that to compare the minimum term with a determinate sentence one should double it: in other words, a minimum term of 15 years

---

[15] There are also some jurisdictions in which capital punishment is discretionary. See generally R. Hood and C. Hoyle, *The Death Penalty: a World-wide Perspective* (4th edn., 2008).

[16] The process of abolishing the death penalty was completed by s. 36 of the Crime and Disorder Act 1998 (dealing with treason and piracy), thus ensuring compliance with Protocol 6 to the European Convention.

[17] The change resulted from the decision of the European Court of Human Rights in *Stafford* v *United Kingdom* (2002) 35 EHRR 1121 and subsequently of the House of Lords in *R (on the application of Anderson)* v *Secretary of State for the Home Department* [2003] 1 AC 837, fundamentally because the Home Secretary cannot be regarded as an 'independent and impartial tribunal' as required by Article 6 of the Convention.

is the equivalent of a determinate sentence of about 30 years.[18] The language of Schedule 21 leaves considerable latitude, however. Although criteria are enumerated for the whole life and 30-year starting points, they are expressed as factors that would 'normally' indicate such a sentence. There is then provision for the court to take account of any further relevant factors, and an explicit statement that 'detailed consideration of aggravating and mitigating factors may result in a minimum term of any length (whatever the starting point)'. The Lord Chief Justice amended the previous guidance to reflect the 2003 provisions when he issued a Practice Direction in May 2004.[19] He has subsequently emphasized that section 269(3) merely states that the judge must specify the minimum term that 'the court considers appropriate', and indeed went on to say that so long as the judge bore in mind the principles set out in Schedule 21, 'he is not bound to follow them'—although an explanation for departing from them should be given.[20] Nonetheless, anomalies can arise: if a farmer's wife chooses to accede to her terminally ill husband's request by shooting him with a shotgun, 30 years is the indicated minimum and premeditation may take the minimum term even higher.[21]

The system introduced by the 2003 Act means that judges can vary the minimum term to reflect degrees of culpability in murder, but the overall framework of the mandatory sentence means that judges cannot set the maximum term to be served, as they do for other serious offences. On expiry of the minimum term, release is determined on public protection grounds by the Parole Board. This constraining effect of the mandatory life sentence means that the justifications for retaining it must be scrutinized afresh. One argument in favour of the mandatory life sentence is that it amounts to a symbolic indication of the unique heinousness of murder. It places the offender under the State's control, as it were, for the remainder of his or her life. This is often linked with a supposed denunciatory effect—the idea that the mandatory life sentence denounces murder as emphatically as possible—and with the supposed general deterrent effect of declaring that there is no way of avoiding the life-long effect of this sentence. It might also be argued that the mandatory life sentence makes a substantial contribution to public safety.

None of these arguments is notably strong, let alone conclusive. The mandatory penalty does indeed serve to mark out murder from other crimes, but whether the definition of murder is sufficiently refined to capture the worst killings, and only the worst killings, remains to be discussed below. As we shall see in section 7.3(c) below, it is sufficient for murder if D killed without intent to kill but with intent to cause serious harm, and the lesser intent is merely a mitigating factor from the various starting

---

[18] As noted by Lord Woolf CJ in *Sullivan* (below, n 20). This is because a determinate sentence of 30 years means 15 years in prison (followed by 15 years on supervised licence), whereas a minimum term for murder is not subject to the general provisions on early release and is served in full.

[19] *Practice Direction (Crime: Mandatory Life Sentences) (No. 2)* [2004] 1 WLR 2551.

[20] *Sullivan* [2005] 1 Cr App R (S) 308.

[21] See the examples discussed by the Law Commission in LCCP 177, *A New Homicide Act for England and Wales? A Consultation Paper* (2005), paras. 1.112–18.

points in Schedule 21 of the 2003 Act. Whether the life sentence is regarded as a sufficient denunciation depends on the public's perception of what life imprisonment means: if it is widely believed that it results in an average of about ten years' imprisonment, the effect will be somewhat blunted, even if the belief is untrue. The same applies to the general deterrent argument: its effectiveness depends on whether the penalty for murder affects the calculations of potential killers at all, and, if it does, whether the prospect of life imprisonment influences them more than the alternative of a long, fixed-term sentence.

As for public protection, this depends on executive decisions with regard to release; it raises the question whether it is necessary for public protection to keep most 'lifers' in for so long.[22] It is sometimes claimed that murderers should be treated differently because they are particularly dangerous: anyone who chooses to kill once can choose to kill again. But this is an over-generalization that takes little account of the situational variations of murder cases. Moreover, the argument will seem less persuasive when we have discussed cases of manslaughter by reason of diminished responsibility: where a murder is reduced to manslaughter, the judge has a wide sentencing discretion and may, according to the facts of the case, select a determinate prison sentence, a hospital order, or life imprisonment. There is no evidence that those who kill and are convicted of manslaughter by reason of diminished responsibility are less dangerous than those convicted of murder, and yet the judge has sentencing discretion in one case and not in the other. Considerations of this kind led the House of Lords Committee on Murder and Life Imprisonment to recommend the abolition of the mandatory sentence for murder.[23] A committee chaired by the former Lord Chief Justice, Lord Lane, reached the same conclusion in 1993.[24] Both committees favoured judicial sentencing discretion to mark the relative heinousness of the murder, subject to review on appeal.[25] A discretionary sentence of life imprisonment would still be available for those cases in which it was thought appropriate. Such a reform could bring improvements in natural justice without loss of public protection, but successive governments have been reluctant to contemplate the abrogation of the mandatory sentence for murder, and the latest reform proposals are premised on the retention of the mandatory penalty.[26]

---

[22] On this, see the cautious words of S. Brody and R. Tarling, *Taking Offenders out of Circulation* (Home Office Research Study No. 64, 1980), 33.

[23] HL Select Committee on Murder and Life Imprisonment (1988–89), HL Paper 78, paras. 101–22, adopting the reasoning of D. A. Thomas, 'Form and Function in Criminal Law', in P. R. Glazebrook (ed.), *Reshaping the Criminal Law* (1978); cf. also M. D. Farrier, 'The Distinction between Murder and Manslaughter in its Procedural Context' (1976) 39 MLR 414.

[24] *Committee on the Penalty for Homicide* (1993).

[25] See further M. Wasik, 'Sentencing for Homicide', in A. Ashworth and B. Mitchell (eds.), *Rethinking English Homicide Law* (2000).

[26] Law Com No 304, *Murder, Manslaughter and Infanticide* (2006), and Ministry of Justice, Consultation Paper 19, *Murder, Manslaughter and Infanticide: proposals for reform of the law* (2008).

(b) THE STRUCTURE OF HOMICIDE LAW

The structure of the law of homicide law varies across jurisdictions,[27] and recent proposals for reforming English law will be discussed below. It must be said that the current structure of the English law of homicide is rather strange. Although formally there are two offences—murder and manslaughter—the latter includes two distinct varieties: 'voluntary' manslaughter (killings which would be murder but for the existence of defined extenuating circumstances); and 'involuntary' manslaughter (killings for which there is no need to prove any awareness of the risk of death being caused, but for which there is thought to be sufficient fault to justify liability for a serious offence). The arguments therefore tend to focus on three borderline questions: what is the minimum fault required for conviction of murder? in what circumstances should murder be reduced to manslaughter? and what is the minimum fault required for a conviction of manslaughter?

(c) REQUIREMENTS FOR MURDER

In English criminal law there are now two alternative fault requirements for murder: an intent to kill, or an intent to cause grievous bodily harm. What do these requirements mean? Do they extend the definition of murder too far, or are they too narrow?

Intent to kill may be regarded as the most obvious and indisputable form of fault element for murder, but to some extent that depends on the meaning of 'intent'. This has been the subject of a number of House of Lords decisions,[28] and yet the definition is still not absolutely clear. A broad definition would be that a person *intends* to kill if it is his or her purpose to kill by the act or omission charged, or if he or she foresees that death is virtually certain to follow from that act or omission; the same applies to an intent to cause grievous bodily harm. In practice, the 'golden rule' is the first to be applied—that intention should be left without description or definition in most cases, and the full definition should be reserved for cases where D claims that his purpose was something other than to cause injury. A fairly typical set of facts is provided by *Nedrick* (1986),[29] where D had a grudge against a woman and had threatened to 'burn her out'. One night he went to her house, poured paraffin through the letter-box and on to the front door, and set it alight. One of the woman's children died in the ensuing fire. When asked why he did it, D replied: 'Just to wake her up and frighten her'. A defence of this kind, a claim that the purpose was only to frighten and not to cause harm, requires the full definition to be put to the jury. The question is: granted that D's purpose was to frighten, did he none the less realize that it was virtually certain that his act would cause death or grievous bodily harm to someone? The jury

---

[27] See J. Horder (ed), *Homicide Law in Comparative Perspective* (2007).
[28] See the discussion of *Moloney* [1985] AC 905, *Hancock and Shankland* [1986] AC 455 and *Woollin* [1999] 1 AC 82 in Ch 5.5(b) above.
[29] (1986) 83 Cr App R 267.

should answer this, as in all criminal cases, by drawing inferences from the evidence in the case and from the surrounding circumstances.

However, as was pointed out in Chapter 5.5(b) above, the decision of the House of Lords in *Woollin*[30] leaves some leeway in the application of the test by holding that, where the jury concludes that D foresaw that death or grievous bodily harm was virtually certain to ensue, it is 'entitled to find' that D had the intention necessary for murder. The test remains a permissive principle of evidence rather than a rule of substantive law, although the Court of Appeal has accepted that, once there is an appreciation of virtual certainty of death, 'there is very little to choose between a rule of evidence and one of substantive law'.[31] However, the test is so formulated in order to leave a degree of indeterminacy,[32] and this could allow juries to make broader moral or social judgements when deciding whether the fault element for murder is fulfilled in a case where death (or grievous bodily harm) was known to be virtually certain.[33]

What about the alternative element in the definition, an intent to cause grievous bodily harm? This has considerable practical importance, since this is all that the prosecution has to prove in order to obtain a verdict of guilty of murder. It must be shown that the defendant intended (which, again, includes both acting in order to cause the result and knowledge of practical certainty) to cause 'really serious injury' to someone, although the use of the word 'really' is not required in all cases.[34] The House of Lords confirmed this rule in *Cunningham* (1981):[35] D struck his victim on the head a number of times with a chair, causing injuries from which the victim died a week later. D maintained throughout that he had not intended to kill, but there was evidence from which the jury could infer—and did infer—that he intended to cause grievous bodily harm. The House of Lords upheld D's conviction for murder: an intent to cause really serious injury is sufficient for murder, without any proof that the defendant even contemplated the possibility that death would result.

Does the 'grievous bodily harm' rule extend the definition of murder too far? If the point of distinguishing murder from manslaughter is to mark out the most heinous group of killings for the extra stigma of a murder conviction, it can be argued that the 'grievous bodily harm' rule draws the line too low. The rule departs from the principle of correspondence (see Chapter 5.4(a)), namely that the fault element in a crime should relate to the consequences prohibited by that crime. By allowing an intent to cause grievous bodily harm to suffice for a murder conviction, the law is turning its most serious offence into a constructive crime. Is there any justification

---

[30] [1999] 1 AC 82. [31] *Per* Rix LJ in *Matthews and Alleyne* [2003] 2 Cr App R 30, at [45].

[32] As the Law Commission has accepted: LCCP 177, *A New Homicide Act for England and Wales?* (2005), para. 3.8.

[33] See the discussion of the views of N. Lacey and A. Norrie, above, Ch 5.5(b)(ii). The Law Commission recommends that the common law approach in *Woollin* should form the basis of a new law: Law Com 304, 57–8.

[34] Cf. *Janjua* [1999] 1 Cr App R 91, where there had been a stabbing with a five-inch knife, with *Bollom* [2004] 2 Cr App R 6, where the Court of Appeal approved a definition in terms of 'seriously and grievously to interfere with the health or comfort of the victim'.

[35] [1982] AC 566.

for 'constructing' a murder conviction out of this lesser intent? One argument is that there is no significant moral difference between someone who chooses to cause really serious injury and someone who sets out to kill. No one can predict whether a serious injury will result in death—that may depend on the victim's physique, on the speed of an ambulance, on the distance from the hospital, and on a range of other medical and individual matters unrelated to D's culpability. If one person chooses to cause serious injury to another, he or she has already crossed one of the ultimate moral thresholds and has shown a sufficiently wanton disregard for life as to warrant the label 'murder' if death results. The counter-arguments, which would uphold the principle of correspondence, are that breach of that principle is unnecessary when the amplitude of the crime of manslaughter lies beneath murder, and also that the definition of grievous bodily harm includes a number of injuries which are most unlikely to put the victim's life at risk. In the leading case of *Cunningham* Lord Edmund-Davies (dissenting) gave the example of breaking someone's arm: that is a really serious injury, but one which is unlikely to endanger the victim's life.[36] So in practice the 'grievous bodily harm' rule goes further than the arguments of its protagonists would support.

Nonetheless, it must be recognized that many other legal systems also have a definition of murder that goes beyond an intent to kill. What other approaches might be taken? The fault element for many serious offences is intent or recklessness: why should this not suffice for murder? One question is whether all killings in which the defendant is aware of a risk of death are sufficiently serious to warrant the term 'murder'. An answer sometimes given is that they are not, because a driver who overtakes on a bend, knowingly taking the risk that there is no vehicle travelling in the opposite direction, should not be labelled a murderer if a collision and death happen to ensue.[37] This example assumes that sympathy for motorists will overwhelm any tendency to logical analysis: the question is whether motorists are ever justified in knowingly taking risks with other people's lives. Yet if the example is modified a little, so that the overtaking is on a country road at night and the risk is known to be slight, it becomes questionable whether the causing of death in these circumstances should be labelled in the same way as intentional killings. This is not to suggest that motorists should be treated differently. The point is rather that, even though knowingly taking risks with other people's lives is usually unjustifiable, taking a slight risk is less serious than intentionally causing death. In discussing the boundaries of murder, we are concerned with classification, not exculpation.

To classify all reckless killings as murder might be too broad, but the point remains that some reckless killings may be thought no less heinous than intentional killings. Can a satisfactory line be drawn here? One approach would be to draw the line by reference to the degree of probability. Murder would be committed in those situations where D caused death by an act or omission which he knew had death as the

---

[36] [1982] AC 582; see also the criticism by Lord Mustill in *Attorney-General's Reference (No. 3 of 1994)* [1998] AC 245 at 258–9, and by Lord Steyn in *Powell and Daniels* [1999] AC 1, at 15.

[37] An example given by Lord Goff, 'The Mental Element in the Crime of Murder' (1988) 104 LQR 30, at 48.

probable or highly probable result. A version of this test of foresight of high probability is used in several other European countries;[38] it was introduced into English law by the decision in *Hyam* v *DPP* (1975),[39] but abandoned in *Moloney* (1985)[40] on grounds of uncertainty. A related approach, applicable to certain terrorist situations, would be to maintain that someone who intends to create a risk of death or serious injury endorses those consequences to the extent that, if they occur, they can fairly be said to be intended.[41]

A second approach is to frame the law in such a way as to make it clear that the court should make a moral judgement of the gravity of the defendant's conduct. Section 210.2 of the Model Penal Code includes within murder those reckless killings which manifest 'extreme indifference to the value of human life'.[42] Scots law treats as murder killings with 'wicked recklessness', a phrase which directs courts to evaluate the circumstances of the killing.[43] Both the Model Penal Code test and the Scots test may be reduced to circularity, however, for when one asks how extreme or how wicked the recklessness should be, the only possible answer is: 'wicked or extreme enough to justify the stigma of a murder conviction'. Admittedly, the Model Penal Code does contain a list of circumstances which may amount to extreme indifference, which assists the courts and increases the predictability of verdicts in a way that Scots law does not, but the essence of both approaches is that there is no precise way of describing those non-intentional killings which are as heinous as intentional killings. Their protagonists argue that the law of murder has such significance that the principle of maximum certainty should yield to the ability of courts to apply the label in ways more sensitive to moral/social evaluations of conduct. Opponents argue that the principle of maximum certainty is needed here specifically to reduce the risk of verdicts based on discriminatory or irrelevant factors, such as distaste for the defendant's background, allegiance, or other activities, especially if the mandatory life sentence is at issue.[44]

A third, more precise formulation now favoured by the Law Commission is that a killing should be classified as murder in those situations where there is an intention to cause serious injury coupled with awareness of the risk of death.[45] Neither an intention

---

[38] See, e.g., A. du Bois-Pedain, 'Intentional Killings: the German Law', in Horder, *Homicide Law in Comparative Perspective*.

[39] [1975] AC 55.   [40] [1985] AC 905.

[41] A. Pedain, 'Intention and the Terrorist Example' [2003] Crim LR 579.

[42] This was recommended as one ground for a murder conviction by the Law Reform Commission of Ireland, *Homicide: Murder and Involuntary Manslaughter* (2008), also requiring that D took a 'substantial and unjustifiable risk' with another's life.

[43] See Sir G. H. Gordon, *Criminal Law of Scotland* (3rd edn., 2001, by M. G. A. Christie), vol. II, 290.

[44] This is particularly relevant to killings resulting from the activities of (allegedly) terrorist groups. The HL Select Committee on Murder etc., para. 76, concluded that: 'It is neither satisfactory nor desirable to distort [general principles] in order to deal with the reckless terrorist and other "wickedly" reckless killers, who will, in any event, be liable to imprisonment for life [i.e. for manslaughter].'

[45] Law Com No 304, *Murder, Manslaughter and Infanticide*, part 3, following the CLRC 14th Report (1980), para. 31, adopted in the draft Criminal Code cl. 54(1) and supported by the HL Select Committee on Murder etc., para. 71.

to cause serious injury nor recklessness as to death should be sufficient on its own, but together they could operate so as to restrict one another and perhaps to produce a test which both satisfies the criterion of certainty and marks out some heinous but non-intended killings.

A fourth approach, adopted by English law until 1957 and still in force in many American jurisdictions, is some form of felony-murder rule: anyone who kills during the course of an inherently dangerous felony should be convicted of murder.[46] Thus stated, there is no reference to the defendant's intention or awareness of the risks: the fact that D has chosen to commit rape, robbery, or another serious offence, and has caused death thereby, is held to constitute sufficient moral grounds for placing the killing in the highest category. Plainly, this is a form of constructive criminal liability: the murder conviction is constructed out of the ingredients of a lesser offence. Presumably the justification is that D has already crossed a high moral/social threshold in choosing to commit such a serious offence, and should therefore be held liable for whatever consequences ensue, however accidental they may be.[47] The objections would be reduced if awareness of the risk of death was also required: in other words, if the test were the commission of a serious offence of violence plus recklessness as to death. The effect of that test would be to pick out those reckless killings which occurred when D had already manifested substantial moral and legal culpability, and to classify them as murder.

Four alternative approaches have been described, and others could be added. The point is that the traditional concept of intention does not, of itself, appear to be sufficiently well focused to mark out those killings which are the most heinous. The law must resort to some kind of moral and social evaluation of conduct if it is to identify and separate out the gravest killings. Some would defend the GBH rule on this basis as a form of 'rough justice,' and that argument could be extended to some of the cases in the fourth category above, as William Wilson has proposed.[48]

At the other end of the spectrum were the Law Commission's provisional proposals, which proposed to deal with the issue by means of a distinction between first degree murder and second degree murder. The mandatory life sentence would remain for first degree murder, the definition of which would be refined by confining it to cases where there is an intent to kill.[49] Second degree murder would then include cases where D is proved to have killed while intending to do serious harm, defined

---

[46] See C. Finkelstein, 'Two Models of Murder: Patterns of Criminalisation in the United States', in Horder, *Homicide Law in Comparative Perspective*.

[47] In their empirical research, P. Robinson and J. Darley found that most of their sample agreed that an accidental killing during a robbery should be punished more severely than other negligent killings, but they did not agree with classifying it as murder: *Justice, Liability and Blame* (1995), 169–81. As the authors express it, the majority view was in favour of a felony-manslaughter rule, not a felony-murder rule.

[48] W. Wilson, 'Murder and the Structure of Homicide', in Ashworth and Mitchell (eds.), *Rethinking English Homicide Law* (2000).

[49] Research shows moderate public support for the mandatory life sentence, but some disagreement about the types of homicide for which the measure is appropriate: see LCCP 177, *A New Homicide Act?*, Appendix A, 'Report on Public Survey of Murder and Mandatory Sentencing in Criminal Homicides', by B. Mitchell.

more tightly than in existing law,[50] and also cases where D is proved to have killed with reckless indifference as to causing death. Second degree murder would carry a maximum sentence of life imprisonment, together with the label 'murder', and is an attempt to allow some 'moral elbow-room' in the definition of murder outside the mandatory penalty.[51] However, in its final report the Law Commission sought a compromise that enlarges first degree murder beyond intention to kill and yet does not encounter the objections made against the GBH rule. In effect, the Commission adopts the third approach above, arguing that first degree murder should extend beyond an intent to kill to those cases where there is an intent to cause serious injury coupled with an awareness of a serious risk of causing death.[52] The Law Commission's view is that cases involving both these elements are morally equivalent to cases of intent to kill, or at least are closer to those cases than to cases placed in the other offence of murder in the second degree.

What cases would fall within murder in the second degree? The Law Commission identifies two types of case—where D kills with an intention to do serious injury (those not accompanied by an awareness of the risk of death and therefore not within murder in the first degree), and where D 'intended to cause injury or fear or risk of injury aware that his or her conduct involved a serious risk of causing death.' The latter category is designed to capture bad cases of reckless killing and to sweep them into an offence with the label murder (in the second degree); whether the breadth of the concepts of 'injury' and 'serious risk' enables the proposal to distinguish fairly between these cases and others that fall into manslaughter will be one of the issues to be debated in the coming years, as the Ministry of Justice intends to leave the offence of murder untouched while it promotes legislation on the partial defences.[53]

7.4 DEFINING MURDER: THE EXCLUSIONARY QUESTION

Even in a legal system which had the narrowest of definitions of murder—say, premeditated intention to kill—there would still be an argument that some cases which fulfil that criterion should have their labels reduced from murder to manslaughter

---

[50] For the broad definition now adopted, see n 37 above; the new definition would relate serious harm to either endangering life or causing permanent or long-term damage to physical or mental functioning— LCCP 177, *A New Homicide Act?*, para. 3.144.

[51] For discussion, see W. Wilson, 'The Structure of Criminal Homicide' [2006] Crim LR 471, and A. Norrie, 'Between Orthodox Subjectivism and Moral Contextualism: Intention and the Consultation Paper' [2006] Crim LR 486.

[52] Law Com No 304, *Murder, Manslaughter and Infanticide* (2006), Part 3, discussed by A Ashworth, 'Principles, Pragmatism and the Law Commission's Recommendations on Homicide Law Reform' [2007] Crim LR 333. Cf. Law Reform Commission of Ireland, *Homicide: Murder and Involuntary Manslaughter*, recommending retention of an intent to cause serious injury as sufficient for murder.

[53] Ministry of Justice, *Murder, manslaughter and infanticide: proposals for reform of the law* (2008), para 9.

because of extenuating circumstances. Just as the discussion of the *inclusionary* aspect of the definition of murder travelled beyond the concepts of intent and recklessness, so the discussion of the *exclusionary* aspect (i.e. which killings fulfilling the definition should be classified as manslaughter rather than murder?) must consider the circumstances in which the killing took place and other matters bearing on the culpability of the killer.

(a) THE MANDATORY PENALTY

The existence of the mandatory penalty has significant effects on the shape of the substantive law of homicide. One argument is that the main reason for allowing such matters as provocation to reduce murder to manslaughter is to avoid the mandatory penalty for murder: if the mandatory penalty were abolished, it would be sufficient to take account of provocation when sentencing for murder. However, this argument neglects the symbolic function of the labels applied by the law and by courts to criminal conduct. Surely it is possible that a jury might decline to convict of murder a person who intentionally killed under gross provocation, even though they knew that the judge could give a lenient sentence, because they wished to signify the reduction in the defendant's culpability by using the less stigmatic label of manslaughter. Since there are two offences—and particularly in jurisdictions where there are three or more grades of homicide—surely it is right and proper to use the lesser offence to mark significant differences in culpability. This may be seen as an application of the principle of fair labelling. When a jury takes the decision between the two grades of homicide, this may also assist the judge in sentencing, and help the public to understand the sentence imposed.[54] A second major effect of the mandatory penalty for murder derives from the long minimum terms (plus the detention for public protection and then the licence for life) imposed for murder, as compared with the considerably shorter sentences for manslaughter upon provocation or by reason of diminished responsibility. Thus the sentencing guidelines for manslaughter upon provocation indicate a starting point of twelve years' imprisonment where the degree of provocation is low, and starting points of eight and three years for greater forms of provocation.[55] The difference between the highest starting point for manslaughter upon provocation—twelve years (release on licence after six years)—and the lowest starting point for murder—fifteen years (which means fifteen years at least before release on licence)—is so considerable that, in practice, 'there is the greatest of pressure to distort the concepts of provocation and diminished responsibility to accommodate deserving or hard cases. This pressure will continue as long as each case of murder carries the mandatory life sentence.'[56]

---

[54] This was the view of the HL Select Committee on Murder etc., paras. 80–83, agreeing with the CLRC, 14th Report (1980), para. 76.

[55] Sentencing Guidelines Council, *Manslaughter upon Provocation* (2005).

[56] Law Com No. 290, *Partial Defences to Murder* (2004), para. 2.68.

(b) MANSLAUGHTER UPON PROVOCATION

Provoked killings are generally thought to be less heinous than unprovoked killings, and provocation has long been accepted as a ground for reducing to manslaughter a killing which would otherwise fulfil the definition of murder.[57] From time to time there are cases where the provocation is so gross and so strong that a court imposes a very short prison sentence or even a suspended sentence for the manslaughter—typically, cases where a wife, son, or daughter kills a persistently bullying husband or father—and such cases may come close to self-defence. The issues here, however, are whether provocation should remain a qualified defence to murder, and, if so, how far it should extend.

In English law the doctrine of provocation has two main elements, which emerge from s 3 of the Homicide Act 1957:

Where on a charge of murder there is evidence on which the jury can find that the person charged was provoked (whether by things done or by things said or by both together) to lose his self-control, the question whether the provocation was enough to make a reasonable man do as he did shall be left to be determined by the jury; and in determining that question the jury shall take into account everything both done and said according to the effect which, in their opinion, it would have on a reasonable man.

This was not intended to be a complete statement of the law on provocation, but it settles the form of the main requirements. First, there must be evidence that D was provoked to lose self-control and kill. Then the jury must decide whether the provocation was enough to make a reasonable man do as D did. D is not required to prove any of this: in a murder trial, if there is sufficient evidence that D was provoked to lose self-control, the judge is bound to leave provocation to the jury, even if D has not raised this defence,[58] and the burden of disproving it beyond reasonable doubt lies upon the prosecution.

(i) *The Subjective Requirement:* The first requirement of the qualified defence of provocation is predominantly subjective—evidence that D was provoked to lose self-control and kill. This requirement contributes to the excusatory component of the provocation doctrine, the idea being that a person who has lost self-control is less responsible for subsequent conduct. Without this, there would be no way of excluding planned revenge killings, and the argument is that they should be excluded from the defence because a person who coolly plans a response to an affront or a wrong ought to ensure that the response conforms with the law. The genuinely provoked killer, on the other hand, is in such a disturbed state of mind that such calculation does not occur.

This requirement may be divided into two elements, that D was (a) *provoked* to (b) lose self-control. Thus, in respect of (a), it is not enough simply to argue that D lost control. The cause must have been some form of provocation, and s 3 includes things

---

[57] See generally, J. Horder, *Provocation and Responsibility* (1992).
[58] Confirmed by the House of Lords in *Acott* [1997] 2 Cr App R 94.

said or done by persons other than the deceased,[59] and acts done against persons other than D (e.g. where D is provoked to kill someone who has just committed a sexual offence upon D's son, daughter, wife, etc.). The word 'provoked' seems to require a human act that can be regarded as a provocation, rather than any kind of event which leads D to lose self-control. What is required, stated Lord Steyn in *Acott* (1997),[60] is 'some evidence of a specific act or words of provocation resulting in a loss of self-control', whereas 'a loss of self-control caused by fear, panic, sheer bad temper or circumstances (e.g. a slow down of traffic due to snow) would not be enough'. There is good reason for insisting that the loss of control be provoked, since anger may be justified and that may strengthen the grounds for partially excusing what follows.[61] However, what may properly be defined as 'provocation' in this context is controversial: in *Doughty* (1986)[62] the crying of a 17-day-old child was held to be sufficient to fall within the requirement, even though such an infant is incapable of moral judgement and is patently unaware of the significance of what he or she is doing. Applying Lord Steyn's well-founded distinction between 'acts or words of provocation' and mere 'circumstances', one might well place *Doughty* in the latter category.

Turning to element (b), how much disturbance amounts to a sufficient loss of self-control? Richard Holton and Stephen Shute argue that the paradigm case is where D normally had sufficient self-control to suppress violent inclinations, but that the provocation aroused those inclinations and undermined D's controls.[63] They go on to argue that commonly-used phrases such as 'loss of temper' or 'heat of passion' are not true synonyms, since they do not necessarily connote even a partial loss of self-control. They also insist that the motive for the attack during loss of self-control is usually revenge, and therefore that a simple dichotomy between revenge killings and uncontrolled killings is false. However, for centuries courts have drawn a distinction between revenge killings and others where D was not 'the master of his own understanding' and where there had not been 'time for the blood to cool and for reason to resume its seat'.[64] In *Duffy* (1949),[65] Devlin J appeared to draw the same contrast but phrased the law's requirement as 'a sudden and temporary loss of self-control'. The word 'sudden', which does not appear in s 3 of the Homicide Act 1957, would narrow the effect of the doctrine considerably. It suggests that the retaliation must occur fairly quickly after the provocation has been received, rather than simply asking whether D was still in an uncontrolled state at the time of the killing. Clearly the length of time that elapses is of evidential importance. Thus in *Ibrams* (1982)[66] there had been considerable ill-treatment and violence by the deceased towards D and his girlfriend,

---

[59] See *Davies* [1975] QB 691.   [60] [1997] 2 Cr App R 94, at 102.

[61] Cf. the detailed discussion by J. Horder, *Excusing Crime* (2004), ch 2.

[62] (1986) 83 Cr App R 319, on which see J. Horder, 'The Problem of Provocative Children' [1987] Crim LR 654.

[63] R. Holton and S. Shute, 'Self-Control in the Modern Provocation Defence' (2007) 27 Oxford JLS 49.

[64] *Hayward* (1833) 6 C and P 157, per Tindal CJ. For detailed historical discussion, see Horder, *Provocation and Responsibility*, chs 4 and 5.

[65] [1949] 1 All ER 932.   [66] (1982) 74 Cr App R 154.

and this led them eventually to plan and carry out a night-time raid on the deceased's flat, during which they attacked and killed him. The Court of Appeal confirmed that the defence of provocation was unavailable; this was a planned attack and not a case in which it could be said that D had been provoked to lose self-control by the acts of the deceased, not least because they crept up on the victim when he was asleep. This amount of planning is inconsistent with loss of self-control, and that (rather than 'revenge') is the true point of distinction.[67]

Distinguishable from *Ibrams* are the many cases where 'cumulative provocation' has been directed towards D over a period of time, and then some minor act sparks off the loss of self-control and killing.[68] In cases of this kind the last act of the provoker, even though minor in itself, may be placed in the context of the previous provocation in order to explain the loss of self-control. Whether in these cases the loss of self-control needs to be 'sudden' has been questioned in a number of appeals, but with little success. In *Ahluwalia* (1993)[69] Lord Taylor CJ accepted that the length of time between the provocation and the killing was a relevant but not a determinative factor. He concluded, somewhat ambiguously, that the subjective requirement in provocation 'would not as a matter of law be negatived simply because of a delayed reaction in such cases, provided that there was at the time of the killing a "sudden and temporary loss of self-control" caused by the alleged provocation'.[70] There are other decisions that seem less to broaden than to ignore the 'sudden and temporary' test: in *Pearson* (1992)[71] the Court of Appeal allowed the defence of provocation in a case where D took a sledgehammer, asked his brother to switch the light on, and then bludgeoned their sleeping father to death. The trial judge's direction to the jury to take account of the father's violent bullying over the preceding years was not questioned, even though there was no 'final act'.

The development of the law relating to the subjective requirement is most unsatisfactory. First, the idea that loss of self-control must be 'sudden' arrived in *Duffy* without support from the precedents, and has been presented as if it is the only way to avoid reducing all revenge killings to manslaughter. Secondly, the suddenness test is objectionable in principle because it favours those with quick tempers over others with a slow-burning temperament (but no less intensity of emotion), and it favours those with the physical strength to act quickly. In this way it may favour some ethnic groups over others, and may favour men over women. It is one thing to exclude cases like *Ibrams* from the defence—not merely was there a gap of some five days between provocation and killing, but there was evidence of planning and premeditation; it is another thing to exclude defendants with slow-burning temperaments, who do not react straight away to an insult or wrong, but go away and then react after minutes or even hours of festering anger. However, the problem then is that allowing lapse of time between the provocation and the retaliation—as suggested in *Ahluwahlia*—not

---

[67] Holton and Shute, 'Self-Control', 61.

[68] See M. Wasik, 'Cumulative Provocation and Domestic Killing' [1982] Crim LR 29.

[69] (1993) 96 Cr App R 133.　　[70] Ibid., at 139. Cf. also *Thornton (No. 2)* [1996] 2 Cr App R 108.

[71] [1992] Crim LR 193; see also *Baillie* [1995] Crim LR 739.

only helps women defendants but also broadens the time-frame for men, and may thus weaken the excusatory force that derives from acting in uncontrolled anger.

The proposal of the Law Commission is to remove the subjective requirement as such, and to stipulate simply that the partial defence should not apply where 'the defendant acted in considered desire for revenge'.[72] This can be opposed on the ground that it seeks to detach the provocation defence from one of its true rationales, which is that a good reason for partially excusing such defendants is that they acted during a distinct emotional disturbance resulting from what was done to them. The Ministry of Justice has now proposed that the requirement of 'loss of self-control' should be retained, regarding it as problematic that a partial defence should be provided to someone who kills 'while basically in full possession of his or her senses': the Ministry would broaden the partial defence by removing any requirement of suddenness so as to allow cases of delayed reaction or 'slow-burn temperament' to be included.[73] This is a sensible change, but it does not deal with the vagueness of the concept of loss of self-control, well exposed by Holton and Shute. Neither the draft clause, although elaborately defined in other respects, nor the Ministry of Justice's paper contains anything to guide the courts towards a desirable and consistent application of this key concept.

(ii) *The Objective Condition:* Once the court is satisfied that there is evidence that D was provoked to lose self-control, it must go on to consider the second requirement: was the provocation enough to make a reasonable man do as D did? This is English law's rather clumsy attempt to reflect the element of partial justification in the doctrine of provocation. The clumsiness is evident in the standard of 'the reasonable man', an anthropomorphic (and male) standard which might be taken to suggest a paragon of virtue if it were not for the context of partially exculpating a killing by such a person. The underlying point is that it is not every act of provocation which should be allowed as the basis of this qualified defence, but only those serious enough to unbalance the behaviour of a person with reasonable self-control. Thus, provocation operates as a partial excuse for murder, but the main reason provocation excuses is the element of partial justification for the anger or loss of control.

In earlier times the judge would rule on the sufficiency of the provocation, and the result of this was rather narrow and legalistic categories of sufficiency (e.g. violence or finding a spouse in adultery was enough, but insulting words or a confession of adultery were not). The Homicide Act 1957 deprived judges of their power to give authoritative rulings on the sufficiency of provocation, and the question must now be left to the jury in the terms of s 3 (set out above), even where the judge is strongly of the opinion that there is no basis for the defence.[74] There appears to be no time-limit on the matters to be considered, so that not only the final act but also the whole course of conduct may be taken into account.[75] This should ensure that those cases of

---

[72] Law Com No. 290, *Partial Defences to Murder,* paras. 1.13 and 3.135.

[73] Ministry of Justice, *Murder, manslaughter and infanticide: proposals for reform of the law* (2008), paras. 35–7 and Annex A; Coroners and Justice Bill 2009, cl. 41(2).

[74] E.g. *Doughty,* above n 63; the leading authority is *Acott* [1997] 2 Cr App R 94.

[75] *Burke* [1987] Crim LR 336; *Pearson* [1992] Crim LR 193; *Thornton (No. 2)* [1996] 2 Cr App R 108.

cumulative provocation that satisfy the subjective requirement (see above) are seen and judged in their proper context.

The objective requirement in provocation—was the provocation enough to make a reasonable man do as D did?—may be subdivided into three questions for the court: how grave was the provocation in this case? How adequate was the level of self-control in response to it? And was the provocation grave enough to make an ordinary person 'do as [the defendant] did'? The first question, on the assessment of the gravity of the provocation, is approached by a version of 'reasonable person' test. In *Bedder v DPP* (1954)[76] D, who was sexually impotent, was taunted about his impotence and kicked in the groin by a prostitute with whom he had been attempting to have sexual intercourse, whereupon he lost self-control and killed her. The House of Lords held that the jury should consider the effect of these acts on a reasonable man, without regard to the sexual impotence. The Court seemed to be afraid that if it allowed the jury to take account of one characteristic, such as sexual impotence, then it would be illogical to direct them not to take account of other characteristics, such as irascibility or bad temper. It is much more illogical, however, to ask a jury to consider the effect of taunts of impotence on a reasonable person who is *not* impotent,[77] and the *Bedder* approach was overruled by the House of Lords in *DPP v Camplin* (1978).[78] Lord Diplock held that a court should consider the effect of the provocation on 'a person having the power of self-control to be expected of an ordinary person of the sex and age of the accused, but in other respects sharing such of the accused's characteristics as they think would affect the gravity of the provocation to him'.

This test demonstrates that the illogicality alleged in *Bedder* does not exist: some characteristics of each individual defendant must be considered by the jury in assessing the gravity of the provocation (even though, as argued below, the level of self-control must be kept fairly constant). In *Newell* (1980)[79] the Court of Appeal developed the *Camplin* test in two ways, purporting to follow New Zealand law on the point.[80] First, it held that only permanent characteristics such as race, ethnic origin, disability, and, probably, religion may be taken into account, whereas transient conditions such as intoxication and exhaustion may not. Secondly, it held that for a characteristic to be relevant the provocation must have been aimed at it. The necessity for either requirement must now be in some doubt. The second has been abandoned in New Zealand.[81] The first was criticized as overly strict by Lord Goff in *Morhall* (1996).[82] In that case D, a glue-sniffing addict, was taunted about his glue-sniffing by the victim, whom D subsequently stabbed. The Court of Appeal held that in applying the objective test the jury should be directed not to take account of discreditable characteristics such as glue-sniffing (or paedophilia). The House of Lords disagreed, and held that a jury should be directed to take account of any matter relevant to an assessment of the strength of the provocation.

---

[76] [1954] 2 All ER 201.   [77] See A. Ashworth, 'The Doctrine of Provocation' [1976] Camb LJ 292.
[78] [1978] AC 705.   [79] (1980) 71 Cr App R 331.
[80] The Court cited extensively from *McGregor* [1962] NZLR 1069.
[81] *McCarthy* [1992] 2 NZLR 550.   [82] [1996] 1 AC 90.

Does this mean that there are no boundaries at all to what personal attributes may be taken into account in assessing the gravity of the provocation? What about the case of a racist who believes that it is gravely insulting for a non-white person to speak to a white man unless spoken to first?[83] Lord Taylor in *Morhall* put the case of 'a paedophile upbraided for molesting children',[84] which raises similar issues. The implication of the House of Lords decision in *Morhall* is that the judgement of such matters must be left to the jury without much guidance. The submission here is that that is unsatisfactory: there ought to be a normative element that excludes attitudes and reactions inconsistent with the law or inconsistent with the notion of a tolerant, pluralist society that upholds the right to respect for private life without discrimination (Articles 8 and 14 of the Convention). Finally, the common law excludes self-induced provocation and the Law Commission proposes that the defence should not apply where 'the provocation was incited by the defendant for the purpose of providing an excuse to use violence'.[85]

Once the court has assessed the gravity of the provocation, the second part of the objective condition requires D to have shown a reasonable standard of self-control. If the function of the 'reasonable man' test in s 3 of the Homicide Act is to insist on a reasonable degree of self-control, it seems to follow that individual factors should be left out of account and that the degree of self-control required should be constant. Thus in *Camplin* Lord Diplock stated that the test is that of the 'ordinary person... possessed of such powers of self-control as everyone is entitled to expect that his fellow citizens will exercise in society today', although the standard should be lowered for the young (in that case, the standard of a reasonable boy aged 15). What other grounds for a varying standard might be asserted? It is widely accepted that bad temper should be left out of account, for that is plainly inconsistent with the standard of reasonable self-control.[86] It would simply be contradictory to refer to a person with reasonable self-control who has a bad temper, whereas it is not contradictory to refer to a person with reasonable self-control who is black, blind, Catholic, one-legged, or whatever. The doctrine of provocation is a limited concession to human passions, the limitation being the requirement that everyone should show a reasonable amount of self-control. Any condition inconsistent with this limitation must therefore be rejected unless, as in the case of young people, there is good reason to maintain that a lower standard may be accepted. What about people from different cultural backgrounds? Such a background would rightly be taken into account in assessing the gravity of the provocation, but in principle it is difficult to see that there is a strong argument for lowering the expected standard of self-control, unless a particular form of cultural pluralism is thought to have higher claims than the requirement of reasonable self-control. The High Court of Australia has taken the view that the standard of self-control should be

---

[83] An example from Horder, *Provocation and Responsibility*, 144.
[84] (1994) 98 Cr App R 108, at 113 (CA).
[85] Law Com No. 290, *Partial Defences to Murder*, paras. 1.13 and 3.18.
[86] This was accepted by Lord Hoffmann in *Smith (Morgan)* [2001] 1 AC 146, at 173.

lowered for the young, but not for women or for members of ethnic minorities, and this seems right.[87]

A related and controversial question is whether a mental condition or personality disturbance that affects D's capacity for self-control may be taken into account, and again the answer—in strict logical terms—must be in the negative. Thus in *Luc Thiet-Thuan v R* (1997)[88] the Privy Council held that the objective requirement should not be lowered in the case of a man who had suffered brain damage that impaired his capacity for self-control. Now this may appear harsh, not least because it was argued earlier (in the context of negligence as a basis for liability) that there should always be a capacity exception for those incapable of attaining the standard normally required.[89] But the ruling would only be harsh if it condemned such defendants to conviction for murder, whereas the law of homicide contains another partial defence for those suffering from 'abnormality of mind', the defence of diminished responsibility.[90] Thus *Luc Thiet-Thuan v R* upheld the distinction between the doctrine of provocation, partly excusing those who were understandably[91] provoked to lose their self-control, and diminished responsibility, catering for those whose loss of control stemmed from mental instability.

The majority of the House of Lords in *Smith (Morgan)* (2001)[92] took a different view. There had been an altercation between D and V about the alleged theft of D's work tools, which culminated in D stabbing V fatally. D introduced evidence that he suffered from a depressive illness, but the trial judge held that this was relevant only to D's defence of diminished responsibility (which failed) and not to his defence of provocation. A majority of the House of Lords disagreed, holding that juries should be allowed to take account of all characteristics (including mental disorder) when applying the test laid down by s 3 of the Homicide Act. However, Lord Hoffmann (for the majority) emphasized that the question for the jury was whether the circumstances were such as to make the loss of control sufficiently excusable:

In deciding what should count as a sufficient excuse, they have to apply what they consider to be appropriate standards of behaviour; on the one hand making allowance for human nature and the power of the emotions but, on the other hand, not allowing someone to rely on his own violent disposition.... So the jury may think that there was some characteristic

---

[87] *Stingel v R.* (1990) 171 CLR 312. See further I. Leader-Elliott, 'Sex, Race and Provocation: in Defence of *Stingel*' (1996) 20 Crim LJ 71, and S. Yeo, 'Sex, Ethnicity, Power of Self-Control and Provocation Revisited' (1996) Sydney LR 304. For a discussion situated in political theory, see D. Ivison, 'Justifying Punishment in Intercultural Contexts: Whose Norms? Whose Values?', in M. Matravers (ed.), *Punishment and Political Theory* (1999).

[88] [1997] AC 131.   [89] Ch 5.5(f).

[90] For the possibility that provocation and diminished responsibility may both apply to the same case, see section 7.4(e) below.

[91] This term is chosen ahead of 'reasonably', but it is not intended to suppress the need for some socially justifiable reason for being provoked into anger by what was said or done. See further T. Macklem and J. Gardner, 'Provocation and Pluralism' (2001) 64 MLR 815 for a discussion of partial justification and good reasons for anger.

[92] [2001] 1 AC 146, on which see J. Gardner and T. Macklem, 'Compassion without Respect? Nine Fallacies in *R v Smith*' [2001] Crim LR 623.

of the accused, whether temporary or permanent, which affected the degree of control which society could reasonably have expected of *him* and which it would be unjust not to take into account. If the jury take this view, they are at liberty to give effect to it.[93]

Although the majority judges in *Morgan Smith* varied in the degree of normative content they found in s 3, they insisted that the jury should ultimately determine this. In *Weller* (2003)[94] the Court of Appeal held that *Morgan Smith* required the jury to be instructed to take all the circumstances into account, including 'matters relating to the defendant, the kind of man he is and his mental state'. In that case there was evidence that D, who had killed his ex-girlfriend, was unduly possessive and jealous. The Court held that the jury must take this into account, in deciding 'what society expects of a man like this defendant in his position'. The inability of judges to place any restrictions on what juries should take into account led to what John Gardner and Timothy Macklem criticized as an 'evaluative free-for-all',[95] but the law was soon to change again.

In *Attorney-General for Jersey* v *Holley* (2005)[96] D was an alcoholic who had been in a stormy relationship with V for many years. One night both of them had been drinking heavily and, following some sexual taunting by V, D struck V with an axe, killing her. The Privy Council sat in a bench of nine Lords of Appeal in Ordinary, in order to resolve the conflict between the *Luc Thiet-Thuan* and *Morgan Smith* decisions. By a majority of six to three, the former decision was preferred. Lord Nicholls, speaking for the majority, held that *Morgan Smith* should not be followed because in that decision the House of Lords had departed from s 3 of the 1957 Act, and that was an improper use of judicial authority. By holding that the test was the degree of control that could reasonably be expected of this defendant, the majority in *Morgan Smith* had wrongly introduced a 'significant relaxation' of the objective standard in s 3. In this case, therefore, the instruction to the jury not to take account of D's alcoholism, even if it did amount to a mental disorder, was correct.

The intended effect of *Holley* is therefore to return the objective condition in provocation to the position in *Luc Thiet-Thuan* and indeed *Camplin*.[97] This means that *Weller* is also overruled, and that some Court of Appeal decisions in the 1990s can no longer stand. Perhaps the high water mark of the flexibility then introduced into the objective standard was reached in *Humphreys* (1995),[98] where the Court held that D's abnormal immaturity and attention-seeking behaviour should have been taken into account. In that case the Court commented that psychological conditions of this kind are 'in no way repugnant to or inconsistent with the concept of the reasonable person'.[99] However, as *Holley* now confirms, they are and always were. The essence of the provocation doctrine is that the defendant should be partly excused

---

[93] At 173 (italics in original).   [94] [2003] Crim LR 724.

[95] In 'Compassion without Respect' (above, n 91), at 631.   [96] [2005] 2 AC 580.

[97] That *Holley* binds English courts was decided by the Court of Appeal in *James* [2006] QB 588.

[98] [1995] 4 All ER 1008; see also *Dryden* [1995] 1 All ER 987 ('eccentric and obsessional personality traits'), *Thornton (No. 2)* [1996] 2 Cr App R 108, and the remarks in *Ahluwalia* (1993) 96 Cr App R 133, at 141.

[99] [1995] 4 All ER at 1022.

because there was some justification for the anger and loss of self-control that led to the killing. If there was insufficient justification, and the cause of the uncontrolled killing lay in some psychological or psychiatric condition of the defendant, then the appropriate qualified defence is diminished responsibility. The distinction between the two ought logically to be based on causal grounds. Finally, it should be noticed that D's intoxicated state, whether or not linked to alcoholism, is not a factor to be taken into account when asking whether the provocation was enough to make a reasonable man do as he did. Even the decision in *Morgan Smith* deferred to the criminal law's general objectivism when confronted with intoxication as a ground of excuse, and *Holley* reaffirms this.

(iii) *The Third Part of the Objective Test:* At common law the famous case of *Mancini* v *DPP* (1942)[100] held that the mode of retaliation must bear a reasonable relationship to the provocation. The idea was that only an extremely grave provocation ought to mitigate a killing with a deadly weapon, whereas a lesser provocation might be allowed to mitigate other killings. S 3 of the 1957 Act requires the jury to consider whether the provocation was enough to 'make a reasonable man do as he did', the last four words harking back to *Mancini*. Although the Court of Appeal has held that the reasonable relationship rule in *Mancini* is no longer a rule of law,[101] the model direction in *Camplin* requires the judge to ask the jury not merely whether the reasonable man would be provoked to lose self-control, but also 'whether he would react to the provocation as the accused did'.[102] The precise meaning of this formulation is unclear: does it mean 'lose self-control and kill', or 'lose self-control and kill in the way D did'? In *Clarke* (1991)[103] the Court of Appeal held that the jury had rightly been instructed to take account of the whole circumstances of the incident, during which D had head-butted V, strangled her and then placed live wires in her mouth in order to electrocute her, when applying the statutory test. In *Van Dongen* (2005)[104] the Court of Appeal held that, if provocation had been left to the jury, they would surely have concluded that no reasonable man could have been provoked (by being struck once) into inflicting fifteen head injuries on V while he lay defenceless on the ground. These decisions appear to confuse two propositions. It is right to suggest that people may reasonably be expected to lose self-control to an extent that reflects how grave the provocation was, as the Privy Council held in *Phillips* v *R*.[105] But there is surely no warrant for asking whether a reasonable person would have done the precise acts that D did, since acts after loss of self-control are *ex hypothesi* uncontrolled. Courts sometimes infer loss of self-control from the frenzied nature of the attack, but it makes no sense to ask whether a reasonable person would have 'retaliated in the same way as the person charged in fact did'—that is much too particularistic.[106]

---

[100] [1942] AC 1.   [101] *Brown* [1972] QB 229.   [102] *Camplin* [1978] AC 705, at 718.
[103] [1991] Crim LR 383.   [104] [2005] Crim LR 971.
[105] [1969] 2 AC 130, on which see Holton and Shute, 'Self-Control', 71.
[106] As is the test proposed by the Ministry of Justice, based on the Law Commission's recommendation: 'might have reacted in the same or a similar way': Ministry of Justice, *Murder, manslaughter and infanticide*, Annex A, cl. 1(1)(c) and now Coroners and Justice Bill 2009, cl. 41(1)(c).

Surely a jury should not be asked whether a reasonable person would have put live wires into V's mouth (*Clarke*) or would have kicked V in the head fifteen times (*van Dongen*), but rather whether a reasonable person would have lost self-control to the extent that D did.

(iv) Reforming the Partial Defence of Provocation: In its 2004 report on *Partial Defences to Murder*, the Law Commission proposed a reshaped partial defence of provocation. This carefully-argued proposal has three main features. First, it removes the subjective condition as such, and instead excludes the defence where D acted 'in considered desire for revenge'. Secondly, it explicitly includes two possible triggers to the homicide, gross provocation and/or fear of serious violence. Thirdly, it imposes the standard of a person of D's age and 'of ordinary tolerance and self-restraint', adding that in applying that standard the court may take account of all circumstances 'other than matters whose only relevance to the defendant's conduct is that they bear simply on his or her general capacity for self-control'. Those recommendations were incorporated in the Law Commission's report on *Murder, Manslaughter and Infanticide* (2006),[107] and have been broadly accepted by the Ministry of Justice as a basis for legislation—subject to certain changes discussed below. It was argued in paragraph (i) above that the Law Commission was wrong not to insist on some element of emotional disturbance or loss of control, and the proposal by the Ministry of Justice to retain a requirement of loss of self-control was broadly welcomed. The Law Commission's proposed extension of the partial defence to gross provocation or fear was designed to deal, *inter alia*, with cases of excessive defence (see (d) below) and with the gender bias in the existing law. Women who have endured repeated violence or other abuse may kill out of fear, rather than upon provocation, and the case for a qualified defence in such circumstances may be no less strong. The initial argument in many such cases will be the defence of self-defence, which would lead to a complete acquittal. Thus Aileen McColgan and others have argued that there may be cases in which a battered woman should construct a case out of her fear of imminent serious injury, the fact that she was in her home and therefore should not be expected to retreat, and the right of pre-emptive strike.[108] To succeed on self-defence would require some reformulation of the concept of 'imminent harm' and an adaptation of the notion of 'reasonableness of response' so as to take account of both the history of violent abuse and the reasonableness of belief that there will be further and unavoidable attacks.[109] The Ministry of Justice makes it clear that it intends the law of self-defence to remain undisturbed by its proposals,[110] and it departs from

---

[107] Law Com No 304, Part 5.

[108] A. McColgan, 'In Defence of Battered Women who Kill' (1993) 13 Oxford JLS 508; see also S. Edwards, 'Abolishing Provocation and Re-Framing Self-Defence—the Law Commission's Options for Reform' [2004] Crim LR 181.

[109] Cf. Ch 4.6 above, and compare J. Dressler, 'Battered Women Who Kill their Sleeping Tormentors', with J. Horder, 'Killing the Passive Abuser', both in S. Shute and A. P. Simester (eds.), *Criminal Law Theory: Doctrines of the General Part* (2002).

[110] Ministry of Justice, *Murder, Manslaughter and Infanticide*, para 30.

the Law Commission's recommendations by treating 'killing in response to a fear of serious violence' as a separate trigger and insisting on loss of self-control as an element of it.[111]

The Ministry of Justice proposes to have a separate and narrower partial defence of 'killing in response to words and conduct which caused the defendant to have a justifiable sense of being seriously wronged.' The term 'provocation' is to be discarded on the ground that it carries 'negative connotations' (not spelt out, but presumably that it implies an over-broad defence), although the title of this new partial defence is likely to be shortened to provocation anyway. The Ministry adopts the Law Commission's formulation of 'a justifiable sense of being seriously wronged' but aims to tighten the partial defence by removing the Law Commission's reference to 'gross provocation' in favour of the narrower 'circumstances of an extremely grave character' as the trigger.[112] Clause 42(6)(c) of the Coroners and Justice Bill 2009 states that 'the fact that a thing done or said constituted sexual infidelity is to be disregarded'. Thus for this partial defence 'a partner having an affair' will not of itself be sufficiently exceptional, 'even if sexual infidelity is present in combination with a range of other trivial [sic] and commonplace factors.' Such situations may be 'devastating for the individuals concerned', but they are essentially commonplace and 'people need to be able to deal with them without resorting to violence.'[113] This is a stronger normative approach than the law has taken hitherto, and the Ministry's intention is that this partial defence will be used much less frequently than provocation under existing law.

Provided that one of the partial defence's two triggers applies, by fear or by things done or said or indeed by both, it must satisfy an objective standard which is a refined version of that in the existing law.[114] The Law Commission endorsed the kind of two-stage test that was subsequently affirmed by the Privy Council in *Holley*.[115] Draft clause 41(1)(c) of the Coroners and Justice Bill 2009 states the requirement that:

'a person of D's sex and age, with a normal degree of tolerance and self-restraint and in the circumstances of D, might have reacted in the same or a similar way to D.'

To emphasize the point, clause 41(3) states that the reference to 'the circumstances of D' refers to 'all of D's circumstances other than those whose only relevance to D's conduct is that they bear on D's general capacity for tolerance and self-restraint.' The reference to a 'normal degree of tolerance', combined with the requirement of a 'justifiable sense of being wronged', comes close to the proposal by Victoria Nourse of a concept of 'warranted excuse' which would sharpen the normative demands on the defendant by directing courts to consider the extent to which D's loss of self-control

---

[111] Ibid., paras. 26–37.   [112] Ibid., Annex A; cf Law Com No 304, Part 5.

[113] Ibid., paras. 31–4.

[114] See also Law Reform Commission of Ireland, *Consultation Paper on Homicide: The Plea of Provocation* (CP 27, 2003).

[115] Above, n 95.

was warranted or justified—thereby excluding from the partial defence those such as the racist, the paedophile, and the male who expects female servility.[116]

There remain those who argue that it is neither normatively defensible nor practically possible to deal separately with what were identified above as the first and second objective questions—how grave the provocation is, and whether D's response displayed a reasonable level of self-control. Thus Mackay, Mitchell and Brookbanks argue that the law should revert to the much looser objective test in *Morgan Smith*: the test should be 'whether D's normal thinking, reasoning and judgment had been distorted by the provocation', measured by the standard of 'what should reasonably be expected of D, taking account of his characteristics and circumstances.'[117] Their argument is that personalities cannot be picked apart in the way that the stricter objective test restored in *Holley* supposes, and that it is consequently unjust to deny the partial defence of provocation to those incapable of meeting a strict objective standard. The law would not be making an adequate concession to human frailty. However, the Ministry's proposals are designed to abolish the partial defence of provocation and, with it, the idea of a general 'concession to human frailty': the explicit aim is to narrow the grounds for a partial defence based on things said or done, but whether juries will be willing to convict of murder in cases that currently fall into manslaughter by provocation—especially if the government retains the mandatory sentence—is difficult to predict. One effect of the recommendations, and of the Privy Council's decision in *Holley*, is that defendants with a mental disturbance that bears on their 'general capacity for tolerance or self-restraint' will be excluded from the new partial defences and will be left to argue their cases on the ground of diminished responsibility—where, under existing law, defendants bear the burden of proving mental abnormality.[118] Combined pleas of 'killing in response to fear of violence or things said or done' and diminished responsibility will probably be rarer, since it will be unusual for someone who is substantially impaired by mental abnormality to meet the objective standard in the new partial defences.[119]. The scope of diminished responsibility is to be widened somewhat, as we shall see in part (e) below; but whether some defendants who suffer from a mental disturbance that explains their violent response will fall outside both the new partial defences and diminished responsibility—a fear raised by the arguments of Mackay, Mitchell and Brookbanks[120]—remains to be seen.

[116] V. Nourse, 'Passion's Progress: Modern Law Reform and the Provocation Defense' (1997) 106 Yale LJ 1331; also, the arguments of C. Wells, 'Provocation: the Case for Abolition', in Ashworth and Mitchell (eds), *Rethinking English Homicide Law* (2000), and H. Power, 'Provocation and Culture' [2006] Crim LR 871.

[117] R. D. Mackay, B. J. Mitchell and W. Brookbanks, 'Pleading for Provoked Killers: in Defence of *Morgan Smith*' (2008) 124 LQR 675, at 692.

[118] Homicide Act 1957, s. 2(2); in provocation, once the defence has adduced credible evidence of a provoked loss of self-control, it is for the prosecution to prove beyond reasonable doubt that the provocation was not grave enough to make a reasonable person do as D did.

[119] See R. D. Mackay, *Mental Condition Defences in the Criminal Law* (1995), 198–202. In LCCP 177, *A New Homicide Act?*, para. 6.142, the Commission proposes that it should remain possible to run the defences in tandem.

[120] See n 117 above.

Whereas the Law Commission placed its proposal for a reformed partial defence of provocation within a new structure of murder in the first degree or second degree,[121] the Ministry of Justice says nothing about that new structure and proposes that its new partial defences will reduce murder to manslaughter, as under existing law. Any reforms of the law of murder itself will be tackled later, not in the Coroners and Justice Bill.

(c) DURESS AS A PARTIAL DEFENCE

In 1987 the House of Lords in *Howe*[122] held that duress should not be available as a defence to murder. Their Lordships devoted little of their speeches to the possibility of allowing duress to function as a qualified defence to murder, reducing the crime to manslaughter and leaving the judge to pass an appropriate sentence. This would preserve the principle that a person who is threatened must be prepared to undergo heroic self-sacrifice rather than take the life of a third party, just as the provocation doctrine preserves the principle that citizens ought always to retain self-control. However, the House of Lords preferred to see a conviction for murder in these cases, with the use of executive discretion to secure an early release from the mandatory sentence of life imprisonment for offenders who killed when under duress, and thus appear to have reduced culpability.[123] This is surely an unsatisfactory solution, since the degree of emotional disturbance is likely to be no less than that involved in most provocation cases. The normative requirements of the defence of duress (discussed in detail in Chapter 6.3) ensure that it is restricted to dire and realistic threats which a citizen of reasonable firmness could not be expected to resist. A high degree of emotional pressure on the defendant can almost be taken for granted in these cases. In its 2005 consultation paper the Law Commission proposed that duress should be available as a defence that reduced first degree to second degree murder,[124] but in its final report it supports duress as a complete defence to murder or manslaughter.[125] It is right to state that 'arguments of principle and morality' support this, particularly where the strict conditions now required for duress are satisfied,[126] but it is unsatisfactory to place the burden of proving these strict conditions on the defendant, as the Law Commission recommends unconvincingly.[127]

(d) KILLINGS BY THE USE OF EXCESSIVE FORCE ON A JUSTIFIED OCCASION

In the Australian case of *McKay* (1957),[128] a chicken farmer found an intruder stealing chickens and shot at him five times, killing him. The farmer's defence was that he

---

[121] Law Com No. 304, discussed in 7.3 above.   [122] [1987] AC 817, above, Ch 6.3(c).

[123] See particularly the speeches of Lords Hailsham and Griffiths.

[124] LCCP 177, *A New Homicide Act?*, para. 7.32.   [125] Law Com No 304, Part 6.

[126] *Hasan* [2005] 2 AC 467; see also para. 21(1), where Lord Bingham stated that the case in favour of allowing duress as a defence to murder was 'irresistible'.

[127] See the critique in Ashworth, 'Principles, Pragmatism and the Law Commission', at 340–2.

[128] [1957] VR 560.

intended only to wound the thief, and thought he was entitled to do so. In another Australian case, *Howe* (1958),[129] D was attacked by a man, in an isolated place, who he believed was trying to force him to commit sodomy. D took a gun and, fearing that this stronger man would renew his attack, shot and killed him. In both cases it was held that the alternative of a manslaughter verdict ought to be left to the jury where the occasion justifies action in self-defence, or to prevent a crime, or to apprehend an offender, but where the defendant acts beyond the necessity of the occasion. Three reasons may be advanced for not labelling these cases as murder. First, cases of 'excessive defence' have a grounding in legal justification, in that the occasion was one which justified the use of some force, and this places them on a higher level morally than killings with no element of justification at all. Secondly, the defendant has what one might term a 'lawful motivation', believing that the actions taken were right and proper. This is a subjective, motivational factor which corresponds to the objective moral distinction identified as the first reason. Thirdly, in some cases the defendant acts instinctively in response to an unexpected situation, completely misjudging the proper reactions in the heat of the moment: this is a similar reason to the second, but adds the element of emotional disturbance, which may explain the over-reaction in certain cases. Both the second and, more strongly, the third reason show that the doctrine of excessive defence may include a substantial element of excuse in its rationale,[130] even though its theoretical foundation lies squarely in the concept of legal justification.

The Australian initiative was rejected by both the Privy Council and the English courts,[131] largely on the grounds that the common law precedents were not compelling, that the full defence of self-defence should be applied indulgently in favour of those who use such force as they instinctively think necessary, and that the doctrine of provocation might be used to accommodate other cases. The Criminal Law Revision Committee disagreed, recommending that a verdict of manslaughter should be possible where the use of some force was justified by the occasion and where D honestly believed that the force he used was reasonable in the circumstances.[132] History then took a strange twist, for in *Zecevic v DPP* (1987)[133] the Australian High Court denounced the doctrine of excessive force as too complicated for juries and removed it from Australian law.

The question came before the House of Lords in *Clegg* (1996),[134] where a soldier in Northern Ireland had been convicted of murder as a result of shooting at a car which drove through a checkpoint. The House upheld the conviction and stated that the introduction of a doctrine of excessive defence to reduce murder to manslaughter was a matter for the legislature, not for the courts. Lord Lloyd, delivering the major speech, seemed sympathetic towards the argument that those who use *excessive* force on an occasion that justified the use of *some* force should not be liable to conviction

---

[129] (1958) 100 CLR 448.
[130] See further above, Ch 4.6(g), on justifiable force and the emotions, and also Ch 6.4.
[131] In *Palmer v R.* [1971] AC 814 and *McInnes* (1971) 55 Cr App R 551.
[132] 14th Report (1980), para. 288; see also the Irish case of *AG v Dwyer* [1972] IR 416.
[133] (1987) 162 CLR 645.   [134] [1996] 1 AC 482.

for murder. A subsequent government review of the law recognized the power of this reasoning but concluded that there was not a strong enough case for introducing further complexity into the law of homicide,[135] an argument taken up in section (i) below. However, it seems wrong to return convictions for murder in these cases, whether or not the mandatory penalty is retained. The Law Commission's recommendation, endorsed by the Ministry of Justice, is that murder may be reduced to manslaughter where D acts out of 'fear of serious violence', provided that D lost self-control and that a person of normal tolerance and restraint would have reacted similarly.[136] This partial defence, designed chiefly to deal with abused women who kill from fear of further violence, seems unlikely to encompass the facts of either *Clegg* or *McKay*, given its emphasis on loss of self-control.

(e) MANSLAUGHTER BY REASON OF DIMINISHED RESPONSIBILITY[137]

Diminished responsibility was formerly one of the most frequently used qualified defences to murder, but in recent years the numbers have fallen from eighty per year in the early 1990s to around twenty per year (22 in 2004, for example). Diminished responsibility was introduced into English law only in 1957, in response to long-standing dissatisfaction with the insanity defence. Insanity was, and still is, a complete defence to crime, as we saw in Chapter 5.2 above, but its confines are narrow, and on a murder charge a verdict of not guilty by reason of insanity requires the court to make a hospital order with restrictions.[138] Diminished responsibility has a wider ambit, but its effect is merely to reduce murder to manslaughter. The judge then has a discretion in sentencing, and in recent years about half of the cases have resulted in hospital orders without limit of time.[139]

The wording with which the Homicide Act 1957 introduced diminished responsibility is rather unsatisfactory, but judges, counsel, doctors, and juries have approached it with a compassionate pragmatism rather than with rarefied verbal analysis. Section 2(1) of the 1957 Act reads:

Where a person kills or is party to the killing of another, he shall not be convicted of murder if he was suffering from such abnormality of mind (whether arising from a condition of arrested or retarded development of mind or any inherent causes or induced by disease or injury) as substantially impaired his mental responsibility in doing or being a party to the killing.

---

[135] Report of the Interdepartmental Review of the Law on the Use of Lethal Force in Self-Defence or the Prevention of Crime (1996), critically reviewed by J. Rogers, 'Justifying the Use of Firearms by Policemen and Soldiers' (1998) 18 LS 486.

[136] Discussed in 7.4(b) above.

[137] For detailed discussion, see Mackay, *Mental Condition Defences in the Criminal Law*, ch 4, and R. Mackay, 'Diminished Responsibility and Mentally Disordered Killers', in Ashworth and Mitchell (eds.), *Rethinking English Homicide Law* (2000).

[138] If the conditions for such an order are fulfilled: see s. 24 of the Domestic Violence, Crime, and Victims Act 2004, and Ch 5.2 above.

[139] See the research by R. D. Mackay in Law Com No. 290, *Partial Defences to Murder*, Appendix B.

The mainstay of s 2 is a wide concept of 'abnormality of mind', interpreted in the leading case of *Byrne* (1960)[140] as 'wide enough to cover the mind's activities in all its aspects', including 'the ability to exercise will-power and to control physical acts' in accordance with rational judgement. This makes it clear that the test is not purely cognitive, as it is for M'Naghten insanity, and that it extends to so-called irresistible impulse.

The words in brackets in s 2(1) specify three ways in which the abnormality of mind may be found to arise if it is to fall within diminished responsibility. 'Arrested or retarded development of mind' includes the categories of mental impairment and severe mental impairment. 'Any inherent causes' seems wide enough to cover virtually all cases in which the mental disorder does not have a clear external cause. Mental abnormality 'induced by disease or injury' refers to organic mental disorders, including disease of the brain. These distinctions emerge from the Court of Appeal's judgment in *Sanderson* (1994),[141] a case in which there was a conflict of psychiatric evidence. Both psychiatrists concluded that D suffered from paranoid psychosis. The prosecution psychiatrist stated that the abnormality of mind arose from taking cocaine. The defence psychiatrist stated that it arose from a childhood characterized by violent abuse and drug-taking since he was 11, an 'inherent cause' perhaps exacerbated by later drug abuse. Reducing D's conviction from murder to manslaughter, the Court held that a jury should be directed only on the part of s 2(1) that is relevant in the case—i.e. no reference to 'arrested or retarded development' was necessary here—and it went on to suggest that the phrase 'any inherent cause' would cover functional mental disorders, whilst 'induced by disease or injury' includes organic disorders. The result, however, is that this judgment represents 'disease' in s 2 as narrower than 'disease of the mind' in insanity at common law, and suggests that psychological injury may not amount to 'injury' within s 2.[142]

Two further requirements arise from s 2(1). First, D must show that the abnormality of mind 'substantially impaired' his mental responsibility. This is plainly a question of degree for the jury in those cases which are contested. In practice, the great majority of diminished responsibility defences are accepted by the prosecution, and only in around a quarter of cases does the prosecution contest the defence evidence and thus require the jury to apply s 2.[143] Secondly, the burden of proving diminished responsibility lies on D, as in cases of insanity.

One class of case where diminished responsibility is quite frequently contested is where alcohol or drugs are involved. There is deep judicial suspicion of any defence based on alcohol or drugs, and so the question is how the courts should respond where D has an underlying mental abnormality and had taken drink or drugs on the day in

---

[140] [1960] 2 QB 396.   [141] (1994) 98 Cr App R 325.

[142] See further R. D. Mackay, 'The Abnormality of Mind Factor in Diminished Responsibility' [1999] Crim LR 117, 122–3.

[143] Research by R. D. Mackay, reported in Law Com No 290, *Partial Defences to Murder* (2004), Appendix B.

question. The House of Lords in *Dietschmann* (2003)[144] had to decide a case in which the underlying clinical condition was a depressive or 'adjustment' disorder, and D had also taken considerable alcohol. The House held that, in a case where it appears that both intoxication and mental abnormality have played a part, the jury should be instructed to answer the question: 'has the defendant satisfied you that, despite the drink, his mental abnormality substantially impaired his mental responsibility for his fatal acts?'[145] This focuses on the 'substantial impairment' element of the partial defence, and the Court of Appeal took the same approach in *Wood*[146] where the underlying clinical condition was alcohol dependency syndrome and D had also drunk much alcohol. The jury should decide whether the clinical condition 'substantially impaired' D's responsibility, discounting any effects of alcohol consumed voluntarily. In effect, the jury are left to determine how much of D's drinking derived from his alcohol dependency and how much was 'voluntary'. This is an even more difficult question than that posed in *Dietschmann*, but it seems inevitable when the defence of diminished responsibility turns on 'substantial' impairment.

Should the qualified defence of diminished responsibility be retained? In principle, a person whose conduct was caused by mental disorder should not be liable to criminal conviction at all, as argued in Chapter 5.2(a) above; but in practice the narrow and antiquated defence of insanity is rarely invoked in England (only around twenty cases each year), and otherwise the courts proceed to conviction and then select a medical disposal where appropriate. In the absence of a workable defence of insanity, it is often assumed that the existence of the mandatory penalty for murder is the essential reason for the s 2 defence. The Butler Committee argued that relatively minor mental disorders may be regarded as falling within s 2 simply because this outcome is thought to be preferable to mandatory life imprisonment. 'The medical profession is humane', commented the Butler Committee, 'and the evidence is often stretched'.[147] The Law Commission recommended a reformulation of the partial defence of diminished responsibility, which is adopted in cl. 39 of the Coroners and Justice Bill 2009. The essence of the defence would be that D was suffering from a 'relevant mental impairment' which 'substantially impaired' D's capacity to understand the nature of his own conduct, to form a rational judgment, or to exercise self-control. The aim is to require the jury to assess whether a substantial impairment was significant in causing the acts that resulted in death. The Law Commission had added a provision for developmental immaturity in cases of defendants under 18, but the Ministry of Justice is unwilling to pursue this.[148]

(f) INFANTICIDE

This is a separate offence from manslaughter, but it is relevant here because of its close links with diminished responsibility. By the Infanticide Act 1922 Parliament created

---

[144] [2003] 1 AC 1209.   [145] *Per* Lord Hutton at [41].   [146] [2008] 2 Cr App R 34.
[147] Report of the Committee on Mentally Abnormal Offenders (1975), para. 19.4.
[148] Ministry of Justice, *Murder, manslaughter and infanticide*, paras 52–5.

this offence to mitigate the application of the law of murder to mothers who kill their new-born babies whilst suffering from the effects of childbirth. Doubts arose over the length of time which might elapse before the child ceased to be regarded as 'newly born', and the Infanticide Act 1938 extended the definition to the killing of a child within twelve months of its birth by a mother whose mind is disturbed either by reason of her not having fully recovered from the effect of giving birth to the child or by reason of the effect of lactation consequent upon the birth of the child. Infanticide is a defence to murder or (it has now been held)[149] to manslaughter, but it is more usual to charge infanticide in the first place. The maximum penalty remains life imprisonment, although almost all cases (only three or four per year on average) are dealt with non-custodially, usually by a community sentence.[150]

We have seen that infanticide depends on a finding of 'mental disturbance'—not clinical mental disorder—resulting either from the effect of giving birth or from the effect of lactation. Three interconnected criticisms of the law may be considered here.[151] First, there has been controversy about the medical foundations of the reference to the effect of lactation, and the social pressures consequent upon the arrival of a new child (such as financial demands, unsuitable housing, effects on family relationships) may be just as likely to lead to the mental disturbance manifest in these cases as any condition linked specifically with the event of giving birth. However, the Law Commission's recent review of the medical evidence indicates that there remains research support for the statutory basis of infanticide: the Commission proposed no change in the law, and the Ministry of Justice agrees.[152]

A second criticism has been that the law is gender-specific, singling out women for more lenient treatment and perhaps suggesting that women generally have weaker characters and are less responsible for their behaviour. However, there is evidence that some women who have given birth do suffer from forms of mental disorder unique to this (female) condition.[153] A third and related criticism is that the definition of infanticide is limited to the killing of the child most recently born, which means that when a mother in a disturbed state kills both her last-born child and another slightly older child, the one killing is infanticide and the other may be murder, whereas D's culpability is surely the same in both cases. If the essence of infanticide lies in the effects of the stresses consequent upon recent childbirth, then it is this, and not the age of the victim, which should be the basis of the law. Similarly, fathers of children may kill whilst overwhelmed by the stress consequent upon the arrival of a new child, and it is questionable whether they should be left outside the law of infanticide.[154] Neither the

---

[149] *Gore* [2008] Crim LR 388.   [150] See *Sainsbury* (1989) 11 Cr App R (S) 533 and *Lewis*, ibid., 577.

[151] See also the Court of Appeal in *Kai-Whitewind* [2005] 2 Cr App R 31.

[152] Law Com No 304, Part 8; Ministry of Justice, *Murder, Manslaughter and Infanticide*. Paras. 111–25 and Annex D. Cl. 44 of the 2009 Bill Confims *Gore* (above, n 149).

[153] Cf. Maier-Katkin and Ogle, 'Rationale for Infanticide Laws', with K. O'Donovan, 'The Medicalisation of Infanticide' [1984] Crim LR 259.

[154] Cf. the case of *Doughty* (above, n 62 and accompanying text).

second nor the third criticism moved the Law Commission or the Ministry of Justice, and so no changes are proposed.

(g) KILLING IN PURSUANCE OF A SUICIDE PACT

Section 4 of the Homicide Act 1957 provides that a person who kills another in pursuance of a suicide pact is guilty of manslaughter not murder. A suicide pact exists where two or more people, each having a settled intention of dying, reach an agreement which has as its object the death of both or all. Some suicide pacts may be regarded as the highest expression of individual autonomy, by means of a mutual exercise of the individuals' rights of self-determination, but the Law Commission reported concern that some cases involve dominant men imposing their will on women for whom they are caring.[155] Whereas the Criminal Law Revision Committee recommended that killings in pursuance of a suicide pact should be a separate offence, on the ground that the stigma and maximum penalty for manslaughter are inappropriate in these cases,[156] the Law Commission has recommended no change until there is a wider review of 'consensual' and 'mercy' killings. It has abandoned its earlier proposal that section 4 should be abolished and all cases dealt with under the partial defence of diminished responsibility, arguing that this would not cater adequately for those whose suicide pact is evidently a rational decision.[157] Suicide and attempted suicide ceased to be criminal when the Suicide Act 1961 became law, in recognition of the right to self-determination, but there remains an offence of aiding, abetting, counselling, or procuring the suicide of another which carries a maximum penalty of fourteen years' imprisonment. Many of the cases involve compassionate assistance, of the kind which may be necessary and justifiable if the right to self-determination is to have any meaning for those who are weak or bed-ridden (e.g. responding to a request to bring pills). Some jurisdictions look favourably on doctors who assist suicide.[158] The rationale for the offence is illustrated by *McShane* (1977),[159] where a woman was convicted of an attempt to counsel her mother's suicide by encouraging her repeatedly to take an overdose, and it was shown that the mother's death would greatly alleviate the defendant's financial problems. There remains a need to protect the vulnerable from persuasion on such a crucial matter as the ending of life, and to recognise cases of genuine compassion connected with the right to self-determination.

(h) MERCY KILLING

This concept has no special significance in English criminal law. Where there is a clear case of mercy killing by a doctor, he or she is likely to avoid prosecution or to benefit

---

[155] LCCP 177, *A New Homicide Act?*, para. 8.68–83.   [156] 14th Report (1980), para. 132.

[157] Law Com No. 304, paras. 7.42–45.

[158] See e.g. J. Griffiths, 'Assisted Suicide in the Netherlands' (1995) 58 MLR 232, and M. Blake, 'Physician-Assisted Suicide: a Criminal Offence or a Patient's Right?' (1997) 5 Medical LR 294.

[159] (1978) 66 Cr App R 97.

from Devlin J's concession to good motive in the *Adams* case.[160] The usual response to a 'genuine' case involving a non-professional defendant is that 'legal and medical consciences are stretched to bring about a verdict of manslaughter by diminished responsibility'.[161] The Criminal Law Revision Committee regarded this bending of the law as unsatisfactory, and tentatively proposed a new offence of mercy killing where a person, out of compassion, unlawfully kills another who is, or is believed by him to be, permanently helpless or in great pain. The proposal attracted strong opposition, some arguing that it might withdraw legal protection from the weak and vulnerable, others arguing that the fundamental ethical problems could not be satisfactorily resolved by legal definition. The difficulty with the counter-arguments is that the practice of 'stretching' diminished responsibility gives a *de facto* defence to mercy killers already. Thus, in Mackay's study of 157 cases in which diminished responsibility was raised, it seems that six were probably cases of mercy killing.[162] Practitioners seem to accept that worthy cases of mercy killing should be eased into diminished responsibility, but this informal approach provides the defendant with no legal basis for a defence—he or she is truly at the mercy of the psychiatrists, the prosecutor, and the judge.[163]

The House of Lords Select Committee on Medical Ethics examined the issues and decided against recommending an offence of mercy killing, largely on the ground that existing provisions are sufficiently flexible to allow appropriate outcomes to be achieved.[164] In respect of doctors, this flexibility is achieved through such distinctions as that between bringing about a patient's death through omission (which may be lawful) and bringing it about by a positive act (which is not),[165] and between intending to cause death and intending to relieve pain while knowingly accelerating death,[166] although even then a 'blind eye' may be turned to the practices of some doctors. But doctors cannot be assured that a 'blind eye' will be turned, and relatives and friends may be exposed to the strict law. In terms of protection for the vulnerable,[167] the chief difference between the present system and the CLRC's proposed offence is that the latter had a maximum penalty of two years' imprisonment, whereas life

---

[160] See Ch 4.5(a) above, and N. Lacey, C. Wells and O. Quick, *Reconstructing Criminal Law* (3rd edn., 2003), 603–24. For a recent (unsuccessful) prosecution of a family doctor for murder by administering high doses of morphine, see Martin, *The Guardian*, 15 December 2005, p. 8.

[161] CLRC 14th Report, para. 115; cf. *Cocker* [1989] Crim LR 740 with Lord Goff, 'A Matter of Life and Death' (1995) 3 Medical LR 1, at 11, and the findings of B. Mitchell, 'Public Perceptions of Homicide and Criminal Justice' (1998) 38 BJ Crim 453, at 460.

[162] Law Com No. 270, *Partial Defences to Murder*, Appendix B: 'The Diminished Responsibility Plea in Operation—an Empirical Study'. The estimate of six cases rests on my inferences from Professor Mackay's descriptions of the relevant features of each case.

[163] On which see S. Ost, 'Euthanasia and the Defence of Necessity' [2005] Crim LR 355.

[164] HL Select Committee on Medical Ethics, *Report* (Session 1993–94), i, paras. 259–60.

[165] The basis of the decision in *Airedale NHS Trust v Bland* [1993] AC 789, discussed in Ch 4.4 above.

[166] The basis of the decision in *Adams* [1957] Crim LR 365, discussed in Ch 4.6 above. See R. Tur, 'The Doctor's Defence and Professional Ethics' (2002) 13 KCLJ 75.

[167] Cf. M. Otlowski, *Voluntary Euthanasia and the Common Law* (1997), and J. Keown, *Euthanasia, Ethics and Public Policy* (2002).

imprisonment is now available even where there is a conviction for manslaughter on grounds of diminished responsibility; and the fundamental ethical problems are now swept under the carpet by a combination of a stretched diagnosis of 'abnormality of mind' and the ample judicial sentencing discretion, whereas the CLRC's proposal attempted to make the issues justiciable. The Law Commission concluded that a separate review and consultation on 'consensual' and 'mercy' killings would be necessary before well-founded proposals could be made, although it points out that its recommended redefinition of diminished responsibility might be adequate to cover some mercy killings.[168]

(i) CONCLUSION: THE MURDER—MANSLAUGHTER BOUNDARY

In this section we have been examining the partial defences which mark out cases where, despite the presence of the mental element for murder, culpability is thought to be sufficiently reduced to warrant a reduction in the class of offence. Our discussion has taken a broad view of partial defences, commenting also on some possible defences which are not (yet) accepted in English law. Various reasons have been advanced for recognizing partial defences to murder. Some regard the mandatory penalty for murder as the chief, even the sole, reason for these doctrines. It has been suggested here that the mandatory penalty is relevant but not critical. The key issues are, on the one hand, the proper legal classification of an offence which contains some exculpatory features, and, on the other, the distribution of decision-making power between the judge and the jury. The label 'murder', and the stigma thought to accompany it, should be reserved for the most heinous group of killings; lesser forms of homicide should be classified differently, especially where the culpability is significantly lower.

Arguments in favour of some seven partial defences have been set out above. Since it is possible that more than one defence might be raised in each case, sometimes in combination with a defence of lack of intent or self-defence, a system of criminal law which offers seven partial defences to murder risks undue complication and confusion in contested cases. The merit of separate partial defences is that they focus the evidence and the legal argument, giving the jury (in contested cases) an opportunity to assess the particular arguments for partial exculpation, and giving the judge fairly precise guidance on the basis for sentencing. Although this may enhance fair labelling, it may also increase the risk of confusing the jury in a contested case, thus eroding that protection. One approach would be to consider amalgamating some of the defences. Three of the partial defences discussed above have an element of justification—provocation, excessive defence, and some cases of duress. Most of the partial defences have an element of excuse—provocation, diminished responsibility, most duress cases, infanticide, mercy killing, and suicide pacts.

---

[168] Law Com No 304, Part 7 and paras 7.34–7.36; Coroners Justice Bill 2009, cl. 39.

One approach would be to adopt a partial defence of killing under extreme emotional disturbance, following the lead of the Model Penal Code.[169] This might encompass all those partial defences with an element of excuse in them. A provoked loss of self-control could fall within this new doctrine—as, indeed, could losses of self-control stemming from non-human sources such as a natural disaster or financial ruin. Diminished responsibility could also be accommodated, although a general defence of mental disorder remains a better way of labelling and dealing with cases of clinical mental disorder. Cases now treated as infanticide often involve extreme emotional disturbance, as do mercy killings, suicide pacts, and cases of duress. One advantage of this amalgamation might be that there would be less potential for the jury to become confused, and yet the jury would still be empowered to reduce murder to manslaughter in appropriate cases. One disadvantage of the change might be that the more precise moral distinctions currently incorporated within the law would become submerged within the sentencing discretion, where the signposts are less clear and the arguments less structured.

The Law Commission's recommendations and the Ministry of Justice's proposals put these debates in a somewhat different perspective. The Law Commission recommends a three-tier structure for the law of homicide which includes two degrees of murder (first degree murder, second degree murder) and manslaughter.[170] Assuming—until we examine the matter in detail in part 7.5 below—that the scope of manslaughter corresponds roughly with the existing law of involuntary manslaughter, the Law Commission's recommendations would have three grades of conviction and therefore three thresholds to consider. To distinguish between first and second degree murder on the basis of the existence of an intent to kill or an intent to cause serious injury with an awareness of a serious risk of causing death may be acceptable, but it would focus much argument on the boundaries of 'serious injury' and of 'serious risk.' Similarly, the proposal that cases of intention to cause injury or fear or risk of injury with an awareness of a serious risk of causing death should qualify for conviction of second degree murder may be acceptable, but it will lead to much argument over the boundaries of 'injury' and of 'serious risk.' The Ministry of Justice's proposals to abolish the partial defence of provocation, to introduce new defences of loss of control resulting from fear of violence and of loss of control resulting from things done or said, may prove to be more acceptable within the present structure of the law (where they reduce murder to manslaughter) than under the Law Commission's revised structure (where they would reduce first degree murder to second degree murder). The broadening of diminished responsibility may compensate in some cases for the narrowing of the other partial defences, but much depends on how restrictively the new partial defences are interpreted.

---

[169] Model Penal Code, s. 210.3.1(b). It must be said, however, that this partial defence is one of the least well received sections of the Code in the United States, with only one or two adoptions: see J. Chalmers, 'Merging Provocation and Diminished Responsibility' [2004] Crim LR 198.

[170] Law Com No 304; above, p 249.

7.5 'INVOLUNTARY MANSLAUGHTER'

The category of killings which has come to be known as involuntary manslaughter has nothing to do with involuntariness, properly so called. These are not cases where the accused has caused death while in an involuntary state.[171] They are cases where death has been caused with insufficient fault to justify labelling it as murder, but with sufficient fault for a manslaughter verdict. The word 'involuntary' is therefore used merely to distinguish these killings from ones which have the necessary intent for murder but which are reduced to manslaughter by one of the doctrines just considered, such as provocation or diminished responsibility. The legal debate in involuntary manslaughter is over the lower threshold of homicide liability—where to draw the line between manslaughter and cases of death by misfortune which are not serious enough to deserve a manslaughter conviction.

There are now three forms of involuntary manslaughter—two at common law (manslaughter by unlawful and dangerous act, manslaughter by gross negligence) and a recent statutory addition, corporate manslaughter. These three offences raise some deep issues of general principle. For example, manslaughter by unlawful act is a species of constructive liability, which was criticized in Chapters 3.6(r) and 5.4(b). In none of these cases was death or grievous bodily harm intended. Can constructive liability be justified by reference to the magnitude of the harm resulting, i.e. death? Or would it be fairer to convict the wrongdoer of a lesser offence, thus ignoring the chance result? The other two forms of involuntary manslaughter are based on liability for negligence, albeit gross negligence: as we saw in Chapter 5.5(f), this is regarded as insufficient for liability for most serious offences. Is it right that liability for the second most heinous crime in English law, which carries a maximum penalty of life imprisonment, should be satisfied by this relatively low grade of fault? These questions will be discussed in more detail once the elements of the offence have been outlined.

(a) MANSLAUGHTER BY UNLAWFUL AND DANGEROUS ACT

This species of involuntary manslaughter is based upon constructive liability. In broad terms, the law constructs liability out of the lesser crime which D was committing, and which happened to cause death. In fact, the courts have progressively narrowed this form of manslaughter over the last century or so:[172] there was a time when the mere commission of a tort or civil wrong sufficed as the 'unlawful act', and when there was no additional requirement of 'dangerousness' to be satisfied. What the prosecution must now prove is that D was committing a crime (not being a crime of negligence or a crime of omission), that in committing this crime he caused V's death, and that what he did when committing this crime was objectively dangerous. Let us examine each of these requirements in turn.

---

[171] On which, see Ch 4.2 above.   [172] R. J. Buxton, 'By Any Unlawful Act' (1966) 82 LQR 174.

First, D must have been committing a crime. In many cases the crime which constitutes the 'unlawful act' will be a battery or an assault occasioning actual bodily harm, arising from a push, a punch, or a kick. The prosecution must establish that all the elements of the crime relied upon as the unlawful act were present: to this extent a mental element is required for this form of manslaughter, and so in assault or battery this would be the mental elements of intent or recklessness. This point had been overlooked by the trial judge in *Lamb* (1967),[173] in assuming that an assault had taken place when two young men were joking with a revolver, without noting that fear was neither caused nor intended to be caused.[174] The point appears to have been overlooked by all the courts, including the House of Lords, in *Newbury and Jones* (1977):[175] two boys caused the death of a railwayman by pushing a paving stone off a railway bridge on to a train below, but none of the judges identified the precise crime which constituted the 'unlawful act'. No doubt the boys' act was a crime (a form of criminal damage, or a specific railway offence), and so this case does not call into question the proposition that all the elements of the crime relied upon must be established. In *Dhaliwal* (2006)[176] D had subjected V to a long course of abuse, including physical assaults. One evening he abused her again, striking her once, and she subsequently committed suicide. The Court of Appeal quashed the manslaughter conviction, on the ground that V's severe emotional trauma caused by D's long course of abuse was not a recognised psychiatric condition and therefore not 'bodily harm'. Thus the abuse was not an unlawful act.

The 'unlawful act' requirement also means that D must not have any defence to the crime relied upon. Intoxication would supply a defence to a crime of specific intent in this context,[177] but in most cases the prosecution will rely on a crime of basic intent or recklessness and therefore intoxication would be no defence.[178] In a case where the prosecution relies on assault or battery as the 'unlawful act' and D claims that it was a justifiable use of force, the court must be satisfied beyond reasonable doubt that the force was not justified if it is to proceed to a manslaughter conviction.[179]

There appear to be two types of crime which will not suffice as the unlawful act—crimes of negligence and crimes of omission. The reasons for excluding crimes of negligence were stated in *Andrews v DPP* (1937),[180] where a driver had killed a pedestrian whilst overtaking another car. There was little dispute that D had committed the offence of dangerous driving, but did that automatically make him guilty of manslaughter when death resulted? The House of Lords held that it did not: since the essence of dangerous driving was negligence, a driver should only be convicted of manslaughter if his driving was so bad as to amount to the gross negligence required under the second head of involuntary manslaughter (see below). Whether or not the decision was motivated by tenderness towards motorists is hard to tell, but there is certainly

---

[173] [1967] 2 QB 981.   [174] For the law of assault, see Ch 8.3(e) below.   [175] [1977] AC 500.

[176] [2006] 2 Cr App R 24, discussed by J. Horder and L. McGowan, 'Manslaughter by Causing Another's Suicide' [2006] Crim LR 1035, who conclude that on the facts a prosecution for manslaughter by gross negligence would have been more likely to succeed.

[177] *O'Driscoll* (1977) 65 Cr App R 50.   [178] *Lipman* [1970] 1 QB 152, and generally Ch 6.2 above.

[179] *Scarlett* (1994) 98 Cr App R 290.   [180] [1937] AC 576.

some logic in keeping offences of negligence out of the 'unlawful act' doctrine when a separate head of manslaughter by gross negligence exists. The logic of the second exception is less evident, and cases of omission have not always been treated differently. In *Senior* (1899)[181] a man who belonged to a religious sect called the Peculiar People refused to call a doctor to his child, who subsequently died; he was held guilty of manslaughter on the ground that he had committed an unlawful act (wilful neglect of the child) which caused death. However, this very reasoning was abjured in *Lowe* (1973),[182] where D failed to ensure that medical help was summoned to his child, and it died. The Court of Appeal held that a manslaughter verdict would not necessarily follow from a conviction for wilful neglect:

if I strike a child in a manner likely to cause harm it is right that if the child dies I may be charged with manslaughter. If, however, I omit to do something with the result that it suffers injury to health which results in death, we think that a charge of manslaughter should not be an inevitable consequence, even if the omission is deliberate.

This passage suggests that the law should, and does, draw a distinction between the blameworthiness of acts and omissions, even where the omission is deliberate. Yet the connection between withholding medical aid and subsequent death is surely closer than that between striking a child once and subsequent death. The father's duty in *Senior* and in *Lowe* is manifest and incontrovertible. If the 'unlawful act' doctrine is thought sound, these cases should fall squarely within it. If the doctrine is thought unsound, it should be abolished. This manifestation of the distinction between acts and omissions is morally untenable.[183]

Once it has been established that D was committing a criminal offence, the second step is to establish that this caused the death. In most cases of battery or actual bodily harm the causal connection will be plain, but cases involving drugs have presented difficulties. In *Kennedy (No 2)*[184] D passed a syringe containing heroin to V, who injected himself and later died. The Court of Appeal upheld D's conviction for manslaughter, on the basis that the unlawful act was causing a noxious substance to be taken by V,[185] and that D was acting in concert with V and therefore bore joint responsibility for the offence. However, the House of Lords overruled this decision,[186] and re-affirmed the principle that a voluntary act (i.e. V's self-administration of the drugs) breaks the causal chain and prevents D from bearing responsibility for the death.

The third requirement is that the defendant's conduct in committing the crime must have been objectively dangerous. This was seen as a slight restriction of the doctrine

---

[181] [1899] 1 QB 283.   [182] [1973] QB 702.

[183] In *Khan and Khan* [1998] Crim LR 830 the Court of Appeal suggested that omissions cases should be dealt with under gross negligence manslaughter.

[184] [2005] 2 Cr App R 23, criticized by D. Ormerod and R. Fortson, 'Drug Suppliers as Manslaughterers (Again)' [2005] Crim LR 819.

[185] Contrary to s. 23 of the Offences Against the Person Act 1861.

[186] [2008] 1 AC 269; for a review of the general topic, see W. Wilson, 'Dealing with Drug-Induced Homicide' in C. Clarkson and S. Cunningham, *Criminal Liability for Non-Aggressive Death* (2008).

when it was imposed in *Church* (1966),[187] where the Court held that 'the unlawful act must be such as all sober and reasonable people would inevitably recognize must subject the other person to, at least, the risk of some harm resulting therefrom, albeit not serious harm'. The House of Lords has declined to narrow this test by requiring that D recognized the risk.[188] The test remains largely objective but not entirely so. The dangers inherent in the situation should be judged on the basis of a reasonable person in that position, endowed with D's knowledge of the surrounding circumstances. Thus an ordinary person who burgled the house of an elderly resident would realize the possible dangers as soon as the age and frailty of the householder became apparent,[189] whereas the ordinary person would not know (if D did not know) that an apparently healthy girl of 15 had a weak heart.[190] However, the reasonable person does not make unreasonable mistakes, and so the mistake of D who carelessly loaded a gun with a live cartridge thinking that it was blank was not taken into account.[191] One element of the *Church* test—'some harm . . . albeit not serious harm'—has been construed restrictively. In *Dawson* (1985) D, wearing a mask and carrying a pickaxe handle, approached a petrol-station attendant and demanded money; D fled when the attendant pressed the alarm bell, but the attendant then suffered a heart attack and died. The Court of Appeal held that the unlawful act would be regarded as 'dangerous' only if it was likely to cause physical harm, not if mere emotional shock (unaccompanied by physical harm) was foreseeable. The manslaughter conviction was quashed, partly because the trial judge had given the impression that conduct likely to produce emotional disturbance would be sufficient.[192]

(b) MANSLAUGHTER BY GROSS NEGLIGENCE

This second variety of 'involuntary' manslaughter has suffered no fewer changes of direction than the first. Gross negligence became well established as a head of manslaughter in the nineteenth century, and then all but disappeared from the law in the 1980s. Thus in *Finney* (1874),[193] where an attendant at a mental hospital caused the death of a patient by releasing a flow of boiling water into a bath, the test was whether he had been grossly negligent. In *Bateman* (1925),[194] where a doctor had attended the confinement of a woman who died whilst giving birth, the Court of Criminal Appeal held that there must be negligence over and above that which is sufficient to establish civil liability, and which shows 'such disregard for the life and safety of others' as to deserve punishment. This test was approved by the House of Lords in *Andrews* v *DPP* (1937).[195] In *Lamb* (1967)[196] two young men were joking with a gun; D pointed it at V and pulled the trigger, believing that it would not fire because neither bullet was

---

[187] [1966] 1 QB 59.   [188] *DPP* v *Newbury and Jones* [1977] AC 500.
[189] *Watson* [1989] 1 WLR 684.   [190] *Carey* [2006] Crim LR 842.   [191] *Ball* [1989] Crim LR 730.
[192] *Dawson* (1985) 81 Cr App R 150; cf. the strange interpretation of this decision in *Ball* [1989] Crim LR 730 and *Watson* [1989] 1 WLR 684.
[193] (1874) 12 Cox CC 625.   [194] (1925) 94 LJKB 791.   [195] [1937] AC 576.
[196] [1967] 2 QB 981.

opposite the barrel. The gun was a revolver, however, and it did fire, killing V. The Court of Appeal held that D might properly be convicted if his belief that there was no danger of the gun firing had been formed in a criminally negligent way.

The beginnings of a change of direction appeared in *Stone and Dobinson* (1977),[197] where two people were convicted of manslaughter for allowing a sick relative, whom they had permitted to live in their house, to die without medical attention. The Court of Appeal's grounds for finding a duty of care in this case are scrutinized elsewhere.[198] The fault element required was expressed as recklessness, and defined thus: 'a reckless disregard of danger to the health and welfare of the infirm person. Mere inadvertence is not enough. The defendant must be proved to have been indifferent to an obvious risk of injury to health, or actually to have foreseen the risk but to have determined nevertheless to run it.' This passage contrasted 'mere inadvertence' with 'indifference to an obvious risk', perhaps foreshadowing the change that was about to take place. In the 1980s it was the concept of recklessness, in the *Caldwell* sense,[199] that came to dominate this variety of manslaughter. Both the House of Lords in *Seymour*[200] and the Privy Council in *Kong Cheuk Kwan*[201] propounded this as the proper test, and it was widely assumed that manslaughter by gross negligence had been absorbed into and replaced by reckless manslaughter.

In *Adomako* (1995)[202] the House of Lords re-established manslaughter by gross negligence, and jettisoned manslaughter by *Caldwell* recklessness. Lord Mackay held that manslaughter by gross negligence requires the prosecution to prove (i) that D was in breach of a duty of care towards the victim, (ii) that the breach of duty caused the victim's death, and (iii) that the breach of duty amounted to gross negligence.

What determines the existence of a duty? Lord Mackay took the view that this was simply a matter of consulting the law of tort, and some decisions can be thus explained. Certain duty situations are well established, such as parent–child and doctor–patient. Others have been recognized in previous decisions: there are the omissions cases where D has a contractual duty to ensure safety,[203] and where D was initially responsible for creating a hazardous situation.[204] New duty-situations may be recognized, as in *R v West London Coroner, ex p Gray* (1988),[205] where the Divisional Court recognized that police officers have a duty of care towards persons they arrest, particularly persons who are intoxicated. In *Prentice* (1994)[206] the Court of Appeal recognized the duty of an electrician to leave the house safe for the householder who employed him. A company has a duty to ensure the health and safety of its employees and of others affected by its activities,[207] for example. More recently, interest has focused on the

---

[197] [1977] QB 354.

[198] A. Ashworth, 'The Scope of Criminal Liability for Omissions' (1989) 105 LQR 424, at 440–5.

[199] Discussed in Ch 5.5(c) above.   [200] [1983] 1 AC 624.   [201] (1986) 82 Cr App R 18.

[202] [1995] 1 AC 171.   [203] *Pittwood* (1902) 19 TLR 37, the operator of a railway level crossing.

[204] *Miller* [1983] 2 AC 161, discussed in Ch 4.4 above.   [205] [1988] QB 467.

[206] [1994] QB 302; this was the case that became *Adomako* in the House of Lords, the other three appellants in the consolidated appeal having had their convictions quashed by the Court of Appeal.

[207] *R v DPP, ex parte Jones* [2000] Crim LR 858.

criminal law's recognition of duties beyond those of the law of torts. This is not a new phenomenon, because the reasons adduced to support a duty to care for a sick relative in *Stone and Dobinson* (e.g. blood relationship, guest in house) remain controversial. In *Wacker* (2003)[208] D was involved in a plan to bring sixty illegal immigrants into the UK in a container on his lorry, and fifty-eight of them died from suffocation. The point was taken that, since the sixty would-be immigrants had concurred in the plan, D did not have an enforceable duty of care towards them because of their voluntary involvement in the illegality. The Court of Appeal responded that, while this may be the situation in the law of tort, the criminal law has the wider function of protecting the public and it is therefore not subject to the same restrictions as the law of tort. In *Willoughby* (2005)[209] D asked V to come to a disused public house that D owned and to help him set fire to it with petrol. The ensuing fire killed V and injured D. The Court of Appeal held that D was rightly convicted of the manslaughter of V, as well as the offence of arson endangering life, because D owed a duty to V. The Court held that the trial judge had been wrong to hold that the duty arose simply by virtue of D's ownership of the pub, but held that the duty stemmed from D's recruiting V to help and assigning him the dangerous task of spreading the petrol. As in *Wacker*, the effect is to go beyond duty-situations recognized by the law of negligence and to impose on D a duty towards people who are willing participants in the same enterprise. The decision in *Willoughby* recognizes that the existence of a duty is a question of law. But, in the absence of criteria for determining duty-situations,[210] this appears to be common law decision-making at its retrospective worst.

Once it is established that there was a duty, that it was breached, and that this caused the death, there is the question of the terms in which the test of gross negligence is to be put to the jury. Lord Mackay LC in *Adomako* held that gross negligence depends:

> on the seriousness of the breach of duty committed by the defendant in all the circumstances in which he was placed when it occurred and whether, having regard to the risk of death involved, the conduct of the defendant was so bad in all the circumstances as to amount in the jury's judgment to a criminal act or omission.[211]

Lord Taylor CJ in the Court of Appeal had earlier stated that there were other types of case that might justify a finding of gross negligence, notably cases where there was actual awareness of a risk combined with indifference to it or a grossly negligent attempt to avoid it.[212] It does not seem difficult to encompass these other cases within the *Adomako* test, so long as the focus remains on 'the risk of death'. If such a risk was reasonably foreseeable, then the jury must decide whether D's conduct fell so far below the expected standard as to justify conviction for manslaughter. It has often been observed that this test is circular: if members of the jury ask how negligent D

---

[208] [2003] QB 1203.   [209] [2005] Crim LR 389.

[210] See the discussion by J. Herring and E. Palser, 'The Duty of Care in Gross Negligence Manslaughter' [2007] Crim LR 24.

[211] [1995] 1 AC at 187.   [212] *Prentice* [1994] QB 302, at 323.

must have been if they are to convict of manslaughter, the answer is 'so negligent as to deserve conviction for manslaughter'. Significant as the circularity point may be, more powerful are the arguments that a) it fails to meet the test of certainty properly required of a criminal law by Article 7 of the Convention, and b) its breadth leads to unfair inconsistencies in prosecution policy. The *Adomako* test was challenged on the former basis in *Misra* (2005),[213] and drew the unconvincing response that the question 'is not whether the defendant's negligence was gross and whether, additionally, it was a crime, but whether his behaviour was grossly negligent and consequently criminal'. This is a distinction without a difference and, despite the Court's discussion of some of the Strasbourg authorities, it should not be the last word on the subject. Indeed, Judge LJ went on to state that 'this is not a question of law, but one of fact'. Lord Mackay's words in *Adomako* make it clear that the jury is, in effect, deciding a question of law when it decides whether the conduct was bad enough to be classed as manslaughter. The second criticism of the *Adomako* test emerges from research by Oliver Quick into the decision-making of prosecutors in cases of fatal errors by medical staff,[214] finding a number of unexplained variations in prosecution decisions that the broad terminology of the offence permits.

(c) CORPORATE MANSLAUGHTER

The Corporate Manslaughter and Corporate Homicide Act 2007 introduced a new form of manslaughter, corporate manslaughter, to English law. It was formerly possible to convict a company of manslaughter by gross negligence at common law, but the 'identification doctrine' (discussed in Chapter 5.3 above) proved so restrictive in practice that only a few convictions of smaller companies were obtained.[215] Public concern at the considerable loss of lives resulting from companies' operations, and belief in the fairness of imposing the censure of homicide convictions (rather than merely of convictions under the Health and Safety at Work Act 1974) in bad cases, led to the lengthy and politically controversial process of bringing forward legislation.[216] The new offence can be committed only by an 'organization', and organizations can no longer be convicted of manslaughter by gross negligence (although individuals can). An individual cannot be held liable for the offence of corporate manslaughter, or for complicity in it.

---

[213] [2005] 1 Cr App R 21, on which see the comments of V. Tadros, *Criminal Responsibility* (2005), 85. Another (unsuccessful) ground of appeal was that the definition of the offence is so uncertain as to be incompatible with Article 7 of the Convention.

[214] O. Quick, 'Prosecuting "Gross" Medical Negligence: Manslaughter, Discretion and the Crown Prosecution Service' (2006) 33 JLS 421.

[215] See generally C. Wells, *Corporations and Criminal Responsibility* (2nd edn., 2001); J. Gobert and M. Punch, *Rethinking Corporate Crime* (2003); and C. Wells, 'Corporate Manslaughter: Why Does Reform Matter?' (2006) 122 SALJ 646.

[216] C. Wells, 'Corporate Manslaughter: Why does Reform Matter?' (2006) 122 SALJ 646.

The provisions of the Act are beset with considerable technicality,[217] but five key elements of the definition may be identified—(i) an 'organization' must (ii) owe a relevant duty of care and (iii) the way in which the activities were managed or organized must amount to a gross breach of that duty, (iv) a substantial element in that gross breach being the way that the organization's activities were organized by senior management, and (v) death must be caused by the way in which the activities were managed or organized. First, what qualifies as an 'organization' for the purpose of the Act? The definition goes well beyond companies and includes partnerships, some unincorporated associations, and most public bodies (such as hospital trusts, the police and government departments).[218] The practical implications of these broad categories are considerably narrowed down by the second requirement, that the organization must owe a relevant duty of care to the deceased person. The concept of duty of care, elaborated in section 2, is confined to duties recognized by the law of negligence.[219] Liability for deaths in custody has been a matter of concern and contention: the government intends to delay for three years the introduction of liability for various forms of detention and custody (as specified in section 2(2)). There are also several exclusions in sections 3 to 7 from duties that would otherwise apply—exclusions dealing with public bodies' decisions on resource allocation and public policy, military activities, the operations of emergency services, and duties under the Children Act 1989. Whether there was a relevant duty of care is a question of law for the judge; the technicality of the tests and the exclusions may give rise to considerable legal argument.

Once the prosecution has satisfied the court that the defendant is an organization to which the Act applies, and that there was a relevant duty towards the deceased, the third element is that the way in which its activities were managed or organized amounted to a gross breach of the organization's duty. How can this be established? A breach is gross if the conduct allegedly amounting to the breach 'falls far below' what could reasonably be expected of the organization in the circumstances. This is a question of degree for the jury, similar to that which has to be decided when determining whether negligence is 'gross' for the purposes of manslaughter by gross negligence (above, 7.5(b)). In this connection section 8(2) requires the jury to consider whether there was a breach of health and safety legislation. If there was, then jury should take account of how serious the breach was, how much of a risk of death it posed, and (by section 8(3)) any evidence of what is often termed corporate culture, i.e. evidence of 'attitudes, policies, systems or accepted practices within the organization that were likely to have encouraged' any breach of safety legislation. This broadens the

---

[217] For analysis, see J. Gobert, 'The Corporate Manslaughter and Corporate Homicide Act 2007' (2008) 71 MLR 413; D. Ormerod and R. Taylor, 'The Corporate Manslaughter and Corporate Homicide Act 2007' [2008] Crim LR 589; and C. Clarkson, 'Corporate Manslaughter: Need for a Special Offence?', in C. Clarkson and S. Cunningham, *Criminal Liability for Non-Aggressive Death* (2008).

[218] See s 1(2) and Schedule 1 to the Act.

[219] Compare the law of manslaughter by gross negligence (above, Ch 7.5(b), where the courts have based liability on duties not recognised by the law of torts.

time-frame of the new offence, by reducing the possibility that the grossness of the breach is assessed simply on a 'snapshot' taken at the time of the fatal incident.

The fourth element in the definition is that the way in which the organization's activities 'are managed and organized by its senior management is a substantial element in the breach.' The term 'senior management' refers (s. 1(4)) to persons who play 'significant roles' in either decision-making about or actual managing of the whole or a substantial part of the organization's activities. This may prove to be a fairly restrictive definition, especially in relation to large organizations, since scrutiny falls only on those who play a significant role in relation to a substantial part of all the organization's activities. The test is probably a factual one (who played a significant role?), and courts are unlikely to be deflected by nomenclature. But then, once the persons who are senior managers are identified for the purposes of the Act, the jury must also be satisfied that those persons' role in the activities was a 'substantial element in the breach', a restrictive phrase that invites argument about the role of a particular employee's fault, and thereby revisits some of the problems of the 'identification doctrine' in corporate liability generally.[220]

The fifth requirement is that the way in which the organization's activities were managed caused the death. The issue of causation is not straightforward: presumably a 'more than minimal' cause is sufficient,[221] and, since there is no provision in the Act to prevent the application of normal principles, a voluntary intervening act (such as the conduct of an employee) would break the causal chain,[222] clearly not the intention behind the Act.

The new offence of corporate manslaughter is an important step towards recognition that corporate liability in this sphere is fair and that it has to be constructed differently from individual liability. There are, however, various respects in which the Act could have been improved. The Act combines great technical complexity in some respects with considerable open texture in key terms, such as 'gross', 'significant' and 'substantial.' Moreover, it remains to be seen whether its application is easier and more extensive than the identification doctrine that applied previously: the notion of 'senior management' still requires the court to identify people within an organization who had a certain amount of influence and whose failure was a substantial element in the breach. On the other hand, if the test proves to be applicable without difficulty to larger organizations, the kernel of this approach could and should be adapted to other forms of corporate liability. The requirement of the consent of the Director of Public Prosecutions for any prosecution is regrettable, since the possibility of private prosecution could have operated to prevent any official 'cover-ups'. The relationship between the new offence and offences under the Health and Safety at Work Act 1974 remains to be worked out:[223] a reconsideration of that legislation, with a view to reformulating

---

[220] Gobert, 'Corporate Manslaughter', at 418.

[221] See the discussion of *Cato* [1976] 1 WLR 110 in Ch 4.5 above.

[222] See the discussion of *Kennedy (No. 2)* [2008] 1 AC 269 in Ch 4.5 above.

[223] F. Wright, 'Criminal Liability of Directors and Senior Managers for Deaths at Work' [2007] Crim LR 949.

its offences, would be a sensible next step. In the meantime, the Sentencing Guidelines Council intends to issue sentencing guidelines on both corporate manslaughter (for which only three forms of sentence—fines, remedial orders and publicity orders—are possible) and offences under the Health and Safety at Work Act resulting in death.

(d) THE CONTOURS OF INVOLUNTARY MANSLAUGHTER

The English law of manslaughter exhibits a tension between the significance of the harm caused and various principles of fairness such as the principles of correspondence and fair labelling. It is the resulting harm (death) which still dominates, and the enormous moral distance between D's conduct and the fatal result is evident from the fact that in many situations there may be nothing more than a conviction for common assault if death does not result (manslaughter by unlawful act if death results) or even no criminal offence at all (manslaughter by gross negligence if death results). Much is made of the unique significance of human life and the need to mark out, and to prevent, conduct which causes its loss. But does this really justify the present contours of the law of involuntary manslaughter?

It is important not to neglect the fact that manslaughter currently covers a wide range of culpability. The focus thus far has been on the lower borderline, but there are some forms of manslaughter that fall little short of murder. Indeed, there is probably a separate category of reckless manslaughter in existing law, based on subjective recklessness as to a risk of serious injury or death,[224] although cases are very rare. There is no doubting the substantial culpability of the person who embarks on a course of conduct knowing that there is a risk of death or serious injury to another (e.g. the man who administered carbon tetrachloride to the woman in *Pike*,[225] knowing the danger of physical harm to her). We noted earlier that the Law Commission has recommended that some forms of reckless killing (where D intended to cause injury or fear or risk of injury, knowing that the conduct involved a serious risk of causing death) should be included in the new offence of murder in the second degree,[226] with lesser varieties falling within the offence of manslaughter.[227]

The main focus of our discussion above was on the lower threshold of manslaughter, where its minimum requirements form the boundary with accidental (non-criminal) homicide. To apply the label 'manslaughter' to the conduct of a person who envisaged no more than a battery, e.g. by a single punch, is both disproportionate and unfair. It is only luck that makes the difference between the summary offence of common assault (maximum, six months' imprisonment) and the grave offence of manslaughter (maximum, life imprisonment). The manslaughter label grossly exaggerates the amount of culpability, producing an extreme form of constructive liability.[228] The Law Commission originally accepted this reasoning and recommended the abolition

---

[224] D. Ormerod, *Smith & Hogan's Criminal Law* (12th ed, 2008), 532–3.   [225] [1961] Crim LR 547.
[226] Law Com No 304, Part 2, discussed at 7.3(b) above.   [227] Ibid., paras. 3.52–3.56.
[228] See Ch 3.6(r) above.

of unlawful act manslaughter,[229] but this has now been replaced—without detailed justification—by a recommendation that adopts the Government's own formulation of a possible offence of manslaughter based on death caused by an act that D intended to cause injury or was aware carried a serious risk of injury.[230] This reversal will be welcome to those who argue that D's responsibility for the death cannot be avoided: it is something D did (he killed by acting dangerously), and he bears some moral responsibility for it.[231] It will also be welcome to those who maintain that a person who changes his or her normative position by attacking another ought to be held liable for manslaughter if death results. Any 'bad luck' in holding the attacker guilty is clearly traceable to the offender's fault in making the attack.[232] However, it can be strongly counter-argued that the language of 'attack' and 'change of moral position' fails to address the enormous gulf between what was intended and what (by mischance) resulted.[233] Statistically speaking, the risk of death from a single punch is far too remote to enter into reasonable contemplation, and it is not clear how significant the proposed restriction to causing 'injury' would be. Death would not be an 'intrinsic risk' when injuring another, rather than injuring another seriously. It remains wrong to attribute too much weight to chance: 'the offender's fault falls too far short of the unlucky result. So serious an offence as manslaughter should not be a lottery'.[234] If D's conduct was not serious enough to constitute reckless manslaughter (as described in the previous paragraph), and does not amount to manslaughter by gross negligence, the proper course is simply to convict D of whatever other offence he has committed and to pass sentence for that.

Where does this leave the crime of manslaughter by gross negligence? Negligence is not usually a sufficient fault element for serious offences. The Law Commission, after a review of the arguments, concluded that it is justifiable in homicide cases to criminalize gross negligence where D unreasonably takes a risk of causing death, where the failure to advert to the risk is culpable because the risk is obviously foreseeable and D has the capacity to advert to the risk.[235] The Commission recommends an offence of killing by gross negligence, with the following elements:

(1) a person by his or her conduct causes the death of another;

(2) a risk that his or her conduct will cause death would be obvious to a reasonable person in his or her position;

---

[229] Law Com. No 237, *Involuntary Manslaughter*, paras. 5.14—5.16.

[230] Law Com No 304, paras. 3.46–3.49, adopting Home Office, *Reforming the Law on Involuntary Manslaughter: the Government's Proposals* (2000).

[231] For development of this view, see J. Gardner, 'On the General Part of the Criminal Law', in R. A. Duff (ed.), *Philosophy and the Criminal Law* (1998), 236–9.

[232] C. Clarkson, 'Context and Culpability in Involuntary Manslaughter', in Ashworth and Mitchell (eds.), *Reforming English Homicide Law* (2000), esp. 159–63.

[233] A. Ashworth, 'A Change of Normative Position: Determining the Contours of Culpability in Criminal Law' (2008) 11 New Crim LR 232; see above, Ch 3.6(q) and (r).

[234] CLRC 14th Report, para. 120.

[235] Law Com No 304, paras. 3.50–3.60, amending only slightly Law Com No. 237, *Involuntary Manslaughter*, Part 4.

(3) he or she is capable of appreciating that risk at the material time; and

(4) either

    (a) his or her conduct falls far below what can reasonably be expected of him or her in the circumstances; or

    (b) he or she intends by his or her conduct to cause some injury, or is aware of, or unreasonably takes, the risk that it may do so, *and* the conduct causing (or intended to cause) the injury constitutes an offence.[236]

This formulation has a number of good features. It incorporates a capacity requirement (3), and now insists that the objective risk must be one of death (2).[237] There is no special provision for omissions, but such cases should fall within (4) and the criteria for deciding whether or not there was a duty to act will continue to be left for development at common law. The formulation of condition (4)(a) does not go far in the direction of maximum certainty, but the Commission argues that at least the new test would not be circular (a criticism levelled at the *Adomako* test), and that the only alternative to leaving 'a large degree of judgment to the jury' would be 'to define the offence in such rigid and detailed terms that it would be unworkable'.[238] As for the second limb of (4), this is advanced as a test that may be simpler for juries to apply than the test in (4)(a), and one that is likely to be co-extensive in practice with (4)(a). It does not, of course, make any explicit reference to gross negligence, and its form is similar to the existing 'unlawful act' doctrine—a doctrine whose abolition the Law Commission originally recommended but whose retention, in modified form, the Commission now supports. The difference in this context is that condition (2) must be satisfied before condition (4)(b) would be applied. The Law Commission envisages that the maximum penalty for killing by gross negligence would be a determinate sentence, not life imprisonment, but no conclusions are reached on its precise grading. However, before we leave the question of how the law of involuntary manslaughter should be structured, it is important to assess various other homicide offences and to consider their proper place.

7.6 CAUSING OR ALLOWING THE DEATH OF A CHILD OR VULNERABLE ADULT

There has long been concern about the difficulty of achieving a homicide conviction when the death of a young child has been caused by one of the child's parents or carers but it cannot be proved which. Parliament has responded by introducing the offence

---

[236] Law Com No 237, para. 5.34.

[237] This is the slight amendment made in Law Com No 304, although it sits rather awkwardly with the Commission's view of unlawful act manslaughter. Cf. the Law Reform Commission of Ireland, *Homicide*, paras. 5.68–5.69, accepting a capacity requirement but not the objective risk of death.

[238] Law Com No. 237, *Involuntary Manslaughter*, para. 5.32.

of causing or allowing the death of a child or vulnerable adult, contrary to section 5 of the Domestic Violence, Crime and Victims Act 2004. The essence of the complex statutory definition can be conveyed by making four points.

First, the victim must be a child (under 16) or a vulnerable person over 16, i.e. someone unable to protect themselves from abuse by reason of physical or mental disability. *Secondly,* the defendant must have been a member of the same household as the victim at the time of the death, and someone who 'had frequent contact' with V. The definition of 'member of the same household' includes a person who visits often and for lengthy periods of time, for example, a boyfriend of the child's mother who does not actually live in the house. *Thirdly,* D must have either committed an act or omission causing V's death or—and this is the key element—have failed to take reasonable steps to protect V from the risk of significant physical harm from another member of the household. Thus the offence can be one of omission, in terms of a failure to protect. *Fourthly,* the offence is satisfied by negligence—that D ought to have known that there was a significant risk of serious physical harm to V from a member of the household.

The creation of this offence, with its maximum sentence of 14 years' imprisonment, may be seen as an important step against child abuse, particularly in respect of those cases that have long gone without conviction or punishment at an appropriate level. However, there are various concerns about the drafting of the offence and its potential use.[239] The drafting is loose in some respects ('household' is left undefined) and demanding in others (a 'significant risk of serious harm', i.e. of grievous bodily harm). And there is the possibility that the offence will be used against women who themselves have been abused and have not been able to prevent their abusive partners from killing their young child.[240] Once again, we see a combination of intricate drafting on some points and wide discretion on others. Whether the creation of a new offence was necessary, as distinct from special procedural means of bringing such cases within mainstream homicide offences, warrants further examination.[241]

7.7 CAUSING DEATH BY DRIVING

English law now contains some five offences of causing death by driving:

(1) causing death by dangerous driving, contrary to s 1 of the 1988 Act;

(2) causing death by careless driving when under the influence of drink or drugs, contrary to s 3A of the 1988 Act.

(3) causing death by careless driving, contrary to s 2B of the 1988 Act;

---

[239] For fuller analysis, see L. Hoyano and C. Keenan, *Child Abuse* (2007), 158, and J. Herring, 'Familial Homicide, Failure to Protect and Domestic Violence–Who's the Victim?' [2007] Crim LR 923.

[240] E.g. *Stephens and Mujuru* [2007] 2 Cr App R 26.

[241] Cf. Law Com No. 279, *Children: their Non-Accidental Death or Serious Injury* (2003).

(4) causing death by driving when unlicensed, disqualified or uninsured, contrary to s 3ZB of the 1988 Act;

(5) causing death by aggravated vehicle taking, contrary to s 1 of the Aggravated Vehicle-Taking Act 1992.

Each of these offences is now discussed briefly, before their overall effect and proper place is reviewed.

The offence of *causing death by dangerous driving* replaced the former offence of causing death by reckless driving and, unlike that offence, is defined in the legislation. This is a considerable step towards greater certainty in the criminal law. In outline, section 2A(1) provides that a person drives dangerously if '(a) the way he drives falls far below what would be expected of a competent and careful driver; and (b) it would be obvious to a competent and careful driver that driving in that way would be dangerous'. Section 2A(2) adds that a person also drives dangerously if it would be obvious to a competent and careful driver that driving the vehicle in its current state would be dangerous—for example, driving an obviously defective vehicle or driving with an unsteady load.[242] Section 2(3) defines 'dangerous' in terms of danger either of injury to any person or serious damage to property, and provides that any special knowledge possessed by the driver should be taken into account. This is an objective standard, but its extension to cases where only serious damage to property (and not death or injury) is foreseeable may be considered too wide. Since it applies to conduct on the road that falls 'far below what would be expected', the standard may therefore be higher than that of negligence in the law of tort, and is approaching (or equivalent to) a standard of gross negligence. The maximum for this offence is fourteen years, following the Criminal Justice Act 2003, compared with a maximum of 5 years for the offence of dangerous driving. It remains possible to convict drivers of murder where the required fault element can be proved,[243] and likewise of manslaughter where the prosecution can establish, following *Adomako*,[244] that D was grossly negligent as to the risk of death, compared with a high degree of negligence as to injury or damage, as required for causing death by dangerous driving.

The offence of *causing death by careless driving when under the influence of drink or drugs* also has a maximum sentence of 14 years' imprisonment. Its constituent offences are careless driving (maximum sentence, fine) and driving with excess alcohol or drugs (maximum sentence, 6 months' imprisonment), but of course it is the consequence of death that has led to the high maximum sentence. The primary fault element in this offence is probably driving while unfit to do so, and the rationale for that offence is to increase safety by reducing the risk of injuries and deaths on the road. In practice sentence levels for this offence tend to be as high as those for causing death

---

[242] Cf. *Crossman* (1986) 82 Cr App R 333.

[243] S. Cunningham, 'The Reality of Vehicular Homicides' [2001] Crim LR 679.

[244] [1995] 1 AC 171, discussed in part 7.5(b) above.

by dangerous driving; and public opinion research supports this, taking the view that it is the decision to drive when intoxicated that is the major wrong.[245]

The Road Safety Act 2006 has introduced two further offences, (c) and (d). The first is *causing death by careless driving*, with a maximum sentence of five years' imprisonment. The Act states that careless or inconsiderate driving means driving that 'falls below what would be expected of a competent and careful driver,'[246] and this contrasts with the dangerous driver whose driving must fall 'far below' that standard. However, the offence of careless driving is chiefly intended to penalize small errors of judgment, and it can hardly be said that the offence is intended to protect people's lives (unlike dangerous driving). Thus it can be said that the moral distance between the underlying offence of careless driving—for which Parliament has provided only a fine as the penalty—and causing death by careless driving, with its maximum of five years, is too great, and that this is an improper use of a homicide offence. This is not to downplay the concern and grief of the families of victims of these offences; but that must be responded to in a different way, rather than by excessive punishment of someone whose error was evidently little more than other drivers might commit from time to time.

The second new offence is *causing death when driving while unlicensed, disqualified, or uninsured*. The essence of this offence is simply causation: if the driver causes death when he is committing one of these three other offences (no valid licence, disqualified from driving, no insurance), he is guilty of this homicide offence without proof of any fault in the driving. Indeed, if there were fault in the driving, one would expect a prosecution for one of the three offences with higher maxima. The reason for creating a homicide offence for deaths caused in these circumstances is that the driver should not have been on the road at all: his or her decision to drive when not permitted to do so was a *sine qua non* of the incident that caused death. Parliament regarded this as the least serious of the offences, assigning it a maximum penalty of two years' imprisonment. That may be taken as an indication of the absence of a fault requirement for the actual driving. However, research among members of the public shows unequivocally that this view is widely rejected: where a disqualified driver takes to the road, and happens to cause death through no fault in the manner of driving, most people regard this as more serious than causing death by careless driving[247]—whereas Parliament evidently viewed it as less serious by a factor of 2 to 5. This research was commissioned in order to assist with the drafting of guidelines for sentencers, but in fact it made that task more difficult, once it became apparent that there was widespread public rejection of the hierarchy of maximum penalties that had been created. Most people, it seems, would wish to see a reversal of the maxima for causing death by careless

---

[245] J. V. Roberts *et al.*, 'Public Attitudes to the Sentencing of Offences involving Death by Driving' [2008] Crim LR 525.

[246] Road Safety Act 2006, s 30 (inserting a new s 3ZA into the Road Traffic Act 1988).

[247] Roberts et al, 'Public Attitudes'.

driving and causing death when driving while unlicensed, disqualified or uninsured; but the sentencing guidelines must reflect the law as it stands.[248]

Finally, there is the little-prosecuted offence of *causing death by aggravated vehicle-taking*, resulting from an amendment to section 12 of the Theft Act 1968 by the Aggravated Vehicle-Taking Act 1992. Essentially, the 1992 Act created an offence of aggravated vehicle-taking where a person takes a vehicle unlawfully and is involved in an accident. The maximum penalty is two years' imprisonment, but rises to five years' imprisonment where death is caused. Once again, it is the unlawfulness of the taking that supplies the fault for this offence; no fault need be provided in relation to the accident that results in death.

Is this structure of offences justifiable? Is there a need for these separate homicide offences? The first offence of causing death by dangerous driving was introduced in 1956, largely because juries were unwilling to convict culpable motorists of such a serious-sounding offence as manslaughter. Ever since its introduction there have been those who have pointed to its 'illogicality'.[249] The difference in practice between an offence of dangerous driving (maximum penalty of five years) and one of causing death by dangerous driving (maximum penalty of fourteen years) may simply be one of chance. Bad driving may or may not lead to an accident, depending on the chance conjunction of other factors and other people's behaviour. And an accident may lead to death (in which case the more serious offence is committed) or merely to serious injuries or to minor damage. The response to this 'illogicality'—which is, of course, the very problem with the law of involuntary manslaughter too—has varied. Both the James Committee in 1976[250] and the Criminal Law Revision Committee in 1980[251] recommended the abolition of the offence of causing death by dangerous driving, thereby accepting the 'illogicality' argument. This accords with the CLRC's proposal that 'unlawful act' manslaughter should be abolished.[252] However, the North Report on road traffic law reversed this trend. The report accepted the principle that, in general, persons should be judged according to the intrinsic quality of their driving rather than its consequences, but argued that the law should depart from this in cases where death is caused and the driver's culpability is already high.[253] There is a well-known risk in motoring that certain kinds of driving may cause accidents, and that accidents may cause death. The rules of the road are designed not only to produce the orderly and unhampered movement of traffic, but also to protect property, safety, and lives. One who deviates so manifestly from these rules as to drive dangerously ought to realize—because the driving test requires a driver to realize—that there is a considerable risk of an accident. If an accident happens as a result of driving which falls well below the

---

[248] Sentencing Guidelines Council, *Causing Death by Driving Offences* (2008).

[249] Sir Brian McKenna, 'Causing Death by Reckless or Dangerous Driving: a Suggestion' [1970] Crim LR 67.

[250] Report of the Interdepartmental Committee on the Distribution of Criminal Business between the Crown Court and the Magistrates' Courts (1975), App K.

[251] 14th Report (1980), paras. 140–148.   [252] Ibid., paras. 116–123.

[253] Road Traffic Law Review (1988), ch 6.

proper standard, then that may well be a case of culpable negligence even if the driver had never thought of the risk in that particular case, because the driver is presumed to know the Highway Code.

Sound as this reasoning may be where it is dangerous driving that results in death, it is significantly less convincing in other cases.[254] Perhaps the next most serious cases would be those where D drives after taking considerable alcohol or drugs, and cases where D drives after being disqualified from driving, and with both of these it is debatable whether the fault is sufficient to justify conviction and sentence for a homicide offence. One view is that it is sufficient—a decision to drive while intoxicated flies in the face of widely advertised safety campaigns, and a decision to drive while disqualified ignores the road safety reasons that led to the disqualification. Another view is that, in these cases and more generally, the current trend places far too much emphasis on the occurrence of death. These are not cases in which death is intended or knowingly risked: many of them are cases of negligence, to a greater (dangerous) or lesser (careless) degree, albeit that the risks to safety involved in motoring are well known. The great significance attributed to the accident of death is more appropriate to a compensation scheme than to a system of criminal law. Yet if the criminal law in motoring cases were to focus on 'intrinsic' fault rather than the consequences of the bad driving, it would come down much harder on many people who by good fortune did not cause any or much harm even though their driving fell appallingly below the required standard. Those who think it wrong that the courts should respond so readily to the 'accident of death' would equally have to harden themselves to reject the pleas of drivers who say 'at least I did no harm'. If the courts were to focus on the intrinsic fault in a defendant's driving, sentencing would become more difficult in itself and more controversial in the view of the mass media.

Many of the issues involved here are similar to those raised by the law of involuntary manslaughter. The offences of causing death by dangerous driving and causing death by careless driving are essentially negligence offences, and must be assessed on the same criteria as manslaughter by gross negligence. The offences of causing death by careless driving when unfit through drink or drugs and, more particularly, of causing death when driving while unlicensed, disqualified or uninsured, are essentially forms of constructive crime, and should be assessed on the same criteria as manslaughter by unlawful act. In line with the arguments presented on unlawful act manslaughter above, it is argued here that there is too great a moral distance between a decision to drive when unlicensed, disqualified or uninsured and the chance causing of death to justify conviction of a homicide offence. However, some would say that the moral distance is narrowed by evidence that unlicensed drivers are between 3 and 9 times more likely to be involved in an accident than other drivers[255]—the whole structure of road traffic law is designed to enhance safety. That cannot be disputed; but whether it indicates that conviction of a homicide offence is a fair response is a different matter, to

---

[254] See S. Cunningham, 'Punishing Drivers who Kill: Putting Road Safety First?' (2007) 27 LS 288.
[255] Home Office, *Review of Road Traffic Offences involving Bad Driving* (2004), ch 4.

be discussed in the context of the financial and other problems of passing the driving test, the use and enforcement of disqualification from driving, and so forth.

7.8 REVIEWING THE STRUCTURE OF
THE LAW OF HOMICIDE

In this chapter we have discussed a wide array of different homicide offences. Towards the end of the chapter, questions about the proper contours and boundaries of the law of homicide have become more and more pressing. Although some suggestions and criticisms have been ventured at appropriate points above, we may conclude the chapter with some broader reflections on the structure of the law of homicide.

Let us begin by mentioning the two extremes. First, there is the law of murder, or murder in the first degree. Its aim is to identify certain offences as generally the most culpable kinds of killings. We have debated the various ways of defining this category—whether, and if so in what way, it should extend beyond killings with intent to kill—and we will not revisit that controversy here. The important point is that there should be a category of the worst killings that justify application of the worst label, murder. Secondly, at the opposite extreme may be found many offences of endangerment, offences that do not require proof of the causing of death but which aim to penalize the creation of a dangerous situation (whatever its outcome). English law does not follow the Model Penal Code in having a general endangerment offence (recklessly engaging in conduct which places another person in danger of death or serious injury).[256] It has some broad endangerment offences, notably section 33 of the Health and Safety at Work Act 1974, which is used after both fatal and non-fatal incidents involving companies. It also has general offences under legislation such as the Explosives Act 1883, the Firearms Act 1968, and section 1(2) of the Criminal Damage Act 1971 (damaging property intending or being reckless as to the endangerment of the life of another). Not only is this kind of offence found in relation to road traffic, in offences such as dangerous driving and careless driving, but there are also offences of operating an unsafe ship (sections 30–31 of the Merchant Shipping Act 1988) and placing on an aircraft a device likely to destroy or damage the aircraft (section 2(2) of the Aviation Security Act 1982). The point is that, even without a general endangerment offence, English law contains a large number of offences penalizing (often with high maximum penalties) the creation of dangerous situations. The existence of this body of law sharpens the question whether we need such extensive and numerous homicide offences. What criteria should determine the proper extent of the law of homicide?

---

[256] Model Penal Code, s 211.2; cf. K. J. M. Smith, 'Liability for Endangerment: English Ad Hoc Pragmatism and American Innovation' [1983] Crim LR 127, and D. J. Lanham, 'Danger Down Under' [1999] Crim LR 960.

Three main interlinked issues present themselves—questions about appropriate fault requirements, questions about appropriate labels, and questions about appropriate sentence levels.[257] Let us begin with fault: the principle should be that of equal treatment of offences of equal seriousness. There should therefore be an alignment of the minimum culpability requirements for homicide offences, unless there are strong reasons to the contrary. For example, manslaughter by gross negligence requires the risk of death to have been obvious, whereas causing death by dangerous driving may be committed if there was danger of injury or serious damage to property—requirements which are surely far too low for a homicide offence. The offence of corporate manslaughter is rather reticent on the whole issue, although section 8 of the Corporate Manslaughter and Corporate Homicide Act 2007 does state that, where the death arose from a breach of health and safety regulations, the jury should consider how serious a risk of death existed.[258] However, we find major departures from this principle when it comes to the two new homicide offences of causing death by careless driving and causing death when driving while unlicensed, disqualified or uninsured. Causing death by careless driving falls significantly below the threshold of fault required for manslaughter by gross negligence, and for causing death by dangerous driving. Moreover, the rationale for having an offence of careless driving is not so much to save lives (one purpose of the offence of dangerous driving) as to protect from injury and damage to property, so the claims for the new offence to be admitted as a form of criminal homicide are low. The arguments relating to causing death when driving while unlicensed, disqualified or uninsured are different, because it is the initial criminal act of driving when not permitted to do so that colours the consequences. The parallel is therefore with manslaughter by unlawful act, and the question is whether the moral distance between the originating criminal act and the tragic (accidental) result is too great to justify its inclusion as a homicide offence. This does not mean that the defendant is not convicted, since the underlying criminal offence is still there, and the legislature could create another (non-homicide) offence if it were thought morally and socially appropriate. The chief argument in favour of including these as homicide offences is that the deliberate commission of a criminal offence changes D's normative position such that it is fair to hold him liable for the fatal (if unanticipated) consequences—a view which, as we have seen, begs enormous questions, such that the original progenitor of the 'change of normative position' reasoning no longer supports it.[259]

Even if the principle of equal treatment of offences of equal seriousness is accepted, it would leave two major questions for discussion. One is what the minimum threshold for a homicide offence should be. The drift of the critique in this chapter has been

---

[257] For fuller argument, see the chapters by Ashworth, Duff and Tadros in Clarkson and Cunningham, *Non-Aggressive Death*.

[258] It is not known how many cases will not involve a breach of health and safety regulations. If such cases exist, there appears to be no duty on the jury to consider the risk of death; if such cases do not exist, why beat about the bush?

[259] See the debate between Gardner, Ashworth and Gardner, discussed in Ch 3.6(q) and (r).

that unlawful act doctrines, based on the 'change of normative position' reasoning, should be rejected, both in principle and because the moral distance between the originating criminal act and the fatal result is too great. But that leaves the claims of gross negligence, qualified by a capacity exception, to be considered. There are rule-of-law concerns arising from the vagueness of the test of gross breach or conduct that falls far below what is reasonably expected: in some situations, people will not have fair notice of what their duty is and in what circumstances its breach would be accounted gross. There are also rule-of-law concerns arising from the vagueness of the test and the consequent inconsistency of interpretations by prosecutors, leading to variable enforcement policies. It would be best to try to resolve these uncertainties before abandoning the idea of gross negligence as a sufficient culpability requirement for homicide offences: although gross negligence is not usually sufficient for criminal liability for serious offences, it does not seem unfair to impose homicide liability where there was an obvious danger of a tragic outcome that D ought to have taken more seriously. On the other hand, Oliver Quick's powerful arguments in favour of a minimum threshold of recklessness before medical professionals become liable for a homicide offence deserve careful attention, as does his fall-back position that, if there is to be homicide liability based on a lower level of culpability than recklessness, the condemnatory term 'manslaughter' should be avoided.[260]

This leads us into the second general issue, that of labelling. In principle the label applied to an offence should be a fair representation of the degree of culpable wrongdoing typically disclosed by the offence. It also seems fair that the labels used should be consistent. At present the term 'manslaughter' is used both for killings reduced from murder by a partial defence and for killings stemming from gross negligence or from an unlawful and dangerous act, as well as corporate manslaughter. The Law Commission has recommended that this common law confusion should be resolved by labelling the former as murder in the second degree while retaining the term manslaughter for the latter, and some counter-arguments were raised earlier.[261] Our present concern is at the lower boundary, where there is a contrast between manslaughter by gross negligence and causing death by dangerous driving (different labels, similar culpability), and where there are three other Road Traffic Act offences that use the formula, 'causing death by . . .' In terms of nomenclature, it can be argued that the condemnatory term 'manslaughter' should be reserved for killings with more than the minimum culpability requirement—killings that currently amount to reckless manslaughter, not merely gross negligence, and certainly not unlawful and dangerous act cases.[262] This would mean that a fresh term should be sought for any group of killings that are considered sufficiently culpable to warrant

---

[260] O. Quick, 'Medical Killing: Need for a Specific Offence?' in Clarkson and Cunningham, *Non-Aggressive Death*.

[261] In part 4(i) above.

[262] Part of this argument would be that this group should includes killings reduced from murder by provocation or diminished responsibility: see Ashworth, 'Principles and Pragmatism', 340.

a homicide conviction—perhaps a term such as 'culpable homicide', not hitherto used in English law.

Might there be good reasons for having separate offences, with separate labels, for killings in certain types of situation? Despite the lobbying of victims' families' movements, decisions on the contours of homicide ought to avoid responses that confuse the proper interests of the wider public in a sensibly calibrated law of homicide with the need to ensure that victims' families are properly supported and compensated. It may be argued, however, that the *circumstances* of certain killings mean that they should have a separate label. This has been part of the debate about corporate homicide: some would have preferred to see a new form of corporate liability for the existing offence of manslaughter by gross negligence, using a procedural change to bring these offences into the mainstream, rather than offence of corporate manslaughter that is differently conceived and might come to be differently viewed. Quick argues that homicide during medical procedures might also justify a different approach. On the other hand, some would have wished the 'duty to protect' cases, which gave rise to the offence under section 5 of the Domestic Violence, Crime and Victims Act 2004, to be brought into the mainstream by a procedural change rather than give rise to a separate offence. One of the main historical reasons for the creation of the offence of causing death by dangerous driving was that juries were reluctant to convict drivers of manslaughter. This should now be revisited: Sally Cunningham doubts whether this reluctance still obtains,[263] and in practice many offences of causing death by dangerous driving result in longer prison sentences than does manslaughter at common law—a position that has given rise to criticism.[264] It is a strong criticism of the codification movement in this country that the interface between manslaughter and causing death by dangerous driving has been studiously ignored. A proper legal structure should involve re-assessment of all forms of criminal homicide.

This brings us to the third set of issues, relating to the sentencing of homicide offences. In principle there should not be a significant disparity between the condemnatory force of the offence label and the normal range of sentences. We should therefore reject the idea of a conviction for manslaughter by unlawful act, resulting from a single punch after an argument, that is followed by a community sentence or short custodial sentence. The sentence correctly indicates that the offence did not warrant that label in the first place.[265] On the other hand, as we have observed, sentence levels for causing death by dangerous driving are often higher than for gross negligence manslaughter. This difference calls for re-examination, as Michael Hirst argues,[266] but we may decide that it is right—in which case that would be a strong argument in favour of bringing the offence into an appropriate mainstream homicide offence. These are

---

[263] S. Cunningham. 'Vehicular Homicide: Need for a Specific Offence?' in Clarkson and Cunningham, *Non-Aggressive Death*.

[264] M. Hirst, 'Causing Death by Driving and Other Offences: a Question of Balance' [2008] Crim LR.

[265] Compare V. Tadros, 'The Limits of Manslaughter', in Clarkson and Cunningham, *Non-Aggressive Death*, 48.

[266] Above, n. 264.

all questions that need to be examined on a wide canvas, and the starting point should be a general review of homicide offences—in other words, a wider review than the Law Commission has hitherto been able to carry out.

FURTHER READING

C. M. G. CLARKSON and S. CUNNINGHAM (eds), *Criminal Liability for Non-Aggressive Death* (2008).

A. ASHWORTH and B. MITCHELL (eds), *Rethinking English Homicide Law* (2000).

J. HORDER (ed), *Homicide Law in Comparative Perspective* (2007).

8

NON-FATAL VIOLATIONS
OF THE PERSON

8.1 INTRODUCTION: VARIETIES OF PHYSICAL VIOLATION

In this chapter we shall be discussing two main forms of physical violation: the use of physical force, and sexual interference. There may be considerable variations of degree: physical force can be anything from a mere push to a brutal beating which leaves the victim close to death, and sexual interference may be anything from a brief touching to a gross form of sexual violation. One problem for the criminal law, therefore, is how to grade the seriousness of the various forms of conduct: to have just a single offence of non-fatal harm and a single offence of sexual violation would contravene both the principle of fair labelling (see Chapter 3.6(s)) and the principle of maximum certainty (see Chapter 3.5(i)). Not only would it be contrary to principle, but it would also leave little to be decided at the trial and would transfer the effective decision to the sentencing stage.

The scheme of the chapter is to discuss non-fatal physical offences (offences against the person) first, including the contested question of the limits of consent, and possible reforms of the law. The second half of the chapter is devoted to the recently reformed law of sexual offences under the Sexual Offences Act 2003, focussing on the main offences and the definition of consent, and concluding with a review of the successes and failures of the new law.

8.2 REPORTED PHYSICAL VIOLATIONS

Crimes of violence constitute about one-fifth of all crimes reported to, and recorded by, the police. Figures from the British Crime Survey show that the overall number of incidents of violent crimes doubled between 1981 and 1996, but since then has declined quite sharply, so that the figure for 2007/08 is very similar to that for 1981. Around half of all incidents of violence involve no injury.[1] Studies have begun to uncover the full extent of so-called 'domestic' violence,[2] and although police forces are moving towards more consistent policies of recording such incidents and dealing with them as true offences of violence,[3] different approaches are still found.[4] Much of the remaining violence takes place in the street, around transport facilities, or in pubs and clubs, the vast majority of both involving young men. It seems that the use of a weapon is important in determining the legal classification of offences (not surprisingly, since offences involving weapons may tend to have more serious consequences): some three-quarters of the serious woundings involved a weapon, whereas the proportion was only one-fifth for the less serious offences.[5]

Two particular points may be made about offences of physical violation. First, there is evidence of a strong correlation between drinking and violence: the 2007–08 British Crime Survey found that the victim said the offender was under the influence of drink in 45 per cent of cases and under the influence of drugs in a further 19 per cent of violent incidents, with higher averages in cases of stranger violence.[6] Even though most drinkers do not erupt into violence, the figures make it clear that the special rules relating to fault and intoxication, discussed in Chapter 6.2, come into play frequently. Thus in Nigel Fielding's research into cases of violence that come to court, the defendant had been intoxicated at the time of the alleged offence in about a third of his sample of cases, and usually the degree of intoxication was considerable.[7] A second general point is that many offences of violence have consequences for the victim which extend well beyond any injury caused. There are psychological effects of fear and depression, which may significantly impair the victim's enjoyment of life long after the physical wounds have healed. Such effects are well documented in the case of female victims of 'domestic' violence,[8] but many other victims of violence suffer

---

[1] C. Kershaw *et al.*, *Crime in England and Wales 2007/08* (2008), 62–5.

[2] C. Mirrlees-Black, *Domestic Violence: Findings from a British Crime Survey Self-Completion Questionnaire* (Home Office Research Study No. 191, 1999).

[3] S. Grace, *Policing Domestic Violence in the 1990s* (Home Office Research Study No. 139, 1995); C. Hoyle, *Negotiating Domestic Violence* (1998); CPS Policy on Prosecuting Cases of Domestic Violence, at <www.cps.gov.uk>.

[4] L. Kelly *et al.*, *Domestic Violence Matters* (Home Office Research Study No. 193, 1999).

[5] R. Walmsley, *Personal Violence* (Home Office Research Study No. 89, 1986), 8.

[6] Kershaw., *Crime in England and Wales 2007–08*, 76.

[7] N. Fielding, *Courting Violence: Offences Against the Person Cases in Court* (2006), 98–104.

[8] Hoyle, *Negotiating Domestic Violence*, ch 7; cf. Fielding (last note), 104–8, on victims, defendants and courtroom tactics.

lasting social and psychological effects stemming from the offence and from other circumstances (e.g. intimidation, long periods off work) that may follow it.[9]

The values which underlie the offences of physical violation are reflected in various Convention rights, such as Article 3 (the right not to be subjected to 'torture or inhuman or degrading treatment'), Article 5 (the right to liberty and security of person), and Article 8 (the right to respect for one's private life). The value of privacy is central: the body is part of one's private identity, and, apart from any physical hurt inflicted by violence, an assault constitutes a challenge to one's personal identity, peace, and well-being. Yet the principle of individual autonomy has its negative as well as its positive implications, in the sense that one should have the liberty to decide for oneself the level of pain to which one subjects one's body (e.g. in sport, or for pure recreation). Central to this is the issue of the extent to which individuals may lawfully consent to the infliction of harm or injury on their bodies, which (as we shall see) raises questions about the justifications for state interference with the right to respect for one's private life in Article 8.

8.3 OFFENCES OF NON-FATAL PHYSICAL VIOLATION

We have seen something of the various situations in which non-fatal physical harm might occur. How does the law classify its offences? How should it respond to these various invasions of physical integrity? One approach would be to create separate offences to cover different ways of causing injury and different situations in which violence occurs. This was the nineteenth century English approach, and many such offences still survive in the Offences against the Person Act 1861 (relating, for example, to injuries caused by gunpowder, throwing corrosive fluid, failing to provide food for apprentices, setting spring guns). A second approach would be to attempt to rank the offences by reference to the degree of harm caused and the degree of fault in the person causing it. The 1861 Act also contains some offences of this kind, but, as we shall see below, its ranking is impaired by obscure terms, uncertainties in the fault requirements, and some overlapping. Thorough reform of the law is long overdue, and will be discussed in subsection (1) below. A significant development in practice has been the promulgation, by the police and the Crown Prosecution Service, of charging standards for the various offences against the person.[10] The expressed aim is to improve fairness to defendants, through greater uniformity of approach to charging, and to make the criminal justice system more efficient by ensuring that the appropriate charges are laid

---

[9] J. Shapland, J. Willmore, and P. Duff, *Victims in the Criminal Justice System* (1985), ch 6, esp. at 99.

[10] Now incorporated into the legal guidance set out at <www.cps.gov.uk/legal/l_to_o/offences_against_ the_person/>.

at the outset. The guidance will be referred to as each offence is discussed, although its impact in practice is difficult to assess.

(a) ATTEMPTED MURDER

If we were to construct a 'ladder' of non-fatal offences, starting with the most serious and moving down to the least serious, the offence of attempted murder should be placed at the top. There is an immediate paradox here: attempted murder may not involve the infliction of any harm at all, since a person who shoots at another and misses may still be held guilty of attempted murder. What distinguishes this offence is proof of an intent to kill, not the occurrence of any particular harm. The fault element for attempted murder is therefore high—higher than for murder, under English law, since murder may be committed by someone who merely intended to cause really serious injury and not death.[11] Nothing less than an intention to kill suffices to convict someone of attempted murder.[12] Beyond that, all that is necessary is proof that D did something which was 'more than merely preparatory' towards the murder.[13] Although a conviction is perfectly possible where no harm results—and such a case might still be regarded as a most serious non-fatal offence, since D tried to cause death, and the subjective principles[14] confirm the high guilt—there are also cases where D's attempt to kill results in serious injury to the victim. In such cases a prosecution might be brought for attempted murder—and will succeed if the intention to kill can be proved. However, the court might not be satisfied of that 'beyond reasonable doubt', and might find that D only intended to cause grievous bodily harm. In that event, the conviction will be for the offence of causing grievous bodily harm with intent, but both offences carry the same maximum punishment—life imprisonment.[15]

(b) WOUNDING OR GRIEVOUS BODILY HARM WITH INTENT

Section 18 of the Offences Against the Person Act 1861 creates a serious offence which may be committed in a number of different ways. There are two alternative forms of conduct, and either of two forms of intent will suffice. The conduct may be either causing a wound or causing grievous bodily harm. A wound has been defined as an injury which breaks both the outer and inner skin. A bruise or a burst blood-vessel in an eye does not amount to a wound,[16] whereas this requirement of the offence may be fulfilled by a rather minor cut. Grievous bodily harm is much more serious,

---

[11] See the discussion above, Ch 7.3(c), where this is viewed as one argument against the 'GBH' rule for murder.

[12] Confirmed in *Fallon* [1994] Crim LR 519.

[13] This is the conduct requirement of all attempted crimes: see below, Ch 11.3(b).

[14] See above, Ch 5.4(a).

[15] The Sentencing Guidelines Council has conducted a consultation on whether sentences for attempted murder should be linked to those for murder (see Ch 7.3(a) above) or to those for other non-fatal offences: SGC, *Attempted Murder: Notes and Questions for Consultees* (2007).

[16] *C v Eisenhower* [1984] QB 331.

although it has never been defined with any precision and the authoritative description is 'really serious harm'.[17] The harm does not have to be life-threatening or permanent, but it takes far less to cause serious harm to a young child or vulnerable
person than to an adult in full health.[18] The harm may be a sexually transmitted
disease with significant effects: the old case of *Clarence* (1888)[19] was against this,
but *Dica* (2004)[20] establishes that infection with HIV can amount to grievous bodily
harm. The CPS guidance refers to injuries resulting in permanent disability or loss of
sensory function, non-minor permanent visible disfigurement, broken or displaced
limbs or bones, injuries which cause substantial loss of blood, and injuries resulting
in lengthy treatment or incapacity.

Does the concept of 'bodily harm' extend to harm to the mind? This question has
been raised in a number of cases of stalking and, although there is now specific legislation on stalking,[21] the substantive issue remains important under the 1861 Act. In
Ireland and Burstow (1998)[22] the House of Lords heard appeals in two cases in which
the defendants had repeatedly made silent telephone calls to their victims. Burstow
had been convicted under s 20 of the 1861 Act, of which grievous bodily harm is an
element, and the House of Lords confirmed that 'bodily harm' includes any recogniz-
able psychiatric injury. The House adopted the distinction, drawn by Hobhouse LJ in
Chan-Fook,[23] between 'mere emotions such as distress or panic', which are not sufficient, and 'states of mind that are . . . evidence of some identifiable clinical condition',
which may be sufficient if supported by psychiatric evidence.[24] What must be proved,
under either s 18 or s 20, is that the psychiatric injury was 'really serious'.

Turning to the fault requirements, the one most commonly relied on in prosecutions is 'with intent to cause grievous bodily harm'. The meaning of 'intention' here
is the same as outlined earlier.[25] Where an attack involves the use of a weapon,[26] that
may make it easier to establish the relevant intention. On the other hand, where psychiatric injury is alleged, it may be more difficult to prove that D intended to cause
really serious harm of that kind. If the prosecution fails to establish intention, the
offence will be reduced to the lower category, to be considered in section 8.3(c) below,
so long as recklessness is proved. But there is an alternative fault element for section
18: 'with intent to prevent the lawful apprehension or detainer of any person'. Whilst
the policy of this requirement—classifying attacks on persons engaged in law enforcement as especially serious—is perfectly understandable, one result of the wording of s
18 of the 1861 Act is that D can be convicted of this offence (with a maximum penalty
of life imprisonment) if he intends to resist arrest and is merely reckless as to causing

---

[17] *DPP v Smith* [1961] AC 290; cf. *Janjua* [1999] 1 Cr App R 91, where the CA held that 'serious harm',
without the word 'really', was a sufficient direction in a case where a five-inch knife was used.

[18] *Bollom* [2004] 2 Cr App R 50.   [19] (1888) 22 QBD 23.

[20] [2004] Q. B. 1257; see M. Weait, (20050 68 MLR 121; see also the discussion of *Konzani*, below, at n 96.

[21] Protection from Harassment Act 1997, discussed in section 8.3(g) below.

[22] [1998] AC 147.   [23] (1994) 99 Cr App R 147, at 152.

[24] This distinction was affirmed in *Dhaliwal* [2006] 2 Cr App R 348, rejecting any extension to
psychological conditions.

[25] See above, Ch 5.5(b).   [26] See above, n 4 and accompanying text.

harm to the police officer.[27] It seems that consequences so serious as grievous bodily harm need not have been foreseen or foreseeable in this type of case,[28] which confirms this element of the crime as a stark example of constructive criminal liability.[29]

(c) RECKLESSLY INFLICTING A WOUND OR GRIEVOUS BODILY HARM

Section 20 of the Offences Against the Person Act 1861 creates the offence of unlawfully and maliciously wounding or inflicting grievous bodily harm. The conduct element in this offence is similar to that for the more serious offence under s 18, and the meanings of 'wound' and 'grievous bodily harm' are no different.[30] Considerable attention has been focused on the distinction between *causing* grievous bodily harm (s 18) and *inflicting* grievous bodily harm (s 20). Critics have long argued that it is illogical for the more serious offence to have the wider causal basis, but John Gardner has countered that it is perfectly rational to allow a wide causal basis (cause) when the fault element is narrow (intent) whilst restricting the causal basis (inflict) when the fault element is much wider (recklessness).[31] However, the exact meaning of the more restrictive word 'inflict' in s 20 is controversial. For many years it was believed to require proof of a sufficiently direct action by D to constitute an assault. This was decided in the leading case of *Clarence* (1888),[32] where D had communicated venereal disease to his wife during intercourse that was held to be consensual. As she consented, there was no assault, and so there could be no 'inflicting' within s 20. A number of other decisions overlooked this requirement: convictions were returned in *Martin* (1881)[33] for harm caused by placing a bar across the exit to a theatre and shouting 'Fire!', and in *Cartledge* v *Allen* (1973)[34] for injury to a hand when a man threatened by D ran off and smashed into a glass door, although in neither case was there a clear assault. However, the House of Lords in *Wilson* (1984)[35] and subsequent cases[36] has decided that there can be an 'infliction' of grievous bodily harm without proof of an assault. The decisions are unsatisfactory in their reasoning,[37] but may be explained as an attempt by the judiciary to improve the workability of a mid-Victorian statute.

The main difference between ss 18 and 20 lies in the fault element, and it is a considerable difference. Section 18 requires intention. Section 20 requires recklessness, in

---

[27] *Morrison* (1989) 89 Cr App R 17; cf. *Fallon* [1994] Crim LR 519.

[28] The decision in *Morrison* did not clarify this; cf. *Mowatt*, below, n 41 and accompanying text.

[29] On which see Ch 5.4(b) above.

[30] It will be recalled that *Burstow*, just discussed in relation to psychiatric injury as bodily harm, involved a conviction under s. 20.

[31] J. Gardner, 'Rationality and the Rule of Law in Offences against the Person' [1994] Camb LJ 502.

[32] (1888) 22 QBD 23.   [33] (1881) 8 QBD 54.   [34] [1973] Crim LR 530.

[35] *Wilson, Jenkins* [1984] AC 242.

[36] *Savage and Parmenter* [1992] 1 AC 699, *Mandair* [1995] 1 AC 208, *Ireland and Burstow* [1998] AC 147.

[37] The decisions have important procedural as well as substantive implications: see G. Williams, 'Alternative Elements and Included Offences' [1984] CLJ 290.

the advertent sense of the conscious taking of an unjustified risk.[38] The fault element in s 20 was further broadened by the decision in *Mowatt* (1968):[39] there is no need to prove recklessness as to wounding or grievous bodily harm, so long as the court is satisfied that D was reckless as to some physical harm to some person, albeit of a minor character. Not only has this unduly broad fault element been approved by the House of Lords,[40] but any attempt to narrow it down by requiring that D foresaw that the conduct *would* cause some minor physical harm now seems precluded by the courts' insistence of foresight that it *might* do so.[41] The *Mowatt* extension is another example of constructive liability, and it is particularly inappropriate here, in so far as the law is aiming to produce a 'ladder' of offences graded in terms of relative seriousness. However, even without the *Mowatt* extension, one might ask whether the distinction between intention (s 18) and recklessness (s 20) in crimes of violence, which are often impulsive reactions to events, is so wide as to warrant the difference in maximum penalties between life imprisonment and five years' imprisonment.[42]

(d) AGGRAVATED ASSAULTS

Common assault is the lowest rung of the 'ladder' of non-fatal offences, with a maximum penalty of six months' imprisonment, and it is discussed in more detail in (e) below. But certain assaults are singled out by the law as aggravated—assault with intent to rob, assault with intent to prevent arrest, assault occasioning actual bodily harm, racially or religiously aggravated assaults, and assault on a constable. Each of these will be discussed in turn.

Assault with intent to rob, like robbery, carries a maximum of life imprisonment;[43] it is, in effect, an offence of attempted robbery. A*ssault with intent to resist arrest* or to prevent a lawful arrest, contrary to s 38 of the 1861 Act, carries a maximum penalty of two years' imprisonment and may be charged where an assault on the police results in a minor injury.

A third form of aggravated assault, which is usually regarded as representing the rung of the 'ladder' below recklessly inflicting a wound or grievous bodily harm (contrary to s 20) but above common assault, is *assault occasioning actual bodily harm* (contrary to s 47). The conduct element of 'actual bodily harm' has been given the wide definition of 'any hurt or injury calculated to interfere with the health or comfort of the victim' so long as it is not merely 'transient or trifling'.[44] However,

---

[38] See above, Ch 5.5(c).   [39] [1968] 1 QB 421.   [40] *Savage and Parmenter* [1992] AC 699.

[41] *Mowatt* [1968] 1 QB 421, confirmed in *Rushworth* (1992) 95 Cr App R 252. This accords with the normal definition of recklessness: see Ch 5.5(c). Diplock LJ's judgment in *Mowatt* also includes the phrase, 'should have foreseen', which wrongly suggests an objective criterion. The Court of Appeal has pointed this out, but judges occasionally fall into the error.

[42] The maximum sentence is seven years when the s. 20 offence is 'racially or religiously aggravated'. See n 56 below and accompanying text.

[43] Theft Act 1968, s. 8(2); note that robbery itself (discussed in the context of property offences in Ch 9.3 below) may also be classified as an offence of violence.

[44] *Donovan* [1934] 2 KB 498.

in *Chan-Fook* (1994)[45] the Court of Appeal held that in most cases the words 'actual bodily harm' should be left undefined. Where there is no bodily contact it may be necessary to elaborate somewhat, but, as the House of Lords confirmed in *Ireland and Burstow*,[46] it should be made clear that any psychological effect on the victim must amount to psychiatric injury before it can fall within s 47. Merely causing a hysterical or nervous condition is no longer sufficient.[47] This is an unfortunate restriction, even if it is arguably inherent in the word 'bodily', since research shows that immediate fright and lasting fear are produced by many attacks.[48] Harm of this magnitude ought to be given some recognition, but the courts have emphasized that only a clinical psychiatric condition, supported by expert evidence, falls within s 47.[49] However, a kick that causes temporary unconsciousness has been held to be within s 47, since it involves 'an injurious impairment to the victim's sensory functions'.[50] The CPS guidance states that s 47 should be charged where there is loss or breaking of a tooth, temporary loss of sensory function, extensive or multiple bruising, broken nose, minor fractures, minor cuts requiring stitches, and (reflecting *Chan-Fook*) psychiatric injury which is more than fear, distress, or panic.

The fault requirement for the offence of assault occasioning actual bodily harm reveals that it is an offence of constructive liability. All that needs to be established is the fault required for common assault, i.e. intent or recklessness as to an imminent unlawful touching or use of force.[51] This clearly breaches the principle of correspondence (above, Chapter 3.6(q)). The Court of Appeal tried to remedy this deficiency, but the House of Lords overruled it.[52] Constructive liability therefore remains: a person who risks a minor assault may be held guilty of a more serious offence if 'actual bodily harm' happens to result. Moreover, the maximum penalty for the s 47 offence is five years' imprisonment, with no apparent justification for the strange approach of making the penalty equivalent to the higher offence on the 'ladder' (the s 20 offence), and the fault requirement equivalent to the lower offence on the 'ladder' (common assault, with a maximum of six months' imprisonment).[53]

A fourth form of aggravated assault is where an offence of assault occasioning actual bodily harm is *racially or religiously aggravated*. This is one of a group of aggravated offences created in order to signal the social seriousness of assaults that are either

---

[45] [1994] Crim LR 432.   [46] [1998] AC 147, discussed in subsection (b) above.

[47] Dicta in *Miller* [1954] 2 QB 282 are no longer good law.

[48] Shapland, Willmore, and Duff, *Victims of the Criminal Justice System*, ch 6; M. Maguire and C. Corbett, *The Effects of Crime and the Work of Victim Support Schemes* (1987), ch 7.

[49] *Morris* [1998] 1 Cr App R 386 (evidence from general practitioner that V suffered sleeplessness, anxiety, tearfulness, fear, and physical tenseness not sufficient). To the same effect, *Dhaliwal* [2006] 2 Cr App R 348.

[50] *R (on the application of T) v DPP* [2003] Crim LR 622.

[51] Several s. 47 cases raise issues about whether there was an assault or battery, and these are discussed in subsection (e) below on Common Assault.

[52] *Savage and Parmenter* [1992] 1 AC 699.

[53] Gardner, 'Rationality and the Rule of Law', argues that this is not irrational: someone who has chosen to assault or risk assaulting another has crossed a moral threshold and is rightly held liable if more serious consequences result. See further Ch 3.6(r) above.

accompanied by, or motivated by, racial or religious hostility.[54] The essence of these offences 'is the denial of equal respect and dignity to people who are seen as "other"',[55] and in *Rogers* the House of Lords adopted a broad approach to the notion of race, holding that calling a group of women 'foreigners' when assaulting them demonstrated hostility based on a racial group. The effect of the aggravation is to raise the maximum penalty from five to seven years.

Brief mention should also be made of the offence, in s 89 of the Police Act 1996, of *assaulting a police officer in the execution of his or her duty*. Procedurally speaking, this is not an aggravated assault, since it carries the same maximum penalty as common assault (six months' imprisonment) and is also triable summarily only. However, in practice the courts tend to impose higher sentences for assaults on the police, and it is therefore worth noting that this offence is committed even though D was unaware that he was striking a police officer. A decision by a single trial judge in 1865[56] is still regarded as authority for this proposition, but there is surely little justification for this today. The draft Criminal Code is right to require actual or reckless knowledge that the person being assaulted is a constable,[57] leaving the possibility of conviction for common assault in other cases.

(e) COMMON ASSAULT

The lowest offence on the 'ladder' is what is known as common assault. Strictly speaking, the term 'assault' is used here in its generic sense, as including two separate crimes—assault and battery. In simple terms, battery is the touching or application of unlawful force to another person, whereas assault consists of causing another person to apprehend or expect a touching or application of unlawful force. Most batteries involve an assault, and in both popular and legal language the term 'assault' is often used generically to include batteries. However, the Divisional Court in *DPP v Little* (1992)[58] held not only that the two offences are separate in law but also that they are statutory offences and not, as had been assumed, still offences at common law. Each offence is properly charged under s 39 of the Criminal Justice Act 1988, which provides that they are triable summarily only with a maximum penalty of six months' imprisonment. We discuss battery first, and then assault.

The essence of a *battery* is any touching or application of unlawful force to another. Examples might include a push, a kiss, touching another's hair, touching another's clothing,[59] or throwing a projectile or water which lands on another person's body.

---

[54] The definitions are to be found in the Crime and Disorder Act 1998 ss. 29 and 28, and the Anti-Terrorism, Crime and Security Act 2001 s. 39. For discussion of the former, see the sentencing guidelines decision in *Kelly and Donnelly* [2001] 1 Cr App R (S) 341.

[55] Per Baroness Hale in *Rogers* [2007] UKHL 8, at [12].   [56] *Forbes and Webb* (1865) 10 Cox CC 362.

[57] Law Com No. 177, cl. 76; awareness that the constable is or may be acting in the execution of duty is not required.

[58] (1992) 95 Cr App R 28.

[59] *Thomas* (1985) 81 Cr App R 331 (touching the hem of a skirt and rubbing it), and *H* [2005] Crim LR 734, discussed in section 8.5(f) below.

Is it right that the criminal law should extend to mere touchings, however trivial? The traditional justification is that there is no other sensible dividing line, and that this at least declares the law's regard for the physical integrity of citizens. As Blackstone put it: 'the law cannot draw the line between different degrees of violence, and therefore totally prohibits the first and lowest stage of it; every man's person being sacred, and no other having a right to meddle with it, in any the slightest manner'.[60] It is strange that the draft Criminal Code defines assault in terms of applying force to, or causing an impact on the body of, another.[61] Would that include or exclude stroking another's hair or clothing? Individuals have a right not to be touched if they do not wish to be touched, since the body is private. Someone who knowingly touches V without V's consent violates this personal right as surely as if he had taken V's property, but does he use 'force'? The difficulty is most evident in cases of sexual assault, which may be committed by the least unwanted touching or stroking of one person's body by another. These are culpable acts, often regarded as being more serious than thefts of property. Should it be made clear that the offence really concerns the invasion of another's right not to be touched or violated in any way—an aspect of the right to privacy—and is not necessarily an offence of 'violence'?[62] One consequence of defining the offence so widely is that reliance is placed on prosecutorial discretion to keep minor incidents out of court. The CPS guidance attempts to structure that discretion, but focuses more on the dividing line between s 39 and s 47. It states that 'although any injury can be classified as actual bodily harm, the appropriate charge will be contrary to s 39 where injuries amount to no more than the following—grazes, scratches, abrasions, minor bruising, swellings, reddening of the skin, superficial cuts, a "black eye"'.

One disputed point about the ambit of the offence of battery is whether it can be committed by the indirect application of force, such as by digging a hole for someone to fall into. There are long-standing judicial dicta in favour of liability in these circumstances,[63] and the decision in *DPP v K* (1990)[64] now supports them. In this case a schoolboy, frightened that he might be found in possession of acid that he had taken out of a laboratory, concealed it in a hot air drier. Before he could remove it, another boy used the drier and suffered burns on his face. Parker LJ held that K had 'just as truly assault[ed] the next user of the machine as if he had himself switched the machine on'.[65] There are firm statements in two House of Lords decisions that are inconsistent with the possibility of an indirect battery,[66] but the Divisional Court

---

[60] W. Blackstone, *Commentaries on the Laws of England* (1768), iii, 120.

[61] Law Com No. 177, cl. 75; assault and battery are combined in a single offence under the code.

[62] See also Gardner, 'Rationality and the Rule of Law', and the discussion of sexual assaults, below, section 8.5(f).

[63] See *Clarence* (1888) 22 QBD 23, *per* Stephen and Wills JJ.

[64] (1990) 91 Cr App R 23 (reversed on other grounds by the House of Lords in *Savage and Parmenter* [1992] 1 AC 699).

[65] (1990) 91 Cr App R 23, 27; although it was not mentioned, the analysis might have been linked to the principle in *Miller* [1983] 2 AC 161, above, Ch 4.4.

[66] See the argument of M. Hirst, 'Assault, Battery and Indirect Violence' [1999] Crim LR 557, relying on Lord Roskill in *Wilson* [1984] AC 242 and Lords Steyn and Hope in *Ireland and Burstow* [1998] AC 147.

continues to decide otherwise. Thus in *DPP v Santana-Bermudez* (2004)[67] a police officer asked D, before searching him, if he had any needles on him, and D said no. The officer put her hands into a pocket and her finger was pierced by a needle. The Court applied the principle in *Miller*[68] to hold that, since D had created the danger, his failure to avert the danger and its resultant materialization were capable of fulfilling the conduct requirement of battery.

Another problem is that, if the offence is defined so as to include all touchings to which the victim does not consent, it seems difficult to exclude everyday physical contact with others. This could be resolved by assuming that all citizens impliedly consent to those touchings which are incidental to ordinary everyday life and travel; but the judicial preference seems to be to create an exception for 'all physical contact which is generally acceptable in the ordinary conduct of daily life'.[69] The cases decide that this exception extends to touching a person in order to attract attention, although there can be no exception when the person touched has made it clear that he or she does not wish to be touched again. The problem arose in *Collins v Wilcock* (1984),[70] where a police officer, not empowered to arrest D, touched D in order to attract her attention and then subsequently took hold of D's arm. D proceeded to scratch the police officer's arm, having previously made it clear—in colourful language—that she did not wish to talk to the police officer. The Divisional Court quashed D's conviction for assaulting a police officer in the execution of her duty, on the ground that the officer herself had assaulted D by taking hold of D's arm. The key issue here was D's obvious refusal of consent to any touching; in other cases there might be a question of whether the touching goes 'beyond generally acceptable standards of conduct'.[71] A number of decisions have suggested what appears to be an alternative approach: to ask whether D's touching was 'hostile'. This seems to be an inferior method of identifying the boundaries of permissible conduct. There has been disagreement whether this requirement forms part of the criminal law,[72] and the House of Lords applied it in *Brown*[73] whilst emptying it of almost all significance.

The essence of the crime of *assault*, as distinct from battery, is that it consists of causing apprehension of an immediate touching or application of unlawful force. It is therefore possible to have a battery without an assault (e.g. where D touches V from behind), as well as an assault without a battery (e.g. where D threatens to strike V but is prevented from doing so), but most cases involve both. Two disputed questions—whether words alone can constitute an assault, and how imminent the threatened force needs to be—have recently received considerable judicial and academic attention. The preponderance of authority until recently was that mere words,

---

[67] [2004] Crim LR 471.   [68] [1983] 2 AC 161, discussed in Ch 4.4 above.
[69] *Per* Goff LJ, in *Collins* v *Willcock* (1984) 79 Cr App R 229, at 234.   [70] Ibid.
[71] Ibid., 234; cf. *Donnelly* v *Jackman* (1969) 54 Cr App R 229.
[72] A requirement of hostility was reasserted in *Brown* [1994] 1 AC 212, although Lord Goff in *Re F* [1990] 2 AC 1 held that it does not form part of the offence of assault.
[73] [1994] 1 AC 212, discussed in (f) below.

unaccompanied by any threatening conduct, could not amount to an assault,[74] but this was unsatisfactory if a primary purpose of the offence was to penalize the deliberate or reckless creation of fear of attack. As Lord Steyn put the point in *Ireland and Burstow*:[75]

There is no reason why something said should be incapable of causing an apprehension of immediate personal violence, e.g. a man accosting a woman in a dark alley saying 'come with me or I will stab you.' I would, therefore, reject the proposition that an assault can never be committed by words.

In that case the argument was taken further, by recognizing that a person who makes silent telephone calls may also satisfy the conduct requirement for assault. As Jeremy Horder has argued,[76] the emphasis is now rightly placed on the intended or risked *effect* of what D did, rather than on the precise method chosen.

That leaves the question of how immediate or imminent the threatened violence needs to be. In one case the Divisional Court held that assault was committed where a woman was frightened by the sight of a man looking in through the window of her house,[77] although there seems to have been little suggestion that the man was threatening to apply force either immediately or at all. The decision might be explained as a pragmatic attempt to remedy the absence of an offence which penalizes such 'peeping toms'.[78] Similarly in *Logdon v DPP* (1976)[79] D showed the victim a pistol in his desk drawer and said that it was loaded, and the Divisional Court held that this was an assault even though D had not handled the gun or pointed it. Presumably the threat was thought sufficiently immediate. Also in this case, D knew that the gun was a replica and was unloaded, but his actions and words caused the victim to believe otherwise. The fact that no harm was likely is immaterial, since the essence of the offence is the causing of apprehension in the victim.[80] The question of immediacy has been raised sharply by the cases of silent telephone calls, but not answered clearly. In *Ireland and Burstow*[81] Lord Steyn held that a caller who says 'I will be at your door in a minute or two' could satisfy the requirement of immediacy or imminence (Lord Steyn appeared to use the terms interchangeably), and that by the same token a silent caller who causes the victim to fear that he may arrive at her door soon could also satisfy the requirement. Lord Hope concluded that repeated silent telephone calls

---

[74] Cf. *Meade and Belt* (1823) 1 Lew CC 184 with *Wilson* [1955] 1 WLR 493, and the discussion by Glanville Williams, 'Assaults and Words' [1957] Crim LR 216.

[75] [1998] AC 147, at 162; see also *Constanza* [1997] 2 Cr App R 492 for a case involving words, silence, and gestures.

[76] J. Horder, 'Reconsidering Psychic Assault' [1998] Crim LR 392.

[77] *Smith v Chief Superintendent of Woking Police Station* (1983) 76 Cr App R 234.

[78] This would only amount to the offence of voyeurism, contrary to s. 67(1) of the Sexual Offences Act 2003, if D, for the purpose of obtaining sexual gratification, observed V 'doing a private act'.

[79] [1976] Crim LR 121.

[80] Thus if the victim also believes that the gun is a toy or is unloaded, there can be no assault: see *Lamb* [1967] 2 QB 981, above, Ch 7.5(a).

[81] [1998] AC at 161; for reflections on the judicial function in thus developing the law see C. Wells, 'Stalking: the Criminal Law Response' [1997] Crim LR 463.

could satisfy the conduct requirement in assault if they created an apprehension of immediate violence.[82] The question was raised more directly in *Constanza* (1997),[83] particularly in respect of a letter put through V's door by D which caused V to fear that D had 'flipped' and might become violent at any time. D lived fairly close to V. The Court of Appeal contrasted a case where the feared violence would not occur before a time in the distant future, which would fall outside the definition of assault, and held that it would be sufficient 'if the Crown has proved a fear of violence at some time not excluding the immediate future'. In that case the appeal against conviction was dismissed. In *Ireland and Burstow* the House of Lords failed to discuss the *Constanza* test, but the two decisions taken together suggest a loosening of the 'imminence' requirement and perhaps the gentle drift of assault towards an offence of creating fear that does not require proof of a clinical psychiatric condition or proof of immediacy in a strict sense.[84]

The fault element required for assault and battery is either intention or advertent recklessness as to the respective conduct elements.[85] The offence is summary only but, where the offence is racially or religiously aggravated,[86] it becomes triable in the Crown Court and has the higher maximum penalty of two years' imprisonment.

(f) QUESTIONS OF CONSENT

In order to explain why offences of violence are regarded so seriously, reference has been made to the values of physical integrity and privacy, aspects of the principle of individual autonomy. However, individual autonomy has both its positive and negative aspects: on the one hand it argues for liberty from attack or interference, whereas on the other hand it argues for the liberty to do with one's body as one wishes. In principle, just as the owner of property can consent to someone destroying or damaging that property,[87] so individuals may consent to the infliction of physical harm on themselves. We shall see below that consent may constitute the difference between the sexual expression of shared love between two people and serious offences such as rape or sexual penetration.[88] Should consent be given the same powerful role in relation to non-fatal injuries?[89] If a person wishes to give up her or his physical integrity in certain circumstances, or to risk it for the sake of sport or excitement, should the other person's infliction of harm on the willing recipient be criminalized?

A preliminary point in answering this question is whether the absence of consent is an element in the offence or the presence of consent is a defence. It seems

---

[82] [1998] AC 161, at 166.   [83] [1997] 2 Cr App R 492.

[84] See further Horder, 'Reconsidering Psychic Assault'. Law reform proposals are discussed in subsection (m) below.

[85] *Venna* [1976] QB 421, approved in *Savage and Parmenter* [1992] 1 AC 699.   [86] See n 54 above.

[87] Criminal Damage Act 1971, except in circumstances where life is endangered: see above, Ch 7.7.

[88] See above, section 8.5(c).

[89] Cf. C. Elliott and C de Than, 'The Case for a Rational Reconstruction of Consent in Criminal Law' (2007) 70 MLR 225.

more sensible to adopt the former alternative in relation to sexual offences—it would seem odd to suggest that every act of sexual intercourse constitutes the whole conduct element of rape, to which the consent of the 'victim' then provides a defence.[90] Similarly, touchings between lovers, whether or not they might be labelled 'sexual', are surely not *prima facie* wrongs. So it is preferable to understand battery as an (unlawful) touching or application of force without the consent of the person touched. The defendant would normally raise the issue of consent, where relevant, but it should be for the prosecution to disprove it beyond reasonable doubt. The same burden of proof is borne where the defendant argues that the force was lawful, e.g. in self-defence, but there is a significant difference between the two doctrines. Self-defence is one of the justifications, which imply that the conduct was right or acceptable in the circumstances.[91] Consent does not have the same philosophical underpinning: it embodies a recognition that the autonomy of the other person is involved, and that if that person agrees to the conduct there should be no offence. One might relate this to the idea of justification by arguing that the State regards it as right and acceptable that the criminal law should not extend to (most kinds of) conduct to which individuals freely consent;[92] but, even if one is persuaded by that link, all it claims is that respect for individual autonomy is right, not that the conduct which then takes place is right. Some judges have fallen into the error of believing that recognition of consent implies approval of the conduct involved.[93]

The ambit of effective consent in non-fatal offences remains a matter of common law, and it has been determined by the answer of the judges to three questions. First, what counts as consent to physical interference? Secondly, of what offences is the absence of consent an element? Thirdly, even when it is not an element in an offence, can consent be relevant in limited circumstances? The answer to the first question has been altered by recent decisions on the communication of HIV. The old case of *Clarence* (1888)[94] had held that, if V knew that she was consenting to sexual intercourse, her unawareness that D had a sexually transmitted disease did not negative that consent—even though the charge was inflicting grievous bodily harm, and she would clearly not have agreed if she had known the true facts. In *Dica* (2004)[95] the Court of Appeal held that consent to sex did not imply consent to bodily harm from a sexually transmitted disease, and that *Clarence* should not be followed. The crucial

---

[90] Likewise, it would seem strange to say that every appropriation of another's property amounts to theft unless there is the defence that the owner consents—although, as we shall see in Ch 9.2(a) below, the courts appear to have gone even further than that.

[91] See Ch 4.7 above.

[92] The effect of deception, threats, and other possible vitiating factors is considered in the context of sexual offences in section 8.5(d) and (e) below.

[93] Compare the remark of Lord Lowry in *Brown* [1994] 1 AC 212, at 255, to the effect that allowing consent would give a 'judicial imprimatur' to what the defendants had done, with the more thoughtful approach of Lord Mustill.

[94] (1888) 22 QBD 23.

[95] [2004] QB 1257; see M. Weait, 'Criminal Law and the Sexual Transmission of HIV: *R v Dica*' (2005) 68 MLR 121.

question of when consent is taken to be present was soon revisited in *Konzani* (2005),[96] where D (who knew he was HIV positive) had unprotected sex with three people without informing them of his condition. The Court of Appeal held that only fully informed consent will suffice, and that this means that if the other party is not aware of D's condition there can be no valid consent to the transmission of the disease. The Court claimed that it was upholding the principle of autonomy in its decision, but this is open to doubt. If V has unprotected sex with D without asking D any questions about his sexual health, could it not be said that V is exercising autonomy by taking a well-known risk of a sexually transmitted disease? The Court's decision is otherwise: in effect, D must disclose to V his condition, and failure to do so means that no valid consent from V can be forthcoming. Thus the Court imposes the duty on D, making this an offence of omission, but it is arguable that D must also be shown to have some understanding of the modes of transmission of HIV.[97] There will be further discussion of the effect of fraud and threats on consent and autonomy below, in the context of sexual offences.[98]

The answer to the second question has also become clearer in recent years, chiefly as a result of three decisions. In *Attorney General's Reference (No. 1 of 1980)*,[99] the reference concerned a fight in the street between two youths to settle an argument. The essence of the Court of Appeal's answer was that 'it is not in the public interest that people should try to cause or should cause each other actual bodily harm for no good reason'. In other words, the Court held that, if the fight merely involves assault or battery, consent can be effective as a defence. But if the results constitute actual bodily harm—which, as we saw in subsection (d) above, extends to 'any hurt or injury calculated to interfere with the health or comfort of the victim'[100]—consent cannot be a defence. In *Attorney General's Reference (No. 1 of 1980)* Lord Lane CJ suggested that it was sufficient if actual bodily harm was caused, even if D did not intend that consequence, but in *Meachen*[101] the Court of Appeal held that D must intend or be reckless as to actual bodily harm. Thus, where D had consensually penetrated V's anus with his finger for their sexual gratification, his conviction under section 20 (she suffered serious anal injury) was quashed because he only foresaw a simple assault and her consent to that was valid. These decisions continue to place the dividing line between actual bodily harm (presence of consent generally irrelevant) and assault and battery (absence of consent an element). This dividing line was attacked by counsel for the appellants in *Brown* (1994),[102] but by a majority of three to two the House of Lords confirmed it. Whilst Lords Mustill and Slynn (dissenting) took the view that the absence of consent should be an element in any offence not involving grievous bodily harm,

[96] [2005] 2 Cr App R 13; see M. Weait, 'Knowledge, Autonomy and Consent: *R v Konzani*' [2005] Crim LR 673.

[97] Cf. S. Ryan, 'Reckless Transmission of HIV: Knowledge and Culpability' [2006] Crim LR 981 and R. Bennett, 'Should we Criminalize HIV Transmission?' in C. Erin and S. Ost (eds), *The Criminal Justice System and Health Care* (2007).

[98] See section 8.5(h) of this chapter. [99] [1981] QB 715. [100] *Donovan* [1934] 2 KB 498.

[101] [2006] EWCA Crim 2414 [102] [1994] 1 AC 212.

the majority rejected this change as unwise and unworkable.[103] The general rule is thus that consent may negative assault or battery, but not a more serious offence.

Thirdly, in what circumstances can consent be relevant, exceptionally, in relation to harms that might otherwise amount to assault occasioning actual bodily harm or even a more serious offence? The best-known modern statement of the position is that of Lord Lane CJ in *Attorney-General's Reference (No. 6 of 1980)*:

Nothing which we have said is intended to cast doubt on the accepted legality of properly conducted games and sports, lawful chastisement or correction, reasonable surgical interference, dangerous exhibitions, etc. These apparent exceptions can be justified as involving the exercise of a legal right, in the case of chastisement or correction, or as needed in the public interest, in the other cases.[104]

The closing words of this passage demonstrate the unsatisfactory basis of the prevailing judicial approach. How can it be said that dangerous exhibitions such as circus acts or trying to vault over twelve buses on a motorcycle are 'needed in the public interest'? The Supreme Court of Canada has attempted to answer this question by suggesting that stuntmen who agree to perform dare-devil activities are engaged 'in the creation of a socially valuable cultural product', with benefits 'for the good of the people involved, and often for a wider group of people as well'.[105] This is far less convincing than an approach that begins with the high value placed on individual autonomy and liberty, and then examines reasons why particular consensual activities should be criminalized by way of exception to the general principle. This would require judges to look for distinct reasons for criminalizing particular consensual conduct, rather than holding it all to be criminal and then finding exceptions by dint of overblown claims about what is 'needed' in the public interest.

If we examine the exceptional categories in turn, cases of lawful chastisement do not belong here: they are hardly consensual, and in any event are subject to legal restrictions.[106] Cases of reasonable surgical interference encompass all the usual medical operations,[107] but there are unanswered questions about non-essential interference such as plastic surgery (a proper manifestation of individual choice and autonomy?) and about the treatment of various disorders that can result in the voluntary amputations of limbs.[108] The exceptional category of sport has attracted many prosecutions in recent years arising from rugby and association football, but in the leading case of *Barnes* (2005)[109] the Court of Appeal re-asserted the proposition that not every 'foul' committed in breach of the rules amounts to a crime. It is assumed that players do,

[103] For discussion see D. Kell, 'Social Disutility and the Law of Consent' (1994) 14 Oxford JLS 121; M. J. Allen, 'Consent and Assault' [1994] J Crim Law 183.

[104] [1981] QB 715, at 719.

[105] *Jobidon* [1991] 2 SCR 714, cited in the discussion by Kell, 'Social Disutility and the Law of Consent'.

[106] See Ch 4.7 above.

[107] For a recent dentistry case see *Richardson* [1998] 2 Cr App R 200, below, part 8.5(h).

[108] See C. Erin, 'The Rightful Domain of the Criminal Law', in C. Erin and S. Ost (eds), *The Criminal Justice System and Health Care* (2007).

[109] [2005] 1 WLR 910.

and may lawfully, consent to physical force over and above the minimum permitted by the rules. This does not exclude the possibility of convictions for the use of physical force well beyond that which may reasonably be expected in a game: the borderline is vague, but courts should decide particular cases by reference to the degree of violence used, its relation to the play in the game, any evidence of intent, and so on. It is sometimes thought that an intent to cause injury carries a case across the threshold into criminality,[110] but there are examples (such as some short-pitched bowling in cricket) where that would lead to unexpected liability. Moreover, in boxing this is surely what each boxer is trying to do. However, it would be wrong to take the legality of boxing as a benchmark: as more is known about the incidence of brain damage among boxers, and as more deaths result from boxing, the question why boxing is still lawful needs to be approached with circumspection and without preconceptions.[111]

We now turn to two categories that were not mentioned in the passage from Lord Lane's judgment, 'horseplay' and sado-masochism. In *Jones* (1986)[112] the Court of Appeal held that schoolchildren could validly consent to 'rough and undisciplined play' so long as there was no intention to cause injury thereby. In that case boys were tossed in the air by others, and injuries were sustained when the others failed to catch them as they fell. This 'horseplay' exception was taken much further in *Aitken* (1992),[113] where officers in the RAF had been drinking and then began various mess games and pranks. At one stage they poured white spirit on the flying suits of some officers who were asleep and set fire to them, dousing the flames with no ill effects. They then seized V, who resisted only weakly, and poured white spirit on his flying suit. When they lit it, he was engulfed in flames and suffered 35 per cent burns. The Courts Martial Appeal Court quashed their convictions for inflicting grievous bodily harm, contrary to s 20 of the 1861 Act. The reason for the decision was chiefly the judge advocate's failure to direct the jury clearly that a mistaken belief in consent would provide a defence. This implies that actual consent would have provided a defence to conduct that would otherwise amount to inflicting grievous bodily harm.

Before commenting on the 'horseplay' exception recognized in *Jones* and *Aitken*, it is appropriate to move on to the leading case on sado-masochism, *Brown* (1994).[114] Here five men were convicted of assault occasioning actual bodily harm, and three of them also of unlawful wounding.[115] They were found to have indulged in various homosexual sado-masochistic practices in private, involving the infliction of injuries on one another but not requiring medical treatment. Having failed to persuade a majority of the House of Lords to accept that the absence of consent should be an element in the offences of actual bodily harm or unlawful wounding, the appellants' second argument was that consensual sado-masochism should be recognized as an exceptional

---

[110] In *Barnes*, ibid., Lord Woolf CJ remarked that every soccer player tackling another in order to win the ball has the recklessness needed to fulfil a s. 20 offence.

[111] M. J. Gunn and D. Ormerod, 'The Legality of Boxing' (1995) 15 Legal Studies 181.

[112] (1986) 83 Cr App R 375.

[113] (1992) 95 Cr App R 304; see also *Richardson and Irwin* [1999] 1 Cr App R 392.

[114] [1994] 1 AC 212.   [115] Discussed above, n 102 and accompanying text.

category. This received a tart response from the Court of Appeal—'the satisfying of sado-masochistic libido does not come within the category of good reason'[116]—and fared no better with a majority of the House of Lords. Lord Templeman condemned the 'violence' and 'cruelty' of what the defendants had done;[117] Lord Lowry referred to their desire to 'satisfy a perverted and depraved sexual desire';[118] Lord Jauncey was particularly exercised by the possibility that others might follow the defendants' example if their convictions were not upheld. What emerges from these three speeches is an overwhelming distaste for the defendants' activities, and a determination to describe it in language designed to produce the conclusion that it should be criminalized. However, a court that looked for good reason for regarding the conduct as lawful might well find the task more difficult than one which looked for good reason to criminalize conduct that was private, consensual, and imposed no burden on the health service. This point emerges with clarity from the dissenting speech of Lord Mustill, who argued that the case was really about the criminalization of 'private sexual relations', and that the proper question was whether the public interest required this. He, like his fellow dissentient Lord Slynn, found no compelling reasons for criminal liability. To characterize the conduct as 'violence' helped the majority judges to their conclusion; if the infliction of pain had been recognized as a desired part of a consensual sexual experience, the approach should have been different.[119]

Beneath all these particular situations there are conflicting values which claim the law's attention. Respect for the principle of individual autonomy suggests that the liberty to submit to (the risk of) injury, however serious, ought also to be respected. It is an aspect of self-determination: the point is conceded in the fact that suicide is no longer an offence, and it should therefore follow that consent to injury should negative any offence. That argument is not watertight, however, because existing law does not formally allow euthanasia, for a variety of reasons mentioned briefly above.[120] One might have thought that many of those reasons, notably the fear of manipulation by the unscrupulous, would be less pressing and more manageable in respect of non-fatal harms. However, the judiciary has maintained a restrictive approach, with a low threshold for consensual harm (only common assault), and two criteria ('good reason', 'needed in the public interest') for recognizing exceptions that allow consensual harms. Even if the low threshold is accepted, the approach to exceptions is manifestly unsatisfactory. The two criteria adopted by the judges fail to explain, let alone to justify, the categories of conduct included and excluded. There has been no attempt to explain why 'horseplay' should be recognized as an exception when sado-masochism is not. Possible explanations suggest themselves—the disgust of the judges for sado-masochism, the notion that the armed forces contain 'decent people' who sometimes act in 'high spirits'—but these are not principled explanations and are an unworthy basis on which to open a small window of liberty. Plainly the degree of injury caused is not conclusive: in both the 'horseplay' cases there were serious injuries requiring

[116] (1992) 94 Cr App R 302, at 309. [117] [1994] 1 AC at 236. [118] Ibid., at 255.
[119] N. Bamforth, 'Sado-Masochism and Consent' [1994] Crim LR 661. [120] See Ch 7.4(h).

hospital treatment, as there may be in boxing, whereas in *Brown* no medical treatment was required.

A subsequent decision has muddied the waters still further. In *Wilson* (1996)[121] D had branded his initials on his wife's buttocks, at her suggestion, using a hot knife. The trial judge, following *Brown*, ruled that her consent could not be a defence to the charge of assault occasioning actual bodily harm. But the Court of Appeal quashed the conviction, saying that *Brown* does not establish that consent is never a defence to actual bodily harm. Exceptions are allowed, and the conduct in this case was equivalent to tattooing, which is an established exception. The Court added that there is surely no public interest in penalizing consensual activity between husband and wife in the privacy of their own home. However, it is difficult to see what reason there is for confining the privacy argument to husband and wife; and, of course, the approach of asking whether there are public interest reasons in favour of criminalization was the approach of the minority, not the majority, in *Brown*.

The discussion so far has been conducted in the shadow of the European Convention on Human Rights. Article 8 of the Convention declares the right to respect for one's private life: should this not conclude the debate in favour of the minority in *Brown* and the Court of Appeal in *Wilson*? An answer to this question can be given, since the *Brown* case was taken to the European Court of Human Rights, where it became *Laskey et al.* v *UK*.[122] The Court held that the criminalization of consensual sado-masochism does violate the right to respect for one's private life in Article 8.1, but it went on to conclude that the criminal law's interference with the right can be justified as 'necessary in a democratic society . . . for the protection of health'. The Court regarded it as within each State's competence to regulate 'violence' of this kind, even though no hospital treatment was required by these defendants. The Court was urged to recognize that this case involved private sexual behaviour; it replied that, because of the 'significant degree of injury or wounding', the conduct might properly be regarded as violence.[123] The Court was urged to recognize that English law is biased against homosexuals, and it was referred to the *Wilson* case, in which violence in a heterosexual context was not criminalized; it replied that the facts of *Wilson* were not 'at all comparable in seriousness to those in the present case'.

The decision in *Laskey* v *UK* is a considerable disappointment to those who expected a rights-based approach, particularly one that respects privacy and has led to the decriminalization of consensual homosexual conduct, to adopt the view of the minority rather than the majority in *Brown*. However, it is evident that both the European and English courts will adopt a case-by-case analysis,[124] and the framework

---

[121] [1996] 2 Cr App R 241.   [122] (1997) 24 EHRR 39, on which see L. Moran (1998) 61 MLR 77.

[123] 24 EHRR at para. 45, distinguishing the case from consensual non-violent homosexual behaviour in private, the criminalization of which has been held to breach Art. 8 in, e.g. *Dudgeon* v *UK* (1982) 4 EHRR 149.

[124] In *K.A. and A.D.* v *Belgium* (judgment of 17 February 2005, App No. 42758/98) the Strasbourg Court followed its *Laskey* judgment in holding that convictions based on consensual sado-masochism were a justifiable interference with the participants' Art. 8 rights.

of Article 8, supplemented by the Strasbourg jurisprudence, suggests that in future English courts will need to adopt rather more rigorous reasoning than that of the majority in *Brown*. In other respects, too, the approach of the English criminal courts to consent to injury requires re-appraisal. The Court of Appeal in *Wilson* was surely right to declare that the burden of finding strong arguments should lie on those who wish to criminalize consensual conduct, not on those who wish it to be lawful. This would mean that it is no longer necessary for judges to affirm that daredevil stunts are 'needed in the public interest' or that 'manly sports' help to keep people fit to fight for their country if necessary.[125] Instead, the question should be whether consensual boxing and 'horseplay', in so far as they are both expressions of individual autonomy, do not go too far if there is a risk of serious injury resulting. This leads on to a further criticism of the law—the absence of clear boundaries to the exceptions. Fair warning ought to be required, since this 'defence' establishes the boundaries of criminal conduct. The exceptional categories plainly apply to offences more serious than common assault, but no court has ever decided how far they go. If boxing is to remain lawful, then do all the exceptions apply, even to the level of causing grievous bodily harm with intent? The sanctity of life is a weighty value, and preservation from serious injury may not be far behind as a principle of welfare. However, greater attention should be paid to the two aspects—negative and positive—of the principle of individual autonomy. Here, the *negative* element is more important, requiring the state to respect each individual's right to pursue his or her choices consensually with others (subject to such limitations as the absence of a mercy-killing defence, and the protection of the young). In relation to sport this negative autonomy is reasonably well protected, but in some other contexts paternalism, and even disgust, seem to take over.

The Law Commission produced a substantial Consultation Paper in 1995, ranging over many of the detailed topics on which consent to injury is an issue.[126] Although the paper contains much of value, the Commission adopts the rather impoverished starting point of trying to assess 'the prevailing Parliamentary culture' in respect of legislation on 'moral issues', allegedly finding 'a paternalism that is softened at the edges when Parliament is confident that there is an effective system of regulatory control'. Of course there are important issues of public pressure and political viability to be taken into account in making recommendations; but the Commission's primary task should surely be to separate the bad arguments from the good, and to avoid all vague references to 'the public interest'. Whether a quantitative criterion (i.e. the distinction between assault and assault occasioning actual bodily harm) should remain a central feature of the law of consent must also be doubted,[127] not least because of the uncertain dividing line between the two offences which the CPS guidance illustrates.

---

[125] Sir Michael Foster, *Crown Law* (1762), 260.

[126] Law Commission Consultation Paper No. 139, *Consent in the Criminal Law* (1995), on which see S. Shute, 'The Second Law Commission Consultation Paper on Consent' [1996] Crim LR 684; P. Roberts, 'Consent in the Criminal Law' (1997) 17 Oxford JLS 389; D. C. Ormerod and M. Gunn, 'Consent—a Second Bash' [1996] Crim LR 694.

[127] See Roberts (last note).

(g) PROTECTION FROM HARASSMENT ACT 1997[128]

When discussing the range of offences against the person in subsections (b) to (e) above, it was noted that most of those offences have recently been applied by the courts so as to cover various manifestations of 'stalking' in so far as it causes psychiatric injury or, in respect of common assault, fear of violence. More directly aimed at stalking are the provisions of the Protection from Harassment Act 1997. The Act introduced civil remedies for harassment of another, and also created two new criminal offences. One is the summary offence in s 2 of pursuing a course of conduct in breach of the prohibition of harassment in s 1. Section 4 creates an offence, punishable with up to five years' imprisonment, of putting people in fear of violence: there must be 'a course of conduct [which] causes another to fear, on at least two occasions, that violence will be used against him',[129] and the fault element is either an intention to cause such fear or negligence, where 'a reasonable person in possession of the same information would think the course of conduct would cause the other so to fear'.[130] Although there is no doubt that these offences address a serious wrong that can cause considerable distress,[131] the combination of a negligence standard with a maximum penalty of five years is unfortunate. It may also be noted that the phrase 'fear of violence' contains neither an imminence requirement nor the need to show psychiatric injury. Statutory changes have now created an aggravated form of the offences under ss 2 and 4 of the 1997 Act: where the s 2 offence is racially or religiously aggravated, the maximum penalty rises from six months to two years; where the s 4 offence is racially or religiously aggravated, the maximum penalty rises from five to seven years.[132]

(h) OFFENCES UNDER THE PUBLIC ORDER ACT 1986

Despite its title, the Public Order Act creates three serious offences which apply whether the conduct takes place in a public or a private place.[133] Of particular relevance here are those offences which involve violence or the threat of violence. The Act provides a 'ladder' of offences, of which the most serious is riot (s 1). The essence of riot is the use of unlawful violence by one or more persons in a group of at least twelve persons who are using or threatening violence. The maximum penalty is ten years' imprisonment, compared with a maximum of five years for the lesser offence of violent disorder. The essence of violent disorder (s 2) is the use or threat of unlawful violence in a group of at least three persons who are using or threatening violence. Beneath violent disorder

---

[128] See the study by E. Finch, *The Criminalisation of Stalking* (2001).

[129] See *DPP v Dunn* [2001] 1 Cr App R 352.

[130] This negligence standard has no exception for incapacity: *Colohan* [2001] Crim LR 845.

[131] As is evident from the facts of cases such as *Ireland and Burstow* [1998] AC 147, *Constanza* [1997] Crim LR 576, and *Morris* [1998] 1 Cr App R 386. See further Wells, 'Stalking: the Criminal Law Response'.

[132] Section 32 Crime and Disorder Act 1998, s. 39 Anti-Terrorism, Crime and Security Act 2001; for sentencing guidelines see *Kelly and Donnelly* [2001] 2 Cr App R (S) 341.

[133] For general analysis see A. T. H. Smith, *Offences Against Public Order* (1987), and R. Card, *Public Order: the New Law* (1986).

comes the crime of affray (s 3), defined in terms of threatening or using unlawful violence towards another, and carrying a maximum of three years' imprisonment. Affray may be committed by one individual acting alone. The term 'violence' includes conduct intended to cause physical harm and conduct which might cause harm (such as throwing a missile towards someone); and, for the two most serious offences of riot and violent disorder, 'violence' bears an extended meaning which includes violent conduct towards property.[134]

Three aspects of the breadth of these offences should be noted. First, not only are the definitions of 'violence' extended but only one person need use this 'violence' whilst the remainder (eleven others for riot, two others for violent disorder) must be involved in threatening it. There is no barrier to convicting only one person of riot or violent disorder, so long as there is evidence that others were also present and threatening 'violence'.[135] Secondly, despite the label 'public order offences', all the offences can be committed either in public or on private property. And thirdly, although a key element in the offences is that the conduct be 'such as would cause a person of reasonable firmness present at the scene to fear for his personal safety', no such person need have been present. So in one sense these are offences of creating fear (and, in affray, one person causing fear in another)—supplementing common assault, and with much higher penalties—although in another sense they are not, since no person of reasonable firmness need actually be, or be likely to be, present. The odds, to put it bluntly, are stacked in favour of the prosecutor. Sentencing for these offences can result in several years' imprisonment where considerable violence is used and where D was the ringleader or prominently involved.[136]

The three serious offences are underpinned by three summary offences—causing fear or provocation of violence (s 4), causing harassment, alarm, or distress with intent to cause it (s 4A),[137] and causing harassment, alarm, or distress (s 5). These summary offences do not involve actual violence, and the offence under s 4 is inchoate in nature.[138] Where one of these offences is racially or religiously aggravated, it becomes triable on indictment, with a maximum penalty of two years' imprisonment.[139]

Is it necessary to have an extra ladder of offences so closely linked with the general ladder of offences against the person? One reason might be the unsatisfactory state of the law under the Offences Against the Person Act 1861; that Act fails to provide either a clear and defensible gradation of offences or any general offences of threatening violence against another.[140] A more frequent argument is that the provisions of the Public Order Act are needed to cope with 'group offending', which causes fear in ordinary citizens, and causes extra difficulties for the police and for prosecutors (in obtaining

---

[134] Public Order Act 1986, s. 8.   [135] Cf. *Mahroof* [1989] Crim LR 72.

[136] *Keys and Sween* (1986) 8 Cr App R (S) 444, *Beasley et al.* (1987) 9 Cr App R (S) 504.

[137] Inserted by Criminal Justice and Public Order Act 1994.

[138] Cf. Ch 2.1 above for discussion of the use to which s. 5 has been put.   [139] See n 56 above.

[140] It does contain the offence of threatening to kill (s. 16), and we saw in subsection (e) above that common assault may be committed by threatening unlawful force, but there are no general offences: see P. Alldridge, 'Threats Offences—a Case for Reform' [1994] Crim LR 176.

persuasive evidence). Offences committed by groups may well occasion greater fear than offences committed by individuals, and it may also be true that groups have a tendency to do things which individuals might not do: there may be a group bravado, fuelled by peer pressure, which may lead to excesses. On the other hand, the criminal law already makes some provision for such cases. The law of conspiracy is aimed at group offending, but that branch of the law is itself open to criticism.[141] The law of complicity and the new offence of encouraging or assisting crime enable the conviction of people who aid and abet others to commit offences, and spread a fairly wide net in doing so.[142] But the 1986 Public Order Act may be seen as a response to the call for a simplified and more 'practical' scheme of offences for dealing with group disorder. Central to this 'practicality' is the way in which the offence definitions go a long way in smoothing the path of the prosecutor, as we saw in relation to the provision that 'no person of reasonable firmness need actually be, or be likely to be, present at the scene'. This is 'practical' in the sense that the prosecution need not rely on members of the public to come forward and give evidence, which there is often a reluctance to do. But it is manifestly impractical from D's point of view, since it limits the opportunities for the defence to contest the issue.

The most prominent argument for having separate 'public order' offences is that group activities of this kind constitute a special threat to law enforcement and the political system. This argument comes close to a constitutional paradox—that people who are protesting against the fairness of the political system may find themselves convicted of serious offences if they adopt a vigorous mode of protest which may be the only effective one available to them because of their relative powerlessness. Article 11 of the European Convention declares a right of peaceful assembly, and where the *bona fide* exercise of this right happens to lead to some form of disorder it would be contrary to Article 11 to hold the speakers or organizers liable if they did nothing to provoke violence.[143] To deal with such violence there is a whole range of general offences against the person, reviewed in the preceding paragraphs. But violence and threats in a context labelled 'public order' now attract higher sentences and lower evidential requirements under the Public Order Act, not to mention a concept of 'public order' that includes private premises and a definition of 'violence' broadened to include damage to property. Thus, 'public order' is a favoured concept among the powerful, used for political advantage and as a means of introducing wide discretionary powers and offences defined in ways that disadvantage the defence.[144] The more recent term 'public safety' may assume the same role, as a difficult-to-contest reason for introducing sweeping powers that ignore sound principle.

---

[141] See below, Ch 11.4 and 11.5.

[142] See below, Ch 10.3, and particularly *Jefferson et al.* (1994) 99 Cr App R 13; also Ch 11.7 on encouraging and assisting crime.

[143] *Redmond-Bate* v *DPP* [1999] Crim LR 998.

[144] See generally N. Lacey, C. Wells, and O. Quick, *Reconstructing Criminal Law* (3rd edn., 2003), ch 2.

(i) ADMINISTERING NOXIOUS SUBSTANCES

The Offences Against the Person Act 1861 contains a number of crimes concerned with the administration of noxious or toxic substances. Section 22 penalizes the use of any overpowering drug or substance 'with intent to enable the commission of an arrestable offence' (maximum sentence of life imprisonment). Section 23 penalizes the intentional or reckless administration of any poison or noxious thing which results in danger to the victim's life or grievous bodily harm (maximum sentence of ten years' imprisonment). A person who prepares a syringe and then hands it to another, who self-injects, does not administer, cause to be administered, or cause to be taken, within the meaning of the section.[145] Section 24 penalizes the administration of any poison or noxious thing, 'with intent to injure, aggrieve or annoy the victim' (maximum sentence of five years). This section has been applied so as to cover the administration of a drug which causes harm to the victim's metabolism by over-stimulation, if D's motive for this is malevolent rather than benevolent.[146] It has also been held that a substance may qualify as noxious when administered in a large quantity even if it would be harmless in a smaller dose.[147]

The three offences seem to provide a 'ladder' but, once again, the distinctions between them vary considerably, with s 23 being more concerned about the result than about D's fault. Indeed, this section was applied in *Cato* (1976)[148] to the injection of heroin into a consenting adult who was well accustomed to taking it: it was no defence, the Court of Appeal held, that the heroin might not be noxious to a particular person. It seems likely that a redefinition of the principal crimes of physical violation would cover most of these cases anyway, and the Criminal Law Revision Committee saw the need to supplement those general offences with only one special offence—administering to another, without his consent, any substance which D knows to be capable of interfering substantially with the other's bodily functions.[149]

(j) TORTURE

In order to comply with its international obligations, the Government introduced an offence of torture in 1988. Its essence is the intentional infliction of severe pain or suffering by an official or by someone else with the consent or acquiescence of an official, and the maximum penalty is life imprisonment.[150] The offence is committed whether the pain or suffering is physical or mental, and whether it was caused by an act or an omission. In almost all cases this would amount to the general offence of

---

[145] *Kennedy (No. 2)* [2007] UKHL 38, overruling previous authority.

[146] *Hill* (1986) 83 Cr App R 386.   [147] *Marcus* (1981) 73 Cr App R 49.

[148] (1976) 62 Cr App R 41.

[149] CLRC, 14th Report, *Offences Against the Person*, Cmnd 7844 (1980), 84–7, and the draft Criminal Code, Law Com No. 177, cl. 73. Cf. now the offence under s. 61 of the Sexual Offences Act 2003, administering a substance with the intention of overpowering or stupefying V so as to enable the commission of a sexual offence.

[150] S. 134 of the Criminal Justice Act 1988.

wounding or causing grievous bodily harm, but the reason for the separate offence is to mark the distinctive character of official violence, and also to give the offence a wider extra-territorial effect.

(k) NEGLECT OF DUTY

Several of the offences discussed above may be committed by omission. One can cause grievous bodily harm by omission, and a person who does so intentionally in a case where a duty of care exists may be convicted under s 18 of the 1861 Act. An example would be starving a child for whom one has parental responsibility, with the result that the child suffers serious harm.[151]

There are also cases in which the criminal law creates special offences attached to certain duties of care, of which the parent's duty towards a child is one example. Section 1 of the Children and Young Persons Act 1933 contains an elaborately worded offence which may be termed 'child neglect'. It consists, essentially, of wilfully assaulting, ill-treating, neglecting, abandoning, or exposing a child in a manner likely to cause unnecessary suffering or injury to health. The maximum penalty for child neglect is now ten years' imprisonment, which should be sufficient to deal with cases involving considerable fault and actually or potentially serious consequences. The Mental Health Act 1983 contains a somewhat similar offence of ill-treating or wilfully neglecting a patient in a mental hospital, which has a maximum penalty of two years' imprisonment.[152] There is also an offence of misconduct in a public office, which applies where a police officer fails to take action to prevent the continuation of an offence of which he becomes aware.[153]

(l) WEAPONS, RISK AND ENDANGERMENT

Most of the offences considered above involve the occurrence of physical harm plus intention or recklessness. It is also justifiable, however, for the criminal law to penalize conduct which creates the risk of physical harm, particularly in situations where the conduct has little social utility or where the risk is well known. In fact, English criminal law has a wide range of such offences, of which those involving firearms, offensive weapons, motor vehicles, and other endangerment will be outlined here.

The Firearms Act 1968 (as amended) sets out a detailed scheme to control firearms and ammunition, using chiefly offences of possession.[154] The basic offence in s 1 is that of possessing a firearm without a certificate, an offence which (despite elements of strict liability[155]) carries a maximum of three years' imprisonment. Section 5 of

---

[151] *Gibbins and Proctor* (1918) 13 Cr App R 134; see above, Ch 4.4.

[152] Section 127, and the decision in *Newington* [1990] Crim LR 593; cf. s. 27 of the Offences Against the Person Act 1861, an obsolete offence of neglect in providing for apprentices.

[153] *Dytham* [1979] QB 722, *Attorney-General's Reference No. 3 of 2003* [2004] EWCA Crim 868.

[154] On which see ch 4.3(b) above and ch 11 below.

[155] See *Howells* [1977] QB 614, discussed above Ch 5.5(a).

the Act penalizes the possession of self-loading guns, sawn-off shotguns and other prohibited weapons, and now carries a mandatory minimum sentence of five years' imprisonment.[156] The Act also contains a number of aggravated offences of possessing a firearm with various intents (see Chapter 7.7 above), and its scope has been extended by the Firearms (Amendment) Act 1997.[157] Among the added offences is s 16A, inserted into the 1968 Act, which penalizes the possession of a firearm with intent to cause another to fear violence. Lower down the scale comes the offence of possessing an offensive weapon without lawful authority or reasonable excuse, contrary to the Prevention of Crime Act 1953. This offence, now with its maximum penalty of four years' imprisonment,[158] encompasses two classes of weapon: first, an article made or adapted for use as a weapon; and, secondly, any article intended for such use. Much attention has been focused on the concept of 'reasonable excuse', where the courts have attempted to impose a fairly stringent test on persons whose reason for carrying a weapon is said to be fear of attack.[159] Further offences penalizing the possession, marketing, and sale of knives and bladed instruments may be found in sections 139–141 of the Criminal Justice Act 1988, and the Knives Act 1997.[160]

Where motor vehicles are concerned, the problems are different. Although they are no less lethal than firearms in their potential to cause injury or even death, their considerable social utility (indeed, the dependence of much social interaction on them) indicates the need for a different approach. That approach consists of a code of good practice (The Highway Code), a requirement that drivers pass a qualifying test, and a network of offences to penalize those who deviate from proper standards. The more serious offences, from causing death by dangerous driving down to careless driving, were discussed in Chapter 7.7 above, and will not be taken further here. It should be noted, however, that the offences already discussed are underpinned by a multitude of less serious offences directed at promoting road safety by reducing the risk of injury. One of these is exceeding the speed limit, an offence designed to prevent dangers of physical harm from occurring, and in that sense somewhat analogous to possession of an offensive weapon.[161] Other examples would be disobeying a traffic signal and crossing double white lines.

The question of endangerment has already been raised in a general fashion in Chapter 7.8. English criminal law contains a number of discrete offences of endangerment, created in particular circumstances to deal with particular problems. For example, in addition to the road traffic offences, there are offences under ss 32 and 33 of the Offences Against the Person Act 1861 of endangering railway passengers; there

---

[156] Criminal Justice Act 2003, s. 287; the maximum sentence is ten years.

[157] The structure of firearms offences is elaborated in the sentencing guideline judgment in *Avis* [1998] 1 Cr App R 420.

[158] Offensive Weapons Act 1996.

[159] *Evans v Hughes* [1972] 3 All ER 412; *Densu* [1998] 1 Cr App R 400; cf. D. Lanham, 'Offensive Weapons and Self-Defence' [2005] Crim LR 85.

[160] The structure of this group of offences is discussed in the sentencing guideline judgment in *Celaire and Poulton* [2003] 1 Cr App R (S) 610.

[161] See J. R. Spencer, 'Motor Vehicles as Weapons of Offence' [1985] Crim LR 29.

are the offences under s 1(2) of the Criminal Damage Act 1971 of endangering the lives of others by causing damage to property (usually by fire); the Health and Safety at Work Act 1974 penalizes employers for failure to ensure that employees and others affected by their activities are not exposed to risks to their health or safety;[162] and there are offences, such as that under s 12 of the Consumer Protection Act 1987, of selling goods in contravention of safety regulations. These are all offences of endangerment, in the sense that no harm need have resulted from the dangerous behaviour. Their importance lies in the value of freedom from physical violation. However, as with motoring offences, they are out of accord with traditional conceptions of crime—many of them being committed in 'normal' situations. This may tend to obscure their direct relation to the issue of physical safety. Social attitudes may be more influential than legal form, but changing the law may have an effect. The apparent transformation of social attitudes towards drinking and driving in recent years, assisted by publicity campaigns, shows the possibility of changing attitudes. So far as the law is concerned, Chapter 7.8 commended the approach of the American Model Penal Code in creating a general offence of endangerment.[163] An alternative would be to extend criminal liability for negligence in dangerous situations.[164] Such reforms would be effective only if they were accompanied by changes in policing practice and prosecution policy.[165] The point of principle they raise is whether the degree of harm and the amount of culpability involved are sufficient to justify the creation of offences of this kind.

(m) THE STRUCTURE OF THE NON-FATAL OFFENCES

In this part of the chapter we have seen that, generally speaking, the existing range of offences seems to emphasize the result, the degree of foresight, the status of the victim, and any element of racial or religious aggravation as the critical issues in grading crimes of physical violation. The crimes in the 1861 Act form a somewhat shakily constructed ladder, with rather more overlapping of offences than is necessary and more elements of constructive liability than are justifiable.[166] Factors such as the existence of provocation, or the difference between premeditated and impulsive violence, are accorded no legal significance: however, they and other factors affect judgements of seriousness at the stages of prosecution and sentencing.[167] There are two main exceptions to this: the status of certain victims is reflected in separate offences for assaults on police officers and wilful neglect of children, for example, and the social seriousness of racial and religious aggravation is marked by a set of aggravated offences with higher maximum penalties.

---

[162] The Health and Safety (Offences) Act 2008 increases the penalties for these offences.

[163] Model Penal Code, s. 211.2; see, generally, K. J. M. Smith, 'Liability for Endangerment: English *Ad Hoc* Pragmatism and American Innovation' [1983] Crim LR 127.

[164] For discussion, see Ch 5.5(f) and (g).   [165] See above, Ch 2.7.

[166] For some doubts on the latter point see n 31 above.

[167] See E. Genders, 'Reform of the Offences Against the Person Act: Lessons from the Law in Action' [1999] Crim LR 689.

There is an overwhelming case for reform of the 1861 Act. It is unprincipled, it is expressed in language whose sense is difficult to convey to juries,[168] and it may lead judges to perpetrate manifest distortions in order to secure convictions in cases where there is 'obvious' guilt but where the Act falls down. How might the non-fatal offences be reformed? It is important to start by affirming the principle of maximum certainty, the principle of correspondence, and the principle of fair labelling, and in particular to ensure that the new scheme of offences is not so dominated by concerns about efficient administration (usually, prosecutorial convenience) as to produce wide, catch-all offences of the kind found in the public order legislation.[169] Proposals for reform were put forward by the Criminal Law Revision Committee in 1980, and revised by the Law Commission on various occasions culminating in a report and draft Bill in 1993.[170] The new Labour Government proclaimed its commitment to reforming this 'outmoded and unclear Victorian legislation', and a new draft Bill (based on the previous proposals) was circulated for comment in 1998.[171] The structure of the draft Bills places three major offences beneath attempted murder: causing serious injury with intent to cause serious injury; causing serious injury recklessly; and causing injury either with intent or recklessly. Below these three offences would be common assault. Three forms of aggravated assault would be retained: assault on a police officer, causing serious injury with intent to resist arrest, and assault with intent to resist arrest.[172] The scheme depends chiefly on the seriousness of the harm caused and the degree of foresight, though in a much more structured fashion than the 1861 Act.[173]

There were some problems with the 1998 draft Bill. First, what is the meaning of 'injury'? Clause 15 follows the previous Bill in defining it as physical injury (including pain, unconsciousness, or any other impairment of a person's physical condition) and any impairment of a person's mental health. This seems to leave a wide and relatively indeterminate dividing line between causing injury and the lesser offence of assault. Minor cuts and bruises would be included, although the test of impairment of mental health is intended to exclude such conditions as alarm, distress, or anxiety and to be limited to clinical disorders.[174] This leaves various forms of mental distress uncovered, as we saw in the stalking cases discussed in subsections (b), (c), and (d) above, and the definition of assault in the draft Bill makes no reference to fear: it is in the sanitized terminology of causing another 'to believe that such force or impact is imminent'.[175]

---

[168] N. Fielding, *Courting Violence*, 209–12.

[169] See Ch 3.5 and 3.6 above for discussion of the principles mentioned here.

[170] Criminal Law Revision Committee, *Offences against the Person*, 14th Report (1980); Law Com No. 218, *Legislating the Criminal Code: Offences against the Person and General Principles* (1993).

[171] Home Office, *Violence: Reforming the Offences Against the Person Act 1861* (1998).

[172] For criticism on this and other points see J. C. Smith, 'Offences against the Person: the Home Office Consultation Paper' [1998] Crim LR 317.

[173] In Ireland, the Non-Fatal Offences Against the Person Act 1997 follows the scheme of the English Bills to some extent, but includes specific offences of harassment, coercion, and attacking another with a syringe. It has now been in force for a decade.

[174] Cf. the existing test in *Ireland and Burstow*, n 22 above and accompanying text.

[175] Cf. the use of the notions of causing others to fear for their personal safety, and causing fear of violence, in the Public Order Act 1986 and the Protection from Harassment Act 1997.

In other respects the Bill states the law broadly, leaving considerable leeway to prosecutors. Whether the CPS guidance on offences against the person is producing greater consistency in police and prosecutorial practice is not known, but it has no legal status.[176] Secondly, what is the distinction between injury and serious injury? Once again, no attempt is made to achieve certainty of any kind, let alone maximum certainty, and a great deal is left to prosecutorial and judicial discretion. Those who maintain that this scheme would 'cause little problem of interpretation' are surely giving way to unwarranted optimism and prosecution-mindedness.[177] Thirdly, why are there two separate offences of causing serious injury—with intent, or recklessly—when the two mental states are combined in a single offence for mere injury? The CLRC's view was that there is 'a definite moral and psychological difference' between causing serious injury with intent and causing serious injury recklessly, and that this difference should be reflected in separate offences. However, since it is 'not an easy distinction for the police, magistrates and juries to have to make', no attempt should be made to draw such a legal distinction at the lower level of 'injury' offences.[178] In order to support this position, one has to accept (i) that the intention–recklessness distinction is the most significant dividing line for serious injuries, more relevant than such factors as premeditation, provocation, or the use of a weapon; (ii) that this is a workable distinction for the courts, especially in impulsive crimes, where the definition of intention may be fulfilled by a momentary realization of what is happening; (iii) that it is so significant that a difference in maximum penalties between life imprisonment and five years' imprisonment is appropriate; and (iv) that there is not a strong case for phrasing the offences in terms of endangerment rather than of causing physical harm.

The draft Bill has not been put before Parliament. The fact that nothing has happened opens up the opportunity for further consideration of the most appropriate framework for the laws on violence. We have seen in this part of the chapter how the ladder of non-fatal offences in the 1861 Act stands alongside, and in a peculiar relation to, the so-called public order offences in the Public Order Act 1986; and then the Protection from Harassment Act has arrived too. Any reform, let alone a step towards codification, should be grounded in a principled examination of the harms and wrongs that ought to be covered by the law. We should not be satisfied with the idea of a law of non-fatal offences separated from these other statutes, particularly when the Public Order Act rides forward on a tide of support engendered by the term 'public order' or its successor 'public safety'. Wide offences that depart from sound principles and minimize procedural safeguards in order to smooth the path of the prosecution should be opposed. Moreover, considerable discretion is bestowed on the police in respect of certain groups of (relatively powerless) people.[179] In addition, there is the long-standing difference of approach to violence on the streets and

---

[176] See n 10 above and accompanying text.   [177] CLRC, 14th Report (1980), para. 154; cf. 71, n 1.
[178] Ibid., para. 152.
[179] Cf. D. Brown and T. Ellis, *Policing Low-level Disorder* (1994); T. Bucke and Z. James, *Trespass and Protest: Policing under the Criminal Justice and Public Order Act 1994* (Home Office Research Study No. 190, 1998).

violence in the home: improvements have been made in the treatment of child abuse and 'domestic' violence, but there remains some distance to go. In some cases, as the Bristol research showed,[180] it is the victims who decline to co-operate by not reporting the offence or not 'making a complaint'. What the law should aim to do is to reflect the relative seriousness of the offence, in terms of harm, culpability, and any other significant features, and to ensure proper substantive and procedural safeguards. What it cannot do, however, is to alter patterns of reporting and the perspectives of enforcement officers, for which cultural change is required.

8.4 REPORTED SEXUAL ASSAULTS

The major change in the law brought about by the Sexual Offences Act 2003 will be discussed in the remainder of this chapter. However, an upward trend in reported sexual offences has been evident for several years. Among the most serious are rapes:, recorded rapes of women and of men have increased considerably in recent decades,[181] and in the last 10 years rape of a female increased from 6,281 in 1997 to reach 13,327 in 2005/06, dropping back to 11,648 in 2007/08, whereas rape of a male has increased steadily from 347 in 1997 to 1,150 in 2006/07, falling back slightly to 1,006 in 2007/08.[182] However, it is difficult to tell to what extent this represents a real increase in the number of rapes or an increase in the reporting of them. The 2000 sweep of the British Crime Survey found that one in twenty women said that they had been raped since the age of 16, and one in ten had experienced some form of sexual assault (including rape).[183] It is not merely the numbers that have been increasing but also that the contours of rape have been confirmed to be different from the stereotype of attacks by strangers. Research has shown that some 45 per cent of rapes were said to have been committed by the victim's current partner, acquaintances accounted for 16 per cent, ex-partners 11 per cent, 'dates' 11 per cent, 'other intimates' 10 per cent, and strangers only 8 per cent.[184] Merely 20 per cent of the rapes and 18 per cent of all sexual victimization were reported to the police, and then only half of them by the victim.[185] Of rape victims who had contact with the police, 32 per cent were 'very satisfied' and 25 per cent 'fairly satisfied' with the police handling of the matter, compared with 16 per cent 'a bit dissatisfied' and 22 per cent 'very dissatisfied'.[186] Despite improvements made by the police over recent years, there is no doubt that reporting a rape may

---

[180] C. Clarkson et al., 'Assaults: the Relationship between Seriousness, Criminalisation and Punishment' [1994] Crim LR 4; cf. Hoyle, *Negotiating Domestic Violence*, chs 6 and 7.

[181] There were 1,300 rapes reported in 1980, 2,900 in 1988, 4,600 in 1993:, see further Kershaw et al., *Crime in England and Wales 2007–08*, Table 2.04.

[182] Kershaw, ibid., 47.

[183] A. Myhill and J. Allen, *Rape and Sexual Assault of Women: the Extent and Nature of the Problem*, Home Office Research Study 237 (2002), ch 3.

[184] Ibid., 30.   [185] Ibid., 49.   [186] Ibid., 51.

still be a strenuous and harrowing experience.[187] It is therefore likely to continue as an under-reported offence.

Even where a serious sexual offence is reported and recorded, however, there remain particular problems in securing a conviction. Significant numbers of rape complaints are discontinued or taken no further for lack of 'reliable' evidence, and rape convictions have declined as a proportion of reported rapes, as recorded rapes have increased—in 1979 some 32 per cent of reported rapes resulted in conviction for rape, compared with 6 per cent in a 2003–04 study for the Home Office.[188] In that study of some 700 reported rapes, some 13 per cent ended in conviction for an offence (6 per cent for rape, 7 per cent for lesser offences), but around 70 per cent of the original reported cases had already disappeared from the system, mostly on grounds of either withdrawal by the victim or insufficiency of evidence. Although there is now greater reporting of rapes between acquaintances, it cannot be inferred that the decline in conviction rates is because juries are more reluctant to convict in cases of acquaintance rape, and that stranger rapes are easier to prove. Indeed, in the Home Office study, stranger rapes had the same overall conviction rate (11 per cent) as acquaintance rapes, the only higher rate being for parents and other relatives (32 per cent).[189] Among other factors, evidence of injuries to the victim was strongly associated with conviction.[190] Longer sentences are now imposed on convicted rapists, so that whereas in the year before the guideline judgment in *Billam* (1986)[191] some 25 per cent of convicted rapists received sentences of five years or more, that percentage rose to 53 per cent in 1989 and to 74 per cent in 2000.[192] The Court of Appeal handed down new sentencing guidelines for rape in 2003, one effect of which is to increase the starting point for sentences for rape between (former) intimates to the same level as that for stranger rape.[193]

The sentencing guidelines take full account of the practical effects of sexual assault, which can be considerable. There are well-documented consequences of rape for many victims: some authors write of a 'rape trauma syndrome', signifying deep disruption of the victim's life-pattern and thought-processes not just in terms of the physical effects of rape (physical pain, inability to sleep, prolonged distress), but also in terms of the effects on well-being (new-found fears, mistrust of surroundings and other people, embarrassment, and so on). Young's New Zealand report concluded that 'rape is an experience which shakes the foundations of the lives of the victims. For many its effect is a long-term one, impairing their capacity for personal relationships, altering their behaviour and values and generating fear.'[194] The effects of sexual abuse of young children may be similar and long-lasting.[195] Indeed, there is no reason to

---

[187] J. Temkin, *Rape and the Legal Process* (2nd edn., 2002), 3–8.

[188] A Feist et al, *Investigating and Detecting Recorded Offences of Rape*, (2007),

[189] See also Temkin and Krahé, 19–22.   [190] Ibid., Table 4.6.   [191] (1986) 82 Cr App R 347.

[192] Temkin, *Rape and the Legal Process*, 37.

[193] *Milberry* [2003] 2 Cr App R (S) 142, adopting the advice and research findings of the Sentencing Advisory Panel: see <www.sentencing-guidelines.gov.uk>.

[194] W. Young, *Rape Study: A Discussion of Law and Practice* (1983), 34.

[195] J. Morgan and L. Zedner, *Child Victims* (1992), ch 3.

suppose that such effects are confined to the victims of rape as traditionally defined: although sexual assaults vary in their degree, there may be many other forms of sexual assault which are serious enough to create such profound physical and psychological after-effects. Those effects may also tend to spread to the family and close friends of the victim, and then to reflect back on to the victim.[196]

8.5 NON-CONSENSUAL SEXUAL PENETRATION

The Sexual Offences Act 2003 is a major piece of law reform, and its provisions will be central to the discussion in the remainder of this chapter. The focus of this part of the chapter will be upon the new offences of non-consensual sexual penetration. Before those new offences are examined, however, we begin by exploring the rationale for taking sexual offences seriously, and then outline the structure and the aims of the 2003 Act.

(a) THE ESSENCE OF SEXUAL INVASION

What are the interests typically threatened or destroyed by sexual assaults? In section 8.4 above, the serious personal consequences of rape and other sexual assaults were described: in many cases rape causes a great deal of harm, and even lesser sexual assaults may have long-lasting psychological consequences that affect the quality of life. It is strongly arguable, however, that it is not primarily the harmfulness of sexual invasions that makes them serious offences. More significant is the autonomy principle, already described in Chapter 2.1 above as the principle that individuals should be respected and treated as agents capable of choosing their acts and omissions. In the present context, however, that principle plays two different roles. It remains relevant to the conditions of liability, and thus to ensuring that defendants should not be convicted unless they may be said to be at fault for that which they are accused of doing. But it also has two further and particular implications. First, part of the rationale for laws against sexual offending is to protect the autonomy of individuals in sexual encounters, ensuring that there are criminal prohibitions to prevent unwanted sexual interference and to criminalize those who culpably interfere with individuals' sexual autonomy. In human rights terms, states have a positive obligation to have in place laws that protect citizens from unwanted sexual interference.[197] Thus the right to respect for one's private life in Article 8 of the Convention recognizes that sexual choice is 'a most intimate aspect of affected individuals' lives'.[198] For this reason each citizen

---

[196] Shapland, Willmore, and Duff, *Victims in the Criminal Justice System*, 107–8.
[197] *X and Y v Netherlands* (1986) 8 EHRR 235; *MC v Bulgaria* (2005) 40 EHRR 459.
[198] See e.g. *Sutherland and Morris v UK* (1997) 24 EHRR CD22, para. 57.

should have the right not to have others' sexual choices imposed on him or her.[199] The second implication of the principle of autonomy is the (*negative*) requirement that the state's laws should respect each individual's right to pursue his or her sexual choices consensually with others, subject to such limitations as public decency laws and to the protection of the vulnerable.[200] This requires the State to ensure that its laws do not unjustifiably inhibit the expression of sexuality in consensual and non-offensive contexts.[201]

Sexuality is an intrinsic part of one's personality, it is one mode of expressing that personality in relation to others, and it is therefore fundamental that one should be able to choose whether to express oneself in this way—and, if so, towards and with whom. This is where the positive and negative aspects of the principle of individual autonomy come together. The essence of sexual self-expression is that it should be voluntary, both in the giving and in the receiving. Thus, even where a sexual assault involves no significant physical force, it constitutes a wrong in the sense that it invades a deeply personal zone, gaining non-consensually that which should only be shared consensually.[202] Indeed, John Gardner and Stephen Shute argue that the real gravamen of rape is that it amounts to 'the sheer use of a person, and in that sense the objectification of a person'. In their view, rape is 'dehumanizing' because it is 'a denial of [the victim's] personhood'.[203] There is a denial of autonomy and of bodily integrity[204] here that applies in some measure to other sexual offences too. But the physical and psychological effects that typically flow from sexual offences (including humiliation and degradation) are also a large part of the justification for treating them seriously.

(b) THE STRUCTURE OF THE 2003 ACT[205]

The Sexual Offences Act 2003 is the first fundamental reform of the relevant law for over a century, the Sexual Offences Act 1956 having been largely a consolidating measure. Sections 1 to 4 of the Act create newly-defined offences of rape, assault by

---

[199] In England there was a long struggle to establish rape within marriage as an offence: see 4th edition of this work, Ch 8.5(b). Cf. S. J. Schulhofer, *Unwanted Sex: the Culture of Intimidation and the Failure of Law* (1998), for a discussion in the context of US rape laws, which generally require force as an element of the offence.

[200] See J. McGregor, *Is it Rape?* (2005), 111.

[201] Hence the many judgments against states which have criminalized consensual homosexual acts, e.g. *Dudgeon* v *United Kingdom* (1982) 4 EHRR 149, and *ADT* v *United Kingdom* (2001) 31 EHRR 33.

[202] See N. Lacey, *Unspeakable Subjects* (1998), ch 4, and Schulhofer, *Unwanted Sex*, reviewed by M. Childs, 'Sexual Autonomy and Law' (2001) 64 MLR 309. For a different approach, starting from the proposition that every act of sexual intercourse is a *prima facie* wrong, see M. Madden Dempsey and J. Herring, 'Why Sexual Penetration Requires Justification', (2007) 27 OJLS 467.

[203] J. Gardner and S. Shute, 'The Wrongness of Rape', in J. Horder (ed.), *Oxford Essays in Jurisprudence (4th Series)* (2000), 205.

[204] For developments of this notion, see Lacey (above, n 202), 117f, and V. Tadros, 'Rape without Consent' (2006) 26 OJLS 515.

[205] The leading text on the Act is P. Rook and R. Ward, *Sexual Offences: Law and Practice* (2004). For briefer treatment, see J. Temkin and A. Ashworth, 'Rape, Sexual Assaults and the Problems of Consent' [2004] Crim LR 328 (on which much of the following analysis is based); J. R. Spencer, 'Child and Family Offences' [2004] Crim LR 347; and A. A. Gillespie, 'Tinkering with "Child Pornography"' [2004] Crim LR 361.

penetration, sexual assault, and causing sexual activity. All these offences turn on the absence of consent. Sections 5 to 8 create parallel offences in respect of child victims under the age of 13, and to these offences consent is irrelevant. Sections 9–15 then create a number of sexual offences against children under 16, with differing maximum penalties according to whether the offender is an adult or is under 18. Sections 16–24 contain various 'abuse of trust' offences, committed against persons under 18 by those in a position of trust. The new Act contains a number of reformulated familial sex offences, in ss 25–29 and 64–65. Sections 30–44 create a range of offences, committed against persons with mental disorder by others (including care workers). Sections 45–51 amend the law to protect children against indecent photographs, pornography and prostitution. Sections 52–60 alter the law relating to prostitution and trafficking for sexual exploitation. There are three preparatory offences in ss 61–63, and then ss 66–71 contain offences of exposure, voyeurism, sexual penetration of a corpse and sexual activity in a public lavatory. Part 2 of the Act contains new notification requirements for sex offenders, and various new preventive orders for the courts to make.

(c) THE AIMS OF THE 2003 ACT

The 2003 Act is a far-reaching reform that was intended to mark a fresh start in the criminal law's response to sexual misconduct. The Sex Offences Review was instituted in January 1999, consulted widely, and produced its report, *Setting the Boundaries*, in July 2000.[206] The Government then announced its proposals[207] and brought forward a Bill in 2002, the details of which changed considerably as a result of parliamentary scrutiny.[208] The Sexual Offences Act 2003 has some 143 sections, of which the first 71 create offences. It is a very long time since there was a statute creating as many offences as this. At the risk of over-simplification, some seven purposes of the Act may be outlined.

First, the Act is intended to modernize the law of sexual offences and to bring it more closely into line with contemporary attitudes. Thus the Home Office criticized the former law as 'archaic, incoherent and discriminatory', and argued that it failed to reflect 'changes in society and social attitudes'.[209] This refers particularly to the attitudes of some men towards women, and one significant change had already been made a decade earlier when the marital rape exception was finally abolished.[210] But it is open

---

[206] For critical comment, see N. Lacey, 'Beset by Boundaries: the Home Office Review of Sex Offences' [2001] Crim LR 3; P. Rumney, 'The Review of Sex Offences and Rape Law' (2001) 64 MLR 890; and Temkin, *Rape and the Legal Process*.

[207] Home Office, *Protecting the Public* (2002).

[208] See e.g. House of Commons Home Affairs Committee, *Sexual Offences Bill* (5th report, 2003), and the Joint Committee on Human Rights, *Scrutiny of Bills: Further Progress Report* (12th report, 2003).

[209] *Protecting the Public*, para. 4.

[210] *R v R* [1992] 1 AC 599 and s. 142 of the Criminal Justice and Public Order Act 1994.

to question whether high maximum penalties for consensual sexual conduct between children are closely in line with modern attitudes.

Secondly, and related to the first, the Act mostly creates gender-neutral offences. Apart from the offence of rape, which can only be committed by a man as principal, the offences can be committed by a male or female against a male or female. This ensures equality of protection and of criminalization, thereby avoiding discrimination that might violate a person's Convention rights.[211]

Thirdly, clarity was said to be an aim of the new law, so that people could know what behaviour was unacceptable. It may be an advantage that there are many separately labelled offences; but the Act adopts an unusually prolix style of drafting criminal provisions, and there are many overlaps between offences. It is open to question whether this was the best means of trying to achieve the desirable objective of greater clarity.

Fourthly, the Government was very keen to clarify the law relating to consent[212]—a vexed question for many years, and one where the nuances of sexual encounters and the power of ingrained attitudes interact to create considerable problems of applying any definition and standards.[213] However, as we shall see in paragraph (h) below, the new approach fails to fulfil the aspirations to certainty and clarity.

Fifthly, the Act was intended to secure appropriate protection for the vulnerable, and to this end it includes (as we have already noted) several separate offences against children and also several separate offences against persons with mental disorder. One difficulty, to be discussed further in section 8.6 below, is that the Act's enthusiasm to criminalize sexual acts involving children succeeds in bringing many other children into the net of criminality, for what are perfectly normal and harmless teenage interactions. The Government's reply is that prosecutors will use their discretion to ensure that youngsters are not prosecuted unless there is coercion or some other untoward element, but this is an unsatisfactory expedient and may not constitute sufficient protection for young people's right to respect for private life under Article 8. Kissing, fondling and other consensual activities between 15 year olds should surely not put either at risk of prosecution.

Sixthly, one aim of the Act is to provide appropriate penalties to reflect the seriousness of the crimes committed.[214] Many of the maximum sentences are higher than before, and, even though the penalties for young offenders committing offences against children are lower than those for adults committing such offences, they are still disproportionately high for young people.

Seventhly, the Government hoped that the reformed law would play its part in reducing the attrition rate in rape cases and helping to convict the guilty. This was to be done by providing 'a clearer legal framework for juries as they decide on the facts

---

[211] E.g. *Sutherland and Morris* v *United Kingdom* (1997) 24 EHRR CD22 and *ADT* v *United Kingdom* (2000) 31 EHRR 803.

[212] *Protecting the Public*, para. 30; Lord Falconer, HL Deb, vol. 644, col. 772 (13 February 2003).

[213] Cf. the discussions in *Setting the Boundaries*, at paras. 2.7 and 2.10.

[214] *Protecting the Public*, para. 5.

of each case'.[215] With key terms such as 'consent' and 'sexual' under-defined, this aspiration seems unlikely to be met. But the new Act expands the definition of rape, which may be one way of increasing the number of convictions.

Reference will be made to these seven aims as various parts of the 2003 Act are examined. It is important to recall, however, that key concepts such as sexual autonomy and vulnerability cut both ways. As we saw in paragraph 8.5(a) above, a law of sexual offences that respects the principle of individual autonomy and complies with Article 8 of the Convention will attend to both the negative and positive aspects of the principle—that is, it will ensure that the law penalizes those whose conduct amounts to unwanted interference with a person's sexual autonomy, and it will ensure that the law does not penalize those who are engaging consensually in sexual activities (unless they are publicly offensive or involve vulnerable victims). The principle will also be referred to below, particularly in respect of sexual activity involving two children and familial sexual activity.

(d) RAPE

A reformed offence of rape was created by s 1 of the 2003 Act, which provides:

> (1) A person (A) commits an offence if—
>
>   (a) he intentionally penetrates the vagina, anus or mouth of another person (B) with the penis,
>
>   (b) B does not consent to the penetration, and
>
>   (c) A does not reasonably believe B consents.

One change was that rape now includes oral penetration with the penis. Under the old law, forced oral penetration could only be prosecuted as indecent assault, a label that manifestly failed to indicate the seriousness of the wrong. The opportunity to reform the law raised the question whether forced oral penetration should be classified as rape and thus aligned with vaginal and anal penetration, or whether it should be classified as assault by penetration, a new offence (see (e) below) that also carries life imprisonment as its maximum sentence. The Sex Offences Review concluded that penetration of the mouth is 'as horrible, as demeaning and as traumatizing as other forms of forced penile penetration'.[216] The Review decided that the fact that this was penetration by the penis justified placing it within the offence of rape, even though penetration by other objects (included within the offence of assault by penetration) was also an extremely serious violation. Against the argument of principle, some raised the practical argument that bringing oral sex within rape might have the effect of devaluing rape, and that juries might be unwilling to return rape verdicts in such cases. The Home Affairs

---

[215] Ibid., para. 10; Lord Falconer, HL Deb, vol. 644, col. 771 (13 February 2003).
[216] Home Office *Setting the Boundaries* (2000), para. 2.8.5.

Committee concluded that this is unlikely to occur in practice, and supported the principle behind the change.[217]

The prosecution must prove that there was penetration by the penis,[218] and that it was intentional. Since 'penetration is a continuing act from entry to withdrawal',[219] this means that the offence can be committed by intentionally failing to withdraw the penis as soon as non-consent is made clear. The prosecution must also establish the absence of consent (see (h) below). The fault requirement in relation to consent has long been a matter of controversy. At common law a defendant could be convicted if he was reckless as to non-consent, in the sense that he 'could not care less' whether the victim was consenting.[220] However, at common law a defendant could be acquitted if he mistakenly believed that the victim was consenting, according to the *Morgan* decision.[221] There was much debate about whether there should be degrees of rape to reflect differing degrees of fault,[222] but in the end the government opted for the requirement that 'A does not reasonably believe that B consents'. The ramifications of this objective standard will be explored in paragraph (i) below, but it will be observed that the concept of recklessness plays no part in the reformed law.

(e) ASSAULT BY PENETRATION

This new offence carries a maximum sentence of life imprisonment, as does rape, but (like most other offences in the Act) it can be committed by a man or woman as principal. Section 2 of the Act provides:

(1) A person (A) commits an offence if—

    (a) he intentionally penetrates the vagina or anus of another person (B) with a part of his body or anything else,

    (b) the penetration is sexual,

    (c) B does not consent to the penetration, and

    (d) A does not reasonably believe that B consents.

The conduct element of the offence includes penetration with any part of the body (such as a finger, but also including the penis, so that the offence overlaps with rape),[223] or penetration with an instrument, such as a bottle. The penetration must be sexual, a requirement discussed in paragraph (f) below, and it must be without consent. The sentencing guidelines are based on the view that digital penetration, or penetration with an instrument, can cause serious harm to young children and also significant psychological harm to adults, and the starting points are therefore substantial, depending

---

[217] Home Affairs Committee, *Sexual Offences Bill*, paras. 10–14.

[218] For this purpose, the vagina includes the vulva, and surgically reconstructed organs and orifices are included: s. 79(3).

[219] S. 79(2).   [220] This test was supported in *Setting the Boundaries*, paras. 2.12.5–6.

[221] Discussed in Ch 5.3(d) above.

[222] See H. Power, 'Towards a Redefinition of the *Mens Rea* of Rape' (2003) 23 Oxford JLS 379.

[223] Relevant in cases where the victim is unsure what penetrated him or her.

on the age of the victim.[224] The fault element for this offence is that the penetration must be intentional, and that the defendant must not reasonably believe that the victim consents (see paragraph (i) below).

(f) SEXUAL ASSAULT

This offence is committed if A intentionally touches another person (B), the touching is sexual, B does not consent to it, and A does not reasonably believe that B consents. The questions of consent and reasonable belief will be discussed in paragraphs (h) and (i) below. The offence replaces indecent assault, and it will be noticed that both elements of the former crime are replaced. There must be a touching, not an assault; and it must be sexual, not indecent. But the offence of common assault remains, and the concept of assault is wider than touching, since it includes causing a person to apprehend bodily contact (see 8(3)(e) above); the offence of assault can also be committed recklessly, whereas sexual assault requires an intentional touching.

What amounts to a touching? Section 79(8) states that it 'includes touching (a) with any part of the body, (b) with anything else, (c) through anything, and in particular includes touching amounting to penetration'. This is not an exhaustive definition, but it makes it clear that the touching does not have to be with the hands (and may be with an instrument), and that touching through clothes is sufficient. Thus in H[225] D made a sexual suggestion to V and took hold of her tracksuit bottoms, attempting to pull her towards him. She broke free and escaped. The Court of Appeal upheld the conviction for sexual assault, ruling that touching someone's clothing is sufficient to fulfil this requirement of the offence. Although s 79(8) refers to touching through clothing, perhaps implying contact with V's body through clothing, the Court rightly held that this was not an exhaustive definition. Touching the clothes V is wearing is sufficient, Lord Woolf CJ held, so long as the other elements of the offence are fulfilled.

When is a touching 'sexual'? This question is important for the offences under ss 2, 3 and 4 (among others). Section 78 provides that:

Penetration, touching or any other activity is sexual if a reasonable person would consider that—

(a) whatever its circumstances or any person's purpose in relation to it, it is because of its nature sexual, or

(b) because of its nature it may be sexual and because of its circumstances or the purpose of any person in relation to it (or both) it is sexual.

It will be evident that this section provides a framework for the decision but leaves much to the magistrates or jury to determine in each case. The framework involves a threefold division of cases,[226] and the standard is that of the reasonable person. Cases falling within (a) are sexual by their very nature, and presumably include most

---

[224] Sentencing Guidelines Coucnil, *Sexual Offences Act 2003: Definitive Guideline* (2007).
[225] [2005] Crim LR 735.   [226] Largely following the previous leading case of *Court* [1989] AC 28.

touchings of sexual organs and private zones of the body. On this view, even a proper medical examination of the vagina or penis is sexual (since the actor's purpose is irrelevant to this classification), but consent, or necessity, would justify it. Cases falling within (b) are ambiguous by their nature: reasonable people would disagree about whether or not they are inherently sexual. If the jury or magistrates decide that a touching might be sexual, the question whether this touching is sexual therefore depends on whether a reasonable person would consider that either the circumstances or the actor's motive or purpose was sexual. Thus in H[227] the Court held that these questions had been properly put to the jury, resulting in the verdict that pulling at the woman's tracksuit bottoms might be sexual and, because of D's purpose, was sexual. In *Court* (1989)[228] D put a 12 year-old girl across his knee and spanked her on her shorts. He admitted that he had a buttock fetish. Under the 2003 Act, it is for the magistrates or jury to decide whether this falls within (b) in the sense that 'because of its nature it *may* be sexual'; if they so decide, then they could go on to hold that D's motive rendered it sexual.

Although s 78 enumerates only two types of case, (a) and (b), there must logically be a third—cases where the touching is not such that a reasonable person would say that it might be sexual. Any touching of this kind cannot be 'sexual', whatever D's motives and whatever the circumstances. In *George* (1956)[229] D had attempted to remove a girl's shoe from her foot, admitting that this gave him sexual gratification. This was held not to amount to an indecent assault, but under the 2003 Act it could be a sexual assault. Everything turns on whether the jury or magistrates hold that a reasonable person would consider that 'because of its nature it may be sexual'.[230] Different tribunals may reach different conclusions: for example, attempting to remove a shoe might be held non-sexual whereas stroking a shoe might be held to be possibly sexual, within (b). One might ask to what extent interference with a shoe is perceived as an attack on someone's sexual autonomy, as distinct from their personal autonomy as an owner of property (i.e. shoes). Many fetishists do things that normally have no sexual connotation. Should the sexual motivation of the fetishist be sufficient to fulfil the offence, even in the third category? If we accept the 2003 Act's view that it should not, then are we sure that sexual motivation should be sufficient in ambiguous cases falling within (b)? Most of these cases amount to common assault, so it is not a question of conviction or not.[231] The present solution leads to uncertainty and probably inconsistency in practice, but it cannot be otherwise so long as we have category (b) and, by implication, a third category too.

---

[227] [2005] Crim LR 735.   [228] [1989] AC 28.   [229] [1956] Crim LR 52.

[230] The CA in *H* [2005] Crim LR 735 held that this would now be for the court to decide in each case.

[231] It is relevant to labelling, of course, and also to the imposition of notification requirements and other preventive measures under the 2003 Act, as well as to sentencing (on which see the Sentencing Guidelines Council, n 222 above).

(g) CAUSING SEXUAL ACTIVITY

Section 4 of the Act provides that a person commits an offence by intentionally causing another person to engage in an activity that is sexual. As with the offences in
ss 1–3, the victim must not consent and D must not reasonably believe that he or
she consents. The essence of the conduct element is that D must cause the victim to
engage in the sexual activity, and this presumably can be effected by explicit or implicit threats, or by use of a position of authority or dominance (simply by speaking
words), rather than by actual physical coercion. Thus forcing V to masturbate in front
of D, or forcing two people to perform sexual acts for D's pleasure, fall clearly within
this new offence.[232] Similarly, P could be held to cause sexual activity by tricking D
into believing that V wants sex when V does not, even if P cannot be convicted of
complicity in rape.[233] It should probably be held that s 4 creates two separate offences,
since the causing of various penetrative sexual activities carries a maximum sentence
of life imprisonment, whereas the causing of other non-penetrative activities has a
maximum of ten years.

(h) ABSENCE OF CONSENT

Each of the offences in ss 1–4 of the 2003 Act has two requirements that have not yet
been examined—that B (the victim) did not consent, and that the defendant did not
reasonably believe that B was consenting. Here we will discuss the absence of consent:
the new law on reasonable belief, which has a similar structure, will be examined in
paragraph (i) below.

Consent has long been the crucial concept in many sexual encounters: its presence
or absence can mark the difference between shared joy and a serious crime. Yet there
are long-standing problems of defining what amounts to consent and to non-consent,
and problems of proof. Indeed, the complexity of the 2003 Act's 'solutions' has led to
a suggestion that the law should be re-structured so as to place minimal reliance on
such a contested concept as consent.[234] However, the aim of *Setting the Boundaries*[235]
and the 2003 Act was to set out a new approach to the difficult problems of consent.
The Act puts forward a definition of consent in s 74, and also further tackles the problems of definition and proof through lists of rebuttable and conclusive presumptions
in ss 75 and 76. The most straightforward course for the prosecution is to establish
that B, the complainant, manifestly did not agree to the activity. Few cases are so
straightforward, however, and the Act therefore establishes three routes by which
non-consent can be proved in cases of rape, assault by penetration, sexual assault and

---

[232] This was the proposal in *Setting the Boundaries*, para. 2.20.

[233] E.g. *Cogan and Leak* [1976] QB 217, discussed in Ch 10.6 below; under the 2003 Act much would turn
on whether D's mistake would prevent conviction.

[234] V. Tadros, 'Rape without Consent' (2006) 26 OJLS 515.   [235] Part 2.10.

causing sexual activity.[236] The first is to bring the circumstances within one of the conclusive presumptions in s 76. The second is to make use of one of the rebuttable presumptions in s 75. The third, residual approach is to rely on the general definition of consent in s 74.

Conclusive Presumptions: section 76(2) provides two sets of circumstances in which the absence of consent will be conclusively and irrebuttably presumed. If the prosecution can establish the relevant factual basis, the 'presumption' (in reality, a legal conclusion) arises and the defence has no answer. The first circumstance is that '(a) the defendant intentionally deceived the complainant as to the nature or purpose of the relevant act'. The common law also held that deception as to the nature of the act was fundamental, as where young girls had been invited to submit to acts in order to train their voice or to improve their breathing[237] and, unbeknown to them, the act which they were permitting was sexual intercourse. Deception as to the purpose of an act is a significantly wider concept, which applies where D deceives V as to the ulterior reason for or objective of the act. The Court of Appeal held in *Jheeta*[238] that, since the presumption is a conclusive one, it ought to be construed narrowly. In that case B had submitted to intercourse because she had received text messages, allegedly from the police (but actually from D), ordering her to have sex with D; the Court held that this was not a deception as to the purpose of the act. The Court stated that the strongest case of deception as to purpose would be where D has deceived B as to the medical need for the particular procedure.[239] The Court held that there would be no deception as to purpose on the facts of *Linekar*,[240] where D promised to pay a prostitute for intercourse but then reneged on the deal. Sir Igor Judge, P., stated that 'she was undeceived about either the nature or the purpose of the act, that is, intercourse.'[241] Yet in the subsequent case of *Devonald*,[242] the Court held that where B was induced to masturbate in front of a webcam, believing that it was for the sexual pleasure of a woman whom he had 'met' on the internet when in fact D (a man) aimed to humiliate B, this was a deception as to purpose. Unusually, however, it was (in the context of the 2003 Act) a reverse deception—V thought that the purpose was sexual, whereas D intended the purpose to be humiliation. A better decision is *Piper*,[243] where V agreed to be measured for a bikini by D on the (false) basis that it was necessary to determine her modelling potential, whereas in fact it was for his sexual pleasure. D's conviction of sexual assault was upheld. This interpretation is more faithful to the concept of purpose. The question then is whether other ulterior purposes can fall within section 76(2)(a), such as

---

[236] However, it seems that the presumptions in ss 75–76 do not apply to attempts and conspiracy to commit sex offences: Judge Rodwell, 'Problems with the Sexual Offences Act 2003' [2005] Crim LR 290.

[237] *Flattery* (1877) 2 QBD 410; *Williams* [1923] 1 KB 340.   [238] *Jheeta* [2007] EWCA Crim 1699.

[239] As in *Green* [2002] EWCA Crim 1501, where a qualified doctor induced young men to masturbate in front of him, allegedly to assess their potential for impotence but actually for his sexual gratification. A similar view might be taken of the facts of. *Tabassum* [2000] 2 Cr App R 328, where women agreed to D examining their breasts for 'research work', when D represented that he was medically qualified and he was not.

[240] [1995] 2 Cr App R 49.   [241] In *Jheeta* (above, n 238), at [27].

[242] [2008] All ER (D) 241.   [243] [2007] EWCA Crim 2131.

deceiving V into having sex with D by falsely representing that D will i) obtain a lucrative modelling contract for V, or (ii) enter into a marriage or civil partnership with V, or iii) falsify the report of a car accident for which V accepts blame. In principle such cases should be capable of falling within s 76(2)(a); but this is not to go so far as Jonathan Herring, who argues in favour of an expansive notion of purpose, extending to any deception as to what 'this act of sexual intercourse is about.'[244] This is an unduly wide approach to a conclusive presumption that applies to so serious an offence as rape. If there is thought to be no logical dividing line between the *Piper* ruling and Herring's approach, then the Court of Appeal's restrictive interpretation in *Jheeta* would be more appropriate—it does not foreclose the issue, as a conclusive presumption would, but rather transfers it to the general definition of consent under section 74 of the Act (see below). It is the absence of a lesser offence of obtaining sex by deception that causes this problem.[245]

The second circumstance is that '(b) the defendant intentionally induced the complainant to consent to the relevant act by impersonating a person known personally to the complainant'. The previous law extended only to impersonating a spouse or partner,[246] whereas the 2003 Act extends to all impersonations other than those of a person who is not personally known to the complainant, such as a sports or television star. However, in one sense this second conclusive presumption is less powerful than the first, since it requires the prosecution to establish that the impersonation induced V to consent: if the defence can create doubt about the causal link, this may be sufficient to prevent the presumption from arising.

The decision to confine the conclusive presumptions to these types of case suggests that they are believed to be either the clearest or the strongest examples of non-consent, but this can be doubted. The use of 'purpose' in (a) is not absolutely clear. Are these the strongest cases? What about the administration of drugs to V without consent? Or doing a sexual act while V is asleep or unconscious? Or, indeed, immediate threats of violence? It is not clear that putting some deception cases into s 76 as conclusive presumptions, and leaving all others to be dealt with under the general definition of consent, is the wisest approach.

Rebuttable Presumptions: section 75(2) enumerates six sets of circumstances giving rise to a rebuttable presumption of non-consent. Once the prosecution establishes the factual basis for one of the presumptions—i.e. that the circumstance existed and that D knew it existed—that presumption operates against D until the defence adduce sufficient credible evidence 'to raise an issue as to whether he consented'. This does not place a burden of proof on D, but does require the defence to 'satisfy the judge that there is a real issue about consent that it is worth putting to the jury'.[247] Once this is

---

[244] J. Herring, 'Mistaken Sex' [2005] Crim LR 519.

[245] The 2003 Act repealed the offence under s. 3 of the Sexual Offences Act 1956 without replacing it.

[246] See *Elbekkay* [1995] Crim LR 163.

[247] The words of Baroness Scotland, quoted by the Home Affairs Committee, *Sexual Offences Bill*, para. 29. For further discussion, see Temkin and Ashworth, 'Rape, Sexual Assaults and the Problems of Consent', 342–4.

done, the prosecution must prove absence of consent in the normal way, relying on section 74 (see below). The six circumstances are:

(a) any person was, at the time of the relevant act or immediately before it began, using violence against the complainant or causing the complainant to fear that immediate violence would be used against him;

(b) any person was, at the time of the relevant act or immediately before it began, causing the complainant to fear that violence was being used, or that immediate violence would be used, against another person;

(c) the complainant was, and the defendant was not, unlawfully detained at the time of the act;

(d) the complainant was asleep or otherwise unconscious at the time of the relevant act;

(e) because of the complainant's physical disability, the complainant would not have been able at the time of the relevant act to communicate to the defendant whether the complainant consented;

(f) any person had administered to or caused to be taken by the complainant, without the complainant's consent, a substance which, having regard to when it was administered or taken, was capable of causing or enabling the complainant to be stupefied or overpowered at the time of the relevant act.

The prosecution has to prove that D knew that one of the circumstances existed, and does not have to show that it actually negatived consent, this being presumed.

The presumptions in (a) and (b) make an important statement about the effect of violence and threats of violence—although conclusive presumptions would have made a stronger statement—but their ambit is limited to threats of immediate violence to V or to another person, such as a family member or friend.[248] Where the threat is no less realistic but is to use violence in the near future, the case falls outside these presumptions and must be dealt with under the general definition of consent (below). Similarly, other threats—relating, for example, to losing a job or being prosecuted for an offence—are also excluded from the presumptions. However, presumptions (a) and (b) are wider than the conclusive presumptions in one respect, since they contain no requirement that D be the author of the threats or violence. Presumption (c) deals with cases of false imprisonment and kidnap. Presumption (d) applies to cases where V is either asleep or unconscious. The presumption applies not just to sleep but to cases where V was unconscious through alcohol or otherwise. At common law, having sex with a person who was asleep would be rape, and thus there is an argument that this should be a conclusive presumption. However, what of the case where it is contended that V has signified to D that V enjoys being awoken from his or her slumbers by D doing something sexual to V? It must be borne in mind that these presumptions apply to all the offences in ss 1–4, including the broad offence of sexual assault.[249]

---

[248] The use of 'immediate' rather than 'imminent' restricts the range of this provision: cf. *Hasan* [2005] UKHL 22, discussed in Ch.6.4(a) above.

[249] See further Temkin and Ashworth, 'Rape, Sexual Assaults and the Problems of Consent', 337–8.

Presumption (e) refers to V's physical inability to communicate with D: there are already several offences in ss 30–44 of the Act aimed at sexual acts with those suffering some mental incapacity, but one purpose of this presumption may be to ensure that serious cases are treated as rape or assault by penetration.

Presumption (f) was added during the progress of the Bill,[250] and its drafting leaves open several questions. The first requirement is that someone (not necessarily D) administered to V or 'caused to be taken' a form of stupefying substance. Presumably, 'caused to be taken' includes cases where V is deceived into believing that what is being taken voluntarily is a substance with different properties, but it remains unclear whether this captures all forms of deception. Consent presumably bears the same broad and uncertain meaning as it has within the Act generally (below). As for the nature of the substance, the primary target is what are known as 'date rape drugs' such as rohypnol, but the presumption appears to extend to alcohol too. The substance must have been capable of stupefying or overpowering V, but it is not clear what degree of effect this will be held to require. Cases of unconsciousness fall within presumption (d), so a logical scheme would suggest that presumption (f) should apply where the effects of the substance on V's functioning are significant but not total. Once again, there is considerable room for interpretation in this provision, and this will determine the practical application of the law—and the 'messages' it sends out.[251] Finally, it should be reiterated that in order to rebut a presumption D needs only to adduce sufficient credible evidence to raise the issue. Thus even if the presumption is established—and that may depend on a jury question, such as whether V was asleep or unconscious or unlawfully detained—it will disappear if D satisfies the evidential burden and the case must then be fought on the general ground of non-consent.

Definition of Consent: although the prosecution is likely to start by considering the application of the conclusive presumptions and the rebuttable presumptions to the case at hand, the general definition of consent will be relevant if the courts apply the narrow interpretation of the conclusive presumptions urged in *Jheeta* and where the defence satisfies the evidential burden in relation to a rebuttable presumption. Section 74 provides that 'a person consents if he agrees by choice, and has the freedom and capacity to make that choice'. This is intended to be a factual or 'attitudinal' definition, turning on what V felt rather than what V expressed.[252] Unfortunately, however, the section simply describes consent in terms of four other contested concepts—agreement, choice, capacity and freedom. The concept of agreement may be construed either to mean simple assent to an act, or to entail a full consensus based on knowledge of the essential particulars. Similarly, the concept of choice may be construed

---

[250] For detailed analysis, see E. Finch and V. Munro, 'Intoxicated Consent and Drug-assisted Rape Revisited' [2004] Crim LR 789.

[251] Many Government statements at the time of the Bill emphasized that it was intended to send out 'clear messages' about what was acceptable and unacceptable: e.g. Home Office, *Protecting the Public*, para. 5, and Home Affairs Committee, *Sexual Offences Bill*, para. 30.

[252] Cf. P. Westen, 'Some Common Conusions about Consent in Rape Cases', (2004) 2 Ohio State JCL 333, and more fully, P. Westen, *The Logic of Consent* (2005).

to mean that the consent should be informed, so that where D has concealed from V a fact material to their sexual encounter this means that an informed choice was not made and that any consent was apparent and not real. However, the Court of Appeal has declined to accept this doctrine of informed consent in a case where D failed to disclose to V that he was HIV positive,[253] Latham LJ holding that V's consent to the sexual act was not vitiated but that D might be liable for an offence against the person by transmission of disease. The concept of capacity would seem to imply an adequate degree of understanding of the acts and their significance, which is particularly relevant in cases of mental incapacity[254] and in cases where the complainant is intoxicated. In *Bree*[255] both parties had been drinking alcohol for some time before they had sex, and the Court of Appeal held that the proper approach in an intoxication case, where the complainant is not alleged to have been unconscious (and therefore within rebuttable presumption (d)), is whether she had sufficient capacity to choose whether to agree to sex and whether she did so. 'If through drink the complainant has temporarily lost her capacity to choose whether to have intercourse on the relevant occasion, she is not consenting.' The Court took a similar approach in *Hysa*,[256] holding that the case was wrongly withdrawn from the jury where V could not remember what she had said because she was so drunk. In view of the muddled evidence in cases of this kind, the decision will often be difficult.

The central concept of freedom demonstrates how vague and contestable the statutory definition is: freedom of decision-making may be greater or less, depending on the impact of any deception, threats or other perceived pressures, and the question is what degree of impairment should be taken to mean that any apparent consent was not free. Freedom cannot practically be defined in terms of a totally unconstrained choice, and we tend to use the term 'free' only 'to rule out the suggestion of some or all of its recognized antitheses'.[257] This indicates that the law might have been better drafted if it had focussed on the effects of various forms of threat, deception and other pressure in order to try to delimit the proper boundaries of consent. If it is argued that this was the aim of the presumptions in ss 75 and 76, then the answer must be that they leave too many contested situations at large. No doubt the limits of consent will be elaborated in the case law, but the concepts of freedom, agreement, choice and capacity do not provide sufficiently clear signposts to prevent inconsistent outcomes. It was suggested that juries might be told not to assume that V did agree freely just because V did not say or do anything, protest or resist or was not physically injured;[258] that might have urged juries to challenge stereotypes, but no such model direction

---

[253] *E.B.* [2006] EWCA Crim 2945, following the decisions in *Dica* and *Konzani*, above, Ch 8.3(f), on this point.

[254] S. 30(2) of the Act refers to capacity in terms of whether D 'lacks sufficient understanding of the nature or reasonably foreseeable consequences of what is being done.'

[255] [2007] EWCA Crim 804. The conviction was quashed because of non-direction by the judge.

[256] [2007] EWCA Crim 2056.

[257] J. L. Austin, 'A Plea for Excuses', in H. Morris (ed.), *Freedom and Responsibility* (1961), 8.

[258] *Setting the Boundaries*, para. 2.11.5.

has emerged. However, the concept of agreement, in s 74, should be interpreted as emphasizing that it is V's perception of choice and freedom that is crucial.[259]

What are likely to be the practical effects of the section 74 'definition' on jury decision-making? Some clues are provided by research conducted by Emily Finch and Vanessa Munro using mock juries.[260] They found that many jurors latched on to one or more of the four terms in section 74 (agreement, choice, capacity, freedom) in order to justify quite different interpretations. As the authors comment, the fact that these four terms are 'within everyone's understanding does not mean that everyone understands them to mean the same thing, either in the abstract or in specific cases.'[261] Indeed, the terms did nothing to prevent some jurors from applying sexist stereotypes in their reasoning.[262] Thus where the woman complainant was intoxicated, some jurors readily assumed fault and therefore consent.

What are the moot cases on consent? Numerous examples have already been mentioned. Taking deceptions first, if D deceives V into thinking that he intends to marry her and only for this reason does V agree to sex, does V agree by choice? Some jurors may conclude that this is nothing more than naivety, but if V regards it as crucial to her agreement, should a conviction for rape follow? Again, if D runs a modelling agency and promises V a glittering modelling career if he or she will have sex with him, does V agree by choice? Does it matter whether D is or is not likely to advance V's modelling career? What if D goes into a hospital dressed in a white coat and examines patients intimately at, say, a breast clinic or a clinic for testicular cancer?[263] And what of the case of *Linekar*,[264] where D deceived V into thinking that he will pay £25 for sex when he had no intention of doing so: does V agree by choice, in these circumstances? It is easy to say that V would not have agreed if all the circumstances had been known, but is it satisfactory that a requirement of a fully informed choice should lead to conviction of rape?[265] There is a strong argument that many of these cases should amount to a lesser offence, on the ground that the deception was not sufficiently fundamental, but the absence of a lesser offence in the 2003 Act, such as obtaining agreement to sexual activity by deception, may force courts to decide between rape and acquittal.

Turning to threats, we observed above that threats of non-immediate violence (e.g. 'I have some very nasty friends, and we know where you live') fall outside rebuttable presumptions (a) and (b), and so a jury or magistrates would have to decide whether such threats negative agreement by choice. If V, a sex worker who agrees to have sex with D for money, tells D that she has been forced to come to England and to work in this way, D then knows that she cannot be said to be agreeing by choice, and he may be guilty of rape. In other cases, where D's conduct creates an atmosphere of

---

[259] Cf. Lacey, *Unspeakable Subjects* (1998), 114; Westen, above n 252.

[260] 'Sexual Consent in the Jury Room' (2006) 26 LS 303.   [261] Ibid., 315.

[262] For a summary and analysis of research, see Temkin and Krahé, ch 3.

[263] Cf. *Tabassum* [2000] 2 Cr App R 238 with *Richardson* [1998] 2 Cr App R 200, and Ch 8.3(f) above.

[264] [1995] QB 250.

[265] J. Herring, 'Mistaken Sex' [2005] Crim LR 511, at 516; cf. the much criticized concept of deception in *Metropolitan Police Commissioner v Charles* [1977] AC 177, discussed in Ch 9.8(c) below, and R. Williams, 'Deception, Mistake and Vitiation of the Victim's Consent' (2008) 124 LQR 132.

fear, V may submit rather than risk a physical attack, even if there has been no actual violence or threats uttered. What if D tells V, an employee who has committed a disciplinary offence, that V will be dismissed unless willing to allow D to do a certain sexual act? Would the test of 'agreement by choice' be applied differently if V agreed to be fondled, or to be caned on a bare bottom, or to allow full sexual penetration?[266] Would the outcome be different if D were a police officer who stopped a motorist for a minor traffic offence, and said she would not report V if he engaged in a sexual activity with her?[267] One difficulty here is that, if the approach to deception is to require fully informed consent, the corresponding approach to threats cases may be that any credible and significant threat should be sufficient to negative choice or freedom.[268] If that were thought to carry criminal liability too far, then the concepts of 'choice' and 'freedom' would be at large again, without any indication of the degree of constraint needed to negative them.

(i) ABSENCE OF REASONABLE BELIEF IN CONSENT

For all the offences in ss 1–4, it must not only be proved that V did not consent to what was done, but also that D did not reasonably believe that V was consenting. Subsection (2) of all those sections provides that 'whether a belief is reasonable is to be determined having regard to all the circumstances, including any steps A has taken to ascertain whether B consents'. This is clearly intended as a move away from the subjective test in DPP v Morgan,[269] which judged D on the facts as he or she believed them to be, however unreasonable that belief might be. Even if Morgan is defensible as a case on general principles, it is unacceptable as a rape decision. There are certain situations in which the risk of doing a serious wrong is so obvious that it is right for the law to impose a duty to take care to ascertain the facts before proceeding. Moreover, not only are serious sexual offences a denial of the victim's autonomy, but the ascertainment of one vital fact—consent—is a relatively easy matter. The subjective test of mistake has therefore been removed and replaced by a requirement of reasonable belief.

The same structure of conclusive and rebuttable presumptions applies as it does to consent itself. Thus, if any of the circumstances of deception in s 76(2) is established, it is conclusively presumed that D did not believe that V was consenting. Similarly, if any of the six circumstances in s 75(2) is established, D is to be taken not to have reasonably believed that V consented, unless sufficient evidence is adduced to raise an issue as to whether he reasonably believed it. The presumptions in ss 75 and 76 were discussed in paragraph (h) above. The Sexual Offences Bill originally had a third conclusive

---

[266] Cf. McCoy [1953] 2 SA 4.

[267] In Setting the Boundaries, para. 2.10.9, it was suggested that threats such as 'losing a job or killing the family pet' should negative consent.

[268] Also relevant is the subtle difference between threats and inducements: see McGregor, Is it Rape? 169.

[269] [1976] 1 AC 182, discussed in Ch 5.3(d) above.

presumption, for cases where V's willingness to engage in sexual activity with D was indicated only by a third party. If sexual autonomy is to be respected, is it not unreasonable that D should proceed on the basis of consent relayed by someone else, as in the notorious cases of *Morgan*[270] and *Cogan and Leak*?[271] In the end this provision was dropped for various reasons, including the possibility that it discriminated against some people with mental incapacity,[272] but such cases have caused controversy and the Act might have been expected to contain some reference to whether mistakes in such circumstances are reasonable.

The reference in subsection (2) to 'any steps A has taken to ascertain whether B consents' is important, in that it directs the court to consider whether D attempted to verify his assumption or belief about consent. But the more difficult question is whether the injunction to courts to have regard to 'all the circumstances' may undermine the objective test by letting in D's prejudices and belief system, or his beliefs about V's sexual history. While recent decisions of high authority suggest a general restrictiveness towards allowing the defendant's own characteristics to set the tone for what was 'reasonable' in the circumstances,[273] various government statements suggested that courts might properly take account of D's personal characteristics when deciding what was reasonable.[274] It is one thing to take account of a learning disability, but quite another thing to take account of stereotypical beliefs about, for example, women's behaviour. Thus account might properly be taken of the fact that D was suffering from Asperger's syndrome and hence prone to misunderstand V's intentions.[275] But there is a danger, borne out by Finch and Munro's research,[276] that the phrase 'all the circumstances' blunts the objectivity of the reasonableness requirement and allows juries to modify the standard to take account of a particular defendant's belief system. The Act does not indicate the levels or spheres of objectivity or subjectivity required by the test, allowing room for the operation of 'questionable socio-sexual myths'.[277] It is unclear whether as a matter of law 'all the circumstances' would include D's drunken state: in principle it would seem wrong for a test of 'reasonable belief' to be adjusted to take account of drunken beliefs,[278] but the Act is not explicit on this point.

Another moot point is how the 'reasonable belief' test applies where D intentionally penetrates the vagina of someone he believes to be X (who has indicated that she would consent) but who turns out to be V (who does not consent). Although the drafting of the Act may be thought to indicate otherwise (in its references to A and B), such a case of mistaken identity should surely be approached by asking whether D had reasonable

---

[270] See Ch 5.3(d) above.   [271] See Ch 10.6 below.

[272] Further discussed by Temkin and Ashworth, 'Rape, Sexual Assaults and the Problems of Consent', 339.

[273] Notably the major decisions on duress in *Hasan* [2005] UKHL 22, discussed in Ch 6.3 above, and on provocation in *Attorney-General for Jersey* v *Holley* [2005] UKPC 23, discussed in Ch 7.4(b).

[274] See Temkin and Ashworth, 'Rape, Sexual Assaults and the Problems of Consent', 341, for references.

[275] *T.S.* [2008] CLW 08/07/1.   [276] Above, n 260.   [277] (2006) 26 LS at 317.

[278] Cf. *Bree* [2007] EWCA Crim 804, above, n 255 and text.

grounds not only for the belief in consent but also for the belief that it was X whom he was penetrating.[279]

(j) THE EFFECT OF INTOXICATION

We have already noted that the intoxicated state of the complainant may be relevant in various ways—unconsciousness (s 75(2(d)), involuntary stupefaction (s 75(2)(f), or lack of capacity to consent (s 74)—and also that D's intoxication may be relevant when deciding whether he held a reasonable belief in consent. But what is the relevance of D's intoxication to the other matters that must be proved for liability, notably in rape and sexual penetration (*intentional* penetration), in sexual assault (*intentional* touching), and in causing sexual activity (*intentionally* causing another to engage in sexual activity)? The general effect of intoxication on criminal liability is not entirely clear, as we saw in Chapter 6.2 above, but one rule of thumb is that offences of basic intent (where intoxication is no defence) are those for which recklessness is sufficient, whereas offences of specific intent (where intoxication may be a defence) are those where intention alone is sufficient. However, in *Heard*[280] D was convicted of sexual assault for exposing his penis and rubbing it against a police officer's thigh. D's defence was that he was drunk, but the judge ruled that this was inadmissible. The Court of Appeal upheld this ruling, concluding that the requirement of 'intentional touching' in sexual assault is one of basic intent. This looks like a pragmatic decision of the kind that abound in intoxication cases, and the attempts of Hughes LJ to align it with existing doctrine involved strain: his argument that 'a drunken accident is still an accident' may have the effect of blurring the boundaries of recklessness, and his narrowing of the concept of 'specific intent' to cases of purpose is a poor fit with the existing case-law. The failure of the 2003 Act to deal with such an obvious issue as intoxication, while going into extraordinary complexity in other respects, is unfortunate.

8.6 OFFENCES AGAINST THE VULNERABLE[281]

One of the central aims of the 2003 Act is to protect the vulnerable, and to this end Parliament enacted a wide range of overlapping offences against children. We begin by discussing those offences against children under age 13 to which consent is irrelevant, and then consider each of the offences in ss 9 to 15.

---

[279] The point could not be authoritatively decided in *Attorney General's Reference No. 79 of 2006 (Whitta)* [2007] 1 Cr App R (S) 752, an appeal against sentence.

[280] [2007] EWCA Crim 125.

[281] See the critique by J. R. Spencer, 'Child and Family Offences' [2004] Crim LR 347.

(a) OFFENCES AGAINST CHILDREN UNDER AGE 13

Sections 5–8 of the Act create offences parallel to those in ss 1–4, save that they are only committed if the victim is under age 13 and consent is not relevant. Section 5 creates the offence of rape of a child under 13, in the same terms as the offence in s 1 but without any of the consent elements. Section 6 introduces an offence of assault of a child under 13 by sexual penetration, again without any consent requirements. The same approach is taken in respect of sexual assault of a child under 13 (s 7) and causing a child under 13 to engage in sexual activity (s 8). The other elements of these offences were discussed in section 8.5 above.

The main purpose of these offences is to provide for strong censure and punishment for adults who abuse young children. A major difficulty is that, in pursuit of the laudable aim of protecting young children and labelling those who abuse them sexually, these offences may result in the criminalization of other children. Sexual activity between children has long been widespread,[282] and some of it may involve boys and girls as young as 12. The serious offences in ss 5–8 contain no exemptions for young persons, and so the conviction of two 12 year-olds for kissing lustily in public is legally possible. The Government sought to prevent this eventuality by assuring critics that there would be no such prosecutions, and the Crown Prosecution Service has published guidelines designed to ensure that the criminal law is not invoked inappropriately.[283] The CPS guidelines do mention that it is not in the public interest to prosecute children of a similar age (assuming that there was no coercion involved), and that would almost certainly dispose of the example of two 12 year-olds kissing. But there may be circumstances when a young person is prosecuted, and is prosecuted for one of the four 'under 13' offences rather than for one of the lesser child sex offences mentioned in (b) below.

This is evident from G.,[284] where G, aged 15, had sex with a girl of 12 whom he had met. G was charged with rape of a child under 13, contrary to section 5. In the belief that the offence imposes strict liability as to age, G was advised to plead guilty, but he did so on the basis that the girl consented in fact and told him that she was 15 too. Both the Court of Appeal and the House of Lords upheld his conviction for rape of a child under 13. Two principal arguments failed to persuade a majority of judges. First, there is the argument that imposing strict liability for such a serious offence is contrary to the presumption of innocence embodied in Article 6.2 of the Convention. European authority for applying the presumption of innocence to the substantive criminal law, rather than to the burden of proof, is rather scanty, however.[285] This argument might have been better put on the basis of the 'constitutional principle' that 'unless Parliament has indicated otherwise, the appropriate mental element is an unexpressed ingredient of every offence.'[286] The reasons why this principle was

---

[282] Ibid., at 354 and 360.   [283] See <www.cps.gov.uk>.   [284] [2008] UKHL 37.
[285] See the commentary on the Court of Appeal decision at [2006] Crim LR 930.
[286] Per Lord Nicholls in B. v D.P.P. [2000] 2 AC 428, at 460; see also K. [2002] 1 Cr App R 121.

asserted by the House of Lords were directly related to the injustices in cases of this kind; but whether such a judicially created presumption could properly be wielded against a recent legislative enactment which was clearly intended to introduce strict liability as to age in the 'under 13' offences is doubtful. More persuasive is the second argument, that convicting a boy of 15 of such a serious and stigmatic offence in these circumstances violates his rights under Article 8. In many European countries there would have been no criminal law intervention in these circumstances. Here, once the basis of plea was established, the prosecution had the choice of a) dropping the prosecution altogether or b) dropping the section 5 prosecution and charging G under section 13 (and section 9) with sexual activity with a child under 16, a lesser offence with a maximum sentence of 5 years for offenders under 18.[287] The majority in the House of Lords recognized that G's right to respect for his private life was engaged, but held that this was less important than the state's positive obligation to ensure that young people are protected from the sexual attentions of others. Baroness Hale emphasized the dangers of under-age sexual activity, referring to the long-term psychological effects to which it can give rise.[288] This is a powerful consideration, but it should not be regarded as the most powerful element in the case. The question for the courts was whether conviction of this very serious offence, carrying a maximum of life imprisonment, was a disproportionate interference with G's right to respect for his private life. The Court of Appeal had quashed the sentence of detention and substituted a conditional discharge; the gross disparity between conviction of a life-carrying offence and the ultimate sentence is a fair indication of the disproportionality involved. Yet the majority of the House of Lords allowed the conviction under section 5 to stand.

The approach of the Sexual Offences Act 2003 to cases involving children or young people close in age is woefully inadequate and potentially unjust, as *G.* demonstrates. Reliance on prosecutorial discretion is unsatisfactory in principle, and is unpersuasive in European human rights law.[289] Greater efforts should have been made to ensure clarity in the law: if an age difference of up to two years is acceptable so long as no coercion (howsoever defined) is present, then that should be used as a model for legislation, as in other jurisdictions. Faced with the inadequacy of the legislation in this respect, the majority of the House of Lords in *G.* should have followed human rights (and children's rights) reasoning more faithfully by focussing on the fairness of convicting this defendant on these assumed facts of this serious offence carrying life imprisonment.

---

[287] See Home Office, *Sexual Offences Act 2003: a Stocktake* (2006), para. 13, stating that in the first 8 months of the Act coming into force, some 39 per cent of prosecutions for the s 13 offence were for offences against children under 13 (as in the case of G).

[288] [2008] UKHL 37, at [45] to [51].

[289] The risk of prosecution is the key issue: e.g. *Sutherland and Monnell v UK* (1997) 24 EHRR CD22.

(b) OFFENCES AGAINST CHILDREN UNDER 16

Sections 9–15 of the 2003 Act create a range of offences against children under age 16, which remains the age of consent in these matters. The original intention was that the first four of these offences, in ss 9–12, would criminalize acts in respect of children aged 13–15 inclusive and would therefore complement the offences against children under 13 in ss 5–8. When it became clear that this would create procedural difficulties where there was uncertainty about the victim's age, the remedy was to extend ss 9–12 to cover offences against all children under 16.[290] This creates a manifest overlap between the two groups of offences when the victim is under 13, and raises serious questions about the need for such duplication.[291] We will return to this and other general issues after outlining this group of new offences.

Section 9 creates two offences of sexual activity with a child. The subsection (1) offence consists of sexual touching of a person under 16, an offence of enormous breadth that potentially criminalizes many normal touchings between young people. The subsection (2) offence consists of sexual activity involving penetration, with higher maxima. To these offences are added the offences in s 10 of causing or inciting a child under 16 to engage in sexual activity (which run parallel to the offences in ss 4 and 8). Further, s 11 penalizes a person who engages in sexual activity in the presence of a child for the purpose of obtaining sexual gratification; and s 12 creates an offence of causing a child to watch sexual activity, for the purpose of obtaining sexual gratification—such as watching a pornographic film, as in *Abdullahi*.[292] In that case the Court of Appeal confirmed that the sexual gratification need not be immediate, and that the requirement could be fulfilled if the purpose was to 'put the child in the mood' for a later gratification of D's desires.

The offences in ss 9–12 have two common characteristics of note. One is that s 13 states that, where any one of them is committed by a person under 18, the offence is triable summarily and, if tried on indictment, a lower maximum penalty of five years applies. This is a significant step in the direction of recognizing the need for a different approach to youngsters involved in sex cases, but it does not go far enough towards separating teenagers who sexually abuse other children (a significant social problem) from young people who consensually engage in sexual activities that are a fairly normal part of growing up. Once again, supporters of the Act rely on prosecutorial discretion to mark this important difference and, for the reasons outlined above, this is unsatisfactory in general and not rendered more satisfactory by the actual guidelines issued by the CPS.[293]

The other common characteristic is that these offences are committed when 'either (i) B is under 16 and A does not reasonably believe that B is 16 or over, or (ii) B is under 13'. In terms of drafting, this is much clearer than ss 5–8 in indicating strict

---

[290] This explains why it would have been possible to charge G (above, n 284) under sections 13 and 9.

[291] Not least because a provision relating to the age of A (and of B) could easily have been inserted into ss. 1–4.

[292] [2007] 1 Cr App R 14.   [293] Above, n 283.

liability where the child is 12 or under, compared with a reasonableness requirement where the child is aged 13–15 inclusive. But the question is whether it is fair: although there are some justifications for holding adults to strict liability where the child is aged 12 or less,[294] it is arguable that they should not hold sway in a stigmatic offence carrying life imprisonment; and for younger defendants this is unduly draconian, as the facts of G. demonstrate.[295]

There are two further child sex offences in this part of the Act. Section 14 creates a wide-ranging offence of arranging or facilitating commission of a child sex offence (under ss 9–13) in any part of the world. This covers much of the ground that the law of complicity would encompass (see Chapter 10 below), but goes beyond that by applying to offences that others may do. There is no lower penalty for offenders under 18, and yet this offence is committed by a teenager who arranges to meet his girlfriend (aged 15) for sex later in the day. Again, the drafting is so wide as to make no distinction between the abuser/exploiter and the consensual friend.

Section 15 introduces the much discussed offence of meeting a child following sexual grooming. This offence can only be committed by a person aged 18 or over. The conduct consists of either an intentional meeting, or where either party travels to a meeting, involving one person under 16, having met or communicated with that person on at least two previous occasions.[296] The required fault element is intending to do acts that constitute a relevant offence (mostly child sex offences under the Act), and not reasonably believing that the child is aged 16 or over. Proof of the intention to do 'relevant acts' is the principal narrowing feature of the offence: otherwise it is an offence in the inchoate mode, complete when D either intentionally meets a child or either party travels to such a meeting.

Efforts were made in Parliament to narrow the enormous reach of the offences in ss 9–14 by ensuring that, at least, carers, teachers and the medical profession are not drawn into the criminal law by virtue of conduct intended to protect or support children. Thus s 14(3) lists a number of circumstances in which a person is taken to be acting 'for the protection of a child' and does not commit the offence—for once, Parliament did not rely on prosecutorial discretion. Reference may also be made here to s 73, which creates exemptions from conviction for aiding, abetting or counselling several (but not all) offences in the Act for persons acting for the purpose of protecting the child rather than obtaining sexual gratification.

(c) ABUSE OF TRUST OFFENCES AGAINST PERSONS UNDER 18

The offence of abuse of a position of trust, introduced by the Sexual Offences (Amendment) Act 2000, was expanded into four new offences in the 2003 Act.

---

[294] Cf. J. Horder, 'How Culpability Can, and Cannot, be Denied in Under-age Sex Crimes' [2001] Crim LR 15.

[295] Above, n 284 and text.

[296] This reflects the broadened definition: see Criminal Justice and Immigration Act 2008, s 73 and Sch 15.

Essentially, where a person over age 18 stands in a position of trust in relation to a person under 18, there is an offence if the person in trust has sexually activity with V (s 16), causes or incites V to have sexual activity (s 17), engages in sexual activity in the presence of V (s 18), or causes V to watch sexual activity (s 19). It will be seen that the substance of these offences parallels those in earlier sections—the drafting could have been much more concise—but the two key elements are the position of trust and the age of the younger person. Section 21 sets out definitions of 'positions of trust' that rely on the term 'looks after', whether in an educational institution, or in a hospital, or children's home, etc. The provision does not extend to others such as choirmasters, scoutmasters or sports coaches, for whom the normal approach of aggravating the sentence is considered sufficient. Indeed, aggravation of sentence under ss 9–12 would have dealt with all 'abuse of trust' offences in respect of children under 16, since the maximum sentences for those offences are already high. The significance of ss 16–19 is that they apply where the young person is 16 or 17, over the age of consent but still (it is thought) vulnerable to abuse by those trusted to care for them. The question is whether the law should have gone further to attempt to separate abusive relationships from loving ones, or whether it is sufficient to state that there shall be no lawful sexual relationships of any kind between persons of 16 or 17 and those trusted to care for them. English law does not say this, since marriage between such persons is lawful. Other legal systems attempt to penalize those elements of pressure that indicate abusive relationships,[297] whereas English law criminalizes all such relationships and then attempts the necessary differentiation at the sentencing stage.[298]

(d) FAMILIAL SEX OFFENCES

The 2003 Act contains two sets of offences aimed at familial sexual activity. We deal first with ss 25–29 on 'familial child sex offences', which apply where one of the family members is under age 18. Child sexual abuse is not merely a sexual offence, but one of the deepest breaches of trust which can take place in a family-based society. The home ought to be a safe haven, the place where young people can go to get away from fear and violence, and this fundamental feeling of safety can be destroyed by sexual abuse. Incest was introduced into English law as a distinct offence by the Punishment of Incest Act 1908.[299] Although the eugenic risk (that the child of an incestuous relationship between father and daughter or brother and sister will have congenital defects) was known at the time and was probably a factor, most of the arguments of the reformers were based on the protection of children from sexual exploitation. Those

---

[297] Spencer, 'Child and Family Offences', 355–6, referring to French law.

[298] Sentencing Guidelines Council, *Sexual Offences* (2007), pp. 60–61, refers to such factors as the degree of vulnerability of the young person, the age gap between the parties, and the presence of coercion.

[299] See V. Bailey and S. Blackburn, 'The Punishment of Incest Act 1908: A Case Study in Law Creation' [1979] Crim LR 708, and S. Wolfram, 'Eugenics and the Punishment of Incest Act 1908' [1983] Crim LR 308.

arguments have great force today, as increasing evidence of child abuse within the family comes to light and as this hitherto 'private' realm is opened up.[300] Fathers may use their considerable power within the home to lead a daughter into sexual activity from a relatively early age. All kinds of pressure may be exerted on the child to keep quiet about the behaviour, with sometimes disastrous effects on his or her emotional development.

The essence of the two main offences is that s 25 penalizes sexual touching of a family member under 18, with higher penalties where penetration is involved and lower penalties where the offence is committed by a family member also under 18; and that s 26 penalizes the incitement of a family member to engage in sexual touching. As observed in relation to the 'position of trust' offences, the objective of labelling these offences separately could have been achieved much more simply by applying ss 9 and 10 in the relevant sets of circumstances. That would still necessitate a definition of a 'family relationship', and s 26 now expands this beyond close blood relations to cover a range of step-relations and foster parents living in the same household and regularly involved in caring for the young family member. Sexual abuse by such persons remains an important matter, of course, but it is already punishable whenever the child is under 16. So, again, it is a question of criminalizing those who commit offences against family members aged 16 and 17, whom (as a matter of law) they may be free to marry. Section 28 creates an exception for parties who are lawfully married, but that is not a convincing resolution of the issue of consensual sexual relations between adult members of the household and young family members aged 16 and 17. No attempt has been made to identify what is abusive about some of those relationships, and the same applies to sexual relations between young siblings in the same family—some of which are abusive, others not sufficiently wrong or harmful to warrant criminal liability. Again, the discretion to prosecute and the sentencing discretion are regarded as the proper methods of making the necessary distinctions, even though prosecution and conviction are momentous events.

Later in the Act appear two offences of sex with adult relatives. Section 64 creates the offence of sexually penetrating a relative aged 18 or over, and s 65 creates an offence of consenting to being sexually penetrated by a relative aged 18 or over. Both offences have a maximum sentence of two years' imprisonment, and both now apply to adoptive relations.[301] This extends the previous law of incest to cover oral, anal and vaginal sex and to include penetrative acts between consenting males. However, the rationale of punishing exploitation of the young is no longer applicable here, since the parties are adults. The offences appear to go against the Article 8 principle of respecting the right of adults to engage in consensual sex in private, but the Sexual Offences Review concluded that 'the dynamics and balance

---

[300] See L. Zedner, 'Regulating Sexual Offences within the Home', in I. Loveland (ed.), *The Frontiers of Criminality* (1995), on the interaction of the State and the family, privacy, and regulation.

[301] Criminal Justice and Immigration Act 2008, s 73 and Sch 15.

of power within a family require special recognition, and we were concerned to ensure that patterns of abuse established in childhood were not allowed to continue into adulthood'.[302] Thus the relevant sentencing guidelines identify exploitation or long-term grooming as factors that render the offence serious enough for a custodial sentence.[303]

(e) OFFENCES AGAINST PERSONS WITH MENTAL DISORDER

For the protection of these vulnerable people the Act introduces three sets of offences, each set being broadly parallel to the scheme for child sex offences in ss 9–12 (i.e. sexual touching, causing or inciting sexual activity, engaging in sexual activity in the presence of such a person, and causing such a person to watch sexual activity). Thus ss 30–33 contain offences against persons with a mental disorder impeding choice. Section 30(2) defines such persons in terms of being either unable to communicate their choice or lacking the capacity to choose whether to agree. In C.[304] the Court of Appeal held that the mental disorder would usually have to be severe if it were to negative the capacity to choose, and that V's irrational fear of the defendant could not be equated with lack of the capacity to choose. The second set of offences, in, ss 34–37, create offences of using inducement, threat or deception in respect of a person with mental disorder. Sections 38–44 penalize care workers for persons with mental disorder who commit these offences.

It is important to ensure that the mentally disordered are properly protected from sexual abuse, but once again the Act contains prolix drafting and overlapping offences. On the one hand prosecutors are left to decide which of various applicable offences to select; on the other hand prosecutorial discretion is the only means of ensuring that sexual conduct between persons with a learning disability is not prosecuted unless there is strong evidence of coercion or other exploitative elements. As with the child sex offences, the Act fails to deal adequately with 'consensual' conduct between two people who both fall into the 'vulnerable' category. It is not possible to rely on the same principle of sexual autonomy here as with 'normal' adults, but the question remains whether relationships that are non-exploitative should be criminalized.

8.7 OTHER NEW SEXUAL OFFENCES

Attention should be drawn briefly to some of the other crimes in the Sexual Offences Act 2003. Reference has already been made to the offences relating to photographs of children and child pornography in ss 45–51,[305] and to various offences relating to

---

[302] Ibid., para. 5.8.3.   [303] Sentencing Guidelines Council, *Sexual Offences* (2007), pp. 92–3.
[304] *The Times*, 9 June 2008.   [305] See Gillespie, 'Tinkering with "Child Pornography"'.

prostitution and trafficking in ss 52–60. The Act introduces three new preparatory sexual offences: s 61 penalizes the intentional administration of a substance with intent to stupefy or overpower,[306] s 62 creates the very broad crime of committing any offence with intent to commit a sexual offence,[307] and s 63 criminalizes trespass with intent to commit a sexual offence.[308] The new offence of exposure of genitals (s 66) is limited by the requirement that D intends that someone will thereby be caused alarm or distress. Section 67 creates the offence of voyeurism for the purpose of obtaining sexual gratification. Section 69 creates offences of sexual intercourse with an animal (maximum sentence, two years). Sexual penetration of a corpse is criminalized by s 70. And s 71 creates an offence of engaging in sexual activity in a public lavatory.[309]

8.8 RE-ASSESSING SEXUAL OFFENCES LAW

The Sexual Offences Act 2003 marks an important advance in many ways. Reform of the essentially Victorian law was long overdue, and the need to reflect modern attitudes manifest. As we noted in part 8.5(c) above, there were some seven aims of the 2003 Act, many of them laudable. The law of sexual offences is now almost as gender-neutral as it could be. In some respects it goes further towards respecting human rights. And it makes considerable and well-signalled strides towards protecting the vulnerable from sexual exploitation.

There are, however, various respects in which the Act falls short of its promoters' ideals. Both the Sexual Offences Review and the 2003 Act set out to create a law that respects sexual autonomy and protects the vulnerable, but are these goals attained? Respect for sexual autonomy has both its positive and negative sides, as argued earlier, and two significant manifestations of paternalism—the criminalization of consensual sex between adult relatives (see 8.6(d) above), and the failure to recognize consent to sado-masochistic practices as part of sexual offences law[310]—amount to considerable restrictions. Respect for sexual autonomy also requires a clear and sensitive attempt to define 'consent', but it was argued above that the Act's scheme in ss 75 and 76, and particularly the broad 'definition' in s 74, fall well short of the ideal. Too many issues are left to interpretation, risking not only inconsistent decisions but also the infiltration of old stereotypes which are at odds with the Act's aims. Thus the Act fails to give any signposts in relation to three obvious types of case—those involving intoxication,

---

[306] Cf. the terms of the presumption in s. 75(2), discussed in section 8.5(h) above.

[307] This was applied to kidnapping with intent to commit a sex offence in *Royle* [2005] 2 Cr App R (S) 480.

[308] Previously s. 9 of the Theft Act 1968 covered entry as a trespasser with intent to commit rape, whereas the new crime applies to any sexual offence.

[309] For detailed treatment of these and other offences in the Act, see Rook and Ward, *Sexual Offences: Law and Practice*.

[310] Discussed in relation to the *Brown/Laskey* decision in part 8.3(f) of this Chapter.

or non-fundamental deceptions, or non-violent threats. Moreover, the repeal of the former offences of obtaining sex by deception or by threats places even more strain on the general definition of consent and its four opaque elements (freedom, choice, agreement and capacity).[311]

As for the protection of the vulnerable, in part 8.6 above we noted the many new offences protecting children, young people aged 16 and 17 (often referred to in the Act as children), and the mentally disordered. Unfortunately, as also observed above, the Act goes too far in the direction of criminalizing members of these very groups, especially children. Almost all the child offences, and particularly the most serious ones in ss 5–8, apply to young defendants as much as to adults. The injustice to which this can lead is demonstrated by the events and the outcome in *G.*,[312] which fails to give adequate protection to D's human rights. This underlines the inadequacy of the Government's assurances that no children will be prosecuted unless there is coercion or some other untoward feature of the case. Reliance on prosecutorial discretion is insufficient protection of accused children's Article 8 rights under the Convention—making teenagers liable to conviction for normal consensual activities also abridges their sexual autonomy—and the actual guidelines of the Crown Prosecution Service are relatively flexible too. Much more effort should be made, as in other jurisdictions, to give statutory protection to young defendants by means of higher minimum ages or age-gaps.

Related to this reliance on prosecutorial discretion is the reluctance of policy-makers and parliamentary counsel to try to capture the core of the wrongs, resulting in offence definitions that are overly broad. CPS guidance states that sexual activity between teenagers will not be prosecuted unless there is coercion, deception or other untoward circumstances: why cannot something along those lines be put into the statute? The answer may be that it is difficult to prove. And yet in other sections, such as 11, 12, 18 and 19, a person may not be convicted unless the prosecution proves that the acts were done 'for the purpose of sexual gratification'—a requirement that goes to the core of the wrong, and may well be difficult to prove, but which is (rightly) included in the Act.[313]

A further point about autonomy concerns the use of objective standards and strict liability in the Act. It was argued in Chapter 5.4 and 5.5 above that respect for individual autonomy militates in favour of subjective tests for criminal liability (intention, knowledge), and against strict liability, save perhaps in respect of minor offences with low penalties. The Sexual Offences Act 2003 is probably the first major statute to introduce widespread negligence liability for serious offences carrying

---

[311] The Government appears content with the statutory definition as construed by the courts in decisions such as *Bree*: see Office for Criminal Justice Reform, *Convicting Rapists and Protecting Victims: Justice for Victims of Rape* (2006) and *Convicting Rapists and Protecting Victims: Response to Consultation* (2007).

[312] Above, n 284 and text.

[313] The same point may be made about the laudable effort, in ss. 14 and 73, to define the circumstances in which people who are acting in order to protect a child are exempted from liability—rather than leaving it to prosecutorial discretion.

life imprisonment, or 14 or 10 years' imprisonment, in the requirement that 'A does not reasonably believe that B consents'. Is this a justifiable derogation from the subjective principle? It has been argued above and in previous editions that this is justifiable, because of the physical proximity of the parties in these offences and the important values (notably the sexual autonomy of both parties) that ought to be known to be at stake. Does that also justify strict liability as to age when the child is under 13, as ss 5–12 provide? This is much more difficult to justify, particularly for young defendants. Perhaps it was thought too favourable to defendants to adopt a 'reasonable belief' requirement here too, since it is much easier to feign ignorance or mistake in these cases. But that is an assertion that is little tested. The House of Lords' declamations about the 'constitutional principle' of requiring subjective belief[314] may have been unconvincing in their precise application to sexual cases, but the case for requiring reasonable belief on the question of age, as with consent, is much stronger.

Both the Sex Offences Review and the Government made much of the Act's aim of introducing greater clarity into sexual offences law, particularly (as noted in part 8.5(c) above) in respect of consent to sexual activity. Maximum certainty is one aspect of the principle of legality, as we saw in Chapter 3.4(i) above, and serves to protect rule-of-law values for defendants, victims and courts. Unfortunately there are serious doubts about whether the Act goes as far towards achievement of this aim as it should.[315] It is not merely a question of prolix drafting, overlapping offences and reliance on prosecutorial discretion. Key terms such as 'consent' and 'sexual' are not satisfactorily defined, leaving the possibility (which the research of Finch and Munro tends to strengthen)[316] that different juries and magistrates may interpret them differently and that old stereotypes will continue to exert an influence. In a statute with high maximum penalties which undoubtedly takes sexual offending seriously, this is one of several unfortunate shortcomings. The Home Office's 'stock-take' of the Act came before some of the problems indicated above were properly manifest, and even then it was commented that many of the changes in the law could not produce increased conviction rates unless 'stereotypes and myths surrounding rape' are addressed and changed.[317] Thus, even if the definitions and drafting cannot be improved[318]—and that is highly doubtful—steps should be taken to incorporate into model directions some warnings against the use of sexual stereotypes in decisions about consent and reasonable belief.[319] Yet to make significant inroads into

---

[314] In B v DPP and K, discussed in Ch 5.5(a) above.

[315] See C. Elliott and C. de Than, 'The Case for a Rational Reconstruction of Consent in Criminal Law' (2007) 70 MLR 225.

[316] Above, n 260 and text.

[317] Home Office, *Sexual Offences Act 2003: a stocktake of the effectiveness of the Act since its implementation* (2006), paras. 45–6; see also Criminal Justice System, *Convicting Rapists and Protecting Victims— Justice for Victims of Rape* (2007).

[318] For a proposal for radical re-structuring, see V. Tadros, 'Rape without Consent' (2006) 26 OJLS 515.

[319] See further Temkin and Krahé, chs 2, 8 and 9.

the disparities between the attrition rape in rape cases and other crimes, not only is procedural reform likely to be as effective as reforming the substantive law, but changing public attitudes seems to be necessary in order to make any progress at all. Education in its widest sense seems necessary in order to reduce the effect of sexual stereotypes.[320]

FURTHER READING

NON-FATAL OFFENCES

Home Office, *Violence: Reforming the Offences against the Person Act 1861* (1998).

J. GARDNER, 'Rationality and the Rule of Law in Offences against the Person', in J. Gardner, *Offences and Defences* (2007), ch.2.

J. HORDER, 'Reconsidering Psychic Assault' [1998] Crim LR 392.

P. ROBERTS, 'Consent in the Criminal Law' (1997) 17 OJLS 389.

C. ERIN, 'The Rightful Domain of the Criminal Law', in C. Erin and S. Ost (eds), *The Criminal Justice System and Health Care* (2007), ch 14.

SEXUAL OFFENCES

N. LACEY, *Unspeakable Subjects* (1997), ch 4.

J. GARDNER and S. SHUTE, 'The Wrongness of Rape', in J. Gardner, *Offences and Defences* (2007), ch 1.

P. WESTEN, 'Some Common Confusions about Consent in Rape Cases', (2004) 2 Ohio St. LJ 333.

V. TADROS, 'Rape without Consent' (2006) 26 *OJLS* 515.

J. TEMKIN and A. ASHWORTH, 'Rape, Sexual Assaults and the Problems of Consent' [2004] Crim LR 328.

J. R. SPENCER, 'Child and Family Offences' [2004] Crim LR 347.

E. FINCH and V. MUNRO, 'Breaking Boundaries? Sexual consent in the jury room' (2006) 26 LS 303.

---

[320] Ibid., ch 10.

9

OFFENCES OF DISHONESTY

9.1 INTRODUCTION

The principal statutes in this part of the criminal law are the Theft Act 1968 and the Fraud Act 2006. The principal offence in the former statute is referred to as theft or stealing. These terms seem to convey the idea of permanently taking another's property, but in fact the definitions in the Theft Act extend the notion of stealing to a wide variety of dishonest violations of another's property rights. The Theft Act shifted the emphasis of the offence from protecting possession to protecting ownership, and also encompassed a much wider range of property rights than the old law of larceny.[1] Now it is more a question of infringing another's property rights than of taking property. There is no requirement that D should have permanently deprived V of the property, although it must be proved that D *intended* to do so. D's conduct does not have to amount to a potential destruction of V's ability to use the property or act as owner: on the contrary, the courts have held that the merest interference with any right of an owner may suffice, so long as it is accompanied by dishonesty and an intention permanently to deprive. One might therefore say that in broad terms these are crimes of dishonesty rather than property crimes as such. The Fraud Act 2006 is even more wide-ranging: the broad concept of dishonesty is at its core, and its principal offence consists of making a false representation, intending thereby to make a gain or cause a loss. Thus this and the other main offences are inchoate in nature, penalizing the making of the false representation rather than any obtaining of property.

---

[1] For discussion see A. T. H. Smith, *Property Offences* (1994), 1–17.

The great variety of offences of dishonesty, and the breadth of their definitions, raises problems of proportionality and the proper limits of the criminal sanction. The proportionality issues revolve partly round the problem of deciding what concept of property rights should be employed (discussed in the next paragraph) and partly round the prevalence of 'white-collar crime'.[2] For many years there has been criminological interest in the notion of 'white-collar crime', particularly deprivations of property perpetrated in commercial settings, but this has not really been reflected by changes in the law or in enforcement practice. The police have traditionally concerned themselves more with stealing from shops and burglary than with embezzlement and the various forms of frauds upon and by companies. And, although the modernization of property offences achieved by the Theft Act 1968 did have the effect of freeing the law from such constricting notions as thieves having to 'take and carry away' property in order to be convicted, the Act provides little indication of a determination to treat white-collar offences as equivalent to other forms of theft: only ss 17 and 19, on false accounting and on false statements by company directors, point in this direction. It is true that the 1980s saw the creation of several new offences in the spheres of white-collar crime and 'city fraud', but these offences remain outside the Theft Acts and the proposed Criminal Code,[3] making it difficult to claim that they have been integrated into a new scheme of property offences which achieves a realistic proportionality among the degrees of offending. The enactment of the Fraud Act 2006 is significant in extending further into the realm of 'white-collar crime', but the Companies Acts, Financial Services and Management Act, and other legislation are still regarded as 'regulatory' in nature, despite the indictable offences they contain, and despite some maximum penalties (e.g. seven years for misleading statements or practices contrary to s 397 of the Financial Services and Markets Act 2000, and for fraudulent inducement to make a deposit contrary to s 35 of the Banking Act 1987) which are the same as for theft[4] and only slightly less than the maximum for fraud (ten years' imprisonment). This chapter's discussion of the 'traditional' property offences will attempt to keep the 'new' offences of dishonesty well in sight.

The idea of dishonesty, explored in the context of the crime of theft below (see section 9.2(e)), seems to be the notion which binds these offences together. But they are also often grouped together as 'property offences', since they involve some violation of the property rights of another. Personal property is one of the basic organizing features of many modern societies, and it may be defended as an institution on grounds of individual autonomy and rights.[5] Individuals should generally be free to decide how to spend their money; if they choose to purchase property with it, this

---

[2] See e.g. E. H. Sutherland, *White Collar Crime* (1949); M. Levi, *Regulating Fraud: White Collar Crime and the Criminal Process* (1987); H. Croall, *White Collar Crime* (1992); D. Nelken, 'White-Collar Crime', in M. Maguire, R. Morgan, and R. Reiner (eds.), *The Oxford Handbook of Criminology* (4th edn., 2007); S. P. Green, *Lying, Cheating and Stealing: a Moral Theory of White-Collar Crime* (2006).

[3] See Law Com No. 177, cll. 139–177, which cover only the offences under the Theft Act and forgery.

[4] S. 26(1) of the Criminal Justice Act 1991 reduced the maximum for theft from ten to seven years.

[5] See e.g. J. W. Harris, *Property and Justice* (1996).

should be respected in the same way as their own physical integrity. This liberal political philosophy does not exclude the compulsory payment of taxes, and the approach should therefore find room for the notion of state property—property in public ownership, which no individual citizen is free to take for his or her exclusive use. So, the foundation of these property or dishonesty offences is that it is wrong for any person to take more than his or her rightful share—'rightful' being interpreted in the light of legally ordained methods of property distribution (including, at present, such things as earned income, inherited wealth, public funds derived from taxation, state benefits paid to certain citizens, etc.). We return, in parts 9.2(a) and 9.2(e) below, to the question whether these are essentially property offences or dishonesty offences. Simester and Sullivan, who strongly believe that they should be cast as property offences, argue that by penalizing theft 'the criminal law both protects individuals from any particular loss they may suffer and safeguards the regime of property law more generally'.[6] This may be true, but it should not be taken to establish that there are two distinct wrongs in each crime of theft, any more than there are in any other type of crime.

How serious, relatively speaking, are theft and kindred offences? There has long been an allegation that English criminal law is too concerned with property offences—at the expense of offences against the person and against the environment. This cannot be more than a general allegation, since it is easy to construct a comparison between theft of some vital and valuable item of property and a minor assault. In broad terms, however, two points should be made about the proposition that property offences are treated too seriously. First, the allegation may concern enforcement as much as the written laws. The police investigate and prosecute relatively fewer crimes within business and commercial circles. This may, in turn, be because offences are dealt with informally in other ways, by dismissing an employee who has been caught committing an offence, for example.[7] In the 1980s the Serious Fraud Office (SFO) was created as part of a stated determination to pursue commercial frauds more vigorously.[8] The SFO's criteria for accepting a case for investigation are that it involves £1 million or more, that it has significant international dimensions, that widespread public concern is likely, that investigation requires highly specialized knowledge, or that the SFO's special powers are likely to be necessary.[9] The Crown Prosecution Service handles many other fraud cases. The Department of Trade and Industry also investigates and prosecutes some offences relating to the financial markets, including the crime of 'insider dealing' in shares.

Significant as these developments may be, they are on such a comparatively small scale that they do little to redress the imbalance in law enforcement between 'crime in the streets' and 'crime in the suites'. Secondly, there is the question whether the

---

[6] A. P. Simester and G. R. Sullivan, 'The Nature and Rationale of Property Offences', in R. A. Duff and S. P. Green (eds.), *Defining Crimes* (2005), 172.

[7] See Levi, *Regulating Fraud*, and 'Suite Revenge' (2009) 49 B J Crim 1.

[8] J. Wood, 'The Serious Fraud Office' [1989] Crim LR 175; G. Staple, 'Serious and Complex Fraud: a New Perspective' (1993) 56 MLR 127.

[9] See <www.sfo.gov.uk>.

threshold of the criminal law is lower in property offences than elsewhere. Civil law has a far greater involvement in offences of dishonesty than in violent or sexual offences; the very questions of property ownership and property rights are the subject of a complicated mass of rules relating to contracts, trusts, intellectual property, restitution, and so forth. Many property losses could be tackled through the civil courts, by suing under one of these heads of civil law. It may be true that the amounts concerned are often too small to justify the time and expense of civil proceedings, but should that not make us pause to consider whether the criminal sanction is being properly deployed here, and whether adequate weight is being given to the policy of minimum criminalization discussed in Chapter 2.4(b)? If the criminal law is to be reserved for significant challenges to the legal order, should there not be vigilance about the extension of the criminal sanction into spheres in which civil remedies exist, or where some non-criminal procedures might be more proportionate? Is it not true that many dishonest dealings which amount to criminal offences are in practice the subject of nothing more than regulatory action or civil penalties, from commercial frauds to income tax frauds? How, then, can one justify prosecuting ordinary people for the relatively petty thefts that are the everyday business of the criminal courts? These are questions to which we will return at the end of this chapter.

Attention should also be drawn at this introductory stage to the respective roles of the legislature and the courts in property crimes. Parliament has, through the Theft Act 1968 and the Fraud Act 2006, provided some fairly broad offences. The appellate courts have, in dealing with appeals, developed the law in ways which often extend the ambit of already wide offences in order to criminalize persons whose conduct seems wrongful. Although the decisions have not been all one way, there is much evidence here of the relative impotence of the principle of maximum certainty in relation to legislators and of the principle of strict construction in relation to judges.[10]

9.2 THE OFFENCE OF THEFT[11]

Theft is not the most serious of the English offences against property, but it must be discussed first, because it is an ingredient of some more serious offences, notably robbery and burglary. The offence of theft, contrary to s 1 of the Theft Act 1968, may be divided into five elements. The three conduct elements are that there must be: (i) an appropriation; of (ii) property; which (iii) belongs to another. The fault elements are that this must be done: (iv) with an intention of permanent deprivation; and (v) dishonestly. The essence of stealing is the violation of another's property rights; unlike fraud, it does not require a particular wrongful method of achieving this.[12]

---

[10] See the examples given above, Ch 3.5(i) and (k).

[11] The classic study is that of A. T. H. Smith on *Property Offences* (see n 1 above); substantially more up-to-date is *Smith's Law of Theft* (9th edn., 2007, by D. Ormerod and D. H. Williams).

[12] See Green, *Lying, Cheating and Stealing*, ch 6.

Discussion of each of the five elements in turn will demonstrate just how extensive the English law of theft is in some directions, and how restrictive in other directions.

(a) APPROPRIATION

Before the Theft Act 1968, English law used to require proof that D had taken and carried away the property, a requirement far too stringent for some types of property (e.g. bank balances), and yet a requirement which at least ensured that certain overt physical acts had to be established before conviction. The Theft Act broadened the law's basis by requiring merely an appropriation. In most cases this will involve taking possession of someone else's property without consent. Section 3(1) of the Act begins by defining an appropriation as 'any assumption by a person of the rights of an owner', and then extends the concept to cover a case where D has come by the property without stealing it and where D subsequently assumes 'a right to it by keeping or dealing with it as owner'. This includes cases where D finds property which he does not initially intend to keep (perhaps intending to report the finding), but later decides to do so. Thus the wording of s 3(1) implies that a simple change of mind, unaccompanied by any overt act, constitutes appropriation. Put another way, the mere omission to return the goods or to report the finding constitutes (together with the change of mind) the keeping which amounts to an appropriation. This is a dramatic demonstration of how far the law has retreated from the requirement of 'taking and carrying away' which characterized the previous law, and of how little is required in order to constitute the conduct element of theft. It also raises questions about the justification for this omissions liability, and whether citizens have fair warning of it.

Let us explore the ambit of appropriation by returning to the main defining words, 'any assumption of the rights of an owner'. Does this mean that one can appropriate property even if one obtains it with the consent of the owner? On the face of it, this might seem absurd: surely there cannot be any stealing of property if the owner consents to part with it. But the House of Lords has pointed out that the definition of theft does not include the phrase 'without the consent of the owner', as did the previous offence; and in *Lawrence* (1972)[13] it held that a taking can amount to theft, even though the owner consents. The facts in that case were that V, an Italian who spoke little English, arrived in England and wished to hire a taxi to take him to an address in London. He offered D, the taxi-driver, enough money to cover the lawful fare, but D asked for more and, as V held his wallet open, D took more notes from it. The defence argued strenuously that this could not be theft because V consented to D taking the extra money, but the House of Lords held this irrelevant. The definition of theft does not expressly *require* the taking to be without the owner's consent, and the House of Lords held that the term 'appropriates' does not imply an absence of consent. Thus D had appropriated V's property dishonestly and with the intention of depriving V permanently of it. This decision has given rise to much controversy and to diverse

---

[13] [1972] AC 626.

interpretations.[14] One technical question is whether the money still belonged to V when D took it from V's wallet: if it was V's intention that ownership should pass to D, maybe the second element in theft was missing. But perhaps the most regrettable fact is that D was prosecuted for theft at all, since the case seems to be an obvious example of fraud (formerly, obtaining by deception). An English appeal court cannot alter the charge, or order a retrial on the different charge, and so the choice lay between quashing the conviction of a manifestly dishonest person and doing 'rough justice' at the risk of destabilizing the law of theft. The courts preferred the latter course to the former.

Apparently inconsistent with *Lawrence* was the later decision in *Morris* (1984).[15] The essence of the two cases consolidated in the appeal was that D took goods from a supermarket shelf, replaced their existing price-labels with labels showing lower prices, and then took them to the checkout, intending to buy them at the lower price. As in *Lawrence*, the cases proceeded on theft charges rather than on obtaining or attempting to obtain by deception. The House of Lords upheld the convictions, but propounded a more restrictive idea of appropriation. Lord Roskill stated that the concept of appropriation involves 'an act by way of adverse interference with or usurpation of' the owner's rights, and that this will generally require D to have committed some unauthorized act. This was clearly fulfilled in *Morris*, since the attaching of price-labels by customers is unauthorized. However, if the case had proceeded on the *Lawrence* basis that consent is irrelevant, the customers would have been held to have appropriated the goods as soon as they took hold of them, and before tampering with the price-labels.

The conflict between these two decisions was resolved by the House of Lords in *Gomez* (1993).[16] D, an employee at an electrical store, persuaded his manager to sell goods to a friend in exchange for cheques which he knew to be worthless. As in the two previous cases (and several others over the years), facts which obviously supported a charge of obtaining property by deception (now, fraud) resulted in a prosecution for theft. The House of Lords, by a majority, preferred *Lawrence* to *Morris* on the ground that the remarks on appropriation in the latter were *obiter dicta* whereas in the former they were part of the *ratio decidendi*. Not only did the House of Lords therefore hold that whether the act was done with the owner's consent or authority is immaterial, but they also stated this as a general proposition on 'appropriation', not confined to cases in which there is an element of deception.

The result of *Gomez* is that the offence of theft is now astoundingly wide. Any act in relation to property belonging to another constitutes an appropriation of that property, and liability for theft then turns on the presence of dishonesty and of an intention permanently to deprive the owner. The breadth of this test is emphasized by one dictum from *Morris* that was incorporated into the *Gomez* formulation: that 'the

---

[14] See especially G. Williams, 'Theft, Consent and Illegality' [1977] Crim LR 127.

[15] [1984] AC 320.

[16] [1993] AC 442; for analysis of this and other decisions, see A. Halpin, *Definition in the Criminal Law* (2004), 166–86.

assumption of *any* of the rights of an owner in property amounts to an appropriation of the property'.[17] Thus all that D needs to do is to assume any one right of an owner, and the conduct element in theft is complete. A customer who touches a tin of beans in a supermarket has appropriated them, even though the owners of the supermarket are quite content for customers to take goods from the shelves and even to replace them later, provided that when they reach the checkout they pay for the goods that are to be taken away.[18]

The breadth of the *Gomez* test has been confirmed (and, some argue, further extended) in a series of decisions on the receipt of 'gifts'. In *Mazo* (1997)[19] D had received substantial gifts from her employer, an elderly woman whose mental state was apparently deteriorating: the Court of Appeal quashed the conviction and stated that a person cannot be guilty of theft of property received as a valid gift. In *Kendrick and Hopkins* (1997)[20] that proposition was doubted, and the convictions were upheld where defendants who organized the affairs of a confused woman secured several payments to themselves, ostensibly for their services to her. In *Hinks* (2001)[21] D received substantial gifts from a man of limited intelligence whom she had befriended. The House of Lords held, by a majority of three to two, that the conviction of theft should be upheld. It does not matter that there was a valid gift of the property according to the civil law: if D had appropriated the property dishonestly, a conviction for theft may follow.[22] One advantage of the *Hinks* decision is the practical benefit of simplicity, since there is no need to instruct juries on the intricacies of the civil law. However, many critics of the decision are concerned that it brings the criminal law and civil law into conflict, and it is said to be absurd that a person can be convicted of a criminal offence on the basis of what was, according to the law of personal property, the receipt of a perfectly valid gift.[23] But the absurdity reduces to vanishing point if three further points are taken into account. First, the civil law and criminal law may be pursuing different purposes: no contradiction exists, Simon Gardner argues, because 'the civil law is rightly concerned to respect established property rights, even if unsatisfactorily acquired, whilst the criminal law rightly concentrates on penalizing the unsatisfactory manner of acquisition'.[24] Secondly, it could be argued that *Hinks* supports the institution of property by criminalizing those who indirectly threaten the system of property rights by committing a wrong against another,[25] the wrong residing in the dishonest behaviour and the potential harm being further instances of similar conduct. Thirdly, to what extent was the transfer in *Hinks* truly consensual? It can be argued that the criminal law is protecting the vulnerable against exploitation

---

[17] [1984] AC 320, *per* Lord Roskill at 332.

[18] The Court of Appeal in *Gallasso* (1994) 98 Cr App R 284 held that there is only an appropriation if there is a 'taking', but this goes against the preponderance of authority: see *Smith's Law of Theft*, 26–7.

[19] [1997] 2 Cr App R 518.   [20] [1997] 2 Cr App R 524.   [21] [2001] 2 AC 241.

[22] *Hinks* was followed by the Privy Council in *Wheatley* v *Commissioner of Police of the British Virgin Islands* [2006] 1 WLR 1683.

[23] E.g. J. C. Smith in [2001] Crim LR 162; J. Beatson and A. P. Simester in (1999) 115 LQR 372.

[24] S. Gardner, 'Property and Theft' [1998] Crim LR 35, at 42.

[25] S. Shute, 'Appropriation and the Law of Theft' [2002] Crim LR 445.

by penalizing dishonest transactions of this kind, and that it is a separate concern that the civil law fails to accomplish this properly.[26]

A number of other questions arise about the ambit of appropriation, some affected by *Gomez*, others not. First, is appropriation an instantaneous or a continuing act? There is no definite answer, but if the question itself is analysed a plausible answer may be found. The question is not whether the appropriation continues throughout the time when the thief is in possession of the property, and whenever he uses it. That is implausible. The question ought to be whether appropriation is complete as soon as D does an act in relation to the property and, if so, whether it can also be said that the appropriation continues throughout the period when D is engaged on that act. It follows from *Gomez* that D could be convicted of theft on the basis of his first act (e.g. seizing a victim's jewellery, getting into a car hired to him). Is it then inconsistent to hold that the appropriation continues whilst D is engaged on that particular piece of conduct (e.g. whilst D is in the victim's house after seizing the jewellery, whilst D is driving the car hired to him)? There is authority to support the view that appropriation does continue throughout the act or 'transaction',[27] not being exhausted by the first act in relation to the property, and this corresponds with the law relating to the conduct element in rape.[28]

Connected with this is a second point about the time factor in appropriation. The result of *Gomez* and *Hinks* is that a person appropriates property even if the owner's consent is given, yet it remains necessary to establish that the appropriation was of 'property belonging to another' (see the further discussion in (c) below). It seems that the *Gomez–Hinks* position is that at the moment when D appropriates it, or immediately before, the money still belongs to the donor.[29] What of the case where D goes to a restaurant, orders food, and eats it before payment? What if D goes to a petrol station and fills up with petrol? In both cases the owner intends ownership of the food or petrol to pass to D. However, ownership has passed by the time D finishes eating or filling the tank with petrol, and the relevant act of appropriation has taken place. If, therefore, D then decides to leave without paying for the food or petrol, there can be no conviction of theft because the appropriation has ceased before the dishonest intention was conceived.[30] A court might hold that the act or 'transaction' should be construed so as to include paying for the property, so that the dishonest intent would be contemporaneous with the appropriation, but since D did not pay either the restaurant or the petrol station this argument would be based on hypothetical rather than real facts.

---

[26] See the carefully argued article by A. Bogg and J. Stanton-Ife, 'Protecting the Vulnerable: Legality, Harm and Theft' (2003) 23 Legal Studies 402.

[27] *Hale* (1979) 68 Cr App R 415 (below, section 9.3); *Atakpu and Abrahams* (1994) 98 Cr App R 254; *Smith's Law of Theft*, 51–2.

[28] S. 79(2) Sexual Offences Act 2003, discussed in Ch 8.5(a) above.

[29] R. Heaton, 'Deceiving without Thieving?' [2001] Crim LR 712, arguing that there may still be some instances where an obtaining by deception does not amount to theft after *Gomez*; cf. now the Fraud Act 2006, below, Ch 9.8.

[30] *Edwards v Ddin* (1976) 63 Cr App R 218, *Corcoran v Whent* [1977] Crim LR 52.

A third, related point is that the act which constitutes the appropriation does not need to be the act which is intended to deprive the owner permanently. The act of appropriation need only be an act done in relation to the property: so long as it was done with the dishonest intent required, theft has been committed at that point. It does not matter that D's act of swapping the price-labels on two items was part of a plan to offer the higher-priced goods to the cashier with the lower price-label on them, and that that plan had not been executed. *Morris*[31] holds that D does not have to intend permanent deprivation by the act of appropriation; he may intend to deprive by some act in the future. This confirms that the offence of theft in English law criminalizes people at a much earlier point than they would generally suppose. A stark example is provided by *Chan Man-Sin* v *Attorney-General for Hong Kong* (1988),[32] where D wrote unauthorized cheques on his employers' accounts. It was argued that this was not an appropriation since, when the bank discovered that the cheques were forged, it would have to make good the companies' accounts. The Privy Council upheld the theft conviction, stating that D had assumed a right of the owner and that it is not necessary to show that the appropriation would be 'legally efficacious'. The decision penalizes dishonesty, but reduces appropriation to a will o' the wisp.[33]

In exploring the concept of appropriation, the phrase 'act in relation to the property' has been used above. We have already noted that an omission (or, at least, a private decision) can suffice, as in the case of a person who finds property and subsequently decides to keep it: section 3(1). What is the minimum conduct that might suffice? In *Pitham and Hehl* (1976)[34] it was held that a person who went to the house of a man who was in prison and offered to sell that man's furniture to the two defendants had thereby appropriated the furniture: he 'showed them the property and invited them to buy what they wanted'. The Court of Appeal held that it was clear that this amounted to 'assuming the rights of the owner', untroubled by the fact that no hands may have been laid on the furniture. Although there were undoubtedly better ways of framing the charge in this case, it may be said after *Gomez* that the person who offered to sell the furniture was assuming *a* right of the owner. However, in *Briggs* (2004)[35] the Court of Appeal held that there was no sufficient act of appropriation where D ensured that conveyancers transferred to her the proceeds of the sale of a house belonging to two elderly relatives. The case was properly one of fraud, since D had obtained the relatives' consent by deception, but one of the charges was theft and the Court held that appropriation requires a physical act rather than merely ordering another to transfer a credit balance in her favour. The decision in *Gomez*, which would support the opposite conclusion, was not discussed.

Before re-assessing the concept of appropriation, mention should be made of the exception in s 3(2) of the Theft Act. If a person acquires property for value in good faith, no later assumption of the rights D believed he had acquired can amount to an

---

[31] [1984] AC 320. [32] (1988) 86 Cr App R 303.
[33] See the criticism by A. T. H. Smith, *Property Offences*, 162. [34] (1977) 65 Cr App R 45.
[35] [2004] 1 Cr App R 34.

appropriation, even if D then knows that he has not acquired good title. This applies when D keeps the goods or gives them away, but if D sells them and represents expressly or impliedly that he has the title to do so, he will commit the offence of fraud.[36]

Leaving aside this exception, what is the ambit of appropriation? As a result of *Gomez*,[37] any act in relation to property that can be said to assume a right of the owner of the property constitutes appropriation, and the consent of the owner is irrelevant. Courts view this as an 'objective' factual question, but it is arguable that the notion of appropriation (as developed) includes an element of 'proprietary subjectivity', i.e. that a mental act of proprietorship helps to mark the distinction between appropriations and non-appropriations.[38] Nonetheless, the notion of appropriation is now considerably more expansive than its framers could have anticipated, and it can be criticized in four ways. First, the definition is not faithful to the intentions of the Criminal Law Revision Committee or of Parliament. That the CLRC intended the concept of appropriation to cover only unauthorized acts is set out plainly in the dissenting speech of Lord Lowry in *Gomez*. A person can now be guilty of theft even though the transaction was effective in passing ownership to D.[39] As a matter of statutory interpretation the decision of the majority of the House of Lords in *Gomez* is untenable; but it is the law, and the House of Lords in *Hinks* applied it not only to cases where the transfer of property was voidable but also to cases of valid gift.

A second and related criticism is that the new definition violates the principle of fair labelling by lumping together thieves and swindlers. One effect of *Gomez* is that many cases of fraud (formerly, obtaining property by deception) are also cases of theft, except those relating to land.[40] Once again this contradicts the intentions of the CLRC and Parliament: 'obtaining by false pretences is ordinarily thought of as different from theft.... To create a new offence of theft to include conduct which ordinary people would find difficult to regard as theft would be a mistake.'[41] The distinction between the two kinds of conduct is morally relevant: there are situations in which one would think differently of a thief and of a swindler,[42] and the law ought to attach different labels to people who violate property rights in such different ways. This is particularly so in view of the difference in maximum penalties between fraud (ten years) and theft (now seven years).

Thirdly, the *Gomez* definition is so broad that it exhibits no respect for the principle of maximum certainty and, by making conduct criminal when it would not even amount to a civil wrong, fails to give fair warning to citizens about the boundaries of the law of theft. For example, there is no civil wrong involved in eating a

---

[36] See below, Ch 9.8.   [37] [1993] AC 442.

[38] See E. Melissaris, 'The Concept of Appropriation and the Offence of Theft' (2007) 70 MLR 581, although somewhat reliant on *Gallasso* (above, n. 00).

[39] Cf. *Kaur v Chief Constable of Hampshire* [1981] 1 WLR 578.

[40] Cf. Heaton, 'Deceiving without Thieving', for a few contrary possibilities.

[41] CLRC, *Theft (General)* (1965), para. 38.

[42] S. Shute and J. Horder, 'Thieving and Deceiving: What is the Difference?' (1993) 56 MLR 548; C. M. V. Clarkson, 'Theft and Fair Labelling' (1993) 56 MLR 554.

restaurant meal or filling a car's tank with petrol before paying, but both acts amount to appropriation and, if accompanied by a dishonest intent at the time, may result in a conviction for theft.[43] Persuading someone to make a substantial gift in one's favour may lead to a valid gift at civil law, and yet receipt of the gift may constitute appropriation. The point about fair warning might be thought to be overdone: after all, a person who acts dishonestly takes the risk that the conduct will be held to be criminal. But that is an unsatisfactory basis for the criminal law. In everyday life, in business, and in financial dealings, there is often a fine line between unlawful dishonesty and merely exploiting gaps in the law—in taxation matters, this is expressed as the distinction between evasion and avoidance.[44] Whilst it is often impossible to frame a criminal provision precisely, without excluding a number of cases that ought to be included and without rendering the law unintelligible, the result of *Gomez* is that the law of theft incorporates no attempt at precision at all. The appropriation need not be a civil wrong, or involve an unauthorized act, or be an overt act, etc.: in effect, any dishonest acquisition can amount to theft. Appropriation is effectively removed from the equation in most cases: the whole weight falls on the concept of dishonesty,[45] discussed and criticized in subsection (e) below.

A fourth and related criticism is that the judicial approach severely reduces the amount of manifest criminality in the offence of theft.[46] In other words, liability is imposed for conduct that is not manifestly theftuous: s 3 of the Theft Act 1968 contains elements of this, in its reference to a later assumption of rights by a finder of property, but the three House of Lords decisions (*Lawrence, Morris, Gomez*) take it much further by labelling as a thief any person who assumes a right of the owner in respect of another's property, with or without that other's consent, provided that the two fault elements (dishonesty, intention to deprive permanently) can be proved. Some would say that this proviso is sufficient to rebut the criticism, since the dishonest intent should be the key factor. But this raises questions about the ambit of the criminal law: quite apart from the fact that it may exceed the ambit of the civil law here, the offence of theft now has the breadth and the characteristics of an inchoate offence, and yet it is extended further by the crime of attempted theft. The result is an extremely wide conduct element, not distinguished from ordinary honest transactions save by the intent.

This fourth criticism is an argument against the judicial expansion of the conduct element in theft, rather than against the assimilation of deception to theft achieved in *Gomez* itself. The two points are treated differently by Peter Glazebrook, who applauds *Gomez* on the grounds that:

Holding swindlers to be thieves does no injustice, will save much inconvenience in cases where it transpires only late in the day that a crook has resorted to deception, and avoids

---

[43] Cf. the lesser offence of making off without payment, mentioned in section 9.8(f) below.

[44] See Green, *Lying, Cheating and Stealing*, 243–5.

[45] Shute, 'Appropriation and the Law of Theft', 452–3.

[46] M. Giles and S. Uglow, 'Appropriation and Manifest Criminality in Theft' (1992) 56 J Crim Law 179, adapting G. Fletcher, *Rethinking Criminal Law* (1978).

the extreme absurdity of denying the name of thief to those who misappropriate property received as a result of a mistake that they have induced while according it to those who had done nothing to bring about the mistaken transfer: Theft Act 1968, section 5(4).[47]

The point about s 5(4), which is discussed in subsection (c) below, is that no absolutely satisfactory line can be drawn between theft and fraud in all instances. But that does not establish the folly of making the effort to draw that distinction in many other clear cases. Holding swindlers to be thieves obscures a clear category difference in many cases. What has exercized the judges, particularly in appellate courts, has been the prospect of quashing a theft conviction simply because the police and the Crown Prosecution Service have alleged the wrong offence. This is largely a procedural error: it ought to be remediable by procedural means either at the trial or on appeal, rather than being allowed to distort the development of the law.

   Whilst procedural change is needed to avoid the acquittal of swindlers simply because they have been wrongly charged as thieves, the substantive definition of theft ought to be reconsidered too. Glazebrook, following Glanville Williams, argues that since theft is an offence of dishonesty 'legal logic requires that the conduct constituting its external elements be unlawful—either tortious, or a breach of trust, or, if the property belongs to a company, a fraud on its creditors or shareholders'.[48] One desirable effect of this definition would be to state clearly that there can be no theft if the owner consented to D dealing with the property as D has done.[49] On the other hand, the arguments in favour of *Hinks* suggest that any reconsideration of the relationship between civil and criminal liability should not assume that the civil law's approach is correct, or that a divergence between the approaches is indefensible.[50] The links with the concept of dishonesty are also close, and we will return to this issue in subsection (e) below.

(b) PROPERTY

In order to be stolen, the object concerned must be 'property' within the meaning of the Theft Act 1968. Section 4(1) appears to be couched in very broad terms: 'property includes money and all other property, real or personal, including things in action and other intangible property.' Thus in certain circumstances, as we shall see in subsection (c) below, D can steal P's bank balance. But there are limits. There is no property capable of being stolen in a dead body or its parts.[51] Nor does electricity fall within the definition of 'property', although s 13 of the Theft Act 1968 provides an offence of dishonestly abstracting electricity. More importantly, there is no property

---

[47] P. R. Glazebrook, 'Revising the Theft Acts' [1993] Camb LJ 191.   [48] Ibid., 192.

[49] For Glazebrook, however, it would be subject to the rider 'unless that consent is obtained by duress or by deceit, that is, tortiously'. This would perpetuate the overlap between theft and fraud, argued against in the text.

[50] See the arguments of S. Gardner and of Shute, discussed on pp 361–2 above.

[51] See the discussion by A. T. H. Smith, *Property Offences*, 46–9.

in confidential information, such as business secrets and examination papers. Thus, if D purloins a confidential document of this kind, photocopies it, and replaces it, he cannot be charged with theft: not only is it difficult to argue that D has an intention to deprive the owner permanently of the information, but what has been taken does not constitute property.[52] Injunctions may be obtained in the civil courts to prevent interference with, or the abuse of, such secrets, but the criminal offence of theft does not extend so far. The problem has become more pertinent with the increasing use of computers as means of storing information: if D 'hacks into' V's computer system, retrieving from it some confidential information which is then noted down, it appears that no 'property' has been stolen. The House of Lords was invited to extend the law of forgery to cover cases of 'hacking' in *Gold and Schifreen* (1988),[53] and its refusal to extend the law in this direction helped to precipitate specific legislation on the subject. The Computer Misuse Act 1990 created three offences of unlawfully entering another's computer system, with dishonest intent.[54] It is right that this form of property violation should be the subject of special provisions: an artificial extension of the present structure of the law of theft to cover such cases, which lie far from the ordinary stealing of tangible property, would probably be less successful and might have unexpected side-effects. It is also right that the law should criminalize this kind of property violation, which might be much more serious financially than many of the takings which fulfil the basic definition of theft. This is one instance in which there was judicial self-restraint and strict construction, in *Gold and Schifreen*, and it was followed by remedial legislative action.[55]

There are further limitations in section 4. In the first place, the general proposition is that land cannot be stolen. There are some exceptions to this, and of course it is quite possible to convict someone of theft of title deeds or of fraud in relation to them, but the land itself, being of a certain permanence, remains. Section 4(3) effectively excludes from the law of theft the picking of mushrooms or of flowers, fruit, or foliage from plants growing wild, unless the picking is 'for reward or for sale or other commercial purpose'. It should be noted that this exception is confined to wild mushrooms, flowers, etc., and that the term 'picking' would seem to exclude a person who digs up a wild plant or cuts down a tree. Section 4(4) provides that a wild creature cannot be stolen, unless it is ordinarily kept in captivity (e.g. at a zoo) or has already been reduced into possession (e.g. game birds already shot and retrieved by a landowner). Much of the conduct thus excluded from the law of theft falls within long-standing offences of poaching.

---

[52] *Oxford v Moss* (1979) 68 Cr App R 183, and generally R. G. Hammond, 'Theft of Information' (1984) 100 LQR 252.

[53] [1988] AC 1063.

[54] M. Wasik, *Crime and the Computer* (1991); A. T. H. Smith, *Property Offences*, ch 11.

[55] See Ch 3.5(k) above.

(c) 'BELONGING TO ANOTHER'

The old law of larceny was concerned mainly to penalize those who took possession of property from those in possession, whereas there are many other ways of depriving a legal owner of property. How far should the law go in criminalizing appropriations of property from persons other than the legal owner? Section 5 of the Theft Act 1968 succeeds in spreading the net wide: property is regarded as belonging 'to any person having possession or control of it, or having in it any proprietary right or interest (not being an equitable interest arising only from an agreement to transfer or grant an interest)'. The first phrase, 'possession or control', may be wide enough to enable D to be convicted of theft of, say, suits from a dry-cleaning shop even though the suits had only been placed there temporarily by their owners. There is no need to establish the precise legal relationship between the possessor and the supposed owner of the goods; for Theft Act purposes, the goods are treated as belonging to the temporary possessor, too. However, if it appears that property has been abandoned by its previous owner or that the previous owner intended to part with her or his entire interest in it, there can be no theft because the property no longer belongs to another.[56] The same should not be true of the proceeds of unknown crimes.[57]

The second phrase of the definition encompasses various situations in which D might regard himself as owner or part owner of the property. Only three years after the enactment of the Theft Act, s 5(1) led the Court of Appeal in *Turner (No. 2)* (1971)[58] to affirm the conviction of a man who had seized his own car back from a garage that had just repaired it. D certainly intended to avoid paying for the repairs, but the question was whether he had appropriated 'property belonging to another'. The Court held that the garage was clearly in 'possession or control' of the car. It was parked outside the garage, and they had a set of keys for it. However, D would only have appropriated property belonging to another if the garage had a lien over the car, and the Court of Appeal held, unsatisfactorily, that the issue of a lien should be disregarded. Section 5(1) certainly provides that one part-owner of property can be convicted of theft from the other part-owner. For example, a business partner who appropriates partnership property in order to deprive the other partner of it may be liable for theft so long as the other elements (notably dishonesty: there must be no claim of right) are present.[59] A controversial question is whether company controllers may be convicted of stealing the property of the company—meaning by 'company controllers' one or more persons who, between them, own the entire share-holding in a company. If D and E (being the sole shareholders) transfer money from the company's account to their personal accounts, it might seem strained to say that

---

[56] *Dyke and Munro* [2002] 1 Cr App R 30 (members of the public intended to part with their entire interest when putting money in a charity collecting box); see also *Wood* [2002] EWCA Crim 832 (D who takes property believing that it has been abandoned does not commit theft).

[57] Cf. *Sullivan and Ballion* [2002] Crim LR 758, where the commentary by J. C. Smith is more notable than the first instance decision reported.

[58] (1971) 55 Cr App R 336.   [59] *Bonner* (1970) 54 Cr App R 257.

the company's property 'belongs to another' when the sole shareholders are the very persons who are doing the appropriating. However, it has been held[60] that such cases may in principle amount to theft because the company is a separate legal entity from its controllers, and this view has been reinforced by the decision in *Gomez* (1993)[61] to the effect that the owner's consent does not prevent an appropriation in law. Thus in this sphere, too, theft liability turns largely on proof of dishonesty. Whether the same applies to transfers of company property by the controllers in order to put it out of the reach of creditors, in circumstances of actual or pending insolvency, remains doubtful.[62]

In view of the gain and of the dishonesty, company cases are surely as proper a concern of the criminal law as shoplifting. Whether they should be classified as theft or fraud, or dealt with under the Companies Act offence of fraudulent trading,[63] bears on such matters as the stigma of conviction (theft may be more stigmatic than a 'breach' of the Companies Act) and the mode of enforcement. Thus there are arguments in favour of criminalization—and against the marginalization of such offences—by placing them within the Theft Act or Fraud Act. Whether the troubled concept of appropriation and the existing definitions within s 5 are adequate to the purpose is doubtful, and legislative amendment seems desirable.

There is also the question whether there is an appropriation of property belonging to another when D acquires part or the whole of P's bank balance. D does not acquire cash from P, but is the recipient of either a credit transfer or a cheque. In *Hilton* (1997)[64] D, an officer of a charity who was a signatory of the charity's bank account, instructed the bank to transfer some of the charity's money to other accounts in order to pay his debts. The Court of Appeal upheld his conviction for theft, on the basis that he appropriated the charity's chose in action (i.e. its right to sue the bank for the relevant money). He did not *obtain* property belonging to another, because what P had before the transaction was the right to sue P's bank for the relevant amount, and P's right is either diminished or extinguished but it is not P's right that is obtained by D but a new and separate right. However, it was accepted that, as a result of *Gomez*, D appropriated (destroyed) the charity's chose in action in respect of that money. It might alternatively be claimed that he appropriated the money itself, because he did an act in relation to that amount which assumes a right of the owner. This would be so if D instructed a particular person at P's bank to make the transfer, or if the transfer were accomplished automatically by the CHAPS process used in modern banking, so long as D initiated the process. The courts have yet to adopt this reasoning.[65] A similar argument can be constructed where D has obtained a cheque from P which D subsequently pays into his account. On the basis of the wide definition in

---

[60] *Attorney-General's Reference (No. 2 of 1982)* [1984] QB 624, and *Philippou* (1989) 89 Cr App R 290.

[61] [1993] AC 442, particularly the speech of Lord Browne-Wilkinson.

[62] Cf. G. R. Sullivan, [1991] Crim LR 929, replying to D. W. Elliott, 'Directors' Thefts and Dishonesty' [1991] Crim LR 732.

[63] Companies Act 1989, s. 41.   [64] [1997] 2 Cr App R 445.

[65] For further discussion, see *Smith's Law of Theft*, 72

Gomez, it can be argued that D appropriates P's bank balance by his act in relation to it, i.e. presenting the cheque drawn on P's account. This analysis assumes that P's account is in credit, but it is no different if P is overdrawn and has an agreement with the bank for an overdraft, since that too is a contractual right against the bank. The conclusion, then, is that D *appropriates* property belonging to another by dealing with it in any of these ways.

The question has arisen also in the context of train tickets. In *Marshall* (1998)[66] D and others collected from travellers on the London Underground tickets that had been used but were still valid, and re-sold them to other travellers. The Court of Appeal, in upholding the convictions, did not address the question whether the tickets were 'property belonging to another', in particular, whether the ticket belonged (in any sense) to London Underground. Instead it decided the case on the ground that there was an intention permanently to deprive London Underground of the tickets, because when they were finally handed in the virtue would have gone out of them. However, as Sir John Smith argued, the prior question is whether the conduct element in theft was made out. To whom did the tickets belong at the relevant time? Much depends on the conditions of issue, and whether they were brought to the travellers' attention, matters not discussed in *Marshall*.

Turning to the other parts of s 5 of the Theft Act, they elucidate, and perhaps extend, the definition of 'belonging to another' in certain ways. Section 5(2) states that when property belongs to a trust, those entitled to enforce the trust should be treated as owners of the property.[67] Section 5(3) expressly includes property received 'from or on account of another' where the person receiving it is under an obligation to the other 'to retain and deal with that property or its proceeds in a particular way'. This applies to the treasurer of a sports club or a holiday fund who holds money on behalf of others. However, it is to be noted that s 5(3) states that the obligation must be 'to the other,' and in *Floyd* v *DPP* (2000)[68] the Divisional Court upheld D's conviction for theft from a Christmas hamper company, in circumstances where money had been collected from work colleagues over several months and where the obligation to deal with the money was evidently owed to the colleagues, not to the company. Section 5(3) does not extend, in the ordinary way, to the travel agent or other trader who receives a deposit for a purchase and then fails to fulfil the contract.[69] It provides only for those cases where D is responsible for holding a particular sum of money or its proceeds on another's behalf:[70] this case involves an obligation to deal with the money received

---

[66] [1998] 2 Cr App R 282, discussed by J. C. Smith, 'Stealing Tickets' [1998] Crim LR 723.

[67] A provision that appears to have been overlooked when quashing the conviction in *Dyke and Munro* [2002] Crim LR 153 (above, n 56); as Sir John Smith pointed out in the commentary, the Attorney-General has the right to enforce charitable trusts.

[68] [2000] Crim LR 411.

[69] *Hall* [1973] QB 126; *aliter* if the contract provides that the money must be held specifically for this purpose. Cf. *Breaks and Huggan* [1998] Crim LR 349.

[70] In most such cases a trust would be created, and s. 5(1) itself could be applied: cf. *Arnold* [1997] Crim LR 833. Cf. also the use of s. 5(3) in *Klineberg and Marsden* [1999] 1 Cr App R 427 to avoid problems arising from *Preddy* [1996] AC 815.

in a particular way, as part of a distinct fund, whereas payments to a business are usually payments into the general funds of that business. It has also been held that the manager of a public house who made secret profits by selling beers not brewed by his employers fell outside s 5(3), since he was merely accountable for the profits of the public house and was under no obligation to 'retain and deal with' them.[71] Some might argue that this is an arbitrary way to draw the line between criminal liability and mere civil liability, but it tends to be justified on the basis that a remedy for breach of contract is usually sufficient for the latter type of case. However, the civil law has been altered by the Privy Council:[72] a secret profit is now deemed to be held on constructive trust for the principal, and so it seems that the manager of the public house would be convicted of theft since s 5(3) would apply.

Section 5(4) extends the definition of 'belonging to another' to cases where D 'gets property by another's mistake and is under an obligation to make restoration (in whole or in part)'. The obvious example of this is the mistaken overpayment: if money is credited to D's bank account in error, and D resolves to keep it, this amounts to theft of the overpaid sum.[73] If the overpayment is by a bookmaker, there is no legal obligation involved and so s 5(4) cannot be invoked to support a theft conviction.[74]

(d) 'THE INTENTION PERMANENTLY TO DEPRIVE'

It must be proved that D intended that the person from whom he appropriated the property should be deprived of it permanently. We have already seen that permanent deprivation itself is not necessary for theft: a temporary appropriation will suffice. But the ambit of the offence is restricted by the need for an *intention* permanently to deprive. Thus, the essential minimum of the offence is temporary appropriation with the intention of permanent deprivation.

The Theft Act does not define 'intention permanently to deprive'. Intention presumably bears the same meaning as elsewhere in the criminal law,[75] and therefore covers cases where D knows that a virtually certain result of the appropriation will be that the other is deprived of the property permanently. Most cases will fall into place fairly easily, but the requirement of intention 'means that it is still not theft to take a thing realizing that the owner may not, or probably will not, get it back'.[76] Thus there will be no theft where D takes property and then abandons it where it might be found, and the description 'stolen car' is inaccurate if it refers to a car taken from its owner and abandoned some distance away, since it is well known that cars are normally returned

---

[71] *Attorney-General's Reference (No. 1 of 1985)* (1986) 83 Cr App R 70.

[72] *Attorney-General for Hong Kong v Reid* [1994] 1 AC 324, noted by Sir John Smith at (1994) 110 LQR 180.

[73] *Attorney-General's Reference (No. 1 of 1983)* [1985] QB 182; it is arguable whether s. 5(4) is needed to achieve this result after the civil case of *Chase Manhattan Bank NA v Israel-British Bank* [1981] Ch 105.

[74] *Gilks* (1972) 56 Cr App R 734.   [75] See above, Ch 5.5(b).

[76] A. T. H. Smith, *Property Offences*, 187.

to their owners by the police.[77] Section 12 of the Theft Act 1968 provides a special offence of taking a car without the owner's consent, which does not require proof of an intention permanently to deprive (discussed in section 9.3 below). A car *would* be stolen, however, if it were taken with a view to changing its identity marks and then reselling it.

Is there an 'intention permanently to deprive' if D takes someone else's money, intending to repay it before the owner notices its absence? At first sight it would appear not: an intention to repay surely negatives an intention to deprive permanently. Yet if the property taken is money, it is highly unlikely that D intends to replace exactly the same notes (or coins) that were taken. It would therefore be correct to hold that D did intend to deprive the owner permanently of the notes and coins that were taken, and the Court of Appeal confirmed that this is the law in *Velumyl* (1989).[78] A manager had taken money from his company's safe, intending to repay it the following day when a debt was repaid to him. The Court held that an intention to return objects of equal value is relevant on the issue of dishonesty, but does not negative the intention to deprive the owner permanently of the original notes and coins. The Court added that taking someone else's property in these circumstances amounts to forcing on the owner a substitution to which he or she does not consent.[79] Some would argue that this is both pedantic and unrealistic, since money is fungible and one £10 note is for all purposes the same as another. On the other hand, there may be situations in which the owner wants a particular denomination (e.g. £1 coins for a slot machine, whereas D takes ten and leaves a £10 note) or needs to use the money earlier than expected. One merit of the strict rule here is that, by foreclosing what might otherwise be a defence of lack of intent to deprive permanently, it ensures that the wider rights and wrongs are assessed in the context of the dishonesty requirement.

Does it matter if the intention is conditional? One answer to this is that most intentions in theft are conditional in some respect, and so it should not matter greatly. Particular difficulty has been caused in cases of attempted theft, where D has not yet appropriated any property but is searching a container (a pocket, handbag, suitcase, car boot) in order to find something worth stealing. In these circumstances it would be unsatisfactory to convict D of attempting to steal a purse, for example, if D had already examined the purse and decided not to take it. This may explain the rather sweeping statement of the Court of Appeal in *Easom* (1971)[80] that 'a conditional appropriation will not do'. Subsequently the Court of Appeal held that the correct form of indictment in these 'container' cases would be to charge D with attempting to steal 'all or any of the contents' of the bag, vehicle, or other container.[81] However, it has been pointed out that this is hardly more satisfactory in a case like *Easom*, where D had examined all the contents of the handbag and had found nothing worth taking. It is an offence

---

[77] E.g. *Mitchell* [2008] EWCA Crim 850 (no theft committed).   [78] [1989] Crim LR 299.

[79] Adopting the words of Winn LJ in *Cockburn* (1968) 52 Cr App R 134.

[80] [1971] 2 QB 315; for analysis see K. Campbell, 'Conditional Intention' (1982) 2 Legal Studies 77.

[81] *Attorney-General's References (Nos. 1 and 2 of 1979)* [1980] QB 180, *Smith and Smith* [1986] Crim LR 166.

to attempt something that turns out to be impossible,[82] and so the better wording is to charge D with simply attempting to steal from the container.[83]

Neither of the two problems just discussed is mentioned in the Theft Act itself. The Act does not define 'an intention permanently to deprive', but it does provide, in section 6, an extension of the concept. It states, in a poorly drafted compromise provision,[84] that persons are to be treated as having an intention permanently to deprive in certain circumstances. The general principle is that where D's intention is 'to treat the thing as his own to dispose of regardless of the other's rights', this is equivalent to an intention permanently to deprive. The Court of Appeal in *Fernandes* (1996)[85] held that this key phrase applies to 'a person in possession or control of another's property who, dishonestly and for his own purpose, deals with that property in such a manner that he knows he is risking its loss'.[86] Another example is the ransom principle, where D takes V's property, telling V that he will return it only if V pays the asking price. D is clearly treating the property as 'his own to dispose of regardless of the other's rights', in that he is bargaining with the owner (in effect) to sell it back. Thus in *Raphael* (2008),[87] where D drove off in V's car and then offered to return it for a cash payment, the Court of Appeal held that this was a clear case of D treating the car as his own to dispose of regardless of V's rights. It is right to bring such cases within theft, inasmuch as they are takings where, as s 6 puts it, D does not mean 'the other permanently to lose the thing itself', and yet where the substance of D's intended taking and V's intended loss is little different from permanent deprivation. However, the Divisional Court effectively broadened s 6(1) in *DPP* v *Lavender* (1994),[88] where D had taken two doors from a council house undergoing repair and had fitted them to another council house to replace damaged doors. The Court did not refer to the dictionary definition of 'dispose of', but appeared to hold that 'dealing with' the doors could amount to 'disposing of' them. The Court therefore held that D should be convicted of stealing the doors, even though they had simply been transferred from one council property to another. This is unsatisfactory.

Section 6 goes on to deal with two specific types of case. One, set out in s 6(2), is where D parts with V's property under a condition as to its return which D may be unable to fulfil; the obvious example of this is pawning another's property, hoping to be able to redeem it at some time in the future. The other example, in s 6(1), is where D borrows or lends V's property: this may amount to D treating it as his own to dispose of 'if, but only if, the borrowing or lending is for a period and in circumstances equivalent to an outright taking or disposal'. Although this is an extension of the idea of intending permanent deprivation, the final few words may prove fairly

---

[82] See Ch 11.3(c).   [83] *Smith's Law of Theft*, 120.

[84] See J. R. Spencer, 'The Metamorphosis of Section 6 of the Theft Act' [1977] Crim LR 653.

[85] [1996] 1 Cr App R 175, at 188.

[86] Cf. *Mitchell* [2008] EWCA Crim 850 (no theft because D always intended to, and did, abandon the car).

[87] [2008] Crim LR 995.   [88] [1994] Crim LR 297.

restrictive. Their scope was considered by the Court of Appeal in *Lloyd* (1985),[89] where a cinema employee removed films from the cinema for a few hours, thereby enabling others to copy the films with a view to selling 'pirate' copies. The employee always intended to return the films, and always did. Clearly, his conduct in allowing others to make copies did significantly reduce the value of the films, but it is not possible to say, as s 6(1) requires, that his borrowing was equivalent to an outright taking. He did not render the films valueless, even though he did reduce their commercial value by enabling the production of copies. Fewer people might pay to watch the films at the cinema. Lord Lane CJ stated the effect of s 6(1) in these terms: '[a] mere borrowing is never enough to constitute the necessary guilty mind unless the intention is to return the "thing" in such a changed state that it can truly be said that all its goodness or virtue has gone'.[90]

The application of this test may be illustrated by D, who takes V's railway season-ticket, which expires on 31 January, and maintains that it was always his intention to return it on 1 February. His intention clearly is to return the ticket, which may be physically unchanged, but, since it will no longer be valid, it is fair to describe it as being in a 'changed state'. 'All its goodness' will have gone by 1 February and so D is liable to conviction. But if D maintains that it was always his intention to return the ticket on 30 January, it will still be valid for one more day and, on the *Lloyd* test, D would have to be acquitted (if the court believed the story). Thus, by using the word 'all', Lord Lane made it clear that few borrowings will amount to theft. Some might argue that the wording of s 6 is slightly more flexible—'in circumstances making it *equivalent* to an outright taking'—but the only way of introducing greater flexibility would be to hold that an intention substantially to reduce the value of the property would suffice, and such a broad reading would go against the principle of maximum certainty (see Chapter 3.5(i)). The real problem here is that, without a general offence of temporary deprivation, judicial attempts to stretch an offence based on an intention permanently to deprive are likely to produce difficulties.

Is there a strong case for dispensing with the requirement of an intention permanently to deprive? At present there are only two offences of temporary deprivation in the Theft Act—s 12, penalizing the taking of cars, bicycles, etc. without the owner's consent; and s 11, penalizing the removal of an article on display in places open to the public, such as museums and galleries. Among the arguments for penalizing temporary deprivation generally,[91] probably the strongest are that the chief value of many items lies in their use and that many modern objects are intended for fashion or for a relatively short active life. If someone deliberately takes an item for a period and deprives the other of its use for the same period, that is wrong, and there may be far

[89] [1985] QB 928.

[90] Ibid., 836; in *Bagshaw* [1988] Crim LR 321, the Court of Appeal commented that this restrictive reading of s. 6(1) was *obiter*. The convictions in *Marshall* (above, n 66 and accompanying text) for re-selling London Underground tickets were upheld by the Court of Appeal purportedly by applying s. 6(1).

[91] See G. Williams, 'Temporary Appropriation Should Be Theft' [1981] Crim LR 129; A. T. H. Smith, *Property Offences*, 191; Law Com No. 228, *Conspiracy to Defraud* (1994), 32–4.

more gain and loss involved than in many cases of theft in which there is an intention permanently to deprive. In many similar cases where deception is used, there will be an offence of fraud;[92] but if the advantage is gained boldly, without deception, it rarely amounts to an offence at present. The usual counter-argument is that the criminal law would be extended to many trivial 'borrowings' without consent, and that the police and courts would be flooded by such cases. However, this does not appear to have occurred in those European and Commonwealth jurisdictions which have extended their law of theft in this way. Moreover, there could be exceptions to cater for many non-serious cases. The real question is whether a sufficiently strong case for extending the ambit of the criminal law has been made: police and prosecutorial discretion might serve to eliminate minor cases, but are there major cases that justify criminalization? Could any major types of case, such as unauthorized copying of materials and other commercial malpractices, be covered adequately by specific offences? Would this approach not have the further advantage of removing the need for the over-complicated provisions in s 6? These are questions for a broad review of dishonesty offences.

(e) THE ELEMENT OF DISHONESTY

Perhaps the core concept in the Theft Act is dishonesty. The breadth of the definition of appropriation means that the finding of dishonesty may often make the difference between conviction and acquittal. From the fact that there is also the requirement of an intention permanently to deprive, it is evident that 'dishonesty' performs a separate function. The fault necessary for theft is not expressed simply in terms of intent, recklessness or other *mens rea* terms. The dishonesty requirement imports considerations of motivation and excuse directly into the offence conditions. Let us consider the details.

The 1968 Act does not provide a definition of dishonesty, but it does stipulate in s 2 that, in each of three instances, an appropriation may *not* be considered dishonest for the purposes of the crime of theft.[93] The first instance, in s 2(1)(a), is where D believes that he has the legal right to deprive V of it. An example of this is where D seizes money from V, believing that V owes him the money.[94] In many cases under this provision there will be a mistake of law (usually, of civil law), and the main question will be whether the court is satisfied that D actually had the mistaken belief claimed—or, to reflect the burden of proof, whether the prosecution has established beyond reasonable doubt that this was not D's actual belief. The second instance, in s 2(1)(b), is where D believes that V would have consented if V had known of the circumstances. The third, in section 2(1)(c), is where D believes that the owner of the property cannot be

---

[92] See below, Ch 9.7(a).

[93] S. 2 does not apply to the term 'dishonesty' as used in other offences under the Theft Act such as false accounting and handling, nor to conspiracy to defraud.

[94] *Robinson* [1977] Crim LR 173.

discovered by taking reasonable steps. This applies chiefly to people who find property
and conclude that it would be too difficult to trace the owner.

The main feature of s 2, then, is that it removes three types of case from the possible ambit of 'dishonesty,' making it clear that it is the personal beliefs of defendants
which are crucial here. These are, effectively, excuses—which could have been drafted
so as to include objective elements, but were not.[95] The only other legislative clue to
the meaning of 'dishonesty' is the declaration in s 2(2) that an appropriation may
be dishonest even though D is willing to pay for the property. Apart from that, the
definition of dishonesty is at large ('morally open-textured'),[96] and the courts have
been left to develop an approach. Whilst insisting that the meaning of dishonesty is a
matter for the jury or magistrates and not a matter of law, the judges have laid down the
proper approach to the question. It seems that there are three stages. First, the court
must ascertain D's beliefs in relation to the appropriation—the reasons, motivations,
explanations. Secondly, the jury or magistrates must decide whether a person acting
with those beliefs would be regarded as dishonest according to the current standards
of ordinary decent people. Thirdly, if there is evidence that D thought that the conduct
was not dishonest according to those general standards, D should be acquitted if the
court is left in reasonable doubt on the matter.

The first and second stages in the test were laid down in *Feely* (1973),[97] where D
had 'borrowed' money from his employer's safe despite a warning that employees
must not do so. D's explanation was that he intended to repay the sum out of money
which his employer owed him (which amply covered the deficiency). The Court of
Appeal held that the key question for the court should have been whether a person who takes money in those circumstances and with that intention is dishonest
according to the current standards of ordinary decent people. The third stage was
added by *Ghosh* (1982),[98] where the Court of Appeal tried to reconcile two lines of
earlier cases. The example given by the court was of a foreigner failing to pay when
travelling on English public transport in the belief that it is free. However, as has
been pointed out,[99] this is a poor example, which would render the third stage super-
fluous. D's own beliefs are already considered at the first stage, so that, in the example
given, the court would then consider at the second stage whether a foreigner with
that belief would be dishonest according to the ordinary standards of reasonable
and honest people. The answer would surely be no. Moreover, even though the third
stage does not provide a defence where D acts on strong moral or social beliefs which
he knows are not shared by 'reasonable and honest people', it may provide a defence
for the person who thinks that those people would not regard his conduct as dishonest. Whether people who are so out of tune with current standards should be
acquitted is a difficult issue. But the overall complexity makes it hardly surprising
that the Court of Appeal has declared that the third stage should not be mentioned

---

[95] J. Horder, *Excusing Crime* (2004), 49; cf. the discussion of mistaken beliefs in Ch 6.4 and 6.5 above.
[96] Horder, ibid., 49.   [97] [1973] QB 530.   [98] [1982] QB 1053.
[99] See K. Campbell, 'The Test of Dishonesty in *R v Ghosh*' [1984] CLJ 349.

to a jury unless the facts specifically raise it—which is highly unlikely in a case where the dishonesty was obvious.[100]

The three-stage test of dishonesty evolved by the courts is complex and controversial. Moreover, its sphere of operation is enormous: around one-half of all indictable charges tried by the courts include a requirement of dishonesty. The few specific instances covered by s 2 are relevant only to a small minority of theft charges: most theft cases and all other dishonesty offences under the Theft Act are decided on the three-stage judicial test. Yet that test is open to serious objections.[101] The root of the problem has been the assumption, first stated by the Criminal Law Revision Committee[102] and then espoused by the courts in the 1970s,[103] that dishonesty is easily recognized and that the concept should therefore be treated as an ordinary word. Neither part of this assumption is well founded. Dishonesty may be easily recognized in some situations, but it is far more difficult in situations with which a jury or magistrates are unfamiliar—such as alleged business fraud or financial misdealing.[104] Moreover, much depends on who is responsible for characterizing conduct as dishonest. In a multicultural society with widely differing degrees of wealth, it may often happen that someone who is poor or is a member of a minority community may have his or her conduct characterized as honest or dishonest by people who are relatively wealthy and are members of the majority community. There may also be an element of hypocrisy in this, since it is well known that practices which are strictly dishonest abound in the business or private lives of people at all levels.[105] Many, or most, forms of employment have their 'perks' according to which some practices of employees taking or using company property have become so traditional as to be thought of almost as an entitlement, and employers are content to 'turn a blind eye' to this. This all tends to suggest that there are situations in which dishonesty cannot be regarded as an ordinary word with a clear, shared meaning. Yet, because it is not easy to devise a law that includes the culpable and excludes the non-culpable, it has been argued that such an issue is better resolved by a jury or lay magistrates assessing the facts of the case, rather than by inevitably crude legal rules.[106]

This, however, brings us to some strong objections to using the 'ordinary standards of reasonable and honest people' as a test for establishing dishonesty. It derogates from the rule of law in various ways. Its uncertainty may mean that, for some defendants, the judgment of dishonesty comes as an *ex post facto* assessment

---

[100] *Roberts* (1987) 84 Cr App R 117 and *Price* (1990) 90 Cr App R 409, criticized by A. Halpin, 'The Test for Dishonesty' [1996] Crim LR 283, at 289, 291–2.

[101] E. Griew, 'Dishonesty: The Objections to *Feely* and *Ghosh*' [1985] Crim LR 341; Halpin, *Definition in the Criminal Law*, 149–66.

[102] Criminal Law Revision Committee, 8th Report, *Theft and Related Offences* Cmnd 2977 (1966), para. 39.

[103] But strongly criticized in Australia: see e.g. *Salvo* [1980] VR 401.

[104] LCCP 155, *Fraud and Deception*, 7.49–7.53

[105] For readings and commentary on this see N. Lacey, C. Wells and O. Quick, *Reconstructing Criminal Law* (3rd edn., 2003), 328–45.

[106] R. Tur, 'Dishonesty and Jury Questions', in A. Phillips Griffiths (ed.), *Philosophy and Practice* (1985).

of their conduct, not knowable at the time of acting. Its uncertainty also brings it into conflict with the principle of maximum certainty in the criminal law.[107] Under the European Convention on Human Rights, an offence definition does not pass the 'quality of law' test unless it is sufficiently certain, which means that it must 'describe behaviour by reference to its effects' rather than relying solely on a morally evaluative term.[108] That cannot be said of 'dishonesty', and it appears that theft, deception, and other dishonesty offences only satisfy the Convention because 'dishonesty' is merely one of several elements in the definition of the offence[109]—a proposition that overlooks the considerable dependence of theft on 'dishonesty' after *Gomez* and *Hinks*. A further rule-of-law criticism is that the breadth of the concept increases the risk of different courts reaching different verdicts on essentially similar sets of facts, and leaves room for the infiltration of irrelevant factors. The *Feely* problem of borrowing money without permission is not unusual, but differently constituted juries might take a different view of its dishonesty. On the other hand, it is true to say that this alleged inconsistency of practice is not supported by any evidence, and that the impact of the alleged uncertainties of definition should not be exaggerated.[110]

It is far easier to criticize the test, however, than to propose a replacement which overcomes all the objections. Some years ago D. W. Elliott proposed that the requirement of dishonesty should be jettisoned; that the three types of case now covered by s 2(1) should be declared not to be theft; and that the statutory definition of appropriation should exclude all appropriations 'not detrimental to the interests of the owner in a significant practical way'.[111] This would have the advantages of greater simplicity than *Ghosh* and of confining the decisions of juries and magistrates to whether the taking was too trivial to justify conviction, but it would fall well below the principle of maximum certainty until the courts had developed some specific criteria. Somewhat similar are the proposals of Peter Glazebrook, which stem from the proposition that no conduct that is not legally wrongful should be sufficient for theft.[112] From this starting-point, Glazebrook assumes the presence of dishonesty unless the case can be brought within one of a number of listed exceptions. The first three exceptions correspond to those in the existing s 2(1), and two others correspond to s 3(2) (purchasers in good faith) and s 4(3) (pickers of wild produce not for a commercial purpose). Whilst Glazebrook does not list a *de minimis* exception of the kind proposed by Elliott, he deals explicitly with one group of cases that Elliott assumed would be excluded by his *de minimis* exception. Thus one

---

[107] See above, Ch 3.5(i) and (j), and Shute, 'Appropriation and the Law of Theft' [2002] Crim LR at 452–3.

[108] *Hashman and Harrup* v *United Kingdom* (2000) 30 EHRR 241   [109] Ibid., para. 39.

[110] See further Bogg and Stanton-Ife, 'Protecting the Vulnerable', 407–14.

[111] D. W. Elliott, 'Dishonesty in Theft: A Dispensable Concept' [1982] Crim LR 395, adapting the words of McGarvie J in the Australian case of *Bonollo* [1981] VR 633, at 656.

[112] Glazebrook, 'Revising the Theft Acts' [1993] Camb LJ 191.

of Glazebrook's exceptions is that a person who appropriates property is not to be regarded as dishonest if:

the property is money, some other fungible, a thing in action or intangible property, and is appropriated with the intention of replacing it, and in the belief that it will be possible for him to do so without loss to the person to whom it belongs.

What convinces both Elliott and Glazebrook that these 'borrowing' cases should not be theft? Elliott does not deny that they involve civil wrongs, but would exclude them because and in so far as they are not serious enough to justify criminalization. Presumably D's belief in the ability to make repayment is one central factor in this judgement, along with surrounding circumstances about the significance of the event for the owner which may suggest that it is sufficient to treat it as a civil matter. This may, however, mean that the differential treatment of employee 'pilfering' and ordinary small-value shoplifting is perpetuated, though this time under the guise of judgements about relative significance. In theory Elliott's test could become the gateway to the decriminalization of much shoplifting, on the basis that a small-value taking is hardly likely to be detrimental in a significant practical way to the interests of Tesco, Sainsbury, or other major retailers, but courts are unlikely to adopt this reading. Glazebrook's formula is concerned more directly with the 'borrower' of money, and would lead to an acquittal in cases such as *Feely*.[113] Here again, the 'borrower' clearly commits a civil wrong, violating the owner's right to decide how and by whom the property may be used,[114] and so presumably the argument for putting them beyond the criminal sanction is that they are insufficiently serious. The provision is narrower in scope, and would be easier to administer since it requires no normative judgment from the court. But it remains a considerable distance from the existing law. At present we have an extremely wide definition of appropriation which leaves most criminalization decisions to the court's judgement of dishonesty—a judgement with few parameters and much scope for differences of perspective. The Glazebrook approach would confine the definition of appropriation, notably by requiring proof of a civil wrong, with the consequence that a far less flexible and extensive definition of dishonesty would be required. Legal certainty would be enhanced, and legalism would triumph over the variable populism of the *Ghosh* test.

9.3 TAKING A CONVEYANCE WITHOUT CONSENT

Although an appropriation of another's property without an intention to deprive the other of it permanently does not normally amount to an offence under English law, there are a few exceptions. The best known and most frequently invoked is the offence of taking a conveyance without the owner's consent, contrary to s 12 of the

---

[113] Above, n 92 and accompanying text.   [114] Halpin, 'The Test for Dishonesty', 294.

Theft Act 1968. In the early 1990s there was growing public concern over 'joy-riding' by young drivers who took cars in order to race them and to give 'displays', and this concern was heightened when some of the offences ended in the deaths of pedestrians or other road users. In 1992 Parliament passed the Aggravated Vehicle-Taking Act, empowering courts to impose harsher sentences in many such cases. The Act was mentioned in Chapter 7.6 during the discussion of serious motoring offences, and reference will be made to it below since it is an aggravated form of the basic offence under s 12 of the Theft Act.

The offence created by s 12(1) applies to the taking of any 'conveyance', which includes any contraption for carrying one or more persons by land, water, or air. There is a distinct offence in s 12(5) relating to pedal cycles. The offence may be committed in three separate ways: taking a conveyance, driving a conveyance that has been taken, and allowing oneself to be carried in a conveyance that has been taken. The conduct of a passenger in a 'stolen' car will often amount to aiding and abetting the driver (see Chapter 10 below), but s 12 dispenses with the need to prove any encouragement by the passenger and penalizes anyone who 'allows himself to be carried in or on' the conveyance. This is an example of treating offences committed by two or more people as more serious than offences committed by one person acting alone: as in conspiracy,[115] the assumption is that mutual reinforcement and group dynamics will often result in the causing of greater harm.

The offence requires a taking, which is constituted by moving the vehicle but not by merely getting into it.[116] A vehicle can be 'taken' by a person authorized to drive it—for example, an employed van-driver or lorry-driver—if that person deviates significantly (in time or place) from the permitted use.[117] The taking must be 'for his own or another's use': this will easily be fulfilled in most cases, but it has been held that pushing a car round a corner as a prank, to induce the owner to believe that it has been stolen, falls outside s 12.[118] The taking must be 'without having the consent of the owner or other lawful authority', and the controversial issue concerns the obtaining of permission by deception. The wording of s 12 makes no reference to cases of deception, and the courts have vacillated on the issue. Two decisions suggest a rather unconvincing distinction between the person who drives the car on a permitted journey and then subsequently takes the car on an unauthorized jaunt—guilty, according to *Phipps and McGill* (1970)[119]—and the person who has the owner's permission for one journey but instead goes on a completely different journey—not guilty, according to *Peart* (1970).[120] The Court of Appeal's finding of a fresh 'taking' in the first case and not the second makes much out of an insubstantial difference, although it must be said that the statutory provision itself is unhelpful. In *Whittaker and Whittaker v Campbell* (1983)[121] the Divisional Court applied the general principles of contract law and took the firm line that s 12 does not extend and was not intended to extend to cases in which

---

[115] See Ch 11.4 below.   [116] *Bogacki* [1973] QB 832.   [117] *McKnight v Davies* [1974] RTR 4.
[118] *Stokes* (1982) 75 Cr App R 84.   [119] (1970) 54 Cr App R 300.   [120] [1970] 2 QB 672.
[121] (1983) 77 Cr App R 267.

consent was obtained, but was obtained by some deception. Thus D, who obtained the hire of a van by pretending to be another person (whose driving licence he had found), was held not to have taken the van without the owner's consent, since this would not be grounds for holding a contract void in English law. This is a rare instance of the courts recognizing that the law of theft presupposes the general civil law relating to property. That, however, raises the question (already discussed in the context of 'dishonesty') whether it is the civil law, or the criminal law's general approach to consent (e.g. in sexual offences and non-fatal offences against the person),[122] that should supply the guiding principles.

The fault elements required for this offence are few. Taking another person's vehicle can hardly be done by accident, but s 12(6) provides that there is no offence where D believes 'that he has lawful authority to do it or that he would have the owner's consent if the owner knew of his doing it and of the circumstances of it'.[123] This test, similar to s 2(1) of the Act on dishonesty in theft, is entirely subjective. Where the charge is that D drove a vehicle or allowed himself to be carried in it, the prosecution must prove that D knew that the conveyance had been taken without authority.

The offence under s 12 is triable summarily only and has a maximum penalty of six months' imprisonment. All the elements of the basic offence must be proved if D is to be convicted and sentenced under the provisions of the Aggravated Vehicle-Taking Act 1992, technically a separate offence in view of its higher maximum penalties.[124] The 1992 Act inserted a new s 12A into the Theft Act 1968, which has the effect of imposing strict liability on a person who commits the basic section 12 offence and where 'at any time after the vehicle was unlawfully taken (whether by him or another) and before it was recovered, the vehicle was driven, or injury or damage was caused, in one or more of [four] circumstances'. It will be noted that no causal connection is required between D's involvement and the causing of injury or damage, a form of criminalization that goes even beyond the ordinary bounds of strict liability.[125] The four circumstances are:

(a) that the vehicle was driven dangerously on a road or other public place;

(b) that, owing to the driving of the vehicle, an accident occurred by which injury was caused to any person;

(c) that, owing to the driving of the vehicle, an accident occurred by which damage was caused to any property other than the vehicle;

(d) that damage was caused to the vehicle.

The maximum penalty is two years' imprisonment or, where death results under (b) above, fourteen years' imprisonment. This makes clear the impact of the strict

---

[122] See above, Ch 8.3(f) and 8.5(e).

[123] Cf. *McMinn and McMinn* [2006] 3 All ER 87 (employee allowed unauthorised driver to drive employer's vehicle, knowing that employer would not agree; *Phipps and McGill* followed).

[124] Applying *Courtie* [1984] AC 463.

[125] See *Dawes v DPP* [1995] 1 Cr App R 65.

liability—an enormous increase in the maximum penalty without proof of any fault other than that required for the basic offence, and particularly when one considers that one reason for creating this serious offence was that in some of these cases it was impossible to prove which one of two or more occupants was driving. Such problems of proof are not unique to this type of case,[126] and it is questionable whether they justify such egregious strict liability as is imposed by the 1992 Act.

9.4 ROBBERY

Robbery can be one of the most serious offences in the criminal calendar, and average sentences are higher than for any other crime apart from rape and murder. The definition of the offence is within the Theft Act 1968, but the crime involves the use or threat of violence and is triable only in the Crown Court. The number of recorded robberies was around 63,000 in 1997, doubling to 121,000 in 2001 but dropping back to 85,000 in 2007/08.[127] Some of these offences are planned attacks on persons in charge of money or other valuables at banks, building societies, or in security companies. However, as we shall see in the paragraphs that follow, many fairly minor forms of snatching a bag or mobile phone can be charged as robbery. This creates a problem of fair labelling: a sudden, impulsive bag-snatching falls into the same legal category as a major armed robbery. The offence is extremely wide, and its drafting owes more to efficiency of administration than to fairness of labelling. Thus the starting-point when sentencing someone convicted of robbery of a bank or security vehicle in which firearms were carried and no serious injury done has been held to be fifteen years' imprisonment,[128] with smaller scale robberies of building society branches often sentenced in the range from four to seven years, and street robberies in which a weapon is produced having a starting point of four (adults) or three (young offenders) years.[129] However, the detection rate for robbery is very low, with no more than one-fifth of robberies 'cleared up'.[130]

The legal elements of robbery contrary to s 8 of the Theft Act 1968 are theft accompanied by the use or threat of force. It follows from this that if D has a defence to theft, there can be no conviction for robbery. Thus where D took V's car by threat of force, intending to abandon it later (and doing so), this was not robbery because it was not theft, the intention permanently to deprive being absent.[131] Again, where D brandished a knife at V in order to get V to hand over money which D believed he was owed, it was held that this could be neither theft nor robbery if the jury found that D did believe

---

[126] See Ch 10.2.   [127] C. Kershaw *et al., Crime in England and Wales 2007/08*, 49.

[128] *Turner* (1975) 61 Cr App R 67, at 89–92.

[129] See Sentencing Guidelines Council, *Robbery: Definitive Guideline* (2006).

[130] For further analysis see A. Ashworth, 'Robbery Reassessed' [2002] Crim LR 851. Kershaw *et al, Crime in England and Wales 2007/08* report a detection rate of 20 per cent for robbery in 2007/08.

[131] *Mitchell* [2008] EWCA Crim 850; see above, part 9.2(d).

that he had a legal right to the money (and so was not dishonest: section 2(i)(a)).[132] Conviction for another offence, such as possessing an offensive weapon or blackmail, might be possible on these facts. But if there is no theft, there can be no robbery.

Turning to the amount of force needed to convert a theft into a robbery, s 8 of the Act requires it to be proved that, immediately before or at the time of stealing, and in order to steal, D 'used force on a person or put or sought to put any person in fear of being then and there subjected to force'. Several points of interpretation arise here. The force, threat, or attempted threat of force must take place immediately before or at the time of the theft: this seems to exclude the use of force immediately after the offence, but the Court of Appeal has circumvented this limitation by holding that the appropriation element in theft continues while the thieves are tying up their victims so as to make good their escape.[133] The force must be used in order to steal, not merely on the same occasion as the stealing. Where there is a threat of force, the threat must be to subject a person (not necessarily the victim of the theft) to immediate violence—a threat to injure at some time in the future would be insufficient for robbery.

One question which has engaged the attention of the courts is, at first sight, a perfectly simple one: what does the phrase 'uses force on a person' mean? *Dawson and James* (1976)[134] seems to hold that bumping into someone so as to knock him off balance may be sufficient force. The result of *Clouden* (1987)[135] seems to be that pulling V's handbag in a way which causes her hand to be pulled downwards amounts to using force on a person. None of the defendants in these cases could claim any social or moral merit in their activities, but should they be classified as robbers rather than mere thieves? Of course it is difficult to draw the line between sufficient and insufficient force, but if robbery is to continue to be regarded as a serious offence, triable only on indictment and punishable with life imprisonment, surely something more than a bump, a push, or a pull should be required. It may be true that the significant feature of robbery 'is not merely that D usurps V's property rights, but how she does so',[136] but that does not support the existence or structure of the current offence. A radical solution would be to abolish the offence of robbery, leaving prosecutors to charge theft together with an offence of violence at the appropriate level—although, interestingly, there are no general offences of threatening or attempting to threaten the use of force, other than common assault (maximum penalty six months) and threatening to kill. Another solution would be to divide the offence of robbery, so that the use or threat of lesser degrees of force in order to steal is differentiated from major robberies involving

---

[132] *Robinson* [1977] Crim LR 173; cf. *Forrester* [1992] Crim LR 792.

[133] *Hale* (1979) 68 Cr App R 415, above, n 27 and accompanying text.

[134] (1976) 64 Cr App R 150.

[135] [1987] Crim LR 56; the decision also goes directly against the Criminal Law Revision Committee's view (8th Report (1966), para. 65), that 'we should not regard mere snatching of property, such as a handbag, from an unresisting owner as using force for the purpose of the definition, though it might be so if the owner resisted'.

[136] Simester and Sullivan, 'Nature and Rationale of Property Offences', 194; Green, *Lying, Cheating and Stealing*, ch 17.

considerable violence or firearms. The principle of fair labelling (Chapter 3.6(s)) is readily adopted for offences against the person, and no-one would argue in favour of a single offence of using or threatening force (of any degree) against another. The present definition of robbery plainly breaches that principle.[137]

9.5 BLACKMAIL[138]

It was noted earlier that the criminal law does not penalize all threats of violence,[139] although we have just seen that robbery is committed if a person uses a threat of immediate violence in order to steal property. The essence of blackmail contrary to s 21 of the Theft Act 1968 is the making of a demand, reinforced by menaces, with a view to making a gain or inflicting a loss. Blackmail is therefore wider than the other offences committed by threats, since it is not confined to threats of violence. The word 'menaces' has been held to extend to threats of 'any action detrimental to or unpleasant to the person addressed',[140] and may involve a threat to disclose some compromising information. On the other hand, blackmail is narrower than some other 'threat' offences, in that the offence is committed only where D makes the demand 'with a view to gain for himself or another or with intent to cause loss to another'. The definitions of 'gain' and 'loss'[141] are supposed to establish blackmail as a property offence (although the notion of 'gain' has been applied to the obtaining of a pain-killing injection from a doctor),[142] whereas it is surely the use of coercive threats (especially where they involve violence) that constitutes the gravamen of the offence.[143]

It has been said that the criminalization of blackmail creates a paradox: it may be legal to reveal another's secret, and it may be legal to ask another person for money, but when D asks V for money as the price of not disclosing a secret a serious offence, triable only in the Crown Court, is committed. A more plausible analysis, however, would emphasize the element of coercion involved in obtaining something that ought only to be yielded by consent.[144] In practice many prosecutions concern the betrayal or threatened revelation of sexual secrets, so the rationale of the offence may also include the protection of certain forms of privacy.[145]

What, then, are the elements of the offence of blackmail? First, there must be a demand: this is a question of substance not form, and, in an appropriate context, the

---

[137] Ashworth, 'Robbery Reassessed', at 855–7.

[138] See the symposium of articles on blackmail in (1993) 141 U Pa L R 1565–989.

[139] See above, Ch 8.3(e).   [140] *Thorne v Motor Trade Association* [1937] AC 797.

[141] In s. 34(2) of the Theft Act 1968.   [142] *Bevans* (1988) 87 Cr App R 64.

[143] Simester and Sullivan, 'Nature and Rationale of Property Offences', 188.

[144] For deeper discussion see G. Lamond, 'Coercion, Threats and the Puzzle of Blackmail', in A. P. Simester and A. T. H. Smith (eds.), *Harm and Culpability* (1996).

[145] P. Alldridge, '"Attempted Murder of the Soul": Blackmail, Privacy and Secrets' (1993) 13 Oxford JLS 368; see the case of *Davies* [2004] 1 Cr App R (S) 209.

politest words can amount to a demand.[146] Secondly, the exact nature of the demand does not matter, but there must be the elements of gain or loss, discussed above. Thirdly, the demand must be accompanied by menaces. The broad definition of 'menaces' already quoted suggests that this is an objective question, but what approach should be taken to the person who knowingly exploits another's timidity? This point was raised in *Garwood* (1987),[147] and Lord Lane CJ held that there are two situations in which a court may need to go beyond the test of whether the menaces would affect a person of normal stability. One is where the menaces would affect a person of normal stability but did not influence the particular victim: that is sufficient. The other is where the menaces would not affect a person of normal stability but did influence the actual victim: that is sufficient if it is established that D was aware of the likely effect of his conduct on this victim.[148]

Fourthly, it must be established that the demand was 'unwarranted', within the special definition in s 21: 'a demand with menaces is unwarranted unless the person making it does so in the belief—(a) that he has reasonable grounds for making the demand; and (b) that the use of menaces is a proper means of reinforcing the demand'. It will be noticed that this definition incorporates a fault element which focuses on the presence of two beliefs in D's mind. The first element classifies a demand as unwarranted unless D thinks there are reasonable grounds for making the demand. This will usually mean that D believes that he has a right to whatever he is demanding—a provision roughly parallel to s 2(1)(a) of the Theft Act 1968, which holds that there is no dishonesty in theft if D believes that he has a legal right to the property taken. The second element classifies a demand as unwarranted unless D believes that the menaces are a 'proper' means of reinforcing the demand. This element plugs a gap which we noticed in the definition of robbery: someone who threatens another in order to obtain what he believes to be his rightful property is not guilty of robbery—he is not being dishonest—but he may be guilty of blackmail if the second element is fulfilled.

The wording of this second element might seem to be 'doubly subjective'—in that D's own moral standards seem to set the standard of liability. If D has been brought up to think that it is proper to threaten those who do not pay their debts, he would be immune from conviction for blackmail. But it is not certain that this is the correct meaning of this element. The Committee which proposed the test intended the word 'proper' to refer to what was thought to be morally and socially acceptable.[149] This would move away from D's own standards towards a test similar to *Ghosh* (on dishonesty): did D believe that people in general would regard the use of menaces as proper? It seems that both elements should be left to the jury, but that does not settle the issue of whether it is D's own standards or general social standards which are the focus of the second element. One decision went so far as to lay down that if D knows that a threatened act is unlawful, it cannot be maintained that it was believed 'proper'.[150] That favours the

---

[146] *Treacy* v *DPP* [1971] AC 537.   [147] (1987) 85 Cr App R 85.

[148] Ibid., at 88, applying *Lawrence and Pomroy* (1971) 55 Cr App R 73 and *Clear* [1968] 1 QB 670.

[149] CLRC, 8th Report (1966), para. 123.

[150] *Harvey, Vylett and Plummer* (1981) 72 Cr App R 139.

view that it is general social standards which apply here, but one might then go on to ask how one discovers what they are. As with the *Ghosh* test of dishonesty, there is much ambiguity and potential for inconsistent verdicts. One solution would be to confine the offence to cases where the threat is to do something that is independently criminal, which would make the offence narrower but clearer.[151] Another solution would be to place the matter entirely on D's own belief as to what was 'proper': the issue will rarely arise, and where courts have doubts about D's understanding of what was proper, this argues against imposing criminal liability. Of course, this amounts to a deviation from the policy of presumed knowledge of the law[152]—by allowing one individual's standard to set the bounds of the criminal sanction—but it does so at a point where clear objective standards peter out.

9.6 BURGLARY

One of the aims of the Theft Act 1968 was to reduce the earlier mass of prolix offences to a reasonable minimum. The law thus abandoned a definition which distinguished between burglaries of dwellings and other premises. However, by virtue of a change in sentencing law there are now separate offences of burglary in a dwelling and other burglaries again, although they share the same definition. The Criminal Justice Act 1991 reduced the maximum penalty for non-residential burglary to ten years, retaining the fourteen-year maximum for burglary in a dwelling. This separation of maximum penalties has the procedural effect of creating separate offences,[153] and the prosecution must specify which form of burglary is being charged. However, the legal definition continues unchanged, with no reference to the psychological harm which constitutes the *gravamen* of burglary in a dwelling. These psychological effects are well documented: Maguire and Bennett found that about a quarter of victims 'are, temporarily at least, badly shaken by the experience', and that a small minority of victims suffer longer-lasting effects.[154] The offence of burglary contrary to s 9 of the Theft Act 1968 has a wide ambit, but its essence may be summarized thus: it may be committed either by entering a building as a trespasser with intent to steal, or by stealing after entering a building as a trespasser. 'Entry' does not require entry of the whole body: it is sufficient if, say, an arm is put through a broken window to take goods from within.[155] What must be entered is a building or part of a building: this is drafted so as to cover the person who enters the building itself lawfully, but then trespasses by going into a forbidden part of the building. The forbidden part does not have to be a separate room: it has been held that a customer in a shop who goes

---

[151] A principled argument for this approach is made in Green, *Lying, Cheating and Stealing*, ch 17; however, the author recognises (at 234) that there may be good grounds for criminalizing some threats to do lawful things.

[152] See above, Ch 6.5(a).   [153] *Courtie* [1984] AC 463.

[154] M. Maguire and T. Bennett, *Burglary in a Dwelling* (1982), 164.   [155] *Brown* [1985] Crim LR 611.

into the area behind a service counter enters part of a building as a trespasser.[156] The requirement of trespass places a civil law concept at the centre of the offence. There is no general offence of trespass in English law—it is regarded as merely a civil matter between the parties—but a stealing or intent to steal converts trespass into the serious offence of burglary. In broad terms, someone who trespasses in another person's building is one who enters it without permission. Usually the permission will take the form of a direct invitation, but there may be cases of implied permission which raise difficulties of interpretation.

Two Court of Appeal decisions have been responsible for developing the requirement of entry as a trespasser in different, and possibly inconsistent, ways. In *Collins* (1973)[157] it was held that it is not enough that D would be classified as a trespasser in civil law: the criminal offence of burglary requires that D knew that, or was reckless as to whether, he was a trespasser. This protects from conviction the person who enters at the invitation of the householder's daughter, without realizing that she is unauthorized to give such permission. This decision kept the offence fairly narrow, by insisting on a fault element on this point, but the decision in *Smith and Jones* (1976)[158] broadened it by suggesting that the fault element is sufficient in itself. The defendants here had entered the house of Smith's father and stolen two television sets. The father maintained that his son would never be a trespasser in his house, but this did not prevent the Court of Appeal from upholding the convictions. The Court reasoned that Smith had entered 'in excess of the permission' given by his father, since the father's general permission surely did not extend to occasions when his son intended to commit a crime on the premises. The result of this decision seems to be that anyone who enters another person's building with intent to steal is a trespasser by virtue of that intention. This approach has what some would see as the great merit of removing questions of civil law from the centre of the offence and replacing them with a straightforward test more appropriate to criminal trials: did D enter the building with the intention of stealing? More turns on D's intent than on the technicalities of trespass.

Simplicity is a virtue in the criminal law, and yet *Smith and Jones* introduces difficulties. In the first place, it seems inconsistent with *Collins*, where D had a (conditional) intent to rape the woman who invited him in, but this was not held to invalidate her permission. More importantly, the boundaries of burglary are being pushed wider than is necessary or appropriate. Surely the proper label for what was done in *Smith and Jones* is theft, and the availability of the charges of theft and attempted theft makes it unnecessary to strain the boundaries of trespass by inserting unstated reservations into general permissions given by householders. There is no element of suspicion, fear, or threat when the person who enters is someone who is generally permitted to do so. Of course, part of the problem here is that the present definition of burglary includes no reference to the factors which make it such a serious crime in some cases. Convictions for the offence might be rare if the prosecution had to prove that D intended to cause, or was reckless as to causing, fear, alarm,

---

[156] *Walkington* (1979) 68 Cr App R 427.   [157] [1973] QB 100.   [158] (1976) 63 Cr App R 47.

or distress—a burglar might try to avoid such effects by entering a house when the occupier is out and taking property without damaging or ransacking the premises— but even then the crime can cause considerable distress and fear (feelings that one's property has been sullied by another, for example, or that one's home is no longer a safe place).[159] The difficulty is that the real *gravamen* of many burglaries lies in an unintended, unforeseen, or even unwanted effect upon the victim. It is fair to fix the general level of sentences by reference to that element,[160] since the psychological effects ought to be widely recognized, but it is more problematic to make it a requirement in the definition of the offence.

Section 9 creates two forms of burglary. The first, contrary to s 9(1)(a), is a truly inchoate offence: entering a building as a trespasser with intent to steal, etc. The offence is complete as soon as D has entered with the requisite intent. What ordinary people might regard as an 'attempted burglary', since D has not yet stolen anything, is in fact the full offence. The section refers to entry with intent to steal 'anything therein', and in most cases it will not matter that D's intent was a conditional one, to steal only if something worth stealing were found.[161] The second form is, having entered as a trespasser, stealing or attempting to steal, etc. (s 9(1)(b)). Either form of the offence becomes the more serious crime of aggravated burglary (s 10, punishable with life imprisonment) if D is carrying any firearm or imitation firearm, any weapon of offence, or any explosive. In most of these instances there could, in any event, be a conviction for an additional offence in respect of the weapon. Section 10 incorporates the aggravating element into the label, but in one decision the Court of Appeal took this too far when extending the offence to D who, having used a screwdriver to effect entry, then prodded the householder in the stomach with it.[162]

Burglary also has another unexpected element. Not only does it have the inchoate form of entering a building with intent, but it also covers three different intents. The discussion thus far has concentrated on the intent to steal, since that is what one would expect. But, in fact, burglary is also committed by entering a building as a trespasser with intent to inflict grievous bodily harm or to commit criminal damage. This means that s 9(1)(a) burglary functions as an inchoate violent offence, so that a person who enters a house carrying a weapon has committed the offence at that point. This illustrates the considerable reach of s 9(1)(a) burglary, going beyond that of an attempt to commit the substantive crime (e.g. grievous bodily harm or criminal damage). If it can be justified, it is on the ground that entering a building as a trespasser is a non-innocent act which should be sufficient (when combined with evidence of a proscribed intent, often inferred from surrounding circumstances or from the absence of any other plausible explanation) to warrant criminal liability. D has crossed the threshold between conceiving an intent and taking steps to translate the intent into action.

---

[159] See Maguire and Bennett, *Burglary in a Dwelling*, ch 5.

[160] See the sentencing guidelines in *McInerney and Keating* [2003] 2 Cr App R (S) 240.

[161] See *Smith's Law of Theft*, 263, arguing that D might fall outside the section if his intention was only to steal a specific item if, on examination, it had certain characteristics.

[162] *Kelly* (1992) 97 Cr App R 245.

It should also be noted that, where the charge is burglary contrary to s 9(1)(b), only two types of further offence convert the crime into burglary: D must have entered as a trespasser and then have either stolen or inflicted grievous bodily harm, or attempted either offence. Criminal damage is not relevant to this form of burglary.[163]

We have seen that what makes most residential burglaries more serious than most thefts is the element of invasion, with all the possible psychological effects which make it a more personal offence. It should therefore be mentioned that there are other offences which 'protect' the home: the Protection from Eviction Act 1977 (as amended) criminalizes the unlawful eviction or harassment of a residential occupier, and there are various offences in Part II of the Criminal Law Act 1977, which penalize the adverse occupation of residential premises. These offences are restated in the draft Criminal Code.[164]

9.7 HANDLING STOLEN GOODS AND MONEY-LAUNDERING

In this section we deal first with the offence of handling, and then with the money-laundering offences that are also concerned with subsequent dealings with stolen property or its proceeds. It has often been said that if there were fewer receivers of stolen goods, there would be fewer thieves.[165] This may well be true—there are professional 'fences' who act as outlets for stolen goods, and goods are sometimes stolen 'to order'[166]—although it is doubtful whether this is a sufficient justification for keeping the maximum penalty for handling stolen goods at fourteen years, double the maximum for theft. Section 22 of the Theft Act 1968 considerably extended the liability of persons concerned in dealing with stolen goods, creating a broad offence which covers many minor acts of assistance which might more naturally fall within inchoate offences or complicity.

The essence of the offence of 'handling' is dealing with stolen goods. The concept of stolen goods includes goods obtained by means of theft (including robbery and burglary), fraud, or blackmail, and it also covers the proceeds of such goods. Goods may, however, lose their legal classification as stolen if returned to their owner or to police custody, even temporarily.[167] The fault elements required for handling are dishonesty, and that D must 'know or believe' that the property is stolen, terms which

---

[163] There were formerly four offences specified by s. 9(1)(a), the intent to rape being the fourth. This has now been repealed and replaced by s. 63 of the Sexual Offences Act 2003, which penalizes trespass with intent to commit a sexual offence, with a maximum sentence of ten years.

[164] Law Com No. 177, cll. 187–196.   [165] E.g. *Battams* (1979) 1 Cr App R (S) 15.

[166] See C. B. Klockars, *The Professional Fence* (1975), and Maguire and Bennett, *Burglary in a Dwelling*, 70–5. For sentencing guidelines on handling, see *Webbe* [2002] 1 Cr App R (S) 82.

[167] For an example see *Attorney-General's Reference (No. 1 of 1974)* [1974] QB 744.

include 'wilful blindness'[168] but not suspicion, even strong suspicion.[169] The prohibited conduct may take one of four forms, but merely touching stolen property does not amount to the offence. 'Handling' is simply the compendious name for the four types of conduct. Type (i) is 'receiving' stolen property, which means taking control or possession of it. This is the most usual form of the offence, and applies to the 'fence' who takes the property from the thief for resale, and to the person who buys stolen goods from another. Type (ii) is 'arranging to receive' stolen goods, and here we meet the broadening of the offence. If D agrees to buy stolen goods from the thief, who is to deliver them later, D has 'arranged to receive' even before the thief has taken any action to bring the goods to him. Type (iii) is 'undertaking or assisting in their retention, removal, disposal or realization by or for the benefit of another person'. This is an extremely wide provision designed to criminalize those who help a thief or a receiver. It is rendered even wider by type (iv), which penalizes arrangements to do an act or omission within (iii). Thus, a person who does, assists in, or arranges to do or assist in any of the acts or omissions within type (iii) is criminally liable—on one condition. The condition is that it must be 'by or for the benefit of another person'. In the leading case of *Bloxham* (1983)[170] D bought a car, subsequently realizing that it was stolen. He then sold the car to someone else and was charged with type (iii) handling. The House of Lords quashed his conviction, on the ground that he sold the car for his own benefit, not for the benefit of another. He did not sell the car for the benefit of the original thief or handler, of whom he knew nothing; and it would be ridiculous to suggest that he sold it for the buyer's benefit. Moreover, D was originally a purchaser in good faith, and the policy of the Theft Act is not to criminalize such purchasers, even if they later discover the unwelcome truth about their purchases.[171]

The purpose of broadening the definition of handling was 'to combat theft by making it more difficult and less profitable to dispose of stolen property'.[172] This purpose has now been taken further by the enactment of legislation on money-laundering and the disposal of the proceeds of crime. There is now a complex body of law that extends the reach of the criminal law considerably beyond the confines of handling stolen goods. No attempt can be made here to examine the details of this legislation, but it is important to outline the three principal offences of money-laundering under the Proceeds of Crime Act 2002.[173] Section 327 of the Act creates the offence of concealing, disguising, converting, transferring or removing from the jurisdiction any 'criminal property.' Section 328 creates an offence of becoming

---

[168] Discussed above, Ch 5.5(d).

[169] Cf. *Grainge* [1974] 1 WLR 619 with *Brook* [1993] Crim LR 455. See further S. Shute, 'Knowledge and Belief in the Criminal Law', in S. Shute and A. P. Simester (eds.), *Criminal Law Theory: Doctrines of the General Part* (2002), at 172–6.

[170] [1983] 1 AC 109, responding to the promptings of J. R. Spencer, 'The Mishandling of Handling' [1981] Crim LR 682.

[171] S. 3(1) and (2) of the Theft Act; see further *Smith's Law of Theft*, 373–4.

[172] CLRC, 8th Report (1966), para. 127.

[173] For full analysis, see *Mitchell, Taylor and Talbot on Confiscation and the Proceeds of Crime* (3rd edn., 2002); for a critical appraisal of the policy, see P. Alldridge, *Money Laundering Law* (2003), esp. chs 3 and 9.

concerned in an arrangement to facilitate the acquisition, retention, use or control of criminal property by another person. Section 329 creates offences of acquisition, use or possession of criminal property. All the offences are punishable with up to 14 years' imprisonment, the same maximum as handling. There are two key elements in the offences. The first is that they all relate to 'criminal property', defined as 'a person's benefit from criminal conduct' or 'property that directly or indirectly represents such a benefit.' It will be noticed that this goes beyond stolen goods to encompass the proceeds of all crimes, notably drug offences. The second key element also forms part of the definition of 'criminal property'—that D must 'know or suspect that it constitutes such a benefit.' In other words, it only qualifies as 'criminal property' if the launderer has this state of mind. This is the only fault element in the offences under sections 327 and 329; the offence under section 328 additionally requires that D knows or suspects that the arrangement will facilitate the acquisition, retention, use or control of the property. These fault elements are entirely subjective, with the minimum requirement being that D suspects that the property may be 'criminal'—a form of recklessness, requiring D to believe that there is a risk of the property being the proceeds of crime. This use of 'suspects' takes these offences considerably beyond the 'belief' requirement for handling stolen goods; and whereas type (iii) handling is only criminal if done for the benefit of another, a similar requirement applies only to the section 328 offence and not to the other offences.

Offences of money-laundering are required by international conventions, but the extent to which such broad offences are justifiable has been questioned. The confiscation provisions in the Proceeds of Crime Act 2002 are so draconian, and not dependent on a conviction, that it may be thought unnecessary to add further offences to the existing crimes of handling and of encouraging or assisting crime.[174] The ostensible purpose is to catch the 'godfathers' who live off organized crime. But the breadth of the offences is such that it may encourage prosecutors to charge money-laundering when a person appears to have no lawful means of support but plenty of money, even though it cannot be proved what particular offences D has committed or acquired proceeds of.[175]

9.8 OFFENCES UNDER THE FRAUD ACT 2006

The Theft Act 1968 introduced the offences of obtaining property by deception (section 15) and obtaining a pecuniary advantage by deception (section 16). Those offences, and further offences in sections 1 and 2 of the Theft Act 1978 that were designed to plug gaps in the law, have now been repealed and replaced by offences under the Fraud Act 2006. The new offences overlap with a considerable number of other

[174] Alldridge, *Money Laundering Law*, 64–9.
[175] Cf. the conflicting CA decisions in *Craig* [2007] EWCA Crim 2913 and *NW et al* [2008] 3 All ER 533.

offences of fraud scattered through the statute-book and at common law. Among the statutory offences are two under the Theft Act 1968, false accounting (s 17) and false statements by company directors (s 19), several under the Forgery and Counterfeiting Act 1981, the offence of fraudulent trading (Companies Act 1985, s 458), and various offences of false and misleading statements under such statutes as the Banking Act 1987, the Financial Services and Markets Act 2000, and the Enterprise Act 2002. Among the common law offences are cheating the public revenue (which is based on fraud, and does not require deception[176]) and conspiracy to defraud, which will be examined in 9.9 below.

The most prominent characteristic of the Fraud Act offences is that they are drafted in the inchoate mode: they set out to penalize fraudulent conduct, whether or not it succeeds in deceiving anyone and whether or not it leads to the obtaining of any property. In this way two of the main difficulties of the previous law—proving that someone was deceived, and proving that the deception caused the obtaining[177]—are removed, although (as we shall see) there are some problems with the new law. The focus below will be on the four main offences introduced by the Fraud Act: fraud by false representation, fraud by failing to disclose information, fraud by abuse of position, and obtaining services dishonestly. Most of the general concepts will be dealt with in relation to the first offence, which is likely to be the most widely prosecuted.[178]

(a) FRAUD BY FALSE REPRESENTATION

This offence, like those in (b) and (c) below, is created by section 1 of the Act and then defined by a subsequent section, in this case section 2. Thus fraud by false representation is, technically, simply one way of committing the offence of fraud. The maximum penalty under section 1 is 10 years' imprisonment. Section 2(1) provides that this form of fraud is committed if D 'dishonestly makes a false representation, and intends, by making the representation, to make a gain for himself or another, or to cause loss to another or to expose another to the risk of loss.' It will be observed that it is the dishonest making of a false representation with the required intention that constitutes the offence: as stated earlier, there is no requirement that anyone is deceived or that anything is actually obtained, let alone that it must be property rather than services. The conduct element or *actus reus* has two components, a representation that is false; the fault element or *mens rea* has three elements—knowledge, dishonesty, and the intent to cause loss or make a gain.

(i) Conduct Elements: the first point is that the representation made by D must be false. This means, according to section 2(2), that it must be either untrue or misleading. A representation can be untrue if in any particular it is inaccurate; in other words,

---

[176] See *Mavji* (1987) 84 Cr App R 34, *Redford* (1989) 89 Cr App R 1, and the thorough study by D. Ormerod, 'Cheating the Public Revenue' [1998] Crim LR 627, who argues that the offence should be abolished.

[177] See the 5th ed of this work, at 397–401.

[178] For fuller analysis, see D. Ormerod, 'The Fraud Act 2006—Criminalising Lying?' [2007] Crim LR 193, and *Smith's Law of Theft* (9th edn., 2007), ch 3.

it is not necessary that the whole representation is untrue, so long as one element of it is untrue. Any argument to the effect that the untruth was so minor as to be immaterial goes to the dishonesty requirement. The term 'misleading' is different, since it posits a particular effect of what was said or done by D. Presumably the term usually bears an objective meaning, i.e. what is likely to mislead the ordinary person. But if D has any special knowledge of the person to whom the representation is addressed—for example, that that person is particularly gullible, or on the other hand that he is so knowledgeable that he will not be misled—this could be relevant in determining whether the representation is misleading.

The requirement that D makes a representation does not suggest that it must be received by another, let alone acted upon. If the representation is not communicated to its intended recipient (perhaps because that person is deaf, or because a written representation is intercepted before arrival), that does not negative the *actus reus* of the offence. Section 2(3) provides that representations as to fact or law are included, as is a representation 'as to the state of mind of the person making the representation or any other person.' This will be particularly relevant in cases where D promises to make payment next week if goods are delivered today, assuming that it can be proved (usually by inference) that at the time he made the promise D did not intend to pay the following week. Section 2(4) provides that 'a representation may be express or implied.' This applies equally to representations by words and by conduct. Many everyday transactions are conducted on certain assumptions which it would be tedious to spell out to or check on every occasion. We assume that the woman wearing a police uniform is a policewoman, or that the man wearing a Royal Mail uniform is a postman. We also assume that when a person pays by cheque there will be the funds to meet the cheque. The representations implied by giving a cheque in payment have now been formalized in a number of decisions: it is implied (i) that the drawer has an account at the bank; and (ii) that the cheque will be met when presented, which may mean in practice that there are sufficient funds in the account, or that sufficient funds will be paid in before the cheque is presented, or that there is an arrangement with the bank for a sufficient overdraft facility.[179] Finally, section 2(5) is a complicated provision intended to bring representations to machines within the offence: 'a representation may be regarded as made if it is submitted in any form to any system or device designed to receive, convey or respond to communications (with or without human intervention).'

(ii) Fault Elements: the first of the three fault elements is to be found, strangely, in the definition of 'false'. A representation is only false, according to section 2(2)(b), if 'the person making it knows that it is, or might be, untrue or misleading.' This is a requirement of knowledge, which seems (by the words 'or might be') to extend to a form of reckless knowledge. As noted in Chapter 5.5(d) above, some cases of 'wilful blindness' may be held to fall within the requirement of knowledge. The second of the fault elements is dishonesty, and it is clear that this was intended to bear the

---

[179] *Gilmartin* (1983) 76 Cr App R 238.

meaning placed on that concept in *Ghosh*.[180] However, in the law of theft the concept of dishonesty is narrowed by section 2 of the Theft Act, which excludes three kinds of case from its ambit. There is no equivalent of section 2 in the Fraud Act, and so cases of belief in legal right will fall to be dealt with according to the *Ghosh* test of the ordinary standards of reasonable and honest people. In view of the inchoate nature of the offence, and the breadth of the requirement of knowledge that the representation 'might be' misleading, many cases are likely to turn on the magistrates' or jury's view of D's honesty or dishonesty. For example, exaggerated claims by sellers might be commonplace in particular markets: D must know that they might be misleading, but in the circumstances is it dishonest to indulge in such over-statements? Or, to put the matter differently, would it be considered sufficiently dishonest to constitute fraud?[181]

The third fault element for this offence is that D 'intends, by making the representation', to cause a gain or a loss. It should be noted that this incorporates a requirement of causation—that the intention must be to cause the gain or loss 'by making the representation'—so that if D argues that he did not intend the false representation to be a causal factor (merely an embellishment), he may create a doubt that this element of the offence is satisfied. In most cases, however, proof of an intent to make a gain or to cause a loss will not cause difficulty. The definition in section 5 is similar to that for the offence of blackmail (see 9.5 above), extending to temporary or permanent losses of money or property, and also covering cases where D intends only to expose the other to the risk of a loss.

(b) FRAUD BY FAILING TO DISCLOSE INFORMATION

This offence is created by section 1(2)(b) of the Fraud Act and defined in section 3. Its essence is dishonestly failing to disclose information that D has a duty to disclose. It is therefore an offence of omission: it is designed to deal with some cases that presented a difficulty for the previous offence of obtaining by deception, but in doing so it overlaps considerably with the offence in section 2, as we shall see. The fault elements for the section 3 offence are dishonesty and an intention, by the failure to disclose the information, to make a gain or to cause a loss. These run parallel to the corresponding requirements for the offence of fraud by false representation, and will not be discussed further. More significant are the two elements of the *actus reus*, the failure to disclose and the information that D has a duty to disclose. It might be thought that 'failing to disclose' is clear enough, but there may be questions over partial or insufficiently full disclosure in some cases. Essentially, if D does not disclose everything that must be disclosed, the defence may have to rest its case on the absence of dishonesty. Turning to the duty to disclose, this was intended to reflect the duties that exist under statute and at common law. It is as plain as can be that the intention of the legislature was that there

---

[180] See the discussion of theft in part 2(e) of this chapter, above.

[181] This is admittedly a re-formulation of the dishonesty requirement, but it points to the element of uncertainty in the definition and to how it might be resolved. Cf. the discussion of whether the 'definition' of dishonesty complies with the 'quality of law' test in the Convention, below, 9.10.

must be an existing legal duty,[182] and that there is no scope for creating special duties under criminal law (as, for example, in relation to gross negligence manslaughter).[183] It therefore behoves the prosecutor to spell out the duty and its source, and whether the duty did indeed exist is a question of law; whether D fulfilled the duty, or failed to disclose that which was required, is a question for the jury. Some of these cases might be prosecuted under section 2, by arguing that D made an implied representation by conduct or by omission, but in principle it will usually be easier for the prosecution to proceed under section 3.

(c) FRAUD BY ABUSE OF POSITION

This offence, created by section 1(2)(c) of the Act and defined in section 4, is the most controversial of the trio. This is because its key terms crumble away into vagueness when scrutinized. Indeed, it looks distinctly less like a fraud offence than either of the other two. Its central element, dishonest abuse of position, appears not to require any fraud or falsity at all—a brazen taking would seem to suffice.

What are the conduct elements of this offence? Three main requirements may be identified—the occupation of a position, the expectation that financial interests will be safeguarded, and the perpetration of abuse. First, what kind of position must D occupy? It seems plain that the intention of the legislature was that the concept of 'position' should not be restricted to recognized fiduciary positions. Indeed, examples given by the Government include cases where V has allowed D access to his or her financial records, or business records, as well as cases where an employee of a care home deals with a resident's financial affairs.[184] Thus employees or others who stand in a particular relationship to another may be brought within the concept of 'position',[185] a penumbra of uncertainty that fails to give fair warning of the law's impact. Secondly, the position must be one 'in which [D] is expected to safeguard, or not to act against, the financial interests of another person.' Many employees who are not expected to safeguard their organization's financial interests may nevertheless be expected not to act against them. Beyond that, this requirement has all the rigidity of a marshmallow. The statute does not say 'may reasonably be expected' but 'is expected', so the obvious question is: whose expectation is relevant? The meaning would vary too much if it depended on the victim's expectation, and it could hardly turn on D's own expectation, so it seems that the courts may well develop a notion of 'reasonable expectation.' Once again, there is no fair warning of the law's impact. Thirdly, there is the requirement

---

[182] Law Com. No. 276, *Fraud* (2002), paras. 7.28–9.   [183] Above, Ch 7.5(b).

[184] See *Smith's Law of Theft*, 170–3. Cases like *Hinks* [2001] 2 AC 241 (discussed in 9.2(a) above) would fall clearly within the new offence. Cf the extensive definition of 'positions of trust' in the Sexual Offences Act 2003, ss. 21–2.

[185] How would this apply to the facts of *Silverman* (1988) 86 Cr App R 213, where D had done building work for V and her family for many years and D, on request, gave V a quotation for building work that was excessively high? V undoubtedly trusted D. Did D 'occupy a position' in which he was expected not to act against her financial interests? Does actual or reasonable reliance create such a position or expectation?

that D 'dishonestly abuses that position.' This is the only active element in the *actus reus* of this offence, and it may be fulfilled by an act or an omission: section 4(2). An employee who awards contracts to friends or who fails to bid for a particular contract in order to allow a friend to obtain it seems likely to fulfil this requirement. It is not clear whether 'abuse' implies the actual making of a gain or loss, but it may be interpreted more broadly as acting (or failing to act) improperly or against the financial interests of V, irrespective of the outcome.

The fault elements for this offence are twofold—dishonesty, and the intention, by the abuse of position, to cause gain or loss. It is evident that the dishonesty requirement will be particularly important in this offence, in view of the uncertain boundaries of the key *actus reus* elements. However, if there has been an apparent abuse of position (in whatever wide sense that is understood), there is likely to be a whiff of dishonesty in most cases. The employee who deviated from appropriate procedures in order to ensure that a friend obtained a contract—whether a local government official, a chief constable, or a car salesperson—may be confronted with the prospect of conviction for a serious offence carrying a maximum of 10 years' imprisonment. It is not clear how widely known this change in the law is.

(d) OBTAINING SERVICES DISHONESTLY

This offence, created by section 11 of the Fraud Act, replaces the offence of obtaining services by deception contrary to section 1 of the Theft Act 1978. It will be noted immediately that the element of deception required by the previous law has gone, and that the concept of dishonesty is once again the centrepiece of the new offence. There is also a major difference between this offence and the three Fraud Act offences just considered: whereas those offences are drafted in an inchoate mode, this offence requires an actual obtaining.

There are three elements in the *actus reus* of this offence. First, D must obtain services for himself or another by an act. The reference to an act has been taken to imply that an omission will not suffice for this offence.[186] There is no definition of 'services', and it may be construed widely so as to include, for example, the unlawful downloading of music. The ambit of 'services' is restricted by the second requirement, that the services 'are made available on the basis that payment has been, is being or will be made for or in respect of them.' This rules out services provided on a complimentary basis, but will cover most cases. Thirdly, D must 'obtain [the services] without any payment having been made for or in respect of them or without payment having been made in full.' This seems to exclude cases where D pays for services by using a credit or debit card that he is not authorized to use—since the issuing company will make the payment if the card transaction is completed.[187] However, it clearly includes cases

---

[186] *Smith's Law of Theft*, 178.

[187] Most such cases will amount to an offender under section 2, since there will be an implied false representation and an intent to cause loss or the risk of loss.

where D obtains a reduced rate of payment to which he is not entitled (whether or not any fraud or deception is involved).

There are three fault elements for the offence. First, D's act must be dishonest. This is a reference to the *Ghosh* test and is likely, once again, to be a crucial issue for the magistrates or jury in determining whether or not D has committed the offence. Secondly, D must know, when he obtains the services, that either they are being made on a payment basis or 'that they might be'. This introduces a requirement of reckless knowledge, to cover cases where D realizes there is a risk that payment might be required but does not enquire further. And thirdly, D must intend that 'payment will not be made, or will not be made in full.' This requirement of an intent to avoid payment means that this offence does not apply to cases where D's dishonest obtaining of services amounts to getting something to which D is not entitled but intends to pay for fully—as where parents lie about their religion in order to get their child into a faith school, intending to pay the full fees for the child's education. This would not be an offence under section 2 either.

9.9 CONSPIRACY TO DEFRAUD

The elements of the common law crime of conspiracy to defraud were restated in *Scott* v *Metropolitan Police Commissioner* (1975).[188] The offence may take one of two forms. If it is directed at a private person, what is proscribed is an agreement between two or more persons 'by dishonesty to deprive' that person of something to which he or she is or may be entitled, or to injure some proprietary right of that person, with intent to cause economic loss. It seems that an intention to do acts which will defraud is sufficient, and a 'good motive' cannot negative that.[189] If the offence is directed at a public official, what is proscribed is an agreement between two or more persons 'by dishonesty' to cause the official to act contrary to his or her public duty. There seem to be few prosecutions for conspiracy to defraud directed at public officials.[190] The controversies mainly concern the first form of the offence.

It is, in the first place, a crime of conspiracy. Conspiracy is one of the three inchoate offences in English criminal law, to be discussed in Chapter 11 below, but conspiracy may also be charged when the acts agreed upon have actually been committed. The definition of conspiracy to defraud is so wide that it criminalizes agreements to do things which, if done by an individual, would not amount to an offence. In its 1994 report the Law Commission accepted that in principle this is objectionable, but maintained that there are 'compelling' practical reasons for retaining the offence, at least until a general review of dishonesty offences is completed.[191] In its final 2002

---

[188] [1975] AC 819.   [189] *Wai Yu-tsang* [1992] 1 AC 269.   [190] Cf. *Moses* [1991] Crim LR 617.
[191] Law Com No. 228, *Conspiracy to Defraud*, summarized at [1995] Crim LR 97 and discussed by Sir John Smith at [1995] Crim LR 209.

report, it criticized the offence for being 'so wide that it offers little guidance on the difference between fraudulent and lawful conduct', and recommended its abolition as part of the reforms that became the Fraud Act 2006.[192] However, the government declined to put forward a provision abolishing conspiracy to defraud, taking the view that prosecutors needed to have time to determine whether the Fraud Act offences would cover all the types of case or whether some lacunae would exist.[193] The matter is therefore to be reviewed in a few years, and in the meantime prosecutors will continue to enjoy the advantages of rolling together a number of instances into a single charge of conspiracy to defraud, within the guidance laid down by the Attorney-General.[194] In the extradition case of *Norris v United States of America* (2008)[195] the House of Lords emphasized the importance of the certainty requirement under human rights law and held that there was no authority for regarding price-fixing as constituting conspiracy to defraud. There remains a strong argument that the offence is too uncertain to satisfy the requirements of the Convention, an argument accepted by both the Law Commission[196] and the Joint Committee on Human Rights.[197] The government disagrees, and a challenge has yet to be made (necessarily, in a case where the conduct alleged would not amount to conspiracy to commit an existing offence).

9.10 DISHONESTY, DISCRETION, AND 'DESERT'

There is a wide range of issues of principle raised by the approach of the legislature and the courts to offences of dishonesty. The most obvious of these is the government's refusal to accept that the offence of conspiracy to defraud fails to measure up to the principle of legal certainty, and the strong suspicion that the ubiquitous requirement of 'dishonesty' is also lacking in certainty. Apart from the three exceptions in s 2 of the 1968 Act, which apply only to offences of theft, the meaning of 'dishonesty' is left at large, with only the 'ordinary standards of reasonable and honest people' to steer the jury or magistrates towards a conclusion. This ample discretion—which is what it amounts to, since there is no touchstone of social honesty—opens the way to retrospective standard-setting (which derogates from the rule of law because D did not have an opportunity to adjust his conduct to the standard), to inconsistent decisions (which amount to arbitrariness that detracts from the rule of law), and to discriminatory decisions (which detract from equality before the law). No doubt, prosecutors

---

[192] Law Com No. 276, *Fraud* (2002), para 1.6.
[193] See *Smith's Law of Theft*, 219–25, for an examination of the arguments.
[194] Attorney-General, *Guidance on the Use of the Common Law Offence of Conspiracy to Defraud* (2007).
[195] [2008] UKHL 16.   [196] Law Com No. 276, para 5.28.
[197] Joint Committee on Human Rights, *Legislative Scrutiny: Fourteenth Progress Report* (2006).

and some judges regard flexibility as a great virtue in the law, but it runs counter to any principles which regard Article 7 and the principle of legality and respect for individual autonomy as central values.[198] As the Law Commission now accepts, following the Human Rights Act, efforts must be made to redefine at least some of the property offences in a way which cuts down or structures this wide discretion. It is a great irony that the Criminal Law Revision Committee, in the report that preceded and proposed the Theft Act, purported to recognize 'the principle of English law to give reasonable guidance as to what kinds of conduct are criminal'.[199]

The definitions of some of the offences under the Theft Act are notable for their breadth. Theft and robbery cover wide areas of minor and major wrongdoing, without differentiation in the label. Some offences spill over into areas normally occupied by inchoate offences or by law of complicity. The inchoate mode of definition is used with regard to burglary contrary to s 9(1)(a), 'entering as a trespasser with intent to steal', and—more significantly—it is adopted for the crime of theft itself: the main conduct element is an 'appropriation', which may be fulfilled by any assumption of the right of an owner, even if it is with the owner's consent.[200] One consequence is to push back the crime of attempted theft even further, so that in *Morris*[201] theft was constituted by swapping labels on goods in the supermarket, and attempted theft would presumably be committed by such acts as trying to peel off the labels prior to swapping them. This presses criminal liability too far. The Fraud Act 2006 accentuates this tendency, since its main offences are phrased in an inchoate mode. Another example is provided by the offence of handling, for which the legislature has cast the net so wide (assisting in, or arranging to assist in, the retention, removal, disposal, or realization of stolen goods) as to cover conduct which would normally be charged as aiding and abetting, etc.[202] Again, one consequence of this is that the law of complicity applies so as to extend the boundaries of the wide offence of handling still further. Just as attempted theft might be termed a doubly inchoate offence, so aiding and abetting an offence of handling stolen goods might be called a doubly secondary offence.

Thus the flexibility of the 'broad band' approach to definitions in the Theft Act 1968, together with the anomalous contours of criminalization, has meant that the outer boundaries of the law (and particularly the lower boundaries) are uncertain and shifting. One consequence of *Gomez*[203] combined with *Hinks*[204] is that the focus of the law of theft has been moved from the misappropriation of others' property towards the punishment of dishonesty. This has caused a great deal of fuss from those who hold that the criminal law should not punish unless there is also a civil wrong, a point that might also be argued against the present definition of blackmail, whereas the stronger objections to the effects of *Hinks* on the law of theft are the deficit in fair

---

[198] See the fairness principles discussed above, Ch 3.4.
[199] CLRC, 8th Report (1966), para. 99(i).   [200] See section 9.1(a) above, discussing *Gomez*.
[201] [1984] AC 320.   [202] See above, section 9.9.   [203] [1993] AC 442.
[204] [2001] 2 AC 241.

warning that comes from reliance on the term 'dishonesty', a contestable concept that invites variable social and moral judgements and is insufficient to guide citizens in the regulation of their conduct.[205]

The legislative and judicial development of dishonesty offences charted in this chapter shows little attachment to a policy of minimum criminalization, and indicates ready resort to the criminal sanction as 'social defence' against relatively minor forms of dishonesty.[206] The Fraud Act may be a much-needed modernization of the law, but it is also a significant extension of the ambit of the criminal law. No efforts have been made to remove many of the lesser appropriations, frauds and handlings from the criminal law. The problem appears to be that it is hard to find a workable distinction between these minor forms of dishonesty and dishonest appropriations of property which are quite serious. English law has no provision equivalent to the *de minimis* section of the Model Penal Code, allowing a defence where the conduct was not serious enough to warrant conviction.[207] There is a provision in the *Code for Crown Prosecutors in England* which states that it is not in the public interest to bring a prosecution where only a nominal penalty would be likely;[208] but that consigns the matter to discretion once more, leaving the boundaries of the criminal law in a distinctly uncertain state. The point is strengthened by the presence of civil remedies for many acts of dishonesty concerning property. One approach is to regard the value of the appropriated goods or services as the crucial element, and to place all cases below a certain sum into a separate category—cancellation of the offence if the taker repays what was taken within seven days, for example, as in the French bad-cheque law,[209] or a new category of civil infractions.[210] English law has now quietly taken the momentous step of empowering the police to issue a Penalty Notice for Disorder in respect of any retail theft under £200, although the expectation is that thefts of £100 or over will only exceptionally be dealt with by a PND. This echoes a radical proposal made twenty years ago,[211] and may be seen as a small step towards recognizing the minor nature of many shop thefts.[212]

Of course, there are possible objections against each of these alternatives, not least the claim that offences of dishonesty have a significance in one's judgement of people which transcends the sum involved. But this is where we meet serious

---

[205] See above, section 9.2(e), and cf. the further discussion by Bogg and Stanton-Ife, 'Protecting the Vulnerable', with Ormerod, 'Cheating the Public Revenue', 635–41, on the problems of 'dishonesty' in fraud offences.

[206] Cf. Ch 3.2(b) with Ch 3.2(a).   [207] Model Penal Code, s. 212.

[208] *Code for Crown Prosecutors* (5th edn., 2004), para. 5.10(a).

[209] For an outline see C. Anyangwe, 'Dealing with the Problem of Bad Cheques in France' [1978] Crim LR 31.

[210] See the discussion by B. Huber, 'The Dilemma of Decriminalization: Dealing with Shoplifting in West Germany' [1980] Crim LR 621.

[211] See A. Ashworth, 'Prosecution, Police and the Public: A Guide to Good Gate Keeping' (1984) 23 Howard JCJ 621.

[212] There may be disadvantages of such measures, in terms of police power and the treatment of very poor offenders: see A. Ashworth and M. Redmayne, *The Criminal Process* (3rd edn., 2005), ch 6.

problems of proportionality and of social ambiguity or hypocrisy.[213] Many forms of conduct amounting to dishonesty offences are routinely dealt with in some non-criminal manner—large companies required to repay money on government contracts, for example, executives dismissed from employment, tax fraudsters required to pay double the underpaid tax rather than being prosecuted, and so forth. A Law Commission Working Paper argued that there is no need to criminalize those who deliberately use another person's profit-earning property in order to make secret profits, since it is generally adequate to leave the owner to sue the malefactor; yet restaurant bilkers who make off without paying a few pounds are routinely subjected to the criminal sanction.[214] Moreover, as argued above, there are few social standards of dishonesty which do not vary according to the background and circumstances of the group of citizens who are making the judgement. The argument is clearly one of social fairness: the present legal definitions are so broad that they give no clear steer on how the law should be enforced, leaving a large discretion that the police and prosecutors tend to exercise on 'conventional' assumptions. As a result, enforcement practices fail to ensure equality before the law, by subjecting many minor offenders to conviction whilst adopting a different approach to some who dishonestly cause large losses to others.

There are, then, at least five conflicting principles in dishonesty offences. The principle of proportionality militates in favour of a more clearly structured restatement of these offences so as to integrate crimes from the Companies Acts and elsewhere into the general framework and emphasize their seriousness. The principle of maximum certainty urges that such a restatement should be less reliant on such broad terms as 'dishonesty', which affords insufficient guidance to citizens. The principle of fair labelling would suggest that the offence of robbery is far too wide and should be sub-divided, and indeed that the offence of theft (sub-divided in several other European countries) should also reflect the difference between a small taking and a substantial theft. The principle of minimum criminalization argues in favour of a reconstruction of these offences (including the new fraud offences) so as to exclude some minor forms of dishonesty and to include some major ones. On the other hand, the same principle would support the exploration of non-criminal means of dealing with some forms of dishonesty: this has been the pattern for many years, but it has generally meant that companies and well-connected persons have succeeded in avoiding the criminal sanction, when others of lowlier status have been convicted. This goes against the principle of equality before the law, since it discriminates on grounds of wealth and social position. Some propose to resolve this conflict by maintaining non-criminal means of dealing with commercial fraud, since these can be more effective,[215] whilst

---

213 See the sources drawn together by Lacey, Wells, and Quick, *Reconstructing Criminal Law*, 328–45.

214 Pointed out by A. T. H. Smith, 'Conspiracy to Defraud' [1988] Crim LR 508, at 513, commenting on the Law Com. Working Paper No. 104.

215 Cf. J. Braithwaite and B. Fisse, 'The Allocation of Responsibility for Corporate Crime' (1988) 11 Sydney LR 468, with Levi, *Regulating Fraud*.

redoubling efforts to narrow down the ambit of the criminal sanction for minor forms of dishonesty. Unfortunately, the present tendency is towards the former but not the latter.[216]

FURTHER READING

A. T. H. SMITH, *Property Offences* (1994).

D. ORMEROD and D. H. WILLIAMS, *Smith's Law of Theft* (9th edn., 2007).

S. P. GREEN, *Lying, Cheating and Stealing: a Moral Theory of White-Collar Crime* (2006).

---

[216] Royal Commission on Criminal Justice, *Report*, Cm 2263 (1993), para. 7.63; Serious Fraud Office, *Annual Report 1993–94* (1994).

10

COMPLICITY

10.1 INTRODUCTION[1]

The question of complicity arises when two or more people play some part in the commission of an offence. It has already been noted, in discussing the various public order offences,[2] and will be emphasized later, when discussing conspiracy,[3] that the criminal law regards offences involving more than one person as particularly serious—inasmuch as they suggest planning and determination to offend and make it difficult for an individual to withdraw, and because group offences against an individual tend to be more frightening. There are, of course, different degrees of involvement in a criminal enterprise, and one of the main issues in the law of complicity is the proper scope of criminal liability: how much involvement should be necessary, as a minimum.

Let us take a hypothetical example of a burglary, in which A plans the theft of certain valuable articles from a country house: he talks to B and C, who agree to carry out the burglary; they approach D, who has worked at the house, for information which will help them to gain entry; they arrange for E to drive them to the house in a large van and to transport the stolen goods after the burglary; and they agree with F that he should come and position himself near the main gates of the house in order to warn them if anyone approaches. If A, B, C, D, E, and F all do as planned, what should be the extent of their criminal liability?

---

[1] See the monograph by K. J. M. Smith, *A Modern Treatise on the Law of Criminal Complicity* (1991).
[2] See above, Ch 8.3(g).   [3] See below, Ch 11.4.

It is apparent that B and C are the only ones to have fulfilled the definition of the crime of burglary, by entering the house as trespassers and stealing property from it.[4] They are guilty as co-principals. It should then be asked whether there is sufficient justification for bringing A, D, E, and F within the ambit of the criminal law at all. Would the law not be more effective if it concentrated on the major offenders? The main difficulty in answering this question is that, in some crimes, the conduct of the accomplices may be no less serious than that of the principals. Here, A is the 'mastermind' behind the offence and, although B and C freely accept his invitation to become involved, A's planning is a decisive factor. At a lower level D, E, and even F are knowingly involved in advancing a criminal endeavour. They have voluntarily lent their support to, and 'endorsed', the offence: the culpability resides in the decision to support the commission of the principal's crime, and the assistance or encouragement is a practical manifestation of that support. A consequentialist reason for convicting those who help and support a criminal enterprise can also be found: penalizing helpers and other participants should act as a deterrent, thereby making offences less likely to occur. But these general rationales do not resolve difficult questions such as the proper reach of liability for criminal complicity, and the minimum conduct requirements. For the procedural reasons to be discussed in 10.2 below, these are important issues.

There are, broadly speaking, three forms of participating in crime—first, as a principal; secondly, as an accomplice who aids, abets, counsels or procures, or who is liable as a participant in a joint venture; and thirdly, as someone who encourages or assists an offence, contrary to one of the new offences created by sections 44 to 46 of the Serious Crime Act 2007. Discussion of the new offences under the 2007 Act is postponed to Chapter 11.7, since they are essentially inchoate offences. But it will be apparent that those offences overlap considerably with the forms of complicity at common law that are discussed here, and reference to the interaction of the two sources of liability will be made throughout this chapter.

10.2 DISTINGUISHING PRINCIPALS FROM ACCESSORIES

The simplest way of drawing this distinction is to say that a principal is a person whose acts fall within the legal definition of the crime, whereas an accomplice (sometimes called an 'accessory' or 'secondary party') is anyone who aids, abets, counsels, or procures a principal. It does not follow from this that where two or more persons are involved in an offence, one must be the principal and the others accomplices. Two or more persons can be co-principals, so long as together they satisfy the definition of the substantive offence and each of them inflicted wounds on the victim with the required

---

[4] Theft Act 1968, s. 9; see above, Ch 9.5.

fault, for example. Indeed, English law goes further, holding that two or more persons can be co-principals if each of them by his own act contributes to the causation of the conduct element of the offence, if all their acts together fulfil all the conduct elements, and if each of them has the required mental element.[5]

Some criminal offences are so defined that they can only be committed by two or more co-principals. The public order offences of riot and violent disorder are clear examples of this.[6] There can also be accomplices to such offences, casting the net of criminal liability even wider so as to encompass those who encourage and intend to encourage the principals.[7] A related rule, which operates only in the United States, is that all members of a conspiracy are deemed to be co-principals in the offence if it is committed. The rule eliminates from such cases the distinction between principals and accessories, and has led to the conviction, as principal in an offence, of someone who was in prison at the time for another crime. The result is that the conviction misrepresents the nature of the person's participation in the crime: a conspirator is labelled as a perpetrator, which is hardly fair or necessary.[8]

Although English law maintains the distinction between principals and accessories, its practical implications are of limited significance—for example, for offences of strict liability the principal need not have *mens rea* but the accomplice must have, and for offences requiring a particular licence or qualification it is the principal who must have that.[9] The leading statute is the Accessories and Abettors Act 1861, which provides that anyone who 'shall aid, abet, counsel or procure the commission of any indictable offence...shall be liable to be tried, indicted and punished as a principal offender'. This means that a mere aider and abettor is liable to the same maximum penalty as the principal—for murder, the mandatory life sentence. It also means that the prosecution can obtain a conviction without specifying in advance whether the allegation is that D is a principal or an accomplice, or what form the alleged complicity took. This is undoubtedly a great convenience for the prosecution in certain types of case. Thus in *Giannetto* (1997)[10] the prosecution case, based on circumstantial evidence, was that D either killed his wife or was an accomplice by virtue of hiring someone else to kill her. The Court of Appeal upheld the conviction, holding that the jury 'were entitled to convict [of murder] if they were all satisfied that if he was not the killer he at least encouraged the killing'. The Court added that 'the defendant knows perfectly well what case he has to meet',[11] i.e. both those allegations.

Does this amount to adequate notice of the charge(s) to be met? While appellate courts have repeatedly encouraged prosecutors to frame indictments in as much detail

---

[5] K. J. M. Smith, *A Modern Treatise on Complicity*, 27–30; J. C. Smith and B. Hogan, *Criminal Law* (12th edn., 2008, by D. Ormerod), 182.

[6] See above, Ch 8.3(g).   [7] *Jefferson et al.* (1994) 99 Cr App R 13.

[8] It conflicts with the principle of fair labelling (discussed in Ch 3.6(s)) and the principles of 'desert' (Ch 5.2(b)). The leading American decision is *Pinkerton v United States* (1946) 328 US 640.

[9] See further Smith and Hogan, *Criminal Law*, 165–6.   [10] [1997] 1 Cr App R 1.

[11] *Per* Kennedy LJ at 8–9, following (*inter alia*) the Supreme Court of Canada in *Thatcher v R* (1987) 39 DLR (3d) 275, where Dickson CJC asked (at 306): 'why should the juror be compelled to make a choice on a subject which is a matter of legal indifference?'.

as possible,[12] it is also clear that 'if the Crown nail their colours to a particular mast, their case will, generally, have to be established in the terms in which it is put'[13]— which creates a disincentive to framing the indictment in detail. Challenges to these rules of criminal law and procedure under the Human Rights Act, on the basis that the charge fails to satisfy the Article 6(3)(a) requirement to inform a defendant 'in detail of the nature and cause of the allegation against him', have not met with success,[14] but there remains the point of principle whether defendants in such cases receive fair warning.

The 1861 English statute is sometimes compared unfavourably with such systems as the German, which restricts the maximum penalty for an accomplice to three-quarters that of the principal.[15] The comparison is not a straightforward one, however. It is true that accomplices are normally less blameworthy than principals and there-fore deserve less severe sentences. It is also true that a law which produces a conviction of murder and a sentence of life imprisonment for giving relatively minor assistance to a murderer is unjust (though the injustice stems as much from the mandatory pen-alty for murder as from the law of complicity). But systems like the German seem not to provide for those, admittedly rare, cases in which the accomplice is no less culpable, even more culpable, than the principal—as where a powerful figure orders a weak-willed person to commit a certain crime. One way of providing for all degrees of complicity would be to retain the legal power to impose any lawful sentence on the principal; to respect the accomplice's right not to be punished more severely than is proportionate to the gravity of his contribution by declaring a general guideline that accomplices should receive no more than half the sentence of the principal; and to permit courts to exceed this normal level in cases where the accomplice's role was unusually influential, and to sentence below it if the accomplice's contribution was minor. This more regulated approach to sentencing would be a significant step, at least for so long as English law fails to reflect the different degrees of involvement in crime by assigning different legal labels.

Finally, how does the law of complicity cope with cases where it can be proved that each of two defendants was at least an accomplice but cannot be proved which one was the principal? Where, in a case of a child's death caused by drugs, it can be shown that one or other parent administered methadone to their young child, and that both were present throughout, it matters not that the prosecution cannot establish which parent administered it because the other parent must at least be an accomplice, having failed to intervene to save the child.[16] On the other hand, if in such a situation it cannot be

---

[12] *Maxwell v DPP for Northern Ireland* [1979] 1 WLR 1350 (HL); *Taylor, Harrison and Taylor* [1998] Crim LR 582 (CA); cf. P. R. Glazebrook, 'Structuring the Criminal Code', in A. P. Simester and A. T. H. Smith (eds.), *Harm and Culpability* (1996), at 198–200.

[13] *Giannetto* [1997] 1 Cr App R 1, at 9.

[14] *Mercer* [2001] All ER (D) 187 confronted the point directly; *Concannon* [2002] Crim LR 215 dismissed a different and less persuasive argument.

[15] See G. Fletcher, *Rethinking Criminal Law* (1978) 634ff.

[16] *Russell and Russell* (1987) 85 Cr App R 388; *Emery* (1993) 14 Cr App R (S) 394.

established that both parents were present throughout, it cannot be proved that both of them were at least accomplices, and the prosecution must fail.[17] However, as we saw earlier,[18] the Domestic Violence, Crime and Victims Act 2004 introduced a new offence of causing or allowing the death of a child or vulnerable adult, reinforced by inferences from silence, in an attempt to fill this gap.

10.3 THE CONDUCT ELEMENT IN COMPLICITY

We have seen that the 1861 Act refers to those who 'aid, abet, counsel or procure' a crime. As a matter of history, it seems that this Act was intended only to declare the procedure whereby accomplices could be convicted and sentenced as principals, and not to provide a definition of complicity. Earlier statutes had used a wide range of terms—contriving, helping, maintaining, directing—and the wording of the 1861 Act was probably intended merely as a general reference to the existing common law on accomplices. However, the words have taken on an authority of their own. In 1976 the Court of Appeal declared that each of the four verbs should be given its ordinary meaning,[19] but, as we shall see, there are several decisions on the scope of the four terms. One factor that formerly had considerable importance was presence during the commission of the crime. So long as the other conditions for liability were fulfilled, presence turned the accomplice into an aider or abettor, absence into a counsellor or procurer.[20] However, it appears that the distinction no longer has any practical consequences in English law.[21] Whether an accomplice is described as an aider, abettor, counsellor, or procurer seems to depend partly on ordinary language and partly on specific judicial decisions.

(a) AIDING AND ABETTING

It has been traditional to consider the modes of complicity in terms of the two time-honoured pairings: 'aid or abet', and 'counsel or procure'. In fact, the concept of abetment seems to play no independent role now. Abetting involves some encouragement of the principal to commit the offence and this usually accompanies, or is implicit in, an act of aiding. Aid may be given by supplying an instrument to the principal, keeping a look-out, doing preparatory acts, and many other forms of assistance given before or at the time of the offence. As long as it has been shown that the accomplice's conduct helped or might have helped the principal in some way, it does not have to be established that the accomplice caused the principal's offence. Causation requirements

---

[17] *Lane and Lane* (1986) 82 Cr App R 5.   [18] Ch 7.6, above.

[19] *Attorney-General's Reference (No. 1 of 1975)* [1975] QB 773.

[20] See e.g. Lord Goddard CJ in *Ferguson* v *Weaving* [1951] 1 KB 814, and generally J. C. Smith, 'Aid, Abet, Counsel or Procure', in P. R. Glazebrook (ed.) *Reshaping the Criminal Law* (1978).

[21] *Howe* [1987] AC 417, overruling *Richards* [1974] QB 776.

often function so as to fix the threshold of legal liability. However, one cannot, in general, trace causal responsibility through the voluntary act of another person[22]—so it will not usually be possible to hold that an accomplice *caused* the principal to act, save in a rather diluted form of 'causing'.[23] Sanford Kadish has argued that the law does require a form of causation: the courts must be satisfied that the accomplice's help *might* have made a difference to whether the principal's offence was actually committed, in the sense that one could not be sure that it would have been committed but for the accomplice's assistance.[24] However, it is not easy to reconcile all decisions with this approach.

Thus in *Wilcox* v *Jeffery* (1951) a jazz enthusiast attended a concert, applauding the decision of an American jazz musician to give an illegal performance. No point was taken in court about whether the musician was actually encouraged by the defendant's acts.[25] Indeed, in cases where several people applaud or encourage some kind of unlawful spectacle, it would be difficult to maintain that the performer(s) drew actual encouragement from the acts of any one of the spectators. In *Giannetto*[26] the Court of Appeal stated that 'any involvement from mere encouragement upwards would suffice', and did not dissent from the trial judge's suggestion that, if another man had said to D that he was about to kill D's wife, 'as little as patting him on the back, nodding, saying "Oh goody"' would be sufficient to turn D into an aider and abettor. This suggests that even at this late stage a small amount of encouragement, giving moral support to or showing solidarity with the principal, is thought to be sufficient for liability.

What if the principal is unaware of the help given by the secondary party? In the famous American case of *State* v *Tally* (1894),[27] Judge Tally, knowing that his brothers-in-law had set out to kill the deceased, and knowing that someone else had sent a telegram to warn the victim, sent a telegram to the telegraph operator telling him not to deliver the warning telegram. The telegraph operator complied, and the brothers-in-law committed the offence. The judge was convicted of aiding and abetting murder, even though the brothers-in-law were unaware of the judge's assistance when they killed the victim. There was a causal connection in this case, but no meeting of minds between D and P. It is questionable whether this should be sufficient for complicity, although, as we will see below, it amounts to the inchoate offence of encouraging or assisting an offence contrary to section 44 of the Serious Crime Act 2007.

(b) ACCOMPLICE LIABILITY AND SOCIAL DUTIES

We saw in Chapter 4.4 how accomplice liability has been used in English law to establish criminal liability for certain omissions, and the relevant authorities must now be considered in the context of complicity. The cases raise issues of constitutional and social importance, but the key question in accessorial liability is simple to state: can a

---

[22] See above, Ch 4.6(a) and (b).
[23] Cf. H. L. A. Hart and T. Honoré, *Causation in the Law* (2nd edn., 1985), 388.
[24] S. Kadish, *Blame and Punishment* (1987), 162.   [25] [1951] 1 All ER 464.
[26] [1997] 1 Cr App R 1, at 13.   [27] *State* v *Tally* (1894) 15 So 722.

person be convicted as an accomplice merely for standing by and doing nothing while an offence is being committed?

If mere presence at the scene during the principal's offence were sufficient for accomplice liability, this would amount to recognizing a citizen's duty either to leave straight away or to take reasonable steps to prevent or frustrate any offence which is witnessed. The courts have held that non-accidental presence, such as attending a fight or an unlawful theatrical performance, is not conclusive evidence of aiding and abetting.[28] At a minimum there must be an act of encouragement (accompanied by an intention to encourage, discussed in section 10.4 below). Some judgments suggest that it must be shown that encouragement was not just given but also had some effect on the principal,[29] but this has not usually been required. The factual questions are for the jury or magistrates. The requirement of an act of encouragement is not satisfied merely by going to the place where the performance is taking place, but payment and applause may suffice;[30] however, in one case it was held that remaining in a vehicle that was being used to obstruct the police, in circumstances showing that D supported the actions of the driver, might amount to aiding.[31] The position of spectators who happen upon an illegal fight or event and stay to watch it is similar: simply sitting or standing nearby is unlikely to be sufficient for liability, but any cheering or applause would probably tip the balance in favour of conviction. The problems are particularly acute in cases of public disorder. To impose duties on bystanders, even the duty to move away, might be regarded as an incursion on a citizen's right to freedom of assembly (declared in Article 11 of the European Convention). What must be proved, to amount to aiding and abetting one of the offences in the Public Order Act, is that D was present, was giving encouragement, and was intending to encourage others to commit the specified offence.[32] Mere presence should not be sufficient, particularly in view of Article 11.

Are there arguments in favour of the law going further and imposing a duty to take steps to prevent crime? The public disorder example may be complicated by the impotence of individuals to do anything to stop the disturbance and, indeed, the imprudence of their trying to do so. But is it not arguable that there should be at least a duty to alert the police? If so, should failure to do so constitute a distinct offence (as in French law[33]) or complicity in the public disorder? Another example, which does not involve public disorder, occurs where a woman is living with a man who she discovers is dealing in drugs. If the police raid the dwelling and find drugs on the premises, should the law treat her as an accomplice even if there is no evidence of

---

[28] *Coney* (1882) 8 QBD 534.   [29] Hawkins J in ibid., and *Clarkson* [1971] 1 WLR 1402.

[30] *Wilcox* v *Jeffery* [1951] 1 All ER 464.

[31] *Smith* v *Reynolds et al.* [1986] Crim LR 559; for another decision based on voluntary presence, see *O'Flaherty* [2004] Crim LR 751.

[32] *Jefferson et al.* (1994) 99 Cr App R 13, at 22; for a summary of the main public order offences, see Ch 8.3(h) above.

[33] Art. 223(1) of the French Penal Code, discussed by A. Ashworth and E. Steiner, 'Criminal Omissions and Public Duties: the French Experience' (1990) 10 Legal Studies 153.

active assistance or encouragement of the drug-dealing? In the case of *Bland* (1988)[34] the Court of Appeal quashed the woman's conviction as an accomplice. Cases such as this demonstrate a vivid conflict between individuals' rights of privacy in their personal relationships and the social interest in suppressing serious crime. Would it be right for the law to co-opt husbands against wives, parents against children, house-sharing friends against friends in order to increase public protection?[35]

Probably the only way to answer this question is to balance the relative centrality of the right against the seriousness of the offence involved—not a simple exercise, but an inevitable one if the true nature of the problem is to be confronted. The same applies to the situation in *Clarkson* (1971):[36] two soldiers happened to enter a room where other soldiers were raping a woman. It was not found that they did anything other than watch, but they certainly did nothing to discourage continuance of the offence. The Courts Martial Appeal Court quashed their convictions for aiding and abetting, because the judge had not made it clear that there should be proof of both an intent to encourage and actual encouragement. Nothing was said about a duty to alert the authorities immediately in the hope of preventing the crime's continuance. What if three persons came upon one man raping a woman? If it was within their power to put a stop to the offence and to apprehend the offender, should they have a duty to do so—or at least a duty to inform the police?[37] The practical possibilities will vary from case to case, but the real issue is whether there is to be a principle that citizens ought to take reasonable steps to inform the police when they witness an offence. The decision in *Allan* (1965)[38] is against this, emphasizing the requirement of encouragement and adding that, even if D would have joined in if necessary, it would be unacceptable 'to convict a man on his thoughts, unaccompanied by any physical act other than the facts of mere presence'. However, variations in the facts of cases could be accommodated by requiring the citizen only to take 'reasonable steps',[39] and no law should require a person to place his or her own safety in jeopardy. Even if this were accepted, there would remain the question whether it is fairer to convict the defaulting citizen of a new offence of failing to inform the police rather than making the citizen into an accomplice to the principal crime. The former is surely more appropriate in terms of fair labelling.

Can a person be said to aid an offence by an omission?[40] There would surely be no awkwardness in describing the cleaner of a bank who, in pursuance of an agreed plan,

---

[34] [1988] Crim LR 41; cf. also *Bradbury* [1996] Crim LR 808.

[35] Cf. s. 80 of the Police and Criminal Evidence Act 1984, which makes a husband or wife (but not a non-spouse) compellable as a witness on a charge of violence towards a child under 16 in the household; and the offence under s 5 of the Domestic Violence, Crime and Victims Act 2004, which criminalizes any 'member of the same household' (including lodgers and frequent visitors) who fails to take steps to protect a child from the risk of serious harm (below, Ch 7.5).

[36] [1971] 1 WLR 1402.

[37] Cf. the proviso to the new offences in the Serious Crime Act 2007, to be discussed in Ch 11.7 below.

[38] [1965] 1 QB 130; see further G. Williams, 'Criminal Omissions—the Conventional View' (1990) 107 LQR 86.

[39] See n 35 above.   [40] K. J. M. Smith, *Modern Treatise on Complicity*, 39–47.

purposely omits to lock the doors when leaving as 'aiding' a burglary of the bank. In such a case, there is a clear duty and a failure to perform it, and the causation question is answered (in so far as it is relevant to aiding) in the same way as for omissions generally.[41] Another example would be the driving instructor who is supervising a learner driver and who realizes that the learner is about to undertake a manœuvre which is dangerous to other road-users: if, as in *Rubie* v *Faulkner* (1940),[42] the instructor fails to intervene, either by telling the learner not to do it or by physically acting to prevent it, then this failure in the duty of supervision is rightly held to be sufficient to support liability for aiding and abetting the learner driver's offence.

From these cases of duty we turn to cases of legal power, and the so-called 'control principle'. The owner of a car who is a passenger when the car is being driven by another has the legal power to direct this other person not to drive in certain ways;[43] the licensee of a public house has the legal power to require customers to leave at closing-time;[44] the owners of a house have the legal power to direct the behaviour of their children and of visitors to their premises. In the first two cases the courts have held the car owner and the licensee liable as accomplices to the crime of the offender who drives carelessly or remains drinking after hours. What is unusual about these cases is that they rest on the legal *power* of control of, respectively, the car owner and the licensee and not, like *Rubie* v *Faulkner* above, on the existence of a legal *duty* to ensure compliance with the law. A similar analysis is found in *J.F. Alford Transport Ltd* (1997),[45] where the company's convictions for aiding and abetting drivers to falsify their tachograph records were quashed. If the prosecution had proved the power of control, knowledge, and encouragement by non-intervention, that would have been sufficient. The court reasserted the control principle, although this case, unlike the previous two, did not involve D's presence during the commission of the offences; and knowledge, or wilful blindness, was held not to have been established. The control principle departs from the usual approach of not imposing liability for an omission unless a clear duty exists. What the courts have done, in effect, is to assimilate these cases of 'power of control' to cases of duty, thereby creating a new class of public duty.[46] Even though English law does not impose liability for failing to take reasonable steps to prevent an offence which occurs in the street, these cases hold that a property owner will be liable for failing to take reasonable steps to prevent an offence which occurs on or with that property (and with the owner's knowledge). The law has, in effect, co-opted property owners as law-enforcement agents in respect of their own property, and *J.F. Alford Transport* provides for employers to be co-opted in respect of their employees' conduct at work.

---

[41] See above, Ch 4.5(c).

[42] [1940] 1 KB 571, discussed by M. Wasik, 'A Learner's Careless Driving' [1982] Crim LR 411, and D. J. Lanham, 'Drivers, Control and Accomplices' [1982] Crim LR 419.

[43] *Du Cros* v *Lambourne* [1907] 1 KB 40.   [44] *Tuck* v *Robson* [1970] 1 WLR 741.

[45] [1997] 2 Cr App R 326.

[46] Cf. the debate between G. Williams, 'Which of You Did It?' (1989) 52 MLR 179 and D. J. Lanham, 'Three Cases of Accessorial Absurdity' (1990) 53 MLR 75.

The Law Commission rightly recommends the abolition of the control principle, narrowing liability to cases of failure to discharge a legal duty.[47]

Does it amount to aiding if a shopkeeper sells an item to P knowing that P intends to use it in a crime, or if a borrower returns an article to its owner knowing that the owner intends to use it in crime? These could be said to be acts of assistance, in the sense that the physical conduct of selling or returning goods helps an offender: should they, if accompanied by the required mental element, amount to aiding the principal? The problem is that both acts are 'normal': the shopkeeper is simply selling goods in the normal course of business, and the borrower is merely fulfilling a duty to restore the goods to their owner. If the law were to regard either of these acts as 'aiding', it would be requiring the defendants to do something abnormal in the circumstances, and—in effect—punishing them for the omission to do the abnormal thing.

Three approaches to this problem may be considered. The first was described by Devlin J in *National Coal Board* v *Gamble* (1959): 'if one man deliberately sells to another a gun to be used for murdering a third, he may be indifferent whether the third man lives or dies and interested only in the cash profit to be made out of the sale, but he can still be an aider or abettor'.[48] This view criminalizes the shopkeeper as an accomplice in every case where the customer's intention to commit that kind of offence is known. Criminal liability might be justified by arguing that a small sacrifice is properly required of shopkeepers in order to benefit the potential victims of crime. Surely, where an offence against the person is a possibility, it is right to place the potential victim's right not to be subjected to assault or injury above the shopkeeper's liberty to sell to all-comers. After all, the shopkeeper is not being required to intervene or even to notify the police of the customer's intentions. The requirement is not to sell goods when the customer is known to be bent on crime.

Despite the decision in *Gillick* v *West Norfolk and Wisbech Area Health Authority* (1986),[49] the statement in *NCB* v *Gamble* that selling goods in the ordinary course of business can satisfy the conduct element of 'aiding' remains good law. But, as we will see in section 10.4 below, there is also support for a second approach, long upheld in many American jurisdictions, namely, that a shopkeeper should be liable as an accomplice only where it was his or her *purpose* to further the customer's offence.[50] This stresses the notions of free trade and individual autonomy, treating the shopkeeper as a mere trader rather than as a fellow citizen's keeper. A third approach would not involve the law of complicity, but would treat the shopkeeper's liability as a matter of general criminal law—either by creating a special offence of selling goods which are likely to be used in the commission of crime (of which there are some examples now, such as the sale of knives) or through the offence of encouraging or assisting

---

[47] Law Com No 305, *Participating in Crime*, para. 3.41 and draft Bill, cl. 8, p. 160.

[48] *NCB* v *Gamble* [1959] 1 QB 11.

[49] *Gillick* v *West Norfolk and Wisbech Area Health Authority* [1986] AC 112, criticized in Ch 4.9(b) and Ch 5.2(b)(ii) above, and discussed in detail at p. 418 below.

[50] Model Penal Code, s. 2.06(3); see also the reasoning of Glanville Williams, *Criminal Law: the General Part* (2nd edn., 1961), sect. 124.

an offence believing that it will be committed, contrary to section 45 of the Serious Crime Act 2007.[51]

Is there a material difference where someone who has borrowed goods is asked by the owner to return them so that they may be used for a crime? In *NCB* v *Gamble* it was held by Devlin J that returning goods in these circumstances is a 'negative act' rather than a 'positive act': 'a man who hands over to another his own property on demand, although(h)e may physically be performing a positive act, in law is only refraining from detinue'.[52] To invent a distinction between 'positive' and 'negative' acts in order to exempt a borrower who returns goods is unconvincing. In one sense the case is weaker than that of the shopkeeper, since the borrower has a duty to return goods to their owner, whereas a shopkeeper has no duty to sell; but in another sense it is just as strong, since a court would be reluctant to find the borrower liable in tort for failing to return goods in such circumstances, and would be more likely to recognize a defence based on the prevention of crime. Devlin J's analysis, despite the fragility of the positive–negative distinction, may appear to offer a pragmatic solution, but it is inadequate when it comes to dealing with a case where the borrower is returning a gun which is then to be used for killing someone. The potential victim's rights must count for more than the borrower's duty to return goods to their owner. Rather than concealing these conflicts behind Devlin J's unconvincing analysis, a preferable course would be either to allow a defence of 'balance of evils' to any apparently criminal complicity,[53] or to state that D should not be liable for returning property to its owner unless D shares the owner's criminal purpose or unless a crime of violence is known to be in contemplation.[54]

(c) COUNSELLING AND PROCURING

The characteristic contribution of the counsellor or procurer is to incite, instigate, or advise on the commission of the substantive offence by the principal. One way of expressing this is to describe the role as 'encouraging' the perpetrator. Some European legal systems provide a higher maximum penalty for an accomplice who incites or instigates than for a mere helper, and a general justification for this can readily be found. No offence might have taken place at all but for the instigation, and this is surely more reprehensible than assisting someone who has already decided to commit a crime. In practice, however, there are many shades of culpability between helpers and instigators, a point which strikes the English lawyer more forcefully because of the uncertain limits of the terms 'counselling' and 'procuring'. The ordinary meaning of

---

[51] Discussed in Ch 11.7 below.   [52] [1959] 1 QB 11, at 20, discussing *Lomas* (1913) 9 Cr App R 220.

[53] See above, Ch 4.8, and cf. the defence created by s 50 of the Serious Crime Act 2007, discussed at Ch 11.7(d) below, with the defence recommended in Law Com No. 305, *Participating in Crime*, draft Bill, p. 159.

[54] G. Williams, 'Obedience to Law as a Crime' (1990) 53 MLR 445; an alternative advanced by G. R. Sullivan, 'The Law Commission Consultation Paper on Complicity: Fault Elements and Joint Enterprise' [1994] Crim LR 252, is to exempt crimes triable only on indictment.

'counselling' may fall well short of inciting or instigating an offence, and covers such conduct as advising on an offence and giving information required for an offence; whereas the ordinary meaning of 'procuring' is said to be 'to produce by endeavour',[55] which goes beyond mere instigation.

The forms of counselling and procuring recognized by English law probably stretch from the giving of advice or information through encouraging or trying to persuade another person to commit the crime to such conduct as threatening or commanding that the offence be committed. Generally speaking, the accomplice's culpability increases as one proceeds towards the extreme of a command backed by threats. In that extreme situation the principal may have the defence of duress,[56] and may be regarded as an innocent agent of the threatener, who then becomes the principal.[57] There are also cases in which the principal does not realize that someone is trying to bring about an offence: for example, if D surreptitiously laces P's non-alcoholic drink with some form of alcohol and P subsequently drives a car, unaware of the consumption of alcohol, P will be liable to conviction for drunken driving and D could be convicted of procuring the offence, so long as it was shown that D knew P was intending to drive. Such conduct fulfils the ordinary definition of procuring: 'you procure a thing by setting out to see that it happens and taking appropriate steps to produce that happening'.[58]

The ordinary meaning of procuring, 'to produce by endeavour', is not restricted to cases where the principal is unaware of the accomplice's design. One can take the appropriate steps to bring about a crime by persuading another to do the required acts—for example, by shaming someone into committing an offence by taunts of cowardice—but conduct such as hiring 'hit-men' to carry out an offence is probably better described as counselling.[59] It can be said that in cases of procuring there is a causal relationship between the accomplice's procuring and the principal's act, and it is proper to say that the principal acts *in consequence of* the accomplice's conduct.[60] These cases, then, represent the high-water mark of causal connection among the various types of accessorial conduct, headed by the case of procuring an unwitting principal (where D laces P's drink), in which there is no meeting of minds between principal and accomplice. Such a strong causal connection is not found in counselling, which may merely involve the supply of information, advice, or encouragement. This led Professor Sir John Smith to conclude that: 'procuring requires causation but not consensus; encouraging requires consensus but not causation; assisting requires actual help but neither consensus nor causation'.[61] If cases of hiring hit-men are classified as

---

[55] *Attorney-General's Reference (No. 1 of 1975)* [1975] QB 773.   [56] See above, Ch 6.3.

[57] See *Bourne* (1952) 36 Cr App R 125, discussed below, Ch 10.6.

[58] See *Attorney-General's Reference (No. 1 of 1975)* [1975] QB 773. Cf. P. Alldridge, 'The Doctrine of Innocent Agency' (1990) 2 Crim Law Forum 45.

[59] As on the facts of *Richards* [1974] QB 776, and of *Calhaem* [1985] QB 808.

[60] Hart and Honoré, *Causation in the Law*, 51–9, and Ch 4.5(d) above.

[61] J. C. Smith, 'Aid, Abet, Counsel or Procure', 134; perhaps the words 'actual or potential help' might be preferable.

counselling or encouraging, then all that is required is that the accomplice and principal reached some kind of agreement on what was to be done, with the accomplice encouraging the principal (usually by offering money) to carry out the crime.[62]

(d) THE PROBLEMS OF THE CONDUCT ELEMENT

The Law Commission's proposed reforms of complicity will be discussed later, but we should note at this point some of the difficulties of the conduct element. It is not just that the four key terms are opaque and that basic questions of principle and policy (concerning, for example, omissions liability and social duties) are resolved on a case-by-case basis. There are two more fundamental difficulties, stemming largely from the breadth of the concept of 'aiding'. The first is that any contribution by the accomplice seems to suffice for liability, no matter how small. This brings both uncertainty and the potential for injustice. The second and related difficulty is that the element of causation stemming from the accomplice's assistance may be slight. Should cases where D's contribution has no causal impact on P's commission of the offence lead to D's liability for the substantive offence, let alone the sentence for it, particularly if that sentence is mandatory (as in murder)? Where the contribution is small and non-essential—such as driving P to a place close to where the offence is to be committed[63]—the sufficiency of the causal contribution may also be questioned.[64] Under the Serious Crime Act 2007, it would now be a separate offence of encouraging or assisting crime, but the penalty structure is the same.

10.4 THE FAULT ELEMENT IN COMPLICITY

The fault required for conviction as an accomplice differs from that required for all other forms of criminal liability. This is because it concerns not merely the defendant's awareness of the nature and effect of his own acts, but also his awareness of the intentions of the principal. It is a form of two-dimensional fault, which brings with it various complexities: the would-be accomplice's knowledge of the principal's intentions may be more or less detailed, and in any event the principal might not do exactly as planned.

Two basic fault requirements may be outlined. First, the accomplice must intend to do whatever acts of assistance or encouragement are done, and must be aware of their ability to assist or encourage the principal.[65] Secondly, the accomplice must know the 'essential matters which constitute the offence'.[66] The scope of this oft-quoted phrase is unclear. It seems that it includes the facts, circumstances, and other matters that

---

[62] *Calhaem* [1985] QB 808.   [63] As in *Bryce* [2004] 2 Cr App R 35, below n 76.
[64] See the strong arguments by R. Sullivan, 'First degree murder and complicity' (2007) 1 *Crim. Law & Phil.* 271; cf. J. Gardner, 'Complicity and Causality' (2007) 1 *Crim. Law & Phil.* 127, at 137.
[65] K. J. M. Smith, *Modern Treatise on Complicity*, 141.   [66] *Johnson* v *Youden* [1950] 1 KB 544.

go to make up the conduct element of the principal offence; but, as we shall see below, there is uncertainty about the extent to which the accomplice must know the details of the offence. There is authority that knowledge includes wilful blindness: thus if D failed to make enquiries about a fairly obvious illegality he might be convicted on the basis of 'shutting his eyes to the obvious', whereas mere negligence in failing to make reasonable enquiries of others cannot suffice.[67] The requirements of intention and knowledge apply whether the principal's crime is one of recklessness, negligence, or strict liability. Why is the higher degree of fault required for the accomplice than for the principal? The answer, as for inchoate offences (see below, Chapter 11.3(a)), is that as the form of criminal liability moves further away from the actual infliction of harm so the grounds of liability should become narrower. Otherwise, the law would spread its net wide indeed, and all kinds of people who did acts which, unbeknown to them, helped others to commit crimes of strict liability or negligence might find themselves liable to conviction. In fact, the two basic fault requirements are put under strain largely in cases of assisting crime in which D is not present at the commission of the offence, and in cases of encouraging (counselling, procuring) when there is a change of plan. Thus, thirdly, it is not merely that the accomplice must have some awareness of what the principal is doing, but in cases where the accomplice acts before the principal starts to commit the crime there is also the problem of awareness of what will happen in the future. In effect, this is a question of prediction rather than knowledge—or, to put it another way, a question of reckless knowledge, being aware that there is a risk of one or more offences occurring.

Given the emphasis on requiring intention and full knowledge in complicity cases, is there ever a justification for lowering the requirements to a form of recklessness? Perhaps the leading case is *Blakely and Sutton v Chief Constable of West Mercia* (1991):[68] the two defendants had laced P's soft drinks with vodka, intending to inform him of this and thus lead him to stay the night with the first defendant rather than driving home. P left before they could inform him, and was convicted of driving with excess alcohol. The two defendants were charged with procuring P's offence and, although their convictions were quashed, it emerges from McCullough J's judgment in the Divisional Court that it may be sufficient for other forms of complicity, if not for procuring, that D contemplated that his act 'would or might' bring about or assist the commission of the principal offence.[69] There is no evidence that prosecutors have exploited this new-found width in the law of complicity, but it could lead to the conviction of most people who host parties at which alcohol is consumed and after which

---

[67] *J.F. Alford Transport Ltd* [1997] 2 Cr App R at 332, following the High Court of Australia in *Giorgianni v R* (1985) 156 CLR 473 at 483; cf. the discussion in S. Shute and A. P. Simester (eds.), *Criminal Law Theory* (2002), between Shute (196–8) and Sullivan (213–14).

[68] [1991] RTR 405.

[69] This case was unusual in that the prosecution alleged only 'procuring'. Cf. the aiding and abetting case of *Carter v Richardson* [1974] RTR 314, and also *Roberts and George* [1997] Crim LR 209, where the Court of Appeal ruled out 'negligent blindness' and also questioned whether any form of recklessness should suffice. For support for extending liability to recklessness see S. Kadish, 'Reckless Complicity' (1997) 87 J Crim Law and Criminology 369.

guests drive their cars, unless the host keeps a careful check on the drinks consumed by potential drivers.[70] One implication of *Bryce* (2004)[71] is that it is sufficient if D believes, at the time he aids P (in this case, by transporting him by motor-cycle to a place near the proposed venue for the killing), that it is a 'real possibility' that P will go on to commit the offence—a recklessness test. Similarly in *Webster* (2006)[72] the Court of Appeal held that the appropriate test was whether D foresaw that P was *likely* to commit the offence—a restricted form of recklessness.

The interaction of the conduct element and the fault element in complicity has not always operated so as to broaden liability. Cases in which recklessness is relied upon have been rare, and greater attention has been given to the conflict of authority between two leading cases on intention and knowledge. The first is *National Coal Board* v *Gamble* (1959),[73] where a weighbridge operator issued a ticket to a lorry driver certifying the lorry's weight and thus allowing him to take his lorry out of the colliery and on to a public road. The Divisional Court held that the weighbridge operator was liable for aiding and abetting the driver's offence so long as he knew that the lorry was overweight and that it was about to be driven on a public road,[74] with Devlin J explaining that '*mens rea* is a matter of intent only and does not depend on desire or motive'. Thus, it was irrelevant that the weighbridge operator was 'only doing his job' and had no personal interest in what the lorry driver might do thereafter. His *knowledge* of what the lorry driver *was about to do* was sufficient. This approach would also lead to the conviction of a shopkeeper who knows that his customer plans to use a certain item for a crime and who nevertheless sells the item, and it is dissatisfaction with this outcome which led the framers of the American Model Penal Code to impose the more stringent requirement that the accomplice should have acted with the *purpose* of promoting or facilitating the offence.[75] The effect of that narrower doctrine is to ensure that citizens are not treated as their fellow citizens' keepers, a sturdy individualist approach. The wider doctrine of *NCB* v *Gamble*, which imposes accomplice liability wherever a person knows that the recipient intends to commit a certain crime with the property delivered, has the effect of placing a seller, a weighbridge operator, etc. under a duty not to make the sale or issue the ticket in these circumstances. Not only is this consistent with the general assimilation of foresight of practical certainty within intention,[76] but it also supports a more social and less individualistic notion of responsibility.

English courts have not always felt comfortable with the proposition that knowledge of the principal's intention (without purpose) should suffice for accomplice liability—indeed, Slade J dissented on the point in *NCB* v *Gamble*—and in the unusual

---

[70] The attempt of Lord Widgery CJ in *Attorney-General's Reference (No. 1 of 1975)* [1975] QB 773 to argue that the 'generous host' would not be liable was unconvincing then, and is more unconvincing since the *Blakely* case.

[71] [2004] 2 Cr App R 35.   [72] [2006] 2 Cr App R 6.   [73] [1959] 1 QB 11.

[74] See also *Attorney-General* v *Able* [1984] 1 QB 795.   [75] Model Penal Code, s. 2.06(3).

[76] As in *Woollin* [1999] 1 AC 92 and the draft Criminal Code, cl. 18(b), discussed above, Ch 5.5(b).

circumstances of *Gillick* v *West Norfolk and Wisbech Area Health Authority* (1986)[77] the House of Lords held that a doctor who supplies contraceptives to a girl under 16, knowing that this will assist her boyfriend to commit the offence of sexual activity with a child, is not an accomplice to the boyfriend's offence. The reason for this decision seems to be that the doctor's purpose would be not to assist the boy but to protect the girl. This runs directly counter to *NCB* v *Gamble*, where it was held that mere knowledge of assistance is enough and that purpose is not required. *Gillick* should probably not be treated as conclusive on the issue of accomplice liability, since their Lordships did not trouble to examine the existing authorities in their speeches.[78] The doctor's motive evidently overshadowed the case,[79] and a preferable way of dealing with that emerges from *Clarke* (1985).[80] Here the Court of Appeal held that a person who knowingly assists others in a burglary with the intent of ensuring that the police capture both the burglars and the stolen property does satisfy the mental element of complicity (in that he knows that the principals will commit the offence), but may have a defence based on his purpose of assisting law enforcement. That decision keeps the question of the accomplice's knowledge separate from the question of whether there is any justification or other defence.[81]

It is regrettable that the question discussed in *Gamble* and in *Gillick* has been obscured by confusions of terminology (e.g. different meanings of intention) and by a failure to discuss it as an issue of principle—what ought to be the proper scope of the criminal law in this sphere? One might argue that the difficulty in finding a reasonably certain definition of the conduct element in complicity renders it desirable to maintain a narrow fault requirement, and yet the decision in *Blakely and Sutton* v *Chief Constable of West Mercia*[82] has the opposite effect by recognizing advertent recklessness as sufficient.

Further problems on fault arise from the fact that at least two people are involved, the accomplice and the principal, and so it is often a question of one person's knowledge of another person's intentions. Some issues can be resolved by basic propositions. If the aider knows the nature of the offence which the principal intends to commit but does not know when it is to occur, that should be immaterial: time is rarely specified as an element in the definition of a crime. The same applies to the location of the offence: so long as the aider knows that the principal plans to burgle a bank, ignorance as to the particular bank is immaterial to accomplice liability.[83] The real difficulties begin when the aider or counsellor does not know precisely what offence the principal intends to commit, and has only a general idea. Should this be sufficient?

---

[77] [1986] AC 112.

[78] Thus in *J.F. Alford Transport* [1997] 2 Cr App R at 335 the Court of Appeal followed *NCB* v *Gamble* on this point without citing *Gillick*, and in *Powell* [1999] AC 1, 30, Lord Hutton expressly declined to follow the *Gillick* approach.

[79] For discussion of a possible defence of medical necessity, based on *Gillick*, see above, Ch 4.9(b).

[80] (1985) 80 Cr App R 344; below, section 10.7(c).

[81] Cf now the reasonableness defence provided by s. 50 of the Serious Crime Act 2007 to the new offences created by that Act, and discussed at Ch 11.7(d) below.

[82] Above, n 67 and accompanying text.   [83] *Bainbridge* [1960] 1 QB 219.

Let us suppose that D lends P some mechanical cutting equipment, knowing full well that P intends to use it in connection with a forthcoming crime but having no precise idea of the crime intended: D does not ask, and P does not tell. In fact, D uses the equipment in a burglary. On facts similar to these, the decision in *Bainbridge* (1960)[84] held that neither mere suspicion nor broad knowledge of some criminal intention is sufficient: the minimum condition for accomplice liability is knowledge that the principal intends to commit a crime of the *type* actually committed. This decision clearly goes against, or beyond, the basic requirement that the accomplice should know the essential matters that constitute the principal's crime.[85] Should this extension of liability be opposed—knowledge of the particular crime committed ought to be required, because the theory is that the accomplice's liability derives from the principal's offence—or should it be accepted as a pragmatic solution which avoids the acquittals of those who assist willingly without knowing the precise form of offence envisaged? This might depend on the breadth of the term 'type', and some light is thrown on this by the decision of the House of Lords in *Maxwell v DPP for Northern Ireland* (1978).[86] Maxwell was persuaded to drive a car for a group of terrorists, knowing broadly what offences they *might* commit, but not knowing which one or ones they *would* commit. It was held that he was liable as an accomplice to the offence of doing an act with intent to cause an explosion, so long as he contemplated that offence as one of the possible offences and intentionally lent his assistance. As Lord Scarman put it: 'an accessory who leaves it to his principal to choose is liable, provided always the choice is made from the range of offences from which the accessory contemplates the choice will be made'.

It is not difficult to see why the courts reached the decisions in *Bainbridge* and in *Maxwell*. They probably believed that a narrow view of the mental element in complicity might open the door to acquittal for some persons believed to be sufficiently culpable, and in *Maxwell* there was the additional factor of the defendant's knowing involvement in terrorism which may have led the court to avoid a narrow view. Both courts appear to have decided to propound a test which stops short of proclaiming that a general criminal intent is sufficient (i.e. knowledge that the principal was going to commit *some* crime), and yet which goes wider than a requirement of full knowledge of the particular crime. The effect of the *Maxwell* test is to introduce reckless knowledge as sufficient: the accomplice knows that one or more of a group of offences is virtually certain to be committed, which means that in relation to the one(s) actually committed, there was knowledge only of a *risk* that it would be committed—and that amounts to recklessness. Since our discussion began with the principle that accomplice liability should be restricted to cases of full knowledge, the ruling in *Maxwell*—like the subsequent decision in *Bryce*[87]—amounts to a significant departure. Yet there is surely no merit in acquitting a person who willingly gives assistance,

---

[84] Ibid.

[85] See *Johnson v Youden*, above, n 66; the Law Commission was prepared to describe the *Bainbridge* judgment as an 'evasion' of this basic requirement: LCCP, *Assisting and Encouraging Crime*, para. 3.22.

[86] [1978] 3 All ER 1140.   [87] Above, n 76 and accompanying text.

knowing that one of a group of crimes will be committed but not knowing exactly which one. Such a person has surely crossed the threshold of blameworthiness, both in conduct and in the accompanying fault.

The matter is now dealt with by the offence in section 46 of the Serious Crime Act 2007, of encouraging or assisting offences believing that one or more will be committed. As its name suggests, this offence aims to deal with the very situation that arose in *Maxwell*, and it does so by the creation of this new offence in the inchoate mode—an offence committed whether or not the principal goes ahead.[88]

10.5 JOINT VENTURES AND ACCESSORIAL LIABILITY FOR DIFFERENT RESULTS

The essence of accessorial liability is that D, an accomplice, incurs liability for the offence committed by P, the principal. In 10.3 and 10.4 above we discussed the conduct and fault elements required. Now we turn to cases where P commits an offence not envisaged by D—P commits a more serious offence, or the same offence with a different result, or a lesser offence. On the basic principles set out earlier, D should only be liable for the different offence if and insofar as he knew its essential elements, etc. We will see below how that principle, and other general principles, have been applied to these cases.

But there is also a separate doctrine to be considered here, the doctrine of joint enterprise or joint venture. When P, D and E agree to commit a robbery, each of them is liable for the agreed crime, as principal(s) or accomplice(s) according to the nature of their contribution. That is an application of general complicity rules. The analysis differs is when P commits a further and more serious offence. The doctrine operates so that, if it can be said that P, D and E embarked on a joint venture to commit an offence (such as robbery), D and/or E may be held liable for a further offence (such as murder) that P goes on to commit if certain conditions are fulfilled. The conditions appear to be threefold:

(i)   P, D and E had an agreed purpose to commit a particular crime;

(ii) D and/or E knew that there was a real risk that P might go on to commit a further particular crime;

(iii) the further crime that P committed was not fundamentally different from what D and/or E had anticipated.

The authority for these conditions will be discussed in the paragraphs below. There has long been controversy about whether the doctrine of common purpose or joint enterprise amounts to an additional form of complicity liability (beyond aiding,

---

[88] The offence is discussed in Ch 11.7(c) below.

abetting, counselling, or procuring), or was merely a descriptive term without legal consequences.[89] Sir John Smith maintained that there is no separate doctrine of joint enterprise and no separate rules,[90] whereas Professors Simester and Sullivan argue strongly that joint enterprise is a distinct doctrine. Recent decisions of high authority leave little doubt that at common law there is a doctrine of joint enterprise, and that its effect is to broaden D's liability for P's further offences where the three conditions are fulfilled. Of course many other cases of complicity, where D is liable for aiding, abetting, counselling or procuring P's offence, could be described as joint criminal ventures too;[91] but the only type of case where the doctrine has any legal effect is where it extends D's liability for offences that P commits outside the actual agreement with D. The type of case in which this might arise is where A, B and C plan a robbery in which they will carry weapons to frighten but not to use, and C unilaterally decides to use his weapon to kill the victim of the robbery.

What are the justifications for thus extending the normal grounds for accessorial liability? Andrew Simester argues that cases of joint enterprise form a sub-set of complicity cases that are distinguished by D's agreement or common purpose with P to achieve a certain criminal goal. Through this agreement D associates himself with, and affiliates himself to, the joint criminal venture, and gives moral support to and shows solidarity with the other member(s) of the enterprise.[92] It is this change of normative position by D that supplies the justification for extending D's liability, so that D is liable not just for further offences he helped or encouraged P to commit, but also for any further offence that he foresaw a real risk of P committing. The moral significance of the change of normative position does not justify making D liable for any offence that P happens to commit—D's unlawful act is participating in a joint criminal venture does not open the way to wide-ranging constructive liability, only to liability based on recklessness (foresight of a real risk). It remains true that D is being held liable for a further crime he did not intend or endorse or support. But the argument is that D's support for the criminal venture, combined with his recklessness as to the further crime committed, is strong enough, not least because joint criminal ventures tend to have a momentum of their own that makes the commission of crimes more likely.

We now turn to consider three sets of cases in which P commits a different crime than envisaged: the first set, relating to more serious offences, is concerned exclusively with joint enterprise, whereas the second and third sets may or may not involve cases of joint venture.

---

[89] See K. J. M. Smith, *Modern Treatise on Complicity*, chs 7 and 8.

[90] See his 'Criminal Liability of Accessories: Law and Law Reform' (1997) 113 LQR 453, and now Smith and Hogan, *Criminal Law*, 206–19.

[91] For different developments of 'the common purpose principle' in South Africa, see J. Burchell, *Principles of Criminal Law* (3rd edn., 2005), ch 41.

[92] A. P. Simester, 'The Mental Element in Complicity' (2006) 122 LQR 578, broadly adopted in Law Com No 305, *Participating in Crime* (2007), 59–64.

(a) JOINT VENTURE: LIABILITY FOR DIFFERENT, MORE SERIOUS OFFENCE

Where one party (P) deliberately deviates from the common purpose held by one or more others in a joint venture so as to commit a more serious offence, English law has not pursued an unwavering course. More than a century ago Sir James Stephen stated the test as whether the crime committed by P could be regarded as a 'probable consequence' of the joint enterprise—an objective test of foreseeability, to be applied at the point at which the assistance was given or the agreement reached.[93] To allow liability to turn on an objective test of foreseeability was open to criticism on the familiar unfairness grounds,[94] and the modern decisions have moved away from it. Thus in *Chan Wing-Siu* (1985)[95] the defendants had gone to commit a robbery armed with knives, and one of their number used a knife to kill one of the robbery victims. The other defendants argued that the agreement was to commit robbery, using the knives to frighten and not to cause death or injury. However, the Privy Council held that there is a doctrine of common purpose that 'turns on contemplation... or authorization, which may be express but is more usually implied. It meets the case of a crime foreseen as a possible incident of the common unlawful enterprise. The criminal culpability lies in participating in the venture with that foresight.' The element of prior agreement or 'authorization' seems to be rather weak here: in reality, the basis of liability has shifted to (subjective) foresight of a significant possibility, as the Privy Council confirmed when suggesting that a remote possibility would be insufficient, but that foresight of a 'real risk' would be enough. Thus the basis of joint enterprise liability is now a restricted form of (subjective) recklessness, similar in spirit to the *Maxwell* decision.[96]

The House of Lords confirmed this approach in *Powell*.[97] Three men went to a drug dealer to buy drugs and the drug dealer was shot dead. The prosecution could not prove which of the three fired the shot, but the submission was that the two must have known that the other had a gun and might use it. Lord Hutton held that the test to be applied is that 'it is sufficient to found a conviction for murder for a secondary party to have realized that in the course of the joint enterprise the primary party might kill with intent to do so or with intent to cause grievous bodily harm'.[98] It follows that awareness that one of D's confederates might commit murder is sufficient to convict D as an accomplice, with a mandatory sentence of life imprisonment. It was argued strongly in *Powell* that this is unfair, and that it ought to be shown that the accomplice knew that it was virtually certain that P would kill or cause serious injury. However, the House of Lords rejected this, Lord Steyn quoting Sir John Smith's argument that the question is not simply whether the accomplice was reckless whether death or serious injury would result: 'he must have been aware, not merely that death or grievous

---

[93] J. F. Stephen, *A Digest of the Criminal Law*, art. 20.   [94] See above, Ch 5.4(a) and 5.5(a).
[95] [1985] AC 168.
[96] See above, n 86 and accompanying text. For a conviction of aiding and abetting murder based on reckless assistance, see *Bryce* [2004] 2 Cr App R 35.
[97] [1999] AC 1.   [98] Ibid., at 24.

bodily harm might be caused, but that it might be caused intentionally, by a person whom he was assisting or encouraging to commit a crime'.[99]

The House of Lords revisited the doctrine of joint enterprise in *Rahman* (2008),[100] where D and others joined in a fight against another gang with a variety of blunt instruments. The deceased was cornered and beaten by D and several others, but it transpired that the death was caused by a deep stab wound. D's argument was that not only was he unaware that anyone had a knife, but he was also unaware that anyone would kill with intent to kill. The House of Lords held unanimously that P's intent to kill need not be known by others in the joint enterprise: the question is whether they knew there was a real risk of death or grievous bodily harm being caused intentionally. This confirms that the doctrine of joint enterprise has a broad sweep, although here it combines with the broad definition of murder (including an intention to cause grievous bodily harm). Becoming part of a joint enterprise and being aware that others might cause serious injury intentionally is sufficient to convict D of murder, with the mandatory sentence of life imprisonment, Although Schedule 21 of the Criminal Justice Act 2003 draws a distinction between killings with intent to kill and killings with intent to cause grievous bodily harm for the purpose of setting the minimum term,[101] the law of murder brackets them together for the purpose of determining liability.

If D is held not liable as an accomplice to P's conduct, because D did not foresee a 'real risk' that P would do as he did or because it was 'fundamentally different', can D still be convicted of being an accomplice to manslaughter if P's crime was murder? There are conflicting authorities on this point. In favour of a manslaughter conviction are decisions such as *Stewart and Schofield*[102] and the Northern Ireland decision in *Gilmour*,[103] where D was the get-away driver for a petrol-bombing. It was held that there was insufficient evidence that D was aware that the bomb was such a large and potentially destructive one, so his conviction for aiding and abetting murder was quashed; but the Court went on to hold him liable for complicity in manslaughter on the ground that P did the act that had been contemplated (petrol-bombing a house). This decision, however, overlooks the significance of the size of the bomb, about which D was mistaken.[104] Against a manslaughter conviction in these situations are decisions such as *English*,[105] where no manslaughter conviction was substituted when the murder conviction was quashed, and *Attorney General's Reference No. 3 of 2004*,[106] where a manslaughter conviction was held to depend on D's anticipation that P would do an unlawful and dangerous act towards V. The *Reference* case seems correct so far as it goes,[107] but in most cases the prosecution would be wise to charge any relevant lesser offences (e.g. relating to the possession of firearms or other weapons).

---

[99] J. C. Smith, 'Criminal Liability of Accessories', at 464, cited by Lord Steyn at [1999] AC 14.

[100] [2008] UKHL 45.   [101] See Ch.7.3(a) above.

[102] [1995] 1 Cr App R 441, a controversial decision that supports a separate doctrine of joint enterprise.

[103] [2000] 2 Cr App R 407.   [104] For criticism, see Smith and Hogan, *Criminal Law*, 217.

[105] [1999] AC 1.   [106] [2005] EWCA Crim 1882.

[107] It is also clear from this decision that, if P had killed V accidentally, D would have been an accomplice to P's commission of manslaughter. The distinctions here are fine.

(b) SAME OFFENCE, DIFFERENT RESULT

What is the position where P commits the same type of offence as D had envisaged but by some unexpected method? If the different result occurs because of an unexpected miscarriage of some kind, the law takes the same approach towards accomplices as it does to offences by individuals. Thus, where the intended result occurs by an unexpected mode (e.g. death caused by drowning rather than by beating), this does not affect the accomplice's liability;[108] where the principal makes a mistake of identity and commits the offence against the wrong victim, this is also irrelevant;[109] and where the intended offence falls upon the wrong victim because the principal's attempt to harm one person succeeds only in harming another, this too is irrelevant.[110] In so far as the policies of transferred liability and the other rules are sound for individuals, they should apply to principals and accomplices. The same should presumably be said of constructive liability: thus, if D helps P in an assault on V, as a result of which V unexpectedly dies, a law which renders P liable for manslaughter should also apply so as to render D an accomplice to manslaughter.[111] These propositions all apply the logic of English law's 'derivative' theory of complicity, whereby the accomplice's liability derives from that of the principal. Most of the questions could, in theory, be approached in other ways—for example, by making the accomplice's liability turn on what he or she intended the principal to do, rather than attaching liability to what actually happened.[112]

The common factor in the above group of cases is that the result was unexpected by both P and D. The problem of the D's liability is different in cases where P deviates intentionally from the agreed course of conduct. Thus in the old case of *Saunders and Archer* (1573), D had advised P to kill his wife by means of a poisoned apple; P placed the apple before his wife, but the wife passed the apple to their small child, who ate it and died.[113] D was held not to have been an accomplice in the child's murder, on the basis that the events amounted to a deliberate change of plan by P. Although P did not actually give the apple to the child, he sat by and allowed the child to eat the apple when it was his parental duty to intervene. This failure to prevent the miscarriage of the plan was treated as equivalent to approval by P, and thus as a voluntary intervening act (omission) it was enough to negative D's complicity in the actual result.

The issue has re-emerged as a crucial one in relation to joint enterprise and murder. In *English*[114] D joined P in an attack on a police officer with wooden posts, but during the course of the attack P produced a knife and stabbed the officer fatally. D's case was that he did not know P had a knife, and that he should therefore not be liable for aiding and abetting murder. The prosecution argued that D had willingly joined in an attack using wooden posts, clearly realizing that P might cause serious injury, and so

---

[108] For the unforeseen mode see Ch 5.6(b) above.   [109] For mistaken victim see Ch 5.6(c) above.
[110] For transferred fault see Ch 5.6(d) above.
[111] *Baldessare* (1930) 22 Cr App R 70; cf. *Mahmood* [1994] Crim LR 368.
[112] Discussed further in section 10.8 below.   [113] (1573) 2 Plowd 473.
[114] The appeal in this case was consolidated with *Powell* [1999] AC 1.

D knew that P might well have the fault element for murder and should be liable despite the unexpected change of mode. The House of Lords came down in favour of the defence argument, holding that D's conviction should be quashed because 'the unforeseen use of the knife would take the killing outside the scope of the joint venture'.[115] Lord Hutton added:

if the weapon used by the primary party is different to, but as dangerous as, the weapon which the secondary party contemplated he might use, the secondary party should not escape liability for murder because of the difference in the weapon, for example if he foresaw that the primary party might use a gun to kill and the latter used a knife to kill, or vice versa.

This was a new principle. The first question in all such cases is the evidential one: did D know that P was carrying the weapon with which death was caused? If he did, then the case falls within (a) above. If the requisite knowledge is not established beyond a reasonable doubt, then the court may still convict D as an accomplice if P used a weapon which was not 'fundamentally different' from the means of injuring or killing that D had contemplated, or was just as 'dangerous' as the means contemplated.[116] The House of Lords returned to the 'fundamental difference' exception to the doctrine of joint enterprise in *Rahman*.[117] The argument that P's act was fundamentally different from what D contemplated because P intended to kill was not accepted by the House, which regarded the exception as confined to the fundamentally different nature of P's act.

These decisions, spanning over four centuries from 1573, seem to be at odds with English law's general disregard of the identity of the victim and of the method used to effect result-oriented crimes. Accepting all the other rules of complicity, if we are satisfied that D knew that P intended to kill V and gave him assistance or encouragement to do so, why should it matter if either P decided to kill Y instead, or P killed V by a different method from that envisaged by D? Most statements of the *English-Rahman* exception refer to P's act as being 'fundamentally different'; but surely what should matter, particularly in a paradigm result-crime such as homicide, is the consequence that P brought about, not the precise form of the act by which P brought the consequence about. Thus if D realized the risk that P might either kill or cause serious injury intentionally, the method chosen by P should not matter. Perhaps one might reply that liability for complicity is premised on either consensus or causation, and that where P chooses a different victim or a different method this should relieve D of liability as an accomplice—there is no longer a consensus or common purpose, and any causal link between D's assistance and P's conduct is severed by P's voluntary and unexpected

---

[115] Cf. the argument of C. M. V. Clarkson, 'Complicity, *Powell* and Manslaughter' [1998] Crim LR 556 in favour of conviction of manslaughter; English was however guilty of a serious wounding offence.

[116] These concepts have not proved easy to apply: cf. *Uddin* [1998] 2 All ER 744 (flick-knife 'fundamentally different' from shortened billiard cues and shod feet; *Greatrex and Bates* [1999] 1 Cr App R 126 (not clear whether metal bar 'fundamentally different' from shod foot).

[117] [2008] UKHL 45, above, n 94 and accompanying text.

decision. Or one might argue that accessorial liability should be determined on the basis that it is for the parties to stipulate which features of their common design are critical, rather than for the law to declare that neither the identity of the victim nor the method employed is legally relevant. For example, in the South African case of *S v Robinson* (1968)[118] P and two others agreed with V that V should be killed by P so that V could escape prosecution for fraud and the others could obtain insurance monies. V withdrew his consent to the arrangement, not surprisingly, but P killed him nevertheless. The offence was as planned, the victim was as planned, but the element of consent was crucial to the common purpose, and that was absent: should the two others be convicted as accomplices to P's offence? The South African court held them liable as accomplices to attempted murder only, because their complicity in murder was dependent on the consent. Is this not too precious an approach, in that they had made their intended contributions to a planned murder?

There are further arguments against the *English* principle. It is evident elsewhere in this chapter (see subsection (b) and section 10.6 below) that the appellate courts are beginning to move away from the 'derivative' theory of liability in favour of assessing the culpability of the accomplice separately: if that approach had been adopted in *English* and *Rahman*, D's liability would have been assessed on the basis of what D contemplated rather than by reference to the unexpected deviation by P. Further, it may be conceded that the doctrines of transferred fault and unintended mode in English law are defensible pragmatically and not on grounds of principle:[119] in many cases a conviction for attempt could be obtained, and that would be a theoretically more satisfactory response.[120] Moreover, the effect of Part 2 of the Serious Crime Act 2007 is that D could now be prosecuted for encouraging or assisting the crime D anticipated, irrespective of what P subsequently did.[121] But if one were to delve into the possible policy reasons for *English*, a leading contender would be their Lordships' distaste for the 'GBH rule' in murder, evident in the speeches in that case.[122] The 'fundamentally different' exception may simply be a pragmatic means of limiting a doctrine whose consequences their Lordships believe to be excessive in some cases, murder particularly.

(c) DIFFERENT, LESS SERIOUS OFFENCE

The House of Lords decision in *Howe* (1987)[123] holds that, where D aids or counsels the principal to commit a certain offence, and the principal deviates by committing a less

---

[118] 1968 (1) SA 666.   [119] Above, Ch 5.5.

[120] Note the practical importance, following *English*, of prosecutors including lesser counts in the indictment to cater for the possibility that D might be acquitted on the ground that P changed the mode of committing the offence, particularly homicide.

[121] The new law is discussed in Ch 11.7 below.

[122] Cf. Lord Bingham in *Rahman* [2008] UKHL 45, at [25], referring to the 'earthy realism' of the gbh rule.

[123] [1987] AC 417.

serious offence, D may be convicted as an accomplice to the intended (more serious) offence. The previous decision in *Richards*[124] laid down a different rule. In that case a woman paid two men to beat up her husband so as to put him in hospital for a few days. Her hope was that this experience would lead her husband to turn to her for comfort, thus repairing their relationship. The hired men inflicted less serious injuries than she had asked them to, and it was held that she could not be convicted as an accomplice to the higher offence unless she was present at the scene (an ancient rule). The effect of *Howe* was to sweep away such restrictions, and also to move away from the derivative theory: the accomplice is liable although the (intended) higher offence was never committed, and so the accomplice's liability cannot derive from any such offence. The theory underlying the *Howe* ruling is that the culpability of the accomplice should be viewed as a separate issue from that of the principal (contrast the *English-Rahman* approach, above), and based upon what the accomplice intended to happen or believed would happen. This result could be achieved on the facts of *Richards* by charging the wife with assisting or encouraging an offence (see Chapter 11.7 below). Where the prosecution uses the law of complicity, the decision in *Howe* suggests that courts sometimes determine liability according to which of two principles—the derivative or the subjective—has the further reach in a given case.

10.6 DERIVATIVE LIABILITY AND THE MISSING LINK

We now come to another set of cases in which the English courts have departed from, or at least modified, the derivative theory of accessorial liability. If the would-be principal is not guilty of the substantive offence, because of the absence of a mental element or the presence of a defence, does this mean that the accomplice must also be acquitted? A straightforward application of the derivative theory would lead to non-liability; one cannot be said to have aided and abetted an offence if the offence did not take place, for there is nothing from which the accomplice's liability can derive. Yet the would-be accomplice has done all that he or she intended to do in order to further the principal's crime, and, considered in isolation, the accomplice is surely no less culpable than if the principal had been found guilty. It is therefore not surprising that English courts have responded by stretching the doctrine of complicity. In *Bourne* (1952)[125] D threatened and forced his wife to commit bestiality with a dog, and his conviction for aiding and abetting bestiality was upheld despite the fact that his wife would have had a defence of duress if charged as the principal. In *Cogan and Leak* (1976)[126] Cogan had intercourse with Leak's wife, believing, on the basis of what

---

[124] [1974] QB 776, discussed by Kadish, *Blame and Punishment*, 184–6.
[125] (1952) 36 Cr App R 125.   [126] [1976] 1 QB 217.

Leak had told him, that Mrs Leak was consenting. Leak knew that his wife was not consenting. Cogan's conviction for rape was quashed because his defence of mistaken belief in the woman's consent had not been properly put to the jury, but Leak's conviction for aiding and abetting rape was upheld. In *DPP v K and B* (1997)[127] two girls aged 14 and 11 threatened and bullied another girl, aged 14, to remove her clothes and submit to penetration by a boy. The boy was never identified, nor was his age known, and the defence argued that if he was under 14 (as suggested) he may not have been liable to conviction as a principal in rape (because of the presumption of *doli incapax*, which then applied to children aged between 10 and 14[128]). If the boy could not have been convicted as principal, could the two girls be convicted of procuring rape? The Divisional Court held that they could.

The judgments in these cases contain little elaboration of the theoretical basis for conviction, but they could be defended as a mere extension of the derivative theory. The extension would be that a person may be convicted as an accomplice to the commission of an *actus reus* or 'wrongful act' where the reason for acquitting the would-be principal is the absence of a mental element or the presence of a defence. This approach does have theoretical and practical limitations, however. One requirement of accomplice liability is that the accomplice must know the essential elements of the offence (including the principal's mental element); but in these cases the accomplice usually knows that the would-be principal lacks an element necessary for conviction. Bourne knew that his wife was acting because of his threats; Leak knew that Cogan was acting because of his lies.[129] The same difficulty arises in respect of *Millward* (1994),[130] where D was convicted of procuring the offence of causing death by reckless driving by sending an employee out in a tractor with a defective trailer which led to the death of another motorist. The employee was acquitted of the principal offence, but the Court of Appeal upheld the employer's conviction for, essentially, procuring the *actus reus*. This was the explicit ground for finding liability in *DPP v K and B*: 'there is no doubt whatever that W was the victim of unlawful sexual intercourse.... The *actus reus* was proved. The respondents procured the situation which included the sexual intercourse.'[131]

This extension of the derivative theory does not, however, give the courts grounds for overturning the decision in *Thornton v Mitchell* (1940).[132] A bus conductor was directing the driver in reversing a bus when an accident was caused. The driver was acquitted of careless driving, because he was relying (reasonably) on the conductor's guidance, and it was held that the conductor must therefore be acquitted of aiding and abetting. Since the *actus reus* of careless driving was not committed, the suggested extension of the derivative theory would yield the same result.

---

[127] [1997] 1 Cr App R 36.   [128] For discussion see Ch 5.2(a).
[129] The same cannot be said of *DPP v K and B*, where, even if the girls had known the boy's age, they would not have known its legal significance.
[130] [1994] Crim LR 527.   [131] *Per* Russell LJ [1997] 1 Cr App R at 45.
[132] [1940] 1 All ER 339; cf. R. D. Taylor, 'Complicity and the Excuses' [1983] Crim LR 656.

Convictions seem justified for Bourne and Leak, because they both chose to bring about a result which the law prohibits: their behaviour and culpability are as high on the scale of seriousness as many principals'. Granted that, what is the most suitable legal technique for dealing with these cases? The new inchoate offences relate to encouraging or assisting a crime or an offence, so a more fruitful approach may be the doctrine of innocent agency. A clear example would be where an adult urges or orders a child under the age of criminal responsibility to commit crimes, such as stealing from a shop. The young child is deemed 'innocent' in law, and so it is said that the adult commits the crime through the innocent agency of the child. No such notion is possible where two adults are involved, since it is presumed that adults are autonomous beings acting voluntarily, save in exceptional circumstances. One exceptional circumstance would be where the adult is mentally disordered; another would be where the adult is acting under duress. Thus if, as in *Bourne*,[133] a man threatens and forces his wife to commit bestiality with a dog, her defence of duress may be said to establish that her conduct was insufficiently voluntary to be regarded as the cause of the event. In causal terms she 'drops out of the picture' as a mere innocent agent, leaving the person who uttered the threats as the principal responsible for the offence.[134] How much further can the doctrine of innocent agency be taken? If D gives a bottle to the carer attending V, telling her that it contains a prescribed medicine when in fact it contains poison, D should surely be liable as the principal when the carer administers the contents of the bottle to V, who dies. The carer would be regarded as an innocent agent because, although not lacking criminal capacity in the sense of being mentally disordered or overborne by threats, he or she was acting under a mistake which would prevent criminal liability for the acts.[135] If this is accepted, it would seem to follow that where (as in *Cogan and Leak*) D persuades P to have sexual intercourse with D's wife by inducing P to believe that she consents to this, P's mistake would mean that he drops out of the picture as an innocent agent and that D should be liable as a principal for rape.[136]

Various objections might be raised against this conclusion. The major counter-argument is that the doctrine of innocent agency should not be used where it is linguistically inappropriate. It is appropriate to describe D as killing (or, at least, causing the death of) V in the case involving the carer, but it is manifestly inappropriate to describe a person as driving with excess alcohol in his blood if what he has done is to lace the drink of someone else who is about to drive a car,[137] or to describe D as having raped a woman if D tricked another man into having sexual intercourse with that woman,[138] or to describe D as having committed bigamy if she induced someone else

---

[133] (1952) 36 Cr App R 125.

[134] See above, Ch 4.5(b), and Alldridge, 'The Doctrine of Innocent Agency'.

[135] *Michael* (1840) 9 C and P 356, above, Ch 4.5(b)(i).

[136] See generally the discussion by Kadish, *Blame and Punishment*, Essay 8.

[137] *Attorney-General's Reference (No. 1 of 1975)* [1975] QB 773.

[138] *Cogan and Leak* [1976] 1 QB 217; at this time a husband could not be convicted of the rape of his wife, but that rule has now been abrogated: see above, Ch 8.5(d).

to believe (erroneously) that the other person's marriage had been legally terminated and to remarry on the strength of this belief.[139] The conflict here is plain. The law has to be expressed in words, and some verbal formulas are hedged about with linguistic conventions which do not correspond to moral or social distinctions in responsibility. It seems right that D who gives poison to the carer to administer unwittingly should be convicted as the principal in murder, because D was the cause of the death. That element of causation remains prominent in the other examples of the 'lacer' of drinks, the encourager of non-consensual intercourse, and the orchestrators of bigamy, and the moral/social argument for criminal liability seems no less strong; but the conventions of language erect a barrier. Some offences are phrased in terms which imply personal agency (rape is said to be one) or which apply only to the holder of a certain office or licence. There is no reason why the law should be constrained by a barrier that is linguistic rather than substantive. The Law Commission has recommended a set of new clauses designed to overcome these and other problems.[140] There would be a new innocent agency provision, rendering D liable as a principal for causing P (an innocent agent) to commit the conduct element of an offence when not liable because of infancy, insanity or lack of the required fault element. There would also be a new offence of causing another to commit a no-fault offence, designed to cater for cases such as *Attorney-General's Reference (No. 1 of 1975)*.[141] And a special provision is recommended to make it clear that D may be guilty of assisting or encouraging an offence even if the offence is one that may be committed only by someone of a particular description and D does not meet that description. It is arguable that these recommendations are somewhat over-elaborate,[142] but legislation is certainly needed and the Law Commission's scheme (perhaps with some streamlining) would be a significant advance.

10.7 SPECIAL DEFENCES TO COMPLICITY

(a) WITHDRAWAL

Complicity often involves the accomplice in words or deeds prior to the principal's crime. If the accomplice has a change of heart before the principal commits the offence, can the accomplice's liability be removed? It can be argued that withdrawal should be rewarded in so far as it may negative culpability in relation to P's offence, and that the availability of the defence gives the accomplice an incentive to take action to prevent the substantive offence from happening.[143] In some cases

---

[139] *Kemp and Else* [1964] 2 QB 341.   [140] Law Com. No. 305, *Participating in Crime* (2007).
[141] Above, n. 61 and text.
[142] R. D. Taylor, 'Procuring, Causation, Innocent Agency and the Law Commission' [2008] Crim LR 32.
[143] Cf. the unavailability of withdrawal as a defence to criminal attempts, below, Ch 11.3(a).

a withdrawal may indeed amount to a denial of the conduct element of complicity, as where the supplier of an instrument takes it back from the principal or where the giver of encouragement supplants this with discouragement.[144] In most cases, however, the contribution of the accomplice may have some enduring influence over the principal by way of either encouragement or assistance, and one might expect the law to require not merely a change of mind communicated to the principal, but some endeavour to 'undo' the effect of the contribution already made. The older decisions tend to speak in terms of the principal acting with the authority of the accomplice, and withdrawal as a countermanding of that authority.[145] Modern decisions have emphasized the significance of the stage which the principal's actions have reached. Thus, where D's contribution consists of giving information to the principal about property to be burgled, and then, a week or so before the planned burglary, D tells the principal that he does not wish to be involved and does not want the burglary to take place, this may be an effective withdrawal.[146] This rule may be thought unduly favourable to D, since the advice or help may well have assisted or even encouraged P.[147]

In *Becerra and Cooper* (1975),[148] however, the situation was rather different. B had given C a knife to use if anyone disturbed them during the burglary they were carrying out. When B heard someone coming, he told C of this, said 'Come on, let's go', jumped out of a window, and ran off. C did not follow: he stabbed the inquisitive neighbour fatally with the knife. B was convicted as an accomplice to murder, and this was upheld in the Court of Appeal. When events have proceeded so far, an effective withdrawal was held to require far more than a few words such as 'let's go'. The Court held that 'where practicable and reasonable there must be a timely communication of the intention to abandon the common purpose', in such a form that serves 'unequivocal notice' of the withdrawal. In *Becerra* the imminence of danger was taken to require something 'vastly more effective' than the few words spoken: it seems clear that if C had already been using or preparing to use the knife against the inquisitive neighbour, an effective withdrawal might have required B to go so far as to try to restrain C physically. Thus the essence of withdrawal in complicity is that the accomplice must not only make a clear statement of withdrawal and communicate this to the principal, but must also (if the crime is imminent) take some steps to prevent its commission.

The closer the principal's offence is to commission, the more active the intervention required of the accomplice for effective withdrawal. In a sense, the argument is similar to but stronger than the *Miller* principle—that one has a duty to prevent harm resulting from a train of events which one has started[149]—since the accomplice is knowingly involved in initiating the train of events, whereas Miller did so unknowingly, and it

---

144 K. J. M. Smith, 'Withdrawal in Complicity: a Restatement of Principles' [2001] Crim LR 769.
145 E.g. *Saunders and Archer* (1573) 2 Plowd 473, at 476.   146 *Whitefield* (1984) 79 Cr App R 36.
147 Cf. K. J. M. Smith, 'Withdrawal in Complicity', at 779–82.
148 (1975) 62 Cr App R 212; see also *Baker* [1994] Crim LR 444.   149 [1983] 2 AC 161.

may be possible to say that D has some causal responsibility for P's subsequent act(s).[150] The Law Commission recommends that any possible defence of withdrawal should be narrowed, so that the accomplice would have a defence only if 'he or she had negated the effect of his or her acts of assistance, encouragement or agreement before the principal offence was committed.'[151]

(b) THE TYRELL PRINCIPLE

In *Tyrell* (1894)[152] it was held that a girl under 16 could not be convicted as a secondary party to an offence of unlawful sexual intercourse committed with her. Lord Coleridge CJ stated that Parliament could not have intended 'that the girls for whose protection [the Act] was passed should be punishable under it for the offences committed upon themselves'. Although the Court's reasoning was based on statutory interpretation, the decision has subsequently been treated as authority for a general principle that victims, particularly victims of sexual offences, cannot be convicted of complicity if the offence was created for their protection.[153] The Law Commission has recommended a re-statement of this 'protective principle',[154] but whether this will deal satisfactorily with the uncertainties left by the Sexual Offences Act 2003 is doubtful.[155]

(c) CRIME PREVENTION

There is authority that a form of 'choice of evils' defence may be available to someone who would otherwise be an accomplice.[156] In *Clarke* (1984)[157] D's defence was that he joined other burglars once the offence had been planned, and did so in order to assist the police. The Court of Appeal held that this could form the basis for a defence if the jury were satisfied that D's conduct was 'overall calculated and intended not to further but to frustrate the ultimate result of the crime'. However, the law is in confusion, since there are other decisions on analogous points which have effectively denied the defence recognized in *Clarke*.[158] The Law Commission recommends a circumscribed defence of acting to prevent the commission of an offence or to limit the occurrence of

---

[150] See the argument in J. Gardner, 'Complicity and Causality' (2007) 1 *Criminal Law and Philosophy* 127.
[151] Law Com No. 305, *Participating in Crime*, para 3.67.   [152] [1894] 1 QB 710.
[153] E.g. *Whitehouse* [1977] QB 868.
[154] Law Com No. 305, *Participating in Crime*, 114–19 and draft Bill, cl. 6.
[155] M. Bohlander, 'The Sexual Offences Act 2003 and the *Tyrell* Principle—Criminalising the Victims?' [2005] Crim LR 701.
[156] For discussion of such defences see above, Ch 4.9.   [157] (1984) 80 Cr App R 344.
[158] Compare *Smith* [1960] 2 QB 423, discussed in Ch 5.5(b)(ii) above, and *Yip Chiu-Cheung* [1995] 1 AC 111, discussed in Ch 11.5(c) below, both denying the defence. For further discussion see A. Ashworth, 'Testing Fidelity to Legal Values' (2000) 63 MLR 633, at 653–8.

harm,[159] although Parliament has enacted a somewhat broader defence that applies to the new offence of encouraging or assisting crime.[160]

10.8 CONCLUSIONS

It is apparent that the English law of complicity is replete with uncertainties and conflicts. It betrays the worst features of the common law: what some would regard as flexibility appears here as a succession of opportunistic decisions by the courts, often extending the law, and resulting in a body of jurisprudence that has little coherence. It has usually been assumed that there are two fundamental principles underlying the English doctrine—that the liability of the accomplice derives from that of the principal, and that the accomplice is required to have intention or knowledge of the principal's offence. Neither proposition can now be advanced without qualifications. The derivative theory has given way in several situations to liability based on causal or subjective principles, and the fault requirements have in some spheres been relaxed so as to include recklessness and in other spheres narrowed to 'purpose' alone. Moreover, the effect of the doctrine of joint enterprise or joint venture is to extend liability for accomplices, even though the definition of a joint venture remains discreditably opaque.

The early part of this chapter was concerned with the ambit of complicity liability: what forms of conduct should suffice? The old terms 'aid, abet, counsel and procure' continue to be relied upon,[161] and it is hardly true to say that each term bears its ordinary meaning. The variations in the level of accomplices' contributions is great. Someone who procures another to commit an offence by threats or by implanting a false belief may have substantial causal influence. This suggests, by the way, that a rule restricting the penalty for the accomplice to half or three-quarters of the maximum for the principal would be too crude. In contrast, acts of aiding or encouraging may be minor and hardly significant, if any encouragement such as saying 'Oh goody' really is sufficient.[162] It would be difficult to attempt a legislative listing of all the types of conduct which might amount to complicity, although some progress can be made in that direction.[163] Yet the obvious expedient of allowing prosecutorial discretion to determine (in practice) the lower threshold of criminal complicity not only leaves scope for prosecutors to exert pressure on fringe participants in offences

---

[159] Law Com No. 305, *Participating in Crime*, 110–14 and draft Bill, cl. 7.

[160] Serious Crime Act 2007, s. 50, discussed in Ch 11.7 below.

[161] E.g. in s. 50 of the Anti-Terrorism, Crime and Security Act 2001, which penalizes anyone who 'aids, abets, counsels or procures, or incites' an offence relating to biological, chemical, or nuclear weapons outside the United Kingdom.

[162] *Giannetto* [1997] 1 Cr App R 1, above, section 10.3(a).

[163] See the draft produced by Glazebrook, 'Structuring the Criminal Code', in Simester and Smith (eds.), *Harm and Culpability*, 212.

to choose between facing prosecution and testifying in offences against the others, but also accords little weight to the principle of minimum criminalization (see Chapter 3.4(a) above).

Although the chapter began by emphasizing that to be liable as an accomplice D must know the essential elements of P's offence, we have encountered considerable evidence of the dilution of this principle. Thus it has been held sufficient that D believes that it is a real possibility that P will commit a certain offence;[164] that D believes that P will commit one of a group of offences but does not know which one;[165] and that D realizes that P may commit a more serious offence than has been agreed.[166] These are all examples of the expansion of accomplice liability by recognizing forms of recklessness (as to P's intentional acts) as sufficient. General arguments in favour of criminal liability based on recklessness were examined earlier;[167] the problem of applying them directly to the law of complicity is that its reach is so broad and ill-defined that the inclusion of recklessness, defensible in some cases, extends the law considerably in others.

The law of complicity has also become the focal point for a number of arguments about the duties of citizens. The normally restrictive approach of English law towards liability for omissions has already been discussed,[168] but complicity is one sphere in which the courts have abandoned their general reluctance. In a sense, this may be compatible with the idea that the accomplice may be held in some way responsible for the conduct of the principal, a notion implicit in the terminology of 'authority' which is sometimes used, and also in the requirements for withdrawal from complicity. But the idea of legal responsibility as an accomplice for the acts of those whose conduct one has the power to control—rendering the publican, the car owner, and the house owner liable for the conduct of their guests, and employers liable for those of their employees[169]—is a bold step towards omissions liability under the camouflage of the law of complicity.[170] The debate about the liability of the gun-seller as an accomplice to murder turns on somewhat similar considerations of a citizen's duties towards law enforcement, but it has become wrapped up in an analysis of the distinction between intention and purpose. As suggested in Chapter 4.4 above, a more open and more principled solution would be to create some discrete offences to cover those situations in which it is felt that citizens ought to take positive action.

Another respect in which English law on complicity is confused is the relationship between the accomplice's conduct and that of the principal. On the one hand the law gives itself extraordinary width by its procedural rule which draws no distinction between principal and accomplice in point of charge, conviction, and

---

[164] *Bryce* [2004] 2 Cr App R 35, above n 71.

[165] *Maxwell v DPP for Northern Ireland* [1978] 3 All ER 1140, above n 86.

[166] *Powell* [1999] AC 1, above n 97.   [167] See Ch 5.5(c) above.

[168] See above, Ch 4.4(b) and (c).

[169] On the last point, recall *J.F. Alford Transport*, above, section 10.3(b).

[170] See A. Ashworth, 'The Scope of Criminal Liability for Omissions' (1989) 105 LQR at 445–7; Law Com No. 177, cl. 24(3).

maximum sentence. Yet on the other hand it has still not relinquished the idea that the accomplice's liability derives from that of the principal, despite the inadequacies of that theory in dealing with cases where there is a missing link[171] or where the principal deviates from the agreed or understood course of action,[172] for example. In these two types of case the courts have stretched or abandoned the derivative theory—but why? The reason for wishing to secure convictions here is surely that the accomplice is no less culpable than would have been the case if the principal had done as intended. Judicial ambivalence between the two approaches remains evident in the House of Lords: on the one hand *Powell and Daniels* (1999)[173] applied the derivative theory in determining the degree of knowledge required for accessorial liability for a more serious offence than planned, whilst in the same decision the House in *English* introduced new and fine-grained distinctions relating to the comparative dangerousness of modes of committing the principal offence that seem more consistent with the principle that each party's liability should be determined separately.

One approach would be to generalize the latter trend by providing for the independent liability of those who help or encourage others to commit offences, and this has become integral to the Law Commission's recommendations. We will see in Chapter 11.7 below how Parliament, following the Law Commission, has enacted inchoate offences of encouraging or assisting crime; the Law Commission now wishes to integrate those offences into a sharpened law of complicity.[174] The fundamental concepts are to be those of assisting and encouraging crime, and the principle is that there must be parity of culpability between principal and accomplice. Thus the four forms of complicity would be reduced to two, assisting and encouraging. Unfortunately, it is not proposed to define either term, although encouraging is to include threatening or putting pressure on another. The absence of definition is regrettable, since judges will need to direct juries and so the courts and the Judicial Studies Board will be required to establish the scope of each term.[175] The absence of statutory definitions becomes a considerable problem when one moves on to the other limb of the Commission's recommendations, an offence of participating in a joint criminal venture. The essence of this form of liability is that one member of the joint venture (D) is liable for an act done by another (P) if it 'falls within the scope of the venture', and that D's liability is not negatived by his absence from the scene, his being against the venture's being carried out or indifferent to whether it is carried out. Problematic here are the absence of a definition of 'joint criminal venture' and the absence of clear specifications of the degree of awareness needed if D is rightly to be convicted. As Professor Sullivan observes, 'this disregard for minimum standards of clarity and comprehensiveness is unsettling.'[176] The Commission's objective was to remain close to the existing law, but, as argued in this chapter, that is complex, under-theorized and unsatisfactory.

---

[171] See above, Ch 10.6.   [172] See above, Ch 10.5.   [173] [1999] AC 1.

[174] Law Com No. 305, *Participating in Crime* (2007).

[175] See W. Wilson, 'A Rational Scheme of Liability for Participating in Crime' [2008] Crim LR 3.

[176] G. R. Sullivan, 'Participating in Crime: Law Com No. 305—Joint Criminal Ventures', [2008] Crim LR 19, at 21.

FURTHER READING

K. J. M. Smith, *A Modern Treatise on the Law of Criminal Complicity* (1991).

S. Kadish, *Blame and Punishment* (1987), ch 5.

J. C. Smith, 'Criminal Liability of Accessories: Law and Law Reform' (1997) 113 *LQR* 453.

A. P. Simester, 'The Mental Element in Complicity' (2006) 122 *LQR* 578.

Law Commission, *Participating in Crime*, Law Com. No. 304 (2007).

11

INCHOATE OFFENCES

11.1 THE CONCEPT OF AN INCHOATE OFFENCE

The word 'inchoate', not much used in ordinary discourse, means 'just begun', 'undeveloped'. The common law has given birth to three general offences which are usually termed 'inchoate' or 'preliminary' crimes—attempt, conspiracy, and incitement. A principal feature of these crimes is that they are committed even though the substantive offence (i.e. the offence it was intended to bring about) is not completed and no harm results. An attempt fails, a conspiracy comes to nothing, words of incitement are ignored—in all these instances, there may be liability for the inchoate crime. However, the legal landscape is changing in several ways. In the first place, the Law Commission has recommended and Parliament has decided that the inchoate offence of incitement should be abolished and replaced by a more extensive set of offences of assisting or encouraging crime, and these are examined in 11.7 below. Secondly, those new offences take their place alongside others that criminalize conduct at an early stage, well before the stage of a criminal attempt—a prime example being the offence of engaging in 'any conduct in preparation for giving effect to' an intention to commit acts of terrorism in section 5 of the Terrorism Act 2006.[1] Thirdly, we have noted throughout the book that several newly-created offences are defined in an inchoate mode, i.e. doing a certain act with intent to do X—offences under the Fraud Act 2006 being a clear example—and that they may therefore be committed even if no harmful

---

[1] See the discussion in Ch 2.7 above, and V. Tadros, 'Justice and Terrorism' (2007) 11 New Crim LR 658.

result occurs. The law of inchoate offences also applies to these offences defined in an inchoate mode, driving criminal liability even further back. Fourthly, crimes of possession are also essentially inchoate:[2] it is not the mere possession, so much as what the possessor might do with the article or substance, which is the reason for criminalization. Once again, more crimes of possession are being created. These developments in the criminal law will be assessed after a discussion of the two remaining common law inchoate offences—attempt and conspiracy—and the new statutory inchoate offences of encouraging or assisting crime.

11.2 THE JUSTIFICATIONS FOR PENALIZING ATTEMPTS AT CRIMES[3]

(a) INTRODUCTION

Let us begin with three examples: (i) X goes to the house of his rival, V, with a can of petrol, some paper, and a box of matches; he soaks the paper in petrol and pushes it through the letter-box, but he is arrested before he can do anything more; (ii) Y drives a car straight at V, but V jumps out of the way at the last moment and is uninjured; (iii) Z is offered money to carry a package of cannabis into Britain; she accepts, brings the package in, but on her arrest it is found that the package contains dried lettuce leaves. These are all cases in which there may be a conviction for attempt.[4] The first feature to be noticed is that no harm actually occurred in any of them—no damage was done, no injury caused, no drugs smuggled. Normally, criminal liability requires both culpability and harm: X, Y, and Z may appear culpable, but they have caused no harm. Why, then, should the criminal law become involved? The answer is that harm does indeed have a central place in criminal liability, but that the concern is not merely with the occurrence of harm but also with its prevention. According to this view, the first decision for legislators is exactly which harms and wrongs should properly be objects of the criminal law (see Chapter 2). Once this has been decided, and taking the aims of the criminal law into account,[5] the law should not only provide for the punishment of those who have culpably caused such harms but also penalize those who are trying to cause the harms. A person who tries to cause a prohibited harm and fails is, in terms of moral culpability, not materially different from the person who tries and succeeds: the difference in outcome is determined by chance rather than by choice, and a censuring institution such as the criminal law should not subordinate itself to the vagaries of fortune by focusing on results rather than on culpability. There is also a consequentialist justification for the law of attempts, inasmuch as it reduces harm by authorizing law

---

[2] See Ch 4.3(b) above.   [3] R. A. Duff, *Criminal Attempts* (1996), ch 5 and *passim*.
[4] This depends on the accused's intention and beliefs at the time: see section 11.3(a) below.
[5] As discussed in Ch 1.3 above.

enforcement officers and the courts to step in *before* any harm has been done, so long as the danger of the harm being caused is clear.

(b) TWO KINDS OF ATTEMPT

The rationale for criminalizing attempts can best be appreciated by drawing a theoretical distinction (which the law itself does not draw) between two kinds of attempt. First, there are incomplete attempts, which are cases in which the defendant has set out to commit an offence but has not yet done all the acts necessary to bring it about. Our first example, of X putting petrol-soaked paper through the door of V's house, is such a case: he has still to strike a match and light the paper. Contrast this with the second kind of attempt, which will be called a complete attempt. Here the defendant has done all that he intended, but the desired result has not followed—Y has driven the car at V, intending to injure V, but he failed; and Z has smuggled the package into the country, believing it to be cannabis when in fact it is a harmless and worthless substance.

It is easier to justify the criminalization of complete attempts than incomplete attempts, and the two sets of justifications have somewhat different emphases. The justification for punishing complete attempts is that the defendant has done all the acts intended, with the beliefs required for the offence, and is therefore no less blameworthy than a person who is successful in committing the substantive offence. The complete 'attempter' is thwarted by some unexpected turn of events which, to him, is a matter of pure chance—the intended victim jumped out of the way or the substance was not what it appeared to be. These are applications of what were called the 'subjective' principles earlier, the essence of which is that people's criminal liability should be assessed on what they were trying to do, intended to do, and believed they were doing, rather than on the actual consequences of their conduct.[6] Rejection of this approach would lead to criminal liability always being judged according to the actual outcome, which would allow luck to play too great a part in the criminal law. Of course luck and chance play a considerable role in human affairs, and we have already seen how important the chance result of death is in the law of involuntary manslaughter.[7] However, there is no reason why a human system for judging and formally censuring the behaviour of others should be a slave to the vagaries of chance. The 'subjective principle' would also be accepted by the consequentialist as a justification for criminalizing complete attempts: the defendant was trying to break the law, and therefore constitutes a source of social danger no less (or little less) than that presented by 'successful' harmdoers.

What about incomplete attempts? The subjective principle does have some application here, inasmuch as the defendant has given some evidence of a determination to commit the substantive offence—though the evidence is likely to be less conclusive than in cases of complete attempts. There is one distinct factor present in incomplete attempts, which is the social importance of authorizing official intervention before harm is done. Since the prevention of harm has a central place in the justifications

---

[6] See above, Ch 5.4.   [7] Above, Ch 7.5(a).

for criminal law, there is a strong case for stopping attempts before they result in the causing of harm. Detailed arguments about the point at which the law should intervene are discussed in section 11.3(b) below. Once this point has been reached, then the agents of law enforcement may intervene to stop attempts before they go further. The culpability of the incomplete attempter may be less than that of the complete attempter because there remains the possibility that there would have been voluntary repentance at some late stage: after all, it may take greater nerve to do the final act which triggers the actual harm than to do the preliminary acts. But so long as it is accepted that the incomplete attempter has evinced a settled intention to continue, and to commit the substantive offence by doing some further acts, there is sufficient ground for criminalization.

Although there are sufficient grounds for criminalizing both complete and incomplete attempts, it may be right to reflect some differences between them at the sentencing stage. It may be argued that incomplete attempts should be punished less severely than the full offence—because of the possibility of voluntary abandonment of the attempt, because it takes greater nerve to consummate an offence, and because it may be prudent to leave some incentive (i.e. reduced punishment) to the incomplete attempter to give up rather than to carry out the full offence. For complete attempts the case for reduced punishment is less strong, although there may be an argument for some reduction of punishment in order to give the complete attempter an incentive not to try again—otherwise D might reason that there is nothing to lose by this.[8] However, on the objectivist approach to attempts advocated by Antony Duff, lesser punishment for completed attempts would be important to mark the fact that D failed to produce the intended effect in the real world.[9] It will be noticed that these arguments for reduced punishments are consequentialist in nature. Following the principle of 'desert', there is little reason for reducing the punishment of the complete attempter, although there is some reason for recognizing the possibility that the incomplete attempter might yet desist.

11.3 THE ELEMENTS OF CRIMINAL ATTEMPT

The relevant English law is now to be found in the Criminal Attempts Act 1981, which followed a Law Commission report on the subject.[10] It will be discussed by considering three separate aspects of the offence in turn—the fault element, the conduct element, and the problem of impossibility.

---

[8] The longest determinate sentence in English law, 45 years' imprisonment, was given for the offence of attempting to place on an aircraft a device likely to destroy the aircraft: see *Hindawi*, discussed in Ch 7.7 above.

[9] Duff, *Criminal Attempts*, ch 4 and 351–4.

[10] Law Com No. 102, *Attempt, and Impossibility in Relation to Attempt, Conspiracy and Incitement* (1980). See further I. Dennis, 'The Criminal Attempts Act 1981' [1982] Crim LR 5 and A. Ashworth, 'Criminal Attempts and the Role of Resulting Harm under the Code, and in the Common Law' (1988) 19 Rutgers LJ 725.

(a) THE FAULT ELEMENT[11]

It has been said that, where a person is charged with an attempt, 'the intent becomes the principal ingredient of the crime'.[12] The law on this point rarely causes much difficulty: it must be shown that the defendant intended to cause the proscribed harm, and had the necessary knowledge of facts and circumstances. There have been appeals in cases where D has been charged with attempting to cause grievous bodily harm by driving a car at another person, and the defence has been that D did not intend to injure the other. These appeals have led the courts to establish that purpose is not required for the crime of attempt: what is needed, according to James LJ in *Mohan* (1976),[13] is proof of 'a decision to bring about... [the offence], no matter whether the accused desired that consequence of his act or not'. This is supposed to align the meaning of intent here with its meaning in the general law, so as to include foresight of virtual certainty,[14] although those who regard ordinary language as important may have misgivings about this 'extension'.[15]

A wider question of principle is whether attempts liability should be taken further. Those wedded to a linguistic approach insist that the word 'attempt' connotes trying, trying connotes purposeful behaviour, and therefore there can be no such thing as a reckless or negligent attempt. The opposite view focuses on the element of luck in whether behaviour results in the commission of a substantive offence or not. How might these views be applied to cases where D intends to do the prohibited act but is only reckless as to the circumstances? This problem arose under the pre-2003 law of rape. If two men set out to have sexual intercourse with two women, not caring whether they consent or not, would it not be absurd if the one who achieved penetration was convicted of rape, whilst the other, who failed to achieve penetration despite trying, was not liable even for attempted rape? It may be true that the latter committed indecent (now sexual) assault, for which the maximum is ten years' imprisonment, but attempted rape would be a more appropriate label for something so close to the full offence. These strong arguments led the Law Commission to change its mind,[16] and the Court of Appeal in *Khan et al.* (1990)[17] also held that a person could be convicted of attempted rape when only reckless as to whether the victim is consenting. The question now is whether that line of analysis should apply to rape under the 2003 Act, which has lowered the requirement of knowledge of lack of consent from recklessness to negligence. The Law Commission rightly prefers to restrict the crime of attempt to subjective knowledge of circumstances, and therefore proposes that where the charge is attempt, the appropriate requirement of knowledge of circumstances should be a) full knowledge, where the substantive offence requires that, or b) reckless knowledge

---

[11] Duff, *Criminal Attempts*, ch 1.

[12] *Per* Lord Goddard CJ in *Whybrow* (1951) 35 Cr App R 141, at 147.

[13] [1976] 1 QB 1, applied to the 1981 Act in *Pearman* (1985) 80 Cr App R 259.

[14] See now *Woollin* [1999] AC 92, discussed in Ch 5.5(b) above; the Law Commission proposes no change: Law Com. Consultation Paper No. 183, *Conspiracy and Attempts* (2007), 14.32.

[15] Cf. Duff, *Criminal Attempts*, 17–21.   [16] Law Com No. 177, 244.   [17] (1990) 91 Cr App R 29.

in every other case, whether the substantive offence requires only negligence (as in rape) or strict liability (as in rape of a child under 13).[18]

Unfortunately, the Court of Appeal[19] appeared to go further when it held that a person can be convicted of attempted aggravated arson if he intends to cause damage to property while reckless as to whether the life of another would thereby be endangered. The Court purported to follow *Khan*, but there are two respects in which their decision went beyond it.[20] First, *Khan* combined intention with recklessness as to circumstances, whereas this case combines intention with recklessness as to further consequences. Secondly, the type of recklessness required in *Khan* was either advertent or indifferent recklessness,[21] whereas criminal damage involves *Caldwell* (inadvertent) recklessness.[22] Although poorly reasoned, this decision opens up the question whether we should have a general law of reckless endangerment. Such a development might extend the reach of the criminal law considerably, and ought to be contemplated only after thorough enquiry.[23] Until now, English law has resolved the question pragmatically, by creating a few specific offences of endangerment to deal with reckless behaviour on the roads and in other situations where there is a risk, but no actual occurrence, of serious consequences (see Chapter 7.7 and 7.8). Since we are concerned here with preliminary offences which go beyond the definitions of substantive crimes, is it not more judicious to proceed in this piecemeal way, thereby ensuring that the outer boundaries of the criminal law are carefully regulated?

(b) THE CONDUCT ELEMENT[24]

Since the effect of the law of attempts is to extend the criminal sanction further back than the definition of substantive offences, the question of the minimum conduct necessary to constitute an attempt has great importance. The issue concerns incomplete attempts: when has a person gone far enough to justify criminal liability? Two schools of thought may be outlined here. First, there is the fault-centred approach, arguing that the essence of an attempt is trying to commit a crime, and that all the law should require is proof of the intention plus any act designed to implement that intention. The reasoning is that any person who has gone so far as to translate a criminal intention into action has crossed the threshold of criminal liability, and deserves punishment (though, for the reasons given above—the possibility of abandonment, for example—the punishment would be less than for a complete attempt). Secondly, there is the act-centred approach, of which two types may be distinguished. One type bases

---

[18] LCCP 183, *Conspiracy and Attempts*, 14.51.

[19] *Attorney General's Reference (No. 3 of 1992)* (1994) 98 Cr App R 383.

[20] See D. W. Elliott, 'Endangering Life by Damaging or Destroying Property' [1997] Crim LR 382, at 392–5.

[21] Cf. the discussion of fault in rape in Ch 8.5(d) above.   [22] On which see Ch 5.5(c) above.

[23] See also Ashworth, 'Criminal Attempts and the Role of Resulting Harm', 755–7, and Horder, 'Varieties of Intention'.

[24] Duff, *Criminal Attempts*, ch 2.

itself on the argument that one cannot be sure that the deterrent effect of the criminal law has failed until D has done all the acts necessary, since one could regard the law as successful if D did stop before the last act out of fear of detection and punishment. This suggests that only acts close to the substantive crime should be criminalized. The other type of act-centred approach is adopted by those who see great dangers of oppressive official action—to the detriment of individual liberties—if the ambit of the law of attempts is not restricted tightly. If *any* overt act were to suffice as the conduct element in attempts, wrongful arrests might be more numerous; convictions would turn largely on evidence of D's intention, so the police might be tempted to exert pressure in order to obtain a confession; and miscarriages of justice might increase, especially when inferences from silence are permissible (see subsection (c) below). To safeguard the liberty of citizens and to assure people that justice is being fairly administered, the law should require proof of an unambiguous act close to the commission of the crime before conviction of an attempt.[25] Otherwise, we would be risking a world of thought crimes and thought police.

The choices for the conduct element in attempts might therefore be ranged along a continuum. The least requirement would be 'any overt act', but that would be objectionable as risking oppressive police practices and as leaving little opportunity for an attempter to withdraw voluntarily. The most demanding requirement would be the 'last act' or 'final stage', but that goes too far in the other direction, leaving little time for the police to intervene to prevent the occurrence of harm and allowing the defence to gain an acquittal by raising a doubt whether D had actually done the very last act. In the United States the Model Penal Code requires D to have taken a 'substantial step' towards the commission of the full offence.[26] This might appear to breach the principle of maximum certainty,[27] but the Model Penal Code seeks to avoid this by listing a number of authoritative examples of a 'substantial step'. Thus, the approach recognizes the inevitable flexibility in questions of degree such as this but seeks to give some firm guidance. The Criminal Attempts Act 1981 requires D to have done 'an act which is more than merely preparatory to the commission of the offence'. Opinions differ on whether this is closer to the fault-centred approach than is the 'substantial step' test, but it is certainly more vague (since there are no authoritative examples), and the Act leaves the application of the test entirely to the jury, once the judge has found that there is sufficient evidence of an attempt.[28] At the earlier stage of arrest, it leaves much to the judgement of the police officer.[29]

---

[25] This was the clear inference from the empirical research on public opinion by P. Robinson and J. Darley, *Justice, Liability and Blame* (1995), 20–8.

[26] Model Penal Code, section 2.5.01, discussed by Ashworth, 'Criminal Attempts and the Role of Resulting Harm', 751–3.

[27] Discussed above, Ch 3.5(i).   [28] Criminal Attempts Act 1981, ss. 1(1) and 4(3).

[29] Under ss. 24(3)(b) and 24(4)(b) of the Police and Criminal Evidence Act 1984 it is lawful to arrest without warrant a person reasonably suspected of committing an attempted crime; and under s. 24(7)(b) a constable may arrest without a warrant anyone reasonably suspected to be *about to commit* an arrestable offence.

On a plain reading of the Act the proper test is whether D was still engaged in merely preparatory acts, in which case he is not guilty of attempt, or whether his conduct was *more* than merely preparatory. This is inevitably a question of degree, and the Court of Appeal has not been wholly consistent in its classification of different cases. Thus, in *Jones* (1990)[30] D bought a gun, shortened its barrel, put on a disguise, and then jumped into the back seat of his rival's car. D pointed the loaded gun at his rival and said 'You are not going to like this', but his rival then grabbed the gun. The defence argument was that this could not amount to attempted murder: what D had done was not more than merely preparatory, because he still had to release the safety catch, put his finger on the trigger, and pull it. The Court of Appeal dismissed this argument, which was more appropriate to the 'last act' test, and held that once D had climbed into the car and pointed the gun there was ample evidence for a jury to hold that attempted murder had been committed. A more difficult case is *Campbell* (1991)[31] where the police had received information about a planned post office robbery. They watched D in the street outside the post office. They arrested him as he approached the door of the post office, and found him to be carrying an imitation firearm and a threatening note, and carrying (but not wearing) sunglasses. The Court of Appeal quashed D's conviction for attempted robbery, holding that it is extremely unlikely that a person could be convicted of an attempt when he 'has not even gained the place where he could be in a position to carry out the offence'.[32] He had not entered the post office, and was no longer wearing the sunglasses.[33] This decision was followed in *Geddes* (1996),[34] where the Court of Appeal quashed a conviction for attempted false imprisonment. D had been seen loitering around the lavatory block of a boys' school, and the prosecution case rested on a can of cider found in a lavatory cubicle, D's rucksack (containing a large kitchen knife, rope, and masking tape) found in nearby bushes, and evidence from a third party that D was sexually fascinated by young boys. The Court harboured no doubt that D's intentions were as the prosecution alleged, but held ('with the gravest unease') that, since D had not spoken to or confronted any pupil at the school, his conduct had been merely preparatory and no more. On the other side of the line fell *Tosti* (1997),[35] where convictions for attempted burglary were upheld. D and another man were seen crouching by the door of a barn, examining the padlock. When disturbed they tried to run away, and D was caught. His car was found nearby, and there was oxy-acetylene cutting equipment concealed in a hedge. The Court of Appeal took the

---

[30] (1990) 91 Cr App R 351; cf. the earlier decision in *Gullefer* [1987] Crim LR 195.

[31] (1991) 93 Cr App R 350.

[32] D's conduct went beyond 'reconnoitring the place intended for the commission of the offence', which is sufficient for an attempt under the Model Penal Code but was intended to lie outside the English test: Law Com No. 102, para. 2.33.

[33] These decisions were considered in *Attorney-General's Reference (No. 1 of 1992)* (1993) 96 Cr App R 298, where the Court of Appeal held that a conviction for attempted rape could be proper even if the man had not yet attempted penetration.

[34] [1996] Crim LR 894; cf. *Nash* [1999] Crim LR 308, where the Court of Appeal upheld convictions on two counts on facts that were a considerable distance short of the commission of the substantive offence.

[35] [1997] Crim LR 746.

view that D had done an act showing that he had tried to commit the offence, rather than merely putting himself in a position to do so.

The Court of Appeal's various endeavours to reformulate the statutory test so that it can be applied meaningfully to the facts of differing cases have not been conspicuously successful. It is hardly helpful to refer to the steering of a 'mid-way course' between the 'last act' test and the penalization of merely preparatory acts.[36] The Court in *Tosti* rightly emphasized the distinction between preparatory acts, which may constitute an attempt, and *merely* preparatory acts, which may not; but that distinction is difficult to apply to *Campbell*, where one might suggest that D had gone beyond mere preparation, whereas *Geddes* is closer to the dividing line. Sheer physical proximity to the intended victim or targeted property may be the only sensible distinction between the convictions upheld in *Jones* and in *Tosti* and the other decisions.

The Law Commission proposes that the law should penalize 'criminal preparation' by those who are 'in the process of executing a plan to commit an intended offence'; that the test should be 'defined with a degree of imprecision' so as to enable courts to deal fairly with a variety of circumstances; and that there should be a list of statutory examples to guide the courts in applying the new test.[37] The Commission denies that the new test would enlarge the current law of attempts and, since no case for extending the law has been made out, the new offence must be carefully drafted so as to ensure this. The use of examples, pioneered in the United States,[38] may well be a fruitful device for achieving consistency in judicial rulings.

(c) THE PROBLEM OF IMPOSSIBILITY[39]

Just as the conduct element in attempts relates chiefly to incomplete attempts, so the problem of impossibility usually arises in connection with complete attempts. Once again, there are fault-centred and act-centred perspectives to be considered, according to whether one takes the view that D's beliefs or the reality of D's conduct should be the primary determinant of liability.

The fault-centred approach to impossible attempts is a straightforward application of the subjective principle (see Chapter 5.4(a) above): a person should be judged on the facts or circumstances as he or she believed them to be at the time. We have seen how the belief principle operates as a ground of exculpation where D is labouring under a mistake of fact (see Chapter 5.5(c)). Here it operates as a ground of inculpation. In other words, where D *believes* that he is doing acts which amount to an offence, it is justifiable to convict of an attempt to commit that offence. D's state of mind is just as blameworthy as it would be if the facts *were* as they are believed to be.

---

[36] The words of Lord Lane in *Gullefer*, considered by K. J. M. Smith, 'Proximity in Attempt: Lord Lane's Midway Course' [1991] Crim LR 576.

[37] LCCP 183, *Conspiracy and Attempts*, 16.8 to 16.17.

[38] See n 24 above, and I. Dennis, 'The Law Commission Report on Attempt: The Elements of Attempt' [1980] Crim LR 758.

[39] Duff, *Criminal Attempts*, ch 3.

Thus, we are justified in convicting the person who smuggles dried lettuce leaves in the belief that they are cannabis, and the person who puts sugar in someone's drink in the belief that it is cyanide, and the person who handles goods in the belief that they are stolen. In all these cases there is no relevant moral difference between their culpability and the culpability in cases where the substances *really* are cannabis, cyanide, and stolen goods.

The act-centred approach points to the absence of actual danger in these cases. Thus it is argued that there is a risk of oppression if the law criminalizes people in objectively innocent situations.[40] Part of the concern here is that convictions might be based on confessions which are the result of fear, confusion, or even police fabrication.[41] Without the need to establish any objectively incriminating facts, the police might construct a case simply on the basis of remarks attributed to the accused person. Anyone carrying a bag might be liable to be arrested and to have attributed to him or her the remark: 'I thought it contained drugs'. These arguments based on the threat to individual rights are too important to be dismissed peremptorily, particularly since the Criminal Justice and Public Order Act 1994 provides that adverse inferences may be drawn from a suspect's silence in the face of key questions, without also providing that statements attributed by the police to the suspect, which are unrecorded and which the suspect denies, should be inadmissible in evidence.[42] There has been no shortage of research findings to the effect that new controls on the police tend to be manipulated in practice so that the intended goals may not be achieved.[43] It may therefore be unsafe to expect the laws of criminal procedure to prevent any dangers to individual rights: if a fault-centred law leads to police malpractice which cannot otherwise be prevented, it ought to be narrowed. This leaves untouched the fault-centred argument that there really is no difference in terms of moral culpability or dangerousness between persons who actually do make an impossible attempt and many ordinary attempters.[44] However, there are also principled arguments in favour of at least a partly objectivist law of attempts, either allowing impossibility as a defence in those relatively unusual circumstances where D's endeavour fails to connect with the real world, or more broadly developing the view that actual consequences make a significant moral difference.[45]

---

[40] Three expressions of the act-centred view are J. F. Stephen, *History of the Criminal Law* (1883), ii, 225; J. Temkin, 'Impossible Attempts: Another View' (1976) 39 MLR 55; and Lords Bridge and Roskill in *Anderton* v *Ryan* [1985] AC 560.

[41] This is one of the concerns expressed in the lengthy discussion of attempts by G. Fletcher, *Rethinking Criminal Law* (1978), 137ff.

[42] For a review of the case law see I. Dennis, 'Silence in the Police Station: the marginalisation of section 34' [2002] Crim LR 25.

[43] See e.g. I. McKenzie, R. Morgan, and R. Reiner, 'Helping the Police with their Inquiries' [1990] Crim LR 22; T. Bucke and D. Brown, *In Police Custody: Police Powers and Suspects' Rights under the Revised PACE Codes of Practice* (1997).

[44] A view meticulously criticized by Duff, *Criminal Attempts*, chs 9–12.

[45] There is not space here to do justice to the careful arguments of Duff, ibid., especially at 206–36 and 378–84.

There would be little difference between the two approaches over the case of D, who fired a shot at V and missed because his aim was not good enough. That is a classic criminal attempt. But what is the difference between that and a case in which E puts sugar in X's drink in the belief that it is cyanide? On the act-centred approach there is no social danger in the latter case, because sugar is innocuous; yet it is equally true that there is no danger in the first case, because shooting and missing is innocuous. Some might say that D might try again and the shot might not miss; yet it is equally possible that E might try again and might choose an ingredient which actually is poisonous. It seems, then, that the act-centred approach incorporates one limb of the subjective principle—that people should be judged on the consequences they intend to happen—but not the other (belief) limb—that people should be judged on the facts as they believe them to be. There is no principled explanation for accepting one and not the other, apart from the argument about police powers and individual liberty, which ought (if possible) to be tackled directly, and not through a distortion of the law of attempts.

The recent history of English law contains evidence of both approaches. The House of Lords in *Haughton* v *Smith*[46] adopted an act-centred stance, but the Law Commission accepted the arguments above and recommended a fault-centred approach, in which impossibility would be no defence to liability. Debate continued during the passage of the new law, and one result of further changes of mind by the government was two strangely-worded provisions in s 1(2) and (3) of the Criminal Attempts Act 1981. The Act purported to follow the Law Commission and to criminalize impossible attempts, but the House of Lords interpreted the provisions so as not to achieve this result, and it was only in *Shivpuri* (1986)[47] that it was settled that, in the English law of attempts, D is judged on the facts as he or she believed them to be. Thus, if a person buys a video recorder believing that it is stolen when it is not, that constitutes an attempt to handle stolen goods.

The fault-centred approach here has been limited to beliefs about facts. If D is mistaken about the law, believing that certain conduct is an offence when it is not, there is no liability for an attempt. Thus, where D believed that he was smuggling currency into the country but there is no offence of importing currency, there could be no conviction.[48] This is easily explained: there is no crime to be attempted, only an imaginary crime. But it can also be seen as a corollary of the maxim that ignorance of the law is no excuse:[49] a mistake about the criminal law neither exculpates nor inculpates. By contrast, a mistake as to the facts may exculpate (subject to other policies relevant to mistakes)[50] or inculpate (as an impossible attempt), since the general principle is that D is judged on the facts as he or she believed them to be.[51]

---

[46] [1975] AC 476.

[47] [1987] AC 1, overruling the House's own decision of the previous year in *Anderton* v *Ryan* [1985] AC 560. A considerable influence in bringing about this judicial *volte-face* was the article by Glanville Williams, 'The Lords and Impossible Attempts' [1986] Camb LJ 33.

[48] *Taaffe* [1984] AC 539.   [49] Discussed above, Ch 6.6.   [50] See above, Ch 5.5(d), and Ch 6.5.

[51] See above, Ch 5.4(a).

(d) REFORM

The Law Commission has consulted on a set of proposals for reforming the law of attempts, as noted at various points above. The major argument is that completed attempts should be distinguished from incomplete attempts (as this work has always maintained), and that two separate offences should be devised to cater for this—the offence of attempt, for those who are engaged in the last acts towards committing the substantive offence, and 'criminal preparation', for those caught at an earlier stage. The Commission is right to emphasize that the 'ordinary language' approach to criminal attempts is ill-suited to deal with incomplete attempts, but whether the solution of two separate offences is either necessary or practical seems doubtful.[52] On the other hand, the Commission's other proposals—on the fault element, on the use of examples to bring consistency to decisions on the conduct element, and on including attempts by omission—are to be welcomed. However, the Commission acknowledges that the proliferation of statutory offences of preparation has become opportunistic rather than principled, and the question of the overall reach of the criminal law needs to be re-assessed.[53]

11.4 THE JUSTIFICATIONS FOR AN OFFENCE OF CONSPIRACY

The essence of conspiracy is an agreement between two or more persons to commit a criminal offence. The reason for criminalization is largely preventive, as in the law of attempts, since it enables the police and the courts to intervene before any harm has actually been inflicted. Whereas in attempts the doing of a 'more than merely preparatory' act is required as evidence of the firmness of the intent, in conspiracy it is the fact of agreement with others which is regarded as sufficiently firm evidence that the parties are committed to carrying out the crime. Another part of the justification for an offence of conspiracy is that persons who go so far as to reach an agreement to commit a crime, and are caught before the agreement is carried out, may not be significantly less blameworthy or less dangerous than persons who conspire and succeed in bringing about the substantive offence.

However, this fairly traditional analysis of conspiracy as an inchoate offence neglects the other social functions which conspiracy law has been called upon to perform. In the nineteenth century it was accepted that a conviction for criminal conspiracy could be based on an agreement to do any unlawful act, even though that act was not criminal but only a civil wrong, such as a tort or breach of contract. This gave the criminal law a long reach, particularly with regard to the activities of the early

---

[52] Cf. J. Rogers, 'The Codification of Attempts and the Case for "Preparation"' [2008] Crim LR 937.
[53] LCCP 183, *Conspiracy and Attempts*, 16.66.

trade unions, and the courts upheld conspiracy convictions for what were, in effect, agreements to strike until the law was changed by the Conspiracy and Protection of Property Act 1875 and the Trade Disputes Act 1906.[54] In social terms, the criminal law lent its authority to those who wished to suppress organized industrial action. In legal terms, the reasoning seemed to be that acts which were insufficiently anti-social to justify criminal liability when done by one person could become sufficiently anti-social to justify criminal liability when done by two or more people acting in agreement. Such a combination of malefactors might increase the probability of harm resulting, might in some cases increase public alarm, and might in other cases facilitate the perpetration and concealment of the wrong.[55] Prosecutions were often brought in cases where the agreement had been carried out and the unlawful acts done, since there was no substantive criminal offence to be prosecuted (in that the conspiracy was to do an unlawful but non-criminal act). Thus the legal definition turned on an 'agreement', but the social reality centred upon the actual commission of the tort or breach of contract, from which a prior agreement was inferred. In these contexts, conspiracy functioned more as an additional substantive offence than as an inchoate crime.

In the 1960s and 1970s the House of Lords, pursuing a broad policy of social defence, expanded the law of conspiracy considerably by criminalizing various agreements to do non-criminal acts;[56] but in *DPP* v *Withers* (1975)[57] their Lordships called a halt, holding that there was no such offence as conspiracy to cause a public mischief. This presaged the Law Commission's report on conspiracy in 1976, which recommended that the offence of conspiracy should be coextensive with the substantive law.[58] Conspiracies should be criminal only if the conduct agreed upon constitutes a crime when done by one person. The principles of non-retroactivity and maximum certainty were accepted, even to the point of asserting that if some new form of wickedness were to arise which did not fall within existing offences, the proper approach would be to await a response from the legislature rather than for the judges to exploit the elasticity of the law of conspiracy.[59] Parliament adopted the substance of the Law Commission's report, and enacted the Criminal Law Act 1977. Part I of the Act created the offence of statutory conspiracy, limited to agreements to commit one or more criminal offences; Part II provided a handful of offences of trespass on residential premises.[60] An agreement to commit one of these distinct trespass offences

---

[54] For a general account of the social history of conspiracy see R. Spicer, *Conspiracy Law, Class and Society* (1981); see also G. Robertson, *Whose Conspiracy?* (1974).

[55] For further discussion see R. Johnson, 'The Unnecessary Crime of Conspiracy' (1973) 61 Cal LR 1137, and I. Dennis, 'The Rationale of Criminal Conspiracy' (1977) 93 LQR 39.

[56] The high water marks were *Shaw* v *DPP* [1962] AC 220 (conspiracy to corrupt public morals), *Knuller* v *DPP* [1973] AC 435 (conspiracy to outrage public decency), and *Kamara* v *DPP* [1973] 2 All ER 1242 (conspiracy to trespass).

[57] [1975] AC 842.   [58] Law Com No. 76, *Conspiracy and Criminal Law Reform* (1976).

[59] Ibid., paras. 1.8–1.9.

[60] The Criminal Justice and Public Order Act 1994 has now added the offences of aggravated trespass (s. 68), trespassory assembly (s. 70), and unauthorized camping (s. 77).

is a statutory conspiracy, and the common law offence of conspiracy to trespass, upheld in *Kamara*,[61] was abolished.

The 1977 Act did not, however, accomplish a clean sweep of common law conspiracy. The Law Commission had been unable to complete its examination of conspiracy to defraud and any new offences which might be needed to replace it (see Chapter 9.8 above); and another committee was engaged in a review of the laws on obscenity, which led the government to exclude from the 1977 Act conspiracies to corrupt public morals and to outrage public decency.[62] Thus the controversial decision in *Shaw*[63] remains authoritative on conspiracy to corrupt public morals, as does the decision in *Knuller*[64] on conspiracy to outrage public decency, and also *Scott v Metropolitan Police Commissioner*[65] on conspiracy to defraud, whose precepts owe more to the 'thin ice' principle (Chapter 3.4(b)) and the policy of social defence (Chapter 3.5(j)) than to any notion of maximum certainty in criminal law (Chapter 3.5(i)). The only small retrenchment is that conspiracy to outrage public decency is now a form of statutory conspiracy, as a result of the decision in *Gibson* (1990) to the effect that the offence of outraging public decency is a substantive offence that one individual can commit.[66]

Leaving aside the common law conspiracies to defraud, to corrupt public morals, and to outrage public decency, is it true to say that statutory conspiracy functions primarily as an inchoate offence? Few conspiracies can be prosecuted at the stage of agreement, because meetings of conspirators usually take place in private and it is rare for sufficient evidence to become available until some acts in furtherance of the agreement have been done and observed. So the rationale of early prevention, even before an attempt has been committed, is often far from the social facts. However, another function of inchoate offences is to criminalize those who try and fail, as well as those who are caught before they have the chance to succeed or fail. Conspiracy does fulfil this function, being used against those who join together to commit a crime in circumstances in which it is impossible to do so.[67] Yet there remains a way in which even statutory conspiracy also functions as an extra criminal offence. The rules of evidence in conspiracy cases are somewhat wider than those in other trials: for example, the statements of one co-conspirator are admissible in evidence against another if they relate to an act done in furtherance of the conspiracy, by way of exception to the general rule that the admissions of one co-defendant cannot be adduced in evidence

[61] [1973] 2 All ER 1242.

[62] The Williams Committee, which subsequently reported on *Obscenity and Film Censorship*, Cmnd 7772 (1979), but whose recommendations were not adopted in legislation.

[63] [1962] AC 220.   [64] [1973] AC 435.   [65] [1975] AC 819.

[66] [1990] 2 QB 619: the combined effect of this decision and s. 5 of the Criminal Law Act 1977 is that conspiracy to outrage public decency becomes a statutory conspiracy. It is undecided whether the same applies to corrupting public morals.

[67] The 1977 Act contained no provision on impossibility, but s. 5 of the Criminal Attempts Act 1981 makes it clear that impossibility is no more a defence to conspiracy than it is to attempt.

against the other.[68] Moreover, all that has to be proved for conspiracy is the agreement, and that may be inferred from behaviour. Prosecutors who wish to take advantage of these rules may prefer to charge conspiracy instead of the substantive crime even in a case where the substantive offence has been committed: it is bad practice for them to charge both conspiracy and the substantive crime,[69] but it is no answer to a conspiracy charge alone that the substantive offence was in fact committed. In the terminology of English criminal procedure, a conspiracy does not 'merge' with the substantive offence. Thus the prosecution may defend its use of a conspiracy charge as giving a more rounded impression of the nature of the criminal enterprise, in terms of planning and the different roles of the various participants.[70]

Despite this use of the crime of conspiracy as an extra substantive offence, its primary justifications remain those of an inchoate offence. An individual who declares an intent to steal certain property has committed no offence; two or more individuals who agree to do the same thing may be convicted of conspiracy to steal. How strong are the justifications? Three arguments may be considered. First, criminal groups generate a 'special social identity' that leads to loyalty, commitment, and indeed a certain loss of control by individuals as a group dynamic takes over, with individuals being afraid to withdraw and participants spurring each other on. Some psychological research suggests that even hastily-formed groups may quickly generate this kind of identity and loyalty.[71] The implication is that such joint criminal ventures may acquire a momentum of their own and may render the commission of further offences more likely, and that this justifies singling them out.[72] Secondly, where several people are involved, this may enable individual members to distance themselves from the actual harm to be caused by looking little further than their own acts of assistance. This 'technique of neutralization' may make crime easier and cheaper to carry out.[73] Thirdly the involvement of several people in an offence may create greater fear in victims and greater public alarm. Although one could imagine an individual more terrifying than two bungling offenders, this casts little doubt on the qualitative difference between most criminal gangs and the activities of most lone offenders. In many cases group crimes are more terrifying, and sentencers may well be justified in treating this as an aggravating factor.[74]

---

[68] See *Liggins et al.* [1995] Crim LR 45 and commentary. The same rule applies to principals and accomplices.

[69] See the case of the Shrewsbury pickets, *Jones et al.* (1974) 59 Cr App R 120, and the Practice Direction [1977] 2 All ER 540.

[70] This 'rounded impression' argument is much emphasized by prosecutors, but the Law Commission seems unpersuaded that a similar effect could not be achieved by using the existing law of complicity: Law Commission Consultation Paper 155, *Fraud and Deception* (1999), paras. 4.36–4.38. See further Ch 9.9 above.

[71] N. K. Katyal, 'Conspiracy Theory', (2003) 112 Yale LJ 1307, cited in LCCP 183, *Conspiracy and Attempts*, Part 2.

[72] See the discussion of joint enterprise in complicity above, Ch 10.5.

[73] Katyal, 'Conspiracy Theory', 1323.

[74] See the discussion of duress in Ch 6.3(c) above, and more generally A. Ashworth, *Sentencing and Criminal Justice* (4th edn., 2005), ch 5.2.2.

Whether considerations such as these justify the creation of special public order offences aimed at group behaviour, with separate rules of proof favouring prosecutors, was questioned earlier.[75] Do they justify the law of conspiracy, especially now that Part 2 of the Serious Crime Act 2007 has introduced wider-ranging inchoate offences of encouraging and assisting crime?[76] What if the doctrine of merger were extended, so that conspiracy ceased to be chargeable if the substantive offence had been committed? No special characteristic of group criminality would be lost, because there remains the doctrine of complicity. The law of principals and accomplices may lack some of the evidentiary advantages to the prosecution which conspiracy has, but it does favour the prosecution procedurally by not requiring it to charge defendants separately as accomplices or principals.[77] And there is the same discretion at the sentencing stage to reflect the element of aggravation in planned group offending. A similar question about the dispensability of the offence of conspiracy may be asked in relation to its inchoate function. Many conspiracies will already have been carried far enough to fulfil the test for criminal attempt, under the existing or the proposed law, or the new offences of encouraging or assisting crime. Much of the ground might therefore be covered by the law of attempts and by prosecutions for complicity in attempts. This leaves only the few cases where clear evidence is obtained of an agreement to commit a crime, without any action having yet been taken to implement the agreement. The Law Commission argues that the offence remains vital to deal with these cases, particularly where the police or security services possess intelligence about a planned terrorist incident that enables them to prove an agreement and thus to intervene early.[78] Even if this is conceded, it seems likely that the offence of conspiracy will continue to be used much more broadly, in cases where the doctrine of complicity also applies, because prosecutors like having the powers that it gives them.[79] These powers raise a range of other questions, however. Agreements usually involve words, and issues of privacy, freedom of speech, and freedom of association may arise here,[80] in the sense that the existence of this offence might encourage the police to use intrusive tactics (such as bugging premises). To advocate freedom to commit crimes would be unsupportable, but one must avoid the risk of inhibiting the development of controversial ideas. Furthermore, there is the danger of conviction based on inference and mere association, which leave opportunities for prosecutions to be brought without much hard evidence. The offence of conspiracy may be defended as a vital tool against organized crime, but the difficulty is that it may bear oppressively on some of the individuals who are caught within its ample net.

---

[75] See above, Ch 8.3(g).   [76] See below, 11.7.

[77] See further, Ch 10.2 above, and *DPP for Northern Ireland* v *Maxwell* [1978] 3 All ER 1140.

[78] LCCP 183, *Conspiracy and Attempts*, para 2.9.

[79] A consideration surprisingly treated by the Law Commission as a justification for retaining the offence: see ibid., para 2.34.

[80] Arts. 8, 10, and 11 of the European Convention on Human Rights.

11.5 THE ELEMENTS OF CRIMINAL CONSPIRACY

(a) AN AGREEMENT BETWEEN TWO OR MORE PERSONS

Agreement is the basic element in conspiracy. The idea of an agreement seems to involve a meeting of minds, and there is no need for a physical meeting of the persons involved so long as they reach a mutual understanding of what is to be done.[81] Whether the understanding amounts to an agreement may be a matter of degree: if the parties are still at the stage of negotiation, without having decided what to do, no criminal conspiracy has yet come into being. But what if the parties have reached agreement in principle, leaving matters of detail to be resolved afterwards? In *Broad* (1997)[82] there was evidence that the defendants had agreed to manufacture certain substances that would undoubtedly be Class A drugs, even though it was not yet clear or decided which drug would be manufactured by the processes they had commenced. The Court of Appeal held that it was sufficient for conspiracy liability that each defendant had participated in the processes knowing that one of these substances would be produced.[83] What if arrangements have been made, but may be unscrambled later? The judicial tendency is to regard these as conspiratorial agreements, and this is consistent with the rule that there is no defence of withdrawal for a person who has become a party to a conspiracy.[84] Moreover, since all human arrangements are vulnerable to changes in circumstances, the possibility that a planned robbery might be cancelled if there are police in the vicinity at the time does not negate the existence of a conspiracy. Further problems over 'conditional' agreements are discussed in section 11.5(b) below.

Certain agreements are excluded from the law of conspiracy. First, by s 2(2)(a) of the Criminal Law Act 1977, agreements between husband and wife only (without a third person) cannot amount to criminal conspiracies. This rule places the value of marital confidence above the public interest in having conspirators brought to justice, a priority which has been partly abandoned in other areas of the law (e.g. by compelling one spouse to give evidence against the other in certain proceedings).[85] If a husband and wife go so far as to commit an attempt or a substantive offence, they can be convicted jointly of that. Secondly, by s 2(2)(b), agreements in which the only other person is under the age of criminal responsibility cannot result in D's conviction for conspiracy—an application of the rule of criminal capacity. Thirdly, by s 2(2)(c) of the

---

[81] G. Orchard, '"Agreement" in Criminal Conspiracy' [1974] Crim LR 297.

[82] [1997] Crim LR 666.

[83] The Court dismissed the relevance of any defendant's ignorance that the substances were, in law, Class A drugs. See Ch 6.5 above.

[84] Compare. *Mulcahy* (1868) LR 3 HL 306, and *Thomson* (1965) 50 Cr App R 1, with the arguments in 11.8 below.

[85] Police and Criminal Evidence Act 1984, s. 80. The Law Commission rightly propose the abolition of this exemption: LCCP 183, *Conspiracy and Attempts*, Part 9.

Act, agreements in which the only other person is an intended victim cannot result in D's conviction for conspiracy. This parallels the rule that a person who falls within the class protected by the offence (e.g. persons under a given age) cannot be convicted as a party to that crime.[86] Fourthly, s 4(1) provides that a prosecution for conspiracy to commit one or more summary offences requires the consent of the Director of Public Prosecutions. Although this appears to restrict the practical use of conspiracy charges, it should be noted that the crime of attempt does not apply to summary offences at all. Once again, the 'double life' of conspiracy as an inchoate and a quasi-substantive offence is evident. One argument is that the deliberate planning of numerous offences, even if summary only, may justify prosecution as a conspiracy. Presumably, also, the number of persons involved in an agreement to commit summary offences might persuade the Crown Prosecution Service that it is in the public interest to prosecute for a single conspiracy rather than bringing various separate small charges.

Agreement is the basic element in criminal conspiracy, but the evidence offered to a court may often amount to inferences from behaviour rather than direct testimony or recording of a meeting of conspirators. Thus the typical process is to infer a prior agreement from behaviour which appears to be concerted. However, courts sometimes overlook the fact that, if the charge is conspiracy, it is the conduct agreed upon and not the conduct actually carried out that is the basis of the offence.[87]

(b) THE CRIMINAL CONDUCT AGREED UPON

We move now to the subject-matter of the agreement. The Criminal Law Act 1977, s 1(1), provides that a conspiracy is criminal if it is agreed that 'a course of conduct will be pursued which, if the agreement is carried out in accordance with their intentions... will necessarily amount to or involve the commission of any offence or offences by one or more parties to the agreement'. The essence, therefore, is that two or more persons should agree on the commission of a crime. It is well established that they need not know that the agreed course of conduct does amount to a crime— ignorance of the criminal law does not excuse here.[88] The 'course of conduct' includes not only the acts agreed upon but also the intended consequences: conspiracy to murder requires not only an agreement to shoot at a person but also the intention that the shots should cause death.[89]

In interpreting the section, one's eyes are drawn to the word 'necessarily': can it ever be said that, if an agreement is carried out in accordance with the parties' intentions, it will *necessarily* involve the commission of an offence? This unduly concrete term seems to run counter to the proposition that all agreements are conditional in some way or another, and thus to ignore the possibility of an unexpected failure (the bomb

---

[86] *Tyrell* [1894] 1 QB 710, discussed in Ch 10.7(b) above.

[87] For an unsatisfactory decision see *El-Kurd* [2001] Crim LR 234.

[88] *Churchill* v *Walton* [1967] 2 AC 224.

[89] As for attempted murder, an intention to cause grievous bodily harm is not sufficient: see O'Connor LJ in *Siracusa* (1990) 90 Cr App R 340, at 350.

which fails to detonate, the shot which misses, etc.). Does it therefore leave all fallible agreements outside the law of conspiracy? Is it enough for the defence to raise a reasonable doubt that the plan might have miscarried for some reason? Such an argument would put the principles of statutory interpretation to a stern test: should the court apply the plain meaning of 'necessarily' on the principle of strict construction—and acquit—or should it apply the purposive approach and the policy of social defence—and convict? One challenge to the wording was heard in *Jackson* (1985).[90] Four men arranged for one of their number to be shot in the leg; the aim was to provide mitigation in the event of his being convicted at his trial for burglary. He was shot in the leg before the end of the trial. On a charge of conspiracy to pervert the course of justice, it was argued that there was no certainty that he would be convicted and therefore the agreement would not necessarily lead to a perversion of the course of justice. The Court of Appeal rejected the argument, drawing a distinction between the inevitability of the substantive offence being committed (which s 1(1) does not require) and the inevitability that it would be committed if the agreement was carried out in accordance with their intentions. The Court approved the example of two people agreeing to drive from London to Edinburgh within a time that could only be achieved without breaking the speed laws if traffic conditions were particularly favourable, and agreeing to break the speed limits if necessary:[91] this would not be a conspiracy to exceed the speed limit because it would be possible to do everything agreed upon without breaking the law. However, it can be argued that this is too favourable to the parties, who have plainly agreed to commit one or more offences if certain contingencies arise.[92] In principle, these cases should be dealt with through the rules on conditional intention, bearing in mind that most intentions are conditional to some extent.[93]

Section 1(1) of the 1977 Act was amended by s 5 of the Criminal Attempts Act 1981 to make it clear that impossibility is no more a defence to conspiracy than to a charge of attempt. It is sufficient to establish that the agreement *would* have involved the commission of an offence but for the existence of facts which rendered it impossible. The justifications for this follow those outlined in section 11.3(c) above.

(c) THE FAULT REQUIREMENTS

The basic fault requirements for conspiracy would appear to be twofold: first, that each defendant should have knowledge of any facts or circumstances specified in the substantive offence, either knowing that present facts exist or (as the case may be) intending that certain facts or circumstances will exist at the time of the substantive offence; and, secondly, that each defendant should intend the conspiracy to be carried out and the substantive offence to be committed, although we will see below that this requirement is in doubt.

---

[90] [1985] Crim LR 442.   [91] *Reed* [1982] Crim LR 819.
[92] A. P. Simester and G. R. Sullivan, *Criminal Law: Theory and Doctrine* (3rd edn., 2007), 290.
[93] See further LCCP 183, *Conspiracy and Attempts*, Part 5.

Section 1(2) makes it clear that these requirements of full intention and knowledge as to facts and circumstances apply no matter what offence is agreed upon. Thus full knowledge and intent are required, even for conspiracies to commit offences of strict liability, negligence, or recklessness. Why is the fault element for conspiracy kept so narrow? If the substantive offence is satisfied, say, by recklessness as to some elements, why should the crime of conspiracy not likewise be satisfied? The answer seems to lie with the remoteness principle encountered elsewhere: that inchoate crimes are an extension of the criminal sanction, and the more remote an offence becomes from the actual infliction of harm, the higher the degree of fault necessary to justify criminalization. Thus, in *Saik* (2007)[94] D changed large amounts of money at his currency exchange on behalf of others. He pleaded guilty to conspiracy to convert the proceeds of drug trafficking, contrary to section 93(2) of the Criminal Justice Act 1988 (now superseded by the Proceeds of Crime Act 2002), but the basis of his plea was that he merely suspected that the money was the proceeds of crime. The House of Lords held that his conviction should be quashed: although the substantive offence would be committed if D had 'reasonable grounds to suspect' that the money was the proceeds of crime, a charge of conspiracy could only be sustained, on the proper interpretation of section 1(2), by proof of full knowledge. This demonstrates one drawback for prosecutors of the 'double life' of conspiracy as an inchoate and a quasi-substantive offence: here, the doctrinal confusion works in favour of defendants rather than against them by requiring full knowledge and intention even where conspiracy is used as a quasi-substantive offence.

Should such a narrow approach to the fault element in conspiracy be retained? If X and Y agree to go to a woman's room and to have intercourse with her, hoping that she will consent but not caring whether she does or not, are they guilty of conspiracy to rape? The wording of s 1(2) of the 1977 Act suggests not. Yet it was argued earlier[95] that there should be a conviction for attempted rape in parallel circumstances, and that argument might apply no less strongly to conspiracy. The Law Commission takes this view, arguing that X and Y are sufficiently culpable because their agreement shows that they are 'prepared to go ahead with the plan even if it turns out that V does not consent'.[96] On this view, the fault element should be extended to cover cases of an intention to do acts reckless as to whether or not an incriminating circumstance exists. However, in applying the 1977 Act, the concern of the courts has not been with these arguments but with other questions about the meaning of s 1(1). In *Anderson* (1986),[97] the House of Lords chose to reinterpret the words of the section in order to uphold a conviction. It was held, first, that a person may be convicted of conspiracy even without intending the agreement to be carried out; and, secondly, that a person is guilty of conspiracy if, and only if, it is established that he or she intended to play some part in the agreed course of conduct. Both these

---

[94] [2007] 1 AC 18.

[95] See section 11.3(a), discussing *Khan* (1990) 91 Cr App R 29 and *Attorney-General's Reference (No. 1 of 1992)* (1994) 98 Cr App R 383.

[96] LCCP 183, *Conspiracy and Attempts*, para 4.109.   [97] [1986] AC 27.

propositions are open to doubt. It seems extraordinary that a person can be held liable for conspiring to commit an offence when he does not intend it to be committed, particularly since that would mean that none of the conspirators needs to intend the substantive offence to be committed. The Privy Council has now held, in *Yip Chiu-cheung* (1995),[98] that the prosecution must establish that each alleged conspirator intended the agreement to be carried out. This is the better view, although *Anderson* remains high authority to the contrary. The second proposition appears to run counter to one of the rationales of conspiracy, which is to bring those who plan offences but do not take part in them (the 'godfathers') within the ambit of the criminal sanction. The second *Anderson* proposition was later reinterpreted by the Court of Appeal in *Siracusa* (1990)[99] so as to mean the opposite of what the House of Lords said: a passive conspirator who concurs in the activities of the person(s) carrying out the crime without becoming involved himself is guilty of criminal conspiracy. The precedents are therefore in a mess, and the Law Commission rightly proposes clarification that each conspirator should intend that the conduct and any consequence element will occur.[100]

11.6 INCITEMENT

The third of the trio of inchoate offences in English criminal law was incitement. The courts had developed it along rather different lines from those of attempt and conspiracy, both of which have been put into statutory form in recent years. The Law Commission gave several reasons for regarding the offence of incitement in its present form as unsatisfactory and, rather than proposing a revised statutory version of the offence, recommended its abolition and replacement with new and broader offences of assisting and encouraging crime.[101] These new offences, created by Part 2 of the Serious Crime Act 2007, came into force on 1 October 2008 and are examined below. However, it must be noted that there remains a whole range of statutory offences of incitement which are unaffected by the abolition of the common law offence—from long-standing offences such as incitement to disaffection from the armed forces, to the offence under section 1 of the Terrorism Act 2006 of publishing a statement likely to be understood 'as a direct or indirect encouragement' of acts of terrorism.[102]

---

98 [1995] 1 AC 111. This was not a statutory conspiracy contrary to the 1977 Act, but the common law is surely no different on this point.

99 (1990) 90 Cr App R 340.

100 LCCP 183, *Conspiracy and Attempts*, para 4.22 et seq; see also the new offences of encouraging and assisting crime, discussed in 11.7 below.

101 Law Com No. 300, *Inchoate Liability for Assisting and Encouraging Crime* (2006), ch 3.

102 For analysis, see A. Hunt, 'Criminal Prohibitions on Direct and Indirect Encouragement of Terrorism' [2007] Crim LR 441.

11.7   ENCOURAGING OR ASSISTING CRIME

The statutory context of the new offences is instructive: they are set out in Part 2 of the Serious Crime Act 2007, between Part 1 (which introduces Serious Crime Prevention Orders) and Part 3 (entitled 'Other Measures to Prevent or Disrupt Serious or Other Crime'). In other words, the new offences are conceived as part of a raft of measures against serious and organized crime.[103] However, nothing in the statute limits them to such types of crime, and so they take their place as general inchoate offences. Part 2 of the 2007 Act creates three new offences of encouraging or assisting crime, and they will now be considered in turn. The three offences are supported by some 20 sections of further detail, rendering this one of the more complex legislative innovations in the criminal law. The aim here will be to identify and to appraise critically the principles of the new offences, without the distraction of too much detail.[104]

(a)   INTENTIONALLY ENCOURAGING OR ASSISTING AN OFFENCE

The first of the three new inchoate offences is that provided by section 44 of the Serious Crime Act 2007, which is committed if D does an act capable of encouraging or assisting the commission of an offence and D intends to assist or encourage its commission. Many of the features of this offence also apply to the other two offences, and so they will be discussed here. It is immediately obvious that this offence applies independently of whether the principal offence is committed or not: so if D encourages P by using the language of incitement, or if D assists P by lending him equipment, D commits this offence irrespective of whether P is encouraged by D's incitement or whether P actually uses D's equipment or commits the principal offence. This must be right in principle, as argued in 11.2 above: D has crossed the threshold of culpability, whether P responds to his promptings or not. But that principled argument does not necessarily justify the extent of the liability for this offence, which we must now examine.

The conduct element of the s 44 offence is doing 'an act capable of encouraging or assisting the commission of an offence.' Thus it seems that any act will satisfy the section, howsoever small or insignificant, so long as it is *capable of* amounting to encouragement or assistance. We have already noted that there is no requirement that D's act did encourage or assist; that probably means that there is no requirement that P even knew of D's act, since the focus of this offence is on D. What is capable of amounting to encouragement or assistance depends on the meaning of each of those terms, but the Act, replete as it is with all manner of other qualifications and extensions, contains no definition of either of these key words. Thus section 65(1) states

---

[103] Home Office, *New Powers against Organized and Financial Crime* (2006).

[104] For a searching analysis of the new provisions, see R. Fortson, *Blackstone's Guide to the Serious Crime Act 2007* (2008).

that encouragement includes 'threatening another person or otherwise putting pressure on' him or her, but in other respects the concept is left for the courts to develop, presumably along the same lines as the common law of incitement.[105] Assistance will presumably be interpreted in a similar way to 'assist' in complicity, but this would be to duplicate some of the shortcomings of that branch of the law. Thus it was argued in Chapter 10.3 above that small acts of assistance should not open the way to conviction of complicity in a major crime and a high maximum penalty; the argument here is the same, and the maximum penalty for the anticipated offence applies even though the conviction is under section 44 and not for the anticipated offence.[106] So any act, however small, suffices for this offence so long as it is capable of encouraging or assisting the commission of the anticipated offence. Section 65(2) states that 'an act capable of encouraging or assisting' includes taking steps to reduce the possibility of criminal proceedings being brought in respect of that offence (as by helping P to flee the country after his crime) and includes failing to take steps to discharge a duty (as by leaving a window open to help burglars to gain access to premises); section 65(3) excludes a failure to respond to a constable's request to assistance, but that exclusion suggests that in other respects the question whether there was a duty is for the court, applying general principles.

The main fault element required for conviction of the section 44 offence appears to be purpose: subsection (1)(b) states that D must intend by his act to encourage or assist the commission of the anticipated offence, and subsection (2) states that it is not enough that encouragement or assistance was 'a foreseeable consequence of his act.' The implication is therefore that foresight of virtual certainty (oblique intention) will never suffice for liability here: presumably this is intended as a counterweight to the potentially wide reach of the conduct element of this offence. However, since the essence of section 44 is 'encouraging or assisting *an offence*', D must also have fault in relation to the full offence he is encouraging or assisting—an offence means conduct plus fault on the part of P, the perpetrator whose offence it is D's purpose to encourage or assist. The Act's provisions on this are complex. Where P's offence is one that requires fault, it must be proved that D believed that P would do it with the required fault or that D was reckless as to whether or not P would have the required fault, or that D's state of mind was such as that if he (D) had done the conduct that he anticipated P would do, he (D) would have had the required fault.[107] That last provision caters for cases where D tricks P into doing something (such as sexually penetrating V) which is not an offence for P (because P has been tricked and therefore lacks fault): since D has the fault, D is liable for the section 44 offence nonetheless. And that is not all. If the anticipated offence is one requiring proof of particular circumstances or consequences or both, it must be proved that D believed or was reckless as to whether P's conduct would be done in those circumstances or with those consequences.[108] This would

---

[105] Law Com No. 300, para. 5.37.
[106] The term 'anticipated offence' is used to denote the offence that D intended to assist or encourage.
[107] Serious Crime Act 2007, s. 47(5)(a).   [108] Ibid., s 47(5)(b).

have obvious implications for charges of encouraging or assisting offences under the Sexual Offences Act 2003, where many of the offences specify circumstances such as the age (under 13, 13 to 15) or the mental capacity of the complainant.

(b) ENCOURAGING OR ASSISTING AN OFFENCE BELIEVING IT WILL BE COMMITTED

Whereas the essence of the section 44 offence is D's purpose to assist or encourage, the section 45 offence is committed when D believes that the anticipated offence will be committed when he does an act capable of encouraging or assisting it. Thus if D, the Polish-speaking manager of a garden centre, sells weed killer to two customers whom he overheard talking in Polish about using it to poison someone, he will be guilty of the section 45 offence if he has the necessary beliefs, but not if he thinks they were speaking hypothetically or were joking. For section 45, the focus is not D's purpose or desire that P will commit the offence, but D's *belief* that P will commit it. Thus the conduct element for the section 45 offence is the same as that under section 44—an act capable of encouraging or assisting—and all the extensions and exclusions mentioned in (a) above apply equally here. As with section 44, the section 45 offence is committed irrespective of whether P actually commits the anticipated offence or even realizes that D is trying to encourage or assist him to do so.

There are two main fault elements for this offence. First, D must believe that the offence he is encouraging or assisting 'will be committed'. What kind of mental state is believing that something will happen? To act with a belief is to act without any significant doubt on the matter: here, a belief that P is virtually certain to commit the offence should be sufficient. When the term 'belief' is combined with the term 'will', this indicates a high degree of confidence in D's mind that P is going to commit the anticipated offence.[109] Also, as under section 44, D must believe that P will commit the full offence (with its conduct and fault elements), or be reckless as to that; and, as with section 44, if D has the fault element for that offence and knows that P does not, D may be convicted under section 45.[110] Similarly, D must believe that any circumstances or consequences specified in the anticipated offence will be fulfilled.[111] Turning to the second fault element for the section 45 offence, D must believe that his act will encourage or assist P. It is doubtful whether this requirement adds a great deal to the offence, since it will usually be satisfied if the other conditions are fulfilled. Finally, Schedule 3 to the 2007 Act lists a number of offences to which section 45 cannot apply: these include conspiracies and attempts, and several statutory incitement offences. Whereas there can be convictions under section 44 where it is D's purpose to encourage or assist

---

[109] Cf. the test in joint venture cases in complicity, where it is sufficient that D realises there is a risk that a greater offence than D has agreed to will be committed: above, ch 10.5 Note also that s 49(7) of the 2007 Act provides that a conditional belief (that the offence will be committed if certain conditions are met) is enough.

[110] See s 47(5)(a) and the discussion at n 105 above.

[111] See s 47(5)(b) and the discussion at n 106 above.

such offences, liability in cases where D merely believes that P will commit one of those offences is thought to go too far.

(c) ENCOURAGING OR ASSISTING OFFENCES BELIEVING ONE OR MORE WILL BE COMMITTED

Section 46 of the 2007 Act creates an offence aimed at resolving a difficulty in the law of complicity, where D assists or encourages P in a criminal enterprise without knowing which of a number of possible offences P might commit.[112] Thus the essence of the section 46 offence is that D does an act capable of encouraging or assisting one of a number of offences, believing that one or more of those offences will be committed. D may be convicted even if he does not know which of the offences will be committed, and irrespective whether any of them are committed. The conduct element for this offence follows the pattern of sections 44 and 45, requiring an act capable of encouraging or assisting. All the extensions and exclusions mentioned in (a) above apply. The only difference here is that the act must be capable of encouraging or assisting 'the commission of one or more of a number of offences', that number being two or more. The prosecution must specify the offences on which it wishes to rely, but not all the possible offences that D's act might have encouraged or assisted.

The fault element for the section 46 offence is complex. As under section 45, D must believe that his act will encourage or assist the commission of one or more of the offences. D must believe that one or more of the offences 'will be committed', which suggests no substantial doubt on the matter.[113] According to section 47(4), it is sufficient if D believes that one of the group of crimes will be committed, without any belief as to which one. Also, as with sections 44 and 45, D must believe that P will commit the crime with the relevant fault element, or be reckless as to that; and D must believe that any circumstances or consequences specified in the anticipated offence(s) will be present, or be reckless as to that.[114]

(d) SPECIAL DEFENCES

Part 2 of the 2007 Act provides two special defences to the three new crimes, as well as spelling out (in section 47(b)(c) and (d)) that ignorance of the law is no defence, so that if D encourages or assists P in doing certain conduct without being aware that that constitutes a criminal offence D will be liable. The two special defences are a reasonableness defence and an exemption for persons in protected categories.

The ambit of the reasonableness defence is uncertain, since so much will depend on the view taken by the jury or magistrates. The burden of proof is on the defendant, contrary to the presumption of innocence,[115] and what D must prove is that he knew or reasonably believed that certain circumstances existed, and that in those

---

[112] Discussed in ch 10.5 above.   [113] See n 109 above, which applies here.
[114] See discussion at notes 105 and 106 above.   [115] See Ch 3.5(m) above.

circumstances it was reasonable for him to act as he did. Section 50(3) provides that, in determining whether D's conduct was reasonable, the court must consider among other factors the seriousness of the anticipated offence, and any purpose or any authority claimed by D for his conduct. Cases of authority or purpose might include someone acting in order to expose another's wrongdoing, or another's susceptibility to temptation.[116] There are unlikely to be many cases where the elements of an offence under section 44, 45 or 46 are present and there is also a claim of reasonableness, but in the absence of a general 'balance of evils' defence it is better to enshrine this possible defence in legislation than to hope that the courts might create such a defence.

Section 51 provides that an offence under sections 44, 45 or 46 cannot be committed if the anticipated offence is a 'protective offence' and D falls within the particular category of persons whom the offence was designed to protect. Thus if D (aged 12) encourages P to touch him sexually, D does not commit an offence under the 2007 Act because the anticipated offence under section 9 of the Sexual Offences Act 2003 is designed to protect children under 16. However, it is unclear what happens in the situation that arose in G (2008),[117] where both D and P are under 16 and therefore within the protected category; if the act was consensual, is it right that only one of them should have a defence under section 51?

(e) CONCLUSIONS: THE NEW INCHOATE OFFENCES

There are several points in favour of this new group of inchoate offences. They ensure that liability depends on D's culpability, irrespective of whether P goes on to commit the anticipated offence. It was argued in Chapter 5, and in this chapter in previous editions, that to make D's liability turn on whether or not P went on to commit the substantive offence was to allow chance to play too significant a role. Seen as replacements for the common law offence of incitement, the new offences avoid some of the stranger twists and turns of the former case law, and that is beneficial. The offences also remedy some gaps in the law of complicity, a branch of the criminal law that awaits reform.

However, the enactment of Part 2 of the Serious Crime Act 2007 also brings several undesirable features. Creating a statutory offence of incitement, and adding an offence of facilitation of crime, could have been a simpler and no less effective model. Simplicity and clarity were not high on the draftsman's agenda; taken together with the complexities of the Corporate Manslaughter and Corporate Homicide Act, it may be concluded that 2007 was not a good year in this respect.[118] Substantively, there are concerns about the breadth or indeed the virtual absence of the conduct requirement for assisting—any act that is capable of providing assistance is sufficient.

---

[116] See the cases discussed in Ch 4.8(d) above.   [117] [2008] UKHL 37, discussed in Ch 8 6 above.

[118] Without entering into a detailed critique, several of the subsections could have been run together (e.g. subsections (2), (3) and (4) of s 47) and others could have been avoided (e.g. s. 47(7)(b)).

The section 46 offence also spreads its net wide, much wider than the *Maxwell* doctrine.[119] The absence of definition of the two key terms, encouragement and assistance, is an ironic feature of this technically complex edifice. Whether the new extensions to criminal liability have an impact on organized or serious crime remains to be seen, but it seems most likely that they will merely become everyday additions to the prosecutor's armoury.

11.8 VOLUNTARY RENUNCIATION OF CRIMINAL PURPOSE

In view of the inchoate nature of attempt, many conspiracies, and the new offences of encouraging and assisting crime, the question arises of the legal effect of a change of mind before the substantive offence is committed. What if D abandons the attempt or withdraws from the conspiracy? English law has generally taken the view that this cannot alter the legal significance of what has already occurred: there is no defence of voluntary renunciation of criminal purpose, and it is a matter for mitigation of sentence only.[120] On the other hand, many other European systems allow such a defence,[121] the American Model Penal Code also makes provision for it,[122] and of course there is a limited doctrine of withdrawal in complicity.[123] What are the main arguments on either side?

The main argument against allowing such a defence is that it contradicts the temporal logic of the law. The definitions of attempt and conspiracy, and of the new offences of encouraging or assisting crime, are fulfilled once D, with the appropriate culpability, does the 'more than merely preparatory' act, or reaches the agreement, or does an act capable of encouraging or assisting a crime. Anything that happens subsequently cannot undo the offence: it has already been committed. The situation is no different from that of the thief who decides to return the stolen property: theft has been committed and the offence cannot be undone, even though voluntary repentance may well justify substantial mitigation of sentence. A subsidiary argument is that it would in any event be difficult for a court to satisfy itself of the voluntariness of the renunciation of criminal purpose, and that such occasions might well involve a mixture of motives on D's part. This makes the matter much more suitable for the sentencing stage than the trial itself.

Against this, and in favour of a defence of voluntary renunciation, may be ranged various moral and prudential arguments. The principal argument is that it is the intent

---

[119] See Ch 10.4.
[120] *Lankford* [1959] Crim LR 209, and Law Com No. 102 (1980), para. 2.133; cf. M. Wasik, 'Abandoning Criminal Intent' [1980] Crim LR 785.
[121] Fletcher, *Rethinking Criminal Law*, 184–97.   [122] Model Penal Code, s. 5.01(4).
[123] Discussed in Ch 10.7(a) above.

or criminal purpose which is the essence of inchoate offences, and that voluntary renunciation shows that the original criminal purpose was not sufficiently firm. This coincides with the view that it often takes more 'nerve' to go through with a crime than merely to plan or encourage it. Thus, D can be said to 'undo' the offence by a change of mind, because the criminal purpose is a continuing one—not a once-and-for-all mental state—and its effect can be neutralized by subsequent decision or action on D's part. The situation is different from that of the thief who voluntarily decides to return the property to its owner, for theft is a substantive offence and is not criminalized simply because it is one stage on the way to another crime. The argument for allowing a defence of voluntary renunciation becomes stronger as the conduct element in the inchoate offences is taken further back from the occurrence of the harm, as in the new offences of encouraging or assisting crime. A further argument is that if D renounces before the harm is caused, this may show that the threat of the criminal sanction has had a deterrent effect. To punish D none the less would be needless, and the case should be regarded as a success for the law rather than a failure. Both these arguments depart from the principle of contemporaneity (see Chapter 5.4(d)) in favour of a broader time-frame for criminal liability.[124] We have already observed the abandonment of contemporaneity in cases of prior fault (see Chapter 5.4(e)): this deviation would be on the ground of subsequent non-fault.

Those systems which have a defence of voluntary renunciation do not appear to find it problematic,[125] members of the public seem to regard it as fair,[126] and it has not caused great problems in English complicity law.[127] The defence is rarely raised, and the issue usually turns on the voluntariness of the change of mind, which may then be explored in a trial setting rather than at the sentencing stage. At a theoretical level, there is a strong argument for reduced culpability, but this does not conclude the case for a complete defence. The allocation of excuses as between the liability and the sentencing stages turns on questions of degree (see Chapter 6.8), and one might well take the view that voluntary renunciation is not sufficiently fundamental to warrant a complete defence to criminal liability.

11.9 THE RELATIONSHIP BETWEEN SUBSTANTIVE AND INCHOATE CRIMES

We have seen that the general function of inchoate crimes is to penalize preparation, planning, or encouragement towards the commission of a substantive offence. It has also been noted that the crime of conspiracy is sometimes invoked where the

---

[124] See M. Kelman, 'Interpretive Construction in the Substantive Criminal Law' (1981) 33 Stanford LR 591, at 611–14 and 628–30.

[125] See the discussion by Fletcher, *Rethinking Criminal Law*, 184–97.

[126] Robinson and Darley, *Justice, Liability and Blame*, 23–8.   [127] See Ch 10.7(a) above.

substantive offence has occurred, and that 'complete' attempts are cases in which D has done everything intended for the commission of a crime: in both those instances, the inchoate offences come very close to substantive crimes. The same phenomenon also appears the other way round: modern legal systems often define what are essentially inchoate offences in the terms of substantive crimes.

Some five variations of these crimes defined in an inchoate mode, or crimes of ulterior intent, have been distinguished by Jeremy Horder:[128]

(1) committing a lesser crime, intending to commit a greater one;

(2) committing a crime, intending to do some non-criminal wrong;

(3) committing a civil wrong, intending to commit a crime;

(4) doing something overtly innocent intending to commit a crime;

(5) crimes where the intent is by its nature ulterior.

The principal offences introduced by the Fraud Act 2006, and the offence of preparing for terrorism under the Terrorism Act 2006, are examples of the increased use of type (4) offences in recent years. Three related points may be made—the effect of doubly inchoate offences, the case for a general threats offence, and the spread of offences of possession.

(a) DOUBLY INCHOATE OFFENCES

Where the offence is in the third category, such as burglary (entering as a trespasser with intent),[129] or in the fourth category, such as doing an act with intent to impede the apprehension of an offender,[130] the prosecution's task is made easier: they do not have to establish that D caused a certain result if they can persuade the court that he did an act with intent to produce that result. Moreover, since these are substantive offences, liability can be incurred additionally through the inchoate offences. Thus there can be an attempted burglary or an attempted bomb hoax, which criminalizes D's conduct at an even earlier point than the doing of an act with intent to cause harm. There is little evidence that these extensions of the criminal law are carefully monitored, or that the implications of applying the inchoate offences to crimes defined in the inchoate mode have ever been systematically considered. It appears that there may be liability under section 44 of the Serious Crime Act 2007 for encouraging or assisting an attempt or a conspiracy, and perhaps liability for attempting or conspiring to encourage or assist a crime. The reach of criminal liability is pushed further and further, without evidence of an overall scheme.

---

[128] J. Horder, 'Crimes of Ulterior Intent', in A. P. Simester and A. T. H. Smith (eds.), *Harm and Culpability* (1996), 156–7; for other discussions see A. Ashworth, 'Defining Criminal Offences without Harm', in P. F. Smith (ed.), *Criminal Law: Essays in Honour of J. C. Smith* (1987), and Duff, *Criminal Attempts*, 354–8.

[129] See Ch 9.5 above.   [130] Criminal Law Act 1967, s. 4.

(b) THREATS OFFENCES

English law already contains a miscellany of threats offences:[131] for example, it has long been an offence to threaten to kill,[132] and common assault is committed by causing another to apprehend the use of force,[133] but there is no structure of offences of threatening to wound, or to cause grievous bodily harm, etc. Sections 4 and 5 of the Public Order Act 1986 criminalize some threats of harm in some circumstances, but the general issue remains. Peter Alldridge points out that the values of consistency and clarity in the law do not favour the creation of a general inchoate offence of threatening to commit a crime, in place of the present array of *ad hoc* accretions, since one might achieve consistency and clarity by abolishing most threats offences and retaining only a few well-known ones.[134] He identifies two key elements in the making of threats. First, uttering a threat is evidence that D has thought about committing the threatened crime and may be willing to do so. It may therefore appear similar in quality to an attempt, although some threats are conditional. Secondly, a primary characteristic of threats is the creation of fear. Since this should be the main target of threats offences, it is therefore inappropriate simply to regard threats as a fourth form of inchoate liability: consideration must be given to the kinds of fear and of circumstances for which criminalization is necessary.[135] There is already the offence of blackmail, which penalizes the making of unwarranted demands with menaces,[136] and this should be the starting-point. In the meantime, threatening another to persuade him or her to commit a crime may amount to encouraging crime for the purpose of the offences under the Serious Crime Act 2007.[137]

(c) POSSESSION OFFENCES

Another prominent example of offences defined in the inchoate mode is possession—possessing offensive weapons, possessing instruments for use in forgery, and possessing drugs. A major difference here is that many of these articles are non-innocent, in the sense that their possession calls for an explanation at least.[138] That certainly cannot be said of offences defined so as to penalize 'any act done with intent', although it can perhaps be said of an offence of burglary, which penalizes the entering of a building as a trespasser (a civil wrong) with intent to steal. Much depends on the way in which a legal system uses and defines its offences of possession, but there is at least one major objection to them, namely, that they presume a further criminal intent from the very fact of possession. In effect, they are abstract endangerment

---

[131] P. Alldridge, 'Threats Offences—a Case for Reform' [1994] Crim LR 176.
[132] Put into statutory form in s. 16, Offences Against the Person Act 1861.
[133] See above, Ch 8.3(e).
[134] P. Alldridge, 'Threats Offences—a Case for Reform' [1994] Crim LR 176, at 180.
[135] Cf. J. Horder, 'Reconsidering Psychic Assault' [1998] Crim LR 392, discussed in Ch 8.3(e) above.
[136] Above, Ch 9.5.   [137] Above, 11.7, and Serious Crime Act 2007, s. 65.
[138] Cf. the critical questions raised by D. Husak, 'Reasonable Risk Creation and Overinclusive Legislation' (1998) 1 Buffalo Crim LR 599, at 618.

offences, presuming danger (without specifying it) from a given fact.[139] We have seen that the concept of possession itself is artificially wide;[140] some possession offences leave no opportunity for D to argue that the possession was for a non-criminal reason, and so are the ideal offences for police and prosecutors;[141] others, like the offensive weapons law, impose on the defendant the burden of proving 'lawful excuse' or 'reasonable excuse' for the possession.[142] Now it is true, and worth bringing into the calculation, that possession offences often have the merit of certainty; there is nothing vague about the warning they spell out to citizens.[143] Yet it must be questioned whether this is enough to outweigh the remoteness from harm and the absence of a need for the prosecution to prove criminal intent which characterize most crimes of possession.[144] One might have thought that, as with the fault element for attempt and conspiracy, the more remote offences should be confined to cases of proven intention that the substantive crime be committed. Many offences of possession have no such requirement at all.

11.10 THE PLACE OF INCHOATE LIABILITY

There appear to be sound reasons for including inchoate offences within the criminal law, both on the consequentialist ground of the prevention of harm and on the 'desert' ground that the defendant has not merely formed a culpable mental attitude directed towards wrongdoing and harm but has also manifested it. Indeed, our argument has gone further in suggesting that some inchoate offences are no different, in terms of culpability, from substantive offences. This is true of so-called complete attempts, where D has done everything intended but some unexpected—or at least, undesired—circumstance has prevented the occurrence of the harm. The same may apply to some impossible conspiracies, and to some of the new offences of encouraging or assisting crime. The subjective principles (see Chapter 5.4(a)) are fulfilled no less in these cases than in substantive crimes. Various challenges to this approach have been noted, and there are prominent desert theorists who oppose it. Thus Nils Jareborg is sceptical of the prominence given to culpability in this approach, arguing that the criminal law is primarily designed for preventing certain types of harm, that a focus on mental states

---

[139] M. Dubber, 'The Possession Paradigm', in R. A. Duff and S. P. Green (eds), *Defining Crimes* (2005), 101.

[140] Above, Ch 4.3(b).

[141] Dubber, 'The Possession Paradigm', 96. Cf. s. 5(4)(b) of the Misuse of Drugs Act 1971, providing a defence for those who take possession of drugs for the purpose of handing them to the police or other authorities.

[142] Prevention of Crime Act 1953, s. 1; see above, Ch 8.3(j). Despite Art. 6.2 of the Convention, it seems that the burden of proof will remain on defendants for this type of offence: *Lynch v DPP* [2002] Crim LR 320.

[143] On the principle of maximum certainty see above, Ch 3.5(i).

[144] Husak, 'Reasonable Risk Creation', 616–26.

is inappropriate for the large anonymous communities of modern States, and that the proper role of culpability should therefore be to exculpate and not to inculpate.[145] Antony Duff has argued for an objectivist approach that gives fuller recognition to the significance of actual harm.[146] However, shifting the focus to the occurrence or non-occurrence of harm attributes too much significance to matters of chance. This may be appropriate in a system of compensation, but not in a system of public censure such as the criminal law. There is a respectable conception of fairness, connected to principles of individual autonomy, that favours penalizing people who tried and failed—even if, because of some fact unknown to them, their attempt, encouragement or assistance was bound to fail. On the view advanced here, the moral difference between those who fail and those who succeed in causing the harm is too slender to justify exempting the former from criminal liability.

While there is a good in-principle justification for liability, there are five contrary arguments that have greater or lesser strength in particular contexts. First, as recognized in section 11.3(c) above, conditions in a particular jurisdiction may be such that a properly developed law of inchoate offences places too much power in the hands of the police and puts innocent citizens at risk. Unless procedural or other means of rectifying this problem can be found, this is a strong argument against these extensions of criminal liability. Secondly, this argument applies with particular vigour to possession offences. Since they typically require no proof of any further intent, they place considerable power in the hands of the police, and effectively leave D to come up with some mitigating circumstances at sentence, since conviction normally follows on from detection. Thirdly, and connected to this, is the uncertainty of key definitional terms: the conduct element in attempts has been drawn so vaguely in English law that it sacrifices values of legality (see Chapter 11.3(a) and Chapter 3.5(i)), and there are also uncertainties over the conduct element in conspiracy (section 11.5(b)) and in the new offences of encouraging or assisting crime (section 11.7) which, if they cannot be reduced, tell against these extensions of the law. The proposal of statutory examples to promote consistency in dealing with attempts cases is important here, but the Serious Crime Act 2007 contains scant guidance on what should and should not amount to assistance or encouragement.

Fourthly, there seems to be absolutely no principled supervision of the reach of the criminal law. It has been noted that the offences under the Fraud Act 2006 are in the inchoate mode, so that an offence of 'making a false representation' is then extended by the law of attempts to penalize more than merely preparatory steps towards making such a representation. Similarly in *R.* (2008)[147] the question was whether R had attempted the offence under section 14 of the Sexual Offences Act 2003, which penalizes a person who 'arranges or facilitates' something that he intends another to do in

---

[145] N. Jareborg, 'Criminal Attempts and Moral Luck' (1993) 27 Israel LR 213.

[146] Duff, *Criminal Attempts*, particularly ch 12 (criticizing the subjectivist use of 'moral luck' arguments) and ch 13 (constructing an objectivist law of attempts).

[147] [2008] EWCA Crim 619.

contravention of sections 9–13 of the Act. R had twice approached an adult prostitute asking her to find him a girl prostitute of 12 or 13. The Court of Appeal held that asking the adult prostitute was capable of amounting to an attempt to arrange an act of sexual activity with a child. Thus a statutory provision worded so as to catch preparatory acts is extended still further by the operation of the law of attempts. This is not to say that the extension is unjustifiable, only that the effects of the law of attempts on new offences seem to receive little principled appraisal.

Fifthly, there now seems to be acceptance by the Law Commission of the remoteness principle—that the inchoate offences should be subjected to more restrictive fault requirements than other crimes, so that intention and knowledge alone are generally required for the inchoate offences, and recklessness is insufficient.[148] To what extent this should apply in cases of intention as to consequences coupled with recklessness as to circumstances has been discussed above.[149] Section 44 of the Serious Crime Act 2007 requires purpose for its basic offence of encouraging or assisting crime; but on the other hand, lesser forms of fault are sufficient under sections 45 and 46. However, no trace of this principle is to be found in the possession offences. A further principle urged above is that the reach of the inchoate offences should increase with the seriousness of the harm—meaning, for example, that the law should stretch further against crimes of violence than against mere property offences. English law has no such scheme:[150] the title of the Serious Crime Act 2007 has it right, but not the contents of Part 2. The only trace is that the crime of attempt does not apply to summary offences (nor does conspiracy, unless the Crown Prosecution Service decides otherwise); the offence under section 46 of the 2007 Act is triable only on indictment, but no such restriction applies to the offences under sections 44 and 45.

It has long been realized that the way forward is to reconsider the law of inchoate offences together with the law of complicity in order to create a coherent and principled scheme for liability. The Law Commission is making efforts in that direction,[151] but it cannot succeed unless the myriad offences of possession and distinct preparatory offences are brought into the scheme. Appendix C to the Law Commission's Consultation Paper catalogues a multitude of offences of possession and preparation under different statutes.[152] Moreover, as indicated above, there is an increasing trend to define new criminal offences in the inchoate mode—when the general inchoate offences extend them further. Much of this legislation originates from different government departments. The result is an unprincipled whole.

---

[148] LCCP 183, *Conspiracy and Attempts*, paras 1.6 and 4.49; cf para 4.62.

[149] Cf. the treatment of recklessness as to circumstances, above, in sections 11.3(a) (attempt) and 11.5(c) (conspiracy).

[150] See Ashworth, 'Criminal Attempts and the Role of Resulting Harm', 764–6.

[151] See the assessment by W. Wilson, 'A Rational Scheme of Liability for Participating in Crime' [2008] Crim LR 3.

[152] LCCP 183, *Conspiracy and Attempts*, 257–63.

FURTHER READING

R. A. Duff, *Criminal Attempts* (1996).

M. D. Dubber, 'The Possession Paradigm', in R. A. Duff and S. P. Green (eds), *Defining Crime* (2005).

V. Tadros, 'Justice and Terrorism', (2007) 10 *New Crim LR* 658.

R. Fortson, *Blackstone's Guide to the Serious Crime Act 2007* (2008).

Law Commission Consultation Paper 183, *Conspiracy and Attempts* (2007), and the Law Commission's forthcoming report on the topic.

BIBLIOGRAPHY

ALEXANDER, L., 'Criminal Liability for Omissions: An Inventory of Issues', in S. Shute and A. P. Simester (eds), *Criminal Law Theory: Doctrines of the General Part* (2002), Oxford: Oxford University Press.

ALLDRIDGE, P., ' "Attempted Murder of the Soul": Blackmail, Privacy and Secrets' (1993) 13 Oxford JLS 368.

—— 'The Coherence of Defences' [1983] Crim LR 665.

—— 'Dealing with Drug Dealing', in A. P. Simester and A. T. H. Smith (eds), *Harm and Culpability* (1996), Oxford: Oxford University Press.

—— 'Developing the Defence of Duress' [1986] Crim LR 433.

—— 'The Doctrine of Innocent Agency' (1990) 2 Criminal Law Forum 45.

—— *Money Laundering Law* (2003), London: Butterworths.

—— *Relocating Criminal Law* (2000), Aldershot: Dartmouth.

—— 'Rules for Courts and Rules for Citizens' (1990) 10 Oxford JLS 487.

—— 'The Sexual Offences (Conspiracy and Incitement) Act 1996' [1997] Crim LR 30.

—— 'Threats Offences—a Case for Reform' [1994] Crim LR 176.

—— 'What's Wrong with the Traditional Criminal Law Course?' (1990) 10 Legal Studies 38.

ALLEN, M. J., 'Consent and Assault' [1994] J Crim Law 183.

AMERICAN LAW INSTITUTE, *Model Penal Code*, revised edn (with commentaries) (1980), Philadelphia American Law Institute.

ANDANAES, J., '*Error Juris* in Scandinavian Law', in G. Mueller (ed.), *Essays in Criminal Science* (1961), London: Sweet & Maxwell.

ANDREWS, J. A., 'Wilfulness: a Lesson in Ambiguity' (1981) 1 Legal Studies 303.

ANYANGWE, C., 'Dealing with the Problem of Bad Cheques in France' [1978] Crim LR 31.

ARDEN, J., 'Criminal Law at the Crossroads: The Impact of Human Rights from the Law Commission's Perspective and the Need for a Code' [1999] Crim LR 439.

ARLIDGE, A., 'The Trial of Dr. Moor' [2000] Crim LR 31.

ASHWORTH, A., 'A Change of Normative Position: Determining the Contours of Culpability in Criminal Law' (2008) 11 New Crim LR 232.

—— 'Criminal Attempts and the Role of Resulting Harm under the Code, and in the Common Law' (1988) 19 Rutgers LJ 725.

—— 'Criminal Liability in a Medical Context: The Treatment of Good Intentions', in A. P. Simester and A. T. H. Smith (eds), *Harm and Culpability* (1996), Oxford: Clarendon Press.

—— 'Defining Criminal Offences without Harm', in P. F. Smith (ed.), *Criminal Law: Essays in Honour of J. C. Smith* (1987), London: Butterworths.

—— 'The Elasticity of Mens Rea', in C. Tapper (ed.), *Crime, Proof and Punishment* (1981), London: Butterworths.

—— 'Excusable Mistake of Law' [1974] Crim LR 652.

—— 'Four Threats to the Presumption of Innocence' (2006) 123 SALJ 62.

ASHWORTH, A., *Human Rights, Serious Crime and Criminal Procedure* (2002), London: Sweet & Maxwell.

—— 'Interpreting Criminal Statutes: A Crisis of Legality?' (1991) 107 LQR 419.

—— 'Intoxication and the General Defences' [1980] Crim LR 556.

—— 'Is the Criminal Law a Lost Cause?' (2000) 116 LQR 225.

—— 'Principles, Pragmatism, and the Law Commission's Recommendations on Homicide Law Reform' [2007] Crim LR 333.

—— 'Prosecution, Police and the Public: A Guide to Good Gate Keeping' (1984) 23 Howard JCJ 621.

—— 'Reason, Logic and Criminal Liability' (1975) 91 LQR 102.

—— 'Re-Drawing the Boundaries of Entrapment' [2002] Crim LR 161.

—— 'Responsibilities, Rights and Restorative Justice' (2002) 42 BJ Crim 578.

—— 'Robbery Reassessed' [2002] Crim LR 851.

—— 'The Scope of Criminal Liability for Omissions' (1989) 105 LQR 424.

—— 'Self-Defence and the Right to Life' [1975] CLJ 282.

—— *Sentencing and Criminal Justice* (4th edn, 2005), Cambridge: Cambridge University Press.

—— 'Social Control and "Anti-Social Behaviour": The Subversion of Human Rights?' (2004) 120 LQR 263.

—— 'Taking the Consequences', in S. Shute, J. Gardner, and J. Horder (eds), *Action and Value in Criminal Law* (1993), Oxford: Oxford University Press.

—— 'Testing Fidelity to Legal Values' in S. Shute and A. P. Simester (eds), *Criminal Law Theory: Doctrines of the General Part* (2002), Oxford: Oxford University Press.

—— 'Testing Fidelity to Legal Values: Official Involvement and Criminal Justice' (2000) 63 MLR 633.

—— 'Towards a Theory of Criminal Legislation' (1989) 1 Criminal Law Forum 41.

—— 'Transferred Malice and Punishment for Unforeseen Consequences', in P. Glazebrook (ed.), *Reshaping the Criminal Law* (1978), London: Sweet & Maxwell.

—— and BLAKE, M., 'The Presumption of Innocence in English Criminal Law' [1996] Crim LR 306.

—— and MITCHELL, B. (eds), *Rethinking English Homicide Law* (2000), Oxford: Oxford University Press.

—— and REDMAYNE, M., *The Criminal Process* (3rd edn, 2005), Oxford: Oxford University Press.

—— and STEINER, E., 'Criminal Omissions and Public Duties: the French Experience' (1990) 10 Legal Studies 153.

—— and ZEDNER, L., 'Defending the Criminal Law: Reflections on the Changing Character of Crime, Procedure and Sanctions' (2008) 2 Criminal Law and Philosophy 21.

ATIYAH, P. S., *Vicarious Liability in the Law of Torts* (1967), London: Butterworths.

AULD LJ, *Review of the Criminal Courts of England and Wales* (2001), London: The Stationery Office.

AUSTIN, J., *Lectures on Jurisprudence* (5th edn, 1885), London: J. Murray.

AUSTIN, J. L., 'A Plea for Excuses', in H. Morris (ed.), *Freedom and Responsibility* (1961), Stanford: Stanford University Press.

BAILEY, V. and BLACKBURN, S., 'The Punishment of Incest Act 1908: A Case Study in Law Creation' [1979] Crim LR 708.

BAKER, E., 'Human Rights, M'Naghten and the 1991 Act' [1994] Crim LR 84.

—— 'Taking European Criminal Law Seriously' [1998] Crim LR 361.

BALDWIN, R., 'The New Punitive Regulation' (2004) 67 MLR 351.

BALL, C., 'Youth Justice? Half a Century of Responses to Youth Offending', [2004] Crim LR 167.

BAMFORTH, N., 'Sado-Masochism and Consent' [1994] Crim LR 661.

BANKOWSKI, Z., and MacCORMICK, D. N., 'Statutory Interpretation in the United Kingdom', in D. N. MacCormick and R. S. Summers (eds), *Interpreting Statutes: a Comparative Study* (1991), London: Dartmouth.

BAZELON, D., 'The Morality of the Criminal Law' (1976) 49 S Cal LR 385.

BEATSON, J. and SIMESTER, A. P., (1999) 115 LQR 372.

BELL, J., *Policy Arguments in Judicial Decisions* (1983), Oxford: Oxford University Press.

BENNETT, R., 'Should we Criminalize HIV Transmission?', in C. Erin and S. Ost (eds.), *The Criminal Justice System and Health Care* (2007), Oxford: Oxford University Press.

BENTHAM, J., *Introduction to the Principles of Morals and Legislation* (1789), Oxford: Blackwell (1948).

BEYNON, H., 'Causation, Omissions and Complicity' [1987] Crim LR 539.

BINGHAM, LORD, 'A Criminal Code: Must We Wait for Ever?' [1998] Crim LR 694.

BITTNER, E., 'The Police on Skid Row: A Study in Peacekeeping' (1967) 32 Amer Soc Rev 699.

BLACKSTONE, W., *Commentaries on the Laws of England* (1768), London: Apollo Press.

BLAKE, M., 'Physician-Assisted Suicide: A Criminal Offence or a Patient's Right?' (1997) 5 Medical LR 294.

BLOM-COOPER, L. and MORRIS, T., *With Malice Aforethought: A Study of the Crime and Punishment for Homicide* (2004).

BOGG, A. and STANTON-IFE, J., 'Protecting the Vulnerable: Legality, Harm and Theft', (2003) 23 Legal Studies 402.

BOHLANDER, M., 'The Sexual Offences Act 2003 and the *Tyrell Principle*—Criminalising the Victims?' [2005] Crim LR 701.

BOWLING, B. and PHILLIPS, C., *Racism, Crime and Justice* (2002).

BRAITHWAITE, J., *Corporate Crime in the Pharmaceutical Industry* (1984), London: Routledge & Kegan Paul.

—— and FISSE, B., 'The Allocation of Responsibility for Corporate Crime' (1988) 11 Sydney LR 468.

BRETT, P., 'Mistake of Law as a Criminal Defence' (1966) 5 Melb U LR 179.

BRODY, S. and TARLING, R., *Taking Offenders out of Circulation*, Home Office Research Study No. 64 (1980), London: HMSO.

BRONITT, S., 'Spreading Disease and the Criminal Law' [1994] Crim LR 21.

BROOKE, SIR H., 'The Law Commission and Criminal Law Reform' [1995] Crim LR 911.

BROWN, D. and ELLIS, T., *Policing Low-level Disorder: Police Use of Section 5 of the Public Order Act 1986*, Home Office Research Study No. 135 (1994), London: HMSO.

BROWNLEE, I., 'The Statutory Charging Scheme in England and Wales: Towards a Unified Prosecution System?' [2004] Crim LR 896.

BRUDNER, A., 'Agency and Welfare in the Penal Law', in S. Shute, J. Gardner, and J. Horder (eds), *Action and Value in Criminal Law* (1993), Oxford: Oxford University Press.

—— 'A Theory of Necessity' (1987) 7 Oxford JLS 338.

BUCHANAN, A. and VIRGO, G., 'Duress and Mental Abnormality' [1999] Crim LR 517.

BUCKE, T. and BROWN, D., *In Police Custody: Police Powers and Suspects' Rights under the Revised PACE Codes of Practice* (1997), London: The Home Office.

BUCKE, T. and JAMES, Z., *Trespass and Protest: Policing under the Criminal Justice and Public Order Act 1994*, Home Office Research Study No. 190 (1998), London: The Home Office.

BURCHELL, J., *Principles of Criminal Law* (3rd edn, 2005), Lansdowne: Juta.

BUXTON, R. J., 'By Any Unlawful Act' (1966) 82 LQR 174.

—— 'Circumstances, Consequences and Attempted Rape' [1984] Crim LR 25.

BUZZARD, J., 'Intent' [1978] Crim LR 5.

CADOPPI, A., 'Failure to Rescue and the Continental Criminal Law', in M. A. Menlowe and R. A. McCall Smith, *The Duty to Rescue* (1993), Aldershot: Dartmouth.

CAMPBELL, K., 'Conditional Intention' (1982) 2 Legal Studies 77.

—— 'Offence and Defence', in I. Dennis (ed.), *Criminal Law and Criminal Justice* (1987), London: Sweet & Maxwell.

—— 'The Test of Dishonesty in *R v Ghosh*' [1984] CLJ 349.

CARD, R., *Public Order: The New Law* (1986), London: Butterworths.

—— 'Authority and Excuse as Defences to Crime' [1969] Crim LR 359.

CHALMERS, J., 'Merging Provocation and Diminished Responsibility: Some Reasons for Scepticism' [2004] Crim LR 198.

—— and LEVERICK, F., 'Fair Labelling in Criminal Law' (2008) 71 MLR 217.

CHILDS, M., 'Sexual Autonomy and Law' (2001) 64 MLR 309.

CHRISTOPHER, R., 'Self-Defence and Objectivity' (1998) 1 Buffalo Crim LR 537.

—— 'Unknowing Justification and the Logical Necessity of the *Dadson* Principle in Self-Defence' (1995) 15 Oxford JLS 229.

CLARKE, R. V. G., *Situational Crime Prevention: Successful Case Studies* (2nd edn, 1997), New York: Harrow and Heston.

CLARKSON, C., 'Complicity, *Powell* and Manslaughter' [1998] Crim LR 556.

—— 'Context and Culpability in Involuntary Manslaughter', in A. Ashworth and B. Mitchell (eds), *Rethinking English Homicide Law* (2000), Oxford: Oxford University Press.

—— 'Corporate Manslaughter: Need for a Special Offence?', in C. Clarkson and S. Cunningham (eds), *Criminal Liability for Non-Aggressive Death* (2008), Aldershot: Ashgate.

—— 'Necessary Action: A New Defence' [2004] Crim LR 81.

—— 'Theft and Fair Labelling' (1993) 56 MLR 554.

—— CRETNEY, A., DAVIS, G. and SHEPHERD, J., 'Assaults: The Relationship between Seriousness, Criminalisation and Punishment' [1994] Crim LR 4.

—— and CUNNINGHAM, S. (eds), *Criminal Liability for Non-Aggressive Death* (2008), Aldershot: Ashgate.

COGGON, J., 'Ignoring the moral and intellectual shape of the law after *Bland*' (2007) 27 LS 110.

COLB, S., 'Freedom from Incarceration: Why is this Right different from all other Rights?' (1994) 69 NYULR 781.

COLLINS, H., *Marxism and Law* (1982), Oxford: Oxford University Press.

COLVIN, E., 'Exculpatory Defences in Criminal Law' (1990) 10 Oxford JLS 381.

COMMISSIONER FOR HUMAN RIGHTS, *Children and Corporal Punishment: 'the Right not to be Hit', also a 'Children's Right'* (2006) 43 EHRR SE17.

COMMITTEE ON THE PENALTY FOR HOMICIDE, *Report* (1993), London: Prison Reform Trust.

CRIMINAL LAW REVISION COMMITTEE, 8th Report, *Theft and Related Offences*, Cmnd 2977 (1966), London: HMSO.

—— 14th Report, *Offences against the Person*, Cmnd 7844 (1980), London: HMSO.

CROALL, H., *White Collar Crime* (1992), Milton Keynes: Open University Press.

CROSS, R., 'Centenary Reflections on Prince's Case' (1975) 91 LQR 540.

—— 'The Mental Element in Crime' (1967) 83 LQR 215.

—— BELL, J. and ENGLE, G., *Statutory Interpretation* (3rd edn, 1995), London: Butterworths.

CROWN PROSECUTION SERVICE, *Code for Crown Prosecutors* (5th edn, 2004).

CUNNINGHAM, S., 'Punishing Drivers who Kill: Putting Road Safety First?' (2007) 27 LS 288.

—— 'The Reality of Vehicular Homicides: Convictions for Murder, Manslaughter and Causing Death by Dangerous Driving' [2001] Crim LR 679.

—— 'Vehicular Homicide: Need for a Specific Offence?', in C. Clarkson and S. Cunningham (eds), *Criminal Liability for Non-Aggressive Death* (2008), Aldershot: Ashgate.

DE BÚRCA, G. and GARDNER, S., 'The Codification of the Criminal Law' (1990) 10 Oxford JLS 559.

DEMPSEY, M. M., 'Rethinking Wolfenden: Prostitute-Use, Criminal Law and Remote Harm' [2005] Crim LR 444.

—— and HERRING, J., 'Why Sexual Penetration Requires Justification' (2007) 27 Oxford JLS 467.

DENNIS, I., 'The Criminal Attempts Act 1981' [1982] Crim LR 5.

—— 'Duress, Murder and Criminal Responsibility' (1980) 96 LQR 208.

—— 'The Law Commission Report on Attempt: The Elements of Attempt' [1980] Crim LR 758.

—— 'The Rationale of Criminal Conspiracy' (1977) 93 LQR 39.

—— 'Silence in the Police Station: The Marginalisation of Section 34' [2002] Crim LR 25.

DEPARTMENT OF HEALTH, *Protecting Children, Supporting Parents* (2000), London: Department of Health.

DERSHOWITZ, A., *Preemption* (2006), London: W. W. Norton.

DEVLIN, P., *The Enforcement of Morals* (1965), Oxford: Oxford University Press.

—— *Samples of Lawmaking* (1970), London: Oxford University Press.

DICEY, A. V., *Introduction to the Study of the Law of the Constitution* (8th edn, 1923), London: Stevens.

DILLOF, A. M., 'Transferred Intent: An Inquiry into the Nature of Criminal Culpability' (1998) 1 Buffalo Crim LR 501.

DINGWALL, G., *Alcohol and Crime* (2006), Cullompton: Willan.

DODD, T., *et al.*, *Crime in England and Wales 2003/2004* (Home Office Statistical Bulletin 10/04), London: The Home Office.

DRESSLER, J., *Understanding Criminal Law* (3rd edn, 2001), New York: Matthew Bender.

—— 'Battered Women who Kill their Sleeping Tormentors', in S. Shute and A. P. Simester (eds), *Criminal Law Theory: Doctrines of the General Party* (2002), Oxford: Oxford University Press.

—— 'Justifications and Excuses: A Brief Review of the Concept and the Literature' (1987) 33 Wayne LR 1155.

DRESSLER, J., 'Reflections on Excusing Wrongdoers: Moral Theory, New Excuses and the Model Penal Code' (1988) 19 Rutgers LJ 671.

DUBBER, M., 'The Possession Paradigm: The Special Part and the Police Power Model of the Criminal Process', in R. A. Duff and S. P. Green (eds), *Defining Crimes* (2005), Oxford: Oxford University Press.

DUFF, R. A., *Answering for Crime* (2007), Oxford: Hart Publishing.

—— *Criminal Attempts* (1996), Oxford: Clarendon Press.

—— 'The Circumstances of an Attempt' (1991) 50 Camb LJ 100.

—— 'Criminalizing Endangerment', in R. A. Duff and S. P. Green (eds), *Defining Crimes* (2005), Oxford: Oxford University Press.

——'Fitness to Plead and Fair Trials' [1994] Crim LR 419.

—— *Intention, Agency and Criminal Liability* (1990), Oxford: Blackwell.

—— 'Law, Language and Community: Some Preconditions of Criminal Liability' (1998) 18 Oxford JLS 189.

—— *Punishment, Communication and Community* (2001), Oxford: Oxford University Press.

—— 'Whose Luck is it Anyway?', in C. Clarkson and S. Cunningham (eds), *Criminal Liability for Non-Aggressive Death* (2008), Aldershot: Ashgate.

DWORKIN, R., *A Matter of Principle* (1985), London: Duckworth.

—— *Taking Rights Seriously* (1977), London: Duckworth.

EDWARDS, S., 'Abolishing Provocation and Re-Framing Self-Defence—The Law Commission's Options for Reform' [2004] Crim LR 181.

ELLIOTT, C and THAN, C DE., 'A Case for Rational Reconstruction of Consent in Criminal Law' (2007) 70 MLR 225.

ELLIOTT, D. W., 'Criminal Damage' [1988] Crim LR 403.

—— 'Directors' Thefts and Dishonesty' [1991] Crim LR 732.

—— 'Dishonesty in Theft: A Dispensable Concept' [1982] Crim LR 395.

—— 'Endangering Life by Destroying or Damaging Property' [1997] Crim LR 382.

—— 'Necessity, Duress and Self-Defence' [1989] Crim LR 611.

EMBRAHIM, I., *et al.*, 'Violence, Sleepwalking and the Criminal Law: The Medical Aspects' [2005] Crim LR 614.

EMMERSON, B., ASHWORTH, A. and MACDONALD, L. (eds), *Human Rights and Criminal Justice* (2nd edn, 2007).

ENVIRONMENT AGENCY, *Enforcement and Prosecution Policy* (2003), at <www.environment-agency.gov.uk>.

ERIN, C., 'The Rightful Domain of the Criminal Law', in C. Erin and S. Ost (eds), *The Criminal Justice System and Health Care* (2007), Oxford: Oxford University Press.

FARMER, L., '"The Genius of our Law": Criminal Law and the Scottish Legal Tradition' (1992) 55 MLR 25.

FARRIER, M. D., 'The Distinction between Murder and Manslaughter in its Procedural Context' (1976) 39 MLR 414.

FARRINGTON, D., 'Childhood Risk Factors and Risk-Focused Prevention', in M. Maguire, R. Morgan and R. Reiner (eds), *Oxford Handbook of Criminology* (4th edn, 2007), Oxford: Oxford University Press.

FEINBERG, J., *Harm to Others* (1984), New York: Oxford University Press.

FEINBERG, J., *Harm to Self* (1986), New York: Oxford University Press.

—— *Harmless Wrongdoing* (1988), New York: Oxford University Press.

—— *Offense to Others* (1986), New York: Oxford University Press.

FEIST, A., et al., *Investigating and Detecting Recorded Offences of Rape* (2007), London: Home Office.

FERGUSON, P. W., 'Codifying Criminal Law: (1) A Critique of Scots Common Law' [2004] Crim LR 49.

FIELDING, N., *Courting Violence: Offences Against the Person in Court* (2006), Oxford: Oxford University Press.

FINCH, E., *The Criminalisation of Stalking* (2001), London: Cavendish.

—— and MUNRO, V., 'Breaking Boundaries? Sexual Consent in the Jury Room' (2006) 26 LS 303.

—— 'Intoxicated Consent and Drug-Assisted Rape Revisited' [2004] Crim LR 789.

FINGARETTE, H., 'Addiction and Criminal Responsibility' (1975) 84 Yale LJ 413.

FINKELSTEIN, C., 'Involuntary Crimes, Voluntarily Committed', in S. Shute and A. P. Simester (eds), *Criminal Law Theory: Doctrines of the General Part* (2002), Oxford: Oxford University Press.

—— 'Merger and Felony Murder', in R. A. Duff and S. P. Green (eds), *Defining Crimes* (2005), Oxford: Oxford University Press.

—— 'Two Models of Murder: Patterns of Criminalisation in the United States', in J. Horder (ed), *Homicide Law in Comparative Perspective* (2007), Oxford: Hart Publishing.

FINNIS, J., 'Intention and Side-Effects', in R. G. Frey and C. W. Morris, *Liability and Responsibility* (1991), Cambridge: Cambridge University Press.

FISCHER, J., 'Responsibility and Control' (1982) 79 Journal of Philosophy 24.

FISSE, B. and BRAITHWAITE, J., *Corporations, Crime and Accountability* (1993), Cambridge: Cambridge University Press.

FLETCHER, G., *Rethinking Criminal Law* (1978), Boston, Mass.: Little, Brown.

FORTSON, R., *Blackstone's Guide to the Serious Crimes Act 2007* (2008), Oxford: Oxford University Press.

FOSTER, SIR M., *Crown Law* (1762), London: Dodson.

FULFORD, K. W. M., 'Value, Action, Mental Illness, and the Law', in S. Shute, J. Gardner, and J. Horder (eds), *Action and Value in Criminal Law* (1993), Oxford: Oxford University Press.

GALLIGAN, D. J., 'Responsibility for Recklessness' (1978) 31 CLP 55.

GARDNER, J., 'Complicity and Causality' (2007) 1 Crim Law & Phil 127.

—— 'Criminal Law and the Uses of Theory: A Reply to Laing' (1994) 14 Oxford JLS 217.

—— 'On the General Part of Criminal Law', in R. A. Duff (ed.), *Philosophy and the Criminal Law* (1998), Cambridge: Cambridge University Press.

—— 'Justifications and Reasons' in A. P. Simester and A. T. H. Smith (eds), *Harm and Culpability* (1996), Oxford: Clarendon Press.

—— *Offences and Defences* (2007), Oxford: Oxford University Press.

—— 'Rationality and the Rule of Law in Offences against the Person' [1994] Camb LJ 502.

—— and JUNG, H., 'Making Sense of Mens Rea: Antony Duff's Account' (1991) 11 Oxford JLS 559.

—— and MACKLEM, T., 'Compassion without Respect? Nine Fallacies in *R v Smith*' [2001] Crim LR 623.

GARDNER, J., and SHUTE, S., 'The Wrongness of Rape', in J. Horder (ed.), *Oxford Essays in Jurisprudence (4th Series)* (2000), Oxford: Oxford University Press.

GARDNER, S., 'Direct Action and the Defence of Necessity' [2005] Crim LR 371.

—— 'Necessity's Newest Inventions' (1991) 11 Oxford JLS 125.

—— 'Property and Theft' [1998] Crim LR 35.

—— 'Reiterating the Criminal Code' (1992) 55 MLR 839.

GENDERS, E., 'Reform of Offences against the Person Act: Lessons from the Law in Action' [1999] Crim LR 689.

GILES, M., 'Judicial Lawmaking in the Criminal Courts: The Case of Marital Rape' [1992] Crim LR 407.

—— and UGLOW, S., 'Appropriation and Manifest Criminality in Theft' (1992) 56 J Crim Law 179.

GILLESPIE, A. A., 'Tinkering with "Child Pornography"' [2004] Crim LR 361.

GLAZEBROOK, P., 'Criminal Omissions: The Duty Requirement in Offences against the Person' (1960) 56 LQR 386.

—— 'Revising the Theft Acts' [1993] Camb LJ 191.

—— 'Situational Liability', in P. Glazebrook (ed.), *Reshaping the Criminal Law* (1978), London: Sweet & Maxwell.

—— 'Structuring the Criminal Code', in A. P. Simester and A. T. H. Smith (eds), *Harm and Culpability* (1996), Oxford: Oxford University Press.

GOBERT, J. 'The Corporate Manslaughter and Corporate Homicide Act 2007' (2008) 71 MLR 413.

—— and PUNCH, M., *Rethinking Corporate Crime* (2003), London: Butterworths.

GOFF, LORD, 'A Matter of Life and Death' (1995) 3 Medical LR 1.

—— 'The Mental Element in the Crime of Murder' (1988) 104 LQR 30.

GORDON, G.H. *Criminal Law of Scotland* (3rd edn, 2001, by M. G. A. Christie), Edinburgh: W. Green.

GOTTFREDSON, M., *Fear of Crime*, Home Office Research Study No. 84 (1985), London: HMSO.

GOUGH, S., 'Intoxication and Criminal Liability: The Law Commission's Proposed Reforms' (1996) 112 LQR 335.

—— 'Surviving without *Majewski*' [2000] Crim LR 719.

GRACE, S., *Policing Domestic Violence in the 1990s*, Home Office Research Study No. 139 (1995), London: HMSO.

GREEN, S. P., *Lying, Cheating and Stealing* (2006), Oxford: Oxford University Press.

GREENAWALT, K., 'The Perplexing Borders of Justification and Excuse' (1984) 84 Columbia LR 1897.

GRIEW, E., 'Dishonesty: The Objections to *Feely* and *Ghosh*' [1985] Crim LR 341.

—— 'States of Mind, Presumptions and Inferences', in P. Smith (ed.), *Criminal Law: Essays in Honour of J. C. Smith* (1987), London: Butterworths.

GRIFFITHS, J., 'Assisted Suicide in the Netherlands' (1995) 58 MLR 232.

GRUBIN, D., 'What Constitutes Fitness to Plead?' [1993] Crim LR 748.

—— 'A Reply' [1994] Crim LR 423.

GUNN, M. J. and ORMEROD, D., 'The Legality of Boxing' (1995) 15 Legal Studies 181.

HALL, J., *General Principles of Criminal Law* (2nd edn, 1960), Indianapolis, Ind.: Bobbs-Merrill.

HALL, L., 'Strict or Liberal Construction of Penal Statutes' (1935) 48 Harv LR 748.

HALPIN, A., *Definition in the Criminal Law* (2004), Oxford: Hart Publishing.

HALPIN, A., 'The Test for Dishonesty' [1996] Crim LR 283.

HAMMOND, R. G., 'Theft of Information' (1984) 100 LQR 252.

HARRIS, J. W., *Property and Justice* (1996), Oxford: Clarendon Press.

HART, H. L. A., *Law, Liberty, and Morality* (1963), Oxford: Oxford University Press.

—— *Punishment and Responsibility* (2nd edn, by J. Gardner, 2008), Oxford: Oxford University Press.

—— and HONORÉ, T., *Causation in the Law* (2nd edn, 1985), Oxford: Clarendon Press.

HAWKINS, K., *Law as Last Resort* (2002), Oxford: Oxford University Press.

HEATON, R., 'Deceiving without Thieving?' [2001] Crim LR 712.

HEDDERMAN, C. and GELSTHORPE, L. (eds), *Understanding the Sentencing of Women*, Home Office Research Study No. 170 (1997), London: Home Office.

HERRING, J., 'Familial Homicide, Failure to Protect and Domestic Violence—Who's the Victim?' [2007] Crim LR 923.

—— 'Mistaken Sex' [2005] Crim LR 519.

—— and PALSER, E., 'The Duty of Care in Gross Negligence Manslaughter' [2007] Crim LR 24.

HIRST, M., 'Assault, Battery and Indirect Violence' [1999] Crim LR 557.

—— 'Causing Death by Driving and Other Offences: a Question of Balance' [2008] Crim LR 339.

HOFMEYR, K., 'The Problem of Private Entrapment' [2006] Crim LR 319.

HOLMES, O. W., *The Common Law* (1881), Boston, Mass.: Little, Brown.

HOLTON, R. and SHUTE, S., 'Self-Control in the Modern Provocation Defence' (2007) 27 Oxford JLS 49.

HOME OFFICE, *Digest 4: Information on the Criminal Justice System in England and Wales* (1999), London: Home Office.

—— *New Powers against Organized and Financial Crime* (2006), London: The Stationery Office.

—— *No More Excuses: A New Approach to Tackling Youth Crime in England and Wales*, Cm 3809 (1997), London: The Stationery Office.

—— *Protecting the Public*, Cm 5668 (2002), London: The Stationery Office.

—— *Reforming the Law on Involuntary Manslaughter: The Government's Proposals* (2000), London: The Stationery Office.

—— *Review of Road Traffic Offences involving Bad Driving* (2004), London: The Stationery Office.

—— *Setting the Boundaries* (2000), London: The Stationery Office.

—— *Sexual Offences Act 2003: a stocktake of the effectiveness of the Act since its implementation* (2006), London: The Stationery Office.

—— *Violence: Reforming the Offences Against the Person Act 1861* (1998), London: The Home Office.

HONORÉ, T., *Responsibility and Fault* (1998), Oxford: Hart Publishing.

HOOD, R. and HOYLE, C., *The Death Penalty: A World-Wide Perspective* (4th edn, 2008), Oxford: Oxford University Press.

HORDER, J., 'Cognition, Emotion and Criminal Culpability' (1990) 106 LQR 469.

—— 'Crimes of Ulterior Intent', in A. P. Simester and A. T. H. Smith (eds), *Harm and Culpability* (1996), Oxford: Clarendon Press.

—— 'A Critique of the Correspondence Principle in Criminal Law' [1995] Crim LR 759.

—— *Excusing Crime* (2004), Oxford: Oxford University Press.

HORDER, J., 'Gross Negligence and Criminal Culpability' (1997) 47 U Toronto LJ 495.

—— Homicide Law in Comparative Perspective (2007), Oxford: Hart Publishing.

—— 'How Culpability Can, and Cannot, Be Denied in Under-age Sex Crimes' [2001] Crim LR 15.

—— 'Intention in the Criminal Law—a Rejoinder' (1995) 58 MLR 678.

—— 'Killing the Passive Abuser', in S. Shute and A. P. Simester (eds), Criminal Law Theory: Doctrines of the General Part (2002), Oxford: Oxford University Press.

—— 'Pleading Involuntary Lack of Capacity' (1993) 52 Camb LJ 298.

—— 'The Problem of Provocative Children' [1987] Crim LR 654.

—— Provocation and Responsibility (1992), Oxford: Clarendon Press.

—— 'Reconsidering Psychic Assault' [1998] Crim LR 392.

—— 'A Reply' [1999] Crim LR 206.

——— 'Rethinking Non-Fatal Offences against the Person' (1994) 14 Oxford JLS 335.

—— 'Self-Defence, Necessity and Duress: Understanding the Relationship' (1998) XI Canadian J Law & Jurisp 143.

—— 'Strict Liability, Statutory Construction and the Spirit of Liberty' (2002) 118 LQR 458.

—— 'The Subjective Element in the Provocation Defence' (2005) 25 OJLS 123.

—— 'Transferred Malice and the Remoteness of Unexpected Outcomes from Intentions' [2006] Crim LR 383.

—— 'Two Histories and Four Hidden Principles of Mens Rea' (1997) 113 LQR 95.

—— 'Varieties of Intention, Criminal Attempts and Endangerment' (1994) 14 Legal Studies 335.

—— and McGOWAN, L., 'Manslaughter by Causing Another's Suicide' [2006] Crim LR 1035.

HOUSE OF COMMONS HOME AFFAIRS COMMITTEE, Sexual Offences Bill (5th Report, 2003).

HOUSE OF LORDS SELECT COMMITTEE on Murder and Life Imprisonment (1988–9), HL Paper 78.

HOUSE OF LORDS SELECT COMMITTEE on Medical Ethics (1993–4) Report.

HOYANO, L. and KEENAN, C., Child Abuse (2007), Oxford: Oxford University Press.

HOYLE, C., Negotiating Domestic Violence (1998), Oxford: Clarendon Press.

HUBER, B., 'The Dilemma of Decriminalization: Dealing with Shoplifting in West Germany' [1980] Crim LR 621.

HUDSON, B., 'Punishing the Poor: A Critique of the Dominance of Legal Reasoning in Penal Policy and Practice', in W. C. Hefferman and J. Kleinig (eds), From Social Justice to Criminal Justice (2000), Oxford: Oxford University Press.

—— 'Punishing the Poor: A Critique of the Dominance of Legal Reasoning in Penal Policy and Practice', in A. Duff, S. E. Marshall, R. E. Dobash, and R. P. Dobash (eds), Penal Theory and Practice (1994), Manchester: Manchester University Press.

HUNT, A., 'Criminal Prohibitions on Direct and Indirect Encouragement of Terrorism' [2007] Crim LR 441.

HUSAK, D., Drugs and Rights (1992), Cambridge: Cambridge University Press.

—— 'Ignorance of Law and Duties of Citizenship' (1994) 14 Legal Studies 105.

—— Overcriminalization (2008), Oxford: Oxford University Press.

—— Philosophy of Criminal Law (1987), New Jersey: Rowman and Littlefield.

—— 'Reasonable Risk Creation and Overinclusive Legislation' (1998) 1 Buffalo Crim LR 599.

—— 'The Serial View of Criminal Law Defences' (1992) 3 Crim LF 369.

—— 'Transferred Intent' (1996) 10 Notre Dame J Law, Ethics & Public Policy 65.

—— and von Hirsch, A., 'Culpability and Mistake of Law', in S. Shute, J. Gardner, and J. Horder (eds), *Action and Value in Criminal Law* (1993), Oxford: Oxford University Press.

Hutter, B., *Compliance: Regulation and Environment* (1997), Oxford: Clarendon Press.

—— *Regulation and Risk: Occupational Health and Safety on the Railways* (2001), Oxford: Oxford University Press.

Ivison, D., 'Justifying Punishment in Intercultural Contexts: Whose Norms, Which Values?' in M. Matravers (ed.), *Punishment and Political Theory* (1999), Oxford: Hart Publishing.

Jackson, B. S., '*Storkwain*: A Case Study in Strict Liability and Self-Regulation' [1991] Crim LR 892.

Jareborg, N., 'The Coherence of the Penal System', in N. Jareborg, *Essays in Criminal Law* (1988), Uppsala: Iustus Vorlag.

—— 'Criminal Attempts and Moral Luck' (1993) 27 Israel LR 213.

—— 'What Kind of Criminal Law Do We Want?', in A. Snare (ed.), *Beware of Punishment: On the Utility and Futility of Criminal Law*, Scandinavian Studies in Criminology, Vol. 14 (1995), Oslo: Pax Forlag A/S.

Jeffries, J. C., 'Legality, Vagueness and the Construction of Penal Statutes' (1985) 71 Virginia LR 189.

Johnson, R., 'The Unnecessary Crime of Conspiracy' (1973) 61 Cal LR 1137.

Joint Committee on Human Rights, *Scrutiny of Bills: Further Progress Report* (12th Report, 2003), London: The Stationery Office.

—— *Legislative Scrutiny* (14th progress Report, 2006), London: The Stationery Office.

—— *Legislative Scrutiny* (15th Report, 2007–08), London: The Stationery Office.

Jones, T. H., 'Common Law and Criminal Law: The Scottish Experience' [1990] Crim LR 292.

—— 'Insanity, Automatism and the Burden of Proof on the Accused' (1995) 111 LQR 475.

Jones, T., Maclean, D., and Young, J., *The Islington Crime Survey* (1986), London: Gower.

Juratowitch, B., *Retroactivity and the Common Law* (2008), Oxford: Hart Publishing.

Kadish, S., *Blame and Punishment* (1987), New York: Macmillan.

—— 'Reckless Complicity' (1997) 87 J Crim Law & Criminology 369.

Katyal, N. K., 'Conspiracy Theory' (2003) 112 Yale LJ 1307.

Kaveny, M. C., 'Inferring Intention from Foresight', (2004) 120 LQR 81.

Keating, H., 'Protecting or Punishing Children: Physical Punishment, Human Rights and English Law Reform' (2006) 26 LS 394.

—— 'Reckless Children' [2007] Crim LR 546.

Kell, D., 'Social Disutility and the Law of Consent' (1994) 14 Oxford JLS 121.

Kelly, L., *et al.*, *Domestic Violence Matters*, Home Office Research Study No. 193 (1999), London: Home Office, Research, Development and Statistics Directorate.

Kelman, M., 'Interpretive Construction in the Substantive Criminal Law' (1981) 33 Stanford LR 591.

KENNEDY, I. M., *Treat Me Right* (1988), Oxford: Clarendon Press.

KENNY, A., *Freewill and Responsibility* (1978), Oxford: Oxford University Press.

KENNY, C. S., *Outlines of Criminal Law* (1st edn, 1902; 16th edn, 1952), Cambridge: Cambridge University Press.

KEOWN, J., *Euthanasia, Ethics and Public Policy* (2002) Cambridge UP.

KERSHAW, C., NICHOLAS, S. and WALKER, A., *Crime in England and Wales 2007/2008* (2008), London, The Home Office.

KHAN, A., 'Intention in Criminal Law: Time to Change?' (2002) 23 Statute LR 235.

KLOCKARS, C. B., *The Professional Fence* (1975), London: Tavistock.

KUGLER, I., *Direct and Oblique Intention in the Criminal Law* (2002), Aldershot: Ashgate.

LACEY, N., 'Beset by Boundaries: The Home Office Review of Sex Offences' [2001] Crim LR 3.

—— 'A Clear Concept of Intention: Elusive or Illusory?' (1993) 56 MLR 621.

—— 'Community in Legal Theory: Idea, Ideal or Ideology?' (1996) 15 Studies in Law, Politics and Society 105.

—— *State Punishment* (1988), London: Routledge.

—— *Unspeakable Subjects* (1998), Oxford: Hart Publishing.

—— WELLS, C. and QUICK, O., *Reconstructing Criminal Law* (3rd edn, 2003), Cambridge: Cambridge University Press.

LAING, J. A., 'The Prospects of a Theory of Criminal Culpability: Mens Rea and Methodological Doubt' (1994) 14 Oxford JLS 57.

LAMOND, G., 'Coercion, Threats, and the Puzzle of Blackmail', in A. P. Simester and A. T. H. Smith (eds), *Harm and Culpability* (1996), Oxford: Oxford University Press.

—— 'What is a Crime?' (2007) 27 Oxford JLS 609.

LANHAM, D. J., 'Danger Down Under' [1999] Crim LR 960.

—— 'Defence of Property in the Criminal Law' [1966] Crim LR 368.

—— 'Drivers, Control and Accomplices' [1982] Crim LR 419.

—— 'Larsonneur Revisited' [1976] Crim LR 276.

—— 'Offensive Weapons and Self-Defence' [2005] Crim LR 85.

—— 'Three Cases of Accessorial Absurdity' (1990) 53 MLR 75.

LAW COMMISSION, No. 29, *Offences of Damage to Property* (1970), London: HMSO.

—— No. 76, *Conspiracy and Criminal Law Reform* (1976), London: HMSO.

—— No. 83, *Defences of General Application* (1977), London: HMSO.

—— No. 102, *Attempt, and Impossibility in Relation to Attempt, Conspiracy and Incitement* (1980), London: HMSO.

—— No. 143, *Codification of the Criminal Law: A Report to the Law Commission* (1985), London: HMSO.

—— No. 177, *Criminal Law: A Criminal Code for England and Wales* (two vols, 1989), London: HMSO.

—— No. 218, *Legislating the Criminal Code: Offences against the Person and General Principles* (1993), London: HMSO.

—— No. 228, *Conspiracy to Defraud* (1994), London: HMSO.

—— No. 229, *Legislating the Criminal Code: Intoxication and Criminal Liability* (1995), London: HMSO.

—— No. 237, *Legislating the Criminal Code: Involuntary Manslaughter* (1996), London: HMSO.

—— No. 276, *Fraud* (2002) London: The Stationery Office.

—— No. 279, *Children: their Non-Accidental Death or Serious Injury* (2003), London: The Stationery Office.

—— No. 290, *Partial Defences to Murder* (2004), London: The Stationery Office.

—— No. 300, *Inchoate Liability for Assisting and Encouraging Crime* (2007), London: The Stationery Office.

—— No. 304, *Murder, Manslaughter and Infanticide* (2007), London: The Stationery Office.

—— No. 305, *Participating in Crime* (2007), London: The Stationery Office.

—— Consultation Paper 127, *Intoxication and Criminal Liability* (1993), London: HMSO.

—— Consultation Paper 139, *Consent in the Criminal Law* (1995), London: HMSO.

—— Consultation Paper 155, *Legislating the Criminal Code: Fraud and Deception* (1999), London: The Stationery Office.

—— Consultation Paper 177, *A New Homicide Act for England and Wales? A Consultation Paper* (2005), London: The Stationery Office.

—— Consultation Paper 183, *Conspiracy and Attempts* (2007), London: The Stationery Office.

—— Working Paper 104, *Conspiracy to Defraud* (1987), London: HMSO.

LAW REFORM COMMISSION OF IRELAND, *Consultation Paper on Homicide: The Plea of Provocation* (CP 27, 2003), Dublin.

—— *Homicide: Murder and Involuntary Manslaughter* (No 87, 2008), Dublin.

LEADER-ELLIOTT, I., 'Sex, Race and Provocation: In Defence of *Stingel*' (1996) 20 Crim LJ 72.

LEAVENS, A., 'A Causation Approach to Omissions' (1988) 76 Cal LR 547.

LEIGH, L. H., *The Criminal Liability of Corporations in English Law* (1969), London: London School of Economics.

—— 'Manslaughter and the Limits of Self-Defence' (1971) 34 MLR 685.

—— *Strict and Vicarious Liability* (1982), London: Sweet & Maxwell.

LEVERICK, F., 'Is English Self-Defence Law Compatible with Article 2 of the ECHR?' [2002] Crim LR 347.

—— *Killing in Self-Defence* (2006), Oxford: Oxford University Press.

LEVI, M., *Regulating Fraud: White Collar Crime and the Criminal Process* (1987), London: Tavistock.

—— 'Suite Revenge?: The Shaping of Folk Devils and Moral Panics about White-Collar Crimes' (2009) 49 BJ Crim 48.

LIPPKE, R., *Rethinking Imprisonment* (2007), Oxford: Oxford University Press.

LOUGHNAN, A. '"Manifest Madness": Towards a New Understanding of the Insanity Defence' (2007) 70 MLR 379.

LUKES, S., *Individualism* (1973), London: Routledge.

MCAULEY, F. and MCCUTCHEON, J. P., *Criminal Liability: a Grammar* (2000), Dublin: Sweet & Maxwell.

MCBARNET, D. and WHELAN, C., 'The Elusive Spirit of the Law; Formalism and the Struggle for Legal Control' (1991) 54 MLR 848.

MCCOLGAN, A., 'In Defence of Battered Women who Kill' (1993) 13 Oxford JLS 508.

MCCONVILLE, M., HODGSON, J. and PAVLOVIC, A. (eds), *Standing Accused* (1994), Oxford: Clarendon Press.

MACCORMICK, D. N., *Legal Right and Social Democracy* (1982), Oxford: Oxford University Press.

MCGREGOR, J., *Is it Rape?* (2005), Aldershot: Ashgate.

MACKAY, R. D., 'Diminished Responsibility and Mentally Disordered Killers', in A. Ashworth and B. Mitchell (eds), *Rethinking English Homicide Law* (2000), Oxford: Oxford University Press.

—— 'The Abnormality of Mind Factor in Diminished Responsibility' [1999] Crim LR 117.

—— 'Fact and Fiction about the Insanity Defence' [1990] Crim LR 247.

—— *Mental Condition Defences in the Criminal Law* (1995), Oxford: Clarendon Press.

—— 'Non-Organic Automatism—Some Recent Developments' [1980] Crim LR 350.

—— 'On Being Insane in Jersey: Part Two' [2002] Crim LR 728.

—— 'On Being Insane in Jersey: Part Three' [2004] Crim LR 291.

—— and GEARTY, C. A., 'On Being Insane in Jersey' [2001] Crim LR 560.

—— and KEARNS, G., 'More Facts about the Insanity Defence' [1999] Crim LR 714.

—— and MITCHELL, B. J., 'But is this Provocation? Some Thoughts on the Law Commission's Report on Partial Defences to Murder' [2005] Crim LR 44.

—— and MITCHELL, B. J., 'A Continued Upturn in Unfitness to Plead' [2007] Crim LR 530.

—— and MITCHELL, B. J., 'Sleepwalking, Automatism and Insanity' [2006] Crim LR 901.

—— MITCHELL, B. J. and BROOKBANKS, W., 'Pleading for Provoked Killers: in Defence of *Morgan Smith* (2008) 124 LQR 675.

—— MITCHELL, B. J. and HOWE, L., 'Yet More Facts about the Insanity Defence' [2006] Crim LR 399.

—— and REUBER, G., 'Epilepsy and the Defence of Insanity—Time for Change?' [2007] Crim LR 782.

McKENNA, B., 'Causing Death by Reckless or Dangerous Driving: A Suggestion' [1970] Crim LR 67.

McKENZIE, I., MORGAN, R., and REINER, R., 'Helping the Police with their Inquiries' [1990] Crim LR 22.

MACKLEM, T. and GARDNER, J., 'Provocation and Pluralism' (2001) 64 MLR 815.

MAGUIRE, M. and BENNETT, T., *Burglary In a Dwelling* (1982), London: Heinemann.

—— and CORBETT, C., *The Effects of Crime and the Work of Victim Support Schemes* (1987), Aldershot: Gower.

—— MORGAN, R. and REINER, R. (eds), *The Oxford Handbook of Criminology* (4th edn, 2007), Oxford: Oxford University Press.

MAIER-KATKIN, D. and OGLE, R., 'A Rationale for Infanticide Laws' [1993] Crim LR 903.

MANCHESTER, C., 'Knowledge, Due Diligence and Strict Liability in Regulatory Offences' [2006] Crim LR 213.

MELDEN, A. I., 'Willing', in A. R. White (ed.), *The Philosophy of Action* (1968), Oxford: Oxford University Press.

MELISSARIS, E., 'The Concept of Appropriation and the Offence of Theft' (2007) 70 MLR 581.

MENLOWE, M. A. and McCALL SMITH, R. A. (eds), *The Duty to Rescue* (1993), Aldershot: Dartmouth.

MICHAELS, A., 'Constitutional Innocence' (1999) 112 Harv LR 829.

MILL, J. S., *On Liberty* (1859) (1910), London: Everyman's Library.

MINISTRY OF JUSTICE, Consultation Paper 19, *Murder, Manslaughter and Infanticide: Proposals for Reform of the Law* (2008), London: Ministry of Justice.

MIRRLEES-BLACK, C., *Domestic Violence: Findings from a British Crime Survey Self-Completion Questionnaire*, Home

Office Research Study No. 191 (1999), London: Home Office.

—— et al., *The 1998 British Crime Survey*, Home Office Statistical Bulletin 21/98 (1999), London: The Home Office.

MITCHELL, A. R., TAYLOR, S. M. E and TALBOT, K. V., *Mitchell, Taylor and Talbot on Confiscation and the Proceeds of Crime* (3rd edn, 2002), London: Sweet & Maxwell.

MITCHELL, B., 'In Defence of the Correspondence Principle' [1999] Crim LR 195.

—— 'Multiple Wrongdoing and Offence Structure: a Plea for Consistency and Fair Labelling' (2001) 64 MLR 393.

—— 'Public Perceptions of Homicide and Criminal Justice' (1998) 38 BJ Crim 453.

MITCHELL, C.N., 'The Intoxicated Offender—Refuting the Legal and Medical Myths' (1988) 11 Int J Law & Psychiatry 77.

MOORE, M., *Act and Crime: The Philosophy of Action and its Implications for Criminal Law* (1993), Oxford: Clarendon Press.

—— 'Causation and the Excuses' (1985) 73 Cal LR 1091.

—— *Placing Blame* (1997), Oxford: Clarendon Press.

MORGAN, J. and ZEDNER, L., *Child Victims* (1992), Oxford: Clarendon Press.

MORRIS, N., *Madness and the Criminal Law* (1982), Chicago, Ill.: University of Chicago Press.

MORSE, S., 'Deprivation and Desert', in W. C. Hefferman and J. Kleinig (eds), *From Social Justice to Criminal Justice* (2000), Oxford: Oxford University Press.

MYHILL, A. and ALLEN, J., *Rape and Sexual Assault of Women: The Extent and Nature of the Problem*, Home Office Research Study 237 (2002), London: The Home Office.

NELKEN, D., 'White Collar Crime and Corporate Crime', in M. Maguire, R. Morgan, and R. Reiner (eds), *The Oxford Handbook of Criminology* (4th edn, 2007), Oxford: Oxford University Press.

NICHOLAS, S., *et al.*, *Crime in England and Wales 2004/05* (Home Office, 2005).

—— *Crime in England and Wales 2006/07* (Home Office, 2007).

NICHOLSON, D., 'A Citizen's Duty to Assist the Police' [1992] Crim LR 611.

—— and SANGHVI, R., 'Battered Women and Provocation: The Implications of *Ahluwalia*' [1993] Crim LR 728.

NORRIE, A., 'Between Orthodox Subjectivism and Moral Contextualism: Intention and the Consultation Paper' [2006] Crim LR 486.

—— *Crime, Reason and History* (2nd edn, 2001), London: Butterworths.

NOURSE, V., 'Passion's Progress: Modern Law Reform and the Provocation Defense' (1997) 106 Yale LJ 1331.

O'DONOVAN, K., 'The Medicalisation of Infanticide' [1984] Crim LR 259.

OFFICE OF THE COMMISSIONER OF HUMAN RIGHTS, *Report by Mr Alvaro Gil-Robles, Commissioner for Human Rights, on his visit to the United Kingdom*, Comm DH (2005) 6, Strasbourg: Council of Europe, <www.echr.coe.int>.

OFFICE FOR CRIMINAL JUSTICE REFORM, *Convicting Rapists and Protecting Victims—Justice for Victims of Rape* (2007), London: Office for Criminal Justice Reform.

ORCHARD, G., '"Agreement" in Criminal Conspiracy' [1974] Crim LR 297.

—— 'Surviving without *Majewski*—a View from Down Under' [1993] Crim LR 26.

ORMEROD, D., 'Cheating the Public Revenue' [1998] Crim LR 627.

ORMEROD, D., 'The Fraud Act 2006—Criminalising Lying?' [2007] Crim LR 193.

—— and FORTSON, R., 'Drug Suppliers as Manslaughterers (Again)' [2005] Crim LR 819.

—— and GUNN, M. J., 'Consent—a Second Bash' [1996] Crim LR 694.

—— and TAYLOR, R., The Corporate Manslaughter and Corporate Homicide Act 2007' [2008] Crim LR 589.

OST, S., 'Euthanasia and the Defence of Necessity', [2005] Crim LR 355.

—— 'Euthanasia and the Defence of Necessity', in C. Erin and S. Ost (eds.), The Criminal Justice System and Health Care (2007), Oxford: Oxford University Press.

OTLOWSKI, M., Voluntary Euthanasia and the Common Law (1997), Oxford: Clarendon Press.

PACE, P. J., 'Delegation: A Doctrine in Search of a Definition' [1982] Crim LR 627.

PADFIELD, N., 'Clean Water and Muddy Causation' [1995] Crim LR 683.

PEDAIN, A., 'Intention and the Terrorist Example' [2003] Crim LR 579.

—— 'Intentional Killings: the German Law', in J. Horder (ed.), Homicide Law in Comparative Perspective (2007), Oxford: Hart Publishing.

PEERS, S., EU Justice and Home Affairs Law (2nd ed., 2006), Oxford: Oxford University Press.

PHILLIPS, C., and BOWLING, B., 'Ethnicities, Racism, Crime, and Criminal Justice' in M. Maguire, R. Morgan and R. Reiner (eds), Oxford Handbook of Criminology (4th edn., 2007), Oxford: Oxford University Press.

POTAS, I., Just Deserts for the Mad (1982), Canberra: Australia Institute of Criminology.

POWER, H., 'Pitcairn Island: Sexual Offending, Cultural Difference and Ignorance of the Law' [2007] Crim LR 609.

—— 'Provocation and Culture' [2006] Crim LR 871.

—— 'Towards a Redefinition of the Mens Rea of Rape' (2003) 23 Oxford JLS 379.

QUICK, O., 'Medical Killing: Need for a Specific Offence?', in C. Clarkson and S. Cunningham (eds), Criminal Liability for Non-Aggressive Death (2008), Aldershot: Ashgate.

—— 'Prosecuting "Gross" Medical Negligence: Manslaughter, Discretion and the Crown Prosecution Service' (2006) 33 JLS 431.

RACHELS, J., 'Active and Passive Euthanasia' (1975) 292 New England Journal of Medicine 78.

RAZ, J., The Authority of Law (1979), Oxford: Oxford University Press.

—— 'Autonomy, Toleration and the Harm Principle' in R. Gavison (ed.), Issues in Contemporary Legal Philosophy (1987), Oxford: Oxford University Press.

—— The Morality of Freedom (1986), Oxford: Clarendon Press.

REISS, A., 'Selecting Strategies of Social Control over Organizational Life', in K. Hawkins and J. M. Thomas (eds), Enforcing Regulation (1984), Oxford: Oxford University Press.

REPORT OF THE COMMITTEE ON MENTALLY ABNORMAL OFFENDERS, Cmnd 6244 (1975), London: HMSO.

REPORT OF THE COMMITTEE ON OBSCENITY AND FILM CENSORSHIP, Cmnd 7772 (1979), London: HMSO.

REPORT OF THE INTERDEPARTMENTAL COMMITTEE ON THE DISTRIBUTION OF CRIMINAL BUSINESS BETWEEN THE CROWN COURT AND THE MAGISTRATES' COURTS, Cmnd 6323 (1975), London: HMSO.

REPORT OF THE INTERDEPARTMENTAL REVIEW OF THE LAW ON THE USE OF

LETHAL FORCE IN SELF-DEFENCE OR THE PREVENTION OF CRIME (1996), London: The Home Office.

REPORT OF THE ROAD TRAFFIC LAW REVIEW (1988), London: HMSO.

REPORT OF THE ROYAL COMMISSION ON THE LAW RELATING TO INDICTABLE OFFENCES, C.2345 (1879), London: HMSO.

RICHARDS, D. A. J., 'Rights, Utility and Crime' (1981) 3 Crime and Justice: An Annual Review 274.

RICHARDSON, G., 'Strict Liability for Regulatory Crime: The Empirical Research' [1987] Crim LR 295.

ROBERTS, J. V. *et al*, 'Public Attitudes to the Sentencing of Offences involving Death by Driving [2008] Crim LR 525.

ROBERTS, P., 'Consent in the Criminal Law' (1997) 17 Oxford JLS 389.

ROBERTSON, G., *Whose Conspiracy?* (1974), London: National Council for Civil Liberties.

ROBINSON, P. H., 'Causing the Conditions of One's Own Defence: A Study in the Limits of Theory in Criminal Law Doctrine' (1985) 71 Virginia LR 1.

—— 'Competing Theories of Justification: Deeds v. Reasons' in A. P. Simester and A. T. H. Smith (eds), *Harm and Culpability* (1996), Oxford: Clarendon Press.

—— *Criminal Law Defences* (1984), St. Paul, Minn.: West Publishing.

—— 'Criminal Law Defenses: A Systematic Analysis' (1982) 82 Columbia LR 199.

—— *Fundamentals of Criminal Law* (2nd edn, 1995), Boston, Mass.: Little, Brown.

—— 'Legality and Discretion in the Distribution of Criminal Sanctions' (1988) 25 Harvard Journal on Legislation 393.

—— 'The Modern General Part: Three Illusions', in S. Shute and A. P. Simester (eds), *Criminal Law Theory: Doctrines of the General Part* (2002), Oxford: Oxford University Press.

—— 'Rules of Conduct and Principles of Adjudication' (1990) 57 U Chic LR 729.

—— 'Should the Criminal Law abandon the Actus Reus/Mens Rea Distinction?', in S. Shute, J. Gardner, and J. Horder (eds), *Action and Value in Criminal Law* (1993), Oxford: Oxford University Press.

—— *Structure and Function in Criminal Law* (1997), Oxford: Clarendon Press.

—— and DARLEY, J. M., 'Does Criminal Law Deter? A Behavioural Science Investigation' (2004) 24 OJLS 173.

—— and DARLEY, J. M., *Justice, Liability, and Blame: Community Views and the Criminal Law* (1995), Boulder: Westview Press.

—— and DARLEY, J. M., 'Objectivist versus Subjectivist Views of Criminality: A Study in the Role of Social Science in Criminal Law Theory' (1998) 18 Oxford JLS 409.

ROCK, P., *The Social World of an English Crown Court* (1993), Oxford: Clarendon Press.

—— 'The Sociology of Deviancy and Conceptions of Moral Order' (1974) 14 BJ Crim 139.

RODWELL, JUDGE D., 'Problems with the Sexual Offences Act 2003' [2005] Crim LR 290.

ROGERS, J., 'A Criminal Lawyer's Response to Chastisement in the European Court of Human Rights' [2002] Crim LR 98.

—— 'Justifying the Use of Firearms by Policemen and Soldiers' (1998) 18 LS 486.

—— 'Necessity, Private Defence and the Killing of Mary' [2001] Crim LR 515.

ROOK, P. and WARD, R., *Sexual Offences: Law and Practice* (2004), London: Sweet & Maxwell.

ROORDING, J., 'The Punishment of Tax Fraud' [1996] Crim LR 240.

ROYAL COMMISSION ON CRIMINAL JUSTICE, *Report*, Cmnd 2263 (1993), London: HMSO.

RUMNEY, P., 'The Review of Sex Offences and Rape Law' (2001) 64 MLR 890.

RYAN, S., 'Reckless Transmission of HIV: Knowledge and Culpability' [2006] Crim LR 981.

SANDERS, A., 'Class Bias in Prosecutions' (1985) 24 Howard JCJ 176.

SANGERO, B., *Self-Defence in Criminal Law* (2006), Oxford: Hart Publishing.

SCHONSHECK, J., *On Criminalization* (1994), Dordrecht: Kluwer.

SCHOPP, R. F., *Automatism, Insanity, and the Psychology of Criminal Responsibility* (1991), Cambridge: Cambridge University Press.

SCHULHOFER, S. J., *Unwanted Sex: The Culture of Intimidation and the Failure of Law* (1998), London: Harvard University Press.

SCOTTISH LAW COMMISSION, *A Draft Criminal Code for Scotland* (2003), Edinburgh: The Stationery Office.

—— *Report on Insanity and Diminished Responsibility* (Scot Law Com No, 195, 2004), Edinburgh: The Stationery Office.

SELLIN, T. and WOLFGANG, M., *The Measurement of Delinquency* (1978) New York: Wiley.

SENTENCING GUIDELINES COUNCIL, *Attempted Murder: Notes and Questions for Consultees* (2007).

—— *Causing Death by Driving* (2008).

—— *Manslaughter upon Provocation* (2005).

—— *New Sentences: Criminal Justice Act 2003* (2004).

—— *Overarching Principles: Seriousness* (2004).

—— *Reduction in Sentence for a Guilty Plea: Revised Guideline* (2007).

—— *Robbery: Definitive Guideline* (2006).

—— *Sexual Offences Act 2003: Definitive Guidelines* (2007).

SHAPLAND, J., WILLMORE J., and DUFF, P., *Victims in the Criminal Justice System* (1985), London: Heinemann.

SHINER, R., 'Intoxication and Responsibility' (1990) 13 Int J Law & Psychiatry 9.

SHUTE, S., 'Appropriation and the Law of Theft' [2002] Crim LR 445.

—— 'Knowledge and Belief in the Criminal Law', in S. Shute and A. P. Simester (eds), *Criminal Law Theory: Doctrines of the General Part* (2002), Oxford: Oxford University Press.

—— 'The Second Law Commission Consultation Paper on Consent' [1996] Crim LR 684.

—— and HORDER, J., 'Thieving and Deceiving: What is the Difference?' (1993) 56 MLR 548.

—— and SIMESTER, A. P. (eds), *Criminal Law Theory: Doctrines of the General Part* (2002), Oxford: Oxford University Press.

SIMESTER, A. P., (ed.), *Appraising Strict Liability* (2005), Oxford: Oxford University Press.

—— 'Can Negligence be Culpable?', in J. Horder (ed.), *Oxford Essays in Jurisprudence (4th Series)* (2000), Oxford: Oxford University Press.

—— 'Is Strict Liability always Wrong?', in A. P. Simester (ed.), *Appraising Strict Liability* (2005).

—— 'The Mental Element in Complicity' (2006) 122 LQR 578.

—— 'Mistakes in Defence' (1992) 12 Oxford JLS 295.

—— 'On the So-called Requirement of Voluntary Action' (1998) 1 Buffalo Crim LR 403.

—— 'Paradigm Intention' (1992) 11 Law and Philosophy 235.

—— 'Why Distinguish Intention from Foresight?', in A. P. Simester and A. T. H. Smith (eds), *Harm and Culpability* (1996), Oxford: Oxford University Press.

—— and SULLIVAN, G. R., *Criminal Law: Theory and Doctrine* (3rd edn, 2007), Oxford: Hart Publishing.

——— and SULLIVAN, G. R., 'The Nature and Rationale of Property Offences', in R. A. Duff and S. P. Green (eds), *Defining Crimes* (2005), Oxford: Oxford University Press.

SIMPSON, A. W. B., *Cannibalism and the Common Law* (1984), Chicago, Ill.: University of Chicago Press.

SKINNER, S., 'Populist Politics and Shooting Burglars' [2005] Crim LR 275.

SMART, A., 'Responsibility for Failing to Do the Impossible' (1987) 103 LQR 532.

SMITH, A. T. H., 'The Case for a Code' [1986] Crim LR 285.

—— 'Conspiracy to Defraud' [1988] Crim LR 508.

—— 'Error and Mistake of Law in Anglo-American Criminal Law' (1984) 14 Anglo-American LR 3.

—— 'Judicial Lawmaking in the Criminal Law' (1984) 100 LQR 46.

—— *Offences against Public Order* (1987), London: Sweet & Maxwell.

——— 'On Actus Reus and Mens Rea', in P. R. Glazebrook (ed.), *Reshaping the Criminal Law* (1978), London: Sweet & Maxwell.

—— *Property Offences* (1994), London: Sweet & Maxwell.

SMITH, D., 'Crime and the Life Course', in M. Maguire, R. Morgan and R. Reiner (eds), *Oxford Handbook of Criminology* (4th edn, 2007), Oxford: Oxford University Press.

SMITH, J. C., 'Aid, Abet, Counsel and Procure', in P. R. Glazebrook (ed.), *Reshaping the Criminal Law* (1978), London: Sweet & Maxwell.

—— 'Criminal Liability of Accessories: Law and Law Reform' (1997) 113 LQR 453.

—— 'Intoxication and the Mental Element in Crime', in P. Wallington and R. Merkin (eds), *Essays in Honour of F. H. Lawson* (1987), London: Sweet & Maxwell.

—— *Justification and Excuse in the Criminal Law* (1989), London: Stevens.

—— 'Offences Against the Person: The Home Office Consultation Paper' [1998] Crim LR 317.

—— 'The Right to Life and the Right to Kill in Law Enforcement' (1994) NLJ 354.

—— *Smith's Law of Theft* (9th edn, 2007, by D. Ormerod and D. H. Williams), Oxford: Oxford University Press.

—— 'Stealing Tickets' [1998] Crim LR 723.

—— and HOGAN, B., *Criminal Law* (5th edn, 1983), London: Butterworths.

—— HOGAN, B., *Criminal Law* (12th edn, 2008, by D. Ormerod), Oxford: Oxford University Press.

SMITH, K. J. M., 'Duress and Steadfastness: In Pursuit of the Unintelligible' [1999] Crim LR 363.

—— *Lawyers, Legislators and Theorists* (1998), Oxford: Oxford University Press.

—— 'Liability for Endangerment: English *Ad Hoc* Pragmatism and American Innovation' [1983] Crim LR 127.

—— *A Modern Treatise on the Law of Criminal Complicity* (1991), Oxford: Clarendon Press.

—— 'Proximity in Attempt: Lord Lane's Midway Course' [1991] Crim LR 576.

—— 'Withdrawal in Complicity: A Restatement of Principles' [2001] Crim LR 769.

SPENCER, J. R., 'Child and Family Offences' [2004] Crim LR 347.

—— 'Criminal Law and Criminal Appeals: The Tail that Wags the Dog' [1982] Crim LR 260.

SPENCER, J. R., 'Handling, Theft and the Purchaser who Takes a Chance' [1985] Crim LR 92 and 440.

—— 'Helping Others to Commit Crimes', in P. Smith (ed.), *Criminal Law: Essays in Honour of J. C. Smith* (1987), London: Butterworths.

—— 'The Metamorphosis of Section 6 of the Theft Act' [1977] Crim LR 653.

—— 'The Mishandling of Handling' [1981] Crim LR 682.

—— 'Motor Vehicles as Weapons of Offence' [1985] Crim LR 29.

—— and PEDAIN, A., 'Strict Liability in Continental Criminal Law', in A. P. Simester (ed), *Appraising Strict Liability* (2005), Oxford: Oxford University Press.

SPICER, R., *Conspiracy Law, Class and Society* (1981), London: Lawrence & Wishart.

STAPLE, G., 'Serious and Complex Fraud: A New Perspective' (1993) 56 MLR 127.

THE STATIONERY OFFICE, *Social Trends 2000* (2001), London: The Stationery Office.

STEPHEN, J. F., *A Digest of the Criminal Law* (1877), London: Macmillan.

—— *History of the Criminal Law* (1883), London: Macmillan.

STUART, D. R., *Canadian Criminal Law* (4th edn, 2001), Toronto: Carswell.

SULLIVAN, G. R., 'The Attribution of Culpability to Limited Companies' (1996) 55 Camb LJ 515.

—— 'Expressing Corporate Guilt' (1995) 15 Oxford JLS 281.

—— 'First Degree Murder and Complicity' (2007) 1 Crim Law & Phil 271.

—— 'Knowledge, Belief and Culpability', in S. Shute and A. P. Simester (eds), *Criminal Law Theory: Doctrines of the General Part* (2002), Oxford: Oxford University Press.

—— 'The Law Commission Consultation Paper on Complicity: Fault Elements and Joint Enterprise' [1994] Crim LR 252.

—— 'Making Excuses', in A. P. Simester and A. T. H. Smith (eds), *Harm and Culpability* (1996), Oxford: Oxford University Press.

—— 'Participating in Crime: Law Com No. 305—Joint Criminal Ventures' [2008] Crim LR 19.

SUTHERLAND, E. H., *White Collar Crime* (1949), New Haven, Conn.: Yale University Press.

SUTHERLAND, P. J., and GEARTY, D., 'Insanity and the European Court of Human Rights' [1992] Crim LR 418.

TADROS, V., *Criminal Responsibility* (2005), Oxford: Oxford University Press.

—— 'Justice and Terrorism' (2007) 11 New Crim LR 658.

—— 'The Limits of Manslaughter', in C. Clarkson and S. Cunningham (eds), *Criminal Liability for Non-Aggressive Death* (2008), Aldershot: Ashgate.

—— 'Rape without Consent' (2006) 26 Oxford JLS 515.

—— 'Recklessness and the Duty to Take Care', in S. Shute and A. P. Simester (eds), *Criminal Law Theory: Doctrines of the General Part* (2002), Oxford: Oxford University Press.

—— 'The System of the Criminal Law' (2002) 22 LS 448.

—— and TIERNEY, S., 'The Presumption of Innocence and the Human Rights Act' (2004) 67 MLR 402.

TAYLOR, P. and DALTON, G., 'Pre-Menstrual Syndrome: A New Criminal Defense?' (1983) 19 Cal WLR 269.

TAYLOR, R. D., 'Complicity and the Excuses' [1983] Crim LR 656.

—— 'The Nature of Partial Defences and the Coherence of (Second Degree) Murder' [2007] Crim LR 345.

—— 'Procuring, Causation, Innocent Agency and the Law Commission' [2008] Crim LR 32.

TEMKIN, J., 'Impossible Attempts: Another View' (1976) 39 MLR 55.

—— Rape and the Legal Process (2nd edn, 2002), Oxford: Oxford University Press.

—— and ASHWORTH, A., 'Rape, Sexual Assaults and the Problems of Consent' [2004] Crim LR 328.

—— and KRAHÉ, B., Sexual Assault and the Justice Gap: a Question of Attitude (2008), Oxford: Hart Publishing.

THOMAS, D. A., 'Form and Function in Criminal Law', in P. R. Glazebrook (ed.), Reshaping the Criminal Law (1978), London: Sweet & Maxwell.

THOMSON, J. J., 'Self-Defense' (1991) 20 Philosophy and Public Affairs 283.

TOLMIE, J., 'Alcoholism and Criminal Liability' (2001) 64 MLR 688.

TONRY, M. and MOORE M., (eds), Youth Violence (1998), Chicago, Ill: University of Chicago Press.

TUR, R., 'Dishonesty and Jury Questions', in A. Phillips Griffiths (ed.), Philosophy and Practice (1985), Cambridge: Cambridge University Press.

—— 'The Doctor's Defence and Professional Ethics' (2002) 13 KCLJ 75.

—— 'Subjectivism and Objectivism: Towards Synthesis', in S. Shute, J. Gardner, and J. Horder (eds.), Action and Value in Criminal Law (1993), Oxford: Oxford University Press.

UNIACKE, S., Permissible Killing: The Self-Defence Justification of Homicide (1994), Cambridge: Cambridge University Press.

UNHCHR, 'Concluding Observations of the Committee on the Rights of the Child: United Kingdom' (9 October 2002) UN Doc CRC/C/15/Add.188.

VAN BUEREN, G., The International Law on the Rights of the Child (1995), Dordrecht: Martinus Nijhoff.

VON HIRSCH, A., 'Extending the Harm Principle: Remote Harms and Fair Imputation', in A. P. Simester and A. T. H. Smith (eds), Harm and Culpability (1996), Oxford: Oxford University Press.

—— ASHWORTH, A. and ROBERTS, J. (eds), Principled Sentencing: Readings in Theory and Policy (3rd edn, 2009), Oxford: Hart Publishing.

—— and ASHWORTH, A., Proportionate Sentencing (2005), Oxford: Oxford University Press.

—— and BOTTOMS, A. E., WIKSTRÖM, P.-O., and BURNEY, E., Criminal Deterrence and Sentence Severity (1999), Oxford: Hart Publishing.

—— and SIMESTER, A. P., 'Penalising Offensive Behaviour' in A. von Hirsch and A. P. Simester (eds), Incivilities: Regulating Offensive Behaviour (2007), Oxford: Hart Publishing.

WADDINGTON, P. A. J., '"Overkill" or "Minimum Force"?' [1990] Crim LR 695.

WALMSLEY, R., Personal Violence, Home Office Research Study No. 89 (1986), London: HMSO.

WARD, A., 'Making Some Sense of Self-Induced Intoxication' [1986] CLJ 247.

WARD, T., 'Magistrates, Insanity and the Common Law' [1997] Crim LR 796.

WASIK, M., 'Abandoning Criminal Intent' [1980] Crim LR 785.

—— Crime and the Computer (1991), Oxford: Clarendon Press.

—— 'Cumulative Provocation and Domestic Killing' [1982] Crim LR 29.

—— 'Duress and Criminal Responsibility' [1977] Crim LR 453.

—— 'A Learner's Careless Driving' [1982] Crim LR 411.

WASIK, M., 'Partial Excuses in the Criminal Law' (1982) 45 MLR 515.

—— 'Sentencing for Homicide', in A. Ashworth and B. Mitchell (eds), *Rethinking English Homicide Law* (2000), Oxford: Oxford University Press.

—— and THOMPSON, M. P., 'Turning a Blind Eye as Constituting Mens Rea' (1981) 32 NILQ 328.

WEAIT, M., 'Criminal Law and the Sexual Transmission of HIV: *R v. Dica*' (2005) 68 MLR 121.

—— 'Knowledge, Autonomy and Consent: *R v. Konzani*' [2005] Crim LR 673.

WELLS, C., 'Corporate Manslaughter: Why Does Reform Matter?' (2006) 122 SALJ 646.

—— *Corporations and Criminal Responsibility* (2nd edn, 2001), Oxford: Oxford University Press.

—— 'Necessity and the Common Law' (1985) 5 Oxford JLS 471.

—— 'Provocation: the Case for Abolition', in A. Ashworth and B. Mitchell (eds), *Rethinking English Homicide Law* (2000), Oxford: Oxford University Press.

—— 'Restatement or Reform?' [1986] Crim LR 314.

—— 'Stalking: The Criminal Law Response' [1997] Crim LR 463.

—— 'Swatting the Subjectivist Bug' [1982] Crim LR 209.

WESTEN, P., 'An Attitudinal Theory of Excuse' (2006) 25 Law and Philosophy 289.

—— *The Logic of Consent* (2004), Aldershot: Ashgate.

—— 'Some Common Conclusions about Consent in Rape Cases' (2004) 2 Ohio State JCL 333.

WHITE, S., 'The Criminal Procedure (Insanity and Unfitness to Plead) Act' [1992] Crim LR 4.

—— 'Offences of Basic and Specific Intent' [1989] Crim LR 271.

—— 'Three Points on *Pigg*' [1989] Crim LR 539.

WICKS, E., 'Terminating Life and Human Rights: the Fetus and the Neonate', in C. Erin and S. Ost (eds.), *The Criminal Justice System and Health Care* (2007), Oxford: Oxford University Press.

WILKES, M., 'Medical Treatment at the End of Life—a British Doctor's Perspective', in C. Erin and S. Ost (eds), *The Criminal Justice System and Health Care* (2007), Oxford: Oxford University Press.

WILLIAMS, G., 'Alternative Elements and Included Offences' [1984] CLJ 290.

—— 'Assaults and Words' [1957] Crim LR 216.

—— 'Convictions and Fair Labelling' [1983] Camb LJ 85.

—— *Criminal Law: The General Part* (2nd edn, 1961), London: Stevens.

—— 'Criminal Omissions—the Conventional View' (1991) 107 LQR 86.

—— 'The Criminal Responsibility of Children' [1954] Crim LR 493.

—— 'The Definition of a Crime' [1955] CLP 107.

—— 'The Draft Code and Reliance on Official Statements' (1989) 9 Legal Studies 177.

—— '*Finis* for *Novus Actus*' [1989] Camb LJ 391.

—— 'Handling, Theft and the Purchaser who Takes a Chance' [1985] Crim LR 432.

—— 'Homicide and the Supernatural' (1949) 65 LQR 491.

—— 'The Lords and Impossible Attempts' [1986] Camb LJ 33.

—— 'Obedience to Law as a Crime' (1990) 53 MLR 445.

—— 'Oblique Intent' [1987] CLJ 417.

—— 'Offences and Defences' (1982) 2 Legal Studies 233.

—— 'The Problem of Reckless Attempts' [1983] Crim LR 365.

—— 'Statute Interpretation, Prostitution and the Rule of Law', in C. Tapper (ed.), *Crime, Proof and Punishment* (1981), London: Butterworths.

—— 'Temporary Appropriation Should Be Theft' [1981] Crim LR 129.

—— 'Theft, Consent and Illegality' [1977] Crim LR 127.

—— 'The Theory of Excuses' [1982] Crim LR 732.

—— *Textbook of Criminal Law* (2nd edn, 1983), London: Stevens.

—— 'The Unresolved Problem of Recklessness' (1988) 8 Legal Studies 74.

—— 'What should the Code do about Omissions?' (1987) 7 Legal Studies 92.

——— 'Which of You Did It?' (1989) 52 MLR 179.

WILLIAMS, R., 'Deception, Mistake and Vitiation of the Victim's Consent', (2008) 124 LQR 132.

WILSON, W., *Central Issues in Criminal Theory* (2002), Oxford: Hart Publishing.

——— 'Murder and the Structure of Homicide', in A. Ashworth and B. Mitchell (eds), *Rethinking English Homicide Law* (2000), Oxford: Oxford University Press.

—— 'A Rational Scheme of Liability for Participating in Crime' [2008] Crim LR 3.

—— 'The Structure of Criminal Defences' [2005] Crim LR 108.

—— 'The Structure of Criminal Homicide' [2006] Crim LR 471.

—— *et al.*, 'Violence, Sleepwalking and the Criminal Law: The Legal Aspects' [2005] Crim LR 624.

WOLFRAM, S., 'Eugenics and the Punishment of Incest Act 1908' [1983] Crim LR 308.

WOOD, J., 'The Serious Fraud Office' [1989] Crim LR 175.

WOODCOCK, G., *Anarchism* (1962), London: Harmondsworth.

WOOTTON, B., *Crime and the Criminal Law* (2nd edn, 1981), London: Sweet & Maxwell.

WRIGHT, F., 'Criminal Liability of Directors and Senior Managers for Deaths at Work' [2007] Crim LR 949.

YEO, S., *Compulsion in the Criminal Law* (1991), Sydney: Law Book Company.

—— 'Sex, Ethnicity, Power of Self-Control and Provocation Revisited' (1996) 18 Sydney LR 304.

YOUNG, W., *Rape Study: A Discussion of Law and Practice* (1983), Wellington: Department of Justice.

ZEDNER, L., 'Family, Sex and the State: Regulating Sexual Offences Within the Home', in I. Loveland (ed), *The Frontiers of Criminality* (1995), London: Sweet & Maxwell.

INDEX